*A Companion to German Literature*

B

*For*
*Celia*
*and*
*Albert*

# A Companion to German Literature

*From 1500 to the present*

EDA SAGARRA AND PETER SKRINE

First published 1997

2 4 6 8 10 9 7 5 3 1

Blackwell Publishers Ltd
108 Cowley Road
Oxford OX4 1JF
UK

Blackwell Publishers Inc.
350 Main Street
Malden, Massachusetts 02148
USA

*British Library Cataloguing in Publication Data*
A CIP catalogue record for this book is available from the British Library.

*Library of Congress Cataloging-in-Publication Data*
Eda Sagarra
A companion to German literature: from 1500 to the present /
Eda Sagarra and Peter Skrine.
p.    cm.
Includes index.
ISBN 0–631–17122–3 (alk. paper)
1. German literature – History and criticism.
2. Literature, Modern – History and criticism.
I. Skrine, Peter N.   II. Title.
PT236.S55   1997
830.9—dc20                                          96–34992
                                                          CIP

Typeset in 10 on 12 pt Ehrhardt
by Best-set Typesetter Ltd, Hong Kong
Printed in Great Britain by TJ Press Ltd, Padstow, Cornwall
This book is printed on acid-free paper

# Contents

## Contents

# *Preface*

———— · ————

Why choose the year 1500 as the starting-point for a history of German literature written for the general and student reader? Apart from the influence of the millennium, which makes the notion of 500 years an attractive 'unit', the answer lies in the ancient city of Mainz, founded by the Romans at the point where the river Main joins the Rhine and seat of the Primate of the Church in Germany since the Anglo-Saxon St Boniface, for it was here that printing by movable type was invented around 1450. Printing changed people's perceptions of society and of themselves in a way that is perhaps comparable to the information technology revolution of our own time. Within two generations of this invention, on the eve of Germany's Renaissance and Protestant Reformation, a qualitative change was already reshaping the ways in which people saw and understood the universe and its Maker. In the Middle Ages access to information had been determined by institutions, namely the Church and the universities. Printing now opened up not just a new technology but a whole new communications system which allowed access to a far wider range of cultural information. The German reading public was still small, although by the standards of most other countries, the percentage of readers was high; indeed, visitors to Germany after the Lutheran Reformation were astonished at the level of literacy even among women. From the early sixteenth century onwards, literacy in Germany was to become closely identified with the concept of the 'German Nation' or 'Fatherland'. German humanists liked to preface their Latin works with exhortations to their compatriots to take pride in their nationhood, and the artist Albrecht Dürer, their contemporary, voiced the hope that his book in German on the theory of perspective would be of use to the whole German nation.

The vital impulse for the development of a consciously national literature in German came from the Lutheran Reformation, and it is no surprise, therefore, that this new literature arose mainly in those parts which became Protestant. Here, in cities such as Leipzig, Hamburg, Königsberg and Zurich, the eighteenth-century Enlightenment was later to generate the aesthetic and moral climate without which the age of Goethe and Schiller, and that of the German Romantics, would have been unthinkable. Blackwell's *Companion to German Literature* has no intention of minimizing the literary achievements of this, the age of Germany's cultural hegemony in Europe. It is, however, written with a clear awareness of the nationalist slant that was given to interpretations of German literary history by the Prussia-oriented historians of the late nineteenth century, and of the new sense of German identity which has understandably been fostered by the economic supremacy of the Federal Republic. As its frequent references to the broader context of other literatures indicate, German literature is understood by both its authors to mean something even wider, richer and more fascinating.

Blackwell's *Companion to German Literature* sees itself as different from most works of its kind in a number of ways. For one thing, it is not the product of several hands under the guidance of an editor. It is the work of two authors, lifelong friends and colleagues, and arises out of their own teaching and research interests. As such, it is pragmatic in a traditionally 'British' way, despite the multicultural interests and affiliations of its authors, the one English/ Swiss/Manx by descent, educated in England, Switzerland, the Isle of Man and France, the other Irish, educated in Ireland, England, Germany, Switzerland and Austria, and Catalan by marriage. Blackwell's *Companion* has the courage of its conviction that, despite appearances, our so-called 'postmodernist' age does in fact require and indeed wish for synthesis. Yet at the same time, the authors are at least as aware as the readers of their book of the foreshortening that is inevitably involved in any synthetic approach to such a vast topic. The aim of the body of this book is to stimulate its readers' interest in German literature, and to encourage them to explore and understand the social context in which literary texts were created and received. Readers familiar with other histories of German literature will, we hope, welcome some shifts of emphasis. One such is the *Companion*'s focus on book production and publication. Such attention to the literary market and to reading tastes should both amplify and contrast with the concentration of most earlier histories of German literature on its thought content, to the neglect of its entertainment value.

The *Companion to German Literature* is organized chronologically and generically, the focus on particular genres in any given period being determined by the preferences not of modern critics but of the people writing and reading at the time. It is divided into nine chapters, each beginning with an introductory section in which the social and economic context of literary creation and enjoyment in a particular period is exemplified by one or more cultural centres or 'exemplary places', which contemporaries would also have recognized as such. Thus Nuremberg, Breslau, Leipzig, Weimar, Heidelberg, Vienna and Berlin are given special prominence, reminding the reader that literature evolves in place as well as in time, and that the landscape of German literature is complex and varied. The *Companion*'s nine chapters present literary eras which are rounded and distinct. But literature exists in a continuum; themes outlast eras, and motifs recur. This dimension is therefore represented by the book's four central 'thematic surveys', which cover the Faust myth, the role of translators and translations in shaping German literary tastes, political poetry, and the long tradition of popular literature in German for both adults and children.

The modern student of German literature may well need to be reminded of certain broad trends in German culture which tend to get overlooked. Today, post-1989 Germany is the richest nation state in Europe and, with some 80 million inhabitants, the largest and most populous after Russia. Yet these are recent developments. When Germany defeated France in the so-called Franco-Prussian War in 1870–1, few had expected that Germany would win, still less win so convincingly. For two centuries, ever since the outbreak of the Thirty Years War, it had been regarded as a relatively poor country, with a considerably smaller population than its wealthy western neighbour. In 1800, Germany (including Austria, Bohemia and Moravia) had just under 23 million inhabitants, whereas France's population was 40 million. By 1871, their populations were roughly equal; by 1900, the German Empire alone, with over 60 million, had 50 per cent more people than France. Germany was only unified in 1871, under the title of the Second Empire, a nation state which now excluded Austria and her empire as well as

Switzerland, Europe's other mainly German-speaking country. The first German Empire, more usually known as the Holy Roman Empire, had been founded by Charlemagne in 800 (or, to be more accurate, by Otto I in 962) and had lasted for a legendary millennium, until 1806. This fact is enough to explain much of Germany's 'differentness' from nation states born in the fifteenth and sixteenth centuries, such as England, France, Spain or the Netherlands. Its lack of a capital city, about which Herder and Goethe wrote so eloquently, had a profound influence on the kind of literature produced by Germans. But, although nineteenth-century nationalists would not have agreed, the effects of this lack were by no means all negative. One of the most interesting features of German culture, of particular topicality today, is its pluri-central character and the abiding significance of regional centres of literary, musical and artistic life right across the German-speaking lands.

It is vital, in approaching literature in German, to remember that the historical topography of the German literary landscape is not identical with Germany today, or even with the Germany of the Second Empire (1871–1918). Many of the most influential writers in the language were born and brought up – indeed, many lived the whole of their lives – in towns and regions far to the east of the area which we know today as Germany, Austria and Switzerland. One such is Herder, the great philosopher of language and the father of nationalism, who came from Riga, now the capital of Latvia; another is the philosopher Kant, who was born and spent his life in Königsberg, once the capital of East Prussia, though now in Russia. The baroque poet and playwright Andreas Gryphius, the Romantic poet Joseph von Eichendorff, and the Naturalist dramatist Gerhart Hauptmann all came from Silesia, now part of Poland; the twentieth century has Franz Kafka and Rainer Maria Rilke from Prague, Paul Celan and Rose Ausländer from Bukovina (now divided between the Ukraine and Romania), René Schickele from Alsace (now part of France) and Günter Grass from Gdánsk (formerly Danzig) in Poland. For the modern student of German language and literature, to explore the relationship of these men and women to their homelands, to Germany and to the German language, is to achieve more than just to meet great creative minds; it is to get behind the barriers which, from the mid-nineteenth century onwards, have separated the Europe of nationalities from its older roots. In that now almost vanished world, literature and culture shaped identities which were both distinct and patriotic but never exclusively national. The users of one language were not seen as superior or hostile to those who used other languages. In a word, they belonged to a Europe not unrelated or dissimilar to that of our own time: a Europe of nations and regions.

A third important issue which Blackwell's *Companion to German Literature* sets out to explore with its readers was once central to the experience of the Germans, but is now remote to many of them: religion. Religion as here discussed is less concerned with a system of beliefs than with cultural identity. It conditioned what people wrote and read, and often even the genre or manner in which they chose to write. Among the differences between Protestant (that is, Lutheran and Calvinist) and Roman Catholic authors and their respective readerships was the much longer survival in Catholic regions of the moral tale, with its idealized stereotypes as opposed to psychologically motivated characters, when such writing had long since begun to seem old-fashioned to Protestant readers. Educated Catholics continued to read Latin, and to read it intensively, well into modern times, while their Protestant counterparts were reading almost exclusively in German, and extensively; the latter were united by the language of Luther whereas the former tended to favour regional usage, a stance reflected in the homogeneous society in Catholic regions such as Bavaria, Austria and the cantons which formed the nucleus of the Swiss Confederation. Austria and Switzerland have produced literatures which have contributed many interesting impulses to that of their bigger neighbour, yet they still have distinct voices of their own.

A quarter of the *Companion* is given over to a bio- and bibliographical section designed to be read either in conjunction with the main text or for its own sake. It has a dual purpose: it gives supplementary information on the many individual authors mentioned in the main text, and provides the reader with a general sense of a considerable further number of writers, who, for reasons of space, could not be included in the *Companion* itself. Moreover, this section also provides students with an easily accessible source for checking names, titles and dates when writing essays of their own: the date given after a work refers to first publication in book form, unless otherwise indicated, or to first performance, as far as is feasible, in the case of plays.

Finally, and perhaps most importantly, Blackwell's *Companion to German Literature* is the first literary history of its kind to attempt to integrate women writers into the narrative of German literary history, and to treat in a systematic manner the role not only of men but also of women as a literary audience.

# *Maps*

—— · ——

# Note to the Reader

_____ . _____

Most German-language authors mentioned in the text of the *Companion to German Literature* appear in its Biographical Index. Those who do not are given their dates of birth and death in the main text.

Place names are given in their accepted English forms where these exist. Where appropriate, places no longer in a German-speaking country are given their traditional German appellations.

# 1

## The Sixteenth Century

In 1482, a year before the birth of Martin Luther and ten years before the discovery of the New World, craftsmen in the Free Imperial City of Nuremberg were already producing eye-glasses for the commercial market. The hand-held eye-glass, later superseded by spectacles worn on the nose, gave many people access to the world of letters who in earlier times would not have been able to read, and prolonged the active life of many poets and scholars by decades. The date and place are surely not fortuitous. The later fifteenth century, the eve of both Renaissance and Reformation in Germany, marks the transition from a predominantly oral literary culture to one based on the written word, or at least one in which the eye, focused on print and woodcut illustration, came to take precedence over the listening ear. The evolution of Germany's 'national literature' in the eighteenth century can be said to have been located almost exclusively in the Protestant North of Germany, creating in its wake a cultural and hence political division of which vestiges are still to be found today, but the focus of the early modern German book market in the late fifteenth century lay further south. The first paper mill in Germany (1390) was located in Nuremberg, a trading centre situated on the so-called *Bernsteinstraße* or 'amber' trade route, midway between the eastern Baltic and Venice. Despite the ravages of the twentieth century, Nuremberg is still the quintessential old German city, its spacious and opulent half-timbered houses and Gothic churches proclaiming its prosperity and importance 500 years ago as the *prima inter pares* of the Free Imperial Cities in the Holy Roman Empire of the German Nation, and the one privileged to be entrusted with the safe keeping of its imperial regalia. Emperor Maximilian I (1493–1519) loved it and often stayed there.

At Mainz, the seat of the Primate of Germany, a hundred or so miles away to the west, the Strasburg-born Johann Gensfleisch, better known as Gutenberg, invented printing by movable type around 1450; by the late fifteenth century Germany had 250 printing presses, many of them grouped in single locations such as Basle, Augsburg, Strasburg and Nuremberg. In the later fifteenth century, Anton Koberger, a Nuremberg printer and publisher, was already using the barter method for selling his products: it was to dominate the book trade from the mid-sixteenth to the mid-eighteenth century. Meanwhile, in the 1470s, the Pfister workshop in neighbouring Bamberg had pioneered the integration of woodcuts into printed text. As the subsequent history of the Reformation would show, this was a vital step in the transformation of flysheet and pamphlet into the first German mass media. And in 1561 Nuremberg became the

**Map 1**   Literary Germany and the Holy Roman Empire in the sixteenth century

first city in Germany to follow the example of Basle in proscribing unlicensed reprinting, including original woodcuts and copperplate engravings.

Between 1480 and 1520, the German book trade virtually exploded. Books were published at a price the prosperous could afford. They were no longer purely the property of monasteries and of princely or university libraries; private individuals could also own them. Erasmus expressed his appreciation in a letter of 1519: if Ptolemy, he asked, earned immortality by creating the library at Alexandria, are not the craftsmen who daily create whole libraries of books for us a kind of demigod? His contemporaries were equally aware of the revolutionary impact of the new technology on people's lives and of its relevance to the message of the Reformers. Only ten weeks after its publication, all 3000 copies of Luther's 1522 translation of the New Testament, costing the price of twenty-five chickens or a kilogram of pepper, had been sold. The pamphlet he addressed to the Christian nobility of Germany, *An den christlichen Adel deutscher Nation*, had an even more spectacular market success: within five days of its appearance on 18 August 1520, all 4000 copies had been bought. 'Nothing of interest happens in the whole world without its being recorded in print,' wrote one Valentin Ickelsamer in 1534, the year in which Luther's complete translation of the Bible first appeared. Over the next hundred years, eighty-seven High German and nineteen Low German editions of Luther's great work had been published.

Sixteenth-century Nuremberg encapsulates much of the characteristic development of the literary market in early modern Germany. A city of patricians and great master-craftsmen, half the size of Cologne but larger than Vienna or Prague and comparable, with its population of 20,000 inhabitants, to cities such as Danzig and Lübeck on the Baltic, Augsburg in the south and Strasburg in the south-west, it was quick to embrace the Lutheran Reformation. Innumerable illustrated pamphlets and broadsheets advocating the cause of reform issued from the pens of its citizens and the presses of its craftsmen. In this it was typical of many of the German cities which enjoyed a high degree of independence within the Holy Roman Empire and were called Free Imperial Cities for this reason. In the seventeenth century, when that empire was caught up in the turmoils of religious and military conflict, Nuremberg would become a refuge for Protestant victims of the Counter-Reformation in Austria, notable among them the poet Catharina von Greiffenberg. But early sixteenth-century Nuremberg, like Strasburg and Basle, was not only a centre of the Reformation; it was also home, in a special sense, to the Renaissance in Germany. It contributed perhaps more than any other German city to the revival of humanism with its great Latinists, such as Conrad Celtis, the *virgo docta* or learned nun Caritas Pirckheimer, and her brother Willibald, and it was the home of the shoemaker poet Hans Sachs, and of the greatest of German painters, craftsmen, graphic artists and polymaths, Albrecht Dürer.

## A Century of Satire

German literature entered the modern age buoyant and full of promise. Germany's well-ordered late-medieval towns and cities provided a self-contained society with trading links all over Europe, and a potential readership avid for entertainment and education. The language spoken by its urban population had attained a remarkable degree of cohesion and a range which made it suitable as a medium for most purposes and topics. Printing had been invented and developed in a number of German cities during the latter part of the fourteenth century, and an urban culture had evolved which was eager for self-expression in words as well as in paintings, woodcarvings, buildings and other artefacts. German urban society was stable and secure enough to see itself and to be regarded by its writers as a normal contemporary world strong enough to tolerate their ridicule and sometimes even their castigation of its defects and vices. It was relaxed enough to be ready to laugh at itself, yet sufficiently concerned with its own moral and spiritual well-being to agonize over its shortcomings and speculate about its future. This accounts for the great success of the book which most effectively captured the temper of the age: *Das Narrenschiff* ('The Ship of Fools') by Sebastian Brant, an erudite Strasburg lawyer with a caustic view of humanity and a rare ability to speak a language which his contemporaries could understand.

*The Ship of Fools* appeared in 1494, as the new age of Humanism which preceded the Lutheran Reformation was getting under way and German scholars were indicating their readiness to take the intellectual lead in Europe. It is a satire of almost unrivalled scope, and it gave Brant the opportunity to pass in review the minor foibles and more serious shortcomings of the men and women who composed the society of which he, too, formed part. Only loosely held together by the memorable notion of a ship manned by fools and heading no one knows where, it is a survey of an ordered society which ends in apocalyptic warnings of its collapse. Many of Brant's concerns are trivial in the extreme; even the most minor manifestations of human stupidity stand condemned to ridicule. But read on. As the book proceeds through its 112 chapters of doggerel verse, Brant's voice begins to sound more like that of the prophets of old. The political disintegration of the Holy Roman Empire of the German Nation (whose staunch supporter he was), the impending invasion of the Turks, who had captured Constantinople forty years earlier and put an end to the Roman Empire of the East, the ominous symptoms of the decline of Christendom and the collapse of Christian faith – anxieties such as these, expressed with mounting intensity, bring Brant increasingly into line with Dante, despite the fact that Brant never forgets his roots in the common idiom, homespun wisdom and wry humour of the Rhineland cities of Strasburg and Basle where he grew up, studied and pursued his legal and academic career. Though its tone was, in the main, light and its satirical language homely and caustic by turns, there was about this remarkable work a prophetic quality which gripped the minds and imaginations of contemporaries in other countries, too, thanks to its translation into Latin (*Stultifera nauis*, 1497) and its paraphrases into French (1498), English (1509) and other languages. By 1521 Luther's doctrinal break with Rome had become irreparable; in 1525 the Peasants' War, a widespread agrarian uprising, gave a nasty fright to the burghers of the wealthy trading cities of southern and central Germany; and in 1529 the Turks were laying siege to Vienna, the seat of the Habsburg Emperor Charles V in his capacity as ruler of Germany.

The satirical range and the prophetic warnings of *The Ship of Fools* were the keys to its success, as were the woodcuts with which it was illustrated, many of them now attributed to Dürer. But it has also been likened to a lens which gathered up the rays of the medieval past and then refracted them to the period which followed: in this sense it performed a valuable function by ensuring an element of continuity in a period of rapid change. Whatever its literary merits – and it has many – Brant's masterpiece proved him to be the creator of a potent myth which has haunted the European imagination ever since. The very fact that he did not exploit the potential of his vision to the full may help to account for the hold it has retained on the consciousness of people ever since, despite the fact that very few have read the book since the sixteenth century. Certainly no work of the imagination could make a better starting-point for tracing the development of a literature which has always tended to regard the moral education of the human being as one of its central concerns.

Though the Reformation intervened, bringing with it an eruption of literary activity in the polemical, theological and devotional fields, the literature of Germany during the sixteenth century is predominantly one of entertainment. Sometimes it is mildly escapist; more often, and at its most appealing, it presents the comic and curious aspects of human nature within the parameters of contemporary life. From it, the reader gets a richly detailed picture of life in Germany in those distant times: a superficial picture, perhaps, but a vivid one, to which Goethe, for instance, responded readily when as a young man he wrote the sprawling sixteenth-century drama *Götz von Berlichingen* (1773), which made his name, and embarked on his lifelong involvement with Faust, the semi-legendary sixteenth-century sage and con-man who was to become the embodiment of the central myth of modern German literature. The basic unit of the German sixteenth-century author was the anecdote, and his favourite form the *Schwank*, an episode usually humorous in content, retold either for its own sake or as part of a collection. Those surrounding the elusive figure of the scholar-sorcerer Faust, first published in the *Faust-*

*Buch* of 1587, provided the original source for Goethe and for Marlowe, while those that told of the equally legendary practical joker, Till Eulenspiegel, introduced another figure who was to become a recurrent German literary myth: the prankster with an astute eye for the follies of mankind, whose exploits held up a mirror to contemporary folk in the hope of making them wiser. The sixteenth century thus established the restless magus and the impertinent satirist as two complementary authorial personae. The self-absorbed introversion of the one in a world of metaphysical speculation and unfulfilled dreams, and the extrovert snook-cocking of the other at the expense of a complacent community, introduced authorial stances which recur through-out the history of German literature to the present day. Thomas Mann's postwar novels *Doktor Faustus* and *Bekenntnisse des Hochstaplers Felix Krull* ('Confessions of the confidence trickster Felix Krull') are the most famous and fascinating instances in modern fiction of the reappear-ance of the magician and the confidence trickster, while a generation later one of the leaders of the student revolt was described as the 'Eulenspiegel of 1968'.

At the time Brant was writing, Germany was unquestionably the richest part of Europe: its monopolies of mining and the metal market, especially copper, and its command of the princi-pal European trade-routes provided the economic base for a flourishing urban culture which in turn fostered the development of literature in the vernacular language its members used and understood. Luther made a point of appealing explicitly to ordinary people: his translation of the Bible (1522–34) was by no means the first into German, but its idiomatic wording made the central texts of the Christian religion immediately accessible to the general reader and church-goer, while his hymns and theological writings gave confidence and encouragement to his supporters all over the German-speaking area. Brant's *Narrenschiff* and other satirical books written in its wake fostered a general awareness that not all was well in affluent Germany; yet their appeal was so wide and their language so genuinely colloquial and congenial that, para-doxically, they ensured that the secular literature of Germany during the century of the Reformation remained entertaining and light-hearted in its criticism of human foibles and behaviour. This can be seen in the work of Brant's fellow Alsatian, Thomas Murner, a Franciscan friar with a gift for satirical humour and a fertile imagination to carry it. In a string of humorous poems he coaxed and cajoled contemporaries into looking at their conduct and into their motives: his satirical campaign reached its zenith when he took on Luther's Reformation itself in his anti-Lutheran burlesque, *Von dem großen lutherischen Narren* ('The great Lutheran fool', 1522), in which all his well-tried satirical strategies were brought to bear on the new religious ideology which he felt was corrupting the values and institutions of what we today would term the Middle Ages. The Lutheran fool of the title is a grotesque embodiment of the German population, overfed with new-fangled ideas, and grown dyspeptic and constipated with the folly of them. Murner, the author, enters his own poem as the master exorcist who proceeds to evacuate the body politic of a nation besotted with novelty: grandiose are the issues at stake, ludicrous and banal the behaviour and words of the fool caught up in them, and crudely effective the methods adopted by the satirist to expose them. Murner the writer was, of course, unable single-handed to alter the course of history; but with his elder contemporary Brant he was responsible for a remarkable flowering of German satire, whose effects were to last well into the seventeenth century, when, writing in the same broad geographical area, a retired soldier called Grimmelshausen was to draw on his experiences during the Thirty Years War to point the tragicomic follies of humankind in a novel of European as well as German significance: *Simplicissimus Teutsch*, published in 1668.

For a century from Brant's *Narrenschiff* in 1494 to Johann Fischart's loquacious German adaptation of Book I of Rabelais's *Gargantua* in its third expanded edition of 1590, German literature was marked by the predominance of satire. This term was first used in German in 1505 to describe a satirical poem, but satirical aims and methods were invading every genre. Narrative, drama and poetry, all were turned into vehicles for it, and lesser genres, such as the dialogue and the mock or open letter, were cultivated for the same purpose. Sixteenth-century German satire was of the sort that presupposes a close-knit sense of community, and the satirical impulse was often kindled by a perceived departure from the norms of common sense or, in more serious contexts, by the apparent abandonment of commonly acceptable moral and spiritual values. It was therefore frequently directed at the Church and at its clergy, whose peccadilloes, moral laxity and excessive economic and political influence were repeatedly brought to task and made the butt of drastic ridicule. The fact that this anticlerical tendency was a long-standing tradition reinforces the view that, as far as literature is concerned, the Reformation was neither quite as unexpected nor as inevitable as it may now seem. This German fondness for satire may be observed at all levels. It is present in the relatively simplistic popular literature intended for unassuming readers and in the broadsheets and pamphlets which commented, often anonymously, on topical matters, drawing attention to their comical side, but it may also be enjoyed in the *jeux d'esprit* of the humanists, Germany's classically educated intelligentsia, whose members felt increasingly impelled to try their hand at more polished ridicule in the manner of the ancients, while at the same time aiming it, angrily or wittily, at contemporary abuses and shortcomings.

In the early years of the century the possibility of combining topical concerns with the formal and stylistic polish of high art had been demonstrated by the Dutch-born writer Desiderius Erasmus, some seventy of whose Latin works had been translated into German by the time of his death in 1537, making him the most widely read serious author next to Luther himself. Erasmus's deceptively elegant *In Praise of Folly* (*Moriae encomium*, 1511), written in stylish Latin, had delighted a cosmopolitan readership with its brilliant variations on the satirical theme that the true religion of mankind is really nothing more nor less than the cult of stupidity personified by a goddess, Folly, created in our own image. Its German rendition by Sebastian Franck (1534) is indicative of the cross-fertilization of two cultures – the humanist, cosmopolitan, intellectual one favouring Latin as its medium, and the vernacular German one, more rooted in popular tradition but sharing many of the same concerns – which was to give the literary culture of sixteenth-century Germany its characteristic flavour. The convergence of the two was confirmed by the appearance in 1520 of a set of seven satirical dialogues by Ulrich von Hutten. His scenario and its treatment are modelled on the best work of Lucian, a late Greek satirical writer much admired during the Renaissance. He wrote them first in Latin and then, within the year, reproduced four of them in German. These vernacular versions were published in Strasburg in 1521 in what he called his *Gespräch büchlin* or 'Little book of dialogues'; the best of them is called *Die Anschawenden* ('The Observers') and is cast in the form of a dialogue between the Sun God and his son, Phaeton, in which the god explains the curious things they can see going on in the world down below them as they drive the sun chariot across the sky. What is shown up by Hutten here is the state in which Germany finds itself in 1520. Drunkenness and immorality are rife, and dread of an imminent Turkish invasion is present everywhere: the Turks actually reached Vienna within the decade. Then, as the two extraterrestrial spectators focus more sharply on the scene below, they observe the procession bringing the papal legate, Cardinal Cajetan, to Germany to sort out the religious dissension caused by the inflammatory words and writings of Martin Luther. By this means Hutten encompasses at one and the same time the state of the nation, its position on the international scene, and the religious upheaval emanating from it which was about to destabilize the late-medieval status quo of Church and state throughout the whole of Europe. His concentration on one single day, the impartial detachment and longer view suggested by his divine protagonists, and the immediacy generated by his vivid close-ups make *Die Anschawenden* a small-scale satirical masterpiece which is also in many respects the prototype of modern journalistic reporting. With it, as with Luther's Bible translation, printing had come of age.

Hutten's choice of the dialogue form was inspired. No period in intellectual history had ever engaged so whole-heartedly in debate, polemics and discussion as the one during which Hutten and Luther were writing, and no genre was better suited to transmit to its readers the rapid interchange of opinions and counter-opinions than this literary form, borrowed from a distant but still relevant past. It was to remain a particular favourite with German writers for the next fifty years, ensuring that the issues and attitudes of the time are more vividly and comprehensively recorded than those of any earlier period.

## Drama without a Theatre

The dialogue is a form which had a good deal in common with drama, and sixteenth-century Germany was unusually rich in dramatists even though theatres as we now know them were still very much a thing of the future. The cities of sixteenth-century Germany never possessed playhouses of the kind that were to be developed by the London actor-impresarios of the Elizabethan age. As in the Middle Ages, performance remained a corporate or civic matter associated with churches, guilds and city schools and, in Protestant areas especially, with lay groups such as the guilds of Mastersingers whose role in maintaining standards of quality in poetry and drama was seen by contemporaries as analogous to the quality controls and training schemes operated by other crafts and trades. A remarkable fusion of these lay traditions and the controversial new ideas emanating from Luther occurred in the Swiss city of Berne in 1523. Niklas Manuel, a local artist and city councillor, decided to use all the means at his disposal to bring home to the public the burning theological and ecclesiastical issues of the day in a way they could all understand. Manuel's *Vom Papst und seiner Priesterschaft* ('[Play] of the Pope and his Clergy', 1524) uses satirical review, dialogue and burlesque to bring to life the crisis in the Church sparked off by the controversial sale of indulgences; two years later, his brilliant satire *Der Ablaßkrämer* ('The Pardoner') homes in on an indulgence vendor with a zest and eye for the telling detail which had, and still has, the effect of making the play, like its precursor, resemble a series of satirical woodcuts brought to life in the city's streets complete with movement and sound effects.

As the century progressed, the German-speaking countries were building up a sustained and remarkably homogeneous body of vernacular literature in which popular motifs and a sense of fun often blended with an exaggerated attention to detail at the expense of the whole. Its chief characteristic is its down-to-earth vigour both of subject and language, a quality which has been compared, and rightly, with the German visual art of the period, and especially with the woodcuts by artists and craftsmen such as Albrecht Dürer in Nuremberg, Hans Holbein in Basle and Hans Baldung in Strasburg, which raised the skills of design and draughtsmanship to new heights. The black and white contrasts of their woodcuts and engravings have their correlative in the clear-cut directness with which the period's favourite stock themes are treated by its dramatic writers, and which is allowed to coexist happily with an eye for linguistic and narrative detail. Certain subjects recur with such frequency that they may be considered as typical of the literature of the period as they are of its painting and engraving. Most were drawn from the Bible, the Old Testament providing exciting tales for dramatization, the New Testament complementing them with subjects of a more thought-provoking kind based usually on the parables told by Christ, such as 'The prodigal son' and 'Dives and Lazarus'. The first of these was particularly popular during the thirty years from 1527 to 1557. Its successful dramatization by the Dutch neo-Latin writer Gnaphaeus in 1529 was translated into German in 1530, and the subject was later treated by the Swiss playwright Hans Salat in 1537, by Jörg Wickram in Alsace in 1540 and by his Nuremberg contemporary Hans Sachs in 1557, though its most successful dramatic treatment was the one by the former Franciscan monk Burkhard Waldis which inaugurated the lively tradition of post-Reformation plays on biblical subjects. His *De Parabell vam verlorn Szohn* ('The Parable of the Prodigal Son') was performed in the local dialect by the citizens and schoolchildren of Riga in 1527. The prodigal son's attempt to break away from home, his destitution and his welcome back by his father seem to have exerted a strong appeal in the Reformation period, during which this divinely sanctioned account of the themes of filial independence and paternal authority gave a topical Christian relevance to the father–son conflict that is a recurrent theme in German literature. In the second half of the century it was if anything overtaken in popularity by the subject of Dives and Lazarus, which similarly reflected a growing and perhaps disturbing contrast between the rich and the poor. The finest dramatic adaptation of this parable appeared in Magdeburg at the end of the century: Georg Rollenhagen's *Spiel vom reichen Manne und armen Lazaro* of 1590.

Of the favourite Old Testament subjects such as the violent story of Judith and Holofernes and the gentler tale of Tobias and the angel, the enigmatic tale of the virtuous Susanna and her denunciation by the two lecherous elders was especially popular. It was dramatized in 1532 by Sixt Birck and three years later by one of the most gifted of all the mid-sixteenth-century German playwrights, Paul Rebhuhn, an Austrian writer living and working in Saxony, whose more delicate treatment of the Susanna story clearly shows that he was alive to the formal conventions of classically oriented humanist drama, even including the use of a chorus many years before such a feature was tried and accepted in other European vernacular drama traditions. Though not always entirely successful at recreating these semi-classical elements in a literary language much closer to ordinary everyday speech than to Renaissance ideals of stylistic and linguistic correctness, Rebhuhn's tragic play is as close as sixteenth-century German literature comes to the Renaissance ideals that were soon to affect the drama of France and England. Such aesthetic values and formal requirements scarcely impinged on creative writing in German during the sixteenth century. Only the neo-Latin writers, who were mainly to be found in academic circles in Germany, were eager to emulate antiquity, and therefore minded about them. In the world of vernacular entertainment what mattered was clear action, swift repartee, effective dramatic episodes, and a more or less simplistic moral scheme recapitulated for the general benefit of the public at the end of the action.

A past master of this technique was the Nuremberg cobbler Hans Sachs, a man with little Latin and no Greek, but with a sure feel for what his contemporaries required and the natural ability to formulate it in words and phrases which still bear the imprint of his unmistakable voice 500 years after his birth. Sachs's dramatic output is copious, and draws on an extraordinarily wide range of sources. From deft, concise comedies intended for performance at carnival time to plays of considerable length, it uses all the techniques familiar to a German writer of the

period to dramatize some of the most famous tragic and romantic subjects in European literature, such as the myths of Oedipus and Orestes, the Trojan War, Antony and Cleopatra,
Tristan and Isolde, and Griseldis, as well as biblical subjects such as Esther, Adam and Eve, and
Job. Sachs also draws on the rich fund of medieval popular narrative and folklore which printing
was reviving and making accessible to new generations of readers who delighted in the old tales
of Hug Schapler and the Fair Melusina, and the more recent adventures of Fortunatus, whose
wishing cap and bottomless purse had captivated an upwardly mobile and commercially oriented readership in the trading cities of Germany ever since its first appearance in 1508 in
Augsburg, where the merchant banker Jakob Fugger and his family were expanding their
financial empire and industrial interests to hitherto unseen proportions.

Sachs has been called an unproblematic writer and dismissed accordingly. Goethe, however,
responded positively to his creative exuberance and wrote a poem in praise of him, and in *Die
Meistersinger von Nürnberg* (1868) Wagner created great music drama out of his life and works
and even drew implicit analogies between Sachs and himself. Sachs's many serious plays are
dramatizations of stories which were more or less familiar to his audiences, and his artistry lies
in his ability to bring them to life in this new medium. Sometimes, when they lack the necessary
dramatic spark, he lapses into narrative. But where he invents his own plots this weakness
disappears. Certainly the eighty-five carnival comedies he wrote for a group of amateur actors
in his native city of Nuremberg in the middle years of the century are an achievement in the
comic vein which can stand comparison with the best in the German language. With remarkable
economy they present the foibles and failings of ordinary people in a way ordinary people can
understand, preaching more by skilfully dramatized example than by pompous precept, and
their vitality, ingenuity of plot, psychological insight and concision, and above all their ability
to generate effective comic drama out of next to nothing, are qualities which should be
remembered whenever German dramatic literature is faulted for its lack of light-hearted
humour.

## Anecdotes and Stories

The other genre which dominated the literature of the sixteenth century was the short tale or
anecdote known in German as the *Schwank*. Like the drama of the time, this could encompass
violent and sad subjects, but more usually it concentrated on episodes of a humorous or ribald
sort, taking great delight in the narration of practical jokes such as those associated in the
popular imagination with Till Eulenspiegel. The authoritative account of this famous prankster's exploits first appeared in Strasburg in 1515, and he has been as vital a figure on the
German scene as Robin Hood in England ever since. Another favourite figure around whom
stories gathered was Claus, a Saxon court fool, whose merry jests were retold in a collection of
627 anecdotes published in Eisleben in 1572; yet another popular collection is the set of forty-
five anecdotes about the foolish inhabitants of the fictitious town of Lalenburg, which were
collected and published in Strasburg in 1597 under the titles *Das Lalebuch* and *Die Schildbürger*,
and which inaugurated a genre which was to become something of a German speciality. The
semi-humorous satirical depiction of small-town stupidity was to resurface in Wieland's novel
*Die Abderiten* (1774–80), the comedies set in the fictitious town of Krähwinkel by Kotzebue,
Nestroy and other playwrights in the early nineteenth century, and in Gottfried Keller's two
collections of long short stories entitled *Die Leute von Seldwyla* after the inhabitants of a small

fictitious Swiss town of that name. Often, however, collections of anecdotes had no central unifying figure and were only held together by their author's tone or voice. This was the case with the most influential of them all, *Schimpf und Ernst* (1522) by the Alsatian Franciscan monk Johann Pauli. Here, as the title implies, the serious and the scandalous are juxtaposed. To more modern readers these short narratives may often seem unnecessarily crude, childishly repetitive or simply unfunny. Their effect largely depends on their being read and appreciated for what they are: a translation into written prose of an essentially oral narrative tradition, which was made possible by printing and which was ideally suited to the requirements of publishers targeting readers whose means and reading ability were limited, but whose readiness to look, listen and learn was still almost childishly fresh during the first century or so which followed the creation of the book-publishing industry in the German-speaking countries. In this sense the rich heritage of sixteenth-century German anecdote and story, and the enormous output of publications which concentrated on it, is a concomitant of the infinitely more serious purposes to which printing was also being put in the German-speaking countries almost from the moment the new technology was perfected.

## The Bible in German

The period's best-seller was of course the Bible. It, too, is essentially episodic, sometimes satirical and often didactic, and represents a rich store of narrative and of narrative forms ranging from the chronicles of Kings to the parables of Christ and the adventures of the Apostles. The translation of the Bible into German by Martin Luther owed its overwhelming success, and its continuous hold on German readers, in large measure to his readiness to see the communicative potential of well-told episodes which appealed to the reader's or listener's imagination, and in so doing alerted their moral sense and aroused their latent spirituality. It was the work of a great man who profoundly affected the course of European history; but, in terms of Germany's literary development, what is even more important is that he succeeded in 'translating' the historical lore, wisdom and religious revelations of a different age and a distant Middle Eastern culture into a readable German text – or, rather, a vast array of texts employing widely different registers and encompassing many types and degrees of narrative, meditative and analytical writing – and that he did so at a time when Germany was entering a new economic and political era and establishing a new identity for itself.

Like the *Narrenschiff*, Luther's Bible is a link between the traditions of the past and the emergence of the Protestant Germany of the future. There had been German translations of the Bible before: but Luther's was the first to demonstrate the full linguistic and stylistic range which the German language could command in its early modern period. It gave Germany an advantage which was to provide a sense of pride and national unity to offset the tendency towards fragmentation that was itself partly the result of the upheavals which the Lutheran Reformation caused. For the next century or so, Germany led the way at least as far as the possession of an authoritative Bible translation was concerned. Luther's New Testament first appeared in Wittenberg, the centre of the Reformer's activities, in 1522, in an anonymous edition of some 4000 copies which was sold out within three months and had to be quickly reprinted in a revised edition to satisfy the demand: its price was just one half-gulden, the weekly wage of a carpenter's apprentice at the time. Eighty-seven editions of the German New

Testament had already appeared before it was followed by the Old Testament, first published in the Complete Bible (*Vollbibel*) of 1534. In Wittenberg alone 100,000 Bibles were printed in the forty years up to 1574: no figures convey more graphically the effect which printing was having on the production of reading matter and on the relationship between an author and the potential readership. No other printed book in German was to come to the notice of so many people or provide them with such a great incentive to read.

Luther's Bible was without doubt the towering achievement of sixteenth-century German literature, and its presence has made itself felt in that literature ever since. Indeed the Bible and Luther's translation of it are so closely synonymous within the German-speaking world, even including its Roman Catholic areas, that palpable traces of his style and phraseology tend to accompany biblical allusions and references wherever they are made. The work of writers from Andreas Gryphius and Paul Fleming in the seventeenth century to Jeremias Gotthelf and Annette von Droste-Hülshoff in the nineteenth century and to Bertolt Brecht in the twentieth thus owes a great deal to this sixteenth-century achievement, in much the same way as English and American literature are indelibly stamped with verbal traces of Tyndale's translation, done in Germany under Luther's influence between 1525 and 1531, and of the Authorized or King James Version of 1611 which owed much to Tyndale.

By the middle of the sixteenth century the German-speaking lands were well on the way to recovery from the conflict which had been generated by the Lutheran Reformation and its political consequences. That conflict had generated an enormous amount of activity: broadsheets, open letters and polemical works had poured from the presses of Germany, and it has been estimated that more individual items were printed there between 1517 and 1525, the climactic years of the Reformation, than in the entire period which, in England, ran from 1477, when the first book ran off Caxton's printing press, to the end of the Civil War. Relatively few of these items were of a strictly literary nature, however, and a great many were ephemeral or of purely local interest, apart, that is, from the great hymns composed by Luther himself, most of which were published in 1524, although the most famous of them, 'Ein feste Burg ist unser Gott', did not appear until 1529. These laid the basis for the rich German hymn tradition which for the next 500 years provides perhaps the most constant element in a literature characterized by its lack of overall continuity.

## The Later Sixteenth Century

The literature of the sixteenth century's middle years is dominated by Hans Sachs, the most important literary figure of the entire period. His creative activities stretch from before 1523, when he hailed Luther's advent by likening his voice to that of the nightingale in a great visionary poem called *Die Wittenbergisch Nachtigall*, to 1567, when his catalogue poem summing up the entire literary output of his life arrived at a total of over 6000 items. The other most interesting writer of the period, Jörg Wickram, was active in Alsace from 1539 to 1555–6, the years which saw the publication of his two masterpieces, *Das Rollwagenbüchlein* ('The covered waggon booklet'), a collection of anecdotes – the prototypes of the modern short story – expressly written to entertain men and women alike while travelling, and the novel, *Von guten und bösen Nachbarn* ('A tale of good and bad neighbours'), which anticipates the family sagas of the late nineteenth century, such as Thomas Mann's *Buddenbrooks*, by tracing the fortunes of a merchant family over three generations. The mid–century realism of both these writers reflects the return to stability of the German urban middle classes and their dual attachment to wealth-creation and the God-fearing orderly life that went with it.

The easier accessibility of Wickram's style has tended to overshadow the work of his fellow Alsatian, Johann Fischart, who was to be the leading force in German literature in the 1570s and 1580s. A much-travelled and well-educated man (he took his master's degree in law at Basle in 1574), Fischart admired Rabelais and set out to imitate his enormously wide range as a humorist and satirist in German, extending the language to bursting-point as he did so. Like Murner and Luther, he is one of the most inventive and creative users of the German language, as he demonstrated in his much-expanded version of Book I of *Gargantua*, originally published by Rabelais in 1534. When Fischart's adaptation appeared with an aptly gargantuan title in 1575, he pointed out that his preposterous verbal artefact was an obvious imitation of their bewildering but real world.

Before that, Fischart had sensed the way the wind was blowing. The period between 1560 and 1580 was one of climatic change. Known as the 'new ice age', it was particularly severe in Germany, and brought famine and a sudden revival of physical terror accompanied by witch-hunts and a vogue for books on demonology and dire events. Fischart was quick to make fun of this mounting craze for horoscopes and almanacs (then known as *practica*) in his *Aller Practic Großmutter* ('The grandmother of all almanacs'), a grotesque satire in Rabelaisian style published in 1572, and then went on to translate the French philosopher Jean Bodin's *Démonomanie* in 1581. But by far the most lasting memento of this curious post-humanist age of credulity, fear and superstition appeared in 1587: a deceptively simplistic anonymous work which was to be the source of what was destined to become the most powerful of Germany's cultural myths: the *Historia von D. Johann Fausten*, better known as the *Faustbuch* or tale of Dr Johann Faust. Clearly aimed at a popular audience, this unassuming book traces the exploits of a magician and confidence trickster who makes a pact with the Devil in an episodic narrative which owes much to the anecdotal story-telling tradition of the period. It is only when Faust's pact draws to its appointed close that the tall-story tone which marked its earlier episodes begins to take on a more ominous and sombre colouring which brings its account of the events leading up to Faust's death into unexpectedly close affinity with the gospel accounts of Christ's Passion as narrated in Luther's Bible. Within less than two years the *Faust Book* had been turned into one of the most powerful works in Renaissance literature: Christopher Marlowe's *Tragicall History of Dr Faustus*. Faust's virtual disappearance, his rediscovery in the eighteenth century, when the tale had become a typical fairground puppet-play, and his resurrection in the hands of Goethe and of many other writers and composers, are one more indication of the fact that the literature of sixteenth-century Germany is far from dead, although it is little known or read today.

# 2

## The Seventeenth Century

Two students, their plumed hats upon their heads – what person of standing goes bare-headed out of doors? – approach each other. The scene takes place in the mid-1660s in a street outside a German university: it could be the new university at Kiel, founded in 1665 by Duke Christian Albrecht of Holstein-Gottorp, or one of the older universities such as Leipzig, Heidelberg and Strasburg, all of which promising young men from the grammar schools in Silesia and its main city, Breslau, attended because their province had no university of its own. Each student proceeds to doff his hat, for salutation is both a recognition of individual worth ('I acknowledge you as my friend') and the token of an orderly society. Social relationships of every kind in the baroque age – whether between prince and courtier, master and servant, clergyman and parishioner, or parent and child – were in some sense public. They were governed by ritual, whose forms expressed the particular place occupied in society by the individual, as representative of his or her estate or social group. The students in the scene above are sons of honourable families and thus, it is hoped, future pillars of society. This they must express in their dress and in their manners and behaviour in public, that is, in their 'deportment'. Our two students meanwhile continue with their greeting, eyeing each other as they bare their heads with a flourish, and bow low, each meticulously observing and matching the level to which the other inclines his head. To bow lower would be to acknowledge inferiority; to bow less low would be to claim superior rank and hence to insult one's equal. A passing professor, however, elicits an immediate deep bow in unison from the two, acknowledged by a gracious incline of the professorial pate. The students will need his goodwill later, less perhaps as an examiner than as a scholar whose connections can help them to gain 'preferment'. He will surely reward their deference.

This meticulous concern with order, hierarchy and precedence, with the appropriate gesture, word or phrase, and with the expression of social divisions in the very clothes a person wore or was entitled to wear, all contrast with the violence and brutality of the age. War, pestilence and hunger afflicted and decimated the population of seventeenth-century Germany, where the last European wars of religion were fought. The barbarity of marauding soldiers during the Thirty Years War (1618–48), described, grotesquely, in the comic mode by Grimmelshausen in his picaresque novel *Der abentheuerliche Simplicissimus Teutsch* ('The adventurous German Simplicissimus'), was often matched by institutionalized violence. Gruesome forms of legal punishment were favoured by the authorities for crimes of all kinds: torture could be followed by breaking on the wheel or by hanging on the roadside gallows, where the bodies were left to rot as a warning to others. The modern imagination focuses, not surprisingly, with voyeuristic horror on the appalling human degradation of the witch-hunts, which could involve torture such as tearing off the female breast prior to burning at the stake.

During the Thirty Years War, Germany's population fell by an estimated one-third, with regional variations of up to 70 per cent. The length of the war and the devastation it left in its wake promoted an overriding obsession with order, in which literature too had its place. Literature, as the historian Gerhard Oestreich observed, had its part to play in the social disciplining of the population, and its hierarchical structure of genres – epic poetry and tragedy at the top, occasional verse and low comedy at the bottom – mirrored the social hierarchy much as would the design of theatres and opera houses, with their galleries, boxes and pit, for centuries to come. To write within one's social estate (that is, as prince, nobleman, patrician, professional man of letters, or even as self-styled peasant) reinforced the sense of individual and collective worth and the orderly structures of Christian society. Redress against an unjust ruler or overlord was not to be sought in this life but in the next, which the contemporary imagination still pictured as being divided, in hell as in heaven, according to devilish or angelic rank. But even in the here and now, poets such as the Silesian satiric epigrammatist Friedrich von Logau could not refrain from lecturing the mighty on their faults, while Maria Katharina Stockfleth (1634–92), the Nuremberg author of the pastoral novel *Die Kunst- und Tugend-gezierte Macarie* ('The virtuous and artistic Macarie', 1669–73), could contrast her role models, low-born but virtuous, with a wicked queen as representative of the ruling class. For his part, the Austrian country nobleman Wolfgang Helmhard von Hohberg, in his *Georgica Curiosa* (1682), offered a practical compendium of estate management combined with a vision of a utopian society projected back into a golden age and forward into a distant future.

Hohberg's *magnum opus* reminds us that the seventeenth-century German writer embraces both the poetic and the useful, and does not, unlike the modern critic, make clear aesthetic distinctions between them. It is all useful in some way or other. Court and city poets provided a service by promoting the fame of their patrons, and this was understood in a very concrete and direct sense by their contemporaries. Literature, including the courtly novel and the Christian martyr tragedy or indeed the sermon – a literary genre often overlooked today – was a vehicle for improving social mores, and hence part of social discipline. Moreover, despite the parallel existence of a vigorous neo-Latin literature, writers in German regarded the task of enhancing the reputation of their mother tongue as a patriotic and worthy activity, and to that laudable end founded or became members of societies for the promotion of the German language, which they cultivated alongside Latin: bilingual authorship was no exception or anomaly as yet. Latin was still the universal language and the primary language of a European intelligentsia whose activities transcended linguistic boundaries and crossed political frontiers with an ease that later centuries were to lose. The division of Europe on linguistic grounds had scarcely begun.

During the sixteenth century Latin had maintained its position in the German-speaking countries as the language of serious scholarship and poetry, while German, the language of the people, provided the medium for popular literature, much as before. The discovery that German was also a language capable of conveying the sentiments of Renaissance European literary culture took place in the seventeenth century. Religious polemics, which represented the intellectual dimension of religious conflict, had become the staple of successive generations of clergymen in the Protestant areas of Germany, and of priests in the areas which remained loyal to the Roman Catholic Church. Trained in the theological power-houses of the reformed religion, such as the universities of Wittenberg and Helmstedt, the Lutheran clergy had come to be an influential and respected element in German society and one that was connected with the promotion of education in the Protestant grammar schools or *Gymnasien*. It is therefore no surprise that many seventeenth-century German writers and poets were Protestant ministers of religion.

The literary and intellectual standards of most writers, whatever their religious denomination, were formed by the education they had received either in Germany's *Gymnasien* or in their counterparts, the new Catholic colleges: the senior classes of both types of institution provided instruction of near-university standard. Classical studies provided a major element in the curriculum of both, and Latin was still the first language of education and of legal, theological and scholarly communication. Familiarity with it therefore gave educated German men (and sometimes women, too) access to a wide pool of knowledge in which the writings of classical antiquity played a much-admired but by no means exclusive part. Alongside the poets, theorists and thinkers of antiquity, a wide range of modern authors had achieved near-classic status in most literary genres and provided a common currency of thought: men such as Grotius, the Dutch lawyer, Lipsius, the Belgian neo-Stoic thinker, Buchanan, the Scottish biblical dramatist, the modern French literary theorist Julius Caesar Scaliger, the Italian poets Vida and Pontanus and the Welsh epigrammatist Owen, and a great many more, including Germans such as the scholarly Caspar von Barth, who found time to translate Italian and Spanish erotic masterpieces into Latin in order to make them more readily accessible. German thought and literature were to remain very much a part of this intellectual world until the eighteenth century, when French began to replace Latin and even to vie with German as a language of serious communication – a development already reflected in the French and Latin works of Gottfried Wilhelm Leibniz (1646–1716), Germany's first major philosopher and the inaugurator of its reputation as a land of thinkers as well as poets.

Literature in the seventeenth century is characterized by a clear sense of the audience which the writer is addressing. Often enough it is commissioned literature: in the case of the many thousands of occasional poems (*Gelegenheitsgedichte*) we generally know the names of the dedicatees and the occasions which their authors were celebrating. This was literature written to serve a particular purpose which reinforced the norms of society: to mark the birth, marriage or death of a person of standing, the graduation of a student, or victory in battle. In the grammar school (*Gymnasium*) of the period, drama in Latin and German, usually based on themes from classical history and the Bible, was an exercise in public speaking, a training in rhetoric, and useful preparation for a career in the Church or at the bar. Cultivated by Protestant grammar schools and Catholic Jesuit colleges alike, it had for the latter the additional aim of religious proselytism. In Jesuit dramas, which were always written and performed in Latin, the division of the stage into three levels – earth, heaven and hell – and the sensory effects of incense (or stink-bombs, depending on the destiny of the main character) made the message entertainingly accessible even to those – and they were many – who could not understand Latin. Contemporaries saw the functional character of literature as natural and positive: the poet sharpened the senses, enlightened the mind, cautioned the rebellious and consoled the sad. Thus devotional literature could assist the containment of grief, and grief could be articulated in the form of a poem, letter, song, obituary or funeral oration. Examples of the literature of bereavement vary from Gryphius's short poem on the death of his little niece to the often anonymous part-songs which the family of the deceased would sing, each member having an appropriate solo verse in turn to express the feelings of father, mother, wife, husband, child and so on. Such songs were a kind of intimate funeral service which might subsequently be printed for distribution in the circle of family and friends together with a formal necrology. In the seventeenth century, by contrast with the twentieth, death was something to be shared, like birth and every other human event.

Literature was 'useful' in more senses than one. When writing a funeral oration or a graduation poem, the poet looked at the work of established authors and literary models and drew on their poetic and rhetorical devices. It was not the individual voice that mattered so much as the pleasing form given to recognized and authoritative ideas. The poet was, above all else, a learned author. The male writer learnt his poetic craft at school and university or from tutors, whether in the form of private teachers or published manuals on the art of poetry. Women writers learnt theirs from their own reading and private study and were therefore almost always the wives or daughters of men of substance, typical examples being Sibylle Schwarz and Catharina von Greiffenberg. More unusually, they had the benefit of a propitious cultural environment, as was the case with Sibylle Ursula, daughter of the book-loving Duke August of Brunswick-Wolfenbüttel, who was encouraged as a girl to read and translate French courtly novels. Seventeenth-century authors were always conscious of writing in a tradition which drew its authority from classical antiquity and, increasingly, from the writing of the European Renaissance. Hence long years of study often preceded ventures into print. How erudite the seventeenth-century writer could be is exemplified by the brilliant Silesian woman astronomer, Maria Cunitz (1610–64), a passionate devotee of calculus, who used her own methods and findings to update the astronomical tables of Johannes Kepler in her 550-page bilingual *Urania propitia* of 1650, in which she aimed to engage the interest of scholars while making science accessible to ordinary readers.

The impact of war on authors' lives through their own experience and that of their contemporaries provided the stuff of some of the finest and most varied writing of the German seventeenth century. By accelerating the destruction of the feudal nobility's political independence in favour of princes and their absolute estates, the wars of the period also changed the condition of the educated middle classes. Increasingly, as the century advanced, princes recruited noblemen rather than burghers for their armies and emergent civil services. But although so many German princes between 1648 and 1789 aspired to model their courts on that of France, the contrast in terms of cultural life between France's centralism and the fragmentation of the German empire could hardly have been more marked. Similarly, in the second half of the century, the imperial cities (such as Nuremberg and Augsburg) were progressively replaced as patrons and focuses of artistic activity by the princely courts, often situated in smaller towns. It was to the local rulers at small courts such as those at Wolfenbüttel, Eutin and Cöthen, to greater princes, and even to the Emperor himself at the Habsburg court of Vienna, that writers looked for status, honoraria and even, with luck, ennoblement and coronation as a poet laureate, an honour which was in the gift of many German potentates and noblemen. In the early decades of the century non-aristocratic poets such as Opitz, Weckherlin, Zincgref or Fleming were sometimes entrusted with diplomatic missions; by the end of the century, in their function as court poets, some writers of middle-class origin were employed to organize court festivals or to act as librarians and historians. But often enough the writer was a schoolmaster or clergyman with little access to the world of the great, though with an equally evident public function in these professional capacities.

Where, then, are the exemplary places of seventeenth-century German literature? The answer is complicated by twentieth-century history. Many centres of seventeenth-century

German literary life lay on the periphery of the Empire or, indeed, beyond its boundaries. Amongst the most important were Breslau, Danzig and Thorn to the north and east, cities which were German-speaking trading centres, self-governing but under the nominal tutelage of the Polish crown. For many years they have been difficult of access behind the Iron Curtain; some, such as Königsberg (Kaliningrad since 1945) in East Prussia, have been virtually obliterated and live on only in the imagination. The literary landscape of the baroque age thus demands more than a little interest in geography on the part of the contemporary English-speaking reader and student. Today, thanks to the events of the late autumn and winter of 1989, historic places, albeit now with Polish, Czech, Hungarian, Baltic or Romanian names, have recovered their sense of identity, though Breslau is now Wrocław, Danzig Gdánsk, Thorn Torún and Siebenbürgen Transylvania.

The 'exemplary place' of German baroque literature is thus to be found in no one location but scattered all over the map of what, in the seventeenth century, was the German-speaking part of Europe. Often it is a question of literary genre: the pastoral poem, for instance, was associated with the patrician cities of Nuremberg and Königsberg, while the simple song also flourished both in Leipzig and in smaller university towns such as Heidelberg. But of all the provinces of the vast and unwieldy Holy Roman Empire – that monster, as the lawyer and historian Samuel Pufendorf described it in 1667 – it is Silesia (since 1945, part of Poland) that one associates above all with the German literary culture of the period. So many of the most celebrated poets of the age came from Silesia: Opitz and Gryphius, Kuhlmann, Scheffler and Logau, Lohenstein and Hoffmannswaldau, and many more. Breslau, its capital, surely has the best claim to be called the most exemplary place of German baroque literature, not least on account of its remarkable schools, the Protestant grammar schools of St Elizabeth and St Mary Magdalene (known as the Elisabethanäum and Magdalenäum), at which most of Silesia's major authors were educated. It was at these two Breslau schools that virtually all the most important dramas of seventeenth-century Germany were staged, a tradition of public performance for both didactic and entertainment purposes which reached its climax in the 1660s, when masterpieces by Gryphius, Lohenstein and Hallmann were simultaneously premiered. It has been claimed that the dramatic quality of these school plays owed much to the tense political situation of the city. Silesia had owed allegiance to the Bohemian crown for several centuries, but Bohemia had then been incorporated into the territories of the House of Habsburg. The independence of Breslau and other Silesian cities was therefore threatened by Habsburg expansion, for which, in the eyes of many, the Counter-Reformation offensive spearheaded by the Jesuits was preparing the way. Breslau, which had been one of the first major German cities to embrace the Lutheran Reformation, felt it had much to lose. But at least it gained a Catholic university, the Leopoldinum, founded in 1702, after it had finally passed into Habsburg hands. Silesia's lack of a university of its own during the seventeenth century had one significant benefit: it encouraged Silesia's bright young men to travel far afield in pursuit of a higher education and professional experience. Opitz reached the German-speaking Lutheran area of Siebenbürgen in what is now Romania; Gryphius lectured for several years on various erudite humanist and scientific subjects at the Dutch university of Leyden, then the most advanced in Europe, before proceeding to Paris, Venice and Rome; Lohenstein and Hoffmannswaldau both embarked on the grand tours preferred by wealthier young men. When, later, Hoffmannswaldau became the chief education officer for the city council of Breslau, he threw his weight behind the school productions of the morally daring and politically controversial plays which his contemporaries were writing. Small wonder, therefore, that a fascination with political debate and foreign parts are recurrent features of Breslau's seventeenth-century literature.

An understanding of the importance of denominational allegiance is central to the full appreciation of the baroque age. In the Catholic regions of Austria and southern Germany the baroque sermon as delivered by its finest practitioners, such as Abraham a Sancta Clara and Laurentius von Schnüffis, was every bit as much a 'performance' as what was taking place on stage in Breslau's schools. But southern Germany and Austria did not participate in the prosodic and linguistic reforms associated with Martin Opitz. Most educated Catholic authors and their readers retained their preference for Latin, but when they wrote for a larger audience or when their work was intended to be read aloud, they wrote in a German which retained the linguistic features characteristic of west and south Germany. This came to be known as 'upper German' (*Oberdeutsch*) as against the standardized written 'New High German' (*Schriftdeutsch*) favoured throughout Protestant Germany and in Protestant Switzerland, and based on the East Saxon or Meissen usage which Luther had popularized with his translation of the Bible. The reason for the Catholics' reluctance to accept language reforms based on normative linguistic and poetic conventions was not simply prejudice against '*Lutherisch Deutsch*', though that played a part. It derived from a belief that linguistic variety represented the true character of the German Empire and that their own use of language was closer to the people and less elitist than the new Opitzian ideals of stylistic decorum and grammatical correctness; they felt that to inhibit the use of the traditional features and forms of popular literature for the sake of standard but 'elevated' language and poetic diction would stunt creativity and impair communication. Many Catholic baroque writers, including Friedrich Spee von Langenfeld, Abraham a Sancta Clara and Johannes Scheffler (better known as Angelus Silesius or 'the Silesian angel'), proved this point in their ability to appeal both to the common people and to the educated classes. The song-writers of Protestant Leipzig and Königsberg also aimed to write appealingly in unaffected German which conformed to Opitzian grammatical correctness while also remaining true to the easy comprehensibility which was, after all, one of Opitz's prime objectives.

The Habsburg court physician Hippolytus Guarinonius liked to prescribe rhubarb to refresh the stomach and the Italian comedians to delight and stimulate the mind. The Italian players performed their *commedia dell'arte* plays mainly in the courts in the south of the Empire. But there was another type of comedy in seventeenth-century Germany which provided an alternative to the closed society in which the *poeta doctus*, the learned poet, operated and which was to have an important impact on the German theatre of the future by influencing Lessing and Tieck on the one hand and the actor-playwrights of the Viennese popular theatre on the other. These were the strolling players who performed at fairs and who, like the troupe in *Hamlet*, were sometimes invited to display their skills at the courts of princes. Originally they came over from England: one famous troupe was recommended to the Duke of Brunswick by his brother-in-law the King of Denmark in 1592 after it had performed at Elsinore. They acted English plays, including Marlowe's *Doctor Faustus*, and *Der Jude von Venedig*, a simplified adaptation of Shakespeare's *Merchant of Venice*, and they quickly realized that to succeed in Germany they had to perform their plays in German. Seventeenth-century Germans had not yet lost their forebears' sense of fun, and these '*Englische Comödianten*' no doubt owed their popularity most of all to the fact that their plays featured the 'funny man', Pickled Herring (Pickelhering), the forerunner of Hans Wurst (Jack Sausage), the sly fool whom we meet in many guises in later comic theatre. The so-called *Englische Comödianten* were a characteristic feature of German inns and fairgrounds during the seventeenth century. Their theatrical troupes began to include women around 1650.

Nowadays the age of the baroque is the one which is most likely to be excluded from the syllabus of the average university department of German studies outside Germany, and to be underrepresented in German-speaking universities. True, many seventeenth-century texts are long: Lohenstein's novel *Arminius* runs to 5000 pages, while Duke Anton Ulrich of Brunswick, with his unfinished 7000-page novel *Octavia*, rivals the twentieth-century Austrian novelist Robert Musil himself. Most are initially difficult to get into for readers brought up in a culture which offers little training in classical rhetoric and poetics, so crucial to a proper understanding of the character and function of seventeenth-century German literature. For almost two centuries, from Gottsched on, the canon of German literature virtually excluded it, thus depriving it of critical standing. This neglect was exacerbated by the fact that until the second half of the twentieth century, German literary history was based on the Romantic notion of original genius, of which Goethe was seen as the greatest example. A greater understanding of rhetoric and poetics has encouraged scholars, at least, to reappraise it, a process to which English-speaking Germanists, notably in the United States, have made a signal contribution. Despite the learned apparatus in which their texts are embedded, and behind their ponderous mien and gait and their normative, ritualized speech, baroque writers were men or women of passion, committed to the task of persuading, impressing and convincing reader and audience alike. Their originality lies not so much in the novelty of their thoughts, though their thoughts may nowadays seem novel to readers who do not share their intellectual and cultural background. Rather it lies in the ingenious presentation of formulas, themes and arguments so as to move, improve and delight. It should not surprise us that it was not so much antiquarian academics as Expressionist poets who, in the early decades of the twentieth century, began to rediscover this long-lost literature, so unjustly ostracized in the German literary canon. They, and especially the wartime generation that came after them, recognized in the work of poets such as Gryphius and Fleming experiences analogous to theirs: a metaphysical *angst* in the case of the baroque poets, an existential *angst* in their own. They were also fascinated by the linguistic devices and syntactical strategies used by baroque poets such as Quirinus Kuhlmann and Catharina von Greiffenberg to give expression to intense religious experience, and by Opitz and Gryphius to express the harsher experiences of war, hunger, plague, natural disasters and the persecution of the marginalized. After all, was it not a Jesuit, Friedrich von Spee, author of playful religious love poetry, who wrote a powerful tract against witchcraft and who, as chaplain to the wretched victims, saw his own hair whiten prematurely in his thirties at the scenes he witnessed? A generation after the Expressionists, Reinhold Schneider, an opponent of National Socialism who had chosen to stay in Germany, wrote a short story with Spee as its hero: *Der Tröster* ('The comforter', 1934). It was the first literary work to condemn Hitler's concentration camps, and it did so by drawing an implicit analogy between the persecution of the Jews and the seventeenth-century witch-hunts, both of which were initiated by a process which marginalized and then dehumanized its victims.

The German baroque age is not impenetrable to the modern reader. It deserves its place in the syllabus of every university course in German studies. Not least among its appealing features – and one which explains its power to attract some of the leading minds in *Germanistik* from the 1960s on – is its openness to other European literatures and cultures, notably, but not only, those of France, the Netherlands, Italy, Spain and Britain. From these and other countries came powerful and beneficial stimuli which offset that other, destructive, European influence with which seventeenth-century Germany had to contend: the hordes of Spanish, Danish, Swedish, French, Hungarian and Croat troops who made Germany into a battleground from the start of the Thirty Years War in 1618 to 1681, the year when the city of Strasburg, which had contributed so much to Germany's literary culture, was taken by France during Louis XIV's protracted wars of expansion.

## Opitz: The Father of German Literature

The vast majority of German writers from the late Middle Ages right up to the time of Goethe and Schiller were the products of a classical education, and Martin Opitz was no exception. Latin was the language in which their minds had been trained: German did not replace it at school or university until well into the eighteenth century. The effects of this early training are everywhere to be seen. They are especially noticeable in the desire to reappraise the legacy of classical antiquity by selecting from it those elements still relevant to modern times. Its frequent references to classical history and mythology make much seventeenth- and eighteenth-century literature difficult for modern readers, but educated contemporaries responded to them with pleasure. Only in the Church and in the world of business was the vernacular predominant: it was mainly to reach relatively uneducated people that authors needed to have recourse to it. But the uneducated represented a large section of contemporary society and therefore of the potential reading public. They ranged from the landed gentry and the urban merchant class to the artisans and small-town dwellers, and of course the peasantry, which still made up the bulk of the German population. Vernacular literature was therefore aimed at a more popular reader-ship than its Latin counterpart. But for men of letters it also became a matter of personal and national pride to convey their own classically based aesthetic and intellectual awareness to this new readership. After all, this had already been taking place with a large measure of success in neighbouring countries such as France and England, so why not in Germany too? As Opitz soon came to realize, the Netherlands provided a telling model of what could be achieved, for there a language closely related to German had already begun to show itself capable of becoming a satisfactory medium for the expression and transmission of modern Renaissance ideas and subject-matter.

In Germany the literary Renaissance began in earnest with Opitz, justifying the title 'father of German literature' which was given him until well into the eighteenth century. He devised his comprehensive scheme for the adoption of German as a literary language while still at school at Beuthen in Silesia, and formulated it in a long Latin essay, *Aristarchus sive de contemptu linguae teutonicae* (1617), which addressed the contempt in which the 'teutonic language' was held by the educated minority, Aristarchus being the prototype of the judicious critic. In his essay Opitz set about defending and demonstrating its intrinsic qualities to an established intelligentsia which still tended to regard it with suspicion and disdain. Within a few years he had become an admired writer of German, equally at home in all the genres his European contemporaries valued. His works were conceived and presented as tangible examples of the German language's ability to act as the medium for a modern literature capable of standing comparison with those of Italy and France, Europe's two most advanced Renaissance cultures. In this lifelong mission, Opitz was encouraged by the example of Dutch, the language most closely related to German, which was already demonstrating that no thought was too subtle and no form too sophisticated for it to be formulated and handled in the vernacular. Paradoxically, his generation was to witness the final separation between Dutch and German, a development encouraged by the political events of the period, which resulted in the independence of the United Provinces of the Netherlands and the 'Golden Age' of Dutch art and literature. No such positive developments took place in Germany. Although many educated Germans studied in Holland or visited it as tutors to wealthy young men on their European grand tours, its influence on the development of German literary culture decreased once it had served its function as a springboard for the new direction which literature in Germany was beginning to take in the 1620s.

Opitz's reforms, foreshadowed in his 1617 essay and formulated in German in 1624 in his seminal theoretical treatise *Buch von der deutschen Poeterey*, coincided with the outbreak and first phase of the Thirty Years War and the prolonged period of sporadic warfare and political instability which then began to engulf most parts of Germany. Such a climate was hardly conducive to the attainment of his cultural aims. Yet they were shared by many contemporaries. In 1617, the same year as the *Aristarchus* essay, Prince Ludwig of Anhalt-Cöthen, a minor German territorial ruler, founded the *Fruchtbringende Gesellschaft* or 'Fruitbearing Society' on the model of the Florentine Accademia della Crusca of which he was a member. By enlisting noble and aristocratic members all over Germany, as well as commoners with a gift for poetry, this organization became the chief mechanism and mouthpiece for the exchange of secular cultural ideas in a society in many respects hostile to them, yet which attached great importance to rank and status. To consider the prominent authors of the seventeenth century in isolation and ignore the cultural network which linked educational institutions, authors, publishers, learned societies, the higher echelons of society, and the relatively small but widely distributed reading public, is to fail to see them in their true context or to appreciate their aesthetic achievements in an accurate light.

Many wrote in both Latin and German, no doubt feeling that their command of the former was more solid and that in it they were in better company. Such bilingualism was a challenge, however, rather than a drawback; after all, it encouraged attention to grammatical correctness, stylistic variety and respect for classical models, features which soon became almost as characteristic of literature in the vernacular as they were of writing in Latin. The result can be syntactically heavy-going and ponderously erudite, and often out of the reach both of modern readers, who lack a correspondingly learned background, and of less well-educated seventeenth-century readers, too. But writers with an original voice and with something to say were able to rise above the general norm and can still command respect and admiration today. Apart from Opitz himself, one of the first to gain a lasting reputation for his creative work in the medium of German was Paul Fleming, a highly educated Saxon physician who trained at Leipzig and spent his crucial years from 1633 to 1639 as a member of a trade mission to Muscovy and Persia. Fleming's Latin verse proclaimed him to be a writer who identified with the European Renaissance tradition, while his German poems showed his responsiveness to the language of Luther's Bible and the hymns of the Lutheran Church. Collected and published after his early death (*Teutsche Poemata*, 1646), they combine elegance of form with a winning sincerity of tone which set an appropriate model for his age and were admired long after it. Like Opitz, Fleming was soon accepted as a classic. He was urbane, devout, intense and deeply conscious of his obligation to aid the literary renewal of his nation, whose misfortunes he deplored.

Like many of his contemporaries, Fleming wrote poems in a wide variety of forms, the sonnet and the strophic hymn or song being his favourites. Opitz, however, knew that a living literature must achieve excellence in prose and drama, too, and felt it his duty to set an example in these genres as well, although he was not a born novelist or playwright. Because he had relatively little to say or because he knew that big names would make a bigger impression, he turned to translation and by the end of his career had supplied German readers with models of tragic drama, the novel, an operatic libretto and didactic verse which were readily accepted as authoritative. His choice of texts and authors reveals his underlying purpose and sure eye for the requirements of a new and up-to-date cultivated readership such as was coming into existence throughout the German-speaking world. Sophocles and Seneca provided the models for tragic drama; Sir Philip Sidney's pastoral novel *Arcadia* (1590) and John Barclay's Latin political romance *Argenis* (1621) represented two of the favourite types of fiction in contemporary Europe; Petrarch and Ronsard embodied the tradition which dominated love poetry in western and central Europe from the early fourteenth century to the end of the seventeenth century. The effect of Opitz's work amounted to a fundamental revolution in taste. By setting up models and patterns of excellence he encouraged imitation, but by being ready from the early days of his career to write verse to order, he demonstrated that poetry was marketable and that the production of good-quality occasional verse created a solid financial and social basis for a man of letters. Whether they belonged to the aristocracy, the landed gentry or the urban middle class, individuals could become sponsors and consumers of poetry. The result was the emergence of a standard of appreciative competence throughout the German-speaking lands, which in its turn was to provide the essential basis for literature, and especially for poetry, for the next 200 years.

Opitz was essentially an instigator of change and an intermediary between the European literary culture of his day and his fellow countrymen, who had remained largely unaware of the aesthetic impact of the Renaissance. But in his own right he could achieve a degree of excellence which enabled him to retain his authoritative status as a classic well into the eighteenth century. The set of four long poems which were his youthful response to the vicissitudes of the first phase of the Thirty Years War remain a powerful if seldom-read example of their kind: sombre, graphic, indignant and thoughtful by turns, they reflect the circumstances and atmosphere in which they were written. His discursive poems, for their part, reveal the personal interests and thought-processes of the man: perhaps the finest is *Zlatna*, a poem which explores the fragile gift of peace of mind in an unstable world in terms of the poet's happy recollections of the visit he paid to the country estate of a man who was himself a refugee from religious strife in war-torn western Europe, and who befriended him during the year he spent as a young teacher in German-speaking Siebenbürgen (Transylvania) in what is now Romania. But at the heart of Opitz's poetic crusade the sonnet held pride of place. The examples he provided with both original poems and translations established it as the favourite lyric form in Germany until the early eighteenth century, and resulted in a rich output by countless poets and poetasters, their generally competent standard now and then surpassed by the work of an author with something new or more pressing to say, such as Paul Fleming, whose passionate love sonnets are as fine as his impassioned religious ones. Even lesser lyric voices could sometimes create a sonnet which rises above the clichés of expression and rhyme which soon became the common currency of the genre: David Schirmer is an instance, and so too is his female contemporary, the talented but short-lived Sibylle Schwarz. Such minor poets belonged to a generation which also produced the major figures of what modern literary historians, especially in Germany, have called the German baroque age. Among them two are so outstanding that their achievement was not to be equalled, let alone surpassed, for the next hundred years: Andreas Gryphius and Catharina Regina von Greiffenberg.

## Gryphius and Greiffenberg

Both were Lutheran Protestants: he from Silesia, she from Lower Austria; both were highly intelligent, and both possessed a remarkable command of their own language and a sure sense of its expressive potential. Gryphius was a man of wide-ranging interests, who spent ten years studying and teaching in Holland, and then visited France and Italy before returning to his native town of Glogau to take up a senior administrative post. Greiffenberg, too, enjoyed an intensive and wide-ranging education, though in her own home in Lower Austria, but found her freedom circumscribed by Counter-Reformation restrictions and the persistent pressure of an uncle who insisted on marrying her. And both poets made the sonnet form their own by using it to express their most personal concerns. But here the obvious similarity ends. The poetry of Gryphius is pervaded by a sense of impermanence, of time passing and appearances deceiving, and of his own mortality, gloomy preoccupations offset by his intellectual curiosity and his profound belief in the certainty of spiritual values. Greiffenberg's poetry is equally introspective, but the focus of her creativity is the relationship between her personal life and her Christian faith.

The 250 sonnets of Greiffenberg's *Geistliche Sonnette, Lieder und Gedichte* ('Spiritual Sonnets, Songs and Poems'), published in Nuremberg in 1662 when she was 29, explore what she felt was her calling to praise God by probing the mysterious workings of divine providence and observing her own responses to its decrees, responses which ranged from fright to fortitude, and from resistance to resignation and total submission. They are an interior monologue in lyric form which imbues the traditional elements of devotional and mystical writing with a sense of ever-renewed wonder and delight at the natural phenomena of the world around her and a zest for the linguistic potential of the new poetic language Opitz had opened up, with its rich opportunities for creating hitherto unspoken words to express fresh thoughts. Nouns and adjectives are unexpectedly put together to describe the almost ineffable with startling precision, as when in one of her sonnets she captures the essence of divine inspiration in terms of light and movement, colour and shadow, and reflections in water. Not for nothing has she been hailed as the first nature poet in German and as the precursor of Annette von Droste-Hülshoff, Germany's outstanding nineteenth-century Catholic woman poet. Her contemporaries, too, were well aware of her genius: the influential Protestant circle of male writers in Nuremberg welcomed her as their equal, and in Catholic circles, too, her religious poems were studied and admired. These were remarkable achievements for a woman in an age dominated by male values and religious discord; indeed she spent her later years attempting, but in vain, to persuade men of their age's tragic and impious folly, and was not afraid to approach the Emperor, Leopold I, to further her crusade.

Gryphius, too, witnessed religious strife at first hand, and some of his finest poetry is a direct response to his boyhood experiences of war, fire, pestilence and death. During his career he wrote some 270 sonnets, which appeared in various publications between 1637 and 1698, when his son Christian, the headmaster of the school of St Elizabeth in Breslau, issued a posthumous collection. He tended to divide them, according to prevalent convention, into those on secular subjects and those of an explicitly religious kind, though the interpenetration of life and religious faith, and of human and divine love, was as obvious to him as it was to most German writers of the seventeenth century. The range of subjects he treated is wider than Greiffenberg's, as he adopted the fashionable new notion of occasional verse in German and raised it to its highest potential. People, objects and events all kindled his creativity, but the 'sonorous voice' for which his contemporaries most admired him can be heard to best effect in those sonnets and other poems where he broods on the vagaries of life and their deeper, darker implications. His sonnets on the vanity of earthly life and the transience of all human endeavour, and those in which he conveys the protracted agony and fevered fears of the sickbed, are amongst the most powerful of their kind in any language. Yet he can capture the essence of rare, fleeting moments, too, as in his few and highly personal love poems. If Greiffenberg's word-paintings reveal to us the intimate workings of an inner life, Gryphius, in the intense introspections of the sonnets he composed with himself as subject, leaves us with a sequence of penetrating self-portraits that make him a Rembrandt in words.

## Other Poets of the German Baroque

As lyric poets Gryphius and Greiffenberg tower above most of their contemporaries, whose generally competent poems are apt to flounder between the urge to display erudition and the temptation to juggle with the verbal conventions in which they felt stock sentiments should be expressed. Opitz had shown the way, and a great many writers tried to follow, yet the majority of seventeenth-century German poets seldom managed to strike the elegantly easy manner that characterizes the love poetry of their French, English and Dutch counterparts, or to get beyond imitative convention when they turned to the pastoral mode in the manner of the Italians. Much pleasant but unmemorable verse was produced, especially by groups of poets working in places as far apart as Königsberg, Nuremberg and Leipzig, but few achieved anything in the less serious vein to compare with the ornate sophistication and flamboyance of the baroque poets of Spain and Italy who were often their models, or the complex directness of the English metaphysical poets who were their close contemporaries. But there is one exception: Christian Hoffmann von Hoffmannswaldau, a Silesian writer from Breslau, whose brittle show of *joie de vivre* is built with clever verbal artistry over a disenchanted acceptance of life's darker side. Here German seventeenth-century literature found itself in line at last with the prevailing literary culture of Europe, an impression confirmed by Hoffmannswaldau's translation (published in 1679 but completed by 1652) of one of the key works of the baroque age, Guarini's dramatic pastoral poem *Il pastor fido* ('The Faithful Shepherd'), which first appeared in Italy in 1590. Esteemed by his contemporaries (and with good reason) but frowned upon by later generations for his apparent lack of decorum and moral fibre, Hoffmannswaldau successfully showed that even a German could write good amorous and erotic baroque verse. A host of admirers set to work to emulate his manner, though seldom with comparable success: among the best are Heinrich Mühlpfort, Daniel Casper von Lohenstein, and some of the contributors to the poetic anthologies associated with the name of Benjamin Neukirch which appeared during the 1690s.

Seen in the broader European context, there can be little doubt that the German poets of the mid-seventeenth century were most at home in poetry of a more serious kind: on the whole their devotional poems were finer than their love lyrics, and their conceits and word-play more successful when they relied on knowledge rather than wit for their effect. Sometimes, however, they could equal the best of their European contemporaries. Johannes Scheffler, for example, better known as Angelus Silesius, attains a degree of compression, intellectual agility and verbal fire only possible once a language has become the responsive material of an individual temperament or mind. A physician by training (he studied medicine and law at Strasburg and Leyden and took his PhD and MD in Padua) and a Catholic convert, he was able to concentrate his religious experience in the self-contained rhyming couplets or epigrams, some 1600 of them, of his *Geistreiche Sinn- und Schlußreime* (Vienna, 1657), later and better known as *Der cherubinische Wandersmann* ('The cherubic wanderer'), and found expression for his love of the Almighty in the passionate spiritual lyrics of *Heilige Seelen-Lust* ('The holy delight of the soul'), published the same year in his native Breslau.

At the opposite extreme of the period's expressive spectrum and rich vein of devotional poetry is Paul Gerhardt. His work reveals the continuity linking the new-found faith of the sixteenth-century Lutheran reformers and the trust in God and love of the natural world of later writers such as Matthias Claudius and Joseph von Eichendorff. He represents another vital aspect of German seventeenth-century literary activity: he is one of the very greatest of Germany's many fine hymn-writers – some Catholic, most of them Protestant – who ensured the hymn its central and enduring place in the evolution of German literature. It is hardly surprising that in Germany's Protestant churches the *Gesangbuch* or hymn book took the place of the Roman Catholic missal and became their counterpart to the Church of England's Book of Common Prayer. Gerhardt is the master of the art of expressing complex spiritual and theological themes in straightforward unadorned language without forfeiting depth and emotional power. Many of his hymns became as familiar to Germans as their favourite folksongs; indeed for many ordinary German people hymns have been their sole encounter with the language, imagery and sentiments of poetry. And like folksong, hymns are an interface between literary and musical culture: the tunes to which Gerhardt's 'Nun ruhen alle Wälder' and 'O Haupt voll Blut und Wunden' are sung became an inseparable part of the musical world of Johann Sebastian Bach and many other later composers.

## Grimmelshausen and the Novel

It was in the work of a novelist that the finest seventeenth-century poets found their equal. German readers had slowly acquired some familiarity with this new form of prose fiction from translations and original works which presented them with the various types of narrative writing enjoyed by contemporaries all over Europe, from the picaresque tales of the lives and adventures of rogues to the complicated romantic ramifications of courtly pseudo-historical romances, a form particularly popular in France, and the kaleidoscopically rotating love affairs of their pastoral equivalents. The standard of most seventeenth-century German novels, both serious and lightweight, and on every stylistic level, was undistinguished, and their general lack of fluency and narrative momentum have prevented them from surviving as part of the living tradition of German literature. From the mid-eighteenth century on they began to be forgotten – with one extraordinary exception: *Der abentheuerliche Simplicissimus Teutsch* (1668) by Hans Jacob Christoffel von Grimmelshausen. Here a German author outstripped his European contemporaries by writing a fiction which transcends the conventions of its day in the way it skilfully combines the complex artificiality of the fashionable romance with the down-to-earth worm's-eye view of the world associated with the picaresque novel. Grimmelshausen's literary debts were many: Charles Sorel's *Francion* in France, Quevedo's *Sueños* in Spain, even Sir Philip Sidney; but his fusion of his multiple precursors and his own experiences of life generates a narrative which is at one and the same time a vivid portrayal of the Thirty Years War in which it is set, and a pointer to future developments in the German novel from the age of Goethe and the Romantics, who rediscovered Grimmelshausen's anonymous masterpiece, to his twentieth-century admirers, such as Thomas Mann and especially Günter Grass, whose *Die Blechtrommel* ('The Tin Drum') is a masterpiece in the 'Simplician' manner.

*Simplicissimus* purports to be the account of a young man's adventures during a violent and unstable period, when living was a risk and premature death a fact of life. Its graphically recounted central storyline is bleak and boisterous by turns, racy and ironic; but these elements are distributed and controlled in a way that gives the novel a coherence which accounts for its original popularity and the esteem in which it has been held right up to the present day. Not since the *Ship of Fools* had a German author written a work which could exert such a persistent appeal yet be regarded by posterity – despite its unique qualities – as so characteristic of its age: it is now the only work of its entire period with which most Germans are at all familiar. Some of its episodes are clearly rooted in vernacular storytelling and in the satirical writing of the sixteenth and early seventeenth centuries, and bring to it a welcome touch of homely realism; but the episodes in which its central figure finds his clueless personality being filled out by life point in another direction. The unsteady progress of young Simplex towards a partial understanding of his own humanity and the ways in which it relates to the apparently arbitrary nature of life around him and to the immutable but inscrutable will of the Almighty contain elements and episodes which bring it into the vicinity of Bunyan's realistically allegorical *Pilgrim's Progress*, published exactly ten years later in 1678. But when, towards the end of the novel, Simplex retreats to a desert island to live a hermit's life, Grimmelshausen's masterpiece looks forward to Defoe's *Robinson Crusoe* (1719), while at the same time using the episode as an extended metaphor of withdrawal from a deceitful world, a favourite theme of baroque literature all over Europe.

Like Opitz, Grimmelshausen set a precedent and had his admirers. He therefore followed his novel with three sequels, of which the best known is the scurrilously lively mock autobiography of his hero's female counterpart, the army caterer Mother Courage (*Trutz Simplex: oder Ausführliche und wunderseltsame Lebensbeschreibung der Ertzbetrügerin und Landstörzerin Courasche*, 'Counter-Simplex or the arch-cheat and vagrant Courasche's full and very strange account of her life', 1670). His memorably down-to-earth character and her struggle for survival amidst the changing fortunes of the seemingly endless Thirty Years War made a successful twentieth-century comeback in Bertolt Brecht's play *Mutter Courage und ihre Kinder* (1941), which adds extra ideological emphasis and a touch of sentimentality to Grimmelshausen's wry, hard-hitting tale of how a woman develops her survival skills in a barbaric male world. These sequels revitalized the German tradition of satirical writing, but their most notable later imitations are marked by a profound change of tone and purpose, and belong to a different era.

## Silesian Drama

Opitz not only laid the foundations for seventeenth-century lyric poetry and narrative prose; with his fine translations of Seneca's then much-admired tragedy *Troades* ('The Trojan Women') in 1625 and of Sophocles' *Antigone* in 1636, he also provided a model for the serious drama of the decades that followed. This was five-act tragedy with choruses after each of the first four acts and written in six-foot rhyming iambic couplets, a set of formal conventions which he borrowed from the example of the Dutch, and which put to dramatic use the so-called alexandrine or twelve-syllable line divided in the middle which he and they recommended for most serious forms of poetry. The German alexandrine was two syllables longer and also less flexible than the iambic pentameter or five-foot ten-syllable line of English blank verse, and when it was used in drama, as opposed to the sonnet, the result was a species of tragic play in verse heavily laden with words and to modern ears strangely out of keeping with a concept of drama which centres on action and momentum. Its tendency to employ verbose rhetorical devices, to create a sense of drama without having to resort to physical action, seems also oddly out of keeping – at least to modern tastes – with the performers for whom these plays were written and who seem to have been the sole performers of tragedy until the rise of the commercial theatre in the eighteenth century. These were the boys of the leading grammar schools in Breslau and other towns and cities, if and when the plays were taken up elsewhere: documentary evidence is scant, though there are records of performances at German courts and even as far away as Regensburg, the seat of the imperial Diet, and Sitten (now Sion in Switzerland). For a combination of reasons, it was Breslau's two rival schools, the Elisabethanäum and Magdalenäum, that were almost exclusively responsible for the theatrical evolution of seventeenth-century Germany because they trained two of its best playwrights and staged the work of all three.

The 'golden age' of Breslau school drama – and of the baroque theatre in Germany – occurred between 1650 and 1672, and witnessed the artistic rivalry of three authors who managed to bring as near to perfection as they could the somewhat cumbersome form Opitz had recommended: these were Andreas Gryphius and Daniel Casper von Lohenstein, who were professional men also admired as poets, and Johann Christian Hallmann, who was drawn to the stage and attempted to live by his pen. All three nearly always chose historical subjects for their plays, though, unlike their English precursors and more like their French contemporaries, of whom they were hardly aware, they never drew on the history of their own country, preferring to find their material in the world of ancient Rome – but never Greece, and never classical mythology – or to take it from the recent history of other countries on the periphery of their world: thus England provided Gryphius with the tragedy of Charles I and Hallmann with that of Catherine of Aragon, while seventeenth-century Turkey supplied Lohenstein with the bloody end of Sultan Ibrahim. Like their great French contemporary, Pierre Corneille, all three wrote tragedies set in imperial Rome; but the parallels are few despite the similarity of setting and themes.

The central and dominant theme round which Gryphius built his five tragedies is the clash of loyalties that arises as soon as one man tries to wield absolute power. He examines the corrupting influence of absolute power from a legal and moral angle in *Papinianus*, set in the corridors of power in Rome as the Emperor Caracalla murders his brother and seizes the throne and then orders Papinianus, his chief legal adviser, to justify his action. He explores it from a religious and erotic angle in *Catharina von Georgien*, the dramatization of the recent fate of a Christian queen held hostage and finally put to death by the Shah of Persia. And in *Carolus Stuardus*, a play set in London in January 1649 and concentrating on what took place during the few hours leading up to the execution of Charles I, the theme is analysed from the contemporary political point of view: the result is a prototype of modern documentary drama which reveals how well informed its Breslau author was: he even revised it at the Restoration. Common to all three plays is the martyrdom of a human being who is essentially innocent, which gives them their central 'action'. But what really generates their dramatic force is the struggle in men's minds and hearts between the conflicting claims of loyalty, conscience, personal integrity and self-preservation, all of which play their part in Gryphius's first and most complex and ambivalent drama, *Leo Armenius*. This is set on Christmas Eve in orthodox Constantinople in the

Middle Ages, and reveals profound insights into the workings of human motivation, the relativity of guilt and innocence, destiny and divine providence, and a clear awareness of the potential of the stage to create moods and bring out significant contrasts by appealing to the eye and ear as well as to the attentive listening mind. In all Gryphius's plays a great poet speaks – perhaps most personally in the only major serious drama of the seventeenth century to take 'ordinary' events as its subject and 'ordinary' people as its characters: *Cardenio und Celinde*, a tormented study of the negative facets of love as well as of its redeeming features. Yet despite the excellence of such plays, German drama was later to develop along different lines; there may be similarities of theme and structure between Gryphius's *Catharina von Georgien* or *Carolus Stuardus* and Schiller's *Maria Stuart* or *Wallenstein*, but by the time Schiller was writing, a century and a half later, the influence of Shakespeare and the adoption of the five-foot unrhymed line of English high drama had ensured that Gryphius's plays and those of his contemporaries would be prevented from ever constituting a living part of the German repertoire; they were consigned instead to a marginal existence as seldom-studied literary texts.

The plays of Gryphius possess innate vitality and considerable dramatic force, though these are contained not so much in action – which is sparse – as in the crossfire of dialogue and debate. The six plays of Lohenstein are more overtly theatrical, though no less intellectual, in that they are conscious of being theatre and their main characters realize that they are acting out their parts. This is particularly the case in his *Cleopatra* (first performed in 1661), a treatment of a well-known subject which is closely based on historical sources but presented in the highly ornate rhetorical language of its author, one of the few seventeenth-century German writers to achieve the aesthetic aims of contemporary baroque art and literature: the result is disconcerting, and an acquired taste, perhaps, but it can stand up to close examination, as modern analysis has shown, as a penetrating study of what in the last resort makes people 'tick'. Lohenstein's Egyptian queen has to be brought to the extreme of her existential predicament to realize that her love for Antony, even after he is dead, is even more important to her than her hold on her rich kingdom, a hold which she is reluctantly forced to realize she will have to relinquish to the victorious Romans: pride combines with grief and with a desperate instinct for self-preservation which, paradoxically, she can only find in death. No German playwright had written plays of such psychological complexity and emotional range before, and for a century none would do so again. But a more rational age dismissed Lohenstein's six plays as improbable and overblown, and they sank into oblivion unplayed and unread.

The moral intensity of Gryphius and the incisive and passionate intellect of Lohenstein eluded their younger rival, Johann Christian Hallmann, whose efforts to secure the future of German baroque drama ultimately led to a dead end, as he seems to have come to realize. His plays are plays with words, virtuosic in their exuberance, but seldom capable of convincing us that there is any integral link between theatre and life. Increasingly he was drawn to exploit the potential of melodrama to use language, music and staging to forge a new form of entertainment designed to appeal to the senses rather than to the mind. In *Die sterbende Unschuld oder Catharina Königin in Engelland* ('Dying innocence, or Catherine Queen of England'), published in 1684 but performed earlier, he came near to striking a balance between the type of martyr drama he had inherited from Gryphius – we pity the innocent Catherine of Aragon and regard her odious husband, Henry VIII, with terror – and a new type of drama, still a long way in the future, which Wieland was to inaugurate in 1758 with his early tragedy *Lady Johanna Gray*, and in which a renewed and subtler effort was made to apply Aristotle's requirements of tragedy to a subject drawn from sixteenth-century English history and which again highlighted the tragic plight of an innocent woman. Potentially Hallmann's plays mark the apogee of the baroque era in German dramatic literature, but their author, who in the grammar schools of Breslau lacked the wider artistic opportunities available to his contemporaries in Rome, London and Paris, soon found that his aesthetic vision could not compete with the rising vogue of Italian opera. He sank into penurious oblivion and is now no more than a peripheral figure, though an interesting one, in Germany's literary and theatrical history. Even the date and place of his death are uncertain.

## Gryphius and Baroque Comedy

Though the literature of the seventeenth century in Germany may have lacked the exuberance and colour of the Italian baroque and the stylized intensity of French classicism, and preferred to dwell on the darker side of human experience, it was not without its lighter side. Like many another deep pessimist, even its greatest poet, Andreas Gryphius, had a sense of humour. His bewilderment at the incomprehensible vicissitudes of life, which marks his tragedies and introspective sonnets, also found expression in his handling of the misunderstandings and confusions of comedy, which reveals his sense of the absurd, as the title of one of them, *Absurda Comica, oder Herr Peter Squenz*, makes clear. Written around 1649, it parallels Shakespeare's *A Midsummer Night's Dream* in that it, too, presents the rehearsals and performance of the tragedy of 'Pyramus and Thisbe' by a group of craftsmen and artisans: being German, these are also proud to be Mastersingers, and therefore masters, so they suppose, of their own sophisticated art. What is absent from Gryphius's version is the supernatural world of fairyland: instead he gives a satirical, perhaps slightly condescending view of the clumsy efforts of ordinary folk to emulate their betters in a cultural and social setting which links Hans Sachs's sixteenth-century Nuremberg with Kotzebue's fictitious early nineteenth-century small town, Krähwinkel, reminding us that despite the manifold changes of the last 500 years German provincial life and attitudes have altered very little.

In comedy Gryphius never repeated himself. *Verliebtes Gespenst* ('The lovesick ghost') was written in 1660 for performance at the wedding of a Silesian duke and a countess palatine of the Rhine, and is a double play which resourcefully alternates a 'high' romantic comedy in the French manner with a 'low' comedy of peasant love-making, *Die geliebte Dornrose*, which centres on the appealing figure of Lise Dornrose ('hedge-rose') whose name speaks for itself. Derived from a play by his Dutch contemporary, Joost van den Vondel, it also in many ways anticipates Kleist's famous peasant comedy, *Der zerbrochene Krug* ('The broken jug') of 1808. Here, in Gryphius's dual foray into two different types of comedy, even the language preserves the hierarchy of society: one play is in correct Opitzian German, the other in the homely dialect of Silesia. Paradoxically, this is the main reason why the daringly unconventional *Die geliebte Dornrose* is the only seventeenth-century German play to have retained some hold on the modern stage. A different side of Gryphius is shown in his comedy *Horribilicribrifax teutsch*, written as the Thirty Years War, which had done so much to darken his disjointed world, was ending. The braggart soldier was one of the oldest stock characters in European comedy, going back to the *miles gloriosus* of the Roman playwright Plautus, and resurfacing, filled-out, in the person of Shakespeare's Falstaff or, more slimly, in the central figure of the one comedy in which Duke Heinrich Julius of Brunswick, the earliest German patron of English strolling players, came anywhere near to emulating the plays he so admired: his comedy *Vincentius*

*Ladislaus* (1593). But Gryphius goes one better. In his play he confronts one braggart army captain with another: Horribilicribrifax and Daradiridatumtarides are two extraordinarily rumbustious creations, who throw themselves headlong and with torrents of far-fetched oaths into a virtuoso farce involving seven pairs of lovers, some of whom are admirable and are rewarded with their heart's desire, for this is comedy. But among them is the dry-as-dust schoolmaster Sempronius, a classic send-up of German pedantry who looks far forward to Heinrich Mann's *Professor Unrat* of 1905. When he finds himself paired off with an ugly old procuress, cruel justice is done.

# 3

## The Augustan Age of German Literature

The period 1690–1745 was in many ways a golden age in the German-speaking lands. Though the Wars of the Spanish Succession, fought from 1700 to 1714 over the rival claims of the Austrian Habsburgs and the French Bourbons to the crown of Spain, were resolved in favour of Louis XIV's grandson, peace brought an important dividend to the Austrians thanks to their great general, Prince Eugene of Savoy; the Turkish menace was finally defeated and Austria consolidated her rule over the Balkans for the next two centuries. Peace prevailed, prosperity grew, the applied arts flourished, and a spate of building activity took place which has marked the landscape of almost every part of the German-speaking world ever since. Imposing monasteries and onion-domed white and gold city and village churches proclaimed the fervour and zeal of the Counter-Reformation, while princely palaces and country seats underlined the new power of the courts and the nobility. It was a period of architects of genius such as Fischer von Erlach (1656–1723), Johann Dientzenhofer (1663–1726) and Johann Lucas von Hildebrandt (1668–1745); the opulent baroque style they favoured set its imprint on the cultural area over which the House of Austria ruled, giving unity to its disparate territories, and was copied in many different idioms by the courts of Saxony and Bavaria, by the Rhenish and Franconian ecclesiastical princes and by the religious orders in monastery churches as far apart as Silesia and Switzerland, with more modest counterparts in countless towns, villages and country estates.

In the domains of philosophy and the sciences, too, activity was widespread and foundations were being laid for Germany's later achievements in both fields. Gottfried Wilhelm von Leibniz (1646–1716) addressed many aspects of intellectual inquiry from mathematics and calculators to metaphysics and international affairs and artificial language, but did so in French and Latin, while Christian Thomasius and Christian Wolff expounded the new philosophy of rationalism. The fact that much of what they wrote was in German (such as Thomasius's practical introduction to rationalism (1691) and the set of philosophical handbooks on a variety of topics, each entitled *Vernünftige Gedanken* ('Rational thoughts') and published by Wolff between 1719 and 1723) indicates that they were ready to accept the vernacular as a satisfactory alternative to Latin and were writing for a widening readership not necessarily conversant with it. It was a linguistic move which took place gradually over a long period and which resulted in a fruitful fusion of Germany's scholarly, Latin-based humanist tradition with its lively concern with modern issues and developments. While the thinkers were creating an abstract language which,

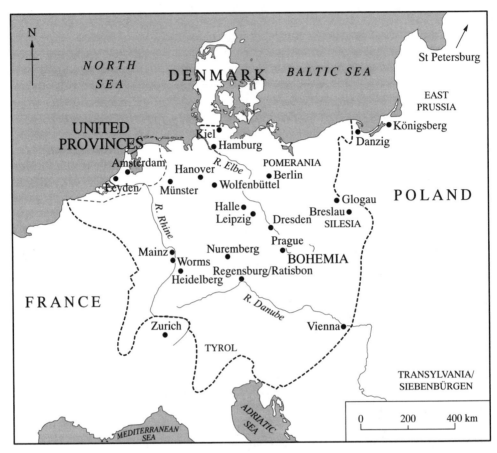

**Map 2**  Literary Germany and the Holy Roman Empire in the baroque and Augustan periods

on the analogy of ancient Greek, could give expression to ideas and was to dominate European philosophy – and increasingly historiography, economics, the natural sciences, and medicine and psychology, too, until well into the twentieth century – a parallel development was taking place in another domain. Drawing on the examples of Italy and France, the two predominant musical cultures of the period, German composers were creating a new musical language or *Tonsprache* which ensured the hegemony of German music for the next two centuries. Thus in the realm of 'classical' instrumental and symphonic music, and to a perhaps lesser degree in that of vocal music, the 'language' of German 'classical' music was to become more easily comprehensible internationally than the German language itself and more widely recognized than the literary masterpieces of Germany's poets, dramatists and prose writers. It is thus hardly surprising that in German literature the composer-musician rather than the poet or painter should so often assume the key role of the 'artist', and that this trend, which was to flourish in the Romantic era and culminate in Thomas Mann's *Doktor Faustus* (1947), was inaugurated in the 1690s by the 'musical' novels of the composer-author Wolfgang Caspar Printz. In the Lutheran parts of the German-speaking world especially, the Augustan age was an age of excellence in music. Every German principality and city prided itself on its musical reputation, and only the best would do. The musical scene in Hamburg was dominated by Georg Philipp Telemann (1681–1767), and Johann Sebastian Bach (1685–1750) occupied the distinguished position of organist and choirmaster at the Thomaskirche in the Saxon city of Leipzig.

It was here in Leipzig that some of the most energetic and best educated of Germany's burgher class helped to project the idea of a particular role for the intelligentsia in civic society and, in the course of time, to identify polite literature as the embodiment of its values. On the eve of the new century, the nascent self-awareness of such men showed itself in terms of convergence, rather than, as later, in terms of a conflict between the nobility and the educated burgher. Christian Thomasius, a young lecturer at Leipzig University in the 1680s, provided a role model for his kind by adopting the style of dress and social intercourse characteristic of the nobility. Thomasius found his place in literary histories as the first man to give lectures in the German language rather than in Latin, and to do so not in stuffy academic gown but modishly dressed in black and gold, a rapier at his side. Like some hippy professor of the 1960s he was making a statement; but it was surely no more than a provocative expression of his determination to carve out a role in the public sphere for an important and growing stratum of society: the educated middle class.

Leipzig was an appropriate setting for such a gesture. Its university was Germany's largest, and the city was one of Germany's most prosperous commercial centres; even though a nobleman could not acquire citizenship there, the city enjoyed special privileges conferred upon it by its territorial prince, Augustus the Strong, Elector of Saxony and sometime King of Poland. In the rationalist age of Leibniz and Wolff, Thomasius offered a programme for the German provincial intelligentsia for decades to come. There is a clear connection between the pioneering character of his German-language journal, the *Lustige und ernsthaftige Monatsgespräche* ('Amusing and serious monthly discourses'), which he edited at Leipzig from 1688 to 1690 as a dialogue between the editor and the reader, and the constant striving in the years to come of men and women as diverse as Gottsched, Gellert, Lessing, Wieland and Sophie von La Roche, in their divergent media of treatise and 'model' tragedy, comedy, lecture and epistolary novel, fable and letter, or indeed as editors of influential journals, to persuade Germans to develop a written language close to the spoken word.

Thomasius was writing at a time when educated burghers still had some chance of entering the service of a prince on the basis of their specialist qualifications. Writers of middle-class background, such as Johann König and Johann von Besser, fulfilled the function of court poet as their predecessors had done in the age of the baroque. Poets were welcome when eulogies were needed.

But the enlightened despotism of the eighteenth century was to become increasingly hostile to burgher ambitions. The territorial princes, including the Emperor, the Elector of Saxony, the rulers of Brandenburg-Prussia and a myriad others, having destroyed the power of the estates of their realms, bought the loyalty of their nobility by creating a system of preferment open only to its members. The effective exclusion of the middle class from access to political power and social status provided not only a central theme but also much of the moral power of literature in German during the eighteenth century. At the same time, the thematic content of polite literature began to move away from the courts and the nobility, and princely patronage of the arts, though still considerable, declined at the same time, the publishers, so often the object of vilification by writers, effectively taking over the role of patrons as far as literature was concerned. Between 1680 and 1745 the German book market expanded, Leipzig publishing houses such as those of Gleditsch, Weidmann and Fritsch leading the way. The link between literary and commercial success was made particularly evident by Christian Fürchtegott Gellert, the most popular poet during the decade 1740–50: his works made the fortune of his Leipzig publisher, Johann Wendler. When Wendler sold his firm to Fritsch in 1766, the exclusive rights to Gellert's works passed into the hands of Philipp Erasmus Reich, who had been one of Weidmann's partners since 1747: at his death, the firm bought them back for 10,000 thalers. But poetry and fiction still represented only a fraction of an output which was still mostly in Latin and aimed at a wider and more international market.

Leipzig and Frankfurt, the twin capitals of the German book trade, lay at the heart of the Holy Roman Empire. For the best part of 500 years, from 1346 to 1806, the seat of the Holy Roman Emperor was situated almost without interruption in Vienna or Prague, in the eastern part of the Empire, but it was to Frankfurt that new Holy Roman Emperors traditionally came to be crowned, an event described by Goethe in a famous passage in his autobiography, *Dichtung und Wahrheit* ('Poetry and Truth', 1811–33). In the age of the Reformation and Counter-Reformation, Frankfurt was home to Germany's most important book fair; its first printed catalogue dates from 1564. Here, too, the imperial censorship or 'book commission' operated, determining what could or could not be published. By 1682, however, Leipzig had overtaken its old rival, largely on account of the Catholic character of these censorship policies. By the first decade of the eighteenth century its annual trade fair was attracting more than four times as many merchant visitors as Frankfurt's, and it was publishing a larger number of books. But the number published in Leipzig was not as significant for the future of German literature as the kinds of book which came to be associated with it in the decades to follow, and which made it the undisputed centre of German publishing.

Leipzig provided a powerful impulse for a whole series of interrelated developments which affected the character of German writing, the reading public, and, in consequence, German society as a whole. Drawing on developments in other cities in the Protestant northern half of Germany such as Halle, the centre of anti-establishment Lutheranism and of Pietist culture between 1680 and 1740, Leipzig University's academics and alumni, its patriotic citizens and its entrepreneurial publishers helped promote a number of fundamental changes in people's reading habits. Among the most important of these changes were: the move from Latin to German as the literary language of educated (North) German readers, institutionalizing, as it were, the impulses set in motion by Opitz from 1617 onwards; the ending of the predominant role of theology and devotional literature and their gradual replacement by secular subjects such as politics, the natural sciences, popular philosophy and, eventually, imaginative literature; and finally, the emergence in the last decades of the century of a large female reading public and increased access for women writers to the literary market. By this time, women were also beginning to hold their own as authors of serious works in many fields and genres. A good example is Maria Sibylle Merian, author of a three-volume standard work on caterpillars and butterflies (*Der Raupen wunderbare Verwandelung*, 'The wondrous metamorphosis of caterpillars', published between 1679 and 1717) for which she made her own copperplate engravings. In her fifties this redoubtable entomologist went to the tropics with her daughter to do fieldwork, the outcome of which was her massive tome on the insects of Surinam, *Metamorphosis insectorum Surinamensium* (1705), published in Amsterdam. A widening vernacular readership wanted access to knowledge, and this need was met by Johann Heinrich Zedler, the compiler of Germany's first great encyclopaedia, the *Großes vollständiges Universal=Lexicon aller Wissenschaften und Künste* ('Great, complete and universal lexicon of all the sciences and arts'). Its sixty-four volumes appeared in Halle between 1732 and 1754, shortly after its English counterpart, Ephraim Chambers's *Cyclopaedia or An Universal Dictionary of Arts and Sciences* of 1728, and well ahead of the French *Encyclopédie* edited by Diderot. The preface to its first volume expressed the hope that it would surpass all other encyclopaedias in Europe. After all, its author explained, a learned man should know everything, and an encyclopaedia should reflect the totality of human knowledge. 'Zwar weiß ich viel, doch möcht' ich alles wissen' ('I know a lot, it's true, but I'd like to know everything'), observes Faust's famulus Wagner in Goethe's drama. The aspiration is a futile one. Yet Zedler's monumental *Universal=Lexicon* laid the foundations for Germany's rise to scientific and intellectual primacy in Europe by the end of the eighteenth century and provides a penetrating insight into Germans taking stock of humanity's achievements at the dawn of the Enlightenment.

Leipzig was located at the convergence of the two main West–East highways across Europe and halfway along the important trading axis between the port of Hamburg and Nuremberg, still South Germany's leading commercial and industrial centre. There were several established universities within a radius of fifty to a hundred miles, among them Erfurt (1392), Wittenberg (1506), Jena (1526) and Helmstedt (1576), as well as two new foundations: Halle (1694) and Göttingen (1736); the two older universities of Rostock (1419) and Greifswald (1450) were less than 200 miles away on the Baltic coast. But Leipzig's own university, founded in 1409, was pre-eminent during this period, and counted among its professors Gottsched, Gellert, and Christian Felix Weiße, the father of German children's literature, and amongst its alumni Lessing, Klopstock and Goethe. Its centrality acted as a magnet for middle-class talent and allowed it to be identified in a special sense with the Enlightenment in Germany. From the late seventeenth century to the 1750s, when Gottsched's disciples were spreading his new ideas on the nature and purpose of literature, and Gellert's lectures, literary works and his 1751 collection of model letters were teaching Germans how to speak urbanely and write with good taste, Leipzig's academics helped shape the way in which ordinary educated (North) Germans saw themselves and their nation, and the function of literature within it. Leipzig was thus both a focus and a centre of communication; through learned treatise, journal and moral weekly, and through the increasingly gregarious forms of eighteenth-century literature, it reached out to Halle, Hamburg, Zurich, Berne, and, later in the century, to Göttingen, where many of Germany's most influential civil servants and jurists trained, to the Königsberg of Kant and Lichtenberg, to Berlin, centre of the late Enlightenment, and finally to the Weimar and Jena of Herder, Goethe, Wieland, Schiller and Humboldt. Even when one of the most celebrated literary feuds of the century – that between Gottsched in Leipzig and Bodmer and Breitinger in Zurich – had been resolved in the latters' favour, it was still to Leipzig that aspiring authors sent their manuscripts. Their readers might be anywhere, but their books were published in Leipzig.

Hamburg was the Augustan age's other main literary and intellectual centre. Neither a vigorous book trade nor a seat of learning promoted Hamburg's status; it owed its influence to the continuity of its prosperity as Germany's major trading city. Located at the mouth of the Elbe, the great river which in the age of the Industrial Revolution was to link Magdeburg, Dresden and northern Bohemia with the North Sea and thus the rest of the world, Hamburg was above all a seafaring city. In the Augustan age its trade encouraged it to face outwards, away from Germany, a hinterland which contributed little to its prosperity, towards London, Amsterdam and further afield; it was the *emporium Germaniae*, the bazaar of Germany, the German city with the readiest access to the lucrative colonial trade, and its great patrician families were wealthier than many with an aristocratic pedigree. Portuguese Sephardic Jews formed a sizeable colony there in the late seventeenth century; Dutch engineers had built its docks and water-ways. Well-born Hamburg citizens liked (and still like) to be 'English'. And in the Augustan age the model of the socially involved, intellectually curious yet critical citizen presented by Steele and Addison in their journals the *Tatler* and the *Spectator* was eagerly copied in the German 'moral weeklies', of which the most influential was *Der Patriot*, published from 1724 to 1726 in Hamburg. These moral weeklies seldom ran for more than a year or two, but are a particularly characteristic feature of the Augustan age because they attempted to provide a forum for promoting useful discussion, disseminating information and educating the moral sense and the good taste of the citizenry; in other words they aimed to create what Germany so patently lacked: a localized public sphere. The places where moral weeklies were published are generally identical with centres of literary life and included, besides Hamburg itself, Leipzig and Zurich, Halle and Berne, Vienna and, later, Göttingen. Moreover, Hamburg was one of the very few German cities to have an opera house (it opened in 1678) without being the capital of a principality; somewhat surprisingly, however, its citizens' efforts to establish a theatre foundered until Lessing's day on the opposition of the orthodox Lutheran clergy. Something of the independence of eighteenth-century Hamburg is conveyed to us in the spirited prose of two of its daughters – in the letters of Meta Moller, determined in 1750 to marry none but her Klopstock ('Heavens, what would I do married to a creature I looked down on?') and, a generation later, in those of Elise Reimarus, who corresponded with relaxed self-confidence with men of the calibre of Lessing and Moses Mendelssohn.

The emergence of Leipzig and Hamburg as significant centres of literary life in the Augustan age was bound up with their commercial status. The case of Halle was different: here August Hermann Francke established his various charitable foundations to assist in spreading the word of God, closely aided and encouraged by Philipp Jakob Spener, the 'father of Pietism'. These included the famous *Waisenhaus* or orphanage and the immensely influential publishing house which bore its name, as well as schools for poor boys and girls and for the sons of noblemen which pioneered new and influential concepts of education and training. Spener was regarded by his followers – who by the 1740s may well have amounted to some 40 per cent of all German Protestants – as a 'new Luther' who would complete the Reformation. Both he and Francke were fired by exemplary zeal for the revival of Protestant Christianity, but they also worked hard towards creating dutiful, hard-working citizens for the state of Brandenburg, which was soon to become better known as the Kingdom of Prussia. In exchange they won important economic and other privileges for their work: in 1694 the Hohenzollerns founded a university at Halle which soon became the essential training ground for young men wishing to enter the Lutheran ministry. By dexterously influencing appointments, Spener, a great organizer as well as an outstanding theologian, saw to it that Pietists were established in key positions in church and state right across Germany, while their mercantile links – the Pietists, non-drinkers themselves, were agents for the distribution of Spanish wines in Germany – brought with them cultural and intellectual contacts between Halle and places as far afield as London, Stockholm and Moscow. The composer Georg Friedrich Handel, born in Halle in 1685 and a law graduate of its new university, left the proceeds from performances of his oratorio *Messiah* to the Foundling Hospital in London when he died in 1759 after a long career in England. The first performance had taken place in Dublin in 1741.

In terms of German literature it would be hard to overestimate the significance of the phenomenon of Pietism. Emanating from Halle and its religious publishing house, but equally strongly represented in Württemberg by the *Cannsteinsche Bibelanstalt* near Stuttgart and later by the university of Tübingen, it propagated devotional and edifying literature in vast quantities to readers at all levels of the social hierarchy, making a powerful contribution to the reading culture of Germany both quantitatively and qualitatively. The Pietists read avidly about the inner life and wrote about their own, scrutinizing their souls and developing the language of feeling which was to achieve its grandest expression in Klopstock's epic poem, *Der Messias*. They also contributed in more secularized form to the sensibility or *Empfindsamkeit* of innumerable minor mid-eighteenth-century authors, diarists and letter-writers and to the autobiographical subjectivity of Goethe and many of the *Sturm und Drang* writers. The delight in letter-writing, the cult of intimate friendship and of reciprocal visits, and the rising fashion for biography and autobiography and for self-observation in the manner of the 'spiritual diaries' kept by Pietist men and women are all part of the powerful impulse emanating from Halle. Its influence makes itself felt in German writers as diverse as Klopstock and Goethe, Hamann, Wieland and Schiller, Hölderlin and the Romantics, and even Büchner.

## The Literary Character of the German Augustan Age

The intellectual and artistic achievements of the period are clear for all to see, yet its literature is generally passed over in silence. But to do this is to overlook a body of writing which has much intrinsic merit. The term 'Augustan' suggests parallels with the 'golden age' of ancient Rome during the reign of Augustus, but its use in describing the literary histories of England and Germany resides rather in its associations with reason and its practical manifestation, common sense, and its aesthetic and critical application, judgement. In both nations, the period between the late 1680s and 1745 was broadly speaking one of political stability and peace at home (in Germany's vast territories there were of course exceptions) in which a new social order developed which sought a balance between the rising urban middle class, the landed property owners, the nobility, and the sovereign or territorial rulers. The closer links between Britain and Germany which followed the succession of the Elector of Hanover to the British throne and the anti-French policies which united it with Austria and Prussia provide a context for the introduction into German literary debate of English ideas and models. These were to affect the evolution of German thought and letters for many decades to come.

The German Augustan age represents a lively, sane and entertaining strand or dimension of German literature which is all too easily overshadowed by the more powerful but often darker and more introverted alternatives which preceded and followed it. Throughout the period 1690–1745 German writing shared many of the chief concerns of literature in the rest of Europe, but it did so with its greatest flowering still before it, not fading or recently over, as was the case in France, Italy, England and Spain. Its writers stated its new identity clearly with their total rejection of the overblown grandiloquence and cleverness of high baroque writing, which they set out to replace by writing of a more balanced and urbane kind which made its points less emphatically and allowed greater scope for humour; one of their prime objectives was better communication with the period's growing and less exclusive readership. This new approach was heralded by a number of influential works of a general critical and informative nature such as Daniel Georg Morhof's *Unterricht von der teutschen Sprache und Poesie* ('Study of the German language and its literature', 1682; revised edition 1700), which gave new impetus to the 'reforms' of Opitz, proclaimed the approaching supremacy of the German language and spoke with approbation of comedy and the novel – two genres whose popularity was soon to place them at the centre of attention. Morhof, who drew, significantly, on his English contemporary, Dryden, for many of his views on 'modern' literature, was also the first German critic to mention Shakespeare and thus the initiator of Germany's 300-year-old tradition of serious Shakespeare criticism. French culture was beginning to exert wide appeal in Germany at the time and affected manners and fashions deeply, but the impulses from England first registered by Morhof were to affect German literature and thought profoundly in the longer term.

The long struggle of these two influences for supremacy in Germany forms the background to the short-term triumph and later defeat of the literary figure who dominated the latter half of the Augustan age: Johann Christoph Gottsched. From the moment he arrived in Leipzig in 1724 he established himself as a name to be reckoned with and exploited the potential of the moral weeklies to broadcast his views, which combined the practical emphasis of educationalists such as Christian Weise with the intellectual originality of Thomasius and the systematic rationalism of Wolff. In Leipzig he soon became the leading light of an association known as the *Deutsche Gesellschaft* or 'German Society' (founded in 1692). In 1730 its first female member, a young widow, was appointed. Her name was Christiane Marianne Ziegler and she had made her reputation with a collection of poems published in two parts in 1728–9, some of which Johann Sebastian Bach used as texts for his cantatas. Her drawing room soon became a hive of cultivated conversation: she was astute enough to point out that she had not always had her literary work vetted by male colleagues, and even brazenly trespassed on male territory by writing satires. In 1731 she took a further pioneering step by publishing a volume of her own letters which displayed the natural idiomatic register she preferred: a century later Germany would pride itself on its wealth of characterful women letter-writers, such as Rahel Varnhagen von Ense, Caroline Schlegel-Schelling and Bettine von Arnim.

Gottsched's major achievement was in the field of critical theory. Always an admirer of Opitz, he proceeded to lay down guidelines on how Germans should both write and appreciate literature: his *Versuch einer critischen Dichtkunst vor die Deutschen* ('An attempt at a critical art of poetry for the Germans', 1729) set out to do for the eighteenth century what Opitz's *Buch von der deutschen Poeterey* had done for the seventeenth almost exactly a century earlier. He admired Boileau, and made 'imitation' his guiding aesthetic principle. But by appearing to ape the French, he shortened his own critical life. By 'imitation', he meant that a poet's creation should literally 'copy' reality, a sensible though limiting view which overlooked the artistic function of the imagination, ruled out fantasy, and soon brought upon itself a critical rejection by his Zurich contemporary Johann Jacob Bodmer. Bodmer was glad to champion the role of the imagination and had by 1750 led his supporters to victory, with far-reaching repercussions for the future of German literature. His critical stance made allowance for the strong imaginative streak in the German artistic mentality, which had recently resurfaced in the Alpine poetry of his compatriot Albrecht von Haller.

Yet though Gottsched's intellectual horizons were flat and his influence short-lived, his writings fulfilled an important critical function. France provided a model which was imitated by all European nations during the Age of Reason, and by shaping his own literary standards on those of modern France, he promoted the commitment to clarity in both thought and expression which was to characterize the literature of Germany's *Aufklärung* or Enlightenment. Without Gottsched the German *Aufklärung* would have been unthinkable. The pride of Leipzig's academic life during the years when Johann Sebastian Bach was in charge of its musical life, he would have been a duller figure had he not shared Opitz's interest in the literature of

Germany's past and enjoyed the support of a wife who translated indefatigably from French and English, shared his belief in the moral and social role of the stage, and wrote plays which were more animated, and have lasted better, than his.

## The Rise of the Novel

By 1700 German readers were able to relax over a steady flow of novels which conducted them on entertaining tours of their comic and curious world in a manner which stressed the amusing and satirical aspect of fiction and openly set out to improve them in the process. Some of the characteristics of Grimmelshausen's *Simplicissimus* were retained, such as its delight in the teeming life of highway, inn and market town, and its keen sense of the unexpected, a narrative quality which it shared with the more cumbersome courtly novels of the baroque and their descendants, the sometimes exotic and often erotic novels which continued to be written until well into the eighteenth century by authors such as Eberhard Werner Happel, Christian Friedrich Hunold and Johann Gottfried Schnabel. Happel, based in Hamburg, devised an effective recipe which combined the complicated storylines of the fashionable late-baroque romances with generous amounts of useful geographical and historical information about foreign parts. Catering for a responsive commercial middle-class readership, his so-called 'history romances' covered key areas of the contemporary world, from Asia and the Ottoman Empire to Hungary and England, and even include a prototype of the campus novel entitled *Der akademische Roman* (1690). A similarly ready response to readers' tastes is seen in Hunold's novels, which indulged middle-class curiosity and prurience by treating recent cases such as that of the charming Frenchwoman who had managed to win the heart and hand of the Duke of Celle-Lüneburg in *Die liebenswürdige Adalie* ('Adorable Adalie', 1702).

Schnabel's most famous work is different: it is an adventure story called *Wunderliche Fata einiger Seefahrer* ('The strange fates of certain seafarers') which recounts the curious adventures of seafarers and benefits from the example of Defoe's *Robinson Crusoe* (1719), the classic of the genre, which had appeared in German translation as early as 1720 in Hamburg, aptly enough. Schnabel's novel was one of the few prose works of the period to survive as something of a classic under its better-known title *Die Insel Felsenburg*, given it by the Romantic writer Tieck in his 1828 edition. In Schnabel's fiction, however, unlike Defoe's, the desert island is a refuge from a cruel and corrupt world rather than a place of lonely and involuntary exile, and it soon turns into a utopian earthly paradise for its hero, who is cast up on it with a nubile young woman aptly called Concordia. Its mood comes closer to the idealizing satirical episodes in Swift's *Gulliver's Travels* (1726) which appeared in German in Hamburg in 1727; indeed, *Die Insel Felsenburg*, which appeared in four volumes between 1731 and 1743, even looks forward to *The Swiss Family Robinson*, the most famous German story of this kind, which appeared in the early nineteenth century.

Novels such as these provided exciting, entertaining reading of an essentially escapist variety specifically intended for a less educated but leisured readership in a period of growing stability and economic property; in many ways they were an equivalent of the romances which, 200 years before, had appealed to the urban middle-class readers of Germany's first capitalist phase. Then there was also the so-called 'low' novel; this was characterized by an earthier, more humorous and satirical vein, and was developed by Christian Weise, a highly influential grammar-school teacher in Saxony. Weise's 'political' novels – that is, humorous and satirical fictions concerned with the contemporary state of society (the 'body politic') – appeared during the 1670s while Grimmelshausen was writing his sequels to his most famous novel, *Simplicissimus Teutsch*. Weise's *Die drey ärgsten Ertznarren in der gantzen Welt* ('The three worst arch-fools in the whole world') and its pendant, *Die drey klügsten Leute in der gantzen Welt* ('The three cleverest people in the whole world') are masterpieces of the genre, and set a high standard. Their ebulliently episodic storylines disguise the author's covert purpose, which is to demonstrate the advantages of a reasonable, open-eyed and honest attitude to what goes on in the world, while their titles also indicate that, like the parallel development in the exotic novel, the genre had had its counterpart in the literature of the sixteenth century, when folly literature flourished and drastic satire appealed to the German sense of humour and fondness for 'poetic' justice. Weise's example was followed by Johannes Riemer in his *Der Politische Maulaffe* ('The political jackanapes', 1679) and *Der Politische Stockfisch* ('The political blockhead', 1681) and adapted to less didactic purposes by Johann Beer, an Austrian Protestant who came to Saxony and whose twenty-one novels were mainly published between 1677 and 1683, and his rival Wolfgang Caspar Printz. It is interesting that in this period of intense musical activity in Germany these two authors were professional musicians: indeed the most interesting of Printz's novels and musical textbooks are the three 'musical' novels he published in 1690–1, which paint a lively picture of the musical life of the period.

One novel of the 1690s survived as a minor classic. This is Christian Reuter's comic story *Schelmuffskys wahrhafftige curiöse und sehr gefährliche Reisebeschreibung zu Wasser und Lande* ('Schelmuffsky's true, curious and very perilous account of his journey on sea and land', 1696), the entertaining first-person account of the larger-than-life journey undertaken by an inveterate liar whose tall stories and extravagant claims ensure him a welcome everywhere except back home, where of course nobody believes him. A humorous variation on the old theme of the prophet being without honour in his own country, Reuter's novel may be seen as the later seventeenth century's contribution to a persistent and rich German narrative tradition (a variant of the Spanish picaresque tale) which looks back to *Fortunatus*, Grimmelshausen's *Der abentheuerliche Simplicissimus Teutsch* and their medieval precursors, and forward to Chamisso's *Peter Schlemihls wundersame Geschichte* ('Peter Schlemihl's strange story', 1814), Keller's *Kleider machen Leute* ('Clothes make people', 1874) and Thomas Mann's *Bekenntnisse des Hochstaplers Felix Krull* ('Confessions of the confidence trickster Felix Krull', 1954). By 1690 there was certainly a very respectable amount of entertaining fiction available in German to set alongside the fiction of the same period elsewhere in Europe. Why so little of it has survived is hard to say. What is certain is that it provided a firm basis for the work of later eighteenth-century novelists such as Wieland, Karl Philipp Moritz and even Goethe himself.

The period's involvement with the novel was given a new direction by Christian Fürchtegott Gellert. What is regarded today as his most remarkable work is his *Das Leben der schwedischen Gräfin von G . . .* (Leipzig, 1747–8), the storyline and narrative structure of which illustrate the period's gradual shift away from the picaresque manner of its earlier writers to the novel of character and manners, with its psychologically subtler presentation of character. The way had been paved for this change of approach by North Germany's enthusiastic reception of Samuel Richardson's epistolary novel *Pamela, or Virtue Rewarded* (1740–1). More importantly, Gottsched in Leipzig and his old critical opponent Bodmer in Zurich were for once united in their praise; its appearance in German translation in 1742 confirmed the supremacy of modern English literature as a model for German writers to follow.

## Poetry and the Return to Reason

The years spanned by German literature's 'Augustan' age were notable for a total change of style and mood in poetry, too. In place of the baroque's brooding or brilliant odes and sonnets, the new generation of poets turned back to Opitz and from him derived their conception of lyric poetry, which, with its insistence on regularity and good sense, was also more in line with the example being provided by France. Amongst the first to do so was Baron von Canitz, whose satirical verse, marked by a new emphasis on urbane, almost conversational balance, established a reputation which was felt until well into the middle of the eighteenth century. Canitz was but the best of a number of poets who laid no great claim to lyric gifts, but who demonstrated that German, too, could be handled and shaped into verse which had all the understated ease of good prose. It is no wonder that Dresden, fast establishing itself as the most fashionable city in Germany during the reign of Augustus the Strong, Elector of Saxony from 1697 to 1733, attracted the best poets of this kind, Johann von Besser and Johann König. Their work, seldom less than elegant, often witty, but rarely profound, reflects the tone of Dresden during its heyday in the early eighteenth century, when its delicate, frivolous china was making its name so well known in the drawing rooms of Europe.

During his earlier years in Hamburg and his period as court poet in Dresden in the 1730s, König came into contact with two poets whose gifts were far greater than his own, and who between them show what German Augustan poetry was really capable of. Johann Christian Günther has often been called the last of the baroque poets because his work retains much of the imagery and many of the formulations that were the hallmark of the mid-seventeenth century. But he uses his gifts to express an intense sense of personal inadequacy offset by fleeting but joyous moments of emotional fulfilment: the autobiographically tangible human being is at the centre of such poetry, not the stylized heart or soul of most later seventeenth-century German erotic and religious verse. His torment, unredeemed by the solace of religious certainty, stemmed from his fraught relationship with his father, who wished him to become a doctor like himself and like his closest model, the poet Paul Fleming: his finest work is the expression of Günther's inability to live up to these expectations, and places him somewhere between the Old Testament's Job and the twentieth century's Kafka, a man ill at ease in the balanced world of rococo elegance and empirical rationalism. He is a poet caught between periods, baroque in the sense that he lacks 'Augustan' composure, 'Augustan' in that for him the values of the baroque age no longer make sense.

The other most original lyric voice of the period was Barthold Heinrich Brockes, whom König met in Hamburg, and who started his literary career by writing the text for an oratorio, *Der für die Sünden der Welt gemarterte und sterbende Jesus* ('Jesus tormented and dying for the sins of the world', 1712), which was set to music by both Handel and Telemann. Brockes's development took a different turn when, in 1724, he became involved in the foundation and organization of a patriotic literary society with a policy of philanthropic rationalism, and produced the first instalment of his masterpiece, a blend of contemplative religious effusion, didactic moral essays in verse and descriptive, painterly poetry, significantly entitled *Irdisches Vergnügen in Gott* ('Earthly delight in God'). The nine volumes to which this remarkable undertaking ran appeared between 1721 and 1748, and provided the second half of Germany's 'Augustan' age with an ongoing example of how to reconcile Christian revelation and Lutheran piety with the pastoral classicism of Virgil, the natural philosophy of Lucretius and the scientific progress being made at the time. It is no coincidence that Brockes also translated two of the masterpieces of contemporary English Augustan literature, Pope's recent philosophical poem *Essay on Man* and Thomson's descriptive poem *The Seasons* (the German versions appeared in 1740 and 1744). His many points of contact with the musical culture and intellectual world of his contemporaries make him a figure of central importance, and one whose poetry, often complacently expansive yet also sometimes capable of sharp, almost oriental concentration, deserves recognition for its intrinsic worth as well as for its role in establishing a tone of voice and a poetic language which were to affect the course of German religious and didactic poetry for many decades.

Brockes had contemplated a career in England: his well-to-do Hamburg compatriot Friedrich von Hagedorn also spent some time in London before returning to his native city to become the most successful and admired poet of his generation on the appearance in 1729 of a collection unassumingly entitled *Versuch einiger Gedichte*. Hagedorn followed this by other collections of verse which built up to a substantial body of well-turned and pleasant poetry that clearly reflects the untroubled, calm contentment which characterizes German art and life in the third decade of the eighteenth century. As Hagedorn's popularity grew, forms and genres which had been fashionable until recently – such as the sonnet and the complimentary poem to mark an occasion – went out of favour to be replaced by the so-called anacreontic ode, a poem made up of short lines in praise of a life of simple contentment, and the fable in verse, which combined narration with generalized satire and moral edification. As a master of this favourite genre of the period, Hagedorn was excelled only by Gellert, whose amiable *Fabeln und Erzählungen* of 1746–8 set forth the Augustan age's ideals of balance and common sense. Here Germany at last achieved its counterpart to the universally admired fables of La Fontaine, which had appeared between 1668 and 1694. Gellert could not match the Frenchman's fastidious wit and lacked his insight into the whole range of human motivation and behaviour; but within their more modest limits his blander fables showed how an urbane manner could be used to point a moral or adorn a tale with verbal and psychological accuracy. His well-reasoned and easily memorized tales and fables appealed to both sexes and all ages, yet some of the most popular such as 'Der Tanzbär' and 'Der Hut' suggest that he was wryly aware of the limitations inherent in the civilized urbanity he was himself responsible for promoting: his dancing bear is told to get lost because he is too clever; his hat achieves the height of elegance and balance yet each generation alters it to suit its different taste.

By the mid-1740s the confident harmony and rationality of the Augustan age was beginning to show signs of giving way to the discovery of the power of sentiment, and its easy intellectuality was being replaced by the new cult of feeling and sensibility. This shift of mood and direction had been anticipated in some important respects by the publication in 1732 of a collection of 'Swiss' poems by the young Albrecht von Haller, who was soon to become the major botanist, neurologist and scientist of the mid-eighteenth century. It contained an ambitious didactic-descriptive poem entitled *Die Alpen*, which was based on the author's own journey into the high Alps in search of botanical samples in 1728. In the field of German and European culture Haller's discovery of the literary potential of the wild mountain landscape of the Alps was to prove momentous, and its resonances have continued to be felt up to the present day. In the context of its own period *Die Alpen* is more important because it presents this discovery within the framework of a rationalist philosophical outlook. The rugged and untamed is shown to be accessible and acceptable because it is part of the natural world, not a figment of the imagination. But Haller's response to it, and the words he found to describe it, evoke a sublime landscape which was to become closely identified with the Romantic age; moreover his appreciative depiction of the life and values of the peasants in the Alps created a model of a simple, honest society not yet contaminated by the malign moral influences and corrupting prosperity of the privileged society of so-called civilization encircling it down below on the plains of Europe. It was a contrast which in 1732 clearly pointed the way to the social thinking of Rousseau over two decades later and to economic and political images which have dominated Western thinking ever since.

## New Directions in Drama

If the German 'Augustan' literature had a shortcoming, it was in the domain of drama. Yet this cannot fairly be held against it, since it was the direct result of the state of the theatre in Germany at the time. In the seventeenth century, dramatic activity had been centred on the Protestant grammar schools and the Catholic colleges, but shifts of emphasis in the teaching curriculum and the moral outlook of society were eroding this tradition. There was, however, one notable exception. The capacity of education to produce rational human beings was widely acknowledged during the Augustan period, but nowhere were the links between education and literary activity more successfully demonstrated than in the Saxon town of Zittau, now situated only a few miles from the Czech and Polish borders.

It is unusual for a satirical novelist to become the headmaster of a reputable school, but that is what happened when Christian Weise was appointed to such a post in his home town in 1678. Weise shared his period's view that education and literature were interconnected. He wrote many educational books and during his headship at Zittau produced some sixty plays (half of which were published) for his boys to perform. As regards both quantity and quality these make him the most important German playwright of his time. His annual drama festival soon acquired the name *Zittauisches Theatrum* and consisted of three plays, one religious or biblical, one a dramatization of some historical episode, and one a comedy of his own invention, usually rich in slapstick and clearly in line with his previous career as a writer of satirical fiction. In all three genres he produced plays of much originality and verve. His first season in 1679 was a statement of artistic and pedagogic intent. *Jephta* is a noble biblical tragedy, albeit in prose; *Der gestürtzte Marggraf von Ancre* ('The fall of the Marshal d'Ancre') is a five-act dramatization of the fall in 1617, some sixty years earlier, of Louis XIII's favourite, the Italian adventurer Concini, who had been created a marquis, offset by *Bäurischer Machiavellus* ('A peasant Machiavelli'), a comedy which remained popular for half a century, and which showed how ordinary German peasants can be just as devious and corrupt as the Italian of whom they have never heard. Weise's emphasis on theatre as entertainment offset the ever-present temptation of the Augustan writer to lapse into moralizing; he had more in common with the Elizabethan theatrical tradition than with his Silesian precursors. He confined himself to prose and avoided high-flown language, features which sometimes bring him close to the translations of Molière's comedies which started to appear as Weise was writing: five comedies by the great comic playwright of Louis XIV's France were published in German in 1670, though the first major translation (fourteen comedies done into prose by Johanna Eleanore Petersen) did not come out until 1694. Like Molière, Weise excelled at comedy in many modes and styles, but was at his best in those plays in which he achieved a vigour and immediacy reminiscent of Dutch genre paintings, such as *Der niederländische Bauer* (1700), a characteristically Weisian reworking of the familiar old theme of the peasant who awakens from his stupor to find himself a prince for a day.

Comedy of a more urban kind had been lacking in seventeenth-century German literature, which in this respect contrasted sharply with the comic traditions of England, France and Spain. However, the turn of the century brought something of a change. The year 1700 saw the publication of *Graf Ehrenfried*, a satirical comedy of money squandered in riotous living, drawn from life by the former Leipzig student Christian Reuter. Reuter had made his name in the 1690s with his novel *Schelmuffsky* and two comedies in which he lampooned his landlady by creating the slipshod character of Frau Schlampampe, a comic figure who both caricatures and embodies the manners and values of ordinary folk in the Leipzig of the period; it is not surprising that the good woman sued Reuter for defamation of character and gave him the opportunity to satirize her further from the relative safety of the university lock-up before he was sent down. On this occasion, town got the better of gown – or did it? His rounded portrayal of her qualifies Frau Schlampampe to be regarded as the first truly individual character in German comedy, and accounts for the amused admiration in which she has been held by Goethe and many others since.

In tragedy the urbane and optimistic Augustan age was less at home. Without much success Gottsched promoted French tragedy as a model, but without being entirely able to escape from the baroque tradition he considered outdated. Indeed that tradition, with its emphasis on argument and debate, lasted until Johann Elias Schlegel's much admired *Canut* in 1746, which transferred Corneille's concept of political and personal tragedy to a nordic setting as King Canute finds himself obliged to condemn his brother-in-law Ulfo to death when, for the second time, he conspires against him. Debates on human conduct in the light of ethical issues were to provide greater moral excitement in Schiller's *Don Carlos* and Goethe's *Iphigenie auf Tauris*. Coincidentally, the Latin rhetorical drama which was in many ways the Catholic counterpart of the German baroque tradition survived even longer. Its keenest champions, the Jesuits, were still writing full-scale plays in Latin until the suppression of the Society of Jesus in 1773 curtailed their activities even in those parts of the German Empire where their role as educators continued to be valued. Schlegel had begun with *Hecuba* (1736), another version of the *Trojan Women*, the play Opitz had recommended as a model for classical tragedy a century before. But his *Hermann* (1743) marked a decisive change. Here for the first time a German figure was the hero of a tragedy: significantly that hero was Arminius or, rather, the legendary Hermann, the Cheruskan chieftain who defeated the Romans in AD 9 and who had already been used to signal an emergent German national identity by Luther's admirer, Hutten. Hermann was soon to reappear in a succession of patriotic, indeed sometimes chauvinist, works including Justus Möser's play *Arminius* (1749), Wieland's unfinished epic, *Hermann* (written around 1750), Klopstock's trilogy of 'bardic' dramas: *Hermanns Schlacht* (1769), *Hermann und die Fürsten* (1784), and *Hermanns Tod* (1787), Kleist's anti-Napoleonic *Die Hermannsschlacht* (1809) and Grabbe's nobly disenchanted play with the same title in 1835. But Schlegel himself was a writer caught between two eras and truly representative of neither. He was aware of the example of the past, and his comparison of Shakespeare with Gryphius, published by Gottsched in 1741, was a decisive contribution to the reception of Shakespeare in Germany, but he was dead by the time Lessing made *Canut*, his best work, one of the bases for a new conception of theatre beyond his reach. His literary survival was in the end due almost solely to *Die stumme Schönheit* ('The dumb beauty', 1747), a one-act comedy deftly turned and written in elegant verse.

The failure of the Augustan age to produce a lasting body of drama was due in large measure to the fact that the Lutheran Church and middle class identified the stage with immorality; it was therefore confined to courtly audiences and the opera houses it was now becoming fashionable to add to palaces. The first clear signs of change and improvement came when Friederike Caroline Neuber (1697–1760) and her husband set about raising the tone and social status of the stage with the encouragement of Gottsched, whose verse tragedy *Der sterbende Cato* their company put on in 1732. Frau Neuber's symbolic expulsion of the harlequin figure from the stage in 1737 exemplified the change in attitude which was to result in the rehabilitation of drama as an integral part of German literature, a status it had not enjoyed since the 1670s. The new development was confirmed when Gottsched's wife, Luise Adelgunde Gottsched, a prolific translator of plays such as Molière's *Le Misanthrope*, began to write comedies of her own, such as *Die Pietisterey im Fischbeinrocke* ('Pietism in hooped petticoats', 1736), a biting satire on the excesses to which false piety can lead. Gellert, too, reclaimed the moral and educational value of the stage by writing straightforward satirical comedies such as *Die Betschwester* ('The female bigot', 1745) and more substantial pieces in the 'French' manner such as *Die zärtlichen Schwestern* ('The tender sisters', 1747), which, with the plays of Johann Elias Schlegel, prepared the way and provided models for Lessing. But amusing satire, deft characterization and a well-turned plot were not enough to offset the pressure of moral and religious disapproval which troubled the harmonious development of drama and of literature in general by the middle of the century. The publication of *Canut* in 1746, followed two years later by that of the first three cantos of Klopstock's epic poem, *Der Messias*, with their lofty Miltonic tone and unquestionable seriousness of purpose, were major literary events which showed that the Augustan age of German literature was over.

## Thematic Survey: Translators and the Literary Canon

'Of all literatures the German has the best as well as the most translations', Carlyle observed in his 1827 essay on the state of German literature. The age of Goethe was indeed rich in translations of great variety and scope, yet the role of translations in shaping the development of a literature is generally overlooked and easily undervalued. Far from being a peripheral activity undertaken mainly to satisfy the curiosity of readers about the outside world, it has sometimes played a leading role in preparing the way for innovation: a few translations have actually achieved a standard of excellence comparable to original works and entered the literary canon of other nations as a result. Throughout Germany's literary history translators have made the cultures of the countries surrounding it accessible to the general reader by overcoming linguistic barriers on their behalf. This was even the case in the eighteenth century when any reasonably well-educated German was capable of reading French, and Latin, too; a spate of translations from the French and from ancient Roman authors testifies to the preference on the part of many readers for books in their own language. From the earliest years of printing, when in 1472/3 Heinrich Schlüsselfelder's translation of the *Decameron* by Giovanni Boccaccio was published in Ulm, the works chosen for translation and successfully published make their own special comment on the constantly shifting interests and tastes of the German reader and on the evolution of the German literary canon.

Long before Opitz in the 1620s held translation up as a ready and effective means of refining, improving and extending the German language and the cultural range of literature written in it, translations had helped to condition the changes of perception, style and taste which literary history records. Luther's translation of the Bible is the major achievement of this kind, and one whose influence up to the present day has been incalculable, but preceding and contemporaneous with it there had appeared German versions of works in the language of the countries which surrounded the Holy Roman Empire and which had already developed literary cultures which, as some Germans realized, were more advanced and more prestigious than their own. Alongside these translations from the leading modern languages of the time – Italian, French and Spanish – another body of translations was steadily growing. These were German versions of texts from Europe's principal cultural reservoir: classical antiquity. The Middle Ages had already seen much activity in this sphere, but with the advent of printing the situation changed. Not only did the reading market grow in size: the reproduction of texts in multiple copies and versions also played its part in creating a more readily available range of translated literature. By 1560, that is, by the end of the first century of printing, German versions existed of key classical works such as Homer's *Odyssey*, Virgil's *Aeneid*, the *Parallel Lives* of Plutarch and Aesop's fables, done into the German prose and verse styles characteristic of the period. Subsequent generations and epochs added to this stock with the result that when Latin's hold on German scholarship began to wane in the eighteenth century, the heritage of antiquity lived on in German. Indeed it was at precisely this juncture that it came into its own and exercised its deepest and most lasting influence on the literature and culture of Germany.

'New' translations of the Greek and Latin classics ensured that antiquity was actively present in Germany's own classical age. Some of them, such as Johann Heinrich Voss's translations of Homer (*Odyssey*, 1781; *Iliad*, 1793), even entered the body of its literature and became German classics in their own right. The nineteenth century built on this achievement. Its scholarship was becoming increasingly specialized, and its translations of literary masterpieces tended to be more accurate but also more heavy-going, yet the indefatigable efforts of gifted translators such as Johann Jakob Christian Donner (1799–1875) should be given their due. Between 1821 and his death Donner single-handedly provided Germany with reliable versions of the tragic dramas of Aeschylus, Sophocles and Euripides and of the comedies of Aristophanes, Plautus and Terence, adding the *Lusiads* of Camoens, the greatest work of Portuguese Renaissance literature, for good measure.

All translations reflect the poetics of the period in which they are written and the taste of the public for which they are intended. This is particularly true of translations from the modern languages, which have always been the principal channel through which foreign literary influences have penetrated the imaginations of German readers and authors. Here, too, translators sometimes added versions of foreign works to the German literary canon. For a variety of interconnected cultural and political reasons Germany has tended throughout the centuries to attach sometimes almost exaggerated importance to the status of other languages and literatures. This was particularly the case during the seventeenth and eighteenth centuries, when Italian, Spanish, French, Dutch and English each acquired for German readers and authors a prestige and appeal which encouraged translation, imitation, and a growing creative rivalry. In the fifteenth century much recent and contemporary foreign prose had already been translated; in the seventeenth century this trend was reinforced by ambitious poetic versions of important modern works such as Diederich von dem Werder's Tasso (*Gottfried von Bulljon, oder Das Erlösete Jerusalem*, 1626) and Tobias Hübner's Du Bartas (an impressive version published in 1622 and 1631 of *La Semaine ou la création du monde* by Tasso's French Protestant contemporary): the originals had been published in 1581 and 1575 respectively. Du Bartas's fame paled with the decline of biblical epic, though his presence may still be felt in Klopstock's *Der Messias*;

Tasso on the other hand became one of Germany's favourite foreign writers when Goethe chose him as the protagonist of his verse play *Torquato Tasso* (1790). Alongside grandiose verse translations such as these there was a steady stream of narrative prose works taken from the Spanish, such as Aegidius Albertinus's *Der Landstörtzer Gusmann von Alfarache* (1615), a version of Mateo Alemán's picaresque novel *Guzmán de Alfarache* (1599), or even from the English, like Opitz's revised version of a German *Arcadia* (1629) translated from the original by Sir Philip Sidney, and his translation of *Argenis* (1626), a once much-admired modern Latin novel by the Franco-Scottish writer John Barclay. Between them these titles provided German authors with models for the increasingly popular picaresque, pastoral and political genres.

The vital cultural role of the translator as mediator became even more marked in the Augustan period of the early eighteenth century, when three German versions of Fénelon's highly influential didactic romance *Télémaque* (1699) appeared between 1700 and 1733, deeply influencing the pedagogic strain that led to the *Bildungsroman*. Half a century later Johann Arnold Ebert's masterly translation of Edward Young's ruminative *Night Thoughts* (published in parallel text format in 1751) gave added impetus to the darker, more introspective side of German *Empfindsamkeit* and *Sturm und Drang*, while a number of German versions of Samuel Richardson's epistolary novels prepared the way for Goethe's genial fusion of both these modern English fashions in his early masterpiece *Die Leiden des jungen Werthers* (1774). Translators also played a key role in Germany's long creative relationship with the plays of Shakespeare. Starting with the early attempts by Wieland (twenty-one in prose and one in verse between 1762 and 1766) and Johann Joachim Eschenburg (*Wilhelm Shakespeares Schauspiele* in thirteen volumes, Zurich, 1775–82), the history of Shakespeare in German culminated with August Wilhelm Schlegel's verse translations, which appeared from 1797 onwards and were finally completed with the help of his wife Dorothea née Mendelssohn and Count Wolf Heinrich von Baudissin in 1833 under the general editorship of Ludwig Tieck: hence the usual German appellation 'Schlegel–Tieck' to the work which more than any other major German translation found its permanent place in the nation's literary canon. Indeed Shakespeare translation has been at the centre of interest from the moment German literature finally became not only good but great in the mid-eighteenth century. Every generation since then has responded to the challenge with new versions, of which the most notable mid- and late-twentieth-century ones are those by Rudolf Alexander Schröder, who also translated Homer, and the exile poet Erich Fried.

Few are the authors of the classical and Romantic period who did not try their hand at translating. Goethe and Schiller are no exception. Their translations range from Goethe's version of the autobiography of Benvenuto Cellini to Schiller's able renderings of plays by Shakespeare, Racine and Gozzi. Herder was an enthusiastic translator of folksongs from many languages and also produced *Der Cid*, the classic German version of the famous medieval Spanish narrative poem. The Romantic writers were equally interested in the potential of translation and adept at it. Tieck, for example, produced the best-known version of *Don Quixote* by Cervantes in 1799–1801, though he had been anticipated by Friedrich Justin Bertuch, a Weimar associate of Goethe's whose version appeared in 1775–7 and again in 1780. Sometimes a trend-setting translation could emanate from a less likely source. This was the case when the *Gedichte Ossians*, a translation of James Macpherson's 'Ossian' poems into German hexameters, was published by the Viennese Jesuit and, later, imperial court librarian, Michael Denis, in 1768–9. Soon Goethe was enthralled by this voice from Scotland's misty past: his own translations of suitably atmospheric Ossian poems are read aloud by Werther to Charlotte at a climactic moment in his novel. There is no more telling example in German literature of translation penetrating the fabric of a major literary text.

Fifty years later, in 1827, Goethe was able to tell his translator, Thomas Carlyle, that anyone who understood and studied German would find himself in a market-place where the nations of the world were offering their wares. Certainly in no other country in Europe did the translator stand in such high regard. Carlyle had translated both parts of Goethe's great novel *Wilhelm Meister*, and his prestige as Britain's leading thinker did much to give German literature a status which it has never regained in Britain and the United States since the early Victorian age. But the exchange was really much more in the other direction. *Yoricks empfindsame Reise* (1771), *Tristram Schandis Leben und Meinungen* (1774) and *Der Dorfprediger von Wakefield* (1776), translated by Lessing's publisher, the talented and indefatigable Johann Joachim Christoph Bode (1720–93), brought the novels of Sterne and Goldsmith to the notice not just of German readers, but of writers who were able to benefit from the lessons in narrative technique they provided. Their example was not lost on writers such as Jean Paul Richter, Wieland, Heine and, later, Raabe and Fontane. By 1800 most major modern works of fiction were available in German translation; so, too, were the towering texts of classical Greece. Sophocles, a writer especially congenial to the German temperament – or so the sustained interest in him in Germany would suggest – was presented in ever more refined and authentic versions by Christian, Count Stolberg (1787) and Karl Wilhelm Ferdinand Solger (1804), but also by Friedrich Hölderlin (1804), whose more daringly imaginative versions, though mocked by Goethe and Schiller, bring home to the twentieth-century reader just how far removed Weimar Classicism was from the art and culture of ancient Greece.

Yet it was Goethe's concept of *Weltliteratur* that gave translation the status it has since held in German-speaking countries. By it he meant an on-going process of cultural exchange based on the assumption that at the core of every great work of literature there is a common human interest which transcends national and linguistic distinctions. By the beginning of the twentieth century it could fairly be claimed that a reader with a good working knowledge of German had access to a range of international writing second to none. To the major authors of France, Spain, England and especially Italy, the foreign country to which German-speakers have always been most attracted, were now added the 'newer' literatures of Russia and Scandinavia. For readers in many countries German translations provided access to the Norway of Henrik Ibsen's dramas and the Russia of Pushkin, Turgenev, Tolstoy and Dostoevsky, as well as to the tormented inner world of August Strindberg in Sweden or the muted symbolism of the Belgian Maurice Maeterlinck as rendered by Friedrich von Oppeln-Bronikowski (1883–1936), his 'official' translator. By 1930 German editions of the collected works of most significant European authors were available, while at the lower end of the market cheap editions of foreign authors were easy to come by, often in parallel text format. It should therefore be remembered that writers of German have been considerably more aware than their English-language counterparts of the achievements of foreign writers. Such competition could be beneficial; but sometimes it could debilitate. Today the proliferation of Anglo-American crime novels and middle-brow fiction in German bookshops may be discouraging German writers from developing their talents in these genres and confining them to a 'high-brow' conception of literature which has relatively little appeal in the English-speaking world. Could this be why modern German, Austrian and Swiss literature is as little known here as the literature of Germany's classical age?

# 4

## The Classical Age of German Literature

'A sea dotted with the islands of princes.' This was the metaphor chosen by Johann Gottfried Herder to describe Germany in an essay of 1781 on the influence of poetry on people's lives in ancient and modern times. It was an apt description of the political geography of the German Empire in the eighteenth century. But it also conveys the potential variety of German literary life during its 'classical age'. The major courts, Frenchified Berlin and Italianate Vienna, did not play the key role in bringing that age into being. That function fell to a handful of the minor, sometimes even minuscule, courts in some of the 340 or more sovereign and semi-sovereign states which made up the German Empire. Of these Weimar was certainly the most important.

How could it be, wrote Friedrich Engels a century later, that a country with such a backward economy could have 'played first fiddle' in the cultural life of Europe, as Germany did in the age of Goethe? When Goethe came to Weimar in 1775 on the invitation of Karl August of Saxe-Weimar, its 18-year-old duke who went on to reign for half a century, it was a small town of 6000 inhabitants, few of whom had any commercial links beyond its confines, and which foreign visitors found sleepy, dull and unfashionable. Eighty years later, when George Eliot visited it with her partner George Henry Lewes, who was collecting material for his pioneering *Life of Goethe*, it had hardly changed. In her evocative essay *Three Months in Weimar* (1855) – the most penetrating account of the Weimar phenomenon in the English language – she records her initial reaction: 'One's first feeling was, How could Goethe live here in this dull, lifeless village? It was inconceivable that the stately Jupiter, in a frock-coat, so familiar to us through Rauch's statuette, could have habitually walked along these rude streets and among these slouching mortals.' But, as Madame de Staël noticed when she visited it in 1802, it was not a small town so much as a large palace, in which a cultivated circle of people took delight in every aspect of the arts. Up to the time of Karl August's majority, Weimar had been ruled by the Duchess Anna Amalia, an enlightened regent and a woman of taste; it was she who had invited the well-known novelist and Shakespeare translator Christoph Martin Wieland to her court in 1772 as tutor to her two sons. She was not alone in being able to express herself with feeling and elegance; so too did her ladies in waiting, Charlotte von Stein and Luise von Göchhausen, whose manuscript copy of Goethe's *Urfaust* saved the work from being lost. Soon Goethe was joined in Weimar by his Strasburg friend Herder, summoned there by Karl August to take charge of its Lutheran churches. In these early years Goethe and the Duke, who enjoyed his role at the centre of a 'court of muses', were constant companions, though protocol had initially forbidden Goethe, as

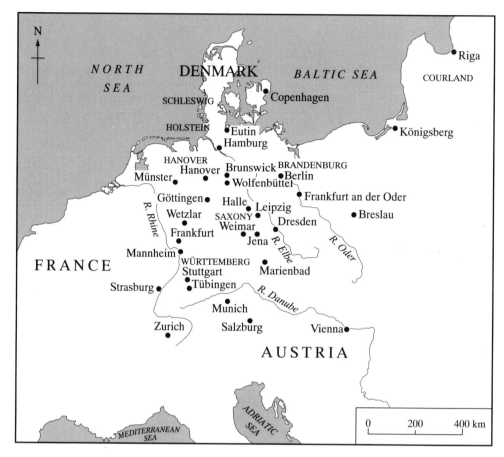

**Map 3**   Literary Germany in the eighteenth century

a commoner, to dine with him in public until he was appointed a Privy Councillor in 1779. Later, relations between the two were often strained, and Goethe, now director of the court theatre, became increasingly involved in cultural rather than political and administrative matters. But that decade from 1775 to 1786 had given him a degree of real power such as no other major German writer of his age enjoyed, or indeed scarcely any after him. This experience is reflected in his self-confidence, the breadth and range of his writings, and his capacity to look after his own interests as a writer.

Weimar was not the only cultural centre in Germany. For instance, there was Darmstadt, residence of the landgraves of Hesse-Darmstadt and home of Goethe's friend Merck, where Herder met his effulgent correspondent and future wife, Caroline Flachsland, and there was Mannheim, to which the influential theatre director Dalberg attracted Iffland, the famous actor, and put on the first performance of Schiller's revolutionary play, *Die Räuber*, in 1782, with Iffland in the role of the villainous Franz Moor. Dalberg, who had sheltered the young author of *Die Räuber* from his despotic overlord, Duke Karl Eugen of Württemberg, then staged the first German production of Beaumarchais' even more revolutionary *Le Mariage de Figaro* just one year after its triumph at the Comédie Française in 1784. The tiny ecclesiastical principality of Eutin in North Germany, home of the Stolberg brothers and of Voss, the translator of Homer, is another such representative centre, and so, too, is the court of the prince bishop of Münster, to which Princess Gallitzin, separated German wife of a Russian ambassador, attracted a distinguished circle of poets and thinkers, amongst them the Dutch philosopher Hemsterhuis, the poet Matthias Claudius, and Johann Georg Hamann, the daring thinker known as the 'Magus of the North', and even, briefly, Goethe. The great commercial centres, such as Hamburg and particularly Leipzig, retained and enhanced their cultural importance, too, while those other academic 'islands', the smaller university towns, provided yet another crucial focus for Germany's diverse and innovative contribution to human culture in the second half of the eighteenth century.

A good example is Königsberg in the remote north-east, where the philosopher Kant spent his whole life and the lawyer Hippel began to challenge received opinion about the place of women in society in *Über die bürgerliche Verbesserung der Weiber* ('The social improvement of women'), a work based on his observation that, though the French Revolution might indeed have liberated men, it had left the condition of women unchanged; it appeared in 1792, the year in which Mary Wollstonecraft published *A Vindication of the Rights of Woman*. Another is the 'English' university of Göttingen, founded in 1737 by George II in his capacity as Elector Georg August of Hanover and home to Lichtenberg, one of the most acute and inquiring minds of the age; here Johann Stephan Pütter and August Ludwig von Schlözer taught the future civil servants who were later to change the course of German history, and here the patriotic yet melancholy *Sturm und Drang* poets of the *Göttinger Hain* studied, as did the Schlegel brothers, leaders of the Romantic movement. Later there was Jena, the university of German classicism and early Romanticism, where Schiller and Fichte taught and many of the Romantics studied. And then there was Zurich. This prosperous Protestant city in the Swiss Confederation had no university as yet, but it had a theological college, the Collegium Carolinum, and its intellectual vibrancy had begun to make itself felt in the 1720s, when Johann Jacob Bodmer and his colleague Johann Jacob Breitinger began to take issue with the narrower rationalism of Gottsched and to replace it with a revaluation of the role and function of the imagination in literary creation, thus replacing Leipzig's French-oriented criteria by ones based on English models. Soon younger German writers were making Zurich a port of call: Klopstock in 1750, Wieland in 1758–60, Goethe in 1775 and again in 1779 and 1797. There, in a beautiful setting that inspired great lake poems by Klopstock and Goethe, they found Salomon Gessner composing the prose idylls that were to be German literature's greatest mid-eighteenth-century international success, Johann Caspar Lavater exploring the links between the face and the psyche and laying the basis for the Romantic fascination with psychology (in his *Physiognomische Fragmente*, 1775–8), and the educationalist Johann Heinrich Pestalozzi researching the concepts of head, heart and hand that underlie his theory of the human being's early development.

How did these 'islands' communicate with one another, given the legendary awfulness of German roads and the multiple brakes on mobility both physical and intellectual imposed by them and by absolute rulers? If you want to communicate your ideas, declared the energetic Berlin rationalist, Friedrich Nicolai, you must publish! He was himself the author of *Sebaldus Nothanker*, the tragicomic story of the involuntary mobility of a modern, tolerant, well-intentioned cleric who falls foul of authority, and he gave a good example to his fellow countrymen as editor of the long-lasting and influential *Allgemeine deutsche Bibliothek* (1765–1805) which, together with its imitator and competitor, the Weimar publisher Bertuch's immensely influential *Allgemeine Literatur-Zeitung* (1785–1849), established the book review in the central place it still holds in the intellectual discourse conducted through the quality press and other media in Germany today.

As though to underline the changing relationship between writer and society in this period of German literary history, the content of polite literature shifted from the world of princes and aristocrats – which still remained the butt of satire – to the concerns of the middle ranks of society, such as the gentry and the lower echelons of the provincial nobility, who were dependent on their own abilities for their living. With some notable exceptions, princely patronage declined as a determining factor in literary production, and publishers, though frequently the object of vilification by writers, took their place. Saxony was the manufacturing centre of late eighteenth-century Germany, and Leipzig, its commercial capital, witnessed the emergence of a modern profit-making book trade. Book production more than doubled between 1760 and 1800, and the number of bookshops grew correspondingly. Moreover, the massive expansion of the book trade after the Seven Years War (1756–63) gave ample opportunities for the rising professions of critic, editor, translator and adapter, and scope for intelligent young men and women to supplement their incomes and even earn their living by the pen. As Rudolf Zacharias Becker, author of one of the most successful books of the late eighteenth century, put it in 1789, 'the writer who wants to free himself from service to a prince must turn his work into merchandise and work for a wage.' Wieland was one of the most adept at doing so, but Sophie von La Roche was also a quick learner who, despite her eight children, became what could be called the first professional woman writer in German history. Indeed there is a good case for seeing late eighteenth-century women's writing more in terms of a 'craft' than writing by men. With La Roche giving the lead, women wrote for specific readerships, shaping and adjusting their texts according to who would read them – and who might censor them before or after publication.

The years between 1740 and 1800 saw remarkable changes in the sorts of books Germans wrote and read. At the beginning of the seventeenth century, books in Latin were twice as numerous as books published in German; a century later the opposite was true. In 1735 books in Latin still counted for about a quarter of total production; by 1800 their proportion was less than 3 per cent. The Leipzig Fair catalogues reflected an equally radical change in the content of books. Whereas in 1740 the arts, including imaginative literature, had counted for a mere 5.8 per cent and theology and devotional reading for 38.5 per cent of books published, by 1800 they amounted to just over 21 per cent, whereas the latter category accounted for little more than 5 per cent of the total. A dynamic book market stimulated demand and gave authors of both sexes greater opportunities: by 1800 imaginative literature was increasingly being written by women as well as being read by them. It is therefore not surprising that the idea that writers should be paid for what they wrote was gaining currency, though the issue remained a controversial one. The concept of intellectual property was explored by legal specialists at Göttingen in the light of the pioneering views of John Locke earlier in the century, and Fichte wrote and lectured on it to his students at Jena in the 1790s. But neither writers nor publishers were protected by the state or by copyright laws (such as the Copyright Act of 1709 in England), nor would they be until Prussia took this important initiative in 1837, and this despite recognition that a buoyant literature presupposes a well-regulated publishing and book trade, as the influential Gotha publisher Friedrich Christoph Perthes pointed out in an important essay on the subject in 1816. In some states, notably Austria, piracy was actually encouraged as a cheap form of enterprise.

Cultures cannot function without an efficient communications system. That of eighteenth-century Germany was provided by its literary and philosophical journals and the letters its inhabitants were constantly writing to each other: the correspondence Goethe and Schiller exchanged between 1794 and 1805 is the most famous example. Alongside Nicolai's and Bertuch's review journals, well-informed persons could subscribe to Wieland's highly successful *Teutscher Merkur*, and the *Berlinische Monatsschrift*, the major organ of the Berlin Enlightenment, in which Kant's famous essay *Was ist Aufklärung?* appeared in 1783. In 1795 Schiller brought out *Die Horen* ('The Graces'), a monthly journal devoted to aesthetic matters, and in the last years of the century Friedrich Schlegel launched his *Athenäum* (1798–1800), the periodical which pioneered Romanticism. But the ubiquitous and elegant *Musenalmanache* were also a vital element in this communications system, and their importance as purveyors and propagators of polite literature and culture until well into the nineteenth century cannot be overestimated. As one of them, Heinrich Christian Boie's *Das deutsche Museum*, put it in 1776, 'such publications are a form of conversation with the public'. Moreover, their role in providing an outlet and means of support for middle-class authors of both sexes was central, as Schiller's career illustrates: at 300 Reichstaler per annum his earnings from his *Musen-Almanach* (1796–1800) were only marginally less than the stipend of his Jena professorship: as he wrote to Goethe, they allowed him to keep going even in poor health and to retain his independence. Like many a small enterprise in this modern economy, Schiller's *Musen-Almanach* helped to create consumer demand: they were popular with women because of their small format, which Schiller reduced still further (to duodecimo) to make them small enough to fit inside a lady's reticule.

The importance of letters as a medium for communicating and exchanging ideas and for making contacts is equally central to a proper understanding of the age. Letters not only helped to create a community of minds, they acted as a form of introduction which might lead to friendships and useful contacts such as those Boie established on his visits to Berlin and Halberstadt in 1769, which later guaranteed him and his editorial successor Johann Heinrich Voss a steady stream of material for the Göttingen *Musen-Almanach* from personalities such as Ramler, Gleim and Anna Louisa Karsch. Even writing not intended for publication, such as letters and autobiographical writings, were composed with an eye on a wider circle. The literary work of women was generally controlled by parents, guardians or even husbands, but the literary fashion of the 1750s and 1760s known as *Empfindsamkeit* or sensibility encouraged an intimate, effusive style; as a result the dividing line between the strictly personal and what could be made public became blurred, as could the boundaries between fact and fiction. Letters were passed around family and friends to provide the stuff of conversation in much the same way as did the letters in the epistolary novels by Richardson and his German imitators borrowed from the circulating libraries. 'Letters must go forth and multiply!' proclaimed Bettine Brentano, a fine representative of women's outstanding skills as letter-writers and correspondents during the Romantic era.

The transformation of Germany from a provincial backwater into a powerhouse of ideas for modern Europe was largely a result of this new system of communications. The key role it now played as leader of what amounted to an intellectual revolution was announced to the wider world in 1813 when Madame de Staël published her pioneering study of Germany's history and modern achievements: *De l'Allemagne*. She had visited Weimar in 1802–3 on an interviewing tour prior to writing her book, and quickly realized its significance as the Athens of Germany, despite its unassuming appearance. It was here, more than anywhere else, that the long story of

Germany's progress towards a classical culture of its own reached fulfilment. She was entertained by Goethe in his famous house in Weimar. He had rented it in 1782, and from 1792 resided there until the end of his life. He was so attached to it that his friend the Duke gave it to him in 1794 in recognition of his tireless service to the administration of Saxe-Weimar, and in it he wrote the major part of his works, which included much more than poetry, novels and plays, since his interests embraced many aspects of the natural sciences and of the visual and applied arts, too. Behind its plain, almost unassuming frontage a suite of six rooms, each opening into the next, seems to illustrate in symbolical form his conviction that each intensely lived phase in life leads on into the next, which only then reveals its mysteries. In one room his collections of prints, gems, cameos, plants and geological specimens were housed in cases fastened by ingenious locking devices he designed himself; in another, overlooking the garden, Christiane Vulpius lived, not far away from the study where he simultaneously dictated his vast correspondence to three secretaries and, left alone, grappled with the ideas and words which, given shape, made him the unquestioned sovereign of a united Germany: the Germany of the mind. Schiller's Weimar house was more modest but is no less eloquent. He did not need to entertain on a grand scale: unlike Goethe he was not an official and privy counsellor, and his requirements were few. But it was in spartan surroundings such as these that his incisive mind shed light on the relationship of morality to beauty and that, stimulated by black coffee, snuff and the smell of rotting apples, he held tuberculosis at bay while his imagination peopled a dramatic world with characters whose passions were equally, and incredibly, the product of that same mind.

The main concerns of the 'golden age' of Goethe and Schiller had been anticipated by many writers and thinkers during the 150 years that preceded it. Its intense reappraisal of the legacy of classical antiquity and its efforts to select from it those elements which were still relevant to the modern world of its own day had behind them a long history of European and German preoccupation with the art and literature of Greece and Rome. Attempts had already been made to translate and adapt antiquity to suit the requirements of Germany, which is hardly surprising, since the study of Greek and Latin, and of classical literature and thought, had provided a major component in the education provided for centuries by the schools, colleges and universities of the German-speaking countries. From the late medieval humanists onwards, the vast majority of German writers were classicists by education, and up until the time of Goethe and Schiller Latin was the language in which their minds had been trained; German did not replace it at school or university until well into the eighteenth century. Only in the Protestant Church and in the world of business was the vernacular predominant, and it was therefore only to reach the uneducated that authors needed to have recourse to the German language. But the uneducated represented a large cross-section of the potential reading public; they ranged from the landed aristocracy and the patrician merchant class to urban artisans, small-town dwellers and the peasantry. Vernacular literature was therefore often synonymous with popular literature, though for men of letters it also became a matter of pride to attempt to relay to sections of this amorphous popular readership something of their own classically based intellectual and aesthetic awareness; this, after all, was a cultural trend that had already been taking place with a large measure of success in neighbouring countries such as France and England, so why not in Germany, too? Their task was underpinned by the achievement of Johann Christoph Adelung, the lexicographer and grammarian whose authoritative and comprehensive dictionary of the German language, based on Saxon usage, appeared in Leipzig between 1774 and 1786. Adelung divided language into five stylistic levels or registers ranging from the elevated to the vulgar and centring, with far-reaching consequences for Germany's literature, on the language of familiar everyday speech. Despite the fact that it did not take the usage of writers after 1760 into account, Adelung's dictionary was highly regarded by the writers of the classical Weimar period and his rejection of the paradigmatic role of Latin did much to promote the perception that German had replaced Latin and was capable of supplanting French as a major European cultural medium in its own right.

The assimilation of the classical legacy into the language and literature of Germany went back to Martin Opitz in the 1620s. Justifying the title 'father of modern German literature' accorded him until well into the eighteenth century, he was the first German writer to tackle Greek tragedy (*Antigone*, 1636, a version of Sophocles) and the first to transfer the pastoral mode to an explicitly German setting. The idealized world of pastoral, and the elegiac yet playful mood associated with it, were to become an important element in the new literature of Germany that was to culminate in the classicism of Weimar. In 1732, a century after Opitz, *Die Alpen*, a discursive poem by the Swiss scientist Albrecht von Haller, evoked an ideal society, but in a setting that was excitingly new: the mountains of Switzerland. Overnight, a traditional classical theme had acquired a contemporary natural setting which, by the end of the eighteenth century, had become closely identified with Jean-Jacques Rousseau, his young German *Sturm und Drang* admirers, and with Romanticism, the first major cultural movement in modern European literature to be closely associated with Germany. Haller's poem pointed forward to the moral landscape of Schiller's last great drama, *Wilhelm Tell* (1804); but it also points further ahead, to the nineteenth century's discovery of the countryside and country folk as an ideal subject for attractively picturesque literature rich in quaint customs and local colour.

The impact of antiquity on late eighteenth-century German literature also took other forms. The long educational tradition of classical studies received potent reinvigoration from another quarter, which confirmed assumptions about the continuing validity of classical culture. In 1755 the art historian Johann Joachim Winckelmann published *Reflections on the Painting and Sculpture of the Greeks* (it was translated into English by the painter Fuseli in 1765), a work which amounted to a rediscovery of the beauty of Greek art, and proclaimed that it was the peak of human aesthetic achievement and therefore a model of perfection which modern artists should imitate. With Winckelmann, the moral and philosophical ideas of antiquity acquired a cultural context, while mythology, long a staple of poetry and painting, now took on added authenticity which, far from making it more remote, actually brought it closer, because underlying the whole cultural trend which Winckelmann's insights had sparked off was the notion that the simplicity, nobility and serenity of Greek art were the visual manifestation of moral and intellectual qualities. Thus Greek art became an object of appreciative imitation as a tangible expression of the humane values which were coming into increasing favour at the time. Thinking individuals such as Lessing's friend, Moses Mendelssohn, and Immanuel Kant, the Königsberg philosopher, led the way with major works including Mendelssohn's *Phädon oder über die Unsterblichkeit der Seele* ('Phaedon or on the immortality of the soul', 1767) and Kant's *Kritik der praktischen Vernunft* ('Critique of practical reason', 1788), in which aesthetic and moral values were seen to converge. The new trend was thus associated from the start with a seriousness of purpose and a strain of lofty idealism, as well as with delicacy of feeling and a preference for the direct and simple which may best be described as neo–classical. Soon it took control of the pure and applied arts, too, in conscious opposition to the flamboyance and bombast of the dying baroque and to the rococo flippancy which still often characterized the culture of the courts, as well as to the facile complacency and optimism which underlay much of the writing of the previous era and the moral license that tended to accompany it. The neo-classicism of Weimar appealed to men and women of taste, but would have been more élitist than was the case had it not upheld values and standards which met with the approval of a steadily expanding section of society, the educated German middle classes with their law-abiding ethos of responsibility and hard work.

The Weimar age was a cultural phenomenon which created a powerful sense that the common European heritage was now safeguarded by German poets and thinkers. It also provided a common bond between the various parts of Germany even if it never came to mark Germany's political institutions as profoundly as the Age of Reason marked those of Britain, France and the United States. In the 'islands' of which it was made up, the old ways had remarkable tenacity; some ruling princes were still drawn to grand displays of their declining authority rather than to the chaster classicism which marked Duke Karl August's Weimar. In Austria and the Roman Catholic areas of southern Germany and Switzerland, the extraordinary flowering of late baroque and rococo architecture in the mid-eighteenth century was in almost every respect the antithesis of Germany's new culture, whereas in Prussia it achieved some of its most notable architectural and decorative successes as Berlin and Potsdam were developed to the designs of Germany's greatest neo-classical architects, Friedrich Gilly (1772–1800) and Karl Friedrich Schinkel (1781–1841). One of the main reasons for such disparities is not far to seek: Enlightenment thought and neo-classical art exerted their greatest appeal in the Protestant parts of the German-speaking world, which were already marked by a long tradition of moral and aesthetic rigour. This tradition now received a new impetus which rendered its values more humane and allowed greater pleasure to be taken in the sensual aspects of culture. Since art, both secular and religious, was now shown to have an essentially moral purpose, it no longer constituted a threat. The composers and musicians of eighteenth-century Germany had already created a musical culture that transcended political and religious differences, and by 1800 German music had become a meaningful and unified concept represented by Gluck, Haydn and Mozart. In 1799 the first German monument to Mozart was erected in the grounds of Schloß Tiefurt, the country residence of Duchess Anna Amalia of Saxe-Weimar, close to the spot where in 1782 Goethe's *Die Fischerin*, an open-air *Singspiel* containing the famous ballad 'Der Erlkönig', had received its first performance. It was Goethe's achievement, and that of many other writers, not least Wieland in the polished yet fantastical stanzas of his once much-read verse romance *Oberon* (1780), to work out ways of making their language a suitable vehicle for expressing a new and fundamentally harmonious conception of the world.

## Poetry in the Mid-Eighteenth Century

The second half of the eighteenth century saw German poetry attain a standard of excellence which helped decisively to win German literature acceptance as one of the great literatures of Europe. By 1800 Germany was widely regarded as a nation of poets, with Goethe and Schiller at their head. The development of German poetry ran in close parallel to that of music in the German-speaking world, and there are many connections between them. By 1800 German music was widely accepted as a central and essential element of Europe's cultural life, and the works and travels of Gluck, Haydn and Mozart carried its reputation far beyond the frontiers of the Holy Roman Empire of the German Nation. The pre-eminence of German poetry, like that of German music, was not achieved overnight. Building sometimes consciously, but often not, on the efforts of Martin Opitz in the seventeenth century to create a basis for a post-Renaissance national literature and to provide models for each of the main conventional poetic genres and forms, the poets of the baroque period and the Augustan age which followed it developed and adapted them to suit changing tastes and times. The elegy, ode and epigram formed the central strands of Germany's lengthening poetic tradition, closely supported by the *Kirchenlied* or hymn, a genre which merged the ode with a more popular vernacular Christian tradition: indeed the language and imagery of religion dominated German verse until well into the eighteenth century, just as works of a theological and devotional nature dominated the German book market.

Running alongside these serious literary genres, the taste for lighter, more profane poetry surfaces time and again as the taste for erotic, convivial and humorous verse took hold of German readers in the period between 1680 and 1750. Outside models – Italian, French and, increasingly, English – were admired and adapted to suit German requirements and much technical versatility was displayed as German verse moved on from the ornate baroque hyperbole of Lohenstein, Hoffmannswaldau and their imitators, to the artificial simplicity and 'art that conceals art' which is so typical of the occasional poetry of Gleim and Uz, and of the amiable fables of Gellert, in the mid-eighteenth century. By the 1740s, however, the onward progress of German poetry was slowing down although its potential was not yet fully explored or realized. The sonnet (which had reached such heights in the hands of Gryphius and his contemporaries) had fallen into disfavour, while the epic failed, despite the efforts of influential critics such as Gottsched and Bodmer, to produce the masterpieces on which the reputation of that noblest and most ambitious kind of poetry depends. To renew the impetus of Germany's poetic development, what was needed was a poet of bold and independent genius.

## The Imagination Set Free

In 1749 the first three cantos of an ambitious epic poem appeared in a short-lived literary journal published in Bremen, a town not often associated with important literary events. Their publication in book form in 1750 was a triumph for their young North German author, Friedrich Gottlieb Klopstock, who had just reached his mid-twenties, and it marked what was in many ways a watershed in the history of German literature and especially of German poetry. Paradoxically, despite the rapturous reception, the poem which precipitated it failed to establish itself as a classic text to set alongside Milton's *Paradise Lost*, the English religious epic which was its literary inspiration and model. Klopstock's *Der Messias*, hailed by contemporary critics and readers as an undoubted masterpiece, never quite achieved the lasting and unqualified success of the string of great works by Lessing, Goethe and Schiller which were soon to follow it. From the vantage-point of the late twentieth century, the reasons for this are not hard to see. Poetry of this committed and affirmative religious kind – unlike the poetry of religious uncertainty and doubt – has been out of favour ever since the rise of positivist thought and Darwinian agnosticism cast doubt on the beliefs which underlie it and which were shared by the vast majority of the reading public until well into the nineteenth century. But there are other reasons, too. Quite apart from the copious biblical knowledge which *Der Messias* presupposes in its readers, questions of tone and style also played their part. By the time of its first complete publication in twenty cantos and 20,000 lines of verse in 1772, the sentiments and language of Klopstock's poem were already beginning to strike some ears as pretentiously high-flown, an impression which was enhanced by his decision to write it in a German equivalent of the hexameter or six-foot line of Latin epic poetry, a line for which there was no precedent in German and which was no more related to the great tradition of medieval German narrative poetry than it was to the epic and didactic poetry of Opitz and Gryphius, borne on the rhythms of the six-foot iambic line so similar and yet so fundamentally different from Klopstock's metre and the new sound of *Der Messias*:

> Sing', unsterbliche Seele, der sündigen Menschen Erlösung,
> Die der Messias auf Erden in seiner Menschheit vollendet [. . .]

('Sing, immortal soul, sinful mankind's redemption / which the Messiah fulfilled on earth when he took on our human nature')

With these commanding lines Klopstock begins his poem – a statement of poetic intent if ever there was one – and often he succeeds in persuading the reader of the validity and urgency of his lofty vision despite the looming threat of monotony as it moves slowly to its foreseeable conclusion. This danger was enhanced by his determination to achieve and maintain a suitably 'elevated' level of diction for his subject, though here the beneficial influence of Luther's noble yet idiomatic Bible translation provided a counterbalance to the chronic tendency of eighteenth-century writers to assume that style and subject must always go hand in hand. Yet although *Der Messias* may make excessive demands on the reader of a modern, secular age, it still deserves recognition and can still stimulate intermittent excitement for some of the same reasons which made it so instantaneously popular in the 1750s. What was new about it was its imaginative scope, its energy, and the sheer volume of words which were generated to convey its author's inner vision. These qualities convinced contemporaries that the language of German poetry had come of age at last, and certainly no serious literary text in German had achieved such a wide readership since Luther's translation of the Bible. *Der Messias* spoke to the hearts and minds of its original readers through its commanding blend of imaginative power and Christian faith, a recipe which did much to help it achieve its short-lived classic status. Its popularity was of course enhanced because it was itself the product of a period of religious revival; it was no mean feat to expand the biblical account of Christ's last days on earth, and to do so without causing offence in pious circles.

Alongside his epic, Klopstock also produced an impressive sequence of odes on personal, political and religious themes: though anchored in a long tradition of Latin and German lyric poetry, these mark the final break with the formal conventions of poetry established by Opitz over a century before. In his shorter lyrics he rejected rhyme and the strict alternation of stressed and unstressed syllables which Opitz had claimed was an innate feature of the German language and therefore natural to German poetry. Instead, he experimented with rhythmic patterns which imitated the scansion of Greek and Latin poetry, dispensing with rhyme in favour of the greater expressive power of 'free' verse carried on the natural rhythms of the German language. The poetic revolution thus brought about was hailed by many as an act of liberation of the poetic imagination from the childish singsong of rhythmic and aural monotony. This struggle between the traditional claims of rhyme and the innovative potential of free verse was to characterize the evolution of German lyric poetry for the next hundred years – the most notable years in its history and ones during which it was to be in a state of almost permanent revolution.

## Gleim and Karsch

The careers and works of Johann Wilhelm Ludwig Gleim and Anna Louisa Karsch give a good idea of what German literary life was like as the eighteenth century entered its second half, and tell us a good deal about the tastes and expectations of the period. Both poets were highly successful. Though Karsch came from an unprivileged peasant background in Silesia and had to fight her way to popularity by sheer determination and an extraordinary talent for writing verse to order, the volume of her selected poems which she published in 1763 earned her more money than any German poet had ever earned before, setting a record which remained unbroken until the next century. Moreover, she had become the darling of fashionable Berlin society and a personal friend of Princess Amalia, the sister of Frederick II of Prussia, a monarch she greatly admired and whose virtues and frequent victories on the field of battle she was adept at praising. She had also met and fallen hopelessly in love with her fellow-poet, Gleim, whose *Versuch in scherzhaften Liedern* ('Experiments in light-hearted song', 1744–58), building on the example of poets such as Hagedorn, had convincingly shown that poetry did not have to be in French in order to capture the delicacy and charm of Dresden china. The 'German Anacreon', as he was called, was adept at imitating the harmlessly playful eroticism associated with the pastoral vein of poetry ascribed to his Greek original. But he was also capable of striking a patriotic and martial strain without having recourse to baroque bombast, as he demonstrated in his collection of Prussian songs of war and victory (*Kriegs- und Siegeslieder der Preußen von einem preußischen Grenadier* or *Preußische Kriegslieder*), published in 1758 and presented as the work of an ordinary grenadier in Frederick's army, and all the more appealing for that reason. Effective yet unassuming, such verse was characteristic of the new taste which marked the poetry of the day.

The match between the German Anacreon and the German Sappho, as he called her, seemed an ideal one, but came to nothing, leaving Gleim to mature into a long-lived and poetically prolific bachelor (he died in 1803), while Karsch, deeply hurt but unable to silence her feelings, discovered a depth of emotional expression which her earlier work, renowned for its facility, had lacked. This new quality was to bring her the admiration of Goethe at a time when he, too, was first discovering the thrill of creating 'spontaneous' poetry in his own natural idiom and free from the deadening restrictions of regularity and correctness. By the time Karsch died, in 1791, Goethe had left his early youthful manner behind to enter the more careful and deliberate 'classical' phase of his career, but in the 1770s, when he and Karsch were vying with one another to demonstrate the liberating effects of commonplace or natural subjects and of rhythmic and stylistic freedom, they had remarkably much in common. If Goethe went on to achieve ever greater stature and Karsch sank into an oblivion from which she is only just being rescued, it was not so much because she was a woman writing in a male-dominated culture – her extraordinary success rather belies that interpretation – as because, despite her unquestionable gift for vigorous and vivid poetry, she never quite managed to compose the sort of poem whose uniquely recognizable qualities ensure it the near-immortality of becoming an anthology piece. Whereas Goethe did.

## Youth, Nature and Love

Klopstock's poems represent a decisive step towards the naturalization of Greek and Roman poetry which was to be one of the major elements in the development of Germany's own kind of classicism in the late eighteenth century. Their aesthetic effect was achieved through his attention to the metrical potential of the German language and his deep-seated belief in the lyric poet's need to display originality of theme and subject. Though much run-of-the-mill verse continued to be written on permutations of stock themes and images by countless authors of modest talent, he had established that an original voice was a prime criterion of literary excellence. For the next century and more, a unique voice was to be the goal of all serious German poets.

The influence of Klopstock manifested itself first, if not always most successfully, in the work of a group of Göttingen students who created something of a stir in the early 1770s and who earned themselves the name *Hainbund* because of their fondness for nocturnal meetings in forest glades in imitation, so they believed, of the 'druids' of ancient Teutonic times, and not without a touch of what would later be called German nationalism. As this was happening, Goethe, a postgraduate law student at the University of Strasburg from 1771 to 1772, was discovering the potential of his own poetic voice. Of course it has elements in common with that of some of his contemporaries, such as the *Hainbund* poet Ludwig Heinrich Christoph Hölty, with his gift for creating moods of intimate melancholy in poems such as *Die Mainacht* (1775), with its delicate evocation of a world poised between day and night:

Wenn der silberne Mond durch die Gesträuche blickt
Und sein schlummerndes Licht über den Rasen geußt
    Und die Nachtigall flötet,
        Wandl' ich traurig von Busch zu Busch.

('When the silvery moon gazes through the leaves and branches/ and pours its slumbering light over the grass/ and the nightingale trills,/ I wander sadly from bush to bush')

At other times Goethe comes closer to Gottfried August Bürger, a close associate of the *Hainbund*, who, aware of the rediscovery of traditional narrative poetry in Britain, succeeded in recapturing its verve and immediacy in ballads such as *Der wilde Jäger* and the more famous *Lenore* (1774), which, to the terror and delight of its early readers, vividly described how a girl's lover returns after he has been killed in battle to claim her and carry her off:

Wie flog, was rund der Mond beschien,
Wie flog es in die Ferne!
Wie flogen oben über hin
Der Himmel und die Sterne! –
'Graut Liebchen auch? – Der Mond scheint hell!
Hurra! die Toten reiten schnell!
Graut Liebchen auch vor Toten?' –
'O weh! Laß ruhn die Toten!' –

While Bürger excelled at the newly rediscovered ballad, his North German contemporary Matthias Claudius realized the potential of the German hymn tradition as a lyric form which could combine love of nature with a contemplative attitude. Their heartfelt directness has kept many of his poems alive, such as the much-loved *Abendlied* of 1779, a poem in which the Lutheran hymn in the style of Paul Gerhardt fuses effortlessly with the elegiac manner associated with Thomas Gray's *Elegy in a Country Churchyard* (1751) and its many imitations: indeed the musicality of the first stanza of Claudius's *Abendlied*, and its evocative power, place it among the supreme achievements of German lyric poetry:

> Der Mond ist aufgegangen,
> Die goldnen Sternlein prangen
> Am Himmel hell und klar;
> Der Wald steht schwarz und schweiget,
> Und aus den Wiesen steiget
> Der weiße Nebel wunderbar.

('The moon has risen and the little stars are blazing bright and clear in the sky; the forest stands black and silent, and up from the meadows the white mist is rising wondrously')

Common to the poems of all these authors was a new flexibility of language. Even in Klopstock's case a closer relationship between poetry and the spoken language of every day underlies the apparent loftiness of his style, while in the case of Goethe and of many of his contemporaries, the freshness and spontaneity of personal responsiveness intensified the relationship between feeling and expression. Indeed in his *Idyllen*, one of the major literary successes of the 1750s, the Zurich writer Salomon Gessner had successfully demonstrated that an open-air mood and the delights of country love-making could be just as effectively conveyed in delicately modulated prose as they could in the polished rhymes of Gleim and the other poets of the so-called Anacreontic school. Goethe was by no means immune to the charm of Gessner's prose poems – for this is what they were, though the term did not yet exist – and nor was Rousseau, the thinker so closely associated with the pre-Romantic slogan 'Back to Nature!' The often highly emotional nature of Goethe's personal responses to the phenomena of the world around him and within him was shared to a greater or lesser degree by all his most talented contemporaries.

Of course there had been subjectivity and flexibility in poetry before – for instance the poetry of Andreas Gryphius embodies the one and that of Christian Hoffmann von Hoffmannswaldau exemplifies the other. But the poetry of later eighteenth-century Germany established a new relationship between reader and poet by extending the reader's range of emotional response: the 'sensibility' or *Empfindsamkeit* which the new poetry presupposed in its readers. As early as the 1740s some writers had begun to play on this responsiveness and even to exploit it, such as the duo of Samuel Gotthold Lange and his friend Immanuel Jakob Pyra with their collection of pseudo-pastoral lyrics published in 1745, and Ewald von Kleist, a Prussian officer whose finer, more fully developed nature poetry touched a chord of sympathetic delight in many contemporaries. Kleist's long poem *Der Frühling* (1749), an evocation of springtime, went further by adopting the subjective approach to nature which James Thomson had made fashionable in and beyond Britain with *The Seasons* (1726–30), and which encouraged a new interpretation of people's relationship to the world around them. By the 1770s the cult of nature, and its corollary, the longing for an idyllic pastoral life, had become established features of the view of the world which German poetry shared with the other literatures of western Europe in the eighteenth century. But in Germany it also prepared the way for a phenomenon which was to have far-reaching consequences for the development of a distinctly German conception of lyric poetry: the discovery of a rich heritage of folksong. This living tradition had sometimes already impinged on literature in the past, but it had never, till now, been appreciated as a poetic phenomenon worthy of genuine admiration in its own right. Now, however, folksong suddenly came to be valued as a form of spontaneous and direct artistic expression untainted by the artificialities of artistic convention and passing fashion. To many discerning eighteenth-century minds, the poetry of the people was the epitome of natural poetry and a clear proof, if any proof were needed, of the innate aesthetic sense of human beings.

The broader implications of this reclamation of the folk heritage was largely the work of Herder, whose *Volkslieder* of 1778–9 consisted of two volumes of folksongs drawn from all parts of Europe; ably translated into German, they demonstrated the wider validity of the ideal of *Naturpoesie* which he had put forward in the collection of essays on the German artistic temper and its heritage which he edited and published in 1773 under the title *Von deutscher Art und Kunst*. Like so many of Herder's far-reaching ideas, the notion of folk poetry, with its great antiquity, simple directness and perennial relevance, quickly caught on, and no one was more naturally adept at capturing its flavour than Goethe. With poems such as 'Der untreue Knabe', 'Der König in Thule' and 'Das Veilchen', all written in and about 1771, Germany's most naturally gifted younger poet – he was barely twenty-five at the time – decisively supplemented Germany's store of folk poetry with poems whose lively imagery and simple language gave them the appearance and feel of authentic folksongs. The perfect example is 'Heidenröslein', with its clear-cut subject, subtle human subtext and simple, unaffected refrain:

> Sah ein Knab' ein Röslein stehn,
> Röslein auf der Heiden,
> War so jung und morgenschön,
> Lief er schnell, es nah zu sehn,
> Sah's mit vielen Freuden.
> Röslein, Röslein, Röslein rot,
> Röslein auf der Heiden.

Goethe was the finest but by no means the only writer whose songs in the folk manner were soon being recited and sung by his fellow-countrymen as folksongs in their own right: this particular vein of nature poetry, with its unaffected lyricism and heartfelt, apparently artless simplicity was to become a constant feature of German lyric poetry from now on.

## The Poetry of Goethe and Schiller

Klopstock was still at the height of his powers and popularity when young Goethe began to attract attention. But Goethe never sounds like Klopstock. From the start, he made it clear that he would not be aiming at the rhapsodic solemnity – the Pindaric strain – which was the great strength of his precursor, nor at the fusion of Greek and German elements which made his poems especially appealing to so many of Goethe's contemporaries, and led to so much imitative poetic activity. Goethe's major poems are distinguished by their individual voice, their technical brilliance and their familiarity to readers in German-speaking countries – their anthologized canon is exceptionally large. Each possesses its own unique contours and radiates its specific and unmistakable aura, yet taken together as the expression of one man's personal responses to life, they convey an ever-changing yet remarkably consistent literary identity. They were written over a period which ranged from Mozart's birth in 1756 to 1832, yet their organic coherence of themes and forms and their diversity in unity account for their central importance in the evolution of German poetry. From the outset, Goethe was endowed with the rare ability to handle the medium of poetry in ways that ensured it a cadence, rhythm and expressive power which distinguish it from the work of his many talented contemporaries, such as Bürger, Lenz, Matthisson and the Stolberg brothers in the eighteenth-century part of his life, or, later, Friedrich Rückert and August von Platen, who shared the delight in the poetry of the Orient which inspired his 'oriental' *West-östlicher Divan* (1819). Being a poet was for Goethe an inescapable destiny, as he knew from very early on; he seldom experienced problems of language and self-expression, but he did know from experience that poetic inspiration is a rare and very precious gift. Self-expression in the medium of poetry – as opposed to the self-exploration of autobiography or the self-revelation of correspondence, at both of which he excelled – was for him a natural urge but also a mysterious blessing.

Goethe is often and understandably seen, especially from outside Germany, as a figure of the Romantic age; but he is more than that. Many of his finest poems are in the Romantic manner: they are folksong-like love poems or ballads. But they often have parallels in a very different manner which goes back to the neo–classicism of Klopstock's odes or back further still to the neo-Latin tradition of the Renaissance humanists and their models, the poets of ancient Rome. From early on he showed a natural receptivity to all the main strands in the living tradition of German poetry from the light verse of Hagedorn, Gleim and the Anacreontics who were fashionable in his youth to the folk tradition his generation rediscovered and the elevated poetry on deep and probing themes which they so admired. 'Ganymed', an ecstatic ode in free metres, has thematic resemblances to the nocturnal gallop of the ballad 'Der Erlkönig' and to the controlled grace and harmony of 'Geweihter Platz', an elegiac poem in imitation of classical metre, and all three tell us much about Goethe's understanding of the relationship between the dimensions of everyday life and the wider, more intense but also more dangerous world of the imagination. But despite such similarities Goethe seldom repeated himself. Having established himself as a master in the folksong idiom he developed an unusually vivid and visual brand of *Gedankenlyrik* – the poetry of ideas so esteemed by his fellow-countrymen – in poems such as 'Das Göttliche' (*c*.1783), which probes deep into the relationship between nature, the gods and humankind, and between freedom of choice and the ineluctable workings of fate, in an abstract argument given shape and colour by images and words drawn from his observation of nature and the universe:

> Denn unfühlend
> Ist die Natur:
> Es leuchtet die Sonne
> Über Bös' und Gute,
> Und dem Verbrecher
> Glänzen wie dem Besten
> Der Mond und die Sterne.

('For Nature is unfeeling: the sun shines on the wicked and the good, and for the criminal as for the best of men shine the moon and the stars.')

Any other European poet treating such a subject during Goethe's lifetime would have given such a theme large-scale discursive treatment, but Goethe adopts an entirely different strategy which immediately reveals the originality of his approach. The poem is pared down to the utmost: each line (there are sixty) is reduced to two stresses – the alexandrines and hexameters of Gryphius and Klopstock contained six – and each verse is condensed into one sentence or thought-span. Thus the whole complex argument – reminiscent of a chorus by Sophocles – is borne on sequences of related words which transmute its profound intellectual argument into sensuous, visual poetry. Such extreme concision is a foretaste of the gnomic style which Goethe was to develop in his later years.

The poetry of Schiller is so different from that of Goethe that it can be hard to understand how, between them, they could embody in their works the essence of the literary and cultural phenomenon known as Weimar classicism. Where in Goethe's poetry feeling ('Gefühl ist alles') is the motive force behind self-expression, in Schiller's poems reasoned rhetoric provides the momentum and excitement; where Goethe distils the abstract from the real, Schiller finds words to embody abstract ideas in vivid, clear-cut images. Such distinctions might suggest that Schiller was cooler than Goethe and more calculating, or that Goethe's visions and insights were more intense than Schiller's. But that would be to underrate the emotive power latent in Schiller's passion for the abstract and to overlook the serene philosophy that emerges from the poems of both men in their maturity. Admittedly Schiller had scant sympathy with poetry of the folksong kind and lacked the common touch of writers such as Bürger, Claudius and Goethe himself: yet, for all that, many of his poems became great favourites with ordinary people. He seldom indulged in the delights of the short lyric, avoided traditional forms such as the sonnet, and in his much shorter career showed few traces of the oriental and gnomic styles to which Goethe increasingly turned after Schiller's death. Where the interests of the two friends converged was in narrative verse and in verse in the neo-classical elegiac or epigrammatic manners as alternative ways of exploring the potential of poetry to crystallize and convey the processes of abstract thought.

Schiller's most popular poems were the ballads he composed in 1797, the so-called *Balladenjahr* or 'year of ballads' which coincided closely with the publication in 1798 of the *Lyrical Ballads* by Wordsworth and Coleridge, and which also saw the composition of some of Goethe's finest contributions to the genre, such as 'Der Zauberlehrling' ('The sorcerer's apprentice'), a colourful, semi-humorous tale of the supernatural, and 'Die Braut von Korinth', a foray into the fashionable subject of vampirism. Schiller's five 1797 ballads, and the two he wrote in 1798, show him moulding a genre inherited from Bürger into something unmistakably his own because their themes are so closely linked to those preoccupying him as a dramatist, such as the human being's urge to tempt providence by going one step too far, thus upsetting the balance of the moral universe as Schiller understood it. Each ballad in its grippingly melodramatic way is an attempt to demonstrate that there is a deeper justice in the apparently fortuitous unfolding of events. Thus, in 'Die Bürgschaft', the readiness of one young man to stand in for his paroled friend and to die for him if need be provides the framework for an exciting account of a man's struggle against unforeseen setbacks to return in time for his own death: a forceful demonstration of the moral virtue humans can sometimes display. In another famous ballad, 'Die Kraniche des Ibykus' ('The cranes of Ibycus'), Schiller's sense of the deep links between tragic drama and the subconscious workings of guilt in the individual are revealed as a tale unfolds of two murderers who seek anonymity in a crowd of spectators watching the awesome performance of a tragedy in ancient Greece, but reveal their guilt when one of them utters the name of their victim as a flock of cranes flies over the auditorium as it did over the scene of the murder.

Die Szene wird zum Tribunal . . . ('The stage becomes a tribunal')

These words from the ballad's final stanza encapsulate Schiller's concept of the stage as a moral institution, a topic he had developed in *Die Bühne als moralische Anstalt* (1802), the famous lecture he had first given in 1784 under a different title. Tragedy – a work of art – can overcome the gap between the abstract and the personal, the imaginary and the real, and in doing so demonstrates the capacity of the stage to act as a moral institution by affecting the workings of an individual conscience in the context of an audience's – that is, a society's – unanimous and innate sense of right and wrong. It was a conception of drama and its moral and social functions which has characterized and, indeed, distinguished the German stage ever since.

The high moral tone of Schiller's poems, combined with their stylistic and narrative force, ensured them a place of honour in the general literary awareness of educated German-speakers at least until the onset of modernism in the twentieth century. None became more popular than 'Das Lied von der Glocke' (1800), Schiller's greatest public success as a poet. It is a long poem made up of quotable lines which develops the multiple analogies and connections between the casting of a bell and the uses to which it will be put to serve the community in joy and adversity, life and death.

As a poet in the late eighteenth-century neo-classical manner Schiller responded to the discipline of rhyming verse, but also favoured the metrical schemes – the hexameters and pentameters – associated with epic and elegiac verse, though he avoided the ode in classical metres championed by Klopstock, who died shortly before him in 1803. His finest elegies are 'Nänie' (1800), a haunting lament on the death of beauty, in which abstract ideas are given the power to affect the reader, and 'Der Spaziergang' (1795), a poem in which he takes up the pastoral mode of Ewald von Kleist's *Der Frühling* (1749) but gradually transmutes it into a medium for philosophical speculation. But as a highly intellectual master of *Gedankenlyrik* he tended to prefer the traditional Germanic discipline of rhyme, which had the added effect of giving his poems on abstract themes wider appeal in an age when learning and reciting poems was an integral part of the educational process and an accomplishment of some value in society. 'Die Götter Griechenlands', an early example written in 1788, is of great importance as a formulation of Schiller's thoughts. It, too, has an elegiac quality: it is a lament for the vanished harmony between man, nature and the divine which ancient Greece enjoyed but which the modern world has lost. In the poem's revised 1800 version this grief is tempered by Schiller's late eighteenth-century cultural optimism: not all is lost, because the artistic expression of our realization that all things must perish endows them, paradoxically, with immortality. The idea is summed up with classical – and quotable – economy in the lines:

Was unsterblich im Gesang soll leben,
Muß im Leben untergehn.

('What is to live in immortal song must perish in real life.')

After Schiller's death in May 1805, Goethe's development as a lyric poet led him into new territory. He had fully subscribed to Schiller's conception of classicism, the programme of which was set out not only by them both but also in thoughtful reviews of their work by contemporaries such as Bürger and Matthisson. But now he first of all took up the sonnet, a lyric form recommended by the poets of the Romantic movement and which he had already begun to take an interest in at the turn of the century when he had declared his intention to explore its symbiosis of artificiality and natural spontaneity in two samples of the genre, 'Das Sonett' and 'Natur und Kunst'. Now, in 1807–8, he composed a collection of sonnets which marked a revival of the form and represent an important link between the great days of the sonnet in the mid-seventeenth century and its return to favour in the hands of George and Rilke during the first quarter of the twentieth. Central to Goethe's conception of the sonnet, and for him its great attraction and challenge, is the notion of *Beschränkung*, that is, limitation or concision, a term he explicitly mentions in two of them. He connected this stylistic notion with the ethos of self-control and willing acceptance of limitations which was the hallmark of his personal philosophy and his mature classicism.

His fascination with oriental poetry, both Persian and Chinese, was a further stage in his pursuit of utmost concision which underlies all his finest poetry and which had already achieved the miraculous simplicity of great art in the twenty-four perfectly balanced and essentially untranslatable words of his second 'Wandrers Nachtlied', written in 1780:

> Über allen Gipfeln
> Ist Ruh,
> In allen Wipfeln
> Spürest du
> Kaum einen Hauch;
> Die Vögelein schweigen im Walde.
> Warte nur, balde
> Ruhest du auch.

Goethe's discovery of the oriental ideal of poetry, which corresponded so closely to his own, was influenced by the translation of the fourteenth-century Persian poet Hafiz by the Austrian writer and scholar Joseph von Hammer-Purgstall published in 1812, but it was inspired in 1814 by his love for Marianne von Willemer (1784–1860). Their deep attachment is the subject of many of the poems in his *West-östlicher Divan* (1819), a title deliberately framed in the Persian manner, and meaning a 'divan' or collection of poems uniting eastern and western traditions, but her identity and her part in its composition – she wrote a number of its finest poems – remained a close secret until after her death. The intensity of their relationship is especially evident in the poems of Books 3 and 8, where the poet's reciprocated love for 'Suleika' (as he called Marianne) is at its height; yet it is also transcended by the intricate construction of the *Divan's* twelve books, the almost mystical feel of the imagery, and the wealth of Islamic and oriental lore offsetting and counterbalancing what Goethe felt was an excessively self-indulgent emphasis on subjectivity in contemporary Romantic literature for which he knew that his earlier writings, such as *Werther*, were partly responsible. Orientalism was in fashion all over Europe (for instance, the Royal Pavilion at Brighton was being rebuilt in oriental style for the Prince Regent), but Goethe's was a good deal more genuine and authentic than that of most of his younger contemporaries; for them it had the alluring charm of the exotic, whereas for him it marked a further stage in a long artistic development. Despite certain similarities, this is the fundamental difference between Goethe's *West-östlicher Divan* and *Lalla Rookh* (1817) by the Irish poet Thomas Moore, a collection of oriental tales in verse which was becoming a favourite with readers in many parts of Europe. On the other hand, Goethe's *Divan* was further confirmation that German literature was not only abreast of current international trends but actually in the forefront of literary achievement and experimentation.

Towards the close of his life Goethe looked even further east. The poems of the *Chinesisch-deutsche Jahreszeiten* ('Chinese-German seasons') he published in 1827 return to the contemplation of the natural world, and give the impression of protracted observation condensed into the minimum of words. He sees no need to imitate Chinese poetry closely: what these poems reveal is that, just as he had come to understand the Greek and Latin poets of antiquity, the sonnet-writers of the Renaissance or indeed the anonymous authors of Germany's folksongs, so, too, he had now finally come to a stage at which he could comprehend the subtle verbal art of the East and use it to the advantage of his own:

Dämmrung senkte sich von oben
Schon ist alle Nähe fern;
Doch zuerst emporgehoben
Holden Lichts der Abendstern!
Alles schwankt ins Ungewisse,
Nebel schleichen in die Höh',
Schwarzvertiefte Finsternisse
Widerspiegelnd ruht der See.

('Twilight has fallen from above and already everything close is far away; but first to be raised on high with its pure clear light is the evening star. Everything swims into indistinctness, mists rise upwards, and darknesses, ever deeper and darker, are mirrored by the still lake.')

Such imagery had been characteristic of his poetry always – he had always been enthralled by the shifting gradations of light and darkness over lake, forest and mountain – but here it reflects the dispassionate serenity of a lifetime's wisdom.

On the way to these ultimate insights into the nature of lyric poetry, Goethe had realized instinctively that the age of the heroic verse epic was over, and that the new German literary renaissance identified with him and his Weimar associates would have to do without one. He was more reluctant to let go of the classical elegy because to him it seemed, as it had done to Schiller, to be the most appropriate form for a theme which was clearly going to dominate modern poetry: lament for loss. In the late 1790s he had displayed his command of the elegiac mode in poems such as 'Euphrosyne', a long threnody written in 1797–8 in remembrance of the young Weimar actress Christiane Becker, in which Goethe's favourite imagery of clearing mist, daybreak and sunlight provides an outlet for his feelings of grief and gratitude. Then, in September 1823, between his two late oriental phases, he returned to the elegiac mode – this time not in classical metre but in rhyming six-line stanzas – for one of his most intense and moving poems. Simply entitled 'Elegie', it is a further example of Goethe's practice of calling what he considered his best achievement in a particular form after the form itself (e.g. *Das Sonett*, *Die Novelle*, *Das Märchen* are all titles of works as well as generic terms). 'Elegie' is a poem of lament and farewell in which reluctant acceptance of the inevitable transcends melancholy, if not anguish and loss; this is because the loved one's lesson is that, though the moment may be fleeting, it can provide direct personal experience of the perfect bliss inherent in the order and beauty of the universe. Perhaps the most remarkable quality of Goethe's last and most personal love poem, written on 1 September 1823 as he drove away from the Bohemian spa of Marienbad, and from Ulrike von Levetzow (1804–99) and the last intense passion of his life, is the sense that here, at last, he has shed that sense of self which can sometimes seem to mar his extraordinary artistic achievement as a lyric poet.

## Classicism or Romanticism in German Poetry? Friedrich Hölderlin

The neo-classical tradition in German poetry which Klopstock inaugurated in the middle of the eighteenth century reached its apogee in the work of Friedrich Hölderlin. No German poet, indeed no modern European writer, ever took the classical ideal to greater lengths or succeeded in identifying himself more closely and exclusively with it: even Keats and Chénier sound less Greek than he. Single-mindedly he confined himself to the metrical schemes and diction of classical prosody as they had been adapted for the German language by Klopstock and Johann Heinrich Voß, the classically trained translator of Homer (*Odüßee*, 1781; *Ilias*, 1793). Even *Der Tod des Empedokles*, Hölderlin's uncompleted tragedy in the style of Sophocles, is conveyed in the medium of a stylized yet supple German written almost as if it were ancient Greek. He developed such a sure command of this medium that he was able to make it the vehicle for poetic ideas and images of great force, profundity and evocative power. But his unremitting fondness for such a rarefied and elevated style could sometimes result in mannerisms which border on self-pastiche: his often unidiomatic syntax and straining after rhetorical effect not only make him sometimes hard to follow, but are also a reminder that German poetry has always run risks when it becomes too far divorced from the language of ordinary people. A poem such as 'Der Neckar' (1800) illustrates the essence of Hölderlin's idea of poetry but also explains why, for all his determined classicism – almost all his poems date from the years 1795 to 1805, a period concurrent with the Napoleonic Wars but also with Weimar classicism – he often had more in common with the authors of the rising Romantic movement. In 'Der Neckar' the river which flows through Hölderlin's native landscape merges imperceptibly with evocations of the unknown vanished landscape of ancient Greece, but in doing so a vividly depicted yet alien world compounded of dreams and learning replaces the one more familiar to him, and the imagined subsumes reality. 'Der Neckar' is an ode in the classical manner: Hölderlin's other great river poem, 'Der Rhein' (1801), is a full-scale hymn in the manner of Pindar, an ode in free verse held together by rhythms, assonances and images if not by any immediately discernible or strictly coherent argument, in which the whole course of Germany's history and its ultimate destiny are conveyed by the geographical metaphor of its greatest river. The idea is given precedence over the object, and the primacy of poetry is threatened. During his schooldays in Tübingen Hölderlin had shared a room with Hegel and Schelling, both of whom became great philosophers, and he was later intimidated by Schiller's formidable intellect. Should the poet philosophize, or should he paint pictures in words? Hölderlin's poetry, like his life, is symptomatic of a conflict of aesthetic and intellectual priorities which has often characterized the literature of Germany and which was to recur time and again in its nineteenth- and twentieth-century culture.

    Hölderlin might have become one of the most successful writers of Germany's classical age. Instead he became one of Germany's most problematic and fascinating poets, and one whose evaluation and interpretation have fluctuated widely. Neglected for a long time, he was hailed and revered as a great precursor by the aesthetic movement at the turn of the century, idolized by the National Socialists, treated as a yardstick to measure literary sensitivity by the authoritative literary critics of the early post-1945 era, and as an intellectual articulating complex responses to political and social revolution by their successors. His contemporaries had found him difficult. He received early encouragement from Schiller, his boyhood hero and role model, and actually reached Weimar. But his psychological make-up contained elements which drew him in a different direction. Like William Blake, his close contemporary, he was a visionary rather than a realist; deeply caught up in the issues raised by the French Revolution, he was acutely aware of the discrepancies between the realities and pressures of his own times and his visions of an idealized Greek past and of a utopian, sometimes even ominously nationalistic future. Hölderlin's collapse into mental illness and growing incoherence comes as no great surprise; from the start of his writing career he was burdened by the thought of the responsibilities of being a poet and the difficulties of living up to his own expectations. For a short time his love for Suzette Gontard, a married woman to whose children he was a tutor, endowed his poetry with a rapt sunlit serenity – most beautifully realized in the poems he addressed to her Platonic ideal, Diotima. Her death in 1802 hastened the breakdown of his carefully constructed poetic world of images, allegories, themes and ideas, and of the sophisticated syntax in which he expressed them. In intention and outward appearance his poems, with their vibrant evocations of season and landscape, were classical indeed, but at a deeper level there was not much in common between the classicism of Goethe and Schiller and Hölderlin's more tormented understanding of poetry and the role of the poet.

## The Golden Century of German Drama

The century that elapsed between the first performance of Lessing's middle-class tragedy *Miß Sara Sampson* in 1755 and the death of the dramatist Friedrich Hebbel in 1863 saw a flowering of theatrical activity and dramatic art in the German-speaking countries which at long last put German drama on a par with that of France, Spain and England. In each of these three countries the theatre had enjoyed a golden age during which the classics of their subsequent repertoires were created and in which drama, both comic and serious, had become the vehicle for some of the profoundest insights on man and society in their literatures. Now it was Germany's turn. A succession of playwrights of genius created a sequence of plays which came to constitute the classical German repertoire, while alongside them a host of secondary theatrical authors, producers, impresarios and actors bore witness to the vitality and variety of the German-speaking stage. Characteristically enough of the German area of Europe, its centre of theatrical activity tended to move from one city to another according to the changing political, cultural and economic circumstances, though this mobility also reflects the growth of a network of theatrical and creative enterprise often linking one place with another.

The golden age dawned in Leipzig, a prosperous trading city with a lively university and a certain cosmopolitan air about it; here an actress of calibre, Caroline Neuber, collaborated with the influential critic and second-rate playwright Gottsched to raise the tone of the German stage by ridding it of burlesque and farcical elements which its potential urban middle-class audience felt it ought to consider distasteful. Their efforts and those of other theatrically minded people such as the poet Gellert encouraged a growing number of minor writers to write plays, though the repertoire mainly consisted of translations from the French or from the Danish of Ludvig

Holberg, the major theatrical author of northern Europe at the time. But then the movement to kindle interest in the theatre and to counteract the disapproval of the civic and church authorities attracted the attention of the young Lessing.

His intellectual interest had already been caught by the paradox which was to occupy him for much of his creative life. French drama had achieved a standard of excellence undisputed on the continent of Europe; yet, despite its great merits in comedy and, especially, tragedy, the French model seemed to Lessing to be inappropriate to Germany. In other words, the effort to emulate French excellence could only lead to second-rate imitations which were already in danger of spoiling the taste of the German middle-class public whom it was necessary to woo to make the stage viable. It was a situation which Lessing strove to remedy; but, despite his success, it was to remain an ever-present factor throughout much of Germany's theatrical golden age. Even when its greatest works were being written and produced, French adaptations of dubious quality held the stage and attracted audiences in pursuit of nothing more demanding than relaxation and diversion. Where could Germany find a model for a theatre more congenial to its own natural tastes and interests? To Lessing the answer was obvious: England – especially the England of Shakespeare. It is ironic that the flowering of German theatre to which this insight led coincided with a period of mediocrity in English drama, which, after Sheridan, was finding itself increasingly incapable of tapping the indigenous tradition Lessing so much admired. Lessing's comparisons between French and English drama constitute the most lively and thought-provoking dramatic criticism of the eighteenth century; his personal interest in play writing, acting and play production and his critical activities culminated in the short-lived Hamburg National Theatre project of 1767–8. The promoters of this enterprise, a consortium of Hamburg citizens, took the bold step of engaging Lessing to be its resident adviser and reviewer, and his write-ups of the productions staged during its brief existence appeared in a kind of house journal and then in book form in 1768. Soon they were recognized as a masterpiece of sustained dramatic criticism, and their pre-eminence in the field is still recognized today. What makes Lessing's *Hamburgische Dramaturgie* such a stimulating and appealing work is the fact that it is a response to a real theatrical situation, not a theoretical work divorced from the challenges and constraints of the playhouse. The repertoire of the Hamburg playhouse ranged widely from Voltaire and Corneille to Shakespeare and Lessing himself, and thus provided ample opportunity for him to air his views on the comparative merits of French and English drama and to develop and try out his own ideas on the future course German drama should take. To a large extent his advice was heeded and his prophecies vindicated.

## Lessing and Middle-Class Drama

Lessing's own work as a dramatist was an integral part of his campaign to set German drama on the course most suitable to it. In 1755 his first important play, *Miß Sara Sampson*, transported its audiences to a fictional England where Sara, a virtuous young woman, daughter of Sir William Sampson, has eloped with Mellefont, a plausible rake whose reluctance to make an honest woman of her is reinforced by the strenuous efforts made by Marwood, his former mistress, to win him back for their small daughter's sake. The play's moral paradoxes are ironic and theatrically effective. The virtuous heroine finds herself cast in the role of the seductive mistress, while the discarded mistress fights for her conjugal and family rights with the determination of a Roman matron and, later, the passion of a Medea. Marwood's explicit allusion to this Greek figure was significant, pointing as it did to Lessing's determination to make the tragic mode of antiquity (Medea's story had been dramatized by Euripides) relevant to a contemporary middle-class audience deficient perhaps in classical scholarship but increasingly attuned to self-scrutiny as a result of the approach to personal morality encouraged by the Pietist movement, forerunner of the Methodist movement in England, which had a similar effect on literature. Meanwhile Sara, caught in a moral dilemma largely of her own making, is torn between the impulses of the heart and the dictates of reason; paradoxically again, her heart counsels the wisdom of virtue whereas reason suggests easier, more instinctual solutions. The play's inversion of conventional social and moral stereotypes reaches its climax when Sara dies, poisoned by Marwood, and in the dingy premises of an inn, yet recognized by her penitent seducer and her forgiving father – another stereotype overturned – as a perfect embodiment of Christian virtue, an impression shared by the play's sobbing audiences, often respectable German burghers who would normally have been shocked by such conduct rather than edified by it.

Lessing's 'English' domestic tragedy demonstrated that a shift of setting and tone from grand, academic subjects and high-flown rhetoric to contemporary locations and speech might be the most effective means to win over the audiences which the German stage needed for its economic viability. This shift to a new register and a new setting for the perennial issues that are the true subject of tragedy went hand in hand with the view he was evolving that modern tragedy would have to appeal to the emotional sensibilities of its audiences if it was to win their hearts. The new audiences he had in mind were no longer likely to be moved by what befell characters quite unlike themselves in situations that were alien to themselves; only if members of the audience could imagine themselves in the same dire situations as the characters in the play, would they be moved to pity and fear – fear lest they might indeed experience something analogously unpleasant, and pity for a person like themselves and with whose plight they could therefore readily identify. The approach Lessing was advocating was Aristotelian, perhaps, but it was Aristotelian with a difference. The difference lay in the fact that tragedy was being brought into line with comedy, which had traditionally always tended to be set in the present and to represent a world more or less consonant with the spectator's own. Gone were the columned antechambers and throne rooms of French classical drama, but gone too was the stage imagined by the spectator's mind, for paradoxically Lessing had dispensed with what many might regard as one of the wonders of Shakespearean drama. But the banishment of both alternatives in favour of prosaic realism, like the abandonment of verse in favour of a more prosaic speech, was to be relatively short-lived. Lessing, though he made no claims to be a poet or imaginative writer, was himself the author of the first major German play in blank verse, *Nathan der Weise* (1779).

Before that, however, Lessing wrote the play that was to be his greatest popular success. *Minna von Barnhelm* has been generally regarded as the finest German comedy ever since it was first performed in Hamburg in 1767. Even in a literature not especially noted for its comic drama, this was a remarkable achievement. The 1760s had seemed to bode well for comedy: in 1759 Lessing had openly ridiculed the banishment of the clown Harlequin from the German stage by the rationalist Gottsched and his associate, the actress Caroline Neuber, in 1737; then in 1761 Justus Möser published his spirited defence of this comic embodiment of the Germans' sometimes drastic sense of humour in his *Harlekin, oder Verteidigung des Grotesk-Komischen* ('Harlequin, or Defence of the comic-grotesque'), a work which introduced the notion of the 'grotesque' to literary discourse. But, while recommending Möser's treatise, Lessing realized there could be no going back to the days of jolly old Hans Sachs and that comedy could no longer be associated with one central clown figure: like tragedy, it was an element of human social life, and in the optimistic Age of Reason it was better suited to raise a smile than a guffaw. New impulses were coming from France in the shape of Marivaux's sophisticated bitter-sweet comedies, and Lessing's play responded to these by adapting them to the emotional and social requirements of the theatre-going public of a country seeking a new identity for itself. By setting it in the immediate aftermath of the Seven Years War (1756–63) between Austria and Prussia, and treating his audiences to the stratagems of Minna, a vivacious young Saxon lady, to win back her proud Prussian lover, Major von Tellheim, by overcoming his negative attitude, he created the classic comedy of German unification: its perennial topicality has been demonstrated on many occasions since. The unique position of Lessing's *Minna von Barnhelm* as a truly national drama played out by recognizably German characters and with a happy ending is reinforced by the fact that no other German playwright has ever managed to equal Lessing's example.

*Minna von Barnhelm* is unique; *Emilia Galotti*, a tragedy first performed in Brunswick in 1772, confirmed a trend. Its appeal to the sensibilities of the period and its immediate literary impact were quickly demonstrated: a copy of the play is found lying open on Werther's desk after he commits suicide in Goethe's best-selling novel; thus the existence of Germany's new drama was brought home to a much wider international public, creating the first symptoms of a taste for German plays which was to last until well into the nineteenth century in English-speaking countries. Lessing's first middle-class tragedy, *Miß Sara Sampson*, had been set in the England of Richardson's novels, *Pamela, or Virtue Rewarded* (1740–1, translated into German in 1743 and again in 1772) and *Clarissa, or The History of a Young Lady* (1748–9, translated in 1753). *Emilia Galotti*, his second play with a contemporary setting, takes place in a small principality in Italy, a choice which was probably dictated mainly by his wish to avoid the charge that he was criticizing corruption and the abuse of privilege in contemporary Germany, in which there were a great many principalities large and small. The play certainly benefits from its more sensual and highly charged setting. The well-paced action gets under way as an effete, morally indifferent prince finds his attention drawn away from affairs of state to the charms of a chaste young middle-class woman whose personal situation – she is about to be married to a nobleman – seems no more than an inconvenient impediment to the pursuit of his own objectives. The clash between Emilia's integrity, which is at once deeply personal and characteristic of her self-respecting class, and the prince's cynical self-indulgence, astutely manipulated by his slippery adviser Marinelli (a role very much in the Jacobean manner), generates an excitement which is dramatically enhanced and made psychologically more problematic by the suggestion that Emilia may not be indifferent to the prince. This weakness in her resolve motivates the drastic, indeed almost melodramatic outcome of the play. Emilia, fearful that she may not be strong enough to withstand the prince, yet loathing him because of this and because he has caused the death of the man she was about to marry, persuades her father, an upright, honourable citizen, to kill her to save her from a fate worse than death. This plot, based on the Roman myth of Virginia, proved that a well-known classical subject could be adapted to the requirements and taste of another age and country. Contemporaries enjoyed it for what it was, an exciting blend of intrigue and sexual passion which, without losing credibility, preserved a high moral tone. But to some, *Emilia Galotti* was more: it was a defiant indictment of corrupt regimes and individuals whose hold on society was based on the abuse of privilege and power. In other words, as early as 1772, twelve years before the first performance of *Le Mariage de*

*Figaro* by Beaumarchais and fourteen years before Mozart's operatic setting of it to a masterly Italian libretto by Lorenzo da Ponte, Lessing was writing drama with clear pre-revolutionary political and social implications. It says much about the separate yet simultaneous development of opera and drama in Germany that Lessing's essentially 'operatic' tragedy was never turned into an opera.

By 1772 Lessing had established himself as Germany's major serious dramatist. His achievement was primarily associated with his two prose tragedies dealing with the social and psychological problems of modern middle-class people, and he has continued to be rightly regarded as the originator of the German tradition of the *bürgerliches Trauerspiel*, which was to continue for most of the next hundred years. But whether this tradition ever really existed is a moot point. It is true that a small number of remarkable plays hark back to the model Lessing created. But they are separated from each other by large gaps of time, and stand out as exceptions to the general trend that the German theatre was in fact taking, isolated examples backed up by a steady output of less distinguished middle-class prose plays by minor playwrights such as Lessing's younger brother Carl Gotthelf Lessing, whose 'serious comedy' *Die Mätresse* ('The Mistress', 1780) turns on the topical and divisive issue of class distinctions, and *Der deutsche Hausvater* by Otto Heinrich von Gemmingen, the popular success of the same year, in which an enlightened aristocratic paterfamilias finally manages to persuade his errant son to marry a lower-class girl to make amends for having seduced her. There had been comic elements even in Lessing's 'weepy' *Miß Sara Sampson*, and plays such as these proved that the new, topical subjects of middle-class tragedy could also be effectively treated with a lighter touch and given a happy ending. The dawning sociological awareness of Lessing's middle-class domestic prose tragedies with their emphasis on the family, child–parent relationships, and social values represents a strand in German drama during its golden age rather than a tradition, and therefore not surprisingly they exhibit qualities that make each one a unique achievement.

## Drama and the *Sturm und Drang*

The years 1773–6 saw an outburst of exciting dramatic activity unequalled in German literary history until the Expressionist breakthrough in 1916–22, and not without parallels with it. In both cases the plays were by young men antagonized by the world they lived in but buoyed up by their wish for change and innovation. Goethe's *Götz von Berlichingen* (1773) led the way. It dramatizes events at a turning-point in German history and involving 'real' historical figures offset by characters of Goethe's imagination. The time is that of the Lutheran Reformation, when the medieval social order was giving way to the particularism and potential despotism of Germany's petty states. The play's turbulent historical setting and vital, down-to-earth hero appealed: the play reached the Berlin stage within a year, and did much to introduce the notion of historical costume drama and prepare the way for the new fashions for plays about knights in armour (*Ritterstücke*) and for Shakespeare, whose dramatic style Goethe was ostensibly imitating in his play's open form and hectic multiplicity of disconnected, even episodic scenes.

*Sturm und Drang* drama quickly abandoned this 'medieval' mode for one more up to date. Soon Goethe's friend J. M. R. Lenz was writing plays which directly reflect the social conditions of the time or, rather, certain social evils which directly affected its younger generation. He instinctively broke the mould of eighteenth-century drama by using the techniques of comedy perfected by Lessing in his comedy *Minna von Barnhelm* (1767) for an intensely serious, indeed tragic purpose. When he turned his attention to the sometimes tragic effects which military garrisons of bored young men can have on a respectable middle-class community in his remarkably informal, colloquial play *Die Soldaten* (1776) or to the social and emotional plight of the many educated but penurious young men who earned their keep tutoring the children of the rich and upper-class in *Der Hofmeister, oder die Vorteile der Privaterziehung* ('The Tutor or The Advantages of Private Education', 1774), his startling fusion of Lessing's dramatic style with the open form and episodic scene-changes of the 'Shakespearean' manner created a new concept of theatre. At the time the appeal of these extraordinarily forward-looking plays was limited: they were not fully appreciated until their gradual rediscovery a century later, or more. Social satire and criticism represented one dimension to Lenz's plays; another was their emphasis on authenticity, a characteristic with little or no parallel in the other European literatures of the period. They are cynical, but they are also moral, indeed even political, and their sceptical avoidance of happy endings stands in sharp contrast to the more popular contemporary plays on domestic themes by writers such as Gemmingen in Germany or Diderot in France; indeed the psychological and social authenticity of Lenz's two master-pieces stands comparison with the probing and influential pre-revolutionary insights of Beaumarchais's *Le Mariage de Figaro*, first performed in 1784 but completed in 1778, the year of the first performance of *Der Hofmeister*. In *Die Kindermörderin* ('The child-murderer', 1776) by Heinrich Leopold Wagner, a gloomy case of infanticide actually comes close to forestalling late nineteenth-century Naturalism, though it is in fact based on the frequent trials and executions of young unmarried mothers which represent the seamier and crueller side of an era too easily associated with ease and elegance. The subject had been taken up by Goethe in *Urfaust*, the first version of his Faust drama, written shortly before. But Wagner's avoidance of rhetoric and theatricality is all the more striking when it is contrasted with the more stylized yet often violent melodrama of Klinger's *Die Zwillinge* ('The twins') and Leisewitz's *Julius von Tarent*. These two plays were submitted for a competition organized by the talent-spotting actor-manager Friedrich Ludwig Schröder in 1775, the same year as Sheridan's first play, *The Rivals*, written when he, like Friedrich Maximilian Klinger and Johann Anton Leisewitz, was in his early twenties. Klinger's play won, but both are fine examples of another speciality of the *Sturm und Drang* movement: the play that highlights a conflict between rival brothers, a genre which was to reach its artistic climax in Schiller's *Die Räuber* ('The robbers') in 1781.

## Blank Verse and the Drama of Ideas

Most German dramatists were pursuing other aims and objectives. Lessing himself sensed the direction in which German serious drama was heading; in 1779 he opted for blank verse as the medium best suited to drama with a high thought-content, and in doing so associated himself with the efforts already made by his contemporary Wieland in *Lady Johanna Gray* (1758) to exploit another facet of the English theatre he so much admired, namely its fondness for subjects taken from history. But *Nathan der Weise* is not really a historical tragedy, despite its ostensible setting in the days of the Crusades. The chivalrous Muslim, Saladin, and his Christian opponent, the over-hasty Knight Templar, are in no way related to the medievalism that was just starting to become popular in Germany. They are simply human beings with widely divergent temperaments and ages caught up in heated yet futile ideological conflict from which they are finally rescued by the selfless intervention of the elderly Jew, Nathan, a memorable embodiment of the human capacity to triumph over suffering and transcend prejudice in pursuit of the peaceful realization of humane ideals. Lessing used the stage to plead for tolerance, and in doing so decisively raised the status of the theatre in the culture of Germany. Except in a rare, inspired performance the play may be tedious to sit through, but it is an enthralling dramatization of the sort of intellectual and moral debate which most eighteenth-century European writers were content to confine to the medium of the moral essay or didactic poem. Contemporary with the work of the philosopher Kant, whose *Kritik der reinen Vernunft* ('Critique of Pure Reason') appeared in 1781, *Nathan der Weise* is Germany's first great drama of ideas. It has retained its pre-eminent position up to the present day because in it Lessing, the outstanding creative intellect produced by Germany during the Age of Enlightenment, was addressing questions which have haunted the German consciousness in the twentieth century. Perhaps the most remarkable feature of the play is that with its central character, reputedly modelled on Lessing's much admired friend, the philosopher Moses Mendelssohn, a Jew was held up as an example of wisdom and understanding to subsequent generations. In no other European literature has a Jew achieved such classical status or a Muslim been presented in such a sympathetic light on the stage.

In the same year which saw the publication of *Nathan* (1779: its first performance followed in Berlin in 1783), the thirty-year-old Goethe wrote and played the male lead in the prose version of what was to be his first great drama in blank verse, *Iphigenie auf Tauris*. He had already made his name with his energetic medieval drama, *Götz von Berlichingen*, but now he had something very different in mind. Like *Nathan der Weise*, his new play was to be a plea for tolerance and understanding, but one which adopted the fashionable neo-classical manner of the period in order to reveal the new ends to which it could be put. The achievement of this objective was to prove a struggle, even for him. The final version of the drama, now in harmoniously fluent blank verse, was not completed until he had experienced the classical world of Italy at first hand, and was not performed until 1800 (Vienna) and 1802 (Weimar).

## Goethe: The Classical Dramatist

With *Iphigenie* the literature of Germany at last achieved a masterpiece in truly classical mould which raised the expressive qualities of the German language to unprecedented heights. Gone was the impression of effort that had marked earlier attempts to mould the German language into the aesthetic unity, flexible yet firm, that was the classical ideal. From the moment Goethe's tragic drama opens and its heroine, the daughter of the Greek general Agamemnon, steps out from her temple into the natural surroundings of her sacred grove in distant Tauris, the ideal unity of art, nature and the human being is established in visual and audible form. *Iphigenie* is a poetic drama created essentially by the sounds and images evoked by its language; characteristically, its lines of blank verse are seldom end-stopped – fluidity is the priority as the poet unfolds his shifting vision of the struggle of a mortal woman to fulfil the dictates of her heart and vindicate her innate sense of the divine by abiding by her emotional truth. Later in the play, she beseeches the gods in momentous words to save their image in her soul. The justification of her faith in them resides in the ability of human beings to achieve harmony, understanding and reconciliation by living up to their moral standards – and Goethe here was in a sense articulating the creed of all those who put their faith in the neo-classical ideal. Iphigenia, exiled against her will and now a priestess in a remote country, finds herself confronted once again by the curse that hangs over her bloodstained family. The unforeseen arrival of her brother, Orestes, who is out of his mind, obliges her to counteract his urge to use violence and deceit in order to rescue her. Sanity must prevail. But at what price? It is a price that to another age might seem slight, but which to the later eighteenth century aroused feelings of intense involvement and appreciative admiration. Rather than allow her brother to have his way and escape from Tauris, she takes the moral initiative and confronts the barbarian king who holds her captive, and who loves her in his way, with an opportunity to show that even an uncivilized savage is a human being and possesses a moral sense. Overcoming his inclination to have his own way, the king lives up to Iphigenia's high expectations of him and all humanity; the handshake that ends the play is a 'happy end' that can and should be deeply moving in performance – indeed its effect has an almost tragic quality in that the spectator is simultaneously conscious of its artistic truth and of the sad fact that, measured against his own experience of life, it may be idealistic wishful thinking.

Goethe followed his first great poetic drama with two more which explore in generalized terms and specific historical settings the tragic predicaments of an idealist in action and a poet hemmed in by restrictions. Both themes represent aspects of his own experience as a poet at the court of Weimar and as a close associate of his friend, its ruling duke. *Egmont* was written between 1774 and 1787, and therefore has its roots in the *Sturm und Drang* period. In broader European context it is a key work in the final phase of the *ancien régime* which was to end with the French Revolution of 1789 and its repercussions abroad. Like Schiller's *Don Carlos*, a verse tragedy completed in the same year, Goethe's prose tragedy looked back for its plot to the struggle of the Netherlands for independence from Spain in the sixteenth century. For both writers freedom of speech, action and personal belief is the central impulse, and it is significant that both plays inspired music by great composers who shared their confidence in the human potential for idealistic action in the struggle against the stranglehold of repression: Beethoven's incidental music for Goethe's play was composed in 1810; Verdi's grand opera *Don Carlos* was written for production in Paris in 1867. In both plays the idealist becomes the victim of realities which thwart his aspirations. Count Egmont's heroism is personal and impulsive: the world in which he finds himself playing an active political part is a world of *Realpolitik*. His love for Klärchen is sincere and affecting, as is his courage in the face of execution; yet he is flawed, and fatally, because he cannot read the signs which ominously signal the impasse into which he is driving himself or, perhaps, being driven by forces in and outside himself. Schiller's treatment of a somewhat analogous subject was a good deal more complex. In his historical drama, set in the same period, the protagonist is split, as it were, into two complementary characters: Carlos, an idealist, is the son of Philip II of Spain, and his freedom to act is restricted by his rank, while the Marquis of Posa, the equally idealistic nobleman who becomes the king's confidant and Carlos's friend, is afforded almost unlimited scope for action, yet neither can succeed without the backing of the other. Their friendship is intense and humanly moving, but historical events and their psychological make-up are in the end too much for them: tragically they go to their doom, highlighting the validity of their aspirations all the more because they fail to convert them into reality.

The insoluble conflict between a human being's inner truth and the external pressures of his situation is the subject of *Torquato Tasso*, completed soon after *Egmont* between 1788 and 1790, though not performed until 1807, when Goethe felt that the Weimar court theatre was technically and stylistically ready to do it justice. It is hard to realize that this intense though outwardly serene blank-verse play set in Ferrara during the Italian Renaissance was a product of the months which witnessed the outbreak of the French Revolution, but it is easier to understand why Goethe decided to centre the play on the great Italian poet whose dreams were admired by his contemporaries but whose personal conduct led him to be certified insane. With this play German literature achieved what in retrospect seems to have been its primary and uniquely characteristic objective: a work of art on the subject of the aesthetic experience itself, seen as the focus of the individual's social, ethical and, above all, emotional life. From now on the predicament of the artist caught between the world of his imagination and the realities of the world in which he lives were to become one of its central and most pervasive themes.

## Goethe and the Weimar Court Theatre

The age of Goethe and Schiller saw the creation of the classical German repertoire and the emergence of a theatrical culture which is, broadly speaking, the one still in evidence in the German-speaking countries today. Theatre reform had been in the air since the days of Frau Neuber and Gottsched in the 1730s, and all through the eighteenth century sporadic efforts were made in many places to raise the tone of the stage in Germany and reduce the influence of foreign actors and playwrights at a time when French cultural hegemony was at its height. The 1767 Hamburg National Theatre project associated with Lessing was one such example; so, too, was the creation of a National and Court Theatre in Vienna in 1776. The great German theatre directors and actor-managers of the period – Dalberg in Mannheim, Schröder in Hamburg and Iffland in Berlin – were doing their best to promote new works and a change in taste. But nowhere did great literature impinge more closely on the stage than at Weimar during the years when Goethe directed its court theatre, that is, from 1791 to 1817. He had played himself in by running an amateur theatre group for the Weimar court and its circle between 1776 and 1781, and had the patience to allow his long-term cultural strategy to take effect slowly. Like all theatre-going publics, the Weimar one wanted to be amused and entertained; 85 per cent of the court theatre's performances were devoted to comedies and short-lived popular plays, operas, and above all *Singspiele*, that is, plays interspersed with music and song, of which hundreds were written and very few are still remembered: Goethe's own (such as *Die Fischerin* and *Jery und Bäteli*) are no exception.

Weimar's most popular playwright during Goethe's twenty-six years as theatre director was the internationally famous August von Kotzebue, a local man: 87 of his plays were staged there in 638 performances. But the Weimar court theatre was also capable of more discriminating taste, and provided a cultural lead for the rest of Germany. Its favourite Schiller verse play was *Wallensteins Lager* (the first part of his *Wallenstein* trilogy), which reached a total of 52 performances; the same period saw 280 Mozart performances in Weimar, including 82 of *Die Zauberflöte* ('The Magic Flute'). Thus, from the start, Weimar classicism was to be closely associated with the music of Mozart, who died in the same year that Goethe took up his theatrical post. Goethe was well aware that he had to tread carefully when it came to serious drama in verse. At all times aesthetic appeal was to take precedence over naturalness of expression because, in his view, beauty of movement and stage grouping was the visual means by which the moral dimension of his plays and those of Schiller could best be conveyed to their spectators. His artistic strategy lay in cultivating ensemble by picking his actors carefully, ensuring adequate rehearsal (which taught him and Schiller much about their art), and encouraging a kind of declamation sensitive to the rhythms and meaning of the text; he also raised the status of his actors by paying them properly and consorting with them socially, thereby rescuing the stage from the opprobrium of society.

Goethe recorded his guiding principles as a director in his *Regeln für Schauspieler* ('Rules for actors', 1803), but they may be largely deduced from his plays and especially those of Schiller, most of which, from *Wallenstein* on, were premiered at Weimar. High points were the premieres of *Maria Stuart* in 1800 and *Wilhelm Tell* in 1804, a cultural triumph for which Goethe paid Schiller 165 thalers, the sum Kotzebue received in Berlin for his farce *Der Wirrwarr* ('The hurly-burly'). Normally playwrights got no other income from a play after this initial payment, and earned nothing from performances after it had appeared in print; fixed royalties and copyright laws were a sequel to the golden age of German drama, not a shaping factor. The great era of the Weimar court theatre set an artistic precedent for towns and cities throughout the German-speaking world, but an economic one too: Goethe introduced the sale of seat tickets, but his court theatre still depended on a subsidy from the Duchy of Weimar of 7000 thalers, and state-subsidized theatre has been a fact of German artistic life ever since. Its leading actress, Caroline Jagemann, earned 100 thalers during her first season after Goethe engaged her in 1796. Within a year she had become the mistress of his friend and patron, Duke Karl August. Goethe finally withdrew from his post as Germany's most distinguished director when she insisted on appearing on stage with a poodle.

## The Plays of Schiller

*Nathan der Weise* and *Iphigenie* had shown how blank-verse drama could convey a moral argument and trace the awakening of moral awareness. *Tasso* had shifted the emphasis from ethics to aesthetics. All three plays proved that ideas can entertain when they are integrated in a powerful human drama. *Don Carlos* indicated that such drama was to be the greatest strength of Friedrich Schiller. He was a more instinctual man of the theatre than either Lessing or Goethe. Though his intellect was powerful and his moral sense a highly developed one, it was the dramatic potential of subjects usually drawn from history that would first arouse his creative imagination. His ability to visualize an unfolding action ensured the stageworthiness of his plays; the dozen or so he wrote soon established themselves as an essential part of the serious German repertoire. Unlike Lessing, he never wrote comedy; unlike Goethe, he never carried his audiences away into the realms of pure poetry. His imagination was of a different order, and his choice of subjects shows that his interests were cosmopolitan rather than patriotic, let alone nationalistic.

Schiller came to prominence overnight when his first play, *Die Räuber*, projected him to the forefront of German and indeed European pre-Romanticism in 1781, when he was only twenty-one. Here was the noble bandit, Karl Moor, a figure who haunted the imagination of the period, betrayed by his devious and jealous brother, Franz, and living an outlaw's open-air life with a band of fellow-students in the forests of Bohemia, a life presented as freer and more honest than that he would be living as a reluctant member of the corrupt society that has disowned him. The play has the turbulent undisciplined quality of an early work, yet far from being imitative it looks far ahead in its championship of the individual's right to an alternative lifestyle when his society has failed him. There is something remarkably modern in this play written before the major political, social and technological revolutions of the late eighteenth century had begun to bring the modern world about. For the young couple at the centre of Schiller's play *Kabale und*

*Liebe* (1784) there is no such attractive alternative. Ferdinand, like the later Don Carlos, is the son of a man with power, Luise is the daughter of a rank-and-file musician, a representative of the unsung class which made possible the extraordinary musical culture of Mozart's age. Their relationship is destroyed by a cabal of opposing interests because it is one which offended the social status quo, though not, it seems, the play's first audiences. Schiller's only attempt at middle-class drama, it prepared contemporaries, as Lessing's *Miß Sara Sampson* had done, for a change in attitude which would be long in coming. It clearly shows Lessing's influence, but Schiller's sense of social history in the making, and his almost operatic flair for strong situations, foreshadow the achievements of the great historical playwright he was to become. *Wallenstein*, a trilogy, is the only one of his dramatic works to be set in the context of German history. Schiller never treated the same type of subject or setting twice. He had a particular fondness for the sixteenth and early seventeenth centuries. He wrote a study of the uprising of the Netherlands against Spain and then, as professor of history at the University of Jena, a history of the Thirty Years War, published in 1791–3. Five of his plays are set in this broad period: *Die Verschwörung des Fiesko zu Genua* ('The conspiracy of Fiesco in Genoa', 1783), *Don Carlos* (1787), *Wallenstein* (1798–9), *Maria Stuart* (1800), and the unfinished *Demetrius*. All five of these 'Renaissance' plays are concerned with crises of national identity and take as their starting-point a moment when the history of a state or nation could have gone either way. He could also use the Middle Ages when it suited him: medieval France in *Die Jungfrau von Orleans* (1801, a dramatization of the deeds – though not the trial – of Joan of Arc), Switzerland's lakes and mountains in *Wilhelm Tell* (1804), both of them studies in myths of nationhood and explorations of the interplay of integrity and self-interest which complicate the nobler theme of liberty that was Schiller's central preoccupation. Both types of historical play lay bare the motivation of violent action and bring home the burden of personal and public responsibility in the shadowy area between constraint and freedom where Schiller the dramatist is most at home. When he turned his hand to neo-classicism, this great exponent of classical aesthetic and moral ideals was less successful. *Die Braut von Messina* ('The bride of Messina', 1803) comes closest of all his plays to the noble model of Sophocles, yet despite the grandeur of its choruses, it is the only Schiller play which can be said to be deficient in the very qualities that have always been associated with the great Greek tragic dramatist, not least his ability to express abstract arguments in human terms.

Unlike Goethe, Schiller was a man cut off from the realities of political life: his career was devoted to writing and historical research even during the final years when he became his great contemporary's close friend and associate at Weimar. Yet he had an uncanny understanding of the workings of the political world and a quite extraordinary imaginative gift for plotting dramas which hold the attention as theatre while plumbing the depths of human character to discover what makes human beings act as they do. Only once, in *Egmont* (1788), did Goethe come near to rivalling his excellence as a historical and political dramatist; but Schiller's review of it and his later adaptation of it in 1796 are clear indications that Goethe's handling of a sixteenth-century historical subject was only superficially akin to his own. Schiller's historical verse dramas owed much to Corneille and more to Shakespeare, but they never turn so exclusively on Corneille's relatively clear-cut conflicts of love and duty or seek to demonstrate a Shakespearean continuum of national history through an epic succession of effective dramatic episodes. It is relatively easy to see them as demonstrations of the conflict of powerful abstractions such as idealism and pragmatism or ambition and passion; but at a deeper level they are always studies in mixed human motivations, and their heroes and heroines are always human beings caught between the confining restrictions of their situation and their dreams of a brighter future of which their own tragic destinies deprive them. Thus the young Spanish prince Don Carlos dreams of becoming the liberator of the Flemings whom his own elderly father, Philip II, rules with a rod of iron; the mature and victorious general Wallenstein sees himself as the arbiter of nations when in fact the course of the Thirty Years War is turning against him and his luck is running out; Joan of Arc naïvely obeys her divine mission to rescue France by force of arms, only to become involved in the ruthlessness of war, the machinations of statesmen and her own love for an enemy officer. Only William Tell, Schiller's last hero, proves not to be a noble failure; instead, he returns to the fastnesses of his mountains and the seclusion of his private life once he has played his crucial part in the unification and liberation of his people. Conscious of this affirmative denouement and of the visual dimension of its dramatic action, Schiller called the play a *Schauspiel*.

Each of Schiller's plays has its own distinctive atmosphere. *Maria Stuart* is the most finely crafted and certainly the most concentrated; here all the virtues of French classical drama – concision, passion and taut intrigue – are miraculously fused with the broad historical sweep and grasp of individual character associated with Shakespeare, a synthesis which put a final and triumphant end to the old eighteenth-century argument about the relative merits of French and English drama as models for the new drama of Germany. And at its heart is a heroine who is very much Schiller's own and the personification of his conception of the tragic hero, a subject on which he wrote a series of notable essays such as *Über das Erhabene* ('On the Sublime', 1793) which provided a characteristically German theoretical foundation for his creative work. The Scottish queen has incurred guilt in the past; she is beautiful still, proud, passionate, and filled with the longing to be free although in reality she is a prisoner about to die; yet within the course of the play's brief time-span she finds within herself a greater strength than any her opponent, Elizabeth of England, possesses: the moral strength to accept her own inevitable destiny not as an arbitrary punishment but as a just reward for an imperfect life which, in death, she is capable of transcending.

Schiller is the great European dramatist of the Age of Revolution. There is a sense in which all the themes which come to crisis-point in his plays had actually surfaced in the contemporary history of Europe: he is much less remote from his own time and ours than the outward appearances may suggest. Privilege, authority, the struggle for independence and human dignity, idealism and its travesty, fanaticism, warfare and the justification for the taking of life: these were intensely topical issues, not just themes for historical costume dramas. He possessed the imaginative power to devise uniquely memorable dramatic actions to explore such themes from various and conflicting angles, and to articulate them in language which may today seem somewhat high-flown, but which is certainly notable for verve and momentum as well as lyric grace. But the quality which, above all, made him Germany's outstanding classical dramatist was his ability to create works which appeal as much to the average theatre-goer as to the intellectual and scholar. Cultured Germans could and can admire him for his command of European history and his successful adaptation of Shakespearean drama to the requirements of a different age and language. But the average spectator, on whom the late eighteenth-century German stage depended, responded to something else in Schiller, and that was his ability to thrill, and to move. For their part, German actors appreciated him because he provided them with great roles. These include the contrasting brothers, Franz and Karl Moor, in *Die Räuber*; the rival queens in *Maria Stuart* who meet and clash in a climactic encounter, not reported by the historians, in the park at Fotheringhay; Joan of Arc, the Dauphin and Talbot the English general in *Die Jungfrau von Orleans*; and of course the most sustained and demanding of all, Wallenstein, the brooding fatalist who is also a man of action, an egotist who has the capacity to inspire loyalty and love. Here at last was an achievement to set alongside that of Shakespeare, whose plays were being authoritatively translated into German verse during the years when Schiller was writing: the classic translation of seventeen Shakespeare plays by August Wilhelm von Schlegel and his associates appeared between 1797 and 1810. Schiller's own translation of *Macbeth* (1800) is no mean achievement either; like his fine attempt at Racine's *Phèdre* (1805) it indicates his awareness of the European traditions he had inherited and which he was intent on fusing into a new German dramatic tradition. For all its innovation and originality, the new literature of Germany which Lessing had largely inaugurated was deliberately cosmopolitan in a way the literatures of France and England were not.

## Thematic Survey: Faust

Faust occupied Goethe's imagination from the moment when, as a boy, he saw a puppet-play loosely based on the original *Faust-Buch* of 1587. The subject was in the air at the time, an expression, perhaps, of the growing urge of many young and intelligent men to break out of the conventions and restrictions of their eighteenth-century culture and to explore the links they felt they had with their precursors, the enlightened humanists of the sixteenth century. These, they felt, were personified in the semi-legendary figure of Faust, a scholar, necromancer and quack doctor who was said to have frequented various German universities in and around the Reformation period. Lessing was the first eighteenth-century writer to be enthralled by what was to become the central myth of modern German literature, but his brilliantly suggestive sketches for a Faust play were not published until 1786, after his death. By then the *Sturm und Drang* writer Friedrich Müller had written a dramatization of episodes in Faust's life; this was published, incomplete, in 1778, and Goethe had begun a play on the subject which was not rediscovered and published until 1887, under the title *Urfaust*. For Goethe, however, Faust was to become much more than a passing craze during his dynamic *Sturm und Drang* phase. *Götz von Berlichingen* (1773), his first great play, was a product of that period in his creative life, and its realistically down-to-earth language, sixteenth-century setting and dual protagonists – Götz, the man of action, and his indecisive friend Weislingen – had already provided a foretaste of his later masterpiece and of the innate duality which runs all through it and characterizes its central figure.

*Urfaust* added important elements to this preliminary scheme. One was Faust himself, the scholar disenchanted with academic life yet unable to prevent himself from turning into the prototype of that essentially German phenomenon which Goethe had no intention of becoming, the eternal student, the product of an educational system which set no deadlines for examinations. Another was the figure of Gretchen, the artless girl who restores his love of life by unwittingly representing an idealized blend of youth, beauty, affection and common sense. For the next century and more, Goethe's Gretchen was to be regarded as the perfect embodiment of young German womanhood, which was no doubt what Goethe intended her to be; but the corruption of that ideal in more modern times, especially by the propaganda of the Third Reich and the ideology of feminism, has inevitably tended to complicate modern interpretations of her, especially in the theatre. Such views are at variance with Goethe's aims; like many a privileged young man in those days, he was as capable as Faust himself of idealizing the woman he was seducing. His personal involvement in his masterpiece is at its most evident in this touching section of the drama.

*Faust Part I*, published in 1808, added yet another element: Faust's pact with the devil, Mephistopheles. According to this pact, Mephistopheles will serve him as long as he continues to strive towards his goal, a beautiful moment lived so intensely that it is worth eternity and is thus the negation of man's temporal nature and its limitations. He will be able to claim Faust, however, if he ever gives up striving or claims that his goal has been achieved. Their relationship is, therefore, not a simple one of right and wrong, or of good and evil; indeed, its significance is that it goes far beyond traditional and simplistic patterns. Its devil is no longer the traditional malevolent embodiment of evil: that sort of devil had been debunked by the Enlightenment in the clear light of reason. He can, of course, be kept for artistic and dramatic purposes, but he cannot force Faust, a human being, to do anything that it is not in his nature to do.

The continuation of the Faust drama in the long and much later play called *Faust Part II* shows us what happens when Faust finds himself confronted not by books and ideas, but by the vested interests at the heart of the 'real' world of politics and economics which he encounters when he attends the Emperor's court. In it, he also meets the classical legacy, when he conjures up and falls in love with Helen of Troy, the mythological beauty made famous by Homer's *Iliad*. Goethe's obsession with both the vitality of the indigenous German tradition embodied in Gretchen and the immortality of classical antiquity represented by Helen is far more than just an aesthetic dream; it is a dichotomy that goes to the heart of modern German, and indeed European culture, and it proves to be too much for Faust, whom his author conceived as the representative of modern western man.

There is one other vital element without which none of Goethe's three *Faust* texts would be complete, for indeed without it their essential issues would not be brought to the surface so effectively. Faust is taken on a journey into life by the devil or, rather, the 'spirit of negation', the mouthpiece of that inner or outer voice which constantly denigrates, mocks and undermines whatever Faust spontaneously or sincerely thinks and feels. Faust's journey to his vision of heaven is through a hell and a purgatory which are less clearly structured and defined than Dante's in the *Divine Comedy* written half a millennium before; Goethe's moral geography is much less certain, and his protagonist's personal involvement very much greater, since what he experiences and sees is largely of his own imagining or making. To frame Faust's journey in a wider symbolical sense, Goethe employs a device more medieval and less sophisticated than any of Dante's. In the manner of a morality play, his drama opens with a prologue in heaven in which God grants Mephistopheles permission to use whatever knavish tricks he likes to seduce Faust from the path towards his intended goal. In Goethe's view that goal resides – and here he comes close to the German Romantics – in the quest for supreme happiness, rather than in its enjoyment, for the latter would be inertia, and therefore life-negating, whereas an unremitting quest is proof positive of being alive. At the end the devil and God dispute the outcome, which turns on the interpretation of Faust's dying words: 'In anticipation of such bliss, I already enjoy this supreme moment.' Far off a voice – the voice of Gretchen, the girl he seduced and who was executed for killing their child in her despair – proclaims Faust's ultimate salvation, for in a sense his journey has taken him back to her. Earlier in the drama, she had prayed in an intensely touching lyric to the Blessed Virgin for assistance, thereby introducing a Christian motif into the play. By identifying Faust's ultimate destination with heaven and his salvation with the loving figure of Gretchen, Goethe, the agnostic, was able to use a point of essentially Christian and Catholic symbolic reference that endowed his work with a timeless and satisfying complete-ness which transcended the latent legacy of Germany's religious disunity since the Reforma-tion. In this respect, too, Goethe overcomes dichotomy because he is prepared to acknowledge, diagnose and, as far as possible, treat it. *Faust* makes it less surprising that nineteenth-century Germany was able, despite its religious and political history, to unite in its veneration for its medieval, gothic, Christian past.

Faust's lifelong search for the true meaning of life, and his ultimate redemption thanks to Gretchen's intercession or, rather, to the presence in his tormented life of *das ewig Weibliche*, the eternal feminine principle so delightfully personified in *Part I* by Gretchen herself, with her wholehearted love and religious faith – these were elements of Goethe's *Faust* to which Romantic artists instinctively responded, especially in music. Robert Schumann's *Scenes from Goethe's Faust* (1844–53), *La Damnation de Faust*, a dramatic legend by Hector Berlioz (1846), and Charles Gounod's internationally successful opera *Faust* (1856) point to the mid-nineteenth-century period around Goethe's centenary as the climax of the work's reception. Some striking musical responses to it transcended words altogether: Wagner's *Faust Overture* (1840) is one example, another is Liszt's *Faust Symphony* (1854), which provided character studies of *Faust*, Gretchen and Mephistopheles, prior to its choral ending. But Faust usually meant *Part I*, even though Schumann's version included an imaginative treatment of the last scene of *Part II*, with its choruses and solo voices (Goethe, a keen opera lover, was never more operatic than here), a scene to which Gustav Mahler turned for the choral second half of his Symphony no. 8 in 1907. Twentieth-century *Fausts* have tended to revert to the starker outlines and antitheses of the original Faust-book, in which Faust is given a fixed time limit in which to achieve his goals: notable examples are Ferruccio Busoni's opera *Doktor Faust* (1916–24), Thomas Mann's reworking of the myth in his novel *Doktor Faustus* (1947), and Alfred Schnittke's opera-oratorio *Historia von D. Johann Fausten*, first performed in Hamburg in 1995.

Responses to *Faust*, especially in its complete form, have varied ever since Goethe published large sections of *Part I* in 1790 under the title *Faust, ein Fragment* in a collection of his works. The completed text of *Part I* followed in 1808, but Goethe never produced it as a play during his term of office as director of the Weimar court theatre from 1791 to 1817. The first performance did not occur until 1829, when it was adapted and staged by Klingemann in Brunswick; some months later Goethe helped with rehearsals when it was put on in Weimar. By then Act III of the second part – Faust's memorable encounter with Helen of Troy – had appeared in print as a *klassische-romantische Phantasmagorie*, a telling title which indicates Goethe's intention to represent his age artistically and to transcend its apparent duality by placing his late medieval German man of action in the world of ancient Greece. The whole vast drama was finally published shortly after his death, as a supplementary volume in the definitive edition of his works, the *Ausgabe letzter Hand*, which he had spent much time preparing during his last years. It finally reached the stage in Weimar in 1875, in the *Gründerjahre* of the Second German Empire. By that time it had become the most hallowed text in the German literary canon, appearing as the first in the celebrated Reclam paperback series in 1867, and had achieved a status which prompted a brilliant parody by the leading aesthetician of the day, Friedrich Theodor Vischer, then a professor at Zurich University. *Faust: Der Tragödie dritter Teil* (1862) adds a third part to Goethe's already enormous drama, in which many of its most familiar phrases and best-known figures reappear in mock confusion, reflecting no doubt the muddled impressions which the original work tends to leave behind it in the minds and imaginations of its readers and spectators. Yet no other work apart from Luther's Bible has given so many familiar phrases and commonplaces to the German language, and none has become so integral a part of the folk memory in German-speaking countries.

Attempts to analyse and interpret *Faust* have been innumerable, and approaches of many different kinds have been adopted. Its unity in diversity has always been central to the debate. In some periods critics have preferred to see it as a unified presentation of its protagonist's journey through life, in line with Goethe's conception of the *Bildungsroman* as exemplified in *Wilhelm Meister*, the other major work which occupied him simultaneously and for almost as long. Other critics and periods have responded more readily to its scintillating medley of stylistic levels and literary forms, which range from the homely manner and rhythms of Hans Sachs's carnival plays to the complex metrical patterns of Sophocles, and include the formality of Italian *opera seria* and some strangely futuristic sequences which anticipate Ibsen's *Peer Gynt* and even the theatrical effects of German Expressionism in the early twentieth century. It is of course both, and much more besides. In tracing Faust's career and destiny, Goethe rejects conventional moral codes and religious doctrines. Instead, and to the work's lasting advantage, he adopts an experimental approach to Faust's encounters with the contingencies of intellectual and emotional life. Like his author, Faust is subject to his individual urges and longings, but at the same time is keenly alive to the often apparently conflicting messages transmitted to him by 2000 years of European civilization. The artistic result is a perfect verbal embodiment of its own subject matter. It is also a fascinatingly responsive and complex diagnosis of human psychology and culture.

## The Novel as Education for Life

By the 1770s, German prose writers had developed a plethora of styles and approaches which indicated that they and their publishers were eager to respond to the requirements of an expanding reading public. Such readiness to explore the potential of most new types of narrative then available in Europe makes German prose writing at the turn of the century particularly fascinating, yet its uncertainty of artistic form and social purpose also inhibited the emergence of any one dominant trend. The pastoral mode developed by the Swiss writer Salomon Gessner in his prose idylls (*Idyllen*, 1756), the first work in German to achieve European fame in the eighteenth century, breathed new life into the shepherds and shepherd-esses of the baroque and rococo by presenting them as unspoilt human beings whose delight in nature is combined with their innate moral virtue in a setting inspired less by classical Greece than by contemporary Switzerland. The freshness of Gessner's style, with its delicate modula-tions and sensitively appreciative response to the natural world, provided a model for the happy opening sections of Goethe's first major prose work, *Die Leiden des jungen Werthers* ('The Sorrows of Young Werther', 1774), a novel in letter form which took the slow-moving narrative style of Richardson's epistolary novels (such as *Pamela*, 1740) and turned it into something very different. Unlike the English novelist's predatory and amoral male protagonists, Werther is a naturally upright and sensitive young man, out of sympathy with the constraints of polite society. When he discovers the innocent delights of the countryside he soon identifies them with Lotte, a young woman whose spontaneous charm is the direct expression of her moral serenity. Goethe realized that the idyll was delicate and could go no further without breaking: Werther's passion swells until it is out of proportion to the harmonious world he has discovered. The earthly paradise in which he revels is one which must exclude him, for Lotte is engaged to

Albert. Soon the sunny pastoral landscape is swept by storms and, as the river bursts its banks, the life-enhancing loveliness takes on a darker, ominous quality. Certainty gives way to confusion, and renunciation replaces self-fulfilment. Werther is caught between the pastoral dream and the dictates of harsh reality, and his mounting tension leads to despair and suicide. From now on, Goethe's primary objective as a creative writer was to work out a viable way to restore moral and emotional balance and thereby discover the way back into the paradise which his hero, a convincingly complex modern man, had lost.

This state of affairs first became evident in the aftermath of the international success of *Die Leiden des jungen Werthers*. Its potent example was hard to resist, but harder still to imitate. In the hands of less sensitive and dynamic writers such as Friedrich Heinrich Jacobi, it quickly degenerated into near-parody as the conflicting facets of the *Sturm und Drang* psyche, such as its tendency to oscillate between euphoria and depression, were allocated to stereotyped characters without the power to convince. Uncertainty of direction, rather than unintentional pastiche, is the dominant characteristic of the most interesting and readable of the many novels which appeared in the wake of *Werther*: *Siegwart* by Johann Martin Miller. Published in 1776 and subtitled *Eine Klostergeschichte*, it attempts to reconcile alternative types of prose fiction in what might best be described as an uncomfortable but entertaining blend of the rural realism of Goldsmith's *The Vicar of Wakefield* (1766), a novel which enjoyed wide resonance in Germany, and the spine-chilling 'gothic' excitement of *The Monk* (1791) by 'Monk' Lewis. Novels such as *Siegwart* were essentially experimental and failed to establish any one discernible tradition congenial to the late eighteenth-century German temperament. But was there no narrative approach in the post-*Sturm und Drang* period that was more amenable to the mood and message of the late Enlightenment and the first stirrings of a new classicism?

If there was, it was the one already represented by the most stylish prose writer of the period, Christoph Martin Wieland. Wieland knew how to combine a satirical eye for human failings with a restrained sense of decorum and an ease of narrative flow which made him far more appealing to most of his contemporaries than any other writer. His first major success as a novelist, *Die Geschichte des Agathon* (1766–7), is set, significantly, in ancient Greece and is a successful revival of the classical Greek tradition of storytelling, with a lightness of touch which its earlier admirers in the baroque period had lacked. Self-interest and idealism contend with each other as young Agathon sets out through life, but gradually he comes to the wise realization that true love and altruistic action are their own reward, and that self-fulfilment in the narrow personal sphere is worth more than the pursuit of unfocused, self-enhancing idealism. With *Agathon*, hailed by Lessing as a work of rare intelligence for readers with classical tastes, the scene was set for the emergence of the form that was to become Germany's favourite during its classical age: the *Bildungsroman*, or novel as education for life.

## *Wilhelm Meister*: The Model *Bildungsroman*

It is a token of Goethe's literary stature that his works in every genre, including prose fiction, were soon perceived to occupy the high ground of literature. This is especially true of the large-scale novel on which he worked off and on for much of his creative life. *Wilhelm Meister* was begun in 1777 and finally completed and published in its entirety in 1829, though its first half, a self-contained novel entitled *Wilhelm Meisters Lehrjahre* ('Wilhelm Meister's Apprenticeship'), had been published in 1795–6. This had quickly been welcomed as a major contribution to contemporary literature, a recognition immortalized in a dictum by the Romantic thinker Friedrich Schlegel to the effect that, along with the French Revolution and the philosophical system of Fichte, it was one of the three motive forces of the age. Despite its wealth of descriptive detail, especially in its earlier sections, *Wilhelm Meister* is essentially a study of the ways in which the central figure, after whom it is named, achieves his own sense of self in the course of a long, varied and sometimes painful process of adaptation, rejection and revision, which depends very largely on his encounters with people and his instinctive or considered responses to them. As a young man Wilhelm sees himself as an actor, whereas his father doesn't; by the end of his apprenticeship to life he has undergone a profound reassessment of himself, though he still requires supervised exposure to the wider range of experience he will gain in Part II, *Wilhelm Meisters Wanderjahre* ('Wilhelm Meister's Travels'). In this long and narratively complex sequel, with its subtle counterpoint of inset, self-contained stories, Wilhelm becomes a journeyman through life and in the painful but also joyful process learns to master both it and himself: his goal is to achieve maturity and qualify for the term 'Meister' (master) already implicit in his surname. It is hardly surprising that the concluding chapters of this vast undertaking, written in Goethe's old age, should take on a strangely visionary quality, for here Goethe, whose semi-autobiographical hero had set out on his journey into life in the eighteenth century, before the Age of Revolution, obliquely confronts the new realities of the post-Napoleonic period and peers into the industrial society of the future.

As a work of narrative fiction, *Wilhelm Meister* had got off to a good start. The early sections, especially in the original unrevised version, *Wilhelm Meisters theatralische Sendung* ('Wilhelm Meister's theatrical vocation'), which only surfaced in 1911, provide an enthralling account of the life of a troupe of strolling actors which has clear links with the eighteenth-century novel tradition. Part II, completed nearly half a century later, adopts a style which has much scanter entertainment value, but this did not prevent the work as a whole from becoming one of the authoritative texts of the nineteenth century both in Germany and in other countries where the influence of German culture was strong. The wisdom of Goethe's profound semi-symbolic insights into the problems with which we are potentially confronted by the world exerted wide appeal. The Scottish philosopher Thomas Carlyle, acutely aware of the difficulties presented to British readers by his translation of it (1824–9), described it in his preface to the second English edition (1839) as 'going on all hands towards infinitude'. Such words, echoed by many a critic since, give a clear indication of the gulf which separates the generally held view of what a good nineteenth-century novel should be from the model Goethe left as his legacy to his novel-writing successors.

Goethe's example towered above his contemporaries and those who came after him, but he was not, of course, alone. Of the relatively few novelists who managed to achieve work of a commensurately high aesthetic and intellectual standard, by far the most original and influential was Johann Paul Friedrich Richter, who wrote fiction to great popular and critical acclaim under the pseudonym 'Jean Paul'. Beginning with *Hesperus* (1795), a *tour de force* of whimsical far-fetched storytelling interspersed with passages of accomplished word-painting, he went on to delight his admirers with *Titan* (1800–3), an even more extraordinary demonstration of over-the-top incident and emotional exuberance controlled, despite extreme prolixity, by his greatest strengths, irony and imagination. *Titan* alternates between a fictitious German setting and evocations of Italy – a formula Jean Paul inherited from some of his eighteenth-century precursors such as Wilhelm Heinse, and which has remained a persistent feature of German prose fiction almost ever since: Thomas Mann's *Der Tod in Venedig* is just one famous example.

The eccentricities of style and presentation in which Jean Paul revelled in *Titan* recur in the humbler and more down-to-earth context of his fictitious account of the life of Quintus Fixlein, a village schoolmaster. First published in 1796, this shorter novel, despite its whimsical excesses, reveals Jean Paul as a writer aware, from his own harsh experience, of the realities of life for well-educated but hard-up people in the fragmented Germany of his day. It also heralded a long tradition of schoolmaster novels which often articulated the pressing anxieties of the day more sharply than most other types of prose fiction because their 'pedagogic' dimension allowed a more definite social purpose and gave greater scope for explicit social criticism and satire than was normally permissible. Examples of this characteristically German sub-genre, which has little or nothing to do with school-stories of the *Tom Brown's Schooldays* type, include *Leiden und Freuden eines Schulmeisters* ('The sufferings and joys of a schoolmaster', 1838–9), the first important work by the Swiss novelist Jeremias Gotthelf and, later, *Die Schriften des Waldschulmeisters* ('The writings of the forest schoolmaster', 1875) by the Austrian Peter Rosegger.

## Goethe's Fiction around 1800

German prose fiction around 1800 presents a very different picture from that of Europe's other major literary cultures. Readers of the other principal literatures of Europe are bound to observe with some puzzlement that the genre which exerted most appeal in Britain, France and Russia, and which provided the format for so many of the major European writers of the new century, was one that was not so highly favoured by writers in the German-speaking countries. The novel of society, which sets out to create a microcosm of contemporary society by focusing on a small group of individually drawn yet representative characters in a clearly recognizable setting, is almost totally absent in German literature at least until the late nineteenth century. Admittedly Goethe came close to it on occasion. The group of characters he selected for the set of stories he entitled *Unterhaltungen deutscher Ausgewanderten* ('Conversations of German refugees', 1795), and the four characters whose interactions he traces in his novel *Die Wahlverwandtschaften* ('Elective affinities', 1809), are clearly to some degree the counterparts of the groupings out of which Jane Austen contructed the novels in which she analysed English society at about the same time. But though there may be superficial similarities, Goethe's purpose was not entirely the same. Like Austen, he wishes to illustrate how personal characteristics, foibles, aspirations, values and responses affect the life of a group of contemporary people; but in the case of the English novelist, character portrayal and narrative episode, though vividly perceived, remain subordinate to the ongoing life of the social group itself, whereas in *Unterhaltungen deutscher Ausgewanderten* the cohesion of the group itself is under threat. Significantly, too, the group merely provides the framework for a sequence of self-contained stories told by its members to deflect their attention from their current preoccupation with the intellectual and political repercussions of the French Revolution by redirecting it towards more basic moral and emotional problems which, Goethe suggests, beset societies at all times and in all places. Goethe's model was to prove very significant for the development of prose fiction in Germany. His relegation of the description of contemporary manners to the periphery, and his emphasis on the timeless issues raised by the encapsulated stories told with economical mastery of form, set a seal of approval on shorter prose fiction as an aesthetically superior genre and helped to demote the novel of society to a less elevated position in the literary perception of

German writers, readers and critics than it occupies in the literary culture of England and France. A whole century was to pass before such priorities were successfully called into question by the novelist Fontane.

The four characters whose interactions form the content of Goethe's masterly novel *Die Wahlverwandtschaften* may seem at first to approximate closely to the familiar non-German model. The setting is a country estate; its well-to-do proprietors, Edward and his wife, Charlotte, for both of whom this is a second marriage, entertain an army captain and a genteel young woman as their house guests. The formula seems familiar enough. But the working out carries the reader into unfamiliar territory as Goethe sets out to prove or, on a deeper and more subtle level, to disprove that human relationships are governed by the processes and formulae of chemistry. Charlotte and her husband produce a child which looks like Ottilie and the Captain; accidentally the child drowns; Charlotte seeks a divorce, Edward agrees, but Ottilie renounces the prospect of marital happiness and social position and starves herself to death instead, the willing victim of a moral conscience more sensitive than any in English prose fiction before George Eliot. The incidents related here, and the issues they raise, are clearly ones which transcend the norms associated with the novel of society. Yet though they are out of the ordinary, and indeed shocking, the setting in which they take place and the tone in which they are related are equally far removed from the style and scenario of the contemporary Gothic romance which, in England especially, was stimulating hitherto neglected areas of the novel-reader's imagination with the *frisson* of terror and suspense. Goethe's novel is as far removed from Mrs Radcliffe as it is from Jane Austen. *Die Wahlverwandtschaften* impresses because it conveys profound emotional truth within a clearly perceived moral landscape devised by Goethe to contain it; but it tells us a great deal more about the complexities of human nature and the moral sensibilities of individual human beings than it does about the social habits and moral climate of a specific place at a given period. Significantly, the actual location of Edward's estate is never specified, though its woodlands, winding paths and lake are vividly described. Though Goethe's novel takes place in a 'real' world, such trivial details are of no relevance to his artistic and moral purpose.

# 5

## *The Romantic Era*

'Always remember what was happening when a young man was twenty.' G. M. Young's celebrated remark in *Portrait of an Age* (1936) applies with particular force to the generation of German writers known collectively as the Romantics. Novalis and Friedrich Schlegel, two leaders of the early Romantic movement, were twenty when in 1792 the decision was taken to guillotine Louis XVI, the anointed king of France; Tieck and Wackenroder, both born in 1773, turned twenty in the year in which that sentence was carried out. When Kleist (born in 1777) reached his twenty-first year, French armies were already occupying Germany; when they in turn reached the same age, the later Romantics, among them Achim von Arnim, the brothers Jakob and Wilhelm Grimm, Joseph von Eichendorff and the political economist Adam Müller witnessed the destruction of the Holy Roman Empire and the temporary annihilation of Prussia. As the Romantics grew to manhood, the repercussions of the French Revolution and the realities of the Napoleonic wars had begun to change the lives of Germans almost everywhere, civilians and soldiers alike, often giving them a sense of unending catastrophe, which, amazingly, left only indirect traces in the vast amount of high-quality writing produced in Germany during those short years. A profounder and more lasting effect was to be left on the German consciousness by the sporadic intellectual and armed uprisings against French supremacy and occupation which, under the somewhat euphemistic name 'the Wars of Liberation', restored the nation's emergent sense of destiny and oneness by demonstrating that it, too, had played its part in the decisive reversal of military fortunes which led up to the battles of Leipzig (1813) and Waterloo (1815). German children learnt that on that famous day it was the arrival of General Blücher and his Prussian army that saved the day for Wellington and Britain. Oxford had conferred an honorary doctorate on him the year before.

Though a number of places may claim the title, among them Berlin, the exemplary places of this unique and hybrid movement are surely the university towns of Jena, in the duchy of Saxe-Weimar, and, in the case of the later Romantics, Heidelberg, capital of the Palatinate, former residence of the Counts Palatine of the Rhine, but incorporated into Baden in 1803. Both were universities with long and famous, sometimes notorious traditions (Heidelberg had associations with the legendary figure of Faust), but in the age of Goethe and Schiller Jena, only twelve miles from Weimar, had become an intellectual centre from which the new philosophy of Kant was beginning to sweep Germany and Europe. The Kantian Schiller had been appointed to its chair of history in 1789, the year of the French Revolution, and the philosopher Johann Gottlieb

Fichte was its professor of philosophy from 1794 to 1799, five years during which he developed and expounded the full range of his philosophy which both built on and rejected Kant's in its proclamation that the ego is the only *Ding an sich* and that the world around it is its own creation. At the same time Fichte raised the temperature of the Romantic generation by suggesting that the Germans might well be the supreme exemplifier of moral superiority. The fact that he was followed at Jena by the philosophers Schelling and Hegel (who in 1818 succeeded him as professor of Philosophy in Berlin) is indicative of the extraordinary range and potential of German Romantic thinking. Seldom if ever have courses of lectures affected the direction of literature quite so radically as they did now: indeed the lecture as a *tour de force* began to appeal beyond academia to a wider public, as was clear when August Wilhelm Schlegel opened up the whole panorama of the history of European drama to a varied and distinguished audience in Vienna in 1808 in a series of lectures whose resonance was soon magnified by publication in three volumes.

Synthesis was the guiding principle of German Romanticism, a cultural and intellectual movement which brought together poetry and philosophy, two disciplines which had made enormous strides during the preceding century, and it was appropriate that universities should be the meeting places of its leading minds and of the young men who were its foremost representatives. Without much experience of adult life, but endowed with extraordinary intuitive and creative intellectual gifts, the writers of this new post-Kantian age, such as Novalis and Friedrich Schlegel, sought to emphasize the universality of feeling and knowledge at a time when the political and social framework in which Germans had lived for centuries was falling apart. They were free-moving intellectuals who disregarded the built-in immobility of its often rigid social and political system and could afford to do so because of the changes then taking place which were affecting the attitudes and literary tastes of their contemporaries. They travelled widely within Germany and sometimes beyond its confines, but even more characteristic of them were the changing constellations of their friendships, the extraordinary range of their intellectual and scientific interests and the agility of their minds. Jena's claim to be the exemplary place of early Romanticism is apt on other counts. It was (and still is) an important medical and scientific university and was to become the centre of the German optics industry: the all-seeing eye had a particular metaphorical significance for the Romantics as, in a different sense, it had for Goethe. Typically Romantic too is the paradox that Jena was at one and the same time both the 'second' literary capital of classicism and the real birthplace of Romanticism. Amongst Fichte's students as he expounded his *Wissenschaftslehre* in 1796–7 was Friedrich Schlegel, who later returned to Jena to join his brother August Wilhelm and sister-in-law Caroline as well as Tieck, and it was there that he produced the last two numbers of his journal *Athenäum* (1798–1800), the main vehicle of early Romanticism and the first of a series of such ventures set up by Schlegel and in which many of the seminal texts of Romanticism appeared. It was in Jena, too, that Novalis read to them from his *Geistliche Lieder* and his long essay, *Die Christenheit oder Europa*, with its retrospective vision of a medieval Europe united by its Christian faith and culture but destroyed by the Lutheran Reformation and the deistic Enlightenment, to rise again one day in a perhaps not too distant future. It was an ideal which was to have far-reaching effects on the Gothic revival in nineteenth-century Germany and further afield, too, after the essay's belated publication in 1826. In a sense it also underlay Konrad Adenauer's vision of the Federal Republic of Germany in 1949.

The past was to seem as important as the future to the Romantic generation, whereas to their precursors in the Enlightenment and, indeed, in the classical world of Goethe's Weimar, the present was the focus of the intellect and the imagination, though it could sometimes be clad in the raiment of antiquity. The simultaneous enthusiasm for classical Athens and a Christian Middle Ages in Romantic Jena is symptomatic of the paradoxes of German Romanticism, as are its seminal influences on both the art and politics of reactionary nostalgia in the nineteenth century and on the development of modern lines of thought and inquiry in fields as diverse as theology, psychiatry, the applied arts and musical composition. The excitement which the ideas of the Jena circle generated accounts for the aura of modernity which, in the eyes of the Victorians, surrounded the Romanticism of Germany, which Coleridge and Carlyle had done much to bring to the awareness of historians, philosophers and a wider general readership in Britain and the United States in works such as Carlyle's *German Romance*, a collection of translations of tales by the leading German Romantic authors published in 1827. This excitement is palpable in Tieck's *Der blonde Eckbert* (1797) and *Der Runenberg* (1804), but it is also present in Gotthilf Heinrich von Schubert's *Ansichten von der Nachtseite der Naturwissenschaften* ('Considerations on the darker side of the natural sciences', 1808) and his *Die Symbolik des Traumes* (1814), as well as in the *Rhapsodien über die Anwendung der psychischen Kurmethode auf Geisteszerrüttungen* ('Rhapsodies on the application of the psychic method of healing mental diseases', 1803) by the pioneering psychologist Johann Christian Reil; these all tantalizingly lifted the curtain on the irrational world of the subconscious which Freud and his contemporaries were to explore and diagnose in detail a century later. There was a spirit of mental exhilaration, too, in Friedrich Schleiermacher's *Reden über die Religion* ('Discourses on religion', 1799), which signalled the end of the rationalist Enlightenment by putting forward the view that religion is based on feeling and emotional experience which provide us with an intuition of a divine reality beyond the reach of rational thought. It was in these ways that, building on the enormous achievements of the generations that preceded them, the thinkers and writers of German Romanticism demonstrated the continuing vitality of Germany to provide the cultural and intellectual leadership of Europe.

The time spent by prominent early Romantics in Jena was relatively short, but 'Romantic' (and 'undergraduate') time is peculiarly subjective, and varies in apparent duration according to the age of those experiencing it and what is experienced: a notion which Tieck metamorphosed into his memorable fairy tale *Die Elfen* ('The elves'). And how intensely they experienced! In the mid-1790s Tieck could read a Gothic romance to his fellow students for a full ten hours at a stretch and become so absorbed that, in his own words, he nearly went out of his mind, a sensation immortalized in his haunting, disturbing tales, which take the long-winded Gothic novel and compress it to its sparsest essentials. The forms of literary expression and communication favoured by the early Romantics were appropriate to the character of their movement. If the short story, fairy tale or novelle was one of their favourites, another was the essay in the manner of a *rêverie* or rhapsody, a genre perfected by Tieck's talented but short-lived friend Wilhelm Heinrich Wackenroder in one of early Romanticism's key works, the collection of essays on pre-Raphaelite and Renaissance Italian and German art with its distinctly Gothic title *Herzensergießungen eines kunstliebenden Klosterbruders* ('Effusions from the heart of an art-loving monk') on which they collaborated and which was published in 1797, the year before his death at the age of 24.

Intense friendships such as theirs and their expression in letter form had been encouraged by the eighteenth-century Pietists and by the disciples of *Empfindsamkeit* and cultivators of sensibility who followed their example. They were to play a key role in Romanticism too. The Romantic writers and their friends and associates felt a great need to communicate, to try out their ideas on each other and to escape from the excessive subjectivity which their philosophy encouraged. As Schlegel put it in one of his many thought-provoking *Fragmente*, 'social life is the right element for all education that aims to cultivate the whole personality'. Schleiermacher even tried to provide a theoretical basis in his essay on the theory of sociability (1799), pointing out that every individual needs partners to help articulate his ideas and act as a spark to set the tinder of the imagination and creativity alight. 'Youth is so *electric*, isn't it?' Bettine von Arnim enthused, and the gregariousness of her circle still seems infectious even across the time-span that separates us from them. And yet – with some notable exceptions, among them Friedrich Schlegel and his wife Dorothea (the daughter of Lessing's friend Moses Mendelssohn) – how many of the typically Romantic pairings and partnerships survived much more than a year? Friedrich Schlegel soon quarrelled with his close friend Novalis, as he did with Schleiermacher; Caroline Michaelis, married first to a doctor called Böhmer and then to August Wilhelm Schlegel, left him for the young philosopher Friedrich Schelling, while Brentano, having enticed Sophie Mereau away from her husband, a Jena professor, tyrannized her and deceived her by turns. Such highly-strung people as the Romantics could rarely get on with each other for long: their quarrels were often more in evidence than the harmony of their souls.

Yet they were essential to each other. Similarly, the *Fragment* is a quintessentially Romantic genre and a particularly apt metaphor for Romantic friendship too. A reincarnation of the classical epigram or baroque apophthegm, it captures a significant *aperçu* remembered from a conversation over a meal or a bottle of wine, lingering on long into the night, perhaps never getting anywhere in particular, but possessing a seemingly infinite capacity to stimulate the mind. At the same time its creator, the poet, retains complete artistic freedom over it: it has no prescribed metrical scheme, unlike the Greek-style verse couplets which Goethe and Schiller were writing and publishing at the same time under the title *Xenien*. The relationships between German Romantic writers were also encouraged but inevitably sometimes broken by their restlessness and their fondness for the peripatetic mode, both literally and in their writing. One famous example is the journey which Wackenroder and Tieck made on foot in 1793 from the university of Göttingen to that of Erlangen, so close to that quintessentially 'German' town Nuremberg, with its half-timbered houses redolent of the medieval culture of Germany and full of reminders of Dürer and Hans Sachs. When Romantics were together they talked; as Friedrich Schlegel wrote to his brother August Wilhelm in 1793, 'one view expressed generates so many others'. Such views then multiplied in conversations and in the letters exchanged and handed around when the circle began to disperse.

Most went to Berlin, where they were invited to the salons of its leading Jewish society hostesses, Henriette Herz and Rahel Varnhagen von Ense. Through them the Schlegels, Schleiermacher and Schelling came into contact with the kind of people they might not otherwise have met, such as Wilhelm von Humboldt, the philologist, translator and educational reformer, and his brother Alexander, the explorer and scientist, or the charismatic and gifted Prince Louis Ferdinand of Prussia, Beethoven's musical friend, killed in battle in 1806. Such constantly changing personal constellations created the kaleidoscopic quality that is so charac-teristic of German Romantic writing and was also the source of the Romantics' fondness for literary and art criticism, the other vital pole of their activity and, in Friedrich Schlegel's words, the pillar on which the whole house of knowledge and language rests. The mental games they played with each other and with each other's ideas stimulated the tendency to extreme intro-spection which finds its most entertaining reflection in the complexities of E. T. A. Hoffmann's unfinished novel *Lebensansichten des Katers Murr* ('The views on life of tomcat Murr') and in the ironies and surprises of Tieck's comedies, and links the Romantics in so many ways with postmodernist criticism.

The early Romantics, and especially Novalis, were preoccupied with the universality of poetry, a concept which informed their view of the world and their artistic vocations, and which they felt was intellectually corroborated by the philosophy of their teacher, Fichte, and brought to its fullest intellectual expression in the philosophical system of his successor at Jena, Friedrich Schelling, first presented in 1799 and 1800 under the headings of *Naturphilosophie* and *Transzendentaler Idealismus*, and extended more fully into the aesthetic field in his *Philosophie der Kunst* (1809), based on earlier lectures. Here the imagination was held up to be as valid as scientific knowledge and to be compatible with it, a view which appealed greatly to Romantic writers, many of whom followed Schelling's own growing penchant for mysticism and Catholicism. The preoccupations of the later Romantics were less with these nebulously intellectual concerns than with the challenge of conserving the heritage of a Germany which seemed to be disintegrating all around them. It was from their lecture rooms and studies at Heidelberg that Arnim and Brentano set forth in quest of the genuine lyrical voice of the German people that resulted in the publication of the 700 and more folksongs and poems in their famous three-volume collection *Des Knaben Wunderhorn* ('The boy's magic horn', 1805–8), the significance of which Goethe quickly recognized. Its appearance in Heidelberg heralded the lead which the south-west of Germany was to take during the later Romantic period with poets such as the 'Swabian Romantics' Ludwig Uhland, Eduard Mörike, Justinus Kerner, Friedrich Gerok, Gustav Schwab and Wilhelm Hauff, as well as with Friedrich Rückert, who worked for a while on the *Morgenblatt für gebildete Stände* ('Morning paper for the cultured classes'), a leading literary periodical published by the firm of Cotta. To the generous but commercially astute patronage of its proprietor Johann Friedrich Cotta, many poets and writers of the period were to owe a great deal. Cotta's, which held the exclusive rights to the works of Goethe and Schiller, had published Hölderlin's novel *Hyperion oder Der Eremit in Griechenland* ('Hyperion or the hermit in Greece') in 1797–9, and Hölderlin (who survived the entire Romantic period in a state of mental withdrawal) was to become the inspiration of the Swabian poets, very different though his work usually was from theirs: in 1829 Uhland and his friend the poet and critic Schwab rescued his name from oblivion with their edition of his poems.

In Heidelberg, with its ruined castle perched picturesquely above the narrow streets that contained the lecture rooms and lodgings of generations of distinguished scholars, Johann Joseph von Görres offered his students a new kind of inspiration, comparable in its stimulating appeal to that of Fichte in Jena in the decade before. Eichendorff recollected getting up at five to learn up his law lecture notes so that he would have time to go to the arts faculty to hear Görres's lectures, which opened up the almost forgotten world of the late medieval Germany and found their way into his influential book on the fiction of that vanished age, *Die teutschen Volksbücher* (1807). To the ears of young contemporaries they seemed a clarion call to revitalize a threatened but not yet vanished past. It was from Heidelberg, too, that the Grimm brothers set out to build up their collections of fairy tales and legends, two works that were to become the centrepieces of the later German Romantic movement and to exert a profound and persistent fascination on the imaginations of children, writers, anthropologists, composers, animated film producers, choreographers and psychologists ever since. The *Kinder- und Hausmärchen* (1812–14) and the *Deutsche Sagen* (1816–18) laid the basis for the extraordinary corpus of scholarship with which Jakob and Wilhelm Grimm, inspired by the early example of Herder, played their incalculable part in the formation of Germany as a nation alive to its cultural inheritance. The fulfilment of this mission came as recently as 1960, when the 32 volumes of their great dictionary of the German language, known as *Grimms Wörterbuch*, which had begun to appear in 1854, finally reached completion.

In the Romantic age reading was synonymous with being part of an intellectually inquiring and culturally aware community whose representatives were dotted all over the German-speaking world. It is therefore not surprising that the genre in which many Romantic writers, and especially the women amongst them, excelled was the letter. Amongst the best letter-writers of the period are Caroline Schlegel, Sophie Mereau and Rahel Varnhagen, whose Berlin literary salon was famous. *Goethes Briefwechsel mit einem Kinde* ('Goethe's correspondence with a child', 1835) by Bettine von Arnim, sister of Clemens Brentano and wife of Achim von Arnim, displayed the imaginative use to which letters could be put, as did *Die Günderode*, a semi-fictional work based on the letters of her friend Caroline von Günderode, who committed suicide in 1806 when her professor lover decided not to dissolve his marriage for her sake. Tactfully Bettine's book did not appear until 1840; in 1979 Caroline von Günderode surfaced again when she became the subject for semi-fictionalized treatment in Christa Wolf's story *Kein Ort: Nirgends* ('No place: Nowhere', 1979), a work which Wolf backed up with an edition of her selected writings. Thus Günderode became a key figure in the mythology of feminism, in which she represents the woman tragically caught between the equally impossible alternatives of self-fulfilment within the norms of her society and outright rejection of them. A characteristic feature of the letters of German women during the Romantic period is that their written words closely reflect the way they spoke: such spontaneity had long since been attained by women such as Madame de Sévigné in seventeenth-century France, but it took longer to break down the stiffness and formality of written German. Both Bettine's breathless syntax and Rahel's Jewish self-deprecation are as much part of Romantic literature as their poems and novels. They show how discriminating they were in their aesthetic judgement and how fertile their imaginations were. Their letters were wide-ranging and sometimes tiresomely self-stylizing, as in Bettine's correspondence with Goethe; but often they were practical too, as when Therese Huber used her immense network of correspondence to create a kind of job agency on behalf of her needy friends and their daughters. The self-awareness of such women was of quite a different order from the tentative expressions of earlier generations. That their menfolk failed to recognize it was equally evident. Even Rahel Varnhagen, who could not complain of a lack of devotion on the part of her husband, could still write to a woman friend in 1819 to say that men 'simply show their ignorance of human nature when they claim that women's minds are different and made for different purposes and say that we ought to be content to be just an extension to the lives of our husbands and sons'. By 1843, when Bettine addressed her advice to the King of Prussia to do something about the misery and oppression in his country, her tone had acquired the confidence of her British Victorian counterparts. Friedrich Wilhelm IV gave her his express permission to dedicate *Dies Buch gehört dem König* ('This book belongs to the King') to himself. A social barrier had been broken down, but by then a new age of German literary history had already begun.

## German Romanticism and the *Bildungsroman*

The conception of the novel as a narrative of fictional, emotionally charged melodramatic events loosely held together by a far-fetched plot seemed to many German authors and readers to be inherent in the term *Roman*, which translates as 'novel' but is actually related to the term 'romance'. As Jean Paul was writing, the Romantic theorist Friedrich Schlegel coined his dictum 'A romance (= novel) is by definition a romantic book', while for a growing and voracious readership his novels were paralleled by the less demanding works of successful writers such as August Lafontaine (1758–1831) and Karl Franz van der Velde (1779–1824). On a more literary level, the romance was cultivated, though with only limited success, by some of the writers associated with the Romantic movement, notably Achim von Arnim, though surprisingly its women writers failed to produce any lasting masterpiece in the genre to set alongside the romances of writers such as Ann Radcliffe. While the romance, often blending with the newly developing historical novel, continued to maintain its hold on the reading public, the aim of many of Germany's serious authors – even those of the Romantic movement – was to produce a successful *Bildungsroman*, that is, a novel which would make its central character aware of the pattern and purpose of his or her life, and in so doing make its readers think seriously about themselves while at the same time being absorbed and entertained. Indeed, for the German Romantic writers the quest for the meaning of life and the emergence of an individual's identity were inextricably bound up with intricate connections and mysterious forces, rather than with the logic of cause and effect that underlies the storylines of the *Bildungsroman* in the hands of more classically and rationally inclined authors. Key examples of this genre were to be published at more or less regular intervals as the nineteenth century progressed, so that in retrospect they form a distinctive strand in nineteenth-century prose fiction, permitting certain inferences to be drawn regarding the changing pattern of readers' preoccupations and writers' responses to them as their often semi-autobiographical protagonists come to terms with themselves and the changing world in which they live.

The first Romantic contribution to the *Bildungsroman* genre was published in 1798 by Ludwig Tieck, one of the leading figures in the Romantic movement. *Franz Sternbalds Wanderungen* ('Franz Sternbald's travels') coincided with *Wilhelm Meisters Lehrjahre*, and shares with Goethe's masterpiece the theme of apprenticeship to life. But Tieck's novel is radically different in that it combines this essentially contemporaneous concern with features which are more easily associated with the rising genre of the historical novel. It is set in the past in that its central figure, Franz Sternbald, is a young painter who is a pupil of the early sixteenth-century Nuremberg artist Dürer. Sternbald's travels in search of himself and in pursuit of artistic excellence take him from Germany to Italy – the Italy of the High Renaissance. In common with what was fast becoming a favourite German formula, found even in Viennese popular comedy and its love intrigues, a series of artistic and erotic encounters put his vocation to the test before he returns to his native land – a goal never reached, however, because Tieck's story breaks off at this point as if to emphasize, in characteristic Romantic manner, that a question mark hangs over the hero's future and over the relationship between Germany's evolving culture and the artistic perfection of the Renaissance in Italy.

The romantic interpretation of the *Bildungsroman* as a study of the individual's quest for a goal that is distant and elusive, which Tieck inaugurated in *Franz Sternbalds Wanderungen*, was developed along more esoteric and mysterious lines by Novalis in his similarly unfinished *Heinrich von Ofterdingen* (1802), though here the reader is invited to enter the world of the German High Middle Ages. Novalis uses its medieval setting and its central figure, a legendary medieval poet, as an extended metaphor to express a romantic view of the world as a creation of the imagination. But the novel is also a creatively critical response to *Wilhelm Meisters Lehrjahre*. Far from being brought, as Wilhelm Meister is, to the sensible realization that his initial vocation was mistaken, Novalis's Heinrich is led by his inner vision to set out in quest of the *blaue Blume*, the slender blue flower which, ever since, has been seen as the quintessential symbol of romantic yearning for the unattainable. Here that longing is personified by Mathilde, whose death, long before the end of the novel is in sight, is symptomatic both of its author's view of life as an impermanent state occasionally transfused with intimations of something beyond, and of the tendency of the major works of German Romanticism to shun completion as a negation of continuity and eternity. These two works were largely responsible for placing the creative artist in the position of central importance which he has held in German literature almost ever since but has seldom enjoyed in the literatures of other nations.

The temptation to indulge in fictionalized autobiography was skirted by making the artist-figure a painter or musician, a device adopted by many writers including the poet Eduard Mörike in his novel *Maler Nolten* (1832), a late-Romantic account of a painter who lacks the will to live. Over a century later, Thomas Mann in his novel *Doktor Faustus* (1947) explores the career of a composer, Adrian Leverkühn, whose successful but self-destructive search for artistic self-realization takes place during a fraught period in twentieth-century German history and depends on a modern version of Faust's pact with the devil. The outstanding nineteenth-century work in this loose yet centrally important Romantic literary tradition is *Der grüne Heinrich* by the Swiss writer Gottfried Keller, published in 1854/5 and in revised form in 1879/80. More strongly autobiographical, much more realistic, and more clearly aware of the model provided by Goethe's *Wilhelm Meister*, this is the enthralling account of a young artist's childhood and adolescence in the period between 1830 and 1848, and of the multiple influences and experiences which shape his life and affect his emergent creative personality. The novel's potential subjectivity is offset by the vivid and close detail with which Keller reproduces the circumstantial reality of the Swiss city of Zurich; indeed the descriptive element is essential to the central theme of the novel since it acts as confirmation of Heinrich's innate eye for outline and colour. Despite initial appearances, *Der grüne Heinrich* owes much more to the tradition established by Goethe than it does to the English tradition of the eponymous novel perfected by Dickens and Thackeray in works such as *David Copperfield* (1850) and *The History of Henry Esmond* (1852). Charting, as it does, the emergence and gradual fulfilment of a creative gift, *Der grüne Heinrich* shares with its great prototype *Wilhelm Meister* a high seriousness of purpose. Yet excessive solemnity is averted by the irony that Heinrich's artistic gifts are not those of a creative genius: the ordinary reader, too, can thus identify with him. It is rich in delightful light-hearted episodes, but these fulfil much the same purpose as the scherzo movements in the symphonies of nineteenth-century German composers: they provide the contrast of light relief, but they do not trivialize. Indeed the analogies between the finest examples of German prose fiction from the 1790s on and the aims and techniques of the symphonic music being written at the same time suggest a closer unity between these different aspects of German culture than is generally realized, especially outside the German-speaking world.

A price was, however, to be paid for the veneration in which the *Bildungsroman* was held. By the very nature of its themes and purpose, it remained an exclusively male domain. Its assumption that the central character is at liberty to experience life to the full made it unthinkable in the social context of the period for that character to be a woman, while his tendency to put even his failures and lapses down to his pursuit of an essentially laudable vocation could hardly be shared by a respectable heroine or be written about by a respectable woman author. Around 1800 some of the more emancipated women associated with the Romantic movement did achieve a degree of expressive freedom which they seldom succeeded in exploiting. Dorothea Schlegel, the wife of the leading Romantic theorist Friedrich Schlegel, began a romance called *Florentin* (1801), but left it unfinished. The life most women led was clearly circumscribed, and no novel aiming to describe it honestly and fairly could properly be termed a *Bildungsroman*. Yet women were avid and often discerning readers and writers of novels, and the history of the nineteenth-century German novel is bound up with their search for appropriate subject matter, and with their readiness – and especially that of their publishers – to produce tales of courtship and marriage. *Eine Ehestandsgeschichte* ('A tale of matrimony', 1830–3), a bold attempt by Therese Huber to face up to the realities of a woman's life within this accepted framework, was not published until after her death. No woman writer was able to produce a *Bildungsroman* to rank alongside the classic examples of the genre: yet in *Meine Lebensgeschichte* (1861–2), an autobiographical account of her upbringing and long, slow, often painful progress towards emotional, social and creative emancipation, the Jewish novelist Fanny Lewald produced a work which can be set alongside the fictional masterpieces of her male contemporaries. It is a pity that this book, like her many novels, is still largely unknown.

## German Romanticism and the Historical Novel

The period which saw the aesthetic triumph of the *Bildungsroman* also saw the emergence of historical fiction. Its rise in popularity continued steadily as the nineteenth century progressed, though it failed to achieve the dominant position that might have been expected for it in the literature of countries with such a rich history and with such a strong sense of the living legacy of the past. Despite some notable artistic and popular successes, historical fiction in German never quite managed to produce a canon of undisputed masterpieces comparable to those which make the genre such an integral part of the mainstream novel tradition in other European countries. Is this because the German countries produced no equivalent of Scott or Manzoni, in whose hands the historical novel became the virtual counterpart of the epic of old? There is no single towering German achievement in the genre to equal theirs, and of no historical novel in the German language, except perhaps Theodor Fontane's *Vor dem Sturm* ('Before the storm'), could it be said that the past was successfully used to illuminate the future. Yet there is in German a fascinating and extremely varied body of historical prose fiction which has much to offer the reader.

The German historical novel of the nineteenth century had its precursors in various forms of semi-historical fiction produced mainly by writers of the second rank in the latter half of the eighteenth century. But a more decisive influence on its development was the ideal of a romance or 'romantic' novel in which past and present would be fused in an evocation of moods, times and places which might have existed or which could be called into existence through the power of the imagination. Often this type of romantic novel was set in what could loosely be termed the Middle Ages, a period whose appeal was becoming widespread and infectious, and whose ideals of valour, chivalry, courtly love and piety could be made to equate with the Romantics' own favourite notions of yearning, innocence, mystery and transfiguration. *Heinrich von Ofterdingen* is a prime example, but Novalis wrote at a level of symbolical sophistication few other novelists have attained. His contemporaries and successors preferred to develop the potential of the pseudo-medieval scenario of his novel in other directions. The most successful, though now the least known, was Friedrich de la Motte Fouqué, a writer of almost inexhaustible imaginative fertility who delighted early nineteenth-century readers in Germany and in Britain with *Undine* (1811), his haunting tale of a watersprite's love for a knight, and with his labyrinthine prose romances *Der Zauberring* ('The magic ring', 1813) and *Sintram und seine Gefährten* ('Sintram and his companions', 1814), best-sellers as the Napoleonic wars were coming to an end. Like Scott, whose first novel, *Waverley*, appeared in the same year as *Sintram*, Fouqué was to exert a decisive and prolonged influence on nineteenth-century taste, and traces of his narrative manner and imaginative world can be detected not only in the late romances of William Morris but in much of today's successful Arthurian and pseudo-medieval fiction.

## History and Local Colour

A different conception of historical fiction was put forward by Tieck in the later part of his long productive career, by which time Scott was already well established throughout Europe as its major exponent. In 1826 Tieck's remarkable, brooding, at times deeply disturbing fictional study of religious fanaticism appeared: *Der Aufruhr in den Cevennen* ('The uprising in the Cévennes') skilfully locates this general phenomenon, together with its attendant symptoms, loyalty and betrayal, religious conviction and metaphysical doubt, in the specific historical and topographical context of the Protestant uprising in southern France in the early eighteenth century. This enables him to introduce a new and fashionable ingredient, local colour, into what had hitherto been a genre which relied on evocative power rather than historical and topographical accuracy.

This trend towards greater authenticity of historical setting, and with it greater reliance on carefully researched background, was also evident in another and even more successful novel published in 1826, *Lichtenstein*, by the young writer Wilhelm Hauff. Tieck had consciously tried not to imitate Scott; Hauff rose to the challenge of providing a German imitation. Significantly, he chose to set his novel in the tense period of social and political upheaval which followed the Lutheran Reformation and which historians have generally agreed was a period of crucial importance in Germany's evolution. Its hero, Georg von Sturmfeder, deserts the rebel cause and the party of progress because his love for Marie von Lichtenstein is of greater importance to him. His devotion to her overlord, the Duke of Württemberg, is ultimately rewarded: Georg gains Marie's hand in marriage. But on the political level life goes turbulently on, conflict continues, and the Duke is forced into exile. Hauff's narrative is an exciting one, and established him in the popular mind as one of Germany's favourite authors right up into the twentieth century. But what makes his achievement particularly revealing are the passages that introduce and end the novel. At the start Hauff states his intention to tell a tale of old Swabia unequalled for its romantic interest; to expect contemporary readers to turn their attention back to the past may, he writes, seem bold, yet they avidly consume the translated novels of writers such as Scott and Fenimore Cooper, whose *The Last of the Mohicans* also appeared in 1826. Their appeal is that of the exotic and unknown, yet Germany's historical landscape is even less familiar than that of Scotland and certainly just as worthy of literary treatment. In fact *Lichtenstein* was to be to the nineteenth-century German historical novel what Goethe's *Götz von Berlichingen* was to German historical drama half a century earlier. Its publication marked another occurrence of a feature that characterizes Germany's literary history: the conscious return to 'national' subject matter in the hope of arousing in readers an awareness of their own nation's particular past and unique destiny. The historical panorama Hauff unfolds – drawn from the same period as Goethe's drama – opened up a vanished world and brought it vividly close to the imaginations of his readers. At its close, Hauff then strikes a note which is at once revealing and unexpected. The novel's final paragraph, a fine passage of sustained writing, is a verbal equivalent of the paintings of Ludwig Richter (1803–84) and Moritz von Schwind (1804–71), and captures the visual quality of German Romanticism. It evokes a custom still practised, the author claims, at the castle of Lichtenstein. Men, women and children ascend its wooded slopes and gaze out at dusk over the countryside spread out below them; at such times, old tales and legends resurface as the last rays of the setting sun cast their glow over the castle on its lonely hilltop. By thus stressing a sense of continuity in landscape and community, Hauff found an imaginative formula for reconciling the challenge of a future rich in potential change with a past whose crucial moments of crisis seemed more distant and less relevant than they actually were.

*Der Aufruhr in den Cevennen* and *Lichtenstein* illustrate two approaches to historical fiction, and the polarity they represent can be observed throughout the subsequent development of the genre. Tieck was at his best in the evocation of foreign places at times of historical and cultural crisis: France is once again the setting of *Der Hexen-Sabbath* ('The witches' sabbath', 1832), his impressive but little-known account of the workings of superstition and mass hysteria in a community that regards itself as civilized and sane. *Dichterleben* ('A poet's life', 1826–31) and its sequels *Das Fest zu Kenilworth* (1828) and *Der Dichter und sein Freund* (1829) are a historically and intellectually convincing treatment of Shakespeare and his circle in which Tieck put to imaginative use his knowledge of the subject (he was one of Germany's most distinguished Shakespearean scholars). Renaissance Rome is evoked powerfully and with a fine sense of period in his later novel *Vittoria Accorombona* (1840). Tieck's cultured, noble-minded heroine is based on the same historical character as Webster's Jacobean drama *The White Devil*, but his depiction of how she becomes caught up in a corrupt and violent world anticipates the cultural pessimism that was later to surface in the stories of Conrad Ferdinand Meyer. By preference Tieck avoided German subject matter and was more at home in France, Italy and England, whose literatures he knew well; his novels depended on his descriptive abilities to make their full impact on readers. Hauff's approach in *Lichtenstein* was essentially narrative and national-istic, which is why it exerted greater appeal, but how he would have developed as a historical novelist is a matter for speculation.

The interest in historical fiction aroused by Hauff and Tieck continued throughout the nineteenth century, producing a number of works of high quality and great popularity which developed the trends they had started. The six main historical novels published between 1840 and 1854 by Willibald Alexis earned him a reputation as the Scott of Prussia because of his ability to bring to life the past of a landscape and society that was near and dear to him. They may contain a strong element of that sentimental local patriotism that was to become the hallmark of most historical fiction associated with specific regional locations all over the German-speaking world, but in his so-called *vaterländische Romane* or 'patriotic novels' this element is held in check by an eye for detail and a sense of whimsical humour seen to particularly good effect in *Die Hosen des Herrn von Bredow* ('Herr von Bredow's breeches', 1846), yet another work set in the Reformation period, but this time in Brandenburg. Alexis tells the readable tale of the adventures of a pair of well-worn leather riding-breeches and their owner, a bluff and bibulous country nobleman, Gottfried von Bredow. A not-quite-vanished world is evoked in which heroic deeds and harsh realities are offset by the author's affectionate depiction of the sights and sounds of familiar places and of a gallery of vividly portrayed characters; his was an art which appealed greatly to Theodor Fontane, who was to become Prussia's major nineteenth-century novelist and whose own career as a writer of prose fiction began in 1878 with the large-scale historical novel *Vor dem Sturm* ('Before the storm'), set in Prussia on the eve of the Wars of Liberation in 1813 and owing much to the example Alexis set with his own long novels about the Napoleonic age, *Ruhe ist die erste Bürgerpflicht oder Vor fünfzig Jahren* ('The Citizen's prime duty is to keep calm', 1852) and its sequel, *Isegrimm* (1854).

Very different is the atmosphere created in *Marie Schweidler, die Bernsteinhexe* ('Marie Schweidler, the amber witch', 1843) by Wilhelm Meinhold. This is an extraordinary example of authorial empathy with characters from a different cultural period. Set on the Baltic coast in the 1630s, it purports to be the work of its central character's father, a country parson during the Thirty Years War. Meinhold totally enters the mind of his elderly narrator, whose sorry tale is full of circumstantial detail and private concerns: he seems only partially aware of what is going on in his daughter's life or of the sinister implications of the incidents he chronicles, so that the elements of sex and superstition which are essential to their motivation are only sparingly and obliquely conveyed – a technique which serves to enhance their threateningly incomprehensible nature in the midst of the harsh and often very graphically described realities of suffering and hardship. The narrator's constant anxiety is that spiritual values will be jeopardized by the sufferings he and his contemporaries have to put up with; only very gradually and out of love for his daughter does he come to realize the horror of her persecution as a witch; even then, his purity of heart seems to make him wonderfully blind to implications which strike the modern reader at once. There is nothing sentimental about this impressive study of prejudice and victimization by an otherwise undistinguished author; with Nathaniel Hawthorne's *The Scarlet Letter* (1850) and Mrs Gaskell's *Lois the Witch* it represents the fascinated interest in cruelty and the supernatural which ruffled the apparent security and calm of early Victorian or *Biedermeier* prose fiction.

That calm is violently disrupted in *Die schwarze Spinne* ('The black spider', 1842) by Jeremias Gotthelf, Switzerland's major novelist during the first half of the nineteenth century. Better known as a writer of realistic novels of peasant life, Gotthelf's imagination was also stimulated by the growing interest in historical fiction. One of his greatest peasant novels, *Wie Anne Bäbi Jowäger haushaltet* ('How Anne Bäbi Jowäger keeps house', 1843–4), brought home the ominous power of superstition to pervert the rational faculties of human beings, but it did so in a modern context. Two years earlier *Die schwarze Spinne*, a shortish, intricately con-structed work, used folk memories of feudal oppression and the Black Death to narrate in flashback two interlinked outbreaks of violence and superstition in the distant past which took place in the same village and which contrast uncomfortably with the prosperous, contented Swiss countryside of the present day that provides the setting in which they are told. By generating both episodes from the instinctive fear of spiders shared by his peasant characters and his middle-class readers, Gotthelf makes the black spider of the title into a terrifying symbol of those dark and evil impulses which are always waiting for an opportunity to break out and gain control of the community when it is morally off its guard. Little did this Swiss chronicler of country life foresee the topical relevance that his story of 1842 would take on a century later.

A very different approach to the contrast between past and present is exemplified in *Witiko* (1865–7), a vast historical novel published by the Austrian writer Adalbert Stifter at the end of his life, which relates at what most modern readers would say was excessive length the some-what repetitious adventures of a young nobleman caught up in the troubles of twelfth-century Bohemia. In keeping with the general tenor of his work, Stifter aimed to fuse the colourful canvas of historical romance with the serious purposes of the *Bildungsroman*. To some critical eyes, the novel is an artistic failure; others see it as a symphony in prose of Brucknerian proportions: the Austrian composer's first symphony was being written at the same time and was first performed in 1868.

The mid-nineteenth century, which saw the gathering momentum of middle-class nationalism overtake the liberal constitutional attitudes of the 1830s and 1840s, found much to its taste in a number of works which developed Hauff's popular model by basing nationalist sentiments or, sometimes, a rather more local patriotism on a foundation of convincingly accurate scholarship. The most widely read example of this trend was *Ekkehard* (1855), by Joseph Viktor von Scheffel. Set in the tenth century, it relates the adventures of a young monk who attracts the interest of his pupil, a widowed duchess. His attempt to give expression to his feelings leads to disaster from which only exile can save him. The novel ends as he returns from his alpine hermitage to become the Emperor's chancellor. Scheffel's achievement – the blend of high romance with scholarship and local colour – corresponded to the taste of the period because it handled some of its key themes in the fashionable format of the medieval revival: in a romanesque setting social barriers leading to noble renunciation are given a positive interpretation as the hero learns from bitter experience to shoulder his mature responsibilities.

The new direction German historical fiction was taking was confirmed shortly after the publication of Scheffel's best-seller by the work of an author who soon became one of the mid-century's favourites: Gustav Freytag. In 1859 the first of his five-volume *Bilder aus der deutschen Vergangenheit* ('Pictures from the German past') established him as a popular historian, a reputation on which he built in *Die Ahnen*, a sequence of seven interlinked novels (published 1873–81) which traces a typical German family over a span of a thousand years from the days of the Goths and their invasion of the Roman Empire to 1848, the year of revolutions. Each novel is set in what Freytag considered to be a crucial moment in the evolution of the German nation (e.g. the Reformation, the Thirty Years War, the Napoleonic era), and his Darwinian portrayal of the heroism of ordinary folk and their struggle for survival flattered and appealed to readers. This ambitious undertaking caught the public imagination. Soon his German family saga had become accepted as the classic prose epic of the newly founded Second Reich.

## Shorter Prose Fiction: The German Novelle

One of the greatest delights of German literature is its wealth of shorter prose fiction. When the other great literatures of Europe were exploring the potential of the full-length novel, most of the major German prose writers were concentrating on the aesthetic challenge of a briefer, more economical type of prose narrative known in German as the novelle. The term 'long short story' is an apt translation, yet it is misleading because it suggests a hybrid unable to find its own proper dimensions. The German novelle is no awkward compromise, however. On the contrary, its aim is to achieve a degree of formal perfection, and this has earned it a higher literary status than the full-length novel. Many writers have specialized in it and achieved their reputations through their handling of it. But the form is deceptively simple; in fact the novelle has usually sought to combine the maximum of range and depth with the greatest economy of means. This demands a degree of brevity and concision alien, some might argue, to a language notable for its lengthy sentences and complex syntax. Perhaps the attraction of the novelle lay in the fact that it contradicts the general tendency of German narrative prose to be long-winded – a feature promoted by the voracious demands of the lending libraries and the need to satisfy the post-1850 popular weeklies such as *Die Gartenlaube* ('The Arbour'). Definitions of the genre have been advanced ever since it came to prominence in the late eighteenth century. It has been described as a tale characterized by an unexpected twist or pivoting on some uniquely memorable yet unlikely event or on some quasi-symbolic motif: it has been likened to drama because it, too, focuses on action and to the lyric poem because it, too, seeks to express the essence of experience or emotion. It has been called the quintessence of narrative art. Such definitions are useful enough; each has its measure of validity. Perhaps the best and certainly the most famous is the one offered by Goethe in his old age: the novelle is nothing more nor less than the retelling of an incident which seems extraordinary yet rings true.

Goethe, late in life, observed that in essence the novelle form is the account of an extraordinary event which has nevertheless actually happened; the reconciliation of the plausible with the unlikely was the artistic objective of most of the finest storytellers writing in German in the nineteenth century. His much-admired paradigm of the genre, entitled simply *Novelle*, was published late in his life, in 1828. In the placid setting of a small German principality a fire breaks out and a lion and tiger escape from a travelling menagerie. Eager to protect the beautiful princess with whom he is hopelessly in love, a young man, Honorio, shoots the tiger; but in response to the entreaties of the distraught owner, a small boy is allowed to coax the lion back into its cage with the innocent melody of his flute. The slightness of the story is obvious enough, less so its allusive depth and profounder relevance which the reader only senses on careful and repeated reading. Goethe's least majestic masterpiece is in fact a crystallization of the themes and tensions which run through his greatest masterpieces – *Werther* and *Tasso*, *Iphigenie* and *Wilhelm Meister* – for here, in the small compass of a story childlike in its simplicity, he expresses his lifelong understanding of human existence. Language, concise and evocative, is used to expose the urges of instinct and to counterbalance them with the restraints of true civilization; the redeeming power of art and tenderness, the products of civilization in harmony with nature, finally subdue the destructiveness of passion and violence in Goethe's mature model of a world in which nature and society learn the need to coexist.

Few novellen attain the numinous insights of Goethe's late essay in the form, but the best of them (and there are a great many that are very fine indeed) share its sense of rounded self-sufficiency. The classic mid-nineteenth-century novelle *Immensee*, written in 1849 by Theodor Storm, is a particularly good example. With its reminders of Goethe's *Die Wahlverwandt-schaften* (1809) in its lakeside setting, the psychology and social behaviour of its characters, and its subtle use of symbolism, it looks backwards to the Romantic period, in which its central episodes take place; yet it also anticipates the experiments with time, memory and form and the intense dramas of the unspoken which were to become the focus of literary attention in the late nineteenth century. It set an example which is as significant within the context of German literature as the weightier novels of Balzac, Dickens and Turgenev are in the literatures of France, England and Russia. Its abiding popularity is a reminder that German Romanticism remains a central strand in the complicated evolution of German literature and culture up to the present day.

## Tales of Mystery and the Imagination

Germany might seem to be the natural habitat for the Gothic novel; curiously it did not make its appearance there until the end of the nineteenth century, and then only in muted form. The full-scale Gothic romance, with its mystery and suspense and its erotic undertones, never materialized; no women of genius set about imitating Mrs Radcliffe or indeed Mary Shelley. Instead, Tieck (the German writer most naturally suited to the genre) quickly abandoned it (*Abdallah*, 1796) on discovering the challenge and force of brevity. In so doing he was largely responsible for inaugurating a fascinating if sporadic tradition of highly accomplished shorter prose fiction unparalleled elsewhere in Europe. Tieck tapped the native German vein of folksong and fairy tale in which Romantic writers and scholars were deeply interested, blending it with a disturbingly acute awareness of the workings of the human psyche and the subconscious that came from close self-scrutiny, itself closely associated with the novel of identity. Thus the focus of the novel of identity on the effects of experience on the emergence of personality during childhood and adolescence, and on the transmission, retention and distortion of sensations and memories, injected a sense of urgency and experimentation, as well as seriousness, into the prose of the Romantic period which freed it from the potential stranglehold of sentimentality, superficiality and sensationalism.

There is nothing sentimental about the episode in Tieck's earliest masterpiece in the new shorter genre, *Der blonde Eckbert* (1797), when young Bertha casually abandons the little dog belonging to the old woman who has given her a home, and something deeply disturbing when, years later (but what is time in a narrative where past and present are so intertwined?), Bertha cannot recall its name, a little detail her memory has suppressed, but which is uncannily supplied by the friend to whom she is divulging her story. What else does he know? Beneath the picturesque surface of such a tale lurks the lure of the unknown, full of promise, yet apt to destroy those who cannot resist it. Even as a little boy, Christian (in *Der Runenberg*, 1804) felt the urge to visit the far-distant mountains. As a young man he achieves his aim: a mysterious woman who dwells in the heart of the mountains grants him untold riches, but such riches are gained at a price. The mandrake he had absent-mindedly pulled from the ground points in another, more disturbing, direction, and this is confirmed when Christian's efforts to lead a 'normal' life are undermined as he loses his hold on reality. His riches are untold, yet to the eyes of those still in the world of normality, the sack he is later seen carrying contains nothing but coloured pebbles. Such tales function on different levels. They may be diagnoses of subconscious states and mental crisis transmuted into art, but they can supply a Gothic *frisson* too, as when in *Liebeszauber* ('Love's magic') the young protagonist, newly arrived in an unknown town one sunny summer's evening, becomes aware that something dreadful is taking place in the house opposite. But such effects depend upon their singularity: repetition blunts them; the challenge to the author's inventiveness and imagination is unremitting. Tieck's early stories, and those of his contemporaries, hover between the childishly naïve, the deliberately archaic, and the penetratingly, disturbingly modern. Their landscapes and locations create moods, but they are more than that, they are also landscapes of the inner mind and the subconscious, where visual detail merges with the sound of language in such a way that the description of a scene, and the fictitious character's response to it, condition the responsiveness of the reader, ensuring his total involvement. Tieck's awareness of his achievement as a writer in a new mode was demonstrated by his inclusion of early masterpieces of concise storytelling in *Phantasus* (1812–17), a large-scale three-volume compendium in which they are set within a framework of conversation and critical discussion deliberately reminiscent of Boccaccio's *Decameron*.

One of the most famous examples of the new romantic kind of storytelling is *Peter Schlemihls wundersame Geschichte* ('Peter Schlemihl's strange story', 1814) by the French-born writer

Adelbert von Chamisso. It is a story which generates a myth for modern times by combining the sixteenth-century tale of Fortunatus and his inexhaustible purse with a Faustian pact with the devil and the personal symbolism of the man who loses his identity by parting with his own shadow. Both here, in his poetry and in his travelogue *Die Reise um die Welt* ('Journey around the world', 1836) – a counterpart of Charles Darwin's account of his voyage on the *Beagle* (1839) – Chamisso is remarkable for his intuitive understanding of the ways in which contemporary technological advances were to change our perceptions of time and space. His sense of the dislocations of time as one of the key experiences of his age was shared by some of his later contemporaries such as Stifter, but its cosmic character has only become fully appreciated in the late twentieth century. As Chamisso observed, even those who stayed at home began to feel restless. Suggestive excursions into the unknown and imaginative fusions of disparate material characterize much of the best shorter fiction of the early nineteenth century period, such as Achim von Arnim's *Isabella von Ägypten* (1812), a more convoluted tale in which a gypsy girl brings a mandrake to ludicrous, sinister life in her efforts to win the heart of the future Emperor Charles V, but is nearly thwarted by the rivalry of a golem, another being brought to life by supernatural means as her soulless double.

The kaleidoscopic interplay here of historical detail and dreamlike fantasy, of emotional intensity and grotesque irony, were also key factors in the success of Arnim's most famous contemporary, E. T. A. Hoffmann. But there was something about Hoffmann's work which gave it an international appeal rivalled only by that of Edgar Allan Poe (1809–49). The tales of Hoffmann are often concerned with musical motifs, but that is hardly surprising: he was one of the Romantic period's most gifted composers and writers on music, and his opera *Undine* (1816), based on the story by Fouqué, marked a decisive step in the development of German Romantic opera. Hoffmann's inventiveness, his strong sense of the supernatural and the grotesque, and the almost palpable reality he can give to even the most unlikely situations were among the factors for his sustained success, and are particularly impressive in stories such as *Ritter Gluck* (1809), *Der Sandmann* (1816) and *Die Bergwerke zu Falun* ('The mines of Falun', 1819). In Hoffmann's imaginative world quirky humour coexists with existential horror; the appeal of his tales can be almost childish, yet they also open up vistas into a disturbing adult, modern world. His irony may have something to do with this, but so, too, does his insight into the symptoms, workings and effects of obsessive and unbalanced mental states (*Das Fräulein von Scuderi*, 1818; *Das Majorat*, 1817): writers such as he were laying the foundations for nineteenth-century German and Austrian psychological and psychiatric research. As a result, Hoffmann's influence on later writers has probably been greater than that of his contemporaries, and may be observed in the theories of Freud and the fictions of Kafka. The 'fortuitous' alternation of a tomcat's life-story with the outpourings of a composer of genius in his unfinished novel *Lebensansichten des Katers Murr* (1820–2) also make Hoffmann one of the most fascinating experimental novelists in German literary history.

Heinrich von Kleist was one of the few playwrights to excel equally at prose narrative. Kleist exploited the sentence structures of written German to such a degree that his stories may almost be said to be created out of its notoriously complicated syntax. But that is to undervalue his imaginative power and his obsessive anxiety regarding the complex make-up of human beings and about the very nature of existence. His stories cast doubt on a stable, comprehensible world. In *Michael Kohlhaas*, the longest of them, a sturdy horse-dealer sets off to market but finds himself drawn into a quite different and destabilizing state of existence when his horses are stolen and he sets out on a mission to get them back. On one level this grandiose tale is an inquiry into the workings, or indeed the existence of justice; on another, it is an analysis of the development of an individual's self-awareness when pitted against the superior forces of random injustice and of the established order that appears to condone it or indeed to be based upon it. Significantly, *Michael Kohlhaas* is also set at the time of the Reformation – indeed it even involves Luther himself, the arch-rebel confronted with the problem of how to cope with a man at odds with the world as it is. It is a powerful story, and its significance is all the greater because it articulates some of the most dominant themes in modern German literature such as the nature of authority, the freedom of the individual within organized society, and the relationship between means and ends. Like the philosophical tales of Voltaire, a writer much admired by Frederick the Great of Prussia, it is in a sense an abstract argument expressed in fictional terms; but Kleist succeeded in reconciling an eighteenth-century intellectual tradition with the new fashion for historical fiction.

The moral sense of the individual is brought into conflict with the corporate ethics of society more intimately in *Die Marquise von O.* (1808), Kleist's uniquely successful exploitation for the most serious of purposes of a double-entendre which might in other hands have lent itself to sophisticated pornography, a genre much in vogue in the politically and morally turbulent late eighteenth century. Dating from the same period as Goethe's *Die Wahlverwandtschaften*, it treats subject-matter of similar delicacy: a beautiful woman finds herself pregnant but unable to account for this fact of nature, and places an advertisement in the paper for the father to present himself. This extraordinary opening soon leads to developments whose serious implications are a reminder that early nineteenth-century literature in German reflects life with a degree of candour unusual in other literatures of the time. The stock topos of appearance and reality plays a major part in the story; Kleist exploits its potential even more fully in his arresting tale of racial and sexual tension on the island of Haiti in the West Indies, *Die Verlobung in St Domingo* ('The engagement in St Domingo', 1811), in which the motives of a half-caste girl are given their obvious yet tragically wrong interpretation by a young Swiss soldier. Kleist's uncomfortable anticipation of the themes and subjects of twentieth-century writing is equally evident in his most economical tale, *Das Erdbeben in Chili* ('The earthquake in Chile', 1807); here the arbitrary destruction wreaked by Nature recreates for a brief moment an earthly paradise which is shattered by the violence of the earthquake's pious yet prejudiced survivors.

## Schiller's Contemporaries and Successors: Kotzebue, Collin and Kleist

For all its originality, the new drama of Germany which Lessing had inaugurated was to a large extent dependent on foreign models. During the middle decades of the eighteenth century it had looked to the middle-class drama of England and France as it addressed themes of general and topical human interest. Even the slow emergence of historical drama inaugurated by *Götz von Berlichingen* was fired by the new enthusiasm for Shakespeare. But by the 1790s a two-way exchange was beginning to take place. The mounting esteem in which Germany's new drama was held in the countries which had provided its models was reflected in a growing number of imitations and translations (Scott's *Götz von Berlichingen*, 1799; Coleridge's *Wallenstein*, 1800; Constant's *Walstein*, 1808). However, in terms of popularity and box-office success these were overshadowed by the international appeal of the plays of August von Kotzebue.

The vogue for Kotzebue is reflected in the episode in Jane Austen's novel *Mansfield Park* (1814), when *Lovers' Vows*, adapted by Mrs Inchbald from his *Das Kind der Liebe* ('The Love-child'), is rehearsed by the young people. He operates on a lower intellectual and aesthetic plane than his greater German contemporaries, yet his deficiencies may be identified with the strengths and qualities which made him the darling of theatrical Europe between 1789 and 1815. *Menschenhaß und Reue* ('Misanthropy and repentance', but known in England as 'The Stranger') took audiences by storm in 1789, the year of the French Revolution; it illustrates the kind of recipe Kotzebue made very much his own. Eulalia, a kind but erring woman, is finally reunited with her embittered and misanthropic husband by a stratagem which involves the heart-rending participation of their two small children. Sentimentality was a device which Kotzebue used in abundance; but he could also employ headier appeals to the emotions, as in his once much-admired *Die Sonnen-Jungfrau* ('The Virgin of the Sun', 1799) and its sequel, *Die Spanier in Peru*, which took the London public by storm when performed in Sheridan's adaptation, *Pizarro*, with Mrs Jordan in the role of Cora. Here exoticism, heroic pathos and grandiloquent expressions of favourite contemporary themes conspired to give audiences the sensation that they were in the presence of great drama. He avoided such effects when he turned with considerable success to comedy in plays of mistaken identity such as *Die beiden Klingsberg* ('The two Klingsbergs', 1801) and, more lastingly, *Die deutschen Kleinstädter* ('German small-town people', 1803), an amiable essay in social satire which sends up typical German provincial middle-class foibles with gentle irony and deft deployment of comic stage techniques; it is the best and in stage terms the sole survivor of his output of 227 plays.

Though Kotzebue longed to be accepted as the equal of Goethe and Schiller, it was evident, when the latter died in 1805, that his succesor was not to be Kotzebue but one of the younger dramatists who were earning the recognition of a more discerning public: Zacharias Werner, Heinrich Joseph von Collin and Heinrich von Kleist. Like his less successful brother, Matthäus von Collin, author of a cycle of Austrian historical dramas charting the eventful saga of the medieval House of Babenberg, Heinrich von Collin represented a new phenomenon, the consciously Austrian writer emulating the achievements of Weimar. With his Roman play, *Regulus* (1801), he scored a short-lived success. Its rhetorically effective presentation of a stark conflict of loyalties was in tune with the times. Regulus, a Roman general taken prisoner by the Carthaginians, is allowed home on parole to plead for peace on enemy terms, but succeeds instead in rousing his demoralized nation to a new sense of purpose knowing that this will seal his own fate: he cannot break his word, so he returns to his captors empty-handed. The predicament of a hostage caught between the interests of his country and the emotional appeals of his family and friends was an adept exploitation of the tension between a topical personal drama and the distancing effect of stylized neo-classical drama in verse. It was a topic soon to take on contemporary relevance when in 1810 the defeated imperial House of Austria found itself forced to give the upstart Napoleon the hand of Marie-Louise, daughter of Emperor Franz I of Austria, in marriage.

A dramatist of considerably greater genius committed suicide in the same year that Collin died: Heinrich von Kleist. But they were contemporaries and their works share something of the same tension; personal conduct and its motivations are as acutely scrutinized in Kleist's tragedies, and in his one comedy, *Der zerbrochene Krug* ('The broken jug', 1808), but analytical precision is offset by flights of poetry that take on meaning of their own, accompanying and enhancing the moral and dramatic action. In Kleist's most rounded play, and the one that has recommended him most strongly to twentieth-century Germans, the hero, Prince Friedrich of Homburg, finds himself compelled by his own moral judgement rather than by external pressure to pay the penalty for his lapse of attention during a military briefing, and the ensuing charge at the wrong moment during battle. The charge may have made the Prince a hero; but its ill-advised rashness made its success smack of luck rather than strategic planning: the 'hero' has to pay the price decreed by a court martial. But he does so in a way that is as unexpected as it is memorable and dramatically effective. On his way to plead for mercy, he catches sight of his own grave, dug to await his dead body the next day. That sight, that experience of the imminence of his own extinction, achieves the moral goal of the drama in a way no death-scene could. The hero's reduction to a forlorn and desperate human being pleading for life at any price presents, in Kleist's tragedy with a 'happy ending', an experience of hubris and a glance into the abyss that is so harrowing and so complete that the execution scene with which the play ends can turn into a scene of resurrection. The ending echoes the beginning (the setting and the atmosphere are the same); but at the beginning the young hero was dreaming of life; at the end he is mature enough to bid the world farewell until suddenly the bandage is lifted from his eyes and he is restored to life and love. Kleist's *Prinz Friedrich von Homburg* is a historical drama of a kind which owes greater allegiance to Goethe's *Egmont* than to Schiller's masterpieces in the genre; it is a paean of praise to Prussian values and Prussian history (the setting is a war between that country and Sweden), but its truer, deeper content can emerge more clearly if it is divorced from the historical context that gave it substance, visual impact and topical relevance: the defeat of Prussia by Napoleon in 1806 had hastened a sense of national demoralization which must have contributed to the drama's moral and political texture, as it also did, but in a form which is now much less appealing, in his uncompromisingly nationalistic play *Die Hermannsschlacht* ('The battle of Hermann'), which gave a new Prussian relevance to the Arminius myth. Like *Prinz Friedrich von Homburg*, it was not published until 1821, ten years after Kleist's suicide. It did not reach the stage until 1839.

Like Schiller, Kleist never repeated himself; his seven dramas, all composed within the short span of nine years, show an exciting development that has its analogy in the creative career of Beethoven the symphonist. Least popular until the turn of this century was *Penthesilea*, a frenetic dramatization in quasi-symbolical terms of the oscillating interplay between violence and love that marks the encounter between Achilles, the Greek hero, and Penthesilea, the Amazon leader. Here neo-classicism loses all its usual frigidity; all is movement, turmoil and passion in this play that seems to be a sort of missing link between the *Bacchae* of Euripides and Strindberg's *Miss Julie*. The tenderness of which Kleist was capable is to the fore in the play of his which has exerted the greatest appeal in Germany: *Das Käthchen von Heilbronn* (1810), a fairy-tale play set in an imaginary medieval Germany, in which a girl, Käthchen (= Kate), follows her knight with trance-like confidence and the sure tread of a sleep-walker, in line with Kleist's conviction that feeling and emotion are surer guides than rational thought can ever be. Kleist's awareness of the vital importance of impulse and of the dangers inherent in logical deliberation enhances his work as a playwright because it endows his dramas with a sense of life unfolding spontaneously. Less quotable than Schiller, his example has been more influential and more frequently followed in modern German literature from the 1890s onwards.

With Kleist as contemporary, Zacharias Werner has paled into insignificance as a romantic playwright whose conception of drama has more in common with Kotzebue in melodramatic vein. An East Prussian by birth, Werner's sometimes almost baroque presentation of the symbolical dimensions of human action, which he saw exemplified in history as he conceived it, had a readier appeal in Vienna than in Berlin. He settled in Vienna, as the North German Friedrich Hebbel was to do some decades later, becoming a Roman Catholic convert and in due course an effective and fashionable preacher. His chief merits as a dramatist are his command of pace and suspense in his fate tragedy or psycho-religious thriller *Der vierundzwanzigste Februar* ('The 24th February', first performed 1810), where past events return to haunt the present in a bleak alpine setting on the fatal 24 February, and his almost operatic fondness for stage spectacle in the fine historical tragedy *Martin Luther, oder die Weihe der Kraft* ('Martin Luther, or The consecration of strength', 1806), qualities which can be seen in fuller, more perfected form in the work of Vienna's major nineteenth-century dramatic poet, Franz Grillparzer.

## Grillparzer

Austria's major nineteenth-century dramatic poet was Franz Grillparzer. He came to fame in 1817 with a masterpiece in the 'fate tragedy' manner much in vogue at the time, Greek tragedy in Gothic disguise, in which suspense is generated by the gradual unfolding of what is predestined to happen. *Die Ahnfrau* ('The Ancestress') captivated audiences with its breathless, doom-laden excitement. Here, even in this first play, there is a sense of vitality and urgency, of life playing tricks on human beings, and of ineluctable fate proceeding remorselessly towards its goal. But, like Kleist, whose first play had something in common with it, Grillparzer refused to be typecast, and followed this romantic melodrama with a controlled and mellifluous essay in neo-classicism, *Sappho* (1818), the tragedy of a poetess whose belated attempt to savour real life and true love to the full leads to her tragic realization that the artist must rise above life, the subject matter of art. Here, too, he treated the poignancy of an older woman's love for a younger man, a theme which was to surface again in Hofmannsthal's libretto for Richard Strauss's opera *Der Rosenkavalier* nearly a century later. Love, rather than art, was to become one of Grillparzer's dominant themes, though he is no romantic playwright in the conventional sense of the term, for to him love is always subordinate to something else, be it the inevitable unfolding of myth in *Das goldene Vlies* ('The Golden Fleece', 1821), a trilogy which follows the legend of the golden fleece to its almost modern conclusion, and *Des Meeres und der Liebe Wellen* ('The waves of the sea and of love', 1831, published 1840), his movingly lyrical treatment of the Hero and Leander story, or the equally inevitable march of history in his masterpieces in the dramatized history vein, *König Ottokars Glück und Ende* ('King Ottokar's good fortune and end', 1825) and the posthumous *Ein Bruderzwist im Hause Habsburg* ('A fraternal conflict in the House of Habsburg', completed around 1848 but not performed or published until 1872), which charts with profound historical and psychological insight the course of events and the dynastic conflict which led up to the outbreak of the Thirty Years War.

   In each and every case, Grillparzer's drama is characterized by a deep-seated mistrust of the human will, an acute sense of the transience of time, and an unremitting awareness of the forward movement of life and history. The will generates action; the consequences of action are unforeseeable; and there is never any hope of a second chance. Frequently in his plays characters reach a point at which they realize that the way forward is blocked for them and that there is no way back. Only in his 'dream play' *Der Traum ein Leben* (1834) does the hero get a chance to experience what no waking mortal ever can: his dream – a fulfilment of his deepest desires and wishes – takes on the reality of life itself until it threatens to reach a denouement so terrible that it is a relief for him to wake up and find it was just a dream. Grillparzer here pinpoints his true place in the evolution of European drama. Despite appearances, he owes less to Shakespeare or to Goethe and Schiller than he does to Calderón and Lope de Vega, the great playwrights of the Spanish Golden Age. Calderón provides one point of reference with his great cosmic comedy *La Vida es sueño* ('Life is a Dream', 1636): the other is provided by *Die Traumdeutung* ('The Interpretation of Dreams', 1900), the seminal study by the Austrian psychoanalyst Sigmund Freud, who was brought up on Grillparzer, and also by Strindberg's surrealistic *Drömspelet* ('A Dream Play', 1902) and the countless twentieth-century plays and films they have inspired. Despite the romantic elements in Grillparzer's work – the Gothic panic of *Die Ahnfrau*, the intense passions of *Sappho* and *Des Meeres und der Liebe Wellen*, the mythological symbolism of his late 'Bohemian' play *Libussa* – he was no German Romantic and disliked the clever intellectualism and disregard for 'human truth' which so many of the German Romantic writers displayed. Instead he deliberately brought to the form the delicate intimation of women as sensual beings, exemplified by the characters of Rahel, the beautiful Jewess who captivates the young king of Spain in *Die Jüdin von Toledo* ('The Jewess of Toledo', a play not published or performed until 1872), and Erny, the young wife in his Hungarian historical play *Ein treuer Diener seines Herrn* ('A loyal servant of his master', first performed in 1828), whose love for her elderly husband proves greater than the other characters or the audience realize or expect.

## The Failure of German Romantic Drama

The German Romantic writers were fascinated by theatre and its artistic possibilities, yet none achieved any real or lasting success as a playwright, with one exception: Ludwig Tieck. A distinguished connoisseur of English Elizabethan and Jacobean drama, he refrained from participating in the vogue for pseudo-Shakespearean plays which obsessed many of his contemporaries in England and Germany, preferring to lend his weight to the completion of the classic translation of Shakespeare's plays known as the Schlegel–Tieck version (1825–33). He also made something of a speciality of plays based on fairy-tale motifs such as Cinderella, Little Red Riding-Hood and especially Puss in Boots: the feline hero of *Der gestiefelte Kater* (1797) finds himself playing his part in a burlesque extravaganza which is part of a more complex and sophisticated satirical comedy ridiculing the shallow, conventional attitudes of philistine middle-class audiences. Brentano, despite his great gifts, disappoints as a dramatist, though he anticipated Büchner's *Leonce und Lena* with his comedy *Ponce de Leon* (1804) and Grillparzer's *Libussa* with his long and pious play *Die Gründung Prags* ('The founding of Prague', 1814) based on the Bohemian legend of the princess who married the city's founder. Neither play entered the repertoire, nor did those of the many other Romantic writers who attempted to write for the stage: not even Eichendorff succeeded, despite the deftness and charm of *Die Freier* ('The suitors', 1833), his romantic comedy of mistaken identities. The most significant contribution to early nineteenth-century German comedy lay elsewhere: in the suburban theatre of Vienna.

## Viennese Comedy

Vienna was the capital of the Austrian Empire from 1804 to 1918, and its Habsburg rulers, who had so long worn the Holy Roman Imperial crown, had often been benevolent if at times despotic patrons of the theatre. The flowering of Viennese comedy did not take place in the court theatres, however, but was located principally in theatres situated on the periphery of the town centre, which is why it is often called 'suburban'. These theatres included the Theater an der Wien, where Mozart's *Magic Flute* and Beethoven's *Fidelio* had their premières, the Josefstädter Theater in the west (home today of what is still probably the leading school of acting in the German-speaking countries) and the Leopoldstädter Theater, situated in the north of the city where poor immigrants congregated and which in 1847 was replaced by the Carl Theater. In the years between 1820 and 1860, before operetta began to oust popular comedy in the public's favour, the Viennese suburban theatre was dominated by two very different but highly talented actor-playwrights: Ferdinand Raimund in the 1820s and 1830s and, from the mid-1830s until his death in 1862, Johann Nestroy. Both men came to writing through acting, and in the framework of the local stage and its requirements. Inspired by Schiller's master-pieces, Raimund aspired in vain to be a great tragic actor; in time he developed his own personal style of acting, between pathos and comedy, and extended his range in the plays which he wrote for himself to act in. A rich imagination guided both the writing and the staging of his 'magic farces', comedies and *Besserungsstücke* or moral pantomimes in which heavenly beings and bodies intervene in human destiny to promote virtue and therefore happiness. Contemporary audiences delighted in the spectacle provided by Raimund's expert handling of the theatrical traditions of Vienna which stretched back to the baroque. His greatest gift, however, is his power to represent stages of human experience and emotional states in scenic terms. Nowhere is this more poignant and intellectually persuasive than in *Der Bauer als Millionär* (1826), especially the scene in which Youth, in the figure of a charming young woman, comes to take farewell of the aptly-named central character, the miserly peasant Fortunatus Wurzel, whom Old Age then comes to join as his new and all too faithful companion. Raimund is at his most powerful in the scene in *Der Alpenkönig und der Menschenfeind* ('The Alp-King and the misan-thropist', 1828), where the misanthropic Rappelkopf encounters his double and falls on this 'enemy' in order to destroy him, anticipating the insights of Freudian psychology. But in this confrontation of the self with its mirror image, Rappelkopf is cured of his mistrust and misanthropy, and his balance is restored. This is comedy where the spectator is the 'customer' and wants to be sent home happy.

In assessing Johann Nestroy's long and successful career it has to be realized that Viennese suburban theatre was a commercial undertaking, and that, unlike the court theatres, it was not subsidized. Plays had to be tailored to an audience whose loyalties were fickle and whose taste changed with its social composition over the period from 1830 to 1860. Moreover, the play-wright had to deal not only with a potentially hostile press, but also with a stringent and exasperating censorship, both suspicious of his satire: stage performances were actually policed. Nestroy was first and foremost a working actor-playwright. He did not 'invent' his plays but generally adapted them from other sources: great European comedy since the days of the Greek Aristophanes and the Roman Plautus has had little difficulty in crossing national and cultural frontiers. Nestroy's frequent reliance on foreign sources, mostly French and English, such as Molière and Dion Boucicault, locates the Viennese suburban theatre, for all its local character, within the framework of the international theatrical life of its day.

The 'Viennese Aristophanes' began his acting career as an opera singer and his writing with magic burlesques and parodies of *Besserungsstücke* such as *Der böse Geist Lumpacivagabundus oder Das liederliche Kleeblatt* ('The evil spirit Lumpacivagabundus or the dissolute trio', 1833), his famous comedy about the trials and tribulations of three good-for-nothing journeyman apprentices. He developed his technique as a brilliant comic author in a series of satirical farces often with interspersed lyrics such as *Der Talisman* (1840), his play about prejudice and the fickle turns of fortune, and *Einen Jux will er sich machen* ('Out for a bit of fun', 1842), known to modern English-speaking audiences as *On the Razzle* by Tom Stoppard (1981). Nestroy was famous for his witty wordplay: audience anticipation would build up to the scenes featuring the author himself displaying the full force of his verbal virtuosity in his famous 'couplets' – deadpan satirical songs on contemporary issues and universal human follies. A great craftsman of plays in which farce, burlesque, satire, melodrama, fairy tale and parody blended, Nestroy is also an extraordinarily sophisticated master of verbal comedy which exploits the interplay between Viennese dialect and standard German. While contemporary social issues are often integrated into his plots (money is often the driving force in them), the plays also function as satirical metaphors of more fundamental aspects of human life: critics have drawn plausible comparisons between the themes of his plays and ideas explored by thinkers from Kierkegaard (as in *Der Zerrissene*, 'The man at odds with himself', 1844) to Wittgenstein (as in *Der Schützling*, 'The protégé', 1847). As the work of its twentieth-century exponents such as Ödön von Horváth and Jura Soyfer confirmed, Viennese suburban comedy forms a central part of German drama, not a minor phenomenon on its dialect periphery.

## Early Nineteenth-Century Poetry

Hölderlin had fallen silent; but his silence was hardly audible at the time because German poetry had entered one of its most exciting and productive periods. New voices were continually joining the chorus of those who were already famous in their own lifetimes, and which was dominated by Goethe, whose achievement was already acknowledged to be phenomenal and whose ability to come up with something new time and again was to continue unabated until his death in 1832. By then the first group of German Romantic poets had come and mainly gone. Tieck, the most productive of the Romantics, was still producing melodically rich but shapeless poems remarkable for their evocative euphony, but their leader, Novalis, mysterious, intense singer of the commingled joys of love, night and death, had died in 1801.

In 1803 Johann Peter Hebel, the only writer of his time to raise poetry in a regional German dialect to the level of high art, had published a much-admired collection of poems which demonstrated that folksong and classical metres could be fused in the broad doric of his native corner of south-western Germany. But despite Goethe's admiration, the *Alemannische Gedichte* of Hebel remained a solitary phenomenon, comparable to that of Burns in Scotland, but with less resonance outside its own region. Hebel is admired in some circles as the founder of modern German dialect poetry, and in his own area he enjoys something of Burns's reputation. But he defies classification. Others, almost too easily grouped in retrospect as Romantics of one kind or another, are also better seen and understood in their own terms and contexts. One thing common to them all, however, was an intense symbiosis with nature. It is the focus of most of the finest German poetry of the period, and is almost invariably the landscape of Germany: wooded, hilly, and vast, it was an infinite source of poetical ideas. Readers of a later era can but marvel at the wealth and variety of the lyric poetry this landscape inspired. It was seldom localized. More often it was stylized: an ideogram, as it were, for moods and emotions whose objective correlative it became. In the hands of lesser talents, the 'pathetic fallacy' of much European Romantic writing could become tiresome, but in the hands of more original writers it could take on a uniquely personal quality. This is evident, for instance, in some of the woodland poems of Joseph von Eichendorff, the ballads and *Wanderlieder* of Ludwig Uhland and the lyrics of Wilhelm Müller.

Uhland, in the early years of the nineteenth century, was most successful with songs such as 'Der gute Kamerad' ('The good comrade'), a war poem reminiscent of Gleim, but so much more intense beneath its outward simplicity:

> Ich hatt' einen Kameraden
> Einen bessern findst du nit,
> Die Trommel schlug zum Streite,
> Er ging an meiner Seite
> In gleichem Schritt und Tritt.

But he was also the author of haunting ballads like 'Das Schloß am Meer', with its deserted, ruined castle by the sea, so romantic and escapist in feel, yet barely concealing the poet's political disenchantment and suppressed anguish, and very much an expression of the general malaise of the period in which it was written.

The rediscovery of the literary potential of German folk poetry had actually reached its climax in the early years of the nineteenth century with the appearance of *Des Knaben Wunderhorn* ('The boy's magic horn'), the collection of the German folksongs edited by Achim von Arnim and Clemens Brentano and published between 1805 and 1808. It confirmed a trend which went back to Herder and Bürger and which had established folk poetry as a central and cherished element of lyric poetry in German, giving it a cultural status it never quite achieved in the other major western European languages and cultural areas. The close relationship between folk and literary poetry continued to make itself felt in many ways. A good example is the *Wanderlied* or 'walking song', a minor genre which originated in the traditional songs sung by journeyman apprentices (*Wanderburschen*) and flourished during the first two decades of the nineteenth century. The *Wanderlied* was associated with the freedom of travel which was lost or restricted in the politically fragmented Germany of the time; in its place a love of country hiking and open-air part-song singing now became a characteristic feature of German social culture which lasted until well into the twentieth century. Uhland himself provided a cycle of eight *Wanderlieder*, and the genre was further popularized by Justinus Kerner, Ludwig Rellstab and many others. The particular blend of pace and mood that characterizes such poetry calls out for musical setting, and inspired Franz Schubert to write many of his finest songs. Their apparent simplicity is underscored by the wistfulness which is often also characteristic of folksong, though here, in Romantic fashion, it indirectly expresses the melancholy and hopelessness of the poet himself, for whom the beauty of the natural world cannot quite compensate for personal disappointment and a growing sense of existential insecurity. Thus the rhythms and images of German folksong combined with the Romantic sensibility to create an aesthetic experience for which the previous sixty years had been the long preparation.

Landscape provided the picturesque setting for a poignant idyll of unreciprocated love in the twenty poems of Wilhelm Müller's cycle *Die schöne Müllerin* (1821, set to music by Schubert in 1823), which make apt use of the favourite German late-Romantic image of the old mill by a stream. But landscape could also become the outward expression of an increasingly desperate state of mind, an aspect captured with extraordinary empathy in Schubert's 1827 setting of *Die Winterreise* (1823), his cycle of twenty-four intensely sombre poems in which any autobiographical element is sublimated in a bleak natural landscape rather than concealed by it. A mere five years elapsed between their publication and the early deaths of the poet (1827) and then the composer (1828), events which foreshadowed the passing of the classic age of German Romanticism.

## Two Catholic Poets: Brentano and Eichendorff

Clemens Brentano was the most gifted artist in sound of the entire Romantic literary movement. Many of his poems date from the period between 1804 and 1812, when he and Achim von Arnim were busy collecting and perfecting *Des Knaben Wunderhorn*. Brentano's own poetry shows the influence of folksong by adopting its characteristic turns of phrase, its rhyme schemes and motifs in order to conceal yet at the same time express his own temperamental oscillations between different facets of his own personality rather than between the different moods most German Romantics cultivated and valued. An amorous romantic, with a strongly sensual streak Germans have liked to ascribe to his Italian ancestry, he was also, and some would claim for the same reason, drawn irresistibly to the rigours and solace of religion, which embraced a love of all creation but also led to bouts of asceticism and self-reproach; later, he found a sort of spiritual balance in mysticism. Of all the Romantics Brentano was the most baroque and, perhaps, the most truly medieval. These tendencies are clearly evident in his most ambitious poetical work, *Die Romanzen vom Rosenkranz*, which did not become available to the wider public until 1852, ten years after his death; like many another German Romantic masterpiece, it was left unfinished. Brentano's 'romances of the rosary' are a sequence of narrative episodes entwined with semi-religious rose symbolism and interlinked to form a pseudo-medieval quasi-religious myth devised by Brentano to illustrate the protracted struggle of mankind to overcome temptation and gain redemption. The first outstanding Catholic religious poems in German since the Reformation, they are an achievement reinforced by their reminiscences of Dante, their setting in medieval Bologna, and a pre-Raphaelite quality that reminds us that they are contemporaneous with the early years of the so-called Nazarene School, founded by a group of German painters of similar religious and artistic outlook who were active in Rome at the time. Brentano's *Die Romanzen vom Rosenkranz* mark a high point in the poetic tradition of Catholic Germany and the literary climax of the Romantic movement's sometimes intense involvement with Roman Catholicism and with the long tradition of European religious and mystical writing. Brentano's romances possess a quality not always associated with devotional verse: a compelling sense of the natural world conveyed by visual detail which often also has symbolical or visionary associations, and by a keen ear for the expressive power of words chosen primarily though seldom exclusively for their sound: it is verse rich in subtle assonances and rhythms.

Besides Brentano, the son of a prosperous Rhineland businessman, the Romantic era produced a second Catholic poet: this was Joseph von Eichendorff, the son of a Silesian nobleman. In Eichendorff's case the profound spiritual impulse which underlies his poems is never their explicit purpose; rather it is an element implicit in nature poems which, instead of painting in verbal detail, evoke the moods of the natural world as economically as possible in words whose symbolical associations add deep layers of meaning to what on the surface seems artlessly simple. Of the two, it was Eichendorff who attracted the notice of composers. They were ever on the lookout for poets who could supply suitable texts for piano-accompanied songs (*Lieder*), a musical genre much in demand by the educated German public of the day and which, ever since Mozart, had become one of the favourite modes of expression for most major and many minor German musicians. Eichendorff's first collection of poems appeared in 1837, and was soon put to good use by Mendelssohn, who appreciated his delicate evocations of woodland and fairy tale ('O Täler weit, O Höhen, O schöner, grüner Wald'); soon Robert Schumann had begun to find inspiration in them, too, responding especially to their magical evocations of nocturnal silence, ineffable sadness and intense ecstasy ('Mondnacht', 'Die Stille'). The combination of Eichendorff's lyricism with their music may rightly be claimed as one of the supreme achievements of German Romantic art.

## Platen and Lenau

The range of German lyric poetry in the first half of the nineteenth century is shown by two writers whose lives and work revealed the more tormented aspects of the Romantic movement associated with European Romanticism rather than with Romanticism in Germany. In all other respects, however, they had very little in common except that they both came from an aristocratic background. August, Graf von Platen-Hallermünde, was a reluctant officer in the Bavarian army at the time, who experienced the disillusionment of the post-Napoleonic era, and was drawn increasingly to scholarship and writing, to art and the cult of beauty. He went into voluntary exile in Italy in order to devote his life to a determined effort to create poems of the greatest possible formal beauty as a bulwark against the uncongenial temper of his age and the emotional untidiness of his own personality. The discipline of the German neo-classical tradition created by Klopstock sixty years earlier, and perfected more recently by Goethe and Hölderlin, offered a way to sublimate himself in the effort to achieve dispassionate, timeless perfection. Yet for all its visionary and rhetorical power, Platen's finely chiselled verse in classical metres can be chilly, except when it is animated by his political indignation at events long since forgotten, or by sights now familiar even to less cultured tourists. More congenial to his poetic temperament was the sonnet, a renaissance lyric form in which, as Shakespeare had shown, formal sophistication could be successfully channelled to the articulation of emotional complexity; he was also drawn to the Persian ghazal, a form which could generate an exciting tension between the obsessive quality of his utterances and their subjugation to the remorseless recurrence of the same rhyme in each alternate line. Platen's Venetian sonnets (*Sonette aus Venedig*) of 1824 represent the highlight of his achievement. Here Venice becomes the objective correlative of the poet's inner and private worlds: a crumbling labyrinth of canals and alley-ways haunted by its glorious past, it is the image of his mounting bewilderment at the baffling complexity of life and of his vain yet perpetual search for a way out of his own inner turmoil. The affirmation of art and beauty is symbolized by the rare perfection of each poem, yet the message beneath the surface is one of intense and confused urgency giving way gradually to the torpor of resignation. Platen may be the first major 'gay' poet in Germany's literature, and his most personal work a discreet revelation of his sexuality; but his visions of beauty owe more to his cultural pessimism and quasi-Islamic fatalism. In his haunting poem 'Tristan', his central theme – the kinship between beauty and death – found perfect expression:

Wer die Schönheit angeschaut mit Augen,
Ist dem Tode schon anheimgegeben.

('He who has beheld beauty with his own eyes is already in thrall to death.')

Like Platen's own death in Sicily, haunted by the fear of cholera, this poem about the seduction of beauty and its associations with death have had far-reaching reverberations in modern German culture. It set the tone for Wagner's music-drama *Tristan und Isolde* (1865), which was written partly in Venice, where Wagner himself was later to die, and it foreshadowed Thomas Mann's analysis of art, sexuality and disintegration in his long short-story about a German writer's death in Venice: *Der Tod in Venedig*, 1912.

For Platen, Italy – and especially Venice – was the landscape of poetry. For his Austro-Hungarian contemporary Nikolaus Lenau, that landscape was the reed-surrounded Neusiedlersee, the desolate lake of his *Schilflieder* ('Songs of the reeds'), and the great plains of his native Hungary beyond it. Written in the year of Goethe's death, these poems, unlike Platen's, are outwardly very simple; as with most of Lenau's poetry the subtlety lies in the fine balance between the expression of personal emotion and the natural settings that seem to be purely descriptive on the surface, yet which hint at deeper symbolical dimensions beneath. Like Eichendorff, Lenau is at his best as a nature poet, and it would be easy to read him as just another late Romantic, rather more intense than his Silesian counterpart, perhaps, but with a basically similar conception of the relationship between shape and symbol, mood and sound, visibility and deeper understanding. What marks Lenau out in the context of German early nineteenth-century poetry is his tone of voice. That is unmistakable. Even his muted evocations of autumnal evenings and misty lakes are saved from lapsing into the rhythms and word patterns of his German contemporaries, which by the 1830s were getting more and more stereotyped with each succeeding year. His poems are different, their often unexpected rhythms and inflections seem sometimes almost to suggest that though they are written in German, their true language is Hungarian. 'Die drei Zigeuner' ('The three gypsies'), brilliantly set to music by his German-speaking compatriot, Franz Liszt, reinforces its vivid Hungarian atmosphere by its deliberate juxtapositions of elongated syllables and jerky rhythms. This linguistic and metrical originality is reinforced by Lenau's avoidance of stock imagery and of the expressive clichés which go with it. In this respect he has much in common with Droste-Hülshoff: like her, he produces poetry shot through with unusual, specific and realistic details which give it a realism untypical of the mainstream of German poets who were already losing their Romantic originality and beginning to give way to mid-nineteenth-century sentimentality.

## Annette von Droste-Hülshoff

Droste-Hülshoff, the outstanding woman poet of nineteenth-century German literature, died in 1848 – the momentous year of revolutions – the same year as Emily Brontë, though twenty years her senior. They have much in common. Both started writing when very young, both wrote poetry that went beyond the conventional poetic language of most women writers of their period (and of many men), and both possessed a vivid imagination counterbalanced by an eye for detail and an awareness of the limitations of reality as they personally experienced it. Both were provincial and drew strength from the landscape around them. Like many of the women writers of their time they were in their own distinctive ways religious. In 1820 Droste-Hülshoff had begun work on *Das geistliche Jahr* ('The spiritual year'), a collection of 72 devotional poems based on and reflecting the calendar of the church year, though it did not appear until 1851, after her death. Droste's 'Spiritual Year' possesses qualities not always present in such poetry. It has a compelling sense of the natural world conveyed through visual detail which also often has symbolical and visionary associations, and a keen ear for the sound of words and their expressive power, normally restrained but sometimes rising to great intensity: indeed her outspoken addresses to the Almighty, with whom she engages in one-sided dialogue – for God's ineffable voice remains implicit only – brought back to German religious poetry a tone of voice which had not been heard since Catharina von Greiffenberg wrote her fervent religious sonnets in the mid-seventeenth century.

Under the influence of her close friend, the writer Levin Schücking, Droste-Hülshoff broke new ground in the *Vormärz* period by writing political and topical poems revealing a sharp eye for the ways of the world, as in her send-up of German nationalist aspirations exemplified by the pan-German campaign to add towers to Cologne's famous cathedral, or her address to the women writers of Germany and France in which she scathingly rejects sentimentality and sexual sensationalism as the wrong avenues for them to follow, and resolutely recommends the lone eagle-like ascent to the moral high ground and the preservation of the human relationships and natural surroundings on which the future of contemporary society and the planet depend.

In her later poems Droste-Hülshoff returns with renewed vigour to her natural surroundings, but the acuteness of observation, the aural effects and her frame of reference now take on an extraordinary subtlety and breadth. Her love of flowers and insects is still there, the product, some say, of her shortsightedness. But, building on the example of Goethe, she explores the uncanny, the terror of nightfall and lonely moorlands (as in 'Der Knabe im Moor') and the shadows of trees in moonlight (as in her famous novelle *Die Judenbuche*), because she knows that the pastoral idyll of meadows in sunshine needs this darker dimension to bring out its beauty and make it ring true. Droste's idylls are always under threat. In her later poems they exist *sub specie aeternitatis*: an eternity at once spiritual and scientific, for this remarkable woman was able to write poems such as 'Die Mergelgrube' ('The marl-pit') in which, surrounded by the peaceful Westphalian scene of a lone shepherd and his flock, she comes across fossils and in her mind's eye witnesses both the beginning of the world and its ending. Aeons are fused into one poetic moment. Transience and eternity coalesce in a fossil: the mystical tradition of Christianity had fused with the scientific revelations of the age of Cuvier and Darwin.

## Heine and Mörike

The Romantic game of hide-and-seek played in their poems by most German Romantic poets became the natural element of two very different writers who both started to publish soon after Goethe's death, and within five years of each other: Heinrich Heine and Eduard Mörike. Each was drawn in his own way to use personal and private experience to give greater cogency and lasting value to the themes they shared with their contemporaries. They, too, experience in their poetry the joy, but more often the hopelessness of love, the transitoriness of happiness and the permanence and beauty of landscape and, in Heine's case, of seascape, too, and the influences of the rich heritage of folk poetry and legend which their precursors had rediscovered and which they now adapted to the needs of their own individual sensibilities and their very different understandings of what it meant to be German.

Heine's versatile and confident treatment of these themes, and his immediately recognizable individual voice with its bitter-sweet mixture of sentimentality and hard-bitten irony, made him one of the most popular poets in Germany. His first major collection, *Das Buch der Lieder*

(1827), made him also one of the best-known abroad. Mörike's reputation grew more slowly. His *Innigkeit* – that is, his inward-looking reticence – was understated, and seemed the hallmark of just another minor regional poet until discerning readers began to realize that his art was one that concealed art and that beneath its simplicity was an intensity which gave the lie to the view that he was no more than a Swabian parson writing in an age of myopic complacency on themes inherited from the past.

Both poets were helped by their composers. In his lifetime Mörike was set by Schumann and by Hugo Wolf after his death. Heine, readier than most of his contemporaries to realize that publicity was important for a freelance writer's career, attracted a large number of composers from early on. Schubert discovered him at the end of his own short life, and in the Heine songs in his late *Schwanengesang* the geniuses of the two artists fused. Schumann was drawn to him and wrote the song-cycle *Dichterliebe*, Mendelssohn's 'On Wings of Song' carried his name into the drawing rooms of the world, and Liszt, Brahms and Richard Strauss added to his reputation as a musician's poet. Apart from Goethe himself, no German poet has ever achieved such a strong hold on the German imagination as Heine, many of whose poems ('Die Lorelei', 'Die Grenadiere', 'Du bist wie eine Blume', 'Der Tod, das ist die kühle Nacht', 'Ein Fichtenbaum steht einsam') are among the most frequently anthologized in the language. No German poet has appealed so widely – or been so disparaged. The claim that Heine's art was cynical and meretricious culminated in the Nazi regime's attempts to expunge this greatest of nineteenth-century poets from its literature on account of his Jewish birth. This exposed a fatal weakness in Germany's culture, but it failed to alter his stature as the writer who, after Goethe and Schiller, did most, through his work and personality, to make other countries aware of Germany as one of them, though very much with a voice of its own. As George Eliot observed in a pioneering essay in 1854, 'he can charm us by a quiet idyll, shake us with laughter at his overflowing fun, or give us a piquant sensation of surprise at the ingenuity of his transitions from the lofty to the ludicrous.' She had put her finger on a quality which was to delight countless readers but which also incurred the displeasure of those of a more pedestrian cast of mind who, unable to appreciate his irony, proclaimed him to be an arch-example of the Jewish inability to be genuinely serious. His deletion from the canon during the Third Reich was a triumph of *Ungeist* from which his reputation, like that of the composer Mendelssohn, is only now recovering.

Heine's range was extremely wide compared with that of Mörike and most of their contemporaries, and extends from the short subjective lyric poem to large-scale satirical verse narrative, and from sharply focused songs and ballads to remarkably modernistic experiments in free verse. Within that range his tone is constantly shifting. His frivolous, slightly offhand humour has often made readers mistake his wit for superficiality, while his ready assumption of romantic postures can be too easily dismissed as an empty pose. Yet faced with a subject that deserved it, Heine's anger could be devastating. His concern with his own woes as an individual may have a good deal of fashionable *Weltschmerz* about it, but his concern with the defects of society was genuine. Unlike the majority of his fellow late Romantics in Germany and elsewhere, Heine had a strongly satirical element in him which he could turn on society but also against himself. The fact that the reader often does not know how seriously to take him, or when to take him seriously, is part of the Heine phenomenon. The poems of the *Buch der Lieder* are predominantly about rejected love and separation, but the monotony of theme is offset by versatility of form and tone and by the inclusion of narrative poems which are as detached as the love poems are emotional, like the laconic ballad 'Belsatzer', which graphically describes Belshazzar's feast and gives the poet the opportunity to prophesy that the writing is on the wall. There is no trace of ironic affectation or modern petrarchism here, nor is there any in the impressive sequence of North Sea pictures (*Nordseebilder*), an experiment in marine poetry which remains almost unique in German literature, or in *Die Götter Griechenlands*, Heine's vision of the Greek gods departing in the clouds to leave the modern, emancipated world to look after itself. Heine's second collection of poetry, *Neue Gedichte*, followed in 1844, and in 1851 he published the last collection, entitled *Romanzero*. They confirmed his reputation as a complex writer with a brilliant technique and plenty still to say.

By comparison with Heine, Mörike seems mild. The golden autumnal landscape revealed as the morning mist rises in 'Herbstmorgen' (1827) may appear placid; but 'Verborgenheit', dated 1832, with its plea to be left alone, betrays the inner complexity and command of language which enabled him in the later poem 'An eine Lampe' to make a lamp, hanging in an almost forgotten room, become what is at one and the same time the profoundest statement in German of the aesthetics of 'art for art's sake' and one of the most perfectly poised poems in Germany's century-long tradition of fine poetry in unrhymed classical metres. Thus Mörike came to be greeted as the great intermediary between the classical tradition of Goethe and late eighteenth-century Germany and the aesthetic symbolism of Conrad Ferdinand Meyer later on in the nineteenth century.

## Thematic Survey: German Political Verse

German political poetry has a long and diverse tradition going back as far as Walther von der Vogelweide in the thirteenth century. In more modern times it has developed two distinct and sometimes opposing traditions. Across the years, and particularly in times of war, it has formed an integral part of a consciously 'national' literature. By contrast, during periods of social, economic and intellectual ferment, as in the later eighteenth century, the 1830s to 1840s, the Weimar Republic and in 1968, during the students' revolt, it has been a means for expressing a critical, even revolutionary message, but one which was long denied a legitimate social function by German society and officialdom.

Elements of both traditions are already audible in the sections towards the end of *Das Narrenschiff* when Brant vents his anger and anxiety about the fate of Germany on the eve of the Reformation. They are present, too, in the poems in which some of the major writers of the seventeenth century, such as Martin Opitz, Andreas Gryphius and Paul Fleming, lamented the fate of their country during the long night of the Thirty Years War, and in the works in which their successors, such as Johann Rist and Johann Klaj, expressed their briefer jubilation when the three nightmare decades of depredation and degradation finally ended in 1648. Patriotic poetry in the consciously national sense goes back in Germany to the Seven Years War (1756–63), which in Lessing's *Minna von Barnhelm* produced what Goethe was to describe as the first work of German literature with an authentic national subject and setting. There was of course no little falsification of history in casting Frederick II of Prussia (1740–86) in the role of national hero, but Gleim's Prussian war songs and Ramler's patriotic odes, like the panegyrics addressed to the victor of Leuthen and Rossbach by Anna Louisa Karsch, proved immediately popular. For their authors, such popularity legitimized the claim of the middle-class poet to be the voice of the nation, just as the common soldier of Gleim's Prussian war songs acquired a new status in literature, if not in life, as representative of the *Volk*.

The influence of such poetry was limited to a relatively narrow spectrum of readers. Nineteenth-century political poetry, however, could count on a much more sophisticated distribution system to reach a much wider audience. Hence Ernst Moritz Arndt, writing against the background of German resistance to Napoleon, could declare in *Geist der Zeit* (4 volumes, 1806–18) that the salvation of the people was in the hands of their writers. Patriotic poetry caught the spirit of the age and gave its readers a sense of citizenship. The stirring lines of Arndt's 'Was ist des Deutschen Vaterland?' ('What and where is the German's fatherland?') with their equally rousing refrain 'As far as the German tongue sounds or God's voice resounds in His heaven!' and the war poems entitled *Leier und Schwert* ('Lyre and sword') by Theodor Körner, a poet turned national hero when he was killed in a skirmish in 1813 at the age of twenty-one, roused ardent enthusiasm especially in the young wherever they were sung, and provided the staple diet of many a male-voice choir for decades to come, notably in the settings by the German Romantic composer Carl Maria von Weber. Women sang them too, as well as patriotic songs to texts by Rückert and Fouqué, Uhland and Schenkendorf, or played the accompaniments which were now often published at the back of the many popular magazines and almanacs intended for female readers. In order to understand the history of German nationalism in the nineteenth century and the role which literature played in its evolution, it is important not to overlook the pleasurable associations it enjoyed among so gregarious a people as the Germans. This continued to be true in a more circumscribed sense when, in the Franco-Prussian War of 1870–1 and in the First World War, patriotic political verse was used to justify and lend respectability to the new form of ideological warfare which involved moral defamation of the enemy.

In the age of Bismarck and national unification the patriotic lyric became a kind of hallmark of loyalty to the nation and to the new authoritarian nation state; such songs were no doubt what Adolf Krola sings in the drawing room of Frau Jenny Treibel in Fontane's novel of that name. After the Franco-Prussian War, Bismarck, now Imperial Chancellor, wrote personally to congratulate the poet Oskar von Redwitz on his *Lied vom neuen deutschen Reich*, a war story told in a sequence of sonnets, hailing him as a 'fellow worker in building our empire'. The degree to which the German literary market had been commercialized by that time is evident in the promptness of publishers as well as authors to respond to a particular situation. The first German anthology of patriotic verse made its appearance in the bookshops 24 days after the declaration of war against France in July 1870. An efficient and extensive distribution network, and the growing role of patriotic texts in schoolbooks, made writing of this kind a major factor in forming and directing opinion in the Second Empire. A comparison between the chauvinistic products of the 1870–1 war and older patriotic verse is also revealing for what it tells us about the gender stereotyping that was taking place at the time, a development that manifests itself, for example, in the growing tendency to stress military rather than civilian and domestic virtues: it is also reflected in and reinforced by the increasing popularity of modern reworkings – not least those by Wagner – of the Nibelungen saga in order to provide a new mythology for the German nation state. Homer's Greek hero Odysseus could weep without loss of manhood whereas Siegfried, the German hero of the Nibelungen myth, has to keep a stiff upper lip to be a man.

By contrast Heinrich Heine's political poetry belongs not to the affirmatively nationalistic but to the critical, even revolutionary, tradition. Here the wit of the satirist is deftly deployed to raise the public's awareness of injustice and to educate what he saw as a potentially influential sector of society: his readers. Its secondary objective is to bring about political change, but partly at least because Germany lacked a capital until 1871 – and satire is a very 'urban' genre – and partly on account of its absolutist form of government, political satire in Germany, which had thrived sporadically for many centuries, still lacked a continuous tradition. Heine was not without precursors. One of the most notable was C.F.D. Schubart, who had been imprisoned for a decade (1777–87) for his forthright criticism in verse of the abuse of power by princes, notably Duke Karl Eugen of Württemberg, the same despot who was making life difficult for the young Schiller. Schubart's poem 'Die Fürstengruft' ('The princely burial-vault'), written in prison, took up the theme with redoubled power and was published elsewhere in Germany in 1781. But Heine was a more polished and deliberate satirist than his late eighteenth-century precursor and one who, not unlike the Viennese playwright Nestroy, delighted in the power of wit to reveal the contradictions between the words of human beings and their thoughts and motivations.

However unique his genius, Heine must be seen in the political climate of the *Vormärz*, the name given retrospectively to the political ferment of the 'springtime' years preceding the outbreak of revolution in 1848, which were not unlike the period which led up to the *Wende* in 1989. Heine might jeer at the tendentious character of the *Jungdeutschland* movement and mock his fellow poets, such as Georg Herwegh, Ferdinand Freiligrath, Franz von Dingelstedt and Hoffmann von Fallersleben (the author of the *Deutschlandlied* which was to become the national anthem of Germany in 1922), and describe their work, not always unjustly, as rhymed newspaper articles, but, for all the aesthetic differences between their poetry and his, they have in common an emblematical quality. In this respect they offer an often exact equivalent to the political caricatures of their day, which were reproduced daily on handbills and flyers circulated in urban centres right across Germany from Königsberg to Karlsruhe, Breslau to Stuttgart, Hamburg to Munich. The hard-hitting poems in which Freiligrath spoke out on behalf of an exploited proletariat and voiced its protest, such as 'Freie Presse' and the cycle entitled 'Ça ira', seemed to contemporaries to herald radical change, while his menacing description in 'Von unten auf' of the sweating soot-blackened stoker rising up through the trap-door in the deck of an elegant Rhine steamer caused horror and dread in many a crinolined or top-hatted middle-class reader. The *Gedichte eines Lebendigen* ('Poems of a man alive') by the once immensely popular Herwegh stirred the emotions of many by their less clearly focused idealism.

Despite the greater sophistication of his verse, Heine desired above all to be as popular as they; hence his choice of a popular eight-syllable metre with four stresses, the trochaic tetrameter, to display his brilliant verbal wit and sovereign command of his craft. As was the case for the *Jungdeutschland* writers and for Nestroy and their other contemporaries in Austria, censorship dogged him throughout his career – between 1835 and 1841 his work was banned throughout Prussia – though his famous battles with the authorities only served to increase popular interest in his work. Perhaps, according to their lights, they were right to try to intimidate and silence a writer who could paint the coming revolution in words and rhythms filled with the terrifying menace of his song of the weavers ('Die schlesischen Weber', 1844), as the inexorable refrain of clacking looms brings home to the reader the realization that they are weaving the death-shroud of feudal Germany, a message which ominously re-echoes fifty years later when Gerhart Hauptmann's Naturalist drama *Die Weber* ('The weavers') takes up Heine's theme. It is no coincidence that at this same time Heine was actively engaged in political and philosophical debate about the state of the contemporary world, and that when he wrote his great mock epic, *Deutschland: Ein Wintermärchen* in 1843, he was on terms of friendship with

Karl Marx. Three years later he conjured up the shade of Gellert's eighteenth-century dancing bear in *Atta Troll*, one of the wittiest of all satirical treatments of political ideology and human frailty. Here classical, Christian, Jewish and German mythology are all made to contribute to an amazing display of Heine's unrivalled metrical and rhetorical virtuosity.

Unlike Nestroy, the 'Viennese Aristophanes', who spoke directly to his audience from the boards of Vienna's theatres, Heine was in exile from 1831, addressing his distant audience from Paris. Always popular in England, where countless translations appeared, he was something of a prophet crying in the wilderness in Germany, and often subject to vilification, especially during the final decades of the Second Empire and again, more virulently, in the Third Reich, on account of his Jewish origin. Yet his success in creating a tradition of political poetry in Germany as an instrument of moral enlightenment was to be eloquently demonstrated in the Weimar Republic, that most metropolitan period in Germany's cultural history, in the work of Brecht, Kurt Tucholsky, Erich Kästner, and others. The cabaret was now the major vehicle for political poetry, alongside the productions of the workers' movement and the pioneering creations of other new media such as Tucholsky's satirical history of the present, *Deutschland, Deutschland über alles* (1929), illustrated with unique photomontages by John Heartfield. Cabaret had its principal centre in Berlin, but it was in Munich, headquarters of the National Socialist Party, that Erika and Klaus Mann (Thomas Mann's children) founded the cabaret *Die Pfeffermühle*, together with the actress Therese Giehse. Symbolically it played both on the night Hitler came to power (30 January 1933) and on the night of the Reichstag fire (27 February 1933), when, as Brecht put it, the biddable German masses trotted off at the behest of Nazi Storm Troopers like little calves to the slaughterhouse.

The German cabaret had its own literary tradition as an effective weapon of political protest, as became evident a generation later in another totalitarian German state in the persons of Wolf Biermann, Volker Braun, Günter Kunert and others. In the 1960s Biermann, the GDR's uncomfortable *chansonnier*, challenged and provoked the authorities who gave official approval to Heine as the 'friend of Karl Marx', by bringing *Deutschland: Ein Wintermärchen* up to date in a mock epic of his own with the same title, in which he suggested intimate links between the regime of his own state and 'brown' Hitlerian Germany. Banned from the public sphere by the mid-1960s, Biermann continued to perform and write for an intimate audience in his East Berlin flat and to publish his verse in the West until that day in 1976 when, following a hugely successful tour of the Federal Republic, he was not allowed home by the East German authorities.

Considering the repressive censorship and harsh reprisals to which GDR poets were subjected, it is ironic that they had a much more clearly defined and accepted social function than poets and intellectuals in West Germany. There they could even be described as pariahs. Yet it was a view which many seemed to share. Hans Magnus Enzensberger, one of the leading politicizers of West German literature in the 1960s, described art as being by its very nature 'opposed to society'. But during the 1960s, building on the Brechtian tradition of 'functional poetry' and coinciding with the end of the Adenauer era of reconstruction and the advent of mass television, a diverse group of writers re-established the role of the political lyric as a vehicle of protest against the Vietnam War, the Springer press and the emergency legislation of the period. They included Enzensberger, Erich Fried, Franz Josef Degenhardt and Peter Rühmkorf. By 1968 and the students' revolt, political poets favoured the forms characteristic of didactic, consciousness-raising poetry, namely the epigram, aphorism, ballad, chanson, protest song and parody. But while the politicization of the universities continued long into the 1970s, the authors of protest and solidarity lyrics moved elsewhere. The *Wende* did not, as might have been expected of such a supremely political event, document its unique character in German history in poetic form.

# 6

## From Biedermeier to Realism

The 'exemplary place' which would best characterize German mid-nineteenth-century literature is more elusive than most; and it would be surprising if it were otherwise. There is a good
case for the argument that Germany itself changed more fundamentally during the nineteenth
century than at any other time in its history. The psychological impact of the dislocations that
accompanied these changes has perhaps not yet been absorbed into the collective consciousness
of Germans. Even at the end of the twentieth century, German literary historians are still
discussing the need to 'overcome' the nineteenth century. In 1900 not only Germans themselves but foreigners, too, looked on Germany with very different eyes than they had a century
earlier. Around 1800 most observant foreign visitors, such as the French novelist Stendhal,
concurred that its people were agreeable if somewhat impractical in character; a hundred years
later they focused on the alleged attributes which made Germany's neighbours feel neither
kindly nor patronizing, but irritated, envious and sometimes anxious. E. M. Butler, a Dublin
student in the pre-1914 Reich who later became professor of German at Cambridge, described
Germany in her autobiography, *Paper Boats* (1959), as being like school: leaving it gave one the
pleasurable sensation of going home for the holidays.

Fundamental political change, disrupting patterns set for centuries, marked the history of
Germany in this period. The French Revolutionary wars and Napoleon's imperialist ambitions
made their impact on Germany. In 1803 the great ecclesiastical princes had been stripped of
their secular territories, which in some cases they had held since the eighth century; then in
1806 the Holy Roman Empire, founded 1006 years earlier by Charlemagne, was abolished at
Napoleon's behest. True, it was by then but a hollow shell – neither holy nor Roman nor an
empire, as Voltaire observed – but its decentralization of power had not only determined the
pattern of German political allegiances, but had also shaped their political nature over the
centuries. The passing of the Empire created a vacuum which would in time be filled by
nationalism and the struggles of individual states for hegemonial domination. The literature of
this period is the literature of Germany between two empires.

The subdivisions of the period which suggest themselves to us today are not very different
from the perceptions of people at the time. Consensus existed then as now about the significance
of the 1848 Revolution even where it failed to deliver. Contemporaries were naturally more
sensitive to political change than to the subtler social and economic transformations which
preceded it: 1870–1 seemed at the time a more evident caesura than perhaps it does today. To

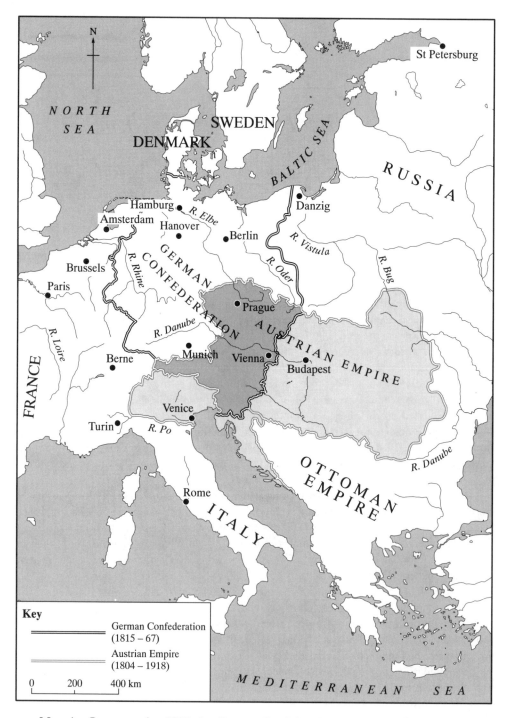

**Map 4**   Germany after 1815: the German Confederation and the Austrian Empire

the late twentieth-century observer of Germany's historical development, 1848 is the more crucial watershed. The first half of the century effectively began in 1814 with the Congress of Vienna and the creation in 1815 of the German Confederation or *Bund* (which lasted until 1867); it ended with the 1848 Revolution. This period is often called the *Restauration* because there was a general wish on the part of the governments of German states to *restore* the old order which had prevailed before their destabilization by the French Revolution. The *Bund* sorely disappointed the hopes of German patriots, for this period proved to be one of acute political repression, with Germany's writers as its chief victims. Two examples from the 1830s are the Lutheran pastor Friedrich Ludwig Weidig, who collaborated with Georg Büchner on a clandestine political pamphlet and was driven to suicide in prison after prolonged interrogation, and the North German novelist Fritz Reuter, who had to serve seven years of detention, three in solitary confinement, for his part in a student demonstration. But, as Heine put it in his mock-heroic epic *Deutschland: Ein Wintermärchen* (1844), it was easier to censor writing than to censor thought: during this period, Germany produced some of the century's most revolutionary thinkers and writers, of whom Karl Marx is the most obvious example.

The *Restauration* was an age in which the authorities attempted to recreate modified forms of the corporate state and to initiate far-reaching programmes of economic and fiscal reform, particularly in a number of states in northern and central Germany. The economy of Prussia was liberalized under the paternalist tutelage of its bureaucrats, many of whom had studied at Göttingen, the enlightened university in the kingdom of Hanover: later in the century this was to prove a powerful factor in Prussia's successful bid for hegemony in Germany. Prussia and its wealthier neighbour Saxony, which in the eighteenth century had been Germany's economically most advanced state, contrasted sharply in ethos and culture with Austria and the states of South Germany. One of the most far-reaching consequences of this contrast was its impact on the north–south cultural divide, still an influential feature of German life in the late twentieth century, although little commented on.

In the 1850s and 1860s, articulate Prussians and members of other German states, such as Württemberg and Saxony, began to register the positive impact of modernization. Economic activity quickened perceptibly after 1848, and is reflected in the rapid and systematic extension of the railway network, itself an important factor in the increasing commercialization of the literary market. The period between 1848 and the three 'wars of unification' – the Prussian-Danish war of 1864, the Austro-Prussian war of 1866 and the Franco-Prussian war of 1870–1 – which culminated in the founding of the Second German Empire (1871–1918) with Prussia's Berlin as its capital, may have seemed lacking in profile. But in economic and intellectual terms the opposite is the case. Although Germany's industrial revolution began in a sporadic and selective way decades earlier, the years 1849–73 constituted a significant cyclical change. Many sections of the population felt the benefits and increasingly began to identify with what was rightly regarded as their principal agency, the State. Though the secularization of intellectual life and of the media in Germany was much less self-consciously ideological than in, say, France or Italy in this period, old tensions were rekindled because this development was associated with the economically powerful and politically vocal Protestant territories of north and middle Germany; even in the Catholic Rhineland the captains of industry and the top administrators were generally Protestant. Even before the long and bitter conflict between the secular state and the Catholic Church known as the *Kulturkampf* (1872–88), the Catholic response was one of deliberate politicization and clericalization. In Catholic Germany, the press became identified with the 'unacceptable face' of modernism, as did socialism. Jakob Grimm's revealing assertion that 'Deutsch ist ein protestantischer Dialekt' ('German is a Protestant dialect') was confirmed in 1871 when the language of Protestant Prussia became the official language of empire. Catholics were not excluded, but, at least until the early 1900s, they felt marginalized, and in many instances actually were. This fostered the emergence of a distinctive German Catholic reading culture which became increasingly and self-consciously denominational. The books offered to Catholic readers were often out of touch with modern ideas. Yet in many ways they were much closer to ordinary people than was the mainstream of German literary culture.

The unification of Germany in 1871, coming as it did after two decades of unprecedented economic growth, was bound to have a centralizing influence on literary life and on book production and distribution. But the developments which, by the end of the century, transformed the German mass reading market into one of the most vibrant and commercially driven in the world rested on a whole series of interrelated factors, ranging from a rise in population and improved schooling to advances in the technology of publishing and the marketing of literature in its broadest sense. After 1871 German literature became increasingly metropolitan. Not unnaturally, its new capital, Berlin, displaced Leipzig from its long-held position as the main centre of the book and newspaper trade. Berlin became the natural focus for ambitious writers from the provinces, as Paris and London had been for centuries. Yet in Germany, during the period from 1800 to 1871, that focus had been in the provinces themselves. A look at a representative sample of the lives and careers of German writers in almost any genre and regardless of differences of class, creed or sex is an object lesson in the rural and small-town geography of nineteenth-century Germany before political unification destroyed its erstwhile amorphous but broader unity. Almost all the main writers in the German language are rooted in a specific landscape and location and draw on it for their creative work: Annette von Droste-Hülshoff in rural Westphalia and the shores of Lake Constance, Gotthelf in the Emmental in the Swiss canton of Berne, Mörike in Swabia, Keller in Zurich, Stifter in southern Bohemia and in Linz, Auerbach in the eastern stretches of the Black Forest, Storm in Husum on the North Sea coast of Holstein. In stark contrast to the imaginative richness and sometimes prophetic character of much mid-nineteenth-century writing, the physical context of their creative lives could be positively convivial and homely: Keller, Raabe and many others favoured the *Stammtisch* or table for 'regulars' at a local hostelry, while others preferred a literary club for amateurs and professionals such as the 'Tunnel über der Spree', where Fontane, Storm, Heyse and Dahn consorted with long-forgotten would-be poets in suburban Berlin, or the *Kränzchen* or 'little circles' which, for all their inadequacies, provided Droste-Hülshoff and other women writers with much-needed encouragement. Although they were often separated by great geographical distances, improvements in the postal service meant that the major writers of the period could be in close touch with each other. Sometimes they left their own localities, travelling far – often by railway – to visit one another: Storm's visit to Mörike in 1855 is one memorable occasion. The literary landscape of mid-nineteenth-century Germany is also crisscrossed by correspondences between writers, their colleagues and their publishers. The correspondences between Keller and Storm and between Storm and Heyse, both spanning many years, are two outstanding examples.

The paradox of high culture coexisting with the dullness of small-town life in a provincial backwater was vividly captured by George Eliot in her accounts of her stay in Weimar in the 1850s. The lack of a capital city and a metropolitan culture, which writers from Herder onwards had lamented, reinforced the importance of two vital literary institutions: the literary periodical, which had been an essential element of intellectual life since the eighteenth century, and the commercial lending or circulating library (*Leihbibliothek*) which had already begun to displace the older, more socially cohesive and hence also more exclusive *Lesegesellschaft* or reading society in the late eighteenth century. By 1800 these had spread across north and central Germany to virtually every town of 2000 inhabitants or more, giving access to literature to a wide and rapidly growing readership. For the next fifty years, such libraries were the most important providers of reading matter. Before 1850 their shelves were stacked mainly with fiction, which earned them the opprobrium of the authorities and the educated; after 1850 they also catered, as did the new family magazines such as *Die Gartenlaube* ('The arbour'), for the mounting demand in a modernizing society for 'useful information'. From the 1880s onwards the circulating libraries, now targeting a more specialized reading public, began to decline, partly in response to the rise of public libraries but also partly because of developments in the printed media. By then they had played out their key role as agents of a reading revolution and the democratization of reading in a society with the smallest proportion of illiterates in the world. A massive increase in newspaper readership also took place in Germany towards the middle of the century, due in part to the fact that after 1830 single issues of newspapers could be bought, whereas previously an annual subscription had been necessary. There was an added reason for the decentralization of the literary market. To avoid censorship, printing often took place far from where the author wrote or the publisher had his office; for example, Julius Campe, Heine's publisher in Hamburg, managed to get Heine's work printed in and distributed from the insignificant central German town of Altenburg (though with Nuremberg as its ostensible place of publication to hoodwink the police further).

As regards imaginative literature, it was the periodical that constituted the real focus of reading culture in mid-nineteenth-century Germany. While the publishing houses were distributing their products to an ever-growing number of bookshops, the literary periodicals were finding subscribers throughout the entire area in which German was spoken, from East Prussia to Switzerland and from Flensburg to Budapest. The number of periodicals increased from some 800 to 1800 in the period between 1833 and 1846 alone. Together with Cotta's liberal *Allgemeine Zeitung*, the most influential literary daily during the first half of the century was the *Morgenblatt für gebildete Stände*, a morning paper for the educated classes published in Stuttgart by Cotta from 1807 to 1865. Two of its literary editors were Therese Huber (from 1816 to 1823) and Wilhelm Hauff's brother, Hermann (from 1827 to 1863); in 1839 it changed its name to *Morgenblatt für gebildete Leser*, and in it important works, such as Droste-Hülshoff's story *Die Judenbuche* and Mörike's earliest poems, made their first appearance. Other journals which had high literary profiles between the revolutions of 1830 and 1848 were the *Zeitung für die elegante Welt*, published in Leipzig from 1801 to 1859, and Gutzkow's *Telegraph für Deutschland*, founded in 1837 and first published in Frankfurt, seat of the Bundestag and already emerging as an important financial centre. Both titles were programmatic. The first was clearly aimed at readers who aspired to a fashionable lifestyle; the second associated modern technology with the 'nation'. The second half of the century saw the rise to dominance of nineteenth-century Germany's most famous illustrated family weekly, *Die Gartenlaube*. Founded in 1853, it lasted until 1918 and numbered among its contributors Raabe, Fontane, Storm, Auerbach and Eugenie Marlitt: its circulation, which stood at 100,000 in 1861, had risen to 382,000 by 1873. The role played by the almanacs and pocketbooks of the *Biedermeier* period should not be overlooked; no publications capture the flavour and literary tastes of their day so well. Notwithstanding their mythological names – such as *Iris, Urania, Penelope* – it was in their pages that some of the period's most important literary works first appeared, such as Grillparzer's *Der arme Spielmann* ('The poor musician'), Tieck's *Des Lebens Überluß* ('The abundance of life') and poems by many important authors.

The so-called *Lesewut* or reading mania already recorded by contemporaries at the start of the nineteenth century accelerated after the end of the Napoleonic wars. In 1813 book production appeared to be on the verge of collapse, but by 1821 it had sprung back to life. This recovery coincided with the first in a series of technical innovations which must be kept in mind in order to understand the explosion of the literary market over the next decades. The cylindrical printing press invented by Friedrich König – the first major technical advance in printing since Gutenberg – was pioneered in England, where *The Times* first used it in 1814; in 1821 the *Haude & Spenersche Zeitung* in Berlin followed suit, the first continental newspaper to do so. The publisher Cotta bought his first König press in 1824, thereby cutting his printing costs by half in the same year; Metzler of Stuttgart and Brockhaus of Leipzig did likewise. As paper was then made from rags, a severe raw material shortage ensued in the 1830s and 1840s, but in 1844 Gottlob Keller patented his process for making paper from wood-pulp, and with remarkable foresight King William I of Württemberg promoted it in his territories, Heilbronn becoming the centre of the industry. In 1866 the addition of cellulose ensured the greater durability and lower price of paper. Re-usable type was introduced by Tauchnitz of Leipzig, a firm which exercised a long-lasting influence on German reading habits with its hugely successful editions of foreign classics in translation. Mechanization of the binding process and the introduction in the late 1830s of lithography from France, and hence of book and periodical illustrations, also contributed to cheaper and more attractive publications, as would colour illustration and the rotary press in the second half of the century.

Alongside these developments, though without the logic that, at least with hindsight, seems to inform the technological revolution in the production and distribution of literature, came long overdue changes of a legal nature. Censorship certainly did not cease after 1848, but it was far less overt: with the signal exception of Austria, most German states had a constitution of sorts by the 1850s which limited or forbade it. However, as the careers of Hauptmann, Wedekind and Panizza demonstrated in the 1890s and the test case of Heinrich Mann's novel *Der Untertan* ('The underling') showed as late as 1914, censorship remained a problem for writers up to the end of the Second Empire in 1918. Paternalist views of the positive role of literature in society, and the state's rejection of criticism as 'unpatriotic' if not 'treasonable', initially precluded any protection for authors. They and their publishers also had little redress against pirates, and until the 1870s book prices therefore remained high, royalties in general low, and editions small. The Act creating the German Federation in 1815 had made provision for the regulation and protection of copyright in its 38 member states (39 after 1818), but in practice this was not implemented. Individual states protected specific works in their own territories, but this did not prevent neighbours or even neighbouring states from pirating them: besides Austria, the Netherlands were a principal offender. Goethe, an exception in most respects, had in 1825 become the first German author to gain such a privilege for his works in all 39 German states. In 1837 Prussia introduced an exemplary copyright law: it was the kind of measure which reconciled so many of Prussia's critics, particularly the intellectuals, to its authoritarianism. Thirty years later, in 1867, the German classics, including Goethe and Schiller, duly came out of copyright, paving the way for a mass readership and the launch of Philipp Reclam's *Universalbibliothek*, small thin paperbacks retailing at two silver groschen apiece (the equivalent of just over one Victorian penny): Thomas Mann recalled purchasing his copy of *Faust*, number 1 in the series, when a schoolboy. In 1886 the German Empire signed the

Berne Convention which afforded further protection to authors, publishers and indirectly to readers; two years later the so-called Kröner Reforms introduced fixed prices throughout the German book trade. The logistics of literary production had made immense strides since the century began.

The growth of Germany's mass market in literature was also shaped by momentous developments in its demography. In 1800 the population of Germany (which then included the Austrian, Bohemian and Moravian crownlands) was no more than 23 million. In 1900, and without these Austrian possessions, it had some 61 million inhabitants. Ninety per cent of the population lived and worked on the land in 1800; in 1848 a mere 3 per cent, with their families could be categorized as industrial workers. By the early 1900s this figure had risen to 43 per cent, and Germany had as many city-dwellers as in 1800 it had had inhabitants. The nature of German society and the industrialization of the media catering for its mass market brought with them a tendency to judge literature by political and nationalistic criteria. This process began in the schools; soon it had invaded every sphere of society and cultural life.

Were women as writers and readers affected by all this? They certainly were. Broadly speaking, the changes taking place in the nineteenth century were beneficial. By the end of it women made up the greater part of the reading public – middle-class men preferred newspapers, and a huge industry competed for their custom – and works of fiction by women and for women were in great and growing demand. Some women with a basic education had managed to exchange the needle for the pen as a means of livelihood or for supplementing their income. One year after the founding of the German Women's Association (*Allgemeiner Deutscher Frauenverein*) in 1865 by Luise Otto-Peters, herself a writer and journalist of rich experience, Eugenie Marlitt's popular novel *Goldelse* appeared in *Die Gartenlaube*. Three years later she was able to purchase a villa on the handsome proceeds of her novels, each serialized before being published in book form. Paul Heyse, the period's most successful male writer of *belles-lettres*, was not in a position to emulate her until shortly afterwards. However, women authors were more liable to be circumscribed by the 'tyranny of genre' than were their male colleagues. Theirs was a kind of secularized form of devotional writing, in which the authoress and her female characters were expected to behave according to conventional stereotypes and women's role in contemporary society was seldom if ever seriously challenged. Over and over again we find instances of women of spirit and imagination, such as Therese Huber, Johanna Schopenhauer and Fanny Lewald, applying self-censorship and tailoring their novels to what the market expected of them. After all, they needed the money. Where they did not conform, as in the cases of Louise Aston, Luise Dittmar or the young Luise Otto, they disappeared from the catalogue. Of course there are exceptions. Droste-Hülshoff's poetry, though generously sponsored by Cotta, did not sell well, and her famous novelle *Die Judenbuche*, though it conformed outwardly to the relatively popular genre of crime literature, might well have been forgotten had Heyse not rescued it for his famous 24-volume anthology, the *Deutscher Novellenschatz* of 1870–6.

By 1850, women with an eye to their niche in the market, a reasonable talent and a capacity for hard work could make a living from writing, as is shown by the success of Luise Mühlbach's popular historical romances. Their opportunities increased with improved access to education such as grammar school, teacher training and the *Abitur*, the school-leaving examination which entitled Germans to matriculate at university. Although this right was only secured for women in Germany and Austria in the twentieth century, it was enjoyed by women in Switzerland from as early as the mid-1860s: many gifted German women chose to study in Zurich, Basle or Berne as a result, a notable literary example being Ricarda Huch, the historian and novelist, who obtained her doctorate at Zurich in 1891. By the 1890s women were prominently represented in the German Naturalist movement, most of them as novelists, notably Helene Böhlau, Gabriele Reuter and Clara Viebig. Elsa Bernstein even invaded male territory by becoming a dramatist of note, though under the male pseudonym 'Ernst Rosmer'. Her success as a playwright renewed a tradition which went back to Frau Gottsched in the eighteenth century, and which in the mid-nineteenth century had produced the actress-manager and popular dramatist Charlotte Birch-Pfeiffer, whose *Die Waise von Lowood* ('The Orphan of Lowood', 1856) earned Charlotte Brontë's *Jane Eyre* the applause of theatre audiences throughout the German-speaking world. Why Germany produced no outstanding woman novelist of the calibre of Charlotte Brontë and her sister Emily is another matter.

The controversies which accompanied Charlotte Birch-Pfeiffer during her career and the high media exposure she attracted, not least at the hands of the caricaturists, brings home the importance of the theatre in the national life of nineteenth-century Germany and Austria. Because of its association with the creation of a German 'national' literature in the age of Lessing, Goethe and Schiller, the stage enjoyed an unusually elevated status in the public mind, and was the nearest thing to a public sphere to be found in Germany, as many writers recognized. One of the consequences was that drama attracted far greater state control than any other literary genre. In the somewhat pompous phrasing of a Prussian civil servant in the 1840s: 'The theatre exercises an extraordinary power over the human mind to promote what is good, noble, great and sublime, but just as great is its power to debase and corrupt.'

Most theatres in the first half of the nineteenth century were court theatres, and some continued to be managed by high-ranking aristocrats until the early twentieth century. Yet middle-class directors also came to exercise considerable influence over repertoire and performance. Among these were Schreyvogel in the Vienna of Grillparzer's early career, Tieck and, later, Gutzkow in Dresden, Immermann in the lively municipal theatre of Düsseldorf in the 1830s, and the former *Jungdeutschland* writer Laube at the Vienna Burgtheater in the 1850s and 1860s. By contrast with France, Britain or Spain, where theatrical life has always tended to centre on the metropolis, the provincial towns of Germany were well provided for. In some cases, even small towns had excellent theatres: Grabbe, for instance, learnt his *métier* as a dramatist from frequenting the court theatre in his little home state of Lippe-Detmold. The theatre of the Saxon capital of Dresden under Tieck's direction (1819–40) was a major centre, and if Weimar retained little more than a nostalgic memory of the great days of Goethe and Schiller, the court and municipal theatres in towns such as Karlsruhe, Oldenburg, Frankfurt and Mannheim were lively centres of theatrical life. A signal contribution towards integrating actors into 'respectable' society was made by the Devrients, Germany's most illustrious nineteenth-century theatrical family, and especially by Emil Devrient, one of the most admired actors of his generation, whose scrupulous attention to the moral tone of his performances in heroic roles such as Goethe's Egmont convinced the middle classes that the stage was indeed a 'moral institution', as their favourite dramatist, Schiller, had claimed, albeit in a rather different sense. Then in the 1870s, Duke Georg, ruler of the petty state of Meiningen, brought great renown to himself and to the German theatre generally by restoring the authority of the text and creating a tradition of historical authenticity in performance which delighted German audiences as it did those who witnessed the Meiningen troupe's highly publicized European tours. In the 1840s, when actors at last began to benefit from fixed contracts, Karl Carl, the Bavarian theatrical entrepreneur and erstwhile employer of Nestroy in Vienna, showed that theatre could be good business too. Increasing and much-criticized commercialization followed, but Berlin acquired nineteen new theatres in the next thirty years, and even then, on Sundays, people were constantly being turned away because they were sold out. As many as 104 new theatres opened during the first fifteen years of the Second Empire, and prices began to drop significantly. Thus, as the century progressed, far more people in all walks of life and in far more geographical locations were able to indulge in playgoing. The lower middle class could afford to go on special occasions, and even working-class people began to feel that the theatre was not just for others. Initially this was thanks to the workers' educational associations, for whom Engels wrote a play in 1847, now lost. By 1890, the *Freie Volksbühne* had been set up with the specific aim of providing theatre for unsalaried workers; 2000 workers and students attended the ceremony.

From 1815 on, despite complaints about 'trivialization', the lowering of intellectual standards, commercialization and the growing desire to appeal to the masses, the theatre continued to exercise its ritual function in German society, particularly as far as the middle classes were concerned. One dressed in one's Sunday best, promenaded around the foyer during the interval, and had a sense of participating in a collective act. The regular theatre-goer sought access to the classical canon of German drama because it was invested with ethical values: German drama was now seen as a manifestation of German nationhood, which largely accounts for the great popularity of historical plays especially, though not only, after 1870. This helps to explain the tremendous appeal of Wagner, his new German mythology and his grand design of making Bayreuth into a great national festival staging *Gesamtkunstwerke* of his own creation, which involved the entire nation in their performance and enjoyment. His dream was realized when the *Festspielhaus* opened its doors in 1876.

## The Novelist and the Contemporary World

The emergence of a nineteenth-century novelist of European stature in Germany seemed likely. All the conditions had been met. As in France and England, social and intellectual change were counterbalanced by the rise of an increasingly prosperous and apparently confident middle class; tradition and innovation coexisted in people's lives and surroundings, and all that was needed, it could be said, was a writer of genius and stamina, like Balzac in France, to forge a literary masterpiece out of the material amply to hand. Even Germany's fragmentation and regionalism did not need to be major obstacles: Balzac himself had realized that scenes of provincial and country life were as integral a part of his great enterprise to paint the full canvas of French society during the first decades of the century as novels set in Paris, the metropolis. Hitherto most German novelists had favoured the *Bildungsroman*, exemplified by Goethe's *Wilhelm Meister*, because it embodied the values of transcendence and idealism and was primarily concerned with the inner development of its protagonist and only secondarily with the circumstances of a particular social world located in time and place. But could this artistic model be reconciled with the accurate observation of the social mores of contemporary society, or should such an aim be relegated to the background in order to concentrate on the great underlying truths of human experience? It was a debate which raged as Scott's historical novels met with a popularity in Germany that demanded explanation. Why did these novels galvanize the German reading public to such a degree during the 1820s and 1830s? It was because Scott's retrospective depiction of Scottish society in the process of change seemed to offer Germans in the aftermath of the Napoleonic era a paradigm of how a historical novelist could both mediate change and create a renewed sense of national identity.

Critical discussion came to a head in 1836 with the appearance of *Die Epigonen* by Karl Immermann. This vast novel was clearly a '*Wilhelm Meister* for modern times', as the critic Heinrich Laube observed in the history of German literature which he wrote during eighteen months' detention for political subversion in 1836–7. But what appeared to sympathetic critics and readers to be a penetratingly accurate analysis of German society in fictional form now strikes us as being an ambitious project flawed by its protagonist, Hermann, who is meant to exemplify the malaise of an age which cannot accept the fact that it is inferior to the one that preceded it (*epigone* is a Greek word meaning 'one born after'). Hermann's travels provide Immermann with a ready opportunity to observe society through his protagonist's eyes: but his descriptions and comments are hindered rather than helped by the fact that his hero is split: he assumed he was a middle-class man but discovers that he is the illegitimate son of an aristocrat. *Die Epigonen* may be an impressive example of nineteenth-century cultural criticism, but this strength is its weakness as fiction. The central figure on which the whole vast picture depends fails to come to life. It was a good idea but an unsatisfactory narrative device on the author's part to create a novel in which a contradictory world is interpreted by a man who shares its contradictions.

Karl Gutzkow, Immermann's younger contemporary, tried to offer an alternative route out of the impasse. He had come to prominence in 1835 with a coolly narrated yet melodramatic short novel, set in Italy, about a woman who loses her faith and her trust in the male sex as a result of the treatment she receives from the men in her life: *Wally, die Zweiflerin*. It shocked many of its readers and led to its author's trial and imprisonment on charges of having brought the Christian religion into contempt. It also caused offence to the susceptibilities of its time because it attributed to a woman the capacity for profound spiritual experience, yet was written by a man. Gutzkow, however, was by nature a narrator on a grander scale, as he demonstrated in two vast novels, each nine volumes in length, called *Die Ritter vom Geiste* ('The knights of the spirit', 1850–1) and *Der Zauberer von Rom* ('The magician of Rome', 1858–61). These addressed respectively the repressive tendencies in contemporary Prussia and what German liberals saw as the alarming growth in the influence of the papacy in contemporary Europe. But their chief interest lies in the innovatory narrative techniques he employs to achieve the sense of diversity and unity which he saw as a fundamental characteristic of his times. His ambitious aim was nothing less than to bring together in one complex text the entire spectrum of themes and social strata which Balzac displays in the many novels of his *Comédie humaine*. In his preface to *Die Ritter vom Geiste* he claimed with some justification that he had invented a new conception of the novel which could do justice to this undertaking: he called it *Der Roman des Nebeneinander* or 'novel of juxtaposition', a formula which attempted to do away both with the parallel plots of the Victorian English novel (as in George Eliot's *Middlemarch*) and with the urge to produce sequels as Trollope did with the Barsetshire novels, the first of which, *The Warden*, appeared in 1855. By then, even Gutzkow himself was beginning to realize that he had paid a heavy price for attempting to paint a panorama of Prussia in a single novel: despite the social realism of much of its detail, *Die Ritter vom Geiste*, with its illegitimate births and tentacular secret society, unintentionally echoes baroque romances and Gothic novels rather than being a creative breakthrough into new narrative territory. Not until Fontane, Germany's great late nineteenth-century novelist, would the German novel succeed in breaking completely free from the stranglehold of plot and discover a subtler and more sensitive definition of storyline.

Gutzkow's narrative experiments, though they are interesting, must be accounted failures. His leading competitors in the novel field were less daring. In the late 1850s Friedrich Spielhagen, who was flatteringly dubbed the German Dickens by contemporaries, was putting his finger on the crux of the problem in an essay on Dickens and Thackeray. Whereas German would-be novelists were forever looking for suitable subject matter, he wrote, their English counterparts were blithely obeying the advice of the *lustige Person* in the prelude to Goethe's *Faust* and coming to grips with life in all its fullness. But could Spielhagen follow their example? He tried indefatigably to overcome the limitations of his simplistic style and fatal lack of authorial irony, but without ever managing to repeat the success of his early novel *Problematische Naturen* (1861). Here, as in Immermann's *Die Epigonen*, a conscientious attempt was made to define the moral and social climate of mid-nineteenth-century Germany in a story which covers a year in the life of Oswald Stein, a young, educated middle-class man, from his appointment in 1847 as a private tutor in a Prussian landed Junker family in Pomerania to his heroic death on the barricades of Berlin during the upheavals of 1848. Had the crisis year in nineteenth-century German history found the writer who would preserve it for posterity? It seemed so to some. Yet despite its merits, not least of which was a keen sense of humour in the delineation of character and manners, Spielhagen's masterpiece failed to maintain its place among the classics of German fiction. In this respect, at least, *Soll und Haben* by Gustav Freytag proved much more successful: indeed it remains one of the very few large-scale novels of this period which are still remembered, if only at second hand.

## A Classic of German Commerce and Industry

In *Soll und Haben* ('Debit and credit', 1855) Freytag adopted another approach to break away from the stranglehold of the *Bildungsroman* and to articulate the tensions of the Germany in which he lived: this was the narrative strategy of two 'parallel lives'. Both are studies in upward mobility. Young Anton Wohlfart grows up to be a loyal employee of the Breslau firm of Schröter, and the reward for the Protestant work ethos he so evidently embodies is that he is able to hobnob with the aristocracy and do Baron von Rothsattel the good turn of saving him from financial disaster. Running alongside Anton's exemplary career, an alternative is presented to the reader: that of Anton's former schoolmate Veitel Itzig. Anton's upward path is closed to Veitel. Being a Jew he has to make his upward way by other means. His rise to material prosperity is a good deal faster, but in the end his career as a financier and dealer crashes. Both Freytag's main characters appear to be embodiments of the period's favourite stereotype, the self-made man. But Freytag's scheme is not as simple as it seems, for he shows us with some subtlety that each of his two characters is dependent on other people for his social and economic rise and that both are products of the subtle workings of social and economic forces and of positive or negative discrimination. Is it perhaps an indication of the German reluctance to wear the cap that fits that Freytag's fine but uneven novel is underrated? In the retrospect of 150 years, its revival of the narrative strategy which Jörg Wickram had pioneered in his topical novels of mid-sixteenth-century middle-class capitalism is an effective artistic device which deserves recognition. The price of prosperity has never been so forcefully yet thoughtfully conveyed in German fiction, and for this *Soll und Haben* deserves credit, even if on the debit side German literary criticism finds fault with it for failing to cover the more unpleasant sides of reality with an adequate veneer of literary style and philosophic depth, and for courting popularity by some unsubtle stereotyping to the detriment of Jews and Poles and the advantage of the national image of the honest, hard-working German. It is not as surprising as it might seem that this 'dated' novel, set in the now 'lost' province of Silesia and in Poland a century before, should have seen its sales rise again during the period of West Germany's postwar economic miracle.

## Gotthelf and the Social Novel of Peasant Life

*Soll und Haben* was published one year after the death of the novelist who is now recognized to be the only one of his contemporaries to warrant mention in the same breath as Balzac and Dickens. Jeremias Gotthelf, a Swiss, succeeded where his German contemporaries failed. *Der Bauernspiegel, oder Lebensgeschichte des Jeremias Gotthelf, von him selbst beschrieben* ('Mirror of the peasantry, or the life story of Jeremias Gotthelf as narrated by himself', 1837), his first novel, had successfully blended autobiographical subject matter and a realistic setting with elements of the *Bildungsroman*, but having written it, he spent the remaining seventeen years of his creative life depicting the peasantry around him rather than the trials and tribulations of an individual like himself. He began to make his name beyond Switzerland with the novel *Uli der Knecht* ('Uli the farm labourer', 1841), in which an ordinary man struggles to gain self-respect and independence; when he followed it with a sequel, *Uli der Pächter* ('Uli the tenant farmer') in 1849, his hero's upward momentum and natural urge to better himself economically is shown to lead to tension in his loving marriage to Vreneli, one of the many vividly drawn women characters in Gotthelf's works. The dangers of nineteenth-century materialism were more evident to him than its benefits, and they disturb the placid surface of his rural world in all his major novels. This is particularly evident in *Zeitgeist und Berner Geist* (1852), a novel whose very title indicates his awareness of the philosophical and sociological thinking of his age, and his readiness to use fiction to address the mounting conflict he saw around him between the materialist and commercial values of the early industrial age and the traditional values of the city and canton of Berne, the part of Switzerland he knew best.

Gotthelf knew how to encapsulate the complexity of social evolution in stories of human proportions, and came nearer than his German contemporaries to anticipating the themes and preoccupations of Naturalist writers half a century later. He has a great humorist's genial verve, but he also knew how to convey the darker visions of the Old Testament prophet whose name he borrowed. These are already apparent in *Wie Anne Bäbi Jowäger haushaltet* ('How Anne Bäbi Jowäger keeps house', 1843–4), one of his most characterful and original novels, where the enlightened figures of the village doctor and parson are relegated to minor roles, while the farmer's wife after whom the novel is named takes centre stage together with her henpecked husband and mollycoddled son in a masterly tale which turns on the twin dangers of a suffocating maternal affection and superstitious ignorance, and the high price to be paid for them both when her sick grandchild dies after she has had well-meaning recourse to a quack. Within a year Gotthelf had completed his third great novel, *Geld und Geist* ('Money and mind', 1843–4), a penetrating study of marital breakdown which loses nothing of its psychological and emotional depth by centring on a peasant couple. Its subtitle, *Die Versöhnung* ('The reconciliation'), indicates that even here not all is hopeless and bitter: indeed the moment when Anneli, the farmer's wife, awakens to the responsibilities and needs of her naturally affectionate person-ality and her Christian conscience is conclusive proof that the inner values of transcendence and idealism, proclaimed to be the essence of the *Bildungsroman*, could in the hands of a novelist of real stature manifest themselves equally tellingly in the circumscribed, regional lives of the Swiss peasantry.

Alone among the German-language novelists of the mid-century, Gotthelf won the approval of readers in his own time and has enjoyed a critical reassessment in recent years which has restored and indeed enhanced his status. His strength lies in his imaginative breadth and his amazing ability to fuse the language of Luther's Bible with the lucid didacticism of Heinrich Pestalozzi, the Swiss educationalist he greatly admired, and the dialect speech of the citizens of Berne and the farming population of the Emmental, the cheese-producing region in which he lived and worked as a Protestant country parson. In his novel *Die Käserei in der Vehfreude* ('The cheese factory', 1850), subtitled 'a tale from Switzerland', cheese-making, and the community whose livelihood depends on it, including the cows, become the subject of literary treatment on an epic scale: the depiction of the cheese fair at Langnau and of what happens after it is a set-piece of description and action that equals Hardy at his best. Passages such as these raise his work to the front rank on linguistic and stylistic grounds alone. It is now clear that of the many nineteenth-century writers in all parts of the German-speaking world who specialized in the novel of peasant life, that characteristic product of cultural or literary regionalism, Gotthelf is the only one to have won himself a lasting readership and growing critical esteem: Auerbach's *Barfüßele* (1856), Ludwig's *Die Heiteretei und ihr Widerspiel* ('Merry Annedorle and her oppo-site', 1857) and Anzengruber's *Der Schandfleck* ('The stigma', 1877) have paled into insignifi-cance by comparison, their gentle sentimentality and loving portrayal of country folk and rural life making them seem dated in a way that Gotthelf's robuster narratives are not: he hoped his peasants would read him, whereas the others were writing primarily for the middle classes. His secret was that he knew full well that the majority of his Swiss readers would spot and scorn any departure from authenticity and truth in favour of the picturesque.

## Wilhelm Raabe

The year which followed the publication of *Soll und Haben* saw the appearance of the first novel by the author whom many German readers, especially in the northern parts of the country, have long considered to be the finest nineteenth-century novelist in the language. Wilhelm Raabe shot to fame with *Die Chronik der Sperlingsgasse* ('The Sperlingsgasse chronicle', 1856), an appealing evocation of Biedermeier Berlin, and for the next half-century he produced novels at regular intervals. Some of his greatest successes appeared relatively early, such as *Der Hungerpastor* ('The breadline pastor', 1864) and *Abu Telfan* (1867); by 1870 his reputation was well established as a writer with a characteristic philosophy of 'positive pessimism' who charted the lives of characterful individuals over adversity. More modern criticism tends to place even greater emphasis on the work of Raabe's later years, in which his prolixity gives way to compression, and his penetrating eye for the irony of events and his confidence in the underly-ing meaningfulness of life come over even more forcefully. *Pfisters Mühle* is an intricate, semi-symbolical study of permanence and mutability set in a spot, an old mill and its pond overshadowed by elm trees, once idyllically romantic but now dilapidated by time and polluted by encroaching industry. Written in 1884, it illustrates Raabe's evolution from Biedermeier

cosiness and whimsicality to a tauter complexity which places him amongst the most individualistic precursors of much of the twentieth century's best writing, a quality particularly evident
in *Horacker* and *Stopfkuchen*, two shorter novels which focus on crime and its detection and
show his sovereign command of action and suspense. With Stopfkuchen himself, the glutton-
ous, laid-back character at the centre of this late masterpiece, Raabe achieved something which
had eluded so many of the German novelists of the mid-nineteenth century, the creation of a
character who takes on a life of his own and remains in the memory long after the intricacies of
his story have been forgotten. Another facet of Raabe's rich literary personality is shown by his
two late novels, *Das Odfeld* and *Hastenbeck*, two unconnected stories both set during the Seven
Years War, which evoke the violence once witnessed by the delightful landscape of a country
whose more turbulent past was experienced by human beings very like those of today. In this
way the continuity of life works its way to the fore as ultimately the most constant theme in the
work of an author who had a much keener eye for the contours of a character and the outlines
of an action than the majority of those contemporaries of his who deliberately preferred the
scope and prolixity of the novel to the concision of the novelle. But his sometimes almost
eccentric personality prevented him from establishing anything like a school.

## Louise von François and Marie von Ebner-Eschenbach

Raabe's way of storytelling, taut and rambling by turns, highly allusive yet never losing the
sense of direct oral narration, was one which was shared to some extent by two remarkable
contemporaries of his, Louise von François, from Saxony, and Marie von Ebner-Eschenbach,
who was a native of Moravia, then part of the Austro-Hungarian Empire. Both women write
with an unflinching eye for detail, and both inhabit the world of the landed aristocracy which
they see both from within and from outside. *Die letzte Reckenburgerin* ('The last of the
Reckenburgs', 1871), hailed by Freytag in the review which made François's name, is a skilfully
organized narrative rich in a harsh irony which is often reminiscent of Hardy. The reader is
constantly misled by her vividly evoked but deceptive appearances, and her bitter tale has to be
read to the end before we and its young central figure, the orphan girl Hardine, find out why.
The aristocratic spinster who brings her up and who, she believes, is her grandmother, is
Hardine von Reckenburg, the last of her line and a penetrating study of a woman obliged by
force of circumstance to take responsibility for her own life: the liberty and emancipation forced
upon her against her will are a corrective to the more stereotyped and sentimental views of
woman's destiny espoused by François's feminist contemporaries. In the process the organic
forward movement of the classical *Bildungsroman* has become a prolonged and uncertain quest
by the two Hardines to make sense of the incomprehensibility of their lives and to understand
their relationship to each other.

François's younger contemporary and friend, Marie von Ebner-Eschenbach, has a rather
similar tale to tell in her novel *Das Gemeindekind* ('The child of the parish'), published in 1887,
but this tale of an orphan boy and girl is set in her own home region of Moravia. Milada is
brought up under the patronage of the lady of a *Schloß*, or country house, while Pavel, being the
son of a murderer, is shunned and driven to crime until rescued by the influence of the village
teacher. As in *Die letzte Reckenburgerin*, there is hope of social and, more important, moral
redemption: but in both novels the way is hard and the narrative uncompromising. In the fiction
of both women the autobiographical element is strong: both were aristocrats by birth, and both

were critical of the aristocracy and showed it either by direct description or more obliquely by adopting the viewpoint of a domestic or other peripheral character in order to reveal the incongruities and defects of a social class and the way of life which it took for granted, as in *Božena* (1876) by Ebner-Eschenbach, a story of family strife in which Božena, the maid, plays a leading part. Neither writer denies her background, but neither conforms to the image which middle-class authors have tended to present of it. There is nothing ladylike about their best work; indeed the opening of François's novel is strong stuff by the standards of the English novel of the 1870s. To read them is to realize that there were psychologically and socially penetrating novels in German before Fontane came on to the scene, and that they were written by women.

## Scenes of Provincial Life

By 1840 a body of highly accomplished shorter prose fiction existed alongside the novel, setting the standard for years to come. But now a decisive change of direction took place with the growing interest in local colour. The fashion was growing for *Lebensbilder* – sketches of life in specific areas – a genre whose vogue swept Europe during the 1840s and marked the decisive advent of realism as the dominant literary mode. The writer's subject now lay immediately around him, and in consequence the sphere of the imagination receded. Accuracy and truth of observation became the watchwords, and commonplace subjects were felt to be as good as any; suddenly the different regions of the country sprang to life as topics for literary treatment as well as locations for artistic activity. Illustrations of this trend are provided by writers in virtually every part of the German-speaking world, and sometimes beyond its periphery: *Die Marzipan-Lise* (1856), by the Austrian dramatic writer Friedrich Halm, is a telling example. Kleist's style is imitated with remarkable success in a story similar to *Die Verlobung in St Domingo* ('The engagement in St Domingo') in intensity and subject matter but set in a realistically conceived Hungarian setting of the kind already perfected by Stifter in *Brigitta* (1844), his 'Hungarian' tale of love misunderstood and inner beauty concealed.

The most influential and widely read pioneer of this new regional genre was Bertold Auerbach, with Heine the most distinguished Jewish writer of the century, though now no longer much appreciated. In 1843 he offered the public the first set of his *Schwarzwälder Dorfgeschichten*, and found that he had tapped a vein which so pleased his readers and publishers that with some reluctance he went on publishing Black Forest stories until 1876. Here was a concept of contemporary narrative fiction which Germany found more to its taste than the satirical social realism of Dickens or the panorama of a whole society being painted by Balzac. Once again, German literature was diverging from the general trend of contemporaneous literature in Europe. The rural setting Auerbach chose for his stories appealed to his readers, and coincided with the growing middle-class enjoyment of tourism which the railways were stimulating. But the setting is not all. Auerbach's sketches of life in an area he knew at first hand are also rich in observation of social relationships and traits of human behaviour he also knew well, such as parochialism, meanness and prejudice. Whether his readers realized it or not, most of his stories deal with prejudice in various forms. This is the case in three of the best of his first set – *Der Tolpatsch* ('The country bumpkin') with its mentally retarded young hero; *Sträflinge* ('Convicts') with its 'rehabilitated' convicts (and early mention of railways); and *Die Frau Professorin*, whose appealing heroine, Lorle, an unaffected country girl who becomes the model and then the wife of a young painter and art teacher, soon finds herself constitutionally unable to adapt to city life and to conform to the conventions of cultured middle-class behaviour.

Prejudice is a key theme in the stories of Auerbach; it offsets the tendency to prettiness and sentimentality which was an ever-present temptation to mid-century authors trying to live on their royalties and therefore having to please a rapidly growing middle-class readership. It is also a potent factor in *Die Judenbuche*, the remarkable tale which at last placed a woman in the front rank of German authors when it was published in the *Morgenblatt für gebildete Leser* in 1842 and in book form nine years later. In what she called a depiction of life and manners in rural Westphalia, Annette von Droste-Hülshoff produced a masterpiece which brings home the fundamental difference between nineteenth-century German fiction and that of most other European countries: it is nothing less than a *Crime and Punishment* in miniature. Like Dostoevsky's vast novel of 1866, Droste-Hülshoff's novelle represents an analysis of criminality in relation to its determining factors and social, psychological and moral consequences. Environment and heredity, factors later to be exploited by Zola and the Naturalist writers, are already present when she deftly set to work to indicate the 'where' as well as the 'why' that made her adolescent central character, Friedrich Mergel, turn into the murderer of a Jew one dark night in the beech woods, and years later made him return to the scene of his crime and to a self-inflicted retribution. An alcoholic father, an incompetent mother and a shady guardian uncle all play their part in conditioning the boy, as do poverty, ignorance and a general lack of moral bearings, factors subtly and effectively suggested in the setting, a remote village and the featureless forest that surrounds it, usually seen at dusk or night-time. Like a wayfarer, the reader can easily lose his bearings in this moral landscape: the author encourages uncertainty about what is actually taking place in this prototype of crime and detection fiction; tantalizingly, she rejects the concept of authorial omniscience and provides only an incomplete account of a sequence of events which leads to violent death but to no ultimate explanation if the reader ignores the reference to Christian forgiveness which is central to the work's moral fabric but figures only as an epigraph.

In the one novelle she completed, Droste-Hülshoff demonstrated how a maximum of action, telling description and thought-content could be contained within a work diminutive in size when set alongside the great novels of foreign contemporaries. No German woman writer was to equal her achievement for the remainder of the nineteenth century; but it had its parallels in other parts of the German-speaking world. In Austria Stifter came to the fore during the 1840s as the exponent of a type of story where action is reduced to the minimum and the moral and emotional meaning of what is taking place between the lines is carried unobtrusively by sustained description. *Der Hochwald* appeared in the same year as *Die Judenbuche*; here, too, a forest provides the moral landscape for a tragic tale. It was to be the first of several stories evoking wooded and mountainous landscapes which reveal Stifter's eye for contour and colour (he was also a landscape painter of some accomplishment). In *Der Hagestolz* ('The bachelor', 1844), *Der Waldsteig* ('The forest path', 1845) and *Der beschriebene Tännling* ('The fir tree with the mark on it', 1845), features of the novel of identity, such as the protagonist's quest for self-knowledge and fulfilment, are miraculously reconciled with a sense of the vulnerability and transience of existence to generate an ideal of personal integrity and almost religious awe in the presence of Nature. The political upheavals of 1848 affected Stifter deeply; in his second creative phase he told his stories to illustrate a more consciously rounded philosophy of life: *Bunte Steine* ('Gemstones', 1853) is a collection of six that sets out to illustrate that things apparently slight and trivial can actually be a truer manifestation of the laws of nature and the human heart than the earth-shaking actions and happenings which usually stimulate the imagination of 'great' writers. On the surface these stories may appear dull, though Stifter's rhythmic and colourful use of language belies any such impression; but they are positively exciting compared with his supreme achievement, the novel *Der Nachsommer* ('Indian summer', 1857), which enshrines an attitude to living in an endlessly protracted account of the slow mellow days of an apparently timeless late summer in an unchanging landscape; in the garden roses bloom, the sounds of music float from the white house aglow with the sunlight: never was the awareness of passing time and imminent mortality more gently concealed than in this understated tale of human relations and aspirations. *Der Nachsommer* is perhaps the least known among the towering peaks of European nineteenth-century fiction.

If the expansive development of themes in Stifter's novels can be likened to nineteenth-century symphonic music, his stories display the genius of chamber music and make much greater aesthetic claims than their narrow compass might suggest. The individual's relationship to other human beings, to natural surroundings and to the divine that is immanent in both, is exemplified with rare sensitivity in the stories that make up *Bunte Steine* and, later, in the mildly humorous, ironic detachment of a late story such as *Nachkommenschaften* ('Inherited traits', 1864), where Stifter's preoccupation with tradition and innovation is identified with the artist's quest for originality and with the intervention of human beings on a timeless landscape, a combination of themes which brings this finely balanced story close to the spirit of Ruskin and makes it an eloquent statement of themes which are again to the fore in the late twentieth century. Few writers were able to achieve the dispassionate intensity and descriptive power of Stifter, and the mid-century novelle was often the vehicle for a less profound kind of realism which has its attractions. The stories of Jewish life in central Europe by Leopold Kompert paint memorable vignettes of individuals and ways of life in an area unfamiliar to the average reader (*Aus dem Ghetto*, 1848), while the *Kulturgeschichtliche Novellen* (1856) by Wilhelm Riehl demonstrated how effectively the novelle could bring to life the feel of other historical periods as well as other places. The unfamiliar and the unexpected had always been the favourite subject matter of the novelle genre: here it took the form of vanished or alien cultures; indeed from 1850 on, all the major exponents of the novelle tried their hand at historical subjects alongside their more overtly 'realistic' aims; the trend was reinforced by the fact that they knew one another's work well and were in more or less close personal contact with one another. Yet they represented quite different parts of the German-speaking world: Gottfried Keller was Swiss; Theodor Storm came from Holstein; while their younger friend and contemporary Paul Heyse was born in Berlin and spent most of his creative life in Munich.

Keller's achievement was to use the restricted compass of the novelle to capture the feel of life in a small town in Switzerland in both past and present. His *Die Leute von Seldwyla*, which consists of two collections of five stories each, published in 1856 and 1873–4, is set in a country town on the border between reality and fiction, and located somewhere between Mrs Gaskell's Cranford and Thomas Hardy's Casterbridge in the evolution of realism. Like Hardy, Keller saw it as the writer's task to present extraordinary episodes in a recognizably authentic setting; it is not surprising that many small places in Switzerland and southern Germany recognized themselves in Seldwyla. The ten stories range from the humorous, even grotesque caricatures of *Die drei gerechten Kammacher* ('The three upright comb-makers'), where the dull probity of three German apprentices is sent up along with the self-satisfied smugness of their Swiss employer's daughter, to the high-spirited depiction of unintentional fraud and innate gullibility in *Kleider machen Leute* ('Clothes make people') and the intimate pathos of *Romeo und Julia auf dem Dorfe* ('A village Romeo and Juliet'), in which the stubborn, self-destructive antagonism of two peasants cannot stifle the love between their two children, though it leads to their deaths. The sequence culminates in *Das verlorene Lachen* ('The lost laugh'), less well known perhaps, but demonstrating Keller's remarkable ability to bring together in the small compass of a novelle all the themes which fascinated him and which in other European literatures of the time would have required the large-scale canvas of a realistic novel. By this last story, the good humour of Seldwyla is severely under threat: modern materialistic values are encroaching upon Keller's little world, faith is suspect, politics corrupt and human relationships are as imperilled as the forests which surround the little town. Thematically, *Das verlorene Lachen* points forward unmistakably to the preoccupations of the late twentieth century. For no writer of the period is the easy assumption that a small scale precludes a wide range more glaringly false.

Keller's close North German contemporary, Theodor Storm, is a more problematic case. Storm is a writer for whom most lovers of German literature have a soft spot. He is a master of atmosphere, unique in his ability to endow the details of realistic description with the fragile aura of transience precisely because they are so vividly captured. His first great success, the short novelle *Immensee* (1850), displays one aspect of his art. In it the heightened moments of childhood and youth surface in the memory of an old man as he sits puzzling over his life and his apparent inability to secure happiness and find fulfilment; it is no paradox that the elusive fulfilment he seeks is to be found in the scenes that rise from the silent, unfathomable depths of his subconscious memory whose objective correlative is found in the still, calm lake of the story's title. Reinhard's childhood love for Elisabeth makes his bachelor life as a scholar worth living even if her love for him erodes what hope she had of happiness as the wife of the staid and prosaic entrepreneur, Erich. No German story has been read so widely, or so it is said: certainly its echoes can be sensed in the work of an early admirer, Turgenev, and, later, in Proust's vast treatment of an analogous theme in *A la recherche du temps perdu*. It has often been described as sentimental by those who do not really know it, yet it is remarkable precisely because of its avoidance of sentimental episodes and for the way in which Storm allows incidents, gestures and utterances to speak for themselves without the interference of an omniscient narrator.

The excellence of *Immensee* set a standard which Storm was understandably not always able to sustain. He can lapse into cliché, and into narrative mannerisms that seem to imitate his own style without achieving the requisite density of content. But, aware no doubt of the dangers of self-parody, he can sometimes astonish his readers by unexpected departures from his usual manner, as in his stark portrayal of a man unable to rebuild his life in *Ein Doppelgänger*, in the semi-autobiographical *Hans und Heinz Kirch*, in which a loving father struggles in vain to save the mind and body of a weak-willed son, or in *Der Schimmelreiter* ('The rider on the white horse', 1888), the famous tale that concluded his career. Here drawing rooms and lakes make way for the windswept marshes of the North Sea coast, and the past comes back to haunt the present in the form of the spectral rider who was once a young man, as 'real' and as human as we are now; Hauke Haien, he was called, and he possessed an inborn understanding of the sea and of how to construct defences against it, but his outstanding qualities were tragically flawed, and his life ended in disaster and in drowning. It is a tale that has haunted the German imagination ever since it appeared in 1888: its central character has been seen by many as the embodiment of the heroic qualities of the German character, but others notice in him the dangerous streak that can call into question German efficiency and inventiveness.

Storm may be a miniaturist, but he is one with a mythopoeic imagination. No such praise is nowadays given to Paul Heyse. More productive than either Storm or Keller, Heyse tried to compensate for his facility by an exaggerated emphasis on the literary quality of his work. His early novelle *L'Arrabbiata* (1855) was long held up as the supreme example of the genre, but can be more properly appreciated as a verbal counterpart to the many highly coloured paintings of Italian life and landscape produced by Heyse's artist contemporaries. His championship of Italy as a setting for the German novelle perpetuated a fashion which culminated in his own lifetime with Thomas Mann's *Der Tod in Venedig*, a masterpiece in the Heyse tradition which coincided with the award of the Nobel Prize for Literature to Heyse himself in 1912 and has as its central figure a fictitious Munich-based author, Gustav von Aschenbach, whose values have much in common with those of Heyse himself. In fact he is seen to better advantage when he allows a streak of irony to bring a carefully composed novelle to life, as in *Der letzte Zentaur*, in which a centaur, the last of these mythological creatures, comes crashing into the contemporary world as if to demonstrate that what may seem pleasing in art may well prove awkward in reality. The ironic *aperçus* of this novelle suggest that Heyse is a writer of very unequal quality and that he knew it; for all its brevity it certainly outweighs his large-scale attempt in the novel *Im Paradies* (1875) to portray the artistic world of Munich, the city in which he lived the part of poet laureate, and which, with Dresden, was the virtual centre of German cultural life until it was overtaken by Berlin towards the turn of the century.

## The *Heimatdichtung* Tradition

The achievement of Keller, Gotthelf, Stifter and many other writers of lesser stature or more regional appeal created a tradition for the German-speaking countries that was truly national in the sense that it was rooted in their landscape and customs. By using the accepted written language of the educated middle classes as its linguistic medium, rather than the dialects still widely spoken in the different areas, readers from all over the German-language area were able to share the experience such writers transmitted, and a sense of community was fostered, rather than a sense of patriotism or nationhood in the more usual political or ideological sense. Here and there a note of more deliberate local patriotism was struck – as in regions whose political identity was less secure, such as Alsace-Lorraine. Sometimes, too, writers aimed at a more overtly regional appeal, in which case their medium was quite likely to be a local dialect: in the case of Fritz Reuter, the strongest and most individual voice to emerge from North Germany in the mid-nineteenth century, a corpus of novels in the Low German of Mecklenburg gained acceptance as 'high' literature on account of their artistic merit and almost Dickensian brand of relaxed good humour. *Ut de Franzosentid* ('In the days of the French', 1859), is set, like so many other works of its time, at the end of the Napoleonic period, while *Ut mine Festungstid* ('My time in prison', 1862) and *Ut mine Stromtid* ('My time as a trainee farmer', 1862–4), as their titles indicate, are closely bound up with their author's own recollections of his anti-authoritarian activities as a student, his imprisonment by the Prussian authorities, and his subsequent attempts to become a farmer at a time of growing agrarian depression which led up to the social and political upheavals of 1848.

The quantity of German regional literature and its wide and persistent appeal to German readers should not be underestimated. Its quality is variable, however, and its popularity does not rest only on stylistic or intellectual merit. It seldom if ever achieves the depth and power of Gotthelf's Swiss novels and stories, the understated subtlety of Stifter's Austrian ones, or the atmospheric magic of Storm's North German novellen. There is no doubt, however, that between 1850 and 1950 it has acted as a barometer of reading taste and can tell us more than other genres about the German-speaking peoples' view of themselves. Much of it was the work of minor writers of limited talent or localized interest. But over the years a body of regional writing grew up which is known in German as *Heimatdichtung* or *Heimatliteratur* and which, at its best, transcended geographical limitations and became a force to be reckoned with in modern prose fiction. The 'classics' of the genre are often, if not always, of a semi-autobiographical kind, which is hardly surprising since they combine the German fondness for the 'novel of identity' with descriptions of natural settings whose appeal for middle-class readers had been so success-fully realized by Auerbach in the 1840s. The skilful yet individualistic blend of the two ensured the success of writers such as Peter Rosegger, the key Austrian representative of the more 'literary' end of the spectrum of this type of writing. By the end of the century Rosegger was much admired at home and abroad: *Die Schriften des Waldschulmeisters* ('The writings of the forest schoolmaster', 1875), a novel in diary form, and the stories collected under the title *Waldheimat* brought his readers the 'feel' of his native Styria, but also made them aware of the human and economic problems of peasant life in a period of change and the intellectual and religious challenges facing an individual emerging from a close-knit community. Indeed Rosegger's concern with growing up, his treatment of religious crisis, and his critical appraisal of Roman Catholicism did much to enhance his reputation among thinking readers, while his increasingly overt appeal to a broad readership fuelled the dream of 'greater German' unity and assured him both posthumous fame and, later, a steady decline in popularity for ideo-logical rather than artistic reasons.

Rosegger had his counterparts all over the German-speaking area. Bavaria, for instance, produced Ludwig Ganghofer and his lighter-hearted contemporary Ludwig Thoma. Ganghofer's *Schloß Hubertus* (1895) achieved long-lasting popularity thanks to its deployment of motifs calculated to please the reading public: an eccentric nobleman besotted with hunting and his collection of antlers, a young painter of peasant stock aspiring to artistic celebrity and social acceptance, a love match between the nobleman's son and an opera star, and one or two stalwart peasants, together with a whole gallery of stereotypes ranging from honest Franzl to the blackguard Schepper, all presented in an alpine lakeside setting, and told in a style rich in cliché and local colour, yet not without humour. Thoma won his readers' hearts with his humorous *Lausbubengeschichten* ('Rascals' tales', 1905), which form a notable addition to South Germany's rich humorous literature, though he could also strike a serious note when he wished. In the Rhineland Rudolf Herzog favoured light historical fiction (*Die Stoltenkamps und ihre Frauen*, 1917) while Wilhelm Schäfer made a name for himself with more serious religious-historical novels and much admired collections of *Anekdoten*, which took up a traditional type of short prose that went back to Johann Peter Hebel's much-loved *Schatzkästlein des Rheinischen Hausfreundes* ('The treasure chest', 1811). Clara Viebig, a finer if now largely forgotten writer perhaps too productive for her own good, made her name at the turn of the century with some powerful descriptions of life in the Eifel region (*Das Weiberdorf*, 'The village of women', 1900), then widened her scope to include stories of urban life in Düsseldorf (*Die Wacht am Rhein*, 'The Rhine watch', 1902) and Berlin (*Eine Handvoll Erde*, 'A handful of soil', 1915). North Germany, too, produced its crop of regional writers, characterized by bleaker visions and the portrayal of flatter, less eye-catching landscapes. Among them, Helene Voigt-Diederichs excelled at short stories stark in subject matter and set in Schleswig-Holstein, but was also capable of producing longer works such as *Dreiviertel Stund vor Tag* ('Just before daybreak', 1905), her memorable account of the bitter-sweet adolescence of a deprived country girl. But the 'classic' North

German example of this genre was *Jörn Uhl* (1901) by Gustav Frenssen, a novel inspired by Storm's *Der Schimmelreiter* and suffused with a similar Nordic starkness. Switzerland, too, was particularly rich in writers able to exploit the local setting for a wider readership and to follow if not outdo the high standard of the model set them by Gotthelf and Keller. Heinrich Federer focused on the human and social implications of the railway-building that was opening up hitherto remote mountain areas in *Berge und Menschen* ('Mountains and men', 1911), while the most successful of Jakob Heer's many novels, *Der König der Bernina* ('The king of the Bernina', 1900), turns on the spate of hotel building which followed the opening up of such areas to tourism.

A recurrent feature in writing of this type is the impact of new ideas and modern technology on hitherto stable communities in settings which inevitably set the handiwork of man against the majestic and imperturbable background of Nature: forest, mountains, boundless plains or northern waters are frequent features of this sort of writing. Not unlike the more sophisticated fiction of their contemporaries Thomas Mann, Hermann Hesse, Jakob Wassermann or Hermann Broch, their novels tend at their best to present the problems of a changing world; the differences between the two are mainly ones of intellectual and stylistic level. Because the best products of *Heimatliteratur* appear to be more straightforward, they achieved a degree of popularity that has led them be rated less highly than they sometimes deserve; paradoxically, they also often tend to perpetuate an image of the countryside which had outlived the reality: what was originally intended as realism and local colour soon acquired a nostalgic charm tinged with escapism. In the hands of ideologists intent on putting the clock back and on preserving traditional values, the works of popular *Heimatliteratur* authors often also lent themselves to the promotion of a concept of total nationhood which was by no means always what their authors had originally intended. By 1933 younger exponents of the tradition such as Hans Friedrich Blunck were ready and able to place their craft at the service of the new order: from 1933 to 1935 Blunck was the president of the *Reichsschrifttumskammer*, and what had been aptly termed *Heimatliteratur* with a slight shift of emphasis became *Blut- und Bodenliteratur* (the literature of blood and soil), a sub-category of regional writing which, for largely non-literary motives, stressed not just the rootedness of ordinary folk in their native soil, but also the healthy continuity of kith and kin, mirroring on the human level the greater organic continuities of topography, climate and vegetation. It is a disturbing irony that Berthold Auerbach, the author of the *Schwarzwälder Dorfgeschichten*, so popular up to the early 1930s, was posthumously excluded because of his Jewish blood from the recognition he so obviously deserved, and that the German *Heimatliteratur* tradition he created acquired associations which have clouded its critical appraisal and obscured the artistic and social importance of its enjoyable contribution to modern fiction in German.

## Conrad Ferdinand Meyer

Comfortably settled in the provincial ambience of his native Zurich, the Swiss poet and historical storyteller Conrad Ferdinand Meyer contradicted the dominant image of the German mid-nineteenth-century realist writer. He had a poet's eye for the detail of landscape, yet his stories, written between 1873 and his death in 1898, are as far removed from the regional literature of his times as they are from the crasser naturalism which overtook it. His fiction is of the historical kind, and owes something to the European tradition of historical fiction inaugurated by Scott, though not much to its representatives in Germany such as Hauff, Scheffel or even Gotthelf. For Meyer history is an escape of a therapeutic as well as an imaginative kind, in which indirect, detached expression can be given to the psychological complexity of his own personality in such a way that his readers are unaware of the subjective elements in the make-up of his distanced historical characters. In this respect, if in no other, he achieved the objectivity prized by Naturalist authors. His art has been called cold and monumental, but seen in the light of his poetry, with its fusions of clear-cut visual imagery and implicit symbolism, its fascination lies in the way it draws its readers into a world of equivocal actions and motivations which seems far-fetched until its underlying psychological truth is grasped. It is seen at its most complex in *Die Hochzeit des Mönchs* ('The monk's marriage', 1883–4), a story invented or improvised in the telling by its narrator, the poet Dante, and in the later *Die Versuchung des Pescara* ('Pescara's temptation', 1887), two long historical novellen set in Italy. Meyer's narrative mastery is at its finest and perhaps most appealing in *Das Leiden eines Knaben*, a story of boyhood suffering at the hands of adults (a modern theme though set in the France of Louis XIV), and, especially for English readers, in his penetrating treatment of the relationship between Henry II and his bosom friend turned implacable enemy, Thomas à Becket – or, rather, between saintliness and selfishness – in *Der Heilige* ('The saint', 1879). This is a psychologically complex tale worthy of Meyer's American contemporary Henry James, but seen, to make the artistic challenge even greater, through the eyes of a Swiss crossbow-maker in the service of the Plantagenet king, a straightforward narrator who is at a loss to understand the full political and emotional significance of what catches his trained and observant eye. With Meyer, what *is* speaks for itself, but great concentration is needed on the reader's part to comprehend what it is saying.

## The Dramatization of Social and Historical Change

Social drama renewed itself in the era of intellectual and political ferment associated with the *Junges Deutschland* movement and known in German as the *Vormärz* because it preceded the revolutions that erupted in Prussia, Austria and other German states in March 1848 in the wake of the February Revolution which toppled the monarchy of Louis-Philippe in France. Like the pre-revolutionary *Sturm und Drang* dramatists, such as Lenz and H. L. Wagner, who had come to maturity during the last two decades of the *Ancien Régime* some seventy years before, the dramatists of the *Vormärz* generation turned their attention to the plight of the socially constrained individual, exploring different ways of presenting it in dramatic terms. It is interesting to compare the various approaches they adopted. Friedrich Hebbel, the least politically involved of them, achieved his most enduring fame by returning to the *bürgerliches Trauerspiel* or middle-class tragedy pioneered by Lessing. Karl Gutzkow in Germany and Friedrich Halm in Austria attempted to infuse conventional types of tragedy with new ideas so as to make it more responsive to the tragic implications of modern life. Otto Ludwig opened up the potential of realistic drama by giving it a symbolic subtext, while Georg Büchner and Christian Dietrich Grabbe wrote the most original and adventurous plays of the period, though their forward-looking qualities did not begin to be fully recognized until the end of the nineteenth century or even later.

Halm's *Griseldis* (1835), based on a well-known medieval tale, uses verse and a romantically Arthurian setting to package a provocatively modern drama which clearly anticipates Ibsen's *A*

*Doll's House* (1879) when Griseldis, a long-suffering wife, awakens to her own identity and walks out on her uncomprehending husband. Four years later, in *Richard Savage oder Der Sohn einer Mutter* ('Richard Savage, or A mother's son'), Gutzkow resurrects a forgotten eighteenth-century English literary figure in order to highlight the plight of the writer misunderstood by society, such as he felt himself to be. Soon both dramas were playing to enthusiastic audiences all over the German-speaking world, proving that new ideas were acceptable even in a time of political and moral censorship if sugared with sentimentality and spiced with melodrama. Gutzkow's *Uriel Acosta* (1846) went even further. A verse tragedy set in seventeenth-century Amsterdam, it was much admired by his thinking contemporaries, while also appealing to mid-nineteenth-century playgoers, which in itself is remarkable, since it dramatizes the struggle of a free-thinking Jew against the bigotry and intolerance of those around him, culminating in his humiliating recantation and its tragic personal consequences. Forgotten it may be, yet it deserves recognition because it marks a crucial midway stage in a development which leads from Lessing's humane ideal of understanding and tolerance embodied in the central figure of *Nathan der Weise* (1779) to the prophetic pessimism of Arthur Schnitzler's *Professor Bernhardi* (1912), in which a Jewish consultant is brought down by the envy of his colleagues and the vested interests behind them. Ludwig's sombre drama *Der Erbförster* ('The hereditary forester', 1850) also looks both forwards and backwards. His effective use of textual reference to intensify dramatic suspense – as when the forester's daughter, Marie, reads random passages from the family bible to her cornered and doomed father – revives a dramatic technique pioneered by the *Sturm und Drang* dramatist Lenz in his tragi-comic play, *Die Soldaten*. On the other hand, while the play's setting in the wooded countryside of Ludwig's native Thuringia makes it the theatrical counterpart of Droste-Hülshoff's novelle *Die Judenbuche*, and is an equally unromantic treatment of the darker side of life in the 'romantic' forests of Germany, its focus on the irreconcilable conflict between the forester's traditional way of life and the modern entrepreneurial attitudes of his new employer, Stein, clearly anticipates key aspects of German Naturalism.

In concentrating on the 'great' plays of this period, the literary historian is particularly liable to overlook the fact that plays were then the main social entertainment of the German population, and that far more writers were providing them than the few 'classics' of the mid-nineteenth century suggest. Sadly, no comedy of the period survives in the repertoire, apart from the masterpieces of Nestroy; even Freytag's *Die Journalisten* (1854), the first play to take as its subject the role of the press, has forfeited the enormous popularity it once enjoyed. When playwrights turned to verse drama and nobler tragic or historical subjects they were understandably apt to fall into the patterns established by Schiller, while never emulating him except in the case of Grillparzer. Yet this does not mean that they are not sometimes interesting and worth rediscovering. For instance there is the case of Halm's grandiloquent later drama *Der Fechter von Ravenna* ('The gladiator of Ravenna'), which caused a storm of controversy at the time of its first performance at the Burgtheater, Vienna, in 1854. In it the Austrian dramatist turned his attention to the Arminius myth which Kleist had dramatized almost half a century before in *Die Hermannsschlacht* ('The battle of Hermann'), but gave it an intriguingly Austrian angle. The hero's son, Sigmar, now known as Thumelicus, is happy in his existence as a Roman gladiator, but his widowed mother Thusnelda pleads with him to return to Germany to lead his countrymen to unity and victory. When he ignores her entreaties she kills him to save the nation's reputation and spare herself the shame of seeing him fight in a Roman arena. Halm's dramatic exploration of the complexities of national identity proved prophetic. Within ten years of the play's publication, defeat by Prussia in the so-called 'German War' of 1866 finally ruled Austria out as the potential leader of a united Germany.

Halm, Gutzkow and Ludwig were writers for their own time, and it is doubtful whether their qualities transcend it. Grabbe is a very different case. Along with Büchner the most naturally gifted playwright working in Germany – outside Austria – between the suicide of Kleist and the emergence of Hebbel, he made his debut with an extraordinary extravaganza of violence and revenge on neo-Jacobean lines called *Herzog Theodor von Gothland* (1827), quickly followed by *Scherz, Satire, Ironie und tiefere Bedeutung* ('Comedy, satire, irony and deeper meaning'), one of German literature's most adroit and entertaining comedies, and one which is still performed. Grabbe's virtuoso send-up of the pretensions and preoccupations of German life and literature is simultaneously a set of inventive object-lessons in the nature and purpose of comedy, ranging, as the title implies, from slapstick and farce to black comedy to existential speculation and philosophical depth. The devil is one of its chief characters, as befits a play published in the same year as Act III of Goethe's *Faust Part II*, and his ironic observation that life is a mediocre comedy written by an angel during his school holidays is a pointer to Grabbe's ability to put 'romantic irony' to effective theatrical use. Like Grillparzer, Grabbe wrote twelve plays which between them show how versatile he was. His two blank-verse dramas on medieval German historical subjects, *Kaiser Friedrich Barbarossa* and *Kaiser Heinrich der Sechste*, make a relative success of a genre to which Ernst Raupach, his more productive contemporary, devoted his lesser skills in sixteen plays to no lasting effect. *Napoleon oder die hundert Tage* ('Napoleon or the hundred days', 1831), written ten years after the French Emperor's death, demonstrates an alternative way of dramatizing history. Not performed until 1895, its kaleidoscope of individual scenes cuts Napoleon down to size as they convey the whole spectrum of events and attitudes in the Paris of 1815: it was an approach rediscovered by twentieth-century cinema and television. *Aschenbrödel* ('Cinderella') shows Grabbe succeeding in a genre where many Romantics failed, fairy-tale drama. *Don Juan und Faust* (1829), the only play of his to be performed in his lifetime, stretches the imagination to its limits by confronting Goethe's Faust with Mozart's Don Giovanni in a verse play which questions the relative validity of words, feelings and actions and exposes the differences between them. Grabbe's last play, *Die Hermannsschlacht* (1838), brings him into direct comparison with Kleist, but here the patriotic chauvinism of Kleist's anti-French play of 1808 (published 1821) is viewed with an ironic and disenchanted eye. Grabbe's treatment of Germany's central 'foundation' myth – the defeat of the Roman army by the German tribes united under the leadership of Hermann – shows the victorious Germans failing to respond to their leader's patriotic call, thus preventing Germany from gaining its hegemony. Such a play was too uncomfortably accurate in its analysis of the contemporary situation, and too lacking in Prussian sentiments, to find favour. It is ironic that the Third Reich chose to make a hero out of an author with such an eye for his nation's pretensions and weaknesses, and a further irony that, as a result, post-1945 critical opinion has tended to play him off against Büchner and to play down his impressive achievement in favour of the slimmer output of the brilliant young writer who survived him by five months.

## Georg Büchner

Georg Büchner is unique in the annals of German, or indeed European, literary history. He died at the age of twenty-three having written three plays and established himself as a promising medical scientist. He admired the work of Lenz, about whom he even wrote a story or, rather, a probing psycho–aesthetic analysis; he was also well aware of the Romantic authors such as Brentano and Tieck, and their whimsical humour, irony and fantasy resurface in his own delicately black comedy *Leonce und Lena*, published by his main champion, Gutzkow, in 1838 but not discovered for the stage until 1885, and not recognized as one of the finest comedies in German until the twentieth century. *Dantons Tod*, written in 1835 and also published by Gutzkow, is a historical drama of sorts. Many other plays are set in the days of the French Revolution, but it leaves them all behind in its acutely observed diagnosis of mixed motives, seemingly arbitrary actions and the responses to them when a group of people becomes caught up in political events which are themselves open to interpretation. He shares Grillparzer's anti-heroic attitude to the characters of history, but unlike him discarded the outward trappings of historical drama which the Austrian inherited from Shakespeare and Schiller: instead, the 'modern' qualities of this extraordinary play projected it to the forefront of critical attention in the early twentieth century and gave it a pre-eminence amongst the classics of historical drama in German in the face of which even Schiller's masterpieces have had to struggle to hold their own.

The modernity of *Dantons Tod* is nothing when compared to Büchner's unfinished drama *Woyzeck*, rediscovered in 1879 and first performed in Munich in November 1913. In *Woyzeck* Büchner renewed techniques which had been pioneered by Lenz and other *Sturm und Drang* writers, such as the fragmentation of the unity of action: it is made up of an apparently disconnected sequence of some twenty-seven scenes. Even in terms of character portrayal and recurring themes, the play owes much to its models. Yet Büchner's portrayal of an ordinary 'little' man victimized until his precarious hold on reality and mental stability gives way, has become as much an icon of the twentieth century as the uncomprehending protagonist of a Kafka story. *Woyzeck* was founded on a true case history, and in this respect anticipated the Naturalist procedures exemplified in *Bahnwärter Thiel* (1887), Gerhart Hauptmann's early account of a lonely railway worker's harrowing descent into psychosis. But *Woyzeck*, like *Wozzeck*, the opera based on it by the Viennese avant-garde composer Alban Berg in 1925, transcends the limitations of Naturalism. In performance its gripping sequence of short scenes – their haphazard order reflecting the incomplete state in which Büchner left it – create a replica of real life so authentic that it leaves all sense of specific time and place far behind.

## Friedrich Hebbel

It is hard to believe that Büchner, this most 'modern' of Germany's classic dramatists, died in 1837, shortly before Queen Victoria came to the throne, and that Wagner, Hebbel and he were born within seven months of each other in 1813. In 1837 neither Hebbel nor Wagner had produced any work of importance; for both, the debut came in 1840 when Wagner's grand opera *Rienzi* received its first performance in Dresden and Hebbel's first play, *Judith*, was premiered in Berlin. The story of their reception and their subsequent reputations brings home some of the paradoxes that underlie modern German cultural history and the ambivalent attitudes which Germans and, in Wagner's case, the international community, have towards it. Nowhere is this shown more clearly than in their treatments of the Nibelungen myth. Wagner completed and published the text of his vast tetralogy *Der Ring des Nibelungen* in 1853, but the complete *Ring* was not performed until 1876 at the first Bayreuth Festival. Hebbel, too, was the author of an ambitious treatment of the Nibelungen myth. Planned in 1855, his dramatic trilogy, *Die Nibelungen: Ein deutsches Trauerspiel*, was first performed in Weimar in 1861, its complete version reaching the stage of the Burgtheater in Vienna in 1871. Their sources were quite different. Wagner's tetralogy is a very personal reworking of an ancient nordic cycle of legends with audible echoes of Fouqué's trilogy *Der Held des Nordens* ('The hero of the north') of 1810; Hebbel based his trilogy on the Middle High German epic *Das Nibelungenlied* and set it in the legendary early Middle Ages. Both works are, however, essentially products of their age and responses to it, and were offered to German theatre-goers at exactly the time when the destiny of Germany and its division into the Second Empire, and Austria-Hungary's exclusion from it, were undermining and at the same time inflating the Germans' understanding of themselves. There is an apt yet ominous irony in the fact that, like Tennyson's *The Passing of Arthur* (1869), the two masterpieces which set the artistic tone for the new German Empire depict an old, heroic order changing and yielding place to new.

There was little doubt in the minds of contemporaries that Hebbel's plays represented the apogee of mid-nineteenth-century German serious drama. But Hebbel's standing has diminished in modern times, and few would still regard him as a dramatist of world stature. Yet there is much to admire in his work. One of his most famous plays, curiously called *Maria Magdalena*, is based not on the New Testament figure but on Hebbel's own boyhood awareness of the tragedy inherent in the parochial restrictions and conventions of a small North German town, where a master joiner's world is shattered when his son is accused of theft and his daughter kills herself to avoid the shame of becoming an unmarried mother. In retrospect it is a pity that Hebbel abandoned realistic drama after this one powerful attempt, leaving his younger Norwegian contemporary, Henrik Ibsen (1828–1906) to fulfil its promise. But it was characteristic of the man and his age that he felt impelled to aim for higher things.

Ibsen's own world view may already have been present in embryo in Hebbel; but as chance would have it, just as Hebbel's grander historical and symbolical dramatic achievements have been upstaged by Wagner, his realistic treatment of low life and common humanity has been increasingly overshadowed by the more 'modern' approach of his other exact contemporary, Büchner. Today, therefore, Hebbel's true genius and originality must be located elsewhere. A man largely self-taught and therefore something of an exception in German literary culture, he advanced the view that the dramatist was the true historian, since only the dramatist can bring to life the complex and interconnecting motivations of human beings at moments of historical and social change. The fullest and most convincing example of this 'Hebbelian' type of drama is to be found in his play *Herodes und Mariamne* (1849), itself the product of a year of upheaval and change in European and German history. Twice Herod leaves his adored wife Mariamne behind in Jerusalem to go off into the dangerous world of international politics during the Roman civil wars; and twice he leaves instructions for her to be put to death should he be killed, in order to prevent her marrying anyone else. On both occasions she finds out from his most trusted confidants what destiny her husband had in store for her. But only once can she forgive. When news reaches Jerusalem that he has been killed, she throws a lavish party at which Herod surprises her. Her response to the news of his murder seems to prove that he was right: she has clearly acted as he foresaw she would, so he condemns her to death. Only when she is dead is he informed that she had vowed to kill herself rather than live without him: indeed the execution he ordered was a suicide in all but name, and the direct result of his failure to live up to the ideal of human trust and partnership she thought they shared. To later readers and playgoers this was obviously a study of modern marriage or of the war between the sexes: indeed it can be presented as a feminist manifesto attacking the male chauvinism of Herod, who regarded his wife as a chattel rather than an equal partner for life. But such an interpretation, while partly valid, must involve the omission of a scene by which Hebbel set great store and which exemplified his conception of drama. As the action draws to its climax, three kings arrive in search of an infant who will bring about a new dispensation for humanity. Irate that a rival has been born in his realm who may even outshine him, Herod orders all new-born males to be killed. It is not so much that he regards babies, too, as things; it is, rather, that Hebbel intended this episode to locate his tragedy at a crucial turning-point in history. With the advent of Christianity, he argues, things could never be the same again. Our retrospect on the intervening years suggests that Hebbel was too easily carried away by grand ideas to see the stark reality of the world around him despite the fact that he grew up in it and that his one realistic masterpiece provides the link between Lessing's middle-class tragedies and the social dramas of Ibsen and Gerhart Hauptmann.

## Mid-Nineteenth-Century Lyric Poetry

Lyric poetry has never been so popular with the German reading public as it was in the years between 1830 and 1890, if the number and appearance of the many albums and anthologies of poetry published in that period are anything to go by. But this popularity was bought at a price. Quality and originality declined, and as a result few areas in German literature are now as unfamiliar, and none since the baroque is so rich in talents and works which were once read and admired, but which are now little more than names.

First and foremost amongst his many contemporaries was Emanuel Geibel, whose sobriquet, the 'Tennyson of Germany', clearly reflects the shifting fortunes of critical favour. Geibel's first collection of verse, simply entitled *Gedichte*, appeared in 1840: by his death in 1884 it had run to 100 editions. His status in the literary world rose fast, as was demonstrated in 1842 by the award of a pension for life by the King of Prussia, followed in 1852 by an invitation from the King of Bavaria to become his poet laureate, a role he played until the late 1860s, when the rise of Prussia persuaded him – he was a North German and came from Lübeck – to become the quasi-official poet of the new German Empire. His rise and fall are easy to appreciate, and so, too, is the popularity he enjoyed amongst his contemporaries, who saw his poems as the artistic fulfilment of the folk lyric trend begun by Goethe and Bürger a century before and representing a quintessentially 'German' type of poetry which owed its accessibility to its 'artless' simplicity of statement and structure and to its fondness for simple human themes. Composers vied with one another to set Geibel to music. 'Der Mai ist gekommen' soon became a modern folksong. Readers responded with alacrity to the optimistic encouragements of 'Vorwärts', a kind of German equivalent to Longfellow's 'Excelsior' but cast in a reassuringly hymn-like mould, which told the reader that progress applies in individual cases, too, and were moved by the gentle, affecting resignation of 'Vorüber ist die Rosenzeit', a mid-nineteenth-century variation on the baroque theme of life's transitoriness. Interspersed with these outwardly unassuming lyrics are poems in ballad and sonnet form and in the classical metres of Goethe and Platen, demonstrating his command of the great tradition he had inherited. Sometimes, as in his *Ostseebilder* ('Baltic sketches'), he could even sound almost like Heine. Here were rich pickings for contributors to the autograph books which mid-nineteenth-century people used to define their cultural identities. He once observed that a poem is like a beautiful dream, and in his own poetry he set out to provide daydreams for the middle classes who read him. But underlying his work were two factors which ultimately contributed to his failure to hold his place as one of the chief poets of Germany: a tendency to lapse into sentimentality and the lack of an immediately recognizable voice.

Geibel had many competitors in the market for lyric poetry in mid-nineteenth-century Germany. Among the most successful were Victor von Scheffel, the author of the popular historical novel *Ekkehard*, whose verse tale *Der Trompeter von Säckingen* (1854) went through innumerable editions. Scheffel's speciality was the appealing evocation of Germany – and especially of Heidelberg – in the good old days of youth, love and laughter, a brand of escapism counterbalanced by that of Friedrich von Bodenstedt, whose pseudo-oriental extravaganza, *Die Lieder des Mirza Schaffy* (1851), supplied daydreams of another sort by transporting its readers to the far-off Caucasus. Almost equally popular, yet almost impossible to take seriously, was Friederike Kempner, a well-meaning and socially aware woman whose *Gedichte* (1873) read like a humorous parody of the work of her least talented contemporaries. Common to all these once popular poets is their new awareness of the need to appeal to a growing readership by giving them what they wanted. Their poetry is essentially escapist. It makes scant demands on the reader and scant reference to emotional truth, preferring to use comprehensible words and pleasing images to convey acceptable sentiments. It was a policy which brought verse closer to popular fiction than is usually the case. This trend was one to which virtually no writer of this period was immune. Now and again, for instance, traces of Geibel and his sentimentality – that is, his all too easy association of certain stock images and phrases with stock emotional responses – may be found even in the lyric poetry of writers whose work has outlived him, such as Theodor Storm and Gottfried Keller.

Keller's first poems appeared in 1846. The difference is audible at once. From the start Keller had a voice of his own, immediately recognizable in the rhythm of his verse, while Storm, who always regarded lyric poetry as the heart of his writing, never forgot his axiom that the art of the lyric poet lies in expressing the most general thoughts and feelings in the most original way – in words and images directly rooted in the poet's own experience and imagination. The achievements of two very dissimilar writers are enhanced when they are appreciated in the context of the poetry their near contemporaries were writing, and which their potential readers most enjoyed. Even the haunting words of Storm's most famous poem, 'Die Stadt', which seem at first simply to evoke any small backwater in Germany, are actually the poet's own very personal evocation of his beloved home town, Husum, on the west coast of Schleswig-Holstein. Keller's equally famous 'Abendlied', on the surface an atmospheric lyric drawing the equation between nightfall and death, is really a personal statement of its author's love of life and of his artistic aim, which was to capture the feel and look of his familiar world in all its vitality and visual detail. Of all the poets of the mid-nineteenth-century period, Keller is also almost the only one who is able to voice patriotic sentiments which sound genuine, and are not carried away by the rhetoric of pompous or sentimental nationalism:

O mein Heimatland! O mein Vaterland! wie so innig, feurig lieb ich dich!

The words of this song, which acquired the popularity of a national anthem in Switzerland, express straightforwardly the relationship between a human being and a nation for which the poet feels genuine affection, indeed passion, while claiming for it nothing more than its natural beauty. Again, it is only in the context of the often inflatedly nationalistic patriotic verse of its day that the full measure of Keller's achievement in this mode can be fully appreciated.

Storm's relationship to nation and homeland was more complicated than Keller's: he was a German, but his love was for a province annexed by Denmark and then by Prussia, yet with its own distinct identity for all that, and it comes through in his nature poems, which capture the magical moments when the transitory seems to partake of the eternal. But he is also the mid-century's most intense and least clichéd love poet. From his poem on a nightingale, with its incantatory opening words

Das macht, es hat die Nachtigall
die ganze Nacht gesungen,

which haunt the memory like a refrain, to the exultation of 'Wer je gelebt in Liebesarmen', the anxiety of 'Beginn des Endes', and the cycle 'Tiefe Schatten' in which he poured out his grief after the death of his wife Constanze in 1865, the subtle modulations of Storm's language hark back to Brentano, whose musicality and ear for assonance he shared. Deceptively simple, like so much of his best prose, Storm's love poetry seems to modern ears to be saying things of which he was not himself fully conscious; for that reason, too, his poetry seldom lapses into the jejune imagery and predictable diction which by his time was depriving much German verse of the freshness and directness that had characterized it ever since the days of Klopstock and Goethe. Indeed, as if to prove his right to be regarded as one of that illustrious tradition, Storm was even able to record the impact of Constanze's death in an elegy in classical metre, entitled simply 'Constanze', one of the finest and most deeply moving poems of its kind in German literature.

There is no doubt that Storm was the strongest lyric voice in North Germany in the mid-nineteenth century. But he was not alone. Not far away from Husum, his exact contemporary Klaus Groth was discovering a different way of avoiding the clichés and the jaded lyricism of the period by using the Low German language still spoken by ordinary folk in North Germany. *Quickborn* (1852), a collection of poems in *Holsteiner Plattdeutsch*, brought him an immediate popularity which spread far beyond his own region because its publication coincided with a wave of patriotic feeling after the defeat of Prussia in 1850 in the first Danish–German War, which had been fought in Schleswig-Holstein. Like the *Poems of Rural Life in the Dorset Dialect* and the *Hwomely Rhymes* of his contemporary William Barnes, Groth's achievement in homely dialect verse outlived a merely topical interest: *Quickborn* grew in size and ran through many editions. Its affectionate and atmospheric lyrics had at last given the North an individual voice which could stand comparison with Johann Peter Hebel's earlier *Alemannische Gedichte* in the dialect of the Swabian South.

The third important poet to represent the revival of North German lyric poetry in the mid-nineteenth century was Friedrich Hebbel, but unlike Groth and Storm, Hebbel had left his native region as a young man to settle in Vienna and become Germany's leading mid-century dramatist. Yet alongside the plays he wrote, he also composed a steady stream of poetry between 1842 and 1857. Though sometimes marred by a straining after profundity and effect, it often achieves a remarkable density of utterance, as in the poem entitled 'Requiem', and an atmospheric quality – for instance in the ballad 'Der Heideknabe', an eerie depiction of childhood terror – which places it somewhere between Annette von Droste-Hülshoff and Storm himself. At their best Hebbel's poems also point forward to the abandonment of cliché in favour of impressionistic detail by the most original poets of the next generation, Detlev von Liliencron in North Germany and Conrad Ferdinand Meyer in Switzerland.

## Thematic Survey: Popular Literature for Adults and Children

The high status which art and artistic endeavour were accorded by the leading German critics and thinkers from the mid-eighteenth century onwards has tended ever since to accentuate the distinction between 'high' literature – the kind with which scholarship and criticism concern themselves – and a 'lower' kind read with pleasure and written and published for profit, but devoid of true artistic integrity and therefore unable to make those higher claims on the moral and aesthetic awareness of its readers that are the hallmark of 'true', 'serious' writing. As a result, middle-brow literature – the 'fiction' of public libraries – is seldom given its due. This is particularly true of the German novel, but it has also affected the evaluation of theatrical works, because the theatre in the German-speaking countries has increasingly made a distinction between the state-subsidized sector and the commercial stage, the one dependent on financial subsidies and artistic reputation for its success, the other relying traditionally on its popular appeal, until its virtual extinction in the post-1945 era. Yet in the case of both genres, the gulf between popular success and serious artistic purpose has not always been quite so marked as we now imagine. Christiane Vulpius (1765–1816), Goethe's partner and, later, his wife, was the sister of one of the most successful authors of the day, Christian August Vulpius, whose Gothic novels, such as *Aurora* (1794–5), share the love of improbable coincidences, supernatural intervention, secret societies, the inscrutable workings of hidden destiny and the exploration of recurrent themes which Goethe discreetly raised to high art in the symphonic structure of the second part of his novel *Wilhelm Meister*. In fact the narrative strategies of the period's more popular novelists are also to be found in the narrative structure of most of the novels produced by the 'respectable' writers of the Romantic movement in Germany. Indeed the popularity of works such as Fouqué's *Der Zauberring* (1813) with the readers of their time has tended to debase their literary value in the eyes of later and more selective critics.

Vulpius's greatest success had come in 1799, when his novel *Rinaldo Rinaldini, der Räuberhauptmann* ('The robber chief') was greeted with such enthusiasm that a dramatic version and two sequels soon followed. It was more than just a pulp novel, as its long hold on its readers proved: by 1858 it had run to eight editions and been translated into over thirty languages, reappearing in many different guises up to the present day; moreover, in theme and subject matter it has more in common with the 'high' art of its period than one might expect. Its noble-minded hero, a Corsican bandit, is a rebel against the conventions of society who displays unexpected moral integrity and philanthropic impulses: in fact a hero cast in the mould of Karl Moor, the protagonist of Schiller's first great stage success, *Die Räuber* ('The robbers', 1782). Thus *Rinaldo Rinaldini* and Vulpius's other popular novels did much to make the broader reading public aware of the issues with which his now more famous contemporaries were concerned, and helped to transmit some idea of them to other countries, such as England, which underwent a short-lived craze for German robber romances around 1800; for example, Lewis, the author of *The Monk*, one of the most famous English Gothic novels, translated the other classic example of the genre, the best-selling *Abällino der große Bandit* (1795) by Heinrich Zschokke, as *The Bravo of Venice* (1805). Schiller himself had signalled his interest in this type of contemporary writing when in 1789 he published his incomplete novel *Der Geisterseher* ('The ghost-seer'), a tale of intrigue, duplicity, mystification and suspense with a Venetian setting, which became the model for many later tales of mystery and horror, and which made a deep impression on the young Byron.

The habit of reading begins in childhood, and the period saw a steady expansion in children's literature. The German Romantics had discovered childhood as an age of innocence but also of natural receptivity to the mysterious world of fairly tale. The Grimms' *Kinder- und Hausmärchen* (1812–15), and the fairy tales of Wilhelm Hauff and Clemens Brentano, took hold in the nursery, while the carefree innocence of Eichendorff's *Aus dem Leben eines Taugenichts* ('From the life of a good-for-nothing', 1826), with its irreverent but engaging rejection of German middle-class behaviour, entranced an older age-group. But the German nineteenth-century market for children's books was dominated by three long-lived authors: Johann Christoph von Schmid, a Catholic priest who spent most of his life in Bavaria, Gustav Nieritz (1795–1876), a Dresden schoolmaster, and Ottilie Wildermuth, a Tübingen teacher's wife. Schmid's voluminous output of stories for children enjoyed popularity for most of the nineteenth century, and not only in Germany: translations made him a much-loved author in many countries including Britain and the United States. *Die Ostereier* ('The Easter Eggs'), the story by which he became best known in Germany, appeared in 1816 and *Das Blumenkörbchen* ('The Basket of Flowers'), his other most successful tale, in 1823. His stories exemplify Christian values and patterns of behaviour in simple, straightforward stories in settings which suggest the hills, forests and meadows, small towns and villages of southern Germany. His ability to combine the commonplace and everyday with the symbolic and distinctive indicates his role in the development of nineteenth-century German literary taste: his stories prepared young readers for the symbolic patterns and moral landscapes of Stifter's *Bunte Steine*, Droste-Hülshoff's *Die Judenbuche* (1842) and the stories of Jeremias Gotthelf, such as *Das Erdbeeri Mareili* ('Mareili the strawberry girl', 1851), in which Schmid's pre-industrial world is found again in subtler and less simplistic form. Gustav Nieritz provided different fare. His stories for young people, such as *Der junge Trommelschläger* ('The young drummer', 1838), *Die Negersklaven und der Deutsche* ('The Negro Slaves and the German', 1841) and *Der Quäker* (1849), exploited the effective recipe of carefully presented historical and geographical facts combined with storylines which allowed their readers to escape from lives circumscribed either by deprivation or by a good upbringing, for they were accessible to all classes thanks to the high level of literacy throughout the German-speaking world; their appeal contributed to the creation of a common literary culture which was to be a decisive factor in its nineteenth-century evolution.

The 1820s, which saw the European vogue for the Waverley novels of Scott, were particularly rich in pseudo-historical romance. The influence of Scott was far-reaching and his example was eagerly taken up by writers and publishers aware of this change of taste, and ready to blend it with already existing German traditions. Of these the most successful was Karl Spindler, whose sixteenth-century novel *Der Bastard* (1826) and fifteenth-century novel *Der Jude* (1827) take up themes already explored with more sophistication but less readably by major Romantic writers such as Tieck and Achim von Arnim. Works such as Spindler's appealed to both sexes; but other writers aimed specifically at a female readership, a good example being August Lafontaine, who was adept at combining the exciting storylines associated with Gothic romance with the sensitivities of middle-class women readers in novels which often set the dastardly deeds of corrupt aristocrats off against the innate virtue of vulnerable ordinary people, especially women.

The image of women in popular fiction had scarcely changed since the late eighteenth century, when Wilhelmine Wobeser (1769–1807) presented her fashionable ideal of woman-hood in her *Elisa oder Das Weib wie es seyn soll* ('Elisa or Woman as she ought to be', 1795), which was complemented by Therese Huber in her more convincing *Ehestandsgeschichte* ('A tale of matrimony', 1804) and by Johanna Schopenhauer in *Gabriele* (1819–20), two novels which make interesting comparison with Susan Ferrier's *Marriage* of 1818. The sweet passivity which characterizes these German portrayals of women by women, as well as by men, was gradually modified as the century went on. Increasingly, the heroines of successful popular novels are caught in a struggle between resignation and self-realization, and in the process one of the most pressing issues of the day, the emancipation of women, becomes the most vital element in many a best-seller. In the 1840s Fanny Lewald, a Jewish merchant's daughter, made the traumas of separation and divorce her speciality (*Eine Lebensfrage*, 1845), while the impoverished aristocrat Ida, Countess Hahn-Hahn, concentrated her attention on the pilgrimage of strong-minded women towards the goal of independence and self-fulfilment (*Gräfin Faustine*, 1840–1).

The growing sense of social realism characteristic of most literature in the 1840s coloured popular fiction, too, but by 1850 the intellectualism of the 1840s, which had done much to offset the stereotyped characterization and storylines of novels aimed at the wider market, was no longer in fashion. Fanny Lewald continued to earn her living by writing novels, but they no longer had the questioning dynamism which had shocked many readers but earned her many more during the previous decade; Ida Hahn-Hahn restricted her range to autobiographically inspired religious and emotional conflicts. The change of mood that followed the political events of 1848–9 is graphically illustrated by the return of popular fiction to two of its staple characteristics: sentimentality and support of an idealized social *status quo*. Ottilie Wildermuth began publishing her homely tales of provincial family life in 1852, and found herself being avidly read in all classes of society; Marie Nathusius scored her first major success in 1854 with her anonymously published *Tagebuch eines armen Fräuleins*; by the late 1860s the market had been captured by Germany's most successful nineteenth-century woman author, Eugenie Marlitt, whose first large-scale novel, *Goldelse*, was published in serial form by the periodical *Die Gartenlaube*: she remained its star author for the rest of her life. Marlitt's stories captivated middle-class German readers and the best of them remained in the best-selling list well on into the twentieth century. Common to all these leading women authors was their sure sense of what their readers, predominantly women, wanted; their knowledge of the literary market enabled them to settle on the narrative recipes which ensured a loyal readership: slow but steady upward mobility for those who deserved it as a reward for their kindness, sincerity and good conduct and, to go with it, slow-moving plots enlivened by vivid, well-told incident and located in recognizable if unspecified German settings. In an age of handbooks on social etiquette and moral conduct, it is no surprise that popular novels of this type also contained a more or less unobtrusive didactic element.

Similar changes of approach and theme, reflecting German society's shifting view of itself, may also be observed in the work of the countless writers who provided reading-matter for an ever-widening and voracious public in the middle and lower classes of society. The nineteenth-century *Volksschriftsteller* or 'writer for the people' regarded the provision of such matter as something of a sacred duty, and approached the task with a clear sense of moral rather than aesthetic responsibility. A critical note could therefore sometimes be struck by drawing out the defects of modern society and their effect on individual morality. Published in uniform series, as well as in the serial form usual for other narrative authors, the works of the leading

*Volksschriftsteller* – whose importance was often regional rather than nationwide – often appeared in numbers which far exceeded the publishing runs of their literary colleagues. In 1850 the average print run for the first edition of a work by a reputable literary author such as Gottfried Keller was 800 copies, a figure which had doubled by the mid-1870s, whereas good *Volksschriftsteller* could expect a run of 5000 and congratulate themselves on the fact that this category of fiction had a share in the market which went up from 15 per cent in the mid-1850s to 40 per cent in the 1870s. Their success was great, but ephemeral; rightly or wrongly even the best of them never achieved the lasting popularity of some of their German and foreign contemporaries whose themes and approaches are quite similar. A good example is *Friedel* (1845) by Wilhelm Oertel, also known as W. O. von Horn, who, like his exact Swiss contemporary Jeremias Gotthelf, was a Protestant pastor throughout his writing career. *Friedel* combines foreign adventure and love of home (in this case the Mosel valley); told by its narrator hero, it is a tale of youthful love, forced enlistment, emigration to South Africa and final return as the benefactor of his native village. In the 1850s, Oertel's stories reflected the general change in taste by adopting a more explicitly moral tone and by turning to topical issues such as alcoholism, declining moral standards and loss of religious faith, negative themes offset by his staunch promotion of Christian ideals of marriage and parenthood. Oertel was highly successful, but he was not unique: like his many competitors, he wrote stories which reflect the general themes and trends of 'higher' literature at the time, but on an artistically less demanding level. Tales of village life were in vogue in the 1840s, and the best authors were writing them, so the *Volksschriftsteller* such as Oertel, Rudolf Oeser and Karl Heinrich Caspari wrote village tales too. But theirs were written for the entertaining improvement of minds and morals rather than for any great wish to be taken seriously as writers. Amongst their more literary contemporaries only Berthold Auerbach could rival them: his Black Forest tales swept him to national and international popularity in the 1840s. The difference was that their tales were actually read by the villagers themselves.

Moral tales were popular in their day, but their appeal has faded with the gradual shift in moral values and attitudes. Two much-loved collections of mid-nineteenth-century verse tales have had a very different fate: the perennial favourites, *Der Struwwelpeter* (1845) by Heinrich Hoffmann (1809–94), and *Max und Moritz* by Wilhelm Busch. Hoffmann, a distinguished child psychiatrist at the Frankfurt mental hospital, wrote his classic collection of cautionary tales because he found the mawkish children's books in the bookshops unsuitable for his small son. His ten *Struwwelpeter* stories present a child's view of the world, in which adult authority is handled with extraordinary discretion by mid-nineteenth-century standards, and is sardonically satirized. Thus Conrad's mother leaves him alone at home (no wonder he is such a suck-a-thumb!) and Harriet's parents (or Paulinchen's in the German original) will come home to find the pussy-cats weeping over their daughter's ashes. The story of the man who went out shooting ('Die Geschichte vom wilden Jäger') and the tale of Cruel Frederick reflect the shift of sensibility that led to the animal welfare and animal rights movements, while the story of the 'Inky Boys' ('Die Geschichte von den schwarzen Buben') is a pioneering indictment of racial and colour prejudice. Hoffmann's own wonderful colour illustrations provide a visual commentary which in a child's eyes far outweighs any didactic message: text and image say it all. No wonder his imitators have been few and unsuccessful, apart perhaps from Hilaire Belloc, whose *Cautionary Tales* in the Hoffmann manner (1907) first delighted British children in the Edwardian era.

A creative conjunction of image and text was also Wilhelm Busch's recipe for success in the nursery and living-room. He, too, knew that the visual can often speak more strongly than words. His stories about the pranks and practical jokes of Max and Moritz, Germany's two favourite 'naughty boys', are rooted in traditions of storytelling going back to Till Eulenspiegel, and, similarly, their satirical purpose is never far away. Drastic and violent Busch's stories may be (and so are his illustrations for them), but their world is one where, as in the American classic tradition of the Hanna-Barbera animated cartoons, all the characters who meet with the direst and most gruesome disasters have an irrepressible ability to bounce back for more. *Max und Moritz* quickly became the comic bible of German-speaking families from the Hohenzollern imperial family downwards. Though it has largely retained its popularity, its full and frequently snook-cocking significance cannot be fully understood if it is read in isolation from the complex set of restrictive social and moral values that are its context.

There was another type of popular fiction, which aimed at a predominantly male readership and which captured the market in the 1840s: novels set in America, the country of promise, opportunity and wide open spaces, where stuffy conventions were unknown. Identifying with the heroes of such fiction, the stay-at-home reader could imaginatively live out his dreams. He had probably been brought up on one of the most influential books for children to come from the German-speaking world, *The Swiss Family Robinson*, a long tale of survival and initiative involving an entire family wrecked on Defoe's desert island, written by the Swiss parson Johann David Wyss and published by his son in 1812–27. Now, in the 1840s, the novels and stories of Friedrich Gerstäcker turned to the adventures and challenges facing settlers beyond the Mississippi (*Die Flußpiraten des Mississippi*, 'The pirates of the Mississippi', 1848) or, even more topically, in the California of the Gold Rush (*Gold*, 1858), while those of his Austrian contemporary Karl Postl, writing under the name of Charles Sealsfield, imaginatively and convincingly transported their readers to contemporary Mexico, Texas and Louisiana (*Das Kajütenbuch*, 'The cabin book', 1841). Both authors knew their settings at first hand, and both paved the way for Karl May, the most extraordinary example of a successful popular writer in German literature. A man of humble background, blind until the age of fifteen and later convicted for theft, May made his reputation as a writer of exotic adventure stories usually set in the Middle East or the Wild West. The best of his enormous output, such as Germany's favourite Red Indian stories, *Winnetou* and *Der Schatz am Silbersee* ('The treasure of the silver lake'), appeared in the 1890s. Perhaps he owed his success to his early disabilities: five years of blindness stimulated his boyhood imagination and extraordinary ability to describe people and places he had never seen, while his brushes with the law gave him insight into the minds of 'baddies' as well as 'goodies'. His storytelling may provoke condescending criticism for its stereotyped situations and macho heroics, but it earned him a loyal and affectionate readership amongst German-speakers everywhere, which it retains to this day.

Between them the work of this group of writers represents the 'colonial' strain in nineteenth-century German writing. Unlike its British counterpart, it was not the fiction of empire but of emigration, and was being written and read at a time when Germany was making a substantial contribution to the expanding population and opening up of the United States, Canada, and other overseas territories, and, in the last decades of the century, also beginning to feel that it had legitimate interests of its own in East Africa and the Middle East. This blend of fact and fiction, of harsh reality and wishful thinking, is clearly reflected in the work of Karl May and the hold it has exerted on the broader adolescent and adult German male reading public for a century and more. The wide open plains and deserts of May's novels, like all his evocations of far-off places and distant climes, are the product of hard money-earning work backed up by scholarly research and a vivid imagination. In this sense they are a remarkably accurate reflection of the characteristic German values of their time and a far cry from the foreign and colonial fiction of his major British contemporaries such as Kipling, Stevenson and Rider Haggard.

What about literature for girls and young women? From the eighteenth century on, an enormous number of books were aimed at this market, most of which propagated 'Kirche, Küche, Kinder' ('Church, cooking and children'), the spheres traditionally apportioned to German women, in tones that were moralizing, escapist or both. Girls' books were even more overtly governed by convention than boys': they were of course likely to be bought by careful parents and guardians or given as rewards for industry and good behaviour by schools. Yet a conventional approach is, paradoxically, not adopted in the most successful of all German-language books for girls: Johanna Spyri's *Heidi* (1880–1). From the start its unkempt, sun-tanned little heroine rejects convention as personified by her German friend Klara's unpleasant governess Fräulein Rottenmeyer; later the story turns on the sickly town girl's return to health in the Alpine air, a therapeutic climax so persuasively yet sensibly handled that it probably did more to shape the outlook of the emancipated young women of the 1890s, who had read *Heidi* as girls, than any feminist tract. Such women remained a minority, however, as is shown by the sustained popularity of Germany's most successful woman novelist, Hedwig Courths-Mahler. Here a narrative recipe is indefatigably deployed in over 200 novels to reassure twentieth-century readers that upward social mobility is possible for disadvantaged women, provided they are resourceful and make the most of themselves, and that, in fiction at least, dreams come true and they will get their man. The success of such novels raises some fundamental questions as to the nature of literary fiction. Looked down on as literature, Courths-Mahler's all too predictable yet readable 'masterpieces', such as *Opfer der Liebe* ('Love's sacrifice') or *Es irrt der Mensch* ('To err is human'), can tell us a lot about the twentieth-century women who avidly read them in preference to the works of her more original female contemporaries. Their roots in the Cinderella myth suggest that the fairy-tale tradition is never far away.

# 7

## The Literature of the Metropolis

If the setting of so much German writing in the age of realism was rural, and the provinces were its exemplary place, its setting in the period which followed is essentially urban, and its exemplary place is the metropolis. German literary modernism, encompassing movements as diverse as Naturalism, Impressionism and neo-Romanticism, *Jugendstil* (the German counterpart of *art nouveau*), Expressionism, Dadaism, surrealism and the new realism known as *Neue Sachlichkeit* or 'new objectivity', had as its setting Berlin, capital of the Second German Empire, and Vienna, capital of the multinational Austro-Hungarian Empire. The changing character of Vienna and, even more, of Berlin was symptomatic of the societies they served and of which they were the centres. Vienna, for centuries the favourite residence of the Habsburg rulers of the Holy Roman Empire (until its demise in 1806), and since 1804 capital of the Austrian Empire, had always enjoyed a metropolitan character and reputation despite its relatively small size by comparison with London or Paris. But Berlin had been little more than a combination of provincial capital and garrison town until 1871 when, following half a century of enlightened economic policies by the Prussian state, military efficiency married to Bismarck's astute political leadership thrust fame and status upon it. Between 1871 and 1910 Berlin grew from a large town of some 400,000 inhabitants to a modern metropolis of 2 million and came to occupy third place among the cities of Europe – a rate of growth comparable to that of American cities such as New York and Chicago during the same period. Vienna, too, expanded. In 1890, when the city was officially extended to include its outer suburbs, its population swelled from 817,000 to 1,364,000 inhabitants. No wonder this was the age of *Großstadtdichtung*: townscape was overtaking landscape as a subject for the painter's and the poet's art. The growth of the metropolis was fed by large-scale migration from the countryside, in Berlin's case from eastern, largely Slav-inhabited provinces now part of Poland, in Vienna's from all over the Dual Monarchy or Austro-Hungarian Empire, as the Austrian Habsburg Empire was known after 1867. In 1870 well over 60 per cent of Germans still lived on the land; by 1910 60 per cent of them were living in towns and cities. In the same period the numbers working in industry doubled and industrial production, which had exceeded that of France in the 1870s, had overtaken that of Great Britain, the 'workshop of the world', by 1900. While France's population remained stable at 40 million during the same period, Germany's increased by some 50 per cent, from 40 million to 60 million. Stendhal's French provincial hero, Julien Sorel, in his novel *Le Rouge et le noir* (1830) had automatically set his sights on the capital, Paris. Now it was the young German's or the young Austrian's ambition to do the same. Vienna acted as a magnet for the gifted and the restless from its vast and diverse catchment area stretching as far as Romania and Moldavia, Hungary and eastern Poland to Bosnia-Herzegovina and the borders of the Ottoman Empire. Some of the most celebrated names of their age came from Bohemia and Moravia (the present Czech Republic) including Sigmund Freud, Karl Kraus and Gustav Mahler; from Hungary came the founder of Zionism, Theodor Herzl.

Berlin was perhaps brasher – and certainly much richer – than Vienna. Its wealth and influence were anchored less in the accumulated treasures of the past than in the goods and services that would underpin its future power, not least in its role as the media centre not just of Germany but of a substantial part of northern and central Europe. It was in Berlin that the impresario and theatre producer Max Reinhardt, the great master of technology in the theatre, began to provide drama for mass consumption, his revolving stages and searchlight-like illumination delighting audiences of thousands, as in his 1910 production of Sophocles' *Oedipus* before a public of 5000. By the 1890s Berlin had ousted Leipzig as the centre of the German publishing industry as well as of the newspaper and periodical press, and, from 1900 onwards, of the new phenomenon of photo-journalism. Even before the First World War it was the focus of German cinema: of the 2000 cinemas in Germany in 1914, 350 were in Berlin. In 1910 a contemporary went so far as to say that Hamburg, Frankfurt, Leipzig, Brussels, Dresden, Cologne, Breslau, and even Vienna, had been turned overnight into suburbs of Berlin. This was hardly true, however, for Vienna at the turn of the century was a city with a uniquely rich and exciting cultural life. There German classical traditions were creatively juxtaposed with a modern culture in which scientists and doctors played a part almost as great as artists and authors in steering the imagination in the new directions confirmed in 1900 by Sigmund Freud's *Die Traumdeutung* ('The Interpretation of Dreams'). As the subconscious yielded up its secrets, psychology took on a new meaning and resonance, and the motivation of fictitious characters was no longer synonymous with logical behaviour. In Germany's buoyant capital progress was made and the future beckoned. In the capital of the Austrian Empire, where serious matters were treated light-heartedly and the apparently trivial was taken seriously, even progress was open to question.

The growth of the cities meant that they now exercised cultural functions once the monopoly of princes. This was evident in the size and scale of their museums, art galleries and particularly in their concert halls and theatres: by 1885 Germany had 600 theatres equipped with up-to-date gas and in some cases electric lighting, an innovation hastened by the disastrous fire that destroyed the Ringtheater in Vienna's most prestigious new boulevard, the Ring, in 1881. This pre-1914 building and cultural boom had much to do with the decentralization of taxation: half of the revenues of German cities came from local taxes, a process later reversed under the Weimar Republic (1919–33). Under Wilhelm II (1888–1918) the state was at pains to promote culture as the repository of the national identity, but on specific and constricting terms, as the stringent theatre censorship and the Kaiser's personal interference demonstrated. Yet until the Weimar years the German educated middle classes or *Bildungsbürgertum*, who, by contrast with their counterparts in Britain, the United States or France, exercised relatively little political power, could claim cultural hegemony over the rest of society. The rise and promotion of working-class literature that is also a phenomenon of Wilhelmine Germany was, by contrast with what was to happen during the Weimar Republic, part of a distinctive sub-culture.

The differences between the craft of writing, still in many ways traditional, and production technology which pointed towards the twentieth century, are epitomized by two figures: the

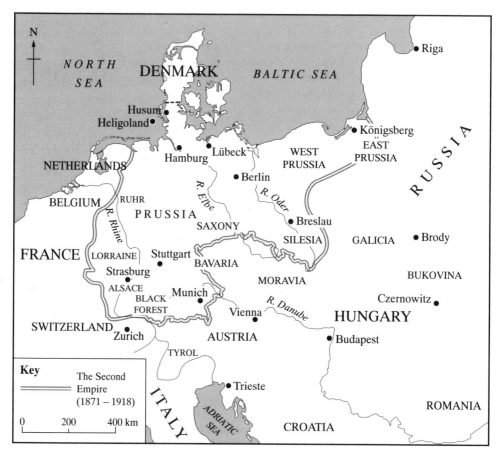

**Map 5**　Literary Germany, 1871–1918: the Second Empire

septuagenarian Emilie Fontane, still copying out her husband's manuscripts in her copperplate hand in the 1890s, for submission to the publisher (including his last novel *Der Stechlin* (1898), which runs to 500 printed pages), and, less than two decades later, Gustav Meyrink dictating his eerie tale *Der Golem* into a dictaphone. By 1900 the writer could see everywhere a burgeoning market for his – and of course now also for her – work. This was evident in the numbers of books now being published and the growing numbers of those who could afford to purchase books and subscribe to journals, and who actually did so. Under 13,000 new books were published in Germany in 1875, but by 1910 the number was over 30,000; furthermore, in the first decade of the new century, the number of copies per edition or print run increased dramatically. In the same time-span journals and magazines proliferated from under 2000 to over 5000, those devoted specifically to literature rising from 27 in 1867 to just under 200 in 1902. Yet it was equally evident that the climate of the literary market had become harsher, and that the number of volumes published was growing more rapidly than the number of authors being published. Their work had become a commodity whose worth was determined by its market value. It had to be tailored to the mass market, and the mass market, the publishers declared, loved some genres and disliked others. Wilhelm Friedrich, the enterprising and generous publisher of less stereotyped writers, pointed out to the poet Liliencron in 1889 that 'from the book trade's perspective even a bad novel is better than the finest collection of novellen', and stated that 'the future lies with the novel: drama and poetry are unsaleable'.

'Who's going to pay?' Bertold Brecht was to ask provocatively in the 1920s: that question was, he said, just as important as 'who's going to read?' Fears that the writer would be prostituted to the public were a constant topic at the turn of the century at a time when to the objective observer of the German literary scene creative talent had rarely been more abundant, more productive and more innovative. Authors were not slow, in view of declining royalties and, in the case of dramatists, of exploitation by theatre agencies, to single out capitalist media entrepreneurs as objects of particular vilification. They had a point. And yet at the same time many now famous writers owed much to individual publishers who acted as generous patrons and influential cultural middlemen. Samuel Fischer (whose son-in-law Bermann Fischer was to rescue the firm of Fischer Verlag and its priceless manuscripts from the Nazis in the 1930s) was the first to make Ibsen and Tolstoy, Dostoevsky and Strindberg widely known in western Europe; he published Thomas Mann's *Buddenbrooks* in 1901, as well as all Mann's subsequent work, and encouraged many women writers including Gabriele Reuter and Clara Viebig. Another Berlin publisher, Kurt Wolff, who was associated with Expressionist writers such as Trakl, Heym, Stadler and Hasenclever, but also with Rilke, Heinrich Mann, Werfel and Meyrink (as well as with Pound and Yeats), declared that it was his policy to publish what the public *ought* to read. Editors played a key role in one of the most innovative areas in German literature in the years just before the First World War, the Expressionist periodical; amongst them was Herwath Walden, editor of *Der Sturm* (1910–32), and Franz Pfemfert, editor of *Die Aktion* (1911–32).

But in the 1890s writers had begun to resort to self-help in order to protect themselves against the arbitrary interventions of government censorship. One such group, which included Samuel Fischer and was headed by Otto Brahm, the critic and theatre director, founded the *Verein Freie Bühne* or 'Free Stage Association' in Berlin. It was a private organization with a small number of active directors, seven of whom were critics; the ordinary members, whose number swelled to 6000, received tickets for a set number of performances of important and controversial new plays each year. This had the advantage that the *Freie Bühne* was not dependent on box-office receipts and as a private organization was not subject to state censorship; as a result Ibsen's *Ghosts* and Hauptmann's *Vor Sonnenaufgang* ('Before sunrise') could be put on in 1889, the *Freie Bühne's* first season, with great success. The critics saw to it that the newspapers took notice: the performances even caught the attention of a nineteen-year-old Dublin student, who spent his summer holidays in 1901 learning German and translating Hauptmann in order to provide the new Irish national theatre, the Abbey, with model modern dramas. His name was James Joyce.

In other ways, too, German and Austrian writers around the turn of the century proved capable of responding as a group to the perceived demands of the growing mass market. Just as the pursuit of sectional interests was as much a feature of political, economic and social life during the reign of Wilhelm II as it was of the last three decades of the reign of Franz-Joseph I (1848–1916), transforming political parties into pressure groups and leading to the ever-greater cartelization and syndicalization of industry and labour, so, too, in the first decade of the twentieth century, writers founded their own professional organizations and developed new initiatives that reflected the growing bureaucratization, professionalization and 'communicative networking' characteristic of modern society. Even lyric poets such as Hofmannsthal and Liliencron proved thoroughly practical in their arguments: verse reproduced in the highly popular (and profitable) anthologies of the day must, they decreed, carry a royalty of 50 pfennigs per line.

Writers now forcefully entered the public sphere in all sorts of other ways; their aim was to construct a counter-culture that would provoke and challenge the prevailing state-approved nationalistic ideology or, in the case of the Expressionists at the end of the period, question the fundamental principles on which German society was founded. A common characteristic of all the very diverse groups and movements subsumed under the general heading of literary modernism was a new relationship to the literary text. That images were to dominate twentieth-century culture was an insight of the German avant-garde from the very outset. If the sixteenth-century German writer could feel that the advances in optics – the invention of the eyeglass and the telescope – had enabled people to see further, clearer and longer, the German artist at the beginning of the twentieth century began to see differently. 'I am learning to see,' declares the artist protagonist in Rilke's novel *Malte Laurids Brigge* in 1910. At one level the massive strides in 'human progress' were making life safer, healthier and materially easier for millions of people who in the last years of the old century and the first years of the new one had gas or electric light installed in their homes, modern sewage systems brought to their streets, and trams and buses to take them on their way, accompanied by a stable currency (the price of a Reclam volume remained the same – 2 *Silbergroschen* – from 1867 to 1917) and the beginnings of a welfare system. Yet writers in the 1880s and 1890s were registering the cost to the human psyche of that progress: the dislocation of centuries-old patterns of rural life and the dehumanizing effects of life in the city.

Though social alienation and atomization formed the essential experience of so much of the work of literary modernism in Germany, its artistic ideas were less likely to be produced in the solitude of the garret or the studio than in the restless noisiness of public places such as cafés and hotels. Thus in Vienna between 1891 and 1897 the Café Griensteidl, where the young Hofmannsthal consorted with Hermann Bahr, Arthur Schnitzler, Richard Beer-Hofmann, Peter Altenberg and other lively minded literary personalities, became synonymous with early Viennese modernism. In Berlin around 1910 the Café des Westens brought together Alfred Döblin, a medical doctor and author of the most famous German big-city novel, *Berlin Alexanderplatz*, George Heym, a pioneer of urban poetry, the graphic artist George Grosz, complete with cane, bowler hat and powdered face, the critic Hiller, the anarchist Mühsam and the pacifist René Schickele, the most gifted Alsatian writer of the period. And in these cafés was to be found another key figure of the epoch: the critic. Critics such as Maximilian Harden and Alfred Kerr in Berlin had their counterparts in Munich's Bohemian Schwabing district alongside Munich's leading writers, such as Thomas Mann and Frank Wedekind, and the emancipated North German aristocrat Franziska zu Reventlow, well known in her day for her unconventional lifestyle. They were also a constituent part of Hans Arp's and Hugo Ball's Dadaist cabaret in Zurich.

## Poetry and the Breakthrough to Modernity

Ernst Bertram's celebrated study *Nietzsche: Versuch einer Mythologie* was published in 1918: the timing was surely fortuitous, yet it coincided with the collapse of the Second German Empire

(1871–1918) whose war aims had appeared to epitomize the bitter aphorism coined by Friedrich Nietzsche at its birth: '*Deutschland, Deutschland über alles* means the end of German philosophy.' Nietzsche was as much a mythological figure for the war generation as he had been for the generation of writers and intellectuals who grew to maturity around the turn of the century. 'We were all of us more or less under his spell,' recalled Hofmannsthal's friend, the otherwise conservatively minded Rudolf Alexander Schröder. Gottfried Benn, who perhaps more than any other twentieth-century German poet was shaped by Nietzsche, used an image favoured by writers as different as Kant and Kleist when he compared Nietzsche's impact on his generation to that of an earthquake. 'If you think about it,' he wrote in a famous essay in 1950, fifty years after Nietzsche's death, 'everything my generation discussed, wrestled with and experienced, had already been expressed and exhaustively formulated by Nietzsche: everything that came afterwards was mere exegesis.'

Nietzsche encapsulates modernity in German literature in its broadest sense. He was one of the many who analysed the sense of cultural crisis which pervaded German literature from the Naturalists in the late 1880s to the late Expressionists in the early 1930s, but he was the most incisive and also the most accessible. Benn called him the greatest master of the German language since Luther, but he was not just a prophet and a magician with words, he was also the poets' philosopher. The reception accorded him was as seminal as it was extraordinarily diverse. At the beginning of the twentieth century his influence was reflected with great immediacy in the vitalism of Richard Dehmel and, later, by the Expressionists and Heinrich Mann; it also became palpable in the work of Heinrich's brother Thomas, making itself tellingly felt in his late novel *Doktor Faustus*. Even Musil, for all his overt distance from the Nietzsche phenomenon, did not escape unscathed; indeed he noted as early as 1902 that Nietzsche was loved by everyone thirsting for new opportunities. That thirst was to become a key concept in Musil's own great novel, *Der Mann ohne Eigenschaften* ('The man without qualities'). But Nietzsche also shaped the modernity of a host of lyric poets such as George, Hofmannsthal and Rilke, where his presence is most clearly felt in the affirmation of life that pervades the late elegies and sonnets.

'Hier liegt Dynamit,' wrote a reviewer of Nietzsche's *Jenseits von Gut und Böse* ('Beyond good and evil') in 1886. To many intellectuals, and particularly to the young of the 1890s and ever since, Nietzsche's notorious declaration that God is dead (the God, that is, of western Jewish and Christian religion) meant liberation from bondage. His forthright destruction of the moral certainties – religion, nation, race, class – which underpinned the élites of the Wilhelmine Empire, was a challenge to Germany in an age which liked to deny its intellectuals their function as critics of society and as its conscience. His subjective metaphysics, his demand that man should be responsible for his own destiny and for the earth on which he lives, had an appeal which has proved even longer-lasting. But the loss of God brought with it an existential loneliness of which Nietzsche's own tragic end in 1900, after collapse and eleven years in a mental home, was a searing example. The poetic forms adopted by poets exploring this loneliness were shaped by their temperaments, personalities, circumstances and their cultural and social origins, which could be very different, as Kafka, Trakl, Rilke and Toller exemplify. Moreover, 'liberation' from God did not mean the abandonment or rejection of the quest for religious meaning, as Rilke's 'angel' in the *Duino Elegies* testifies, and as is borne out by the new 'human religion of love' advocated by Expressionist dramatists such as Toller. Religious symbols pervade the language of early twentieth-century poets far more than that of the generation before: indeed the longing they expressed for *Erlösung* (the term means both 'release', 'rescue' and 'salvation') was to become an essential feature of the modern age and a further reminder of the paradox of Nietzsche's heritage. In the longer term there is a wry but comprehensible irony in the fact that the proud, defiant message of his most widely-read work, *Also sprach Zarathustra* (1883–92), whose lofty cadences with their biblical overtones had inspired Richard Strauss's tone poem in 1896 and Delius's *Mass of Life* in 1909, should later have been used to underpin and justify the National Socialist ideology of the ruthless superman or *Übermensch* – a macho concept with which Nietzsche's thinking seemed superficially to have much in common, but which the lone philosopher-prophet would scarcely have recognized as the fulfilment of his vision of a humanity brave and honest enough to face up to the truth staring modern man in the face. Given the multiple paradoxes associated with Nietzsche, his impact on the mentality of his time, the reactions to him of his contemporaries and, more crucially, of posterity, there is a certain irony in the further paradox that, despite his deliberate exclusion of women from the 'new order' he envisaged for mankind, it was a woman, Lou Andreas-Salomé, who in 1894 provided the first full-length – and sympathetic – study of his work.

The moment at which 'modern' poetry made its first appearance in German has been variously pinpointed, but it certainly took place at the start of Nietzsche's creative lifetime. It has sometimes been identified with the new direction taken by the later poems of the Swiss writer Conrad Ferdinand Meyer (*Gedichte*, 1882), which formed a link between the later Romantics and their contemporaries such as Platen and Mörike in the 1830s, the early poetry of Hofmannsthal, and the Rilke of *Das Buch der Bilder* (1902). But the form-conscious artistry and objectivity of Meyer's poems is not the only or indeed the most obvious characteristic of 'modernity' in lyric poetry. The abandonment of the notion of a worked-out 'subject' in favour of impressionistic verbal images was perhaps an even more telling pointer to twentieth-century developments, and this is what had been taking place in a collection of poems published within a year of Meyer's *Gedichte*, the *Adjutantenritte* ('Rides of the adjutant', 1883) by a former army officer, Detlev von Liliencron. When writing ballads Liliencron is part of a long tradition; but in some of these short lyrics – especially those which express his immediate responses to the enormity of war (he fought and was wounded in the Franco-Prussian War of 1870–1) or to the fleeting memories of loving and dying – we hear something hitherto unheard but something which audibly and visually anticipates the mainstream of poetry to the present day. Liliencron pares poetry down to a minimum. Isolated phrases, single words even, are put together to form patterns which often conceal his unobtrusive use of transitional rhyme. The tension between rhyme and rhythm and between metrical pulse and the figurative implications of images had, it is true, been a constantly recurring feature of German poetry ever since Klopstock and his imitators had adopted classical metres and abandoned rhyme, and others among their contemporaries such as Bürger and the young Goethe had rediscovered the expressive power of folk poetry. Formal and technical issues therefore played a less central part in the emergence of modern German poetry than they did in the poetry of other literatures where the very concept of poetry had been closely associated with one particular level of diction and with specific verse forms, as was the case in France and even in England. In the case of poets using German as their medium the change in the understanding of the means and purposes of lyric poetry which took place towards the end of the nineteenth century therefore concentrated on its subject matter and on the artistic responsibilities of poets towards their readers and the great issues facing a changing world. Thus the writers of the Naturalist movement, which was concerned above all with the nature of society and the influences of environment and heredity, were perfectly able to express themselves in verse, although posterity has tended to subordinate them to the playwrights of the movement and thus restrict our awareness of their true range.

All the major German Naturalist authors wrote poems – and so too did the minor ones. These poems range from the graphic and impressionistic to the visionary and symbolical. But what they have in common is their preoccupation with the present and with the future – utopian or cataclysmic – which awaits it. They saw their task as the elucidation and illustration of the forces and conditions which shape life and make it what it is. One of the masters of the Naturalist lyric was Bruno Wille, whose vivid descriptions of urban life are surpassed only by those of Karl Henckell, whose more confident style comes closer to that of Liliencron, though it lacks Liliencron's self-control and concision. The poems of Arno Holz, the Naturalist movement's leading theorist, now sound closer to those of Heine: he was quick to abandon his efforts to achieve naturalism in poetry (*Das Buch der Zeit*, 1885) in favour of seventeenth-century baroque pastiche (*Dafnis*, 1904). The theoretical essay *Revolution der Lyrik* (1899) put forward another approach: 'inner rhythm' and a 'central axis' were now to be the determinant features of lyric poetry; but it was a revolution that was already being overtaken by the innovations of other writers. Yet *Phantasus* (1898), his self-indulgent collection of poems in extravagantly flamboyant form and language, proclaimed him as one of the main exponents of the *Jugendstil* style which sprang up in antithesis to Naturalism at the turn of the century. By the time its final vast four-volume edition appeared in 1925, it was little more than a reminder of a vanished era.

*Jugendstil* poetry was both a backward turn and a way forward. Its precursors can be identified and its persistent influence is pervasive. Even at the time, the features associated with *Jugendstil* – its combination of youthful exultation, rapt intensity and expansive expression, and its fondness for curvilinear, apparently asymmetrical design – were often shared, though seldom so fully achieved, by the majority of poets writing in Germany and Austria at the turn of the century. Its fusion of foreign impulses such as French symbolism, the English Pre-Raphaelites and European *art nouveau* with traditional German elements such as folksong and fairy-tale motifs, and elements drawn from art and design, such as its obvious delight in eighteenth-century rococo, caught the mood of the cultured classes wherever German was spoken and affected their lifestyle profoundly. This popularity is reflected in the work of poets who were once household names but are now virtually forgotten: an example is Cäsar Flaischlen, whose collection of prose poems *Von Alltag und Sonne* ('Everyday life and sun', 1898) quickly became one of the most loved and frequently reprinted works of contemporary literature during the first decades of the twentieth century. Most of the themes and hallmarks of *Jugendstil* are present here, and many of them were also to surface in the poetry of more important writers: the tension between the seasons: the burgeoning promise of spring ripening into the glowing fullness of summer, summer merging into mellow autumn as winter's shadows gather; such 'natural' imagery cannot escape figurative implications as youthful affirmation of life in the present contends with nostalgic longing for past happiness and presentiments of age and death. Such images, a central element of the 'new' poetry of the turn of the century, are echoed in the sinuous lines of *Jugendstil* architecture seen at its best in the ornamental façades of bourgeois houses and public buildings of the pre-1914 era. They were images which it took from the Romantic German tradition and handed on to many twentieth-century German poets who, for instance, were to make the cult of autumn into a central theme of modern German poetry: Hermann Hesse is just one of many examples. However, as the twentieth century opened, the minor key too easily associated with lyric poetry was frequently drowned by the exuberance of 'inner rhythm' and by a more confident-looking imagery which found its central symbol in the sun. German poets had often tended ever since the baroque and the 'Göttingen

*Hainbund*' to prefer the melancholy of dusk, night-time and moonlight. Now a change of mood occurred, yet continuity was assured. Another pervasive feature of *Jugendstil* art and design is its fascination with plants and vegetation and especially with roses, an age-old image of passion, beauty and transience which recurs time and again in German poetry of this period and which also frequently appears in other genres such as Hermann Sudermann's set of masterly yet dated one-act plays entitled *Rosen* (1907).

## Rilke and George

*Die Weise von Liebe und Tod des Cornets Christoph Rilke* ('How the cornet Christoph Rilke loved and met his death', first published in Prague in 1904) opened the series of slim, finely produced books launched in 1912 by the Insel Verlag under the title 'Insel-Bücherei', which quickly became the quintessence of cultured taste amongst readers of German for the whole century. With it Rainer Maria Rilke made his name and established his reputation as a new voice to be reckoned with. Love and death are recurrent themes in Rilke's breathless account of a young soldier's adventures in the seventeenth century and of his first experience of love. Within a year *Das Stunden-Buch* also appeared, a collection of poems purporting to have been written by a monk which make their way through the pilgrimage of life to poverty, self-abnegation and death. Rilke was to spend the remainder of his life (he died in 1926) extending and developing these themes into a philosophy of life, while at the same time intently exploring new ways of giving expression to a modern sensibility – his own. Central to this is his emphatic reverence for art in relation to life, a topos which owes much to a German Romantic tradition going back to the short-lived but influential writer Wilhelm Heinrich Wackenroder a century before him, and which also deeply influenced the artistic life philosophy of Rilke's contemporary Thomas Mann. The two volumes of *Neue Gedichte* of 1907–8 confirmed Rilke as a creator of the tangible in poetry. Like Conrad Ferdinand Meyer before him, he describes, but in doing so sets out to grasp, the very essence of the signified in words and phrases of maximum precision: 'Römische Fontäne' ('Roman fountain'), a sonnet of 1906, is a famous example. As in Meyer's poem 'Der römische Brunnen', form and content merge. What on the surface seems solely to be a description of an overflowing fountain is also, more subtly yet translucently, an image of the poem itself, whose lines, like the fountain's water, flow over from one into the next.

Rilke's *Das Marienleben* (1913), a sequence of fifteen poems about the Virgin Mary, are his period's semi-secularized contribution to the tradition of German religious and mystical poetry, and reveal how his emergent perception of life was permeated by his Austrian Christian inheritance, despite his more overt allegiance to Greek paganism and German classicism. The titles of his two greatest collections clearly reflect the classical inspiration of his later poetry. In the elegies which he began to write at the castle of Duino on the Dalmatian coast in 1912 (but did not publish until 1923) he uses the appropriate elegiac form to celebrate the transience of life, the inevitability of death, and the subtle ways in which, through acceptance and artistic sensitivity, we can cope with them. In the *Sonette an Orpheus* (1923), a collection addressed to the mythical figure of Orpheus and with clear reminiscences of Goethe, consisting of two linked cycles of 26 and 29 sonnets, he reverts to variations on the Renaissance form of the sonnet in order to proclaim in enigmatic but haunting words the message of the rebirth of life through art and poetry.

During the first decades of the twentieth century, the cult of Stefan George appealed to an even greater following. The George circle included many writers and thinkers who were influential at the time, and the messages that went out from his poetry and from the poet himself were ones of renewal. *Der Teppich des Lebens* ('The carpet of life') and *Die Lieder von Traum und Tod* ('Songs of dream and death', 1899), with their suggestive titles, laid the foundations for the revival of civilization which George envisaged and set in train in later works such as *Der Stern des Bundes* ('The star of the covenant', 1914) and *Das neue Reich* ('The new kingdom', 1928). They illustrate George's conception of the poet's role as priest and prophet, and the reluctance to appeal to a wider public which is visibly evident in their typographical appearance, in which refined graphic art combined with a disdain for the German uses of capital letters for nouns and of commas to separate clauses. Beneath this surface appearance his poetry has features in common with some of his contemporaries in other countries such as Robert Bridges, whose concern for the spiritual needs of the age George shared. Yet his conception of poetry was unashamedly patriotic and German in the senses which the term had come to have in the years which led up to the 1914–18 war. His emphasis on German vigour and manliness coexisted, often uncomfortably, with his equally characteristic effete *fin-de-siècle* mannerisms. Like the recurrent themes of his poetry, these dichotomies reveal the many connections there are between the culture of the Wilhelminian period and the personal and cultural values promoted in Nazi Germany. Stefan George died in December 1933 in Switzerland: he had left Germany soon after the party which saw him as its prophet had come to power.

## Other Poets of the Turn of the Century

George and Rilke seem in retrospect to have dominated the poetry of Germany in the period between 1890 and 1933. But they were in fact surrounded by remarkable contemporaries who make this period into one of the golden ages of German poetry, comparable with the *Sturm und Drang* and early Goethe. Alfred Mombert and Theodor Däubler represented the cosmic aspirations of the period: Mombert made his way from *Tag und Nacht* (1894) to the grandiose, almost neo-Byronic broodings of his dramatic trilogy *Aeon* (1907–11), while Däubler worked steadily on *Das Nordlicht* (1910), a loosely constructed poem of epic proportions which proclaimed his subjective philosophy of cosmic dynamism. The *Attische Sonette* (1924), which Däubler wrote in the sun-drenched Greek landscape of Attica and published a year after Rilke's *Sonette an Orpheus*, are a late example of the sun-cult of the *Jugendstil* period, which D. H. Lawrence was exalting in his poems and later novels. Orientalism was also a passing fashion, seen at its best in the work of Max Dauthendey, whose *Die acht Gesichter am Biwasee* ('The eight visions by Lake Biwa', 1911), a collection of well-told tales set in Japan, proved immensely popular with German readers, for whom he represented something of an amalgam of R. L. Stevenson and Gauguin. And if German poets exulted in degrees of self-indulgence not experienced since, there was also a strong vein of parody and pastiche in the literary make-up of the period to preserve a sense of proportion. Amongst the finest exponents of this was Otto Julius Bierbaum, author of *Prinz Kuckuck* (1907), the story of a would-be superman who finds himself without the stamina and strength to sustain this dynamic Nietzschean role.

For Alfred Soergel, the author of *Dichtung und Dichter der Zeit* (first edition 1911), that impressive survey of what for him was contemporary literature, the greatest living German poet since the death of Liliencron in 1909 was unquestionably Richard Dehmel. It was a view with which many contemporaries agreed. Dehmel's equation of art with love, both of which widen human awareness by overcoming the antinomy between self-consciousness and loss of self, was symptomatic of his 'vitalism' and of his rejection of both aestheticism and asceticism in favour of a positive philosophy of life. His second collection *Aber die Liebe* (1893) suggests his priorities in its title, which leaves it to his reader to add 'is the greatest of these', greater, that is, than faith or hope. His range as an analyst of love in many moods was great, but Dehmel was no mindless love-poet: his respect for Nietzsche saw to that. It was above all his ability to combine his own passionate intensity with philosophical ruminations on the challenges facing the emancipated people who constituted his readership that encouraged them to prize his verse so highly as the twentieth century opened. Yet today, a century on, his voice has sunk into a puzzling obscurity, unlike those of Rimbaud, D'Annunzio, Whitman and Yeats, with each of whom, on the surface, he has something in common.

## Theatre in the Second Reich and the Impact of Naturalism

In 1889 German drama regained the momentum it had lost with the death of Hebbel in 1863. The first performance of Gerhart Hauptmann's social drama *Vor Sonnenaufgang* ('Before sunrise') on 20 October 1889 had often been credited with the sudden change in direction which German dramatic literature now took. But that performance took place before a select audience at a closed matinée organized by the newly founded Berlin free stage society (*Verein Freie Bühne*), a group formed by the progressive theatre director Otto Brahm and his associates to circumvent official censorship by staging private productions in imitation of the famous *Théâtre libre* in Paris: the London Stage Society was founded with similar aims in 1899. These organizations were symptomatic of a wish to bring about change in the theatre, which was the chief source of public entertainment before the cinema began to compete with it a decade later. Their aim was to perform controversial foreign plays, like those of the Norwegian dramatist Henrik Ibsen, and to promote new work even at the risk of offending against decency and the moral and aesthetic susceptibilities of comfortable middle-class society – the group from which late nineteenth-century audiences were mainly drawn. In its aims and methods, the *Freie Bühne* in Berlin was part of a European movement closely identified with the ultra-realistic art promoted by the Naturalist painters and writers. But there the similarity ends. This was because the development of German drama had differed so greatly from that of France or England and the United States. Schiller, Goethe and Hebbel, Germany's classics, were all relatively modern: apart from Shakespeare in the century-old translation by August Wilhelm von Schlegel and Ludwig Tieck, the German serious theatre repertoire consisted almost entirely of plays written within the previous 130 years, and of lighter, shallower entertainment mostly written by foreign playwrights and their German and Austrian imitators.

In Berlin in the late 1880s it seemed that the great German tradition was quite safe in the hands of Ernst von Wildenbruch, the dramatist who had dominated the serious German stage from the moment in 1881 when his historical drama *Die Karolinger* ('The Carolingians') was staged by the court theatre at Meiningen, the provincial company ably run by the theatre-loving Prince Georg of Meiningen, which between 1874 and 1890 became the leading exponent of an 'authentically' historical approach to staging and acting both in Germany and in most of Europe's theatrical capitals. The period was one which had a high regard for historicism, and Wildenbruch's dramas suited it ideally. The new German Empire encouraged a monumental style in all the arts, which reflected the achievement of a unified national state under Prussia's leadership in 1871, and this historical destiny was the overt or hidden agenda of Wildenbruch's patriotic dramas: like Shakespeare's *Henry V* they demonstrated the potential of historical plays in blank verse to convey the inevitability of historical evolution, and audiences in Berlin, the new imperial capital, responded to them with enthusiasm. Such drama was bound to date. Germany's defeat in the First World War put an end to Wildenbruch's claim to be regarded as a major figure in Germany's theatrical and literary history, though not to the intrinsic interest of his work as an artistic response to the demands of public taste and an exercise in the creation of national stereotypes.

The two contradictory concepts of modern serious drama collided in 1888–9. In 1888 Wildenbruch scored his greatest triumph with *Die Quitzows*, a patriotic verse drama in which the first Hohenzollern ruler of Brandenburg-Prussia destroys the power of the noble family which had opposed his accession. Set in the late Middle Ages, the play's Shakespearean parallels with *Richard II* and *Richard III* guaranteed its lofty artistic purpose, while its theme of national destiny reinforced his status as the 'official' dramatist of the new German Empire by drawing clear connections between Germany's destiny and that of the Hohenzollerns, a family to which Wildenbruch was personally related. By the end of 1890 *Die Quitzows* had achieved a hundred performances: but in the meantime, on 20 October 1889, the *Freie Bühne* had premièred Hauptmann's *Vor Sonnenaufgang* and set in motion a development which soon overtook Wildenbruch's success. Hauptmann's first (unpublished) play had been a verse drama on a national theme, the defeat of the Romans by the Germans under Hermann, cast in the Wildenbruch mould. But Hauptmann was a man of the people, without Wildenbruch's establishment connections, and his new play set out to reveal to theatre-going audiences a very different aspect of the new Germany: the appalling conditions of exploitation, degradation and disease prevalent in a country which was beginning to see itself as the dynamic leader of the modern world. *Vor Sonnenaufgang* opens as a young Berlin economist, Alfred Loth, arrives in a remote Silesian village in order to write a fact-finding report on the effects of industrial development on an agrarian community. As he discovers more about his hosts, he finds himself becoming personally involved in the facts he is supposed to be studying objectively. The Krause family are peasants who have become rich overnight because coal deposits have been found under their land. The obvious parallels here were not with Shakespeare but with Ibsen, whose social dramas were exciting both controversy and admiration for their superbly crafted exposure of the ugly realities behind the smug façade of contemporary late-nineteenth-century life. The revelation of the local doctor that the Krauses are degenerate alcoholics leads Loth, who is a non-drinker on principle, to get out and to abandon Helene Krause, the girl he has come to love, to the fate which her environment and her genes have destined her, and from which she saves herself by suicide. The complex motivation of Loth's action gave the play a psychological depth Wildenbruch's dramas lack, and set it apart from the general run of plays on social themes which were being written at the time in other countries, with the exception of those by Ibsen. Loth sees himself as a modern man wedded to scientifically based views about society, industry, health and hygiene, and his decision to abandon Helene was hailed by most of Hauptmann's educated young contemporaries as an act of heroic integrity. But closer interpretations of the play bring out its deeper and darker implications, and Hauptmann himself lived to see the friend on whom he had modelled Alfred Loth turn into one of National Socialism's leading authorities on racial hygiene.

*Vor Sonnenaufgang* and *Die Quitzows* clearly illustrate the dichotomy between the two views of the form and purpose of drama in Germany in the late 1880s. The contrasts between them are profound, yet between them they mark the return of drama to the centre of literary attention. The Naturalist plays which rapidly appeared after *Vor Sonnenaufgang* illustrate the many different ways in which the aims of the new movement could be interpreted. They all share its rejection of literary and theatrical speech in favour of natural, colloquial language, including slang and, where appropriate (as in plays set in regional areas), dialect, and they also share its concentration on the social problems and living conditions of contemporary life, aspects reflected in the Naturalist emphasis on the importance of presenting an authentic 'slice of life' in an accurately described milieu. As Berlin was now the main centre of literary and theatrical activity, many plays are set there. Some, such as *Die Familie Selicke* (1890), written in collaboration by Arno Holz and Johannes Schlaf, and Gerhart Hauptmann's exuberant Naturalist comedy *Der Biberpelz* ('The beaver coat', 1893), are set in squalid urban areas in and around the city, as is his later, more serious play, *Die Ratten* (1911), which juxtaposes theatricality and real-life drama in its virtuoso handling of simultaneous plots. Other plays take their audiences into the more familiar territory of a middle-class milieu, a fine example being *Einsame Menschen* ('Lonely people', 1891), Hauptmann's sensitive study of existential loneliness involving three young people, a research scientist, his meek wife and an ambitious young woman intent on studying medicine. Hermann Sudermann's more conventional social drama *Die Ehre* ('Honour'), also premièred in 1889, exploits a characteristic Berlin feature: the more respectable house in front, facing the street, and the humbler house concealed in the courtyard behind it, the home of humbler folk. Not all Naturalist dramas are Berlin dramas, however. The countryside could also be used as the milieu for a realistic portrayal of contemporary life; Hauptmann's *Rose Bernd* (1903) shows that this involved shedding the 'picturesque' image country life had acquired during the age of Poetic Realism in the mid-nineteenth century.

## Varieties of Naturalism

The extremes encompassed by German Naturalist drama are exemplified in the work of Holz and Sudermann. In his theoretical writing Holz had championed an extreme kind of realism, which he called 'logically consistent Naturalism' (*konsequenter Naturalismus*) because it was its aim to convey total authenticity in every respect, even if this meant the abandonment of the established dramatic conventions. This he set out to achieve in *Die Familie Selicke*, a play which redefined traditional notions of dramatic structure and timing by presenting a near-photographic account of a day in the life of a deprived family in a Berlin tenement. No play of the period comes closer to cinema, but it was a technique which few writers could or wished to emulate. Sudermann was much less innovative, but he had a remarkable flair for late nineteenth-century theatrical techniques and how to combine them with the preoccupations of Naturalism, such as the influence of environment and social pressure on the lives of individuals. This more conciliatory approach worked in the theatre, and his plays did much to make Naturalism arouse applause as well as disapproval. *Heimat* ('Home') touched on some very awkward problems, but it was a well-made play aimed at its audiences and it provided a leading role in which actresses could star; under its alternative name, *Magda*, it soon achieved something which had eluded German playwrights for half a century: international acclaim. The role of Magda, the erring daughter of a retired army officer who returns to her provincial home town as a fêted opera singer, but one with what in those days was called 'a past', was soon taken up by actresses like Sarah Bernhardt, Eleonora Duse, Mrs Patrick Campbell and Helena Modjeska, and as a result German drama was once again world theatre. Like the play itself, the central conflict of *Magda* is a clever compromise between tradition and modernity. Conflicts between fathers and children had been a favourite source of dramatic tension ever since Ferdinand fell out with his father in Schiller's *Kabale und Liebe* ('Intrigue and love') in 1784; by making Magda's return spark off a conflict of wills and attitudes between herself and her father, Sudermann adroitly combines the German theme of paternal authority with the newer issue of a woman's right to come of age and lead her own life.

Sudermann succeeded better than most post-Ibsen dramatists in making theatrically effective drama out of such an issue, but none managed better to give it emotional subtlety and depth than Elsa Bernstein, the most gifted woman dramatist of the Naturalist period. Her play *Dämmerung* ('Twilight'), written under her alias, 'Ernst Rosmer' in open allusion to Ibsen's *Rosmersholm*, was staged by the Berlin *Freie Bühne* in March 1893. It provides two female lead roles, one a young woman threatened with blindness, the other the recently qualified eye specialist who, in diagnosing the problem, discovers that it is directly connected with the syphilis from which her patient's father once suffered. The disease had lurked in the shadows of Ibsen's *Ghosts* (1881), a controversial play which made a crucial contribution to the emergence of the new type of social drama favoured by the Naturalist movement: here it is brought out into the open and named without embarrassment by a woman doctor, the representative of the new woman of the next century.

The sharp concentration on contemporary German life gave the plays of the Naturalist movement a quality German drama had not had since Hebbel's *Maria Magdalene* and Otto Ludwig's *Der Erbförster* ('The hereditary forester') in the 1840s and which was reinforced by their use of a wider range of spoken registers than German drama had ever used before. The theoretical and polemical writing which underpinned them – essays, newspaper articles, and so on – also stressed that the new realism was inspired by specifically German considerations and a return to 'German' notions of simplicity and frankness which were as reminiscent of the *Sturm und Drang* as they were of the many foreign critics and writers who had already brought Naturalism to the centre of debate, and the 'new' disciplines, such as sociology, economics, psychiatric medicine, which provided its intellectual base. The concepts of environment, heredity and the pressure of the moment, which had been advanced by the French social historian Hippolyte Taine earlier in the century, were common currency by the 1890s amongst the German Naturalist generation of intellectuals and writers, but the vigour with which their best work explored them and the social idealism which underlies it is more directly attributable to the fact that they were the first generation to have been educated and to come of age in the Second Reich. Their victory over Wildenbruchian national historicism was the victory of the young over the middle-aged rather than of disenchantment over patriotic enthusiasm, but there was a critical tone to it which could not be overlooked. They aroused the hostility of the establishment as a result, and liked to call themselves *Jüngstdeutsche* ('most modern Germans') in allusion to the *Jungdeutschland* movement of the 1840s. It was precisely to that period of political and social unrest that Hauptmann turned in his most famous Naturalist play, *Die Weber* ('The weavers').

The first performance of *Die Weber* by the *Freie Bühne* in February 1893 marked the high point of German Naturalism, and Hauptmann's masterly handling of the techniques and preoccupations of the movement also make it the supreme embodiment of the Naturalist aesthetic. The fact-finding research which its author, himself the grandson of a poor weaver, put into his play recreates the 'feel' of the mid-1840s in a cloth-making community in the

Riesengebirge area of Silesia, while the meticulous sociolinguistic detail of its dialogue (a quality even more audible in Hauptmann's first version in Silesian dialect) guarantees its sense of authenticity: the fluid action, subtle changes of tempo and sporadic upwellings of tension endow it with the unpredictability of life itself. Yet by going back half a century, aware perhaps that the up-to-date dates very rapidly, Hauptmann was effecting a fundamental shift away from Naturalism's obsessive focus on contemporary issues, while at the same time moving dangerously towards a critique of society by dramatizing a breakdown of industrial relations. *Die Weber* reveals the effects of the lowering of prices for cottage-manufactured cotton cloth forced on German producers by the mass mechanization of the Lancashire cotton industry, and in it he was coming uncomfortably close to writing drama which carried an unmistakably topical political message. Private performances in Berlin and Paris aroused enthusiasm among the avant-garde, but the first public performance at the Deutsches Theater in Berlin under Otto Brahm on 25 September 1894 led to the boycott of its royal box by Emperor Wilhelm II, and to protracted court cases. Translated into many languages and filmed in 1927, *Die Weber* became something of a classic text for progressive readers and theatre-goers and one of the main precursors of twentieth-century socialist realism. Its ending as a chance bullet hits Old Hilse, the weaver least involved in the Luddite uprising and its suppression which form the double climax of the drama, may be criticized for being an anticlimax or a political cop-out, yet its suggestive power restored the element of chance or fatality to a type of literature which was constantly in danger of being written to a 'scientific' formula in order to make a sociological point.

## The Drama of *fin-de-siècle* Neo-Romanticism

The first half of the 1890s marked the heyday of German Naturalism; the second half saw theatre audiences turn with relief to a new kind of drama that was Naturalism's antithesis in every way. Hauptmann had anticipated this trend in 1893 by writing *Hanneles Himmelfahrt* ('Hannele goes to heaven'), a play which begins in the uncompromisingly naturalistic setting of a poor-house in Silesia, but which ends as the delirious dreams of a dying girl come alive, are acted out on stage, and carry the drama away from externals such as the girl's environment to the less tangible but ultimately more significant realities of her subconscious emotional life which her dreams and visions express. Hannele's image of heaven as she dies is childishly sentimental: but the point is made that she has one. Thus the interrelated domains of dream and transience, long absent from the German stage, returned to enthral theatre audiences. One year later, the first and artistically the most successful realization of neo-Romanticism in the theatre came from Elsa Bernstein, whose sensitive play, *Dämmerung*, had made such an outstanding contribution to the drama of Naturalism.

Bernstein's 'German fairy tale' *Königskinder* ('The prince and his princess'), first published in 1894, transported its readers and spectators to a magic forest where a prince falls in love with a goosegirl. The young dreamer and the unspoilt child of Nature present themselves to the citizens of a town as its ideal rulers: but adult realism prevails, and they are chased away and left to die in the cold forest. Their corpses are found by the town's children and its musician, for only artists and children still have the imagination and sensitivity to appreciate what modern society dismisses as irrelevant make-believe and fairy tale. Bernstein's symbolical fairy-tale play was published in 1894 and first performed in 1897. In the meantime Hauptmann had switched allegiance by writing a verse fairy-tale drama of his own, called *Die versunkene Glocke* ('The Sunken Bell', 1896). Here the central character is himself an artist, but one unable to complete his masterpiece until he has fallen in love with the elfin Rautendelein, the incarnation of nature and the antithesis of the loyal wife who shares his life in the valley below. Here, too, the neo-Romantic message carries the seeds of its own destruction. Heinrich, torn between his two alternatives, loses the bell that would have rung out his new message to all mankind. When it had finally sunk beneath the surface of the lake, the play's audiences emerged into Berlin's streets busy with the hubbub of modern life. The theatre had become a means of escape. Escapist fairy-tale drama proved popular and maintained its hold until well into the twentieth century with once well-known plays such as *Tantris der Narr* ('Tantris the fool', 1907), a dramatization of an episode in the Tristan and Isolde story by Ernst Hardt, and Karl Gustav Vollmoeller's *Mirakel* ('The Miracle'), first performed to great acclaim in London in 1911 and in Berlin in 1912 in a production by Max Reinhardt, the famous theatre producer. Such drama was closely associated with the plays of the Belgian poet and dramatist Maurice Maeterlinck, such as *Pelléas et Mélisande* (1892), which were regularly translated from French into German; yet strangely enough German writers never quite managed to transfer their enigmatic, understated quality to the German stage.

## Drama in Austria at the Turn of the Century

Where the more impressionistic and symbolist facets of the new Romanticism did produce drama of high poetic quality was in Vienna, where the young Hugo von Hofmannsthal found his own voice in an eclectic artistic and literary scene with short evocative plays such as *Der Tor und der Tod* ('The fool and death', 1894), a lyric-dramatic monologue spoken by Claudio, a young nobleman, who realizes as Death confronts him that he has never really lived, and who in so doing comes fleetingly to life as he passes away. Here precocious disenchantment finds expression in the delicate cadences of the language and in the associative symbolism of its images. Poetry had found its way back on to the German stage.

Vienna's contribution to the revival of dramatic literature at the turn of the century was second only to that of Berlin. Its Hofburgtheater, which had become almost synonymous with serious drama in the German-speaking world during the nineteenth century, was rebuilt in 1888 to hold an audience of over 1600, but it was at its other theatres, notably the Stadttheater (founded in 1872) and the Deutsches Volkstheater (built in 1889), that innovations began to take place. Here the plays of Ludwig Anzengruber, Austria's most original dramatist between 1870 and 1890, were staged alongside those of Ibsen, whose much wider and more influential appeal was to eclipse him. The parallel such productions offered contemporary audiences highlighted the contrasts between the sort of social drama which the Naturalist school developed and a more indigenous kind of realism which carried the themes and subject matter of the mid-nineteenth-century peasant novel on to the stage in a recognizably Austrian setting. *Der Pfarrer von Kirchfeld* ('The parish priest of Kirchfeld') made Anzengruber's name when it was premièred in Vienna in 1871 by daringly concentrating on topical tensions in the Roman Catholic Church in Austria and doing so in Austrian dialect. His ability to dramatize crises of personal and public conscience in a down-to-earth way is seen at its best in two plays which by comparison with Ibsen were straightforward and unintellectual but certainly no less hard-hitting: *Der Meineidbauer* ('The perjured farmer', 1871), a peasant tragedy of great imaginative power, and *Das vierte Gebot* ('The fourth commandment', 1878), set in Vienna itself, in which realism and didacticism combine to generate dramatic tension from the juxtaposition of three simultaneous plots each involving the treatment meted out by three sets of parents to their adolescent children. Comic incident and dark tragedy interact in this dramatic realization of the social and psychological implications of the Commandment 'Honour thy father and thy mother'. The play's originality is too easily overlooked if it is simply seen as a minor work in which the themes of Hebbel's *Maria Magdalene* and the traditions of Nestroy's Viennese comedies merge in anticipation of later treatments of parent–child relationships such as Frank Wedekind's *Frühlings Erwachen* ('Spring's awakening', 1891) and Max Halbe's *Jugend* ('Youth', 1893). Anzengruber's remarkable achievements were doomed to be underrated because their unashamed regionalism and use of dialect cut them off from the mainstream of German drama. They were also soon to be overshadowed by the work of the more polished writer whose plays and stories have come to personify pre-1914 Vienna: Arthur Schnitzler.

Schnitzler 'arrived' as a playwright in 1895 when his 3-act play *Liebelei* ('Dalliance') opened at the Burgtheater and was taken up by the Deutsches Theater in Berlin: indeed the bitter-sweet Viennese plays with which his name is most closely associated achieved their high standing thanks in no small measure to Otto Brahm's Berlin productions. *Liebelei* presents the then stereotypical relationship between an upper-class young man and a girl who is his social inferior. Fritz inspires in Christine the great love of her life just as, maybe, she does in him: for, as with Schnitzler's Russian near-contemporary Chekhov, it is always possible to see alternative interpretations of characters and plots which seem to capture the feel of life being lived rather than of a dramatic plan unfolding. This quality is shared by all Schnitzler's finest full-length plays, notably *Der einsame Weg* ('The lonely way', 1904) and *Das weite Land* ('The distant country', 1912), in both of which the subtle unforeseeable paths of self-discovery bring characters together in ways which have the potential for tragedy or, sometimes, for farce. It is a quality which is just as evident in the other dramatic form in which Schnitzler, a great short-story teller, excelled: the one-act play or, in the case of *Anatol* and *Reigen*, the sequence of one-acters or cycle of self-contained scenes which turned into an interesting new concept of drama. What distinguishes Schnitzler's central characters (except the shallow Anatol) is their tendency to step beyond the confines of their social and literary context and, in doing so, to carry their audiences into new dimensions of experience, of which freedom or death – or a combination of both – are the most striking and frequent. In *Liebelei*, a sweet Viennese girl turns out to have unexpected emotional depth beyond the comprehension of those around her; in *Der einsame Weg* one character in a close-knit and cultured Viennese set realizes that he must go it alone. In his ability through dialogue and stage movements to suggest the tensions and emotions under the surface of people living an apparently ordered life in an apparently stable society Schnitzler comes closer to Chekhov than to his main contemporaries in Germany, even though the attitudes and social behaviour of his characters, their mix of sentimentality and fatalism, their politeness and the streak of cruelty in them are often diagnosed as quintessentially Austrian. The one-acters and cyclical dramas, for their part, turn on the underlying image of life as a roundabout or round dance, its unexpected twists and turns ironically underlying its remorselessly repetitive monotony as, for example, Anatol flirts with one woman after another without ever achieving a meaningful relationship, or the multiple characters in *Reigen* (written in 1896 but not released for public performance until 1920 in Berlin and 1921 in Vienna) pair off, each with the next, always hopeful, ever unsatisfied, and seldom without their ulterior motives. Like Wedekind's *Lulu* plays, *Reigen* shocked, and its chequered production history and clashes with official and unofficial censorship ensured its continuing relevance throughout the twentieth century.

The full-length Schnitzler plays are now most appreciated for their sensitive depiction of life in the Austro–Hungarian capital on the eve of the Habsburg Empire's collapse, and this theme is also central to *Der grüne Kakadu* ('The green cockatoo', 1899), his most theatrically adventurous play. The year is 1789, the scene Paris: a troupe of out-of-work actors enact a revolution in the Green Cockatoo bistro as a real revolution erupts outside. Which is the reality: the performance or the historical event? Where does make-believe begin and reality end? These are the questions which this *tour-de-force* of theatrical dexterity raises and answers in a way that obliquely brings to the surface the subconscious anxieties of Vienna's psychologically aware cultured classes as the nineteenth century drew to a close. Schnitzler's last major play, *Professor Bernhardi* (1912), was banned in Austria and first performed in Berlin. Based on Schnitzler's personal experience of anti-Semitism as a young doctor in Vienna in the 1880s, it opens up vistas of things yet to come as a distinguished Jewish consultant in a Vienna hospital is brought down by his colleagues in a conspiracy of vested interests ranging from Roman Catholic bigotry and corrupt local politics to personal envy and resentment. In the light of events after his death in 1931, Schnitzler's carefully crafted evocation of the mood of Vienna in his play of 1912 revealed its deeper implications: it was the city to which Adolf Hitler, too, had come in 1908. In 1913 he left it to become a German politician, having been turned down by the Vienna Academy of Art.

## The Theatre of Wedekind

Frank Wedekind was two years younger than Hauptmann and Schnitzler, but in many ways he is a playwright of a later age. They brought the drama of their period to its highest perfection and their plays, whether naturalistic or neo-Romantic, are almost always based on the assumption that they are presenting a 'reality' to their audiences. But for Wedekind drama is always first and foremost theatre: it is play-acting and therefore by definition 'unreal'. For that very reason it is able to generate a surrealistic and satirical force which transcends realism and romanticism. Wedekind's plays gave their audiences new insights into the mechanisms of human motivation and behaviour by holding human beings up like puppets and performing animals for all to see. They also gave censors a headache because instead of criticizing public figures and obvious abuses they questioned the very premises on which contemporary society and its much-vaunted values were based. He began by addressing that vital stage in the life of human beings as social animals: adolescence. His first major play, *Frühlings Erwachen* ('Spring's awakening'), published in 1891 and first performed in 1906 in Berlin, tries hard to be realistic, but even more than Anzengruber's *Das vierte Gebot*, its most effective moments verge on the grotesque, macabre and surreal, for such modes can alone bring out the vital facets of existence. His drama of growing up highlights the social, physical and emotional rigours of the rite of passage to the adult world which few adult writers had ever taken seriously before.

That adult world in turn became the subject of his two closely linked 'Lulu' plays, *Erdgeist* ('Earth spirit') and *Die Büchse der Pandora* ('Pandora's box'). These carried audiences – when they were allowed to see them – into a world which Wedekind hoped they would recognize as having some connection with their own, however much it baffled and offended them. His treatment of the rise and fall of a beautiful woman in a male-dominated world controlled by the values of the marketplace rejects the restrictive earnestness and verisimilitude of realist drama, and for this reason seems more accessible, but just as relevant, to audiences in the later twentieth century whose notions of tragic drama have been tempered or deflated by the theatres of cruelty, silence and the absurd. *Der Marquis von Keith*, written in 1900, conjures up a swindler and confidence trickster who persuades the citizens of Munich to part with large sums of money, but whose unmasking leads neither to exposure, punishment nor suicide. The twentieth-century world the play introduces is as fraudulent as the rogue trickster himself and just as immoral.

Wedekind died just before the defeat of Germany and Austria in 1918. He did not live to see the Weimar Republic and the brave new world of the 1920s for which his plays had helped to set the tone. In broader context, however, his work is the vital link between Naturalism's precursors such as Grabbe and Büchner and the exponents of the new tradition of theatre. Brecht and Dürrenmatt were both to learn much from his example.

## Prose Fiction in the Late Nineteenth Century

In retrospect it is obvious that a change occurred in German literature in or around 1880. The major prose writers of the mid-nineteenth century were reaching the ends of their careers, and who was to take their place? The Prussian Fontane, born in 1819, the Swiss Conrad Ferdinand Meyer, born in 1825, the Austrian Ferdinand von Saar, born in 1833, or a much younger writer? Storm died in 1888, Keller in 1890, but some of their younger contemporaries continued to write well into the early years of the twentieth century: in 1910 their friend Paul Heyse became the first German poet to receive a Nobel Prize, and the ever-productive Friedrich Spielhagen died a year later. But there was a growing sense among the intelligentsia that the ample, leisurely form of the nineteenth-century novel was nearing exhaustion and that the novelle had reached a degree of contrivance and artificiality that prevented it from genuinely reflecting the realities of life. What could be put in the place of the two genres that German prose writers had favoured for half a century?

For the first time since the mid-eighteenth century, Germany began to look beyond itself for literary models; this is shown by the extraordinary spate of translations which now began to sweep the German book market. Soon all the major modern literature of Scandinavia, Russia, France and England was available in translation in German bookshops, and writers such as Ibsen, Zola and Dostoevsky were fast becoming more relevant to modern readers than home-grown authors. But this renewal of interest in foreign achievements was slow to have any practical effect on German writers. It is significant that *Papa Hamlet* (1889) by Arno Holz and Johannes Schlaf, one of the first and most exciting pieces of modern prose written in the late 1880s, appeared under the 'Scandinavian' pseudonym of 'Bjarne P. Holmsen'. An account of a day in the life of a failed actor, it was a bold attempt to devise new narrative strategies that would capture the 'feel' of evanescent reality. Parallel, indeed simultaneous levels of text in different sizes of print and reminiscent of the stage directions and asides of a modern screenplay, scrupulous observation of the actual time-schemes of lived experience in lieu of the contractions and expansions of conventional narrative, and a deliberate effort to exclude the author's presence as narrator, mark it out as a milestone in the emergence of modern fiction. Yet though Holz and Schlaf anticipated James Joyce's approach to fiction in *Ulysses* and the techniques associated with the post-1945 *Hörspiel* or radio play, their experiment proved to be something of a dead end in the context of German prose fiction itself. Here a successful way forward was to be achieved through a different approach, one that built on the indigenous narrative tradition but made it sensitive to the perceptions of a new age and the requirements of a new kind of reader.

## Theodor Fontane

Irony did what experimentation failed to do: tone, rather than form, underwent decisive change. Only irony could provide an adequate means for showing up the realities of the contemporary world; it alone could expose the paradoxes and contradictions of a society characterized by the complacent acceptance of itself and appeal to a new readership that was increasingly critical of the world it lived in. Where daring young authors failed, an elderly writer, Theodor Fontane, succeeded. Among the many writers producing prose fiction at the end of the nineteenth century, Fontane takes pride of place. Yet his emergence as the major novelist of the 1880s and 1890s was long and slow. He had already made a name as a poet in the 1850s and enjoyed a career as a travel-writer and journalist before he turned to the novel with increasing success: *Wanderungen durch die Mark Brandenburg* ('Rambles through Mark Brandenburg'), a masterpiece of topographical writing, appeared in 1862–82. The turning-point came in 1878 with *Vor dem Sturm* ('Before the storm'), a long historical novel set in Prussia and Berlin at the end of the Napoleonic era and located in the landscape and milieu he knew at first hand. By 1883, when he returned to the same period for his shorter novel, *Schach von Wuthenow*, the decisive shift had been made. Here was a historical novel with a difference: no retrospective fictional recreation of past events, but an account of probable events in the past as if they were 'real' and being experienced by human beings perplexed by the often incomprehensible ironies of their own lives and of history in the making. Fontane had already turned to the present of his own day: *L'Adultera* (1880), a novel set in contemporary Berlin, gave him an opportunity to display his closely observed inside knowledge of society and to broach a theme – the failure of a respectable marriage – which had dominated mid-nineteenth-century English fiction and now, at last, entered German literature, too. There are parallels with George Eliot here, and with Trollope, too (her *Daniel Deronda* had appeared in 1876, his *Can You Forgive Her?* in 1865), but it would be wrong to speak of imitation. Fontane developed his own ways of presenting his world, and he possessed the vital knack of being able to create characters who, despite themselves, reveal perplexing facets which German readers recognized in themselves. By finding his subject matter, Fontane was finding himself.

The novels that followed filled out Fontane's picture of Prussian society with increasing subtlety. *Irrungen, Wirrungen* ('Mistakes and confusions', 1888), a taut account of an affair between a young Prussian officer and the adopted daughter of a washerwoman, is the classic treatment of a theme particularly associated with Prussia (and Austria) at the time: the usually futile attempt of human beings to find happiness by overcoming the social barriers between the officer caste and the respectable working class. *Stine* (1890) takes up this theme from another angle: an aristocrat attempts to disregard convention and find happiness with a lower-class woman, but is rejected by her because she has a shrewder idea of what society can accept. The sequence culminates with three works which demonstrate Fontane's total command of the narrative form and social territory he had now made his own. Of these, *Effi Briest* (1895) is the most popular, and understandably so, because it achieves something rare enough in German literature – the creation of credible and rounded characters to set alongside their counterparts in *Middlemarch, Madame Bovary* or *Anna Karenina*. The depiction of provincial life in nineteenth-century Prussia is masterly, but the novel's artistic quality lies first and foremost in Fontane's even-handed treatment of the two human beings around whose relationship the novel is centred. With infinite restraint he prevents his 'heroine' from becoming one: his unobtrusive but unfailingly accurate irony is able to convey both her vitality and her vulnerability, but also her emotional and intellectual shortcomings, while at the same time hinting at the suppressed humanity and sensitivity of her apparently staid, uncomplicated and conventional husband, Baron von Innstetten. *Effi Briest* owes much of its lasting popularity to the fact that it is a love story with a difference, but its deeper fascination lies in its suggestive use of unexplained incidents and enigmatic motifs beneath its surface action. More intangible, and even more delicate, is the diagnosis of loving and being loved that lies at the heart of *Unwiederbringlich* ('Beyond recall', 1891), a novel whose Danish setting reflects the refreshing appeal of the new realist literature of his Danish contemporaries such as Herman Bang.

Fontane returned to the setting he knew best in the two other masterpieces that brought his belated career as a novelist to a close. In *Frau Jenny Treibel* (1892) all suggestion of a 'romantic' novel is discarded: instead the social tapestry of Berlin that surrounds Frau Treibel, the inexhaustible embodiment of successful social mobility, is submitted to an analysis remarkable for its richness of detail and achieved through the interplay of multiple layers of irony, a technique which points unmistakably forward to Thomas Mann, and which established the ironic approach as the most effective means of revitalizing the flagging German narrative tradition. Fontane's revitalization of the novel culminated in 1898 with his crowning work *Der Stechlin*, published when he was nearly eighty. *Der Stechlin* (the title referring to a lake near Neu-Ruppin, Fontane's birthplace) harks back to *Vor dem Sturm* but in doing so it demonstrates the artistic distance he had travelled. Here everything lies between the lines: the sensation of a society living and developing like a living organism is conveyed not by a network of storylines or the interventions of the author: instead conversations about a hundred and one topics take up much of the text, leaving it to the reader to form the connections. Gone is the passively appreciative mid-nineteenth-century reader for whom Fontane's immediate precursors had written; instead, readers of his last novel find themselves having to play an essential part in the creation of the 'other' reality of a fiction which, in his hands, becomes almost more real than the world his readers inhabit and think they understand. As a portrayer of German life and German people Fontane's reputation continues to grow even though the society he described in such fine detail is that of an era which vanished with the First World War.

## Eduard von Keyserling and Ferdinand von Saar

Fontane is the outstanding German novelist of his period, but he was not the only one. There are similarities between his works and the novels and novellen of authors as far apart geographically and culturally as Eduard von Keyserling and Ferdinand von Saar. Keyserling belonged to an old German landed family in Courland (now part of modern Latvia, but then in the Russian Empire) and he retained his Russian nationality throughout his life. However, his creative years from 1899 onwards were spent in Munich, where blind, and slowly dying of syphilis, he dictated his later works to his two unmarried sisters. In them he invoked the heavy, doom-laden atmosphere surrounding the gradual decline of the society, still landed and feudal, to which he belonged, a German ascendancy in the Baltic area whose cool, sometimes cruel correctness contrasts sharply with the easy-going earthiness and sensuality of the Latvian peasants; it is a contradiction which often also surfaces in the psychological make-up of his main characters, such as Günther von Tarniff and the two women in *Beate und Mareile* (1903). He builds up his atmospheric stories with such an impressionistic lightness of touch and unobtrusive satirical powers of observation that his vanished world of decaying Baltic country houses and the doomed people who inhabit them, seen at its best in *Dumala* (1908) and *Abendliche Häuser* ('Twilight houses', 1914), seems to live on in its monotonously haunting setting of wide flat countryside, of woods and lakes, which sometimes take on an almost symbolical quality.

Far away, in Habsburg Austria, the long, slow ending of an era and the transition to a new one had been receiving similarly perceptive treatment in Ferdinand von Saar's two volumes of *Novellen aus Österreich* (1877 and 1897). Here, too, the sense of lived reality is paramount, as is the skilful use of allusion and irony, seen at its most impressive in *Schloß Kostenitz* (published on its own in 1892), the story of a castle, now acquired by a wealthy industrialist, where in previous years an Austrian aristocrat had survived the death of his wife and of the arrogant cavalry officer who was not really her lover after all. The contrasts between what appears to have happened and what really did, and between 'now' and a past which was even more 'present', is brought out with rare narrative subtlety here: *Seligmann Hirsch*, the story of a preposterous parvenu Jew, characteristically turns out to be about a good deal more than the reader at first realizes, thanks to its subtext of observations which point in other, less clear-cut directions. By the time he committed suicide in 1906 after a long illness Saar had become a fêted literary figure much admired by younger Austrian writers such as Schnitzler and Hofmannsthal. The fact that his work in many ways foreshadows theirs should not obscure its originality.

## A Jewish Literature in the East

From the time of the first steps towards their emancipation in Austria (1781–2) and Prussia (1812) to the horrors of the Holocaust in 1935–45, Jews played a prominent part in the cultural life of the German-speaking countries. Their contribution to the artistic and musical life of Germany and Austria is well known, but their contribution to literature in German is in need of reassessment. For a number of reasons, however, it has been slow to take place, and the restoration of many of the major Jewish authors to the German canon has hardly begun. Before 1940, the German-speaking Jews of Europe were scattered across a larger geographical area than any other linguistic group outside Russia; while the Jewish communities in cities such as Berlin, Frankfurt and Vienna were culturally important and influential, many major centres of Jewish population actually lay on the outer periphery of the German and Austro-Hungarian Empires, in areas such as Galicia (with its capital Lemberg or Lvov) and Bukovina (with its capital, Czernowitz) – Austrian provinces until 1918, but now in the Ukraine, Moldavia and Romania. This is why their writers in the nineteenth-century realist mould open up rare and fascinating glimpses of a vanished world. By the second half of the nineteenth century the language of Goethe and Schiller was being used to describe ways of life and social conditions very different from those made familiar by the non-Jewish German writers of the period. Reassessment is made all the harder because the world so lovingly yet often critically evoked by these authors was wiped out when, under German occupation during the Second World War, Eastern European Jewry was exterminated. Since 1945 there has been no great demand in German bookshops for the works of writers who used German to record a German and Yiddish culture destroyed by the Nazis. Post-1945 *Vergangenheitsbewältigung* did not go as far as that.

The first major Jewish prose writer of modern Germany was Bertold Auerbach, the creator of the nineteenth-century *Dorfgeschichte* or village tale. But though Jews appear in his stories and novels, they remain peripheral; Auerbach, a native of south-west Germany, wrote for all Germans, and reaped the reward of popularity with German readers at least until 1933. Heine's unfinished novel, *Der Rabbi von Bacherach* (1840), is generally seen as the first specifically Jewish story in German, but it takes place in a historical German setting. The contemporary Jewish story as a distinct genre was inaugurated in 1848 by Leopold Kompert's collection *Aus dem Ghetto*, followed in 1860 by his *Geschichten aus dem Ghetto*, the Jewish community or ghetto they depicted being that of Prague. During the 1860s equality before the law was being achieved by Jews in one German state after another, and 1867 saw it built into the new constitution of the Austro-Hungarian Empire, where the Jews, at $4\frac{1}{2}$ per cent of the total population, were three times as numerous as in the German Empire. A wave of migration from the ghettos of Eastern Europe to the cities of the west ensued, which led in turn to an expanding and increasingly assimilated readership of educated Jews eager for literature on Jewish themes.

Karl Emil Franzos catered for this new readership. His stories take place further east, in Czortków, his home town in the Austrian crownland of Galicia, which he renamed 'Barnow'. With the subtle, closely observed stories in *Die Juden von Barnow* (1876) the ghetto tale came of age. They were saved from folkloric sentimentality by their author's blend of empathy and detachment, a quality he shares with the Grillparzer of *Der arme Spielmann* (1848) or with Ferdinand von Saar's first set of *Novellen aus Österreich*, also published in 1877. But there the similarity ends. Now more famous as the editor of Büchner's previously unpublished play *Woyzeck*, Franzos was proud of his *Deutschtum* or 'Germanness' and a champion of enlightenment and progress who viewed ghetto life as an anachronism and the orthodoxy of the Hasidim as a self-imposed tyranny. Convinced that modernization was on its way, he took the view that Jewry should adapt to modern culture by adopting the German language; it was a view shared by the parents of the later Nobel Prize winner Elias Canetti, when they decided to abandon their linguistic heritage in order to benefit from the culture of Austro-Germany. Franzos is at his best when writing stories which told of the high price such cultural change involves: a fine example is *Nach dem höheren Gesetz* ('According to a higher law'), where Nathan, a pious Jew, obeys a higher law by releasing his much-loved wife Chane from their childless marriage to marry Negrusz, a Christian, having ensured that her future will be secure should her family and community shun her. His last work, the novel *Der Pojaz* ('The Clown', 1905), is a richly readable and often autobiographical account of a gifted young Jew's attempts to become an actor. Sender, nicknamed 'the clown', is a beggar's son who struggles to learn German, the language of art and culture which will open up the world of the theatre to him, but the only role he plays in his tragically short career is, ironically, that of Shylock in *The Merchant of Venice*. *Der Pojaz* is a kind of Yiddish variation on *Wilhelm Meisters theatralische Sendung* written in the language of Goethe, but such double typecasting (Max Frisch would say stereotyping) also makes it a sensitive study of the painful experience of assimilation.

Franzos was not alone. The late nineteenth century produced a rich flowering of literature in Yiddish (i.e. *Jüdisch*), the everyday language, closely related to German, spoken by Ashkenazi Jews in Eastern Europe. But alongside the great Yiddish realist writers, such as Isaac Leib Perez (1851–1915), Sholem Asch (1880–1957), and the classic humorist Sholem Aleichem (1859–1916), there were also many who followed the example of Franzos. One of these was Jakob Julius David, who chose as his central subject the Jewish immigrants flooding into Vienna from the outer reaches of the Empire, but without forgetting his own roots in Moravia (*Mährische*

*Dorfgeschichten*, 'Moravian village tales', 1910) or the upward mobility of many assimilated Jews described in his family saga *Der Übergang* ('The transition'), a kind of Austrian Jewish counterpart to Thomas Mann's *Buddenbrooks* published in 1902, one year after Mann's novel. By the late nineteenth century the success of the ghetto tale was also stimulating non-Jewish writers: Marie von Ebner-Eschenbach's *Der Kreisphysikus*, a story about a Jewish country doctor in a Galician setting, from her *Dorf- und Schloßgeschichten* of 1883, is a good example; so, too, though in a different way, are some of the stories of Leopold von Sacher-Masoch. Such writers were motivated by a desire to document the process of Jewish assimilation as proof of the success of Jewish emancipation. By contrast, the pathos of Ferdinand von Saar's novelle *Seligmann Hirsch* (in his collection *Schicksale*, 1889), like the socio-psychological complexity of Schnitzler's novel *Der Weg ins Freie* ('The road to the open', 1908), points to its failure.

By the turn of the century the assimilation of Jewish writers and readers into the mainstream of German literary culture seemed complete. Their active involvement in the literary market (the premier publishing house of Samuel Fischer in Berlin was a towering example), and their role in stage production and film-making, personified by figures such as Otto Brahm and Max Reinhardt, made them leaders and promoters of German culture rather than its belated imitators. The abandonment of a traditional Jewish set of values and way of life in the East was to be recorded most graphically by the Austrian novelist Joseph Roth in the late 1920s. By then the map of eastern Europe had changed out of recognition, and Jewish authors no longer needed to feel themselves confined either by preference or by prejudice to Jewish subject matter and themes. But that was to reckon without history. With tragic irony the German ghetto tale was to achieve its masterpiece in 1969 with *Jakob der Lügner* ('Jacob the liar'), the novel which Jurek Becker based on his childhood memories of life in the ghetto at Lodz in German-occupied Poland during the Third Reich.

## Mann and Sudermann

When Fontane died in 1898, just before *Der Stechlin* was published in book form, young Thomas Mann was already working on the novel that was to make his name and remain his most popular work: *Buddenbrooks*. Mann started where Freytag left off. Subtitled 'the decline of a family', his novel covers most of the nineteenth century as it charts the rise of a Lübeck merchant family like his own to wealth and influence, and diagnoses the reasons for its inability to sustain its position. The narrative tone adopted by the young writer (he was in his early twenties) is unexpectedly deliberate, mature and dispassionate, yet also tinged with irony and a dry humour that makes him Fontane's truest successor. The reader becomes absorbed in a storyline involving a large gallery of characters without realizing on first reading that the end is already implicit in the opening, that one of its main characters is present all the way through, and that the comfortable stability which his nineteenth-century family is acquiring is already largely a thing of the past. The Buddenbrooks' prosperity is gradually but remorselessly undermined by a variety of factors ranging from the economic decline of Lübeck in favour of Hamburg to the strains which affluence places on its traditional North German, Protestant work ethos. The move from the gabled merchant's house where commercial activity and family life were almost inseparable to the Victorian villa where 'business' is almost a dirty word is symptomatic of a much deeper change in social attitudes. When a bout of ill health leads Thomas Buddenbrook, the prototype of nineteenth-century probity, to break his normal routine and pick up a volume of Schopenhauer in an unguarded moment, the harm is done. The philosopher's infectious pessimism begins to affect both the family and the text: his only son, Hanno, turns out to be a sensitive and sickly child, and an embodiment, without realizing it, of *fin-de-siècle* decadence, whose absorption in the music of Wagner is symptomatic of his century's terminal disease. As an account of a society undergoing change, *Buddenbrooks* leaves its many competitors behind. Galsworthy's *Forsyte Saga*, begun in 1906 and almost equally popular in Germany, seems almost simplistic by comparison, despite its greater length; in English fiction only George Eliot's *Middlemarch* provides a comparably full and authentic picture of provincial life based on first-hand experience, but there is an added irony in the fact that it was not until the new century that Germany fulfilled its longing to produce a large-scale novel of comparable excellence and status.

The vast span of *Buddenbrooks* is under the close yet unobtrusive control of an author who was to become famous as a master of irony. Irony was in fact becoming a conscious and effective feature of the best fiction of the time; in some writers it resides most obviously in the actual working out of the story; in others, it makes its presence felt in the descriptive passages which form such an integral part of the realistic mode. Fine examples of both types of irony are to be found in the work of Hermann Sudermann, a writer and dramatist no longer always regarded as being in the same league as Thomas Mann and his more satirically and politically inclined elder brother Heinrich Mann. Yet, like them, Sudermann, who is better known as a dramatist, had a remarkably sharp eye for the often ludicrous contradictions inherent both in the human character and in German society before the First World War. *Frau Sorge* (1897), which made his name as a novelist, is a semi-autobiographical story based on his own adolescent attempts to break out of a provincial East Prussian background; but it contains little of the quality and descriptive vividness of later novels such as *Das Hohe Lied* ('The Song of Songs', 1908), whose translation into English caused moral outrage and roused the support of Sudermann's British contemporaries such as Shaw, Bennett and Hardy. The 'Song of Songs' of the title is the score of an oratorio which the novel's central figure, Lilly Czepanek, carries with her through thick and thin as the only relic of her musician father. Her career is a downward spiral, and an opportunity for Sudermann to expose the double standards of modern society, while the oratorio acts as an effective leitmotiv ironically linking cultural creativity and sexual fulfilment as positive values in a society which prostitutes both.

Works of this kind, fusing a critical view of social behaviour with an abiding and arguably typical German respect for culture, must be seen as the background both to Thomas Mann's masterly short early prose works *Tonio Kröger* (1903) and *Der Tod in Venedig* ('Death in Venice', 1912) and to the massive panorama of *Der Zauberberg* ('The magic mountain', 1924) and the darker metaphor of *Doktor Faustus* (1947), which treats Germany's central modern myth – the myth of Faust – as a means of dealing with the traumas of the Third Reich. In contradistinction to most English-language works of the same period, culture and its endangered values constitute an essential element in these works which is often juxtaposed to social position and success, creating an area of tension and an opportunity to weigh up the world as his characters experience it and, perhaps, as he saw it himself. To the ailing Frau Klöterjahn in the story *Tristan* (1903) and the conceited writer she encounters in an alpine sanatorium, the score of Wagner's music-drama *Tristan und Isolde* is, or seems to be, a revelation of the profoundest ecstasy, though to the reader the ludicrously ironic contrasts between their infatuation for each other and the overblown passion of Wagner's mythical romantic figures is as evident and almost as disturbing as the dichotomy between the reader's perception of the reality of an existence poised between life and death and the sense of amused distance encouraged by the very act of reading about it. In *Der Tod in Venedig* the downward spiral into the nether reaches of the self, loss of self-control and death is subtly played off against a successful writer's voyage of discovery into the meaning of artistic perfection and his limited ability to perceive it in his own life: the very fragility of art, and the contradictory images with which Mann surrounds it in his evocation of Venice at the turn of the century, actually enhance it, since it is embodied in the highly wrought text itself, an acknowledged masterpiece of German prose.

With works such as these Mann was rejoining a tradition which goes back to the late eighteenth century's growing preoccupation with the artist as a subject for art and the Romantics' fascination with the meaning of art and the contradictions between its aesthetic and moral dimensions. By the early twentieth century, artist figures were back again at the centre of interest as embodiments of semi-autobiographical experience in a manner reminiscent of the *Bildungsroman*, or as figures through whose receptive and sensitive eyes the world could be described effectively. A good example of the first trend is Hermann Hesse's first success, *Peter Camenzind*, a novel of 1904 which portrays in an appropriately visual Swiss setting the emotional development of a writer as a young man. Schnitzler's novel *Der Weg ins Freie* (1908) is an example of the second approach. It centres on a would-be composer, Georg von Wergenthin, whose artistic and personal development presents an opportunity to portray the social and cultural ambience of Vienna before the First World War, with all its conflicting ambivalences and tensions.

By now male domination of the literary scene was being challenged by some remarkable women. In Florence the emancipated Isolde Kurz was taking the 'Italian' novelle genre associated with Meyer and Heyse to what seemed new heights (*Florentiner Novellen*, 1890), while Gabriele Reuter, brought up in Egypt and daughter of an affluent businessman, found a voice of her own and for a whole generation with her novel *Aus guter Familie* ('From a good family', 1895), the sorry story of Agathe Heidling, a well-brought-up girl whose natural impulses are thwarted by bourgeois values and taboos against which she inwardly rebels, yet which she cannot reject. Visually and intellectually stimulating, Reuter's ironic diagnosis of the makings of a respectable spinster, like her realistically stark short stories, would be acknowledged classics if German readers were as responsive to their nineteenth-century heritage as their English-speaking counterparts. Ricarda Huch, like Reuter (and Fanny Lewald fifty years earlier), was a businessman's clever daughter. Fortunately Zurich University had opened its doors to women: for her this was a liberation later recalled in *Frühling in der Schweiz* ('Spring in Switzerland', 1938). At the turn of the century her *Blütezeit der Romantik* ('The flowering of Romanticism', 1899) and *Ausbreitung und Verfall der Romantik* ('The spread and decline of Romanticism', 1902), two interlinked studies of the German Romantics, made her a key figure in the neo-Romantic movement. As their titles indicate, her perception of cultural development paralleled that of Mann, whose *Buddenbrooks: Verfall einer Familie* appeared in 1901. Huch's feel for the immediacy of the present within an ineluctable cycle of rise and fall permeates the three volumes of *Der große Krieg in Deutschland* ('The great war in Germany'), an imaginative yet scholarly reconstruction of the Thirty Years War published with ominous if unintended aptness in 1912–14. A revered and influential figure during the Weimar Republic years, but profoundly out of sympathy with the crude ideology and crueller realities of the Third Reich, Huch survived to devote her last months to an (unfinished) account of German resistance to Nazi dictatorship and to the rebirth of idealism personified by the Munich students Hans and Sophie Scholl and their courageous circle.

# 8

## *Classical Modernism*

The Great War, to paraphrase the words of the Austrian writer Robert Musil, 'tore reality and thought irreparably asunder'. Defeat in 1918 and the falls of the Russian Empire in 1917 and the German, Austrian and Ottoman Empires in 1918 were followed by the creation of the so-called Weimar Republic, the first truly democratic state in the history of Germany, as a direct consequence of that defeat. In German political, social, economic and intellectual history 1918 was a major watershed. But the same cannot be said of 1918 in the history of German literature, not least in view of the 'prophetic' character of Expressionist writing which, in the most creative decade and a half of its existence (1910–25), straddled the war years, as did Dadaism in a narrower time-span. Both movements helped, however, to shape the cultural climate of Weimar Germany in significant ways. The publication, just before the war ended, of the first volume of Oswald Spengler's *Der Untergang des Abendlandes* (translated as *Decline of the West* in 1926–9) set the tone for the 1920s. Spengler was a rare example of a thinker who reached a vast readership because of his ability to pinpoint the anxiety his readers would soon be feeling; his pessimistic assessment of the future of Western civilization was based on the premise that it had already achieved fruition in the Faustian nineteenth century with its faith in progress, and that it was now in terminal decline. In 1931 Spengler followed it up with a less famous work, *Der Mensch und die Technik*, which argued that technology would destroy Western culture by shifting the economic balance to Asia and Africa; this imminent crisis was given profounder metaphysical significance in the same year in *Die geistige Situation der Zeit* ('The intellectual and spiritual situation of our time') by the philosopher Karl Jaspers, a study of 'man in the modern age' which sought to diagnose the existential predicament arising out of the extinction of man's awareness of the spiritual dimension of life, an inevitable corollary of the technological world view generated by modern science.

The impact of technology, which architects, doctors and social policy makers in the 1920s tried to harness for the common good, had already been addressed with frantic and prophetic terror by Expressionist writers and painters on the eve of the Great War, a war misnamed except for the mechanized mass destruction it caused. The focus on the human body, frenetically epitomized as an image of liberation in the cult of dance which swept through Western countries in the early twentieth century, was itself in a sense an indirect product of changes in technology and social policy in pre-1914 Germany. But it was also a way of commemorating the reality of a war which had robbed artists and writers of so many of their friends and contemporaries – among them Trakl, Stramm, Sorge, Stadler – in circumstances totally at variance with the war-memorials and pious words which afterwards mythologized death for the Fatherland. Otto Dix's triptych 'War' (*Der Krieg*) and his hideous lithographs of pieces of flesh caught on rusty barbed wire in the trenches were, like Erich Maria Remarque's reference to dead soldiers' entrails hanging 'like spaghetti' from their filthy uniforms, a provocative challenge to the army generals, the unreformed judiciary, the landed aristocrats, the right-wing press and the fascist agitators who were seeking to fasten the blame for Germany's and Austria's defeat on those who were the war's victims. They soon became the butt of the wit of satirists and caricaturists as diverse as Karl Kraus, George Grosz, Kurt Tucholsky and Bertolt Brecht.

The seeing eye of the Expressionist artist and writer deformed reality, and with palpable urgency infused the resulting abstraction with a social, religious or existential 'message' aimed at creating the world anew. In common with other avant-garde movements they exploited the visually conceived products of the industrial machine they reviled, such as commercial advertising, posters, industrial design and, especially after 1918, cinema and photomontage, the by-products of the German optics industry. By the end of the Weimar period the National Socialist propaganda machine masterminded by Joseph Goebbels had realized the political capital which such aspects of modern technology and design could have as a means of promoting its utopian ideology. This was not without echoes of German Expressionism despite its calculated appeal to sections of the German public which feared and disliked it. Yet among writers it was perhaps Brecht who responded most systematically and effectively to his own acute understanding of how technology, and particularly the cinema, had changed people's perceptions of the world about them, and how this understanding could be used to change their ways of thinking.

The war had already politicized the masses, including for the first time the rural labourers. Authors responded to this new situation in very different ways. Some developed a fresh understanding of the writer as the conscience of society and of the public as a mass readership; others, particularly the more conservative ones, did their best to shield their readers from harsh reality by providing fiction as an escape route from the modern world they now inhabited and could not escape even when they spurned the city for the countryside. The link between war, defeat and mass culture was evident to writers and artists alike, and mass culture was coming to be seen as an objective worthy of their art. The most creative names during the period, such as Toller and Brecht, were generally found on the left of the political spectrum, but authors of all political and ideological persuasions shared a concern with 'art for the masses' and were convinced of its intrinsic value. Writers on opposing sides of the ideological divide also appreciated the threat to the printed word posed by the new media and pastimes competing for the public's attention: the wireless, the cinema, the modern dance hall and cabaret, and sport for the masses. The additional fact that economic catastrophe – the inflation of 1922–3 and the unemployment of the early 1930s – had occurred twice within half a generation patently made the position of authors more difficult. As Alfred Döblin declared in 1929 in his address for 'German Book Day', there had once been a reasonably large middle-class readership in Germany, but war and inflation had destroyed it. The conclusion he drew was that the growing number of people now flooding into the cities in search of employment constituted a potential new reading public. Books had to be written which would appeal to them; as the Berlin publisher Samuel Fischer observed three years earlier, it was to the new media that people turned after a hard day's work. Literature had to entertain.

The dominant literary genre in the Weimar Republic was theatre. In all its forms, including film, revue and cabaret, it was regarded as pre-eminently up to date. It also happened to be one of the few areas where the revolutionary upheavals which shook Germany in 1918–19 had a lasting effect. German theatres were now largely owned and subsidized by the state: many experimental theatres flourished, not only in Berlin but in regional capitals such as Hamburg, Munich, Frankfurt, Düsseldorf and Dresden. Moreover, the *Volksbühnen* could boast up to half a million members. The boundaries between dramatic literature and the various sorts of stage entertainment were fluid: the *Dreigroschenoper* ('Threepenny Opera') by Brecht and Weill was a great success in 1928 because it combined so many different elements – revue, operetta, pastiche, parody and social criticism, the grotesque and the macabre – and therefore seemed to be a 'statement' of the age. In culture as in politics the characteristic feature of the Weimar era was performance. This was as true for the political rallies of the National Socialists as it was for Erwin Piscator's famous drama productions for the Berlin Volkstheater or Thomas Mann's staged public lectures. Tragedy was out of favour – Hofmannsthal never completed his most ambitious work, a tragedy called *Der Turm*. The entertainment industry favoured something lighter and promoted a return to comedy. In the last years of the Weimar Republic, the *Zeitstück* or 'play for today', as written by playwrights such as Marieluise Fleißer and Friedrich Wolf, became an effective vehicle for debate on the burning issues of the day such as unemployment, abortion, and the corruption of justice.

For the student of German literature during this period, the main focus is obviously urban. In the Weimar Republic years (1919–33) Berlin achieved unprecedented international fame and notoriety as the home of experimental art, innovation – and decadence. Immortalized for readers of English by Christopher Isherwood's *Goodbye to Berlin* (1939), it had by now ex-panded into a metropolis of some four million inhabitants, with a character all its own and an artistic and cultural life second to none. In its theatres Sophocles and Shakespeare, Wedekind and Sternheim, Strindberg and the contemporary Expressionists could all be seen if only because Max Reinhardt dominated its rich theatrical life during the first quarter of the twen-tieth century. In 1905 he had succeeded Otto Brahm as director of the Deutsches Theater; in 1906 he had founded the more intimate Kammerspiele; in 1913 he took over the populist Freie Volksbühne, and in 1919, in an atmosphere of defeatism, he transformed a former market hall into his Großes Schauspielhaus, where his grandiose productions could enthral thousands. By 1920 Reinhardt had virtually abandoned Berlin for Vienna and his newly founded Salzburg Festival, but by then Leopold Jessner was already using the flights of steps that were a feature of his productions to demonstrate that inherent in Expressionism was a neo-classical modernist aesthetic according to which the strongest effects lay in simplicity of form. By the end of the decade Piscator was experimenting in Berlin with his new dramaturgy for a new political age. His 1929 production of *Der Kaufmann von Berlin* by Walter Mehring (1896–1981) with music by Kurt Weill, brought Shakespeare's Shylock to Germany's inflation-ridden capital, creating as mixed a reception as any during the artistically exciting Weimar years.

From Berlin, and to a lesser extent Vienna, new artistic and literary impulses radiated out to the major German cities, which took their cue from their capitals to a degree not known in Germany before. There trends were set and reputations made or lost. Not surprisingly, there-fore, interwar Berlin has taken on an almost legendary quality. But its 1920s image should not blind us to the harsher, uglier realities which some authors preferred to concentrate on, Fallada's *Kleiner Mann – was nun?* ('Little man – what now?', 1932) and Brecht's *Dreigroschenoper* ('Threepenny opera', 1928) being just two well-known examples. Moreover, since literature and culture do not exist in a social and political void, it is also important to bear in mind that the reading culture of Berlin, Vienna and the other major cities was still very different from that of the provinces. It was there that conservative writers such as Hans Grimm, the author of *Volk ohne Raum* ('People without space', 1926), commanded the attention of literally millions of readers who saw in the works of literary modernism, which so few of them either read or understood, the intrusion of an alien, 'un-German' culture into their insecure world. And it was in the provinces – in Bavaria and Thuringia, Saxony and Bremen – that in 1932–3 the vital votes were cast which brought the National Socialists to power.

And so it was that the most potent symbols of literature during the last years of the Weimar Republic – the glamorous revolving stage, or the endlessly revolving door of the hotel foyer – were transformed in the weeks and months after Hitler's seizure of power on 30 January 1933 into the waiting-room of the foreign consulate where Germans no longer welcome or at home in their own country queued to get the exit papers which would take them into exile; for many who put their misplaced trust in the powers of Germany's idealistic cultural tradition, it turned into the attic or cellar in which they would be compelled to hide in order to survive the Third Reich.

## The Theatre after Naturalism

The period from 1910 to 1933 was one of artistic experimentation and excitement, and the theatre reflected this by being the vortex of theoretical debate, technical innovation and new acting styles. Never before in the history of German drama had so many alternatives been championed and explored by so many playwrights and directors, and never had theatregoers in the German-speaking countries been offered such a rich and varied choice. Yet this was also the era during which cinema became the public's main form of entertainment and the average person's favourite escapist pastime. Between 1910 and 1940, and especially during the fifteen Weimar years, the German cinema led the way and enjoyed international acclaim. German directors such as Ernst Lubitsch, Fritz Lang, F. W. Murnau, Max Ophüls and Josef von Sternberg explored film as a new artistic medium and exploited its potential, which was already becoming evident before the outbreak of the First World War. In fact the German cinema had many links and parallels with what was happening in the theatre. From *Der Golem* (1914), *Das Kabinett des Dr Caligari* (1919) and *Dr Mabuse* (1922) to *Der blaue Engel* (1929), film–makers translated the imaginative world of modern German literature into the new medium which was still wordless, but visually all the more eloquent and intense. For the first time in theatre history we therefore have a tellingly vivid if not always entirely accurate record of how the aims and ideals of dramatists and producers were being realized in the theatres of the day. In 1927 Berlin, the artistic and literary metropolis of the period, was itself the subject of a famous film: *Berlin, die Symphonie einer Großstadt*.

German film directors drew heavily on the contemporary theatre, and theatre producers and dramatists in their turn took ideas from the cinema. The interplay of different styles and genres, which was to become a characteristic of the whole period, is already apparent in *Die Ratten*, the 'Berlin tragicomedy' with which Gerhart Hauptmann, still a major creative presence in the theatre throughout the period, scored a major success in 1911. *Die Ratten* revitalized an almost forgotten genre by juxtaposing satire and farce with pathos. But it contrasts other alternatives, too; indeed its whole elaborate structure reinterprets the old image of 'life is a play', and in doing so documents the turning-point in cultural values being reached at the time. In *Die Ratten* the gift of words is personified in the retired theatre director Hanno Hassenreuter, an almost

Shavian character who is never at a loss for them, but is offset by the repressed anxiety of Frau John, the unassuming woman with plenty of maternal affection but no child, and by the linguistically handicapped Polish immigrant whose unwanted child she attempts to adopt regardless of the well-meaning modern social legislation which prevents such old-fashioned solutions. Meanwhile another strand of the play is taking place in the dusty attic above (the scene is an East Berlin tenement house), where Hassenreuter stores his props and costumes. There Hassenreuter is rehearsing his pupils in a chorus from Schiller's most stylized tragedy *Die Braut von Messina*: its lofty style and sonorous language appear ludicrously dated and irrelevant in the context of contemporary social reality, whose pressures provide a more immediate impetus for tragic experience and use urban slang and spontaneous body language to make a tragic point more directly and bluntly. Adorno's post-1945 insights into the relationship of language and silence and the negation of aesthetic beauty in modern art are clearly anticipated by Hauptmann. The traditions of classical drama were making way for drama of a new kind.

Naturalism had led the way. With its emphasis on realistic timing and lighting it was to contribute substantially to cinema and, in due course, to television drama, but its insistence on total realism was something of a dead-end as far as the stage was concerned. Significantly, the early years of the new century saw the rediscovery of other, more fruitful influences, by far the most important of which were the plays written between 1831 and 1836 by Georg Büchner. These now started to be reclaimed by the theatre: *Dantons Tod*, his pioneering drama set in the time of the French Revolution, received its first-ever public performance in Berlin in 1902, and *Woyzeck* followed in Munich in 1913; Büchner's contemporary, Grabbe, was another major rediscovery. The first public performances of the authentic text of *Napoleon oder Die hundert Tage* ('Napoleon or The hundred days') had taken place in 1895, while his comedy *Scherz, Satire, Ironie und tiefere Bedeutung* ('Comedy, satire, irony and deeper meaning') was first seen in Munich in 1907. In the case of both these authors ahead of their times, rediscovery was promoted by people actively associated with contemporary drama, most notably Max Halbe. Halbe had begun his career as a playwright in the naturalist manner, but his once-acclaimed plays such as *Jugend* (1893) and *Der Strom* (1904), with their semi-symbolical treatment of sexuality and suffering, pointed in other directions. Both were themes which Büchner had treated and had been convincingly able to link sixty years earlier, and they were both to be constant elements in the drama of the 1910–40 period, which broke with the 'illusion' of 'reality' and used symbolism and satire as determinants of its stylistic tone and intellectual purpose. All four elements are conspicuous in the plays of Frank Wedekind, its most influential dramatist. They are present from *Frühlings Erwachen* ('Spring's awakening', 1891), his tragic satire of adolescent suffering in the contemporary middle-class world, to his masterpiece, the *Lulu* tragedy, and now lesser-known later plays such as *Simson oder Scham und Eifersucht* ('Simson or Shame and jealousy', 1914) and *Herakles* (1914). Wedekind was dead by 1918, but the potential of his work, with its highly original use of theatrical techniques drawn from music-hall bur-lesque and from older comic traditions, and its resourceful readiness to juxtapose styles and experiment with iconoclastic disruptions of tone, gave many of his plays a new lease of life in the 1920s and made him a living presence among its many gifted playwrights. The Wedekind touch is evident in the plays of Georg Kaiser and Carl Sternheim, and even more so in those of Bertolt Brecht, three of the major playwrights to emerge during the 1910–45 period. Georg Kaiser made his name in 1914 with the publication of his 'medieval' drama *Die Bürger von Calais* and its performance in 1917. An essay in the 'grand' manner, it reveals how six hostages submit to death to preserve the lives of their fellow citizens, while the seventh opts for suicide instead; it was a bitter and moving commentary on the public and private dimensions of heroism and self-sacrifice, manly virtues endorsed on all sides when the play first appeared, but being questioned by the time the play reached the stage. In 1917 Kaiser reinforced his position with a very different play, *Von morgens bis mitternachts* ('From morning to midnight'). Here a humble bank cashier seizes an opportunity to misappropriate funds which seem to offer him an escape from humdrum routine and obscurity and a life in which he can fulfil his potential: he discovers that money cannot buy the things that really matter. Kaiser's early indictments of unquestioning self-sacrifice and the pursuit of material happiness treated two major themes which were to recur in his own work and that of other playwrights. In 1917 Reinhard Goering, a minor writer, wrote a major play, *Seeschlacht* ('Battle at sea'), which presented audiences with the reactions of seven naval ratings in a gun turret of a warship during the Battle of Jutland. In the final months of the Great War its contemporary relevance was brutal. Panic, abject terror, gallantry, idealism, patriotism, selfishness and desperate fatalism blaze up but are finally drowned by the common compulsion to fight on to the end, until the tense drama terminates with an almighty explosion. Like R. C. Sherriff's famous British war-play, *Journey's End* (1928), in which a group of soldiers live and die in their small section of the trenches, Goering's *Seeschlacht* presented a corrective to the stereotyped romantic conception of war. What is remarkable about the German drama is that it opened at the Royal Theatre in Dresden in February 1918, nine months before the war ended, not ten years after its end.

## Expressionism in the Theatre

*Von morgens bis mitternachts* and *Seeschlacht* are very different in almost every respect, yet they are two of the most famous plays associated with a movement which displayed the full force of its vitality in the theatre: German Expressionism. Born of a profound suspicion of the direction in which the twentieth century was heading and often almost too ready to reject modern achievements in the domains of technology and legislation, Expressionism remains perhaps paradoxically the most 'modern' of all twentieth-century artistic and literary movements. Its focus on the individual was a timely corrective to the mass culture emerging at the time, which was geared to the average and promoted by commercial interests. At a time when the horrors of the 1914–18 War were raising urgent and profound questions about the very nature of the Western world's much vaunted civilization, key Expressionist writers felt impelled to adopt pacifist attitudes and to look to the postwar future as a more positive breeding-ground for a new race of individuals united in their common humanity. Utopianism became a characteristic feature of Expressionism, but it never extinguished its critical scepticism or its feel for the existential anguish of the individual in crisis.

For the playwright Expressionism presented a challenge: how could its individualistic vision be communicated to a modern audience? Karl Kraus, a brilliant Viennese satirist, attempted to demonstrate the horrendous enormity of the war in a panoramic drama of enormous proportions, *Die letzten Tage der Menschheit* ('The last days of mankind'). A first version was published immediately after the war: by the time he completed it in 1926 it had swollen to 220 scenes and would, he claimed, take ten evenings to perform. But there were other approaches to the challenge of dramatizing modern experience, and ones more congenial to the avant-garde theatre of the time. In a theatre the audience listens; but it also watches: and the Expressionist playwrights experimented tirelessly with new modes of aural and visual presentation, from the rhythmic prose or free verse of *Seeschlacht* to the laconic colloquialism of *Von morgens bis mitternachts* and from the interplay of light and shade in some productions to the hierarchies of steps and platforms in others. Or they fused and contrasted both. Certainly they set out to make fuller use of the 'theatrical' aspects of drama than any of their precursors had done since the days of Raimund in Vienna in the 1820s. The Naturalist playwrights had written for an audience situated beyond the non-existent fourth wall which separated it from the three-sided acting space on stage: now the Expressionists began to experiment with other approaches to 'reality' by projecting the stage action into the auditorium. Later, Max Reinhardt, the postwar period's greatest producer, successfully experimented with vast audiences seated around a central arena. If theatre in the round was to become one of the legacies of Expressionism, so, too, was the play without scenery, where voice is all, a technique first used to telling effect in *Der Bettler* ('The beggar') by Reinhard Sorge when Reinhardt produced it in Berlin after Sorge's death on the Somme in 1916. These changes in the audience–actor relationship and the relationship between action and setting were as significant as the attempt to get rid of the proscenium arch and the curtain in order to erase the line of demarcation between fact and fiction as in many ways the cinema had done.

Sightlines were one important concern: so, too, was exposition. The gradual revealing of character as the plot unfolds had been a central characteristic of Naturalist drama, but it now gave way to a more 'theatrical' alternative: the revelation of the discrepancy between appearance and reality (*Schein* and *Sein*) achieved in such a way that the audience often senses the difference acutely without knowing which is which. The different levels of dramatic action hitherto marked by prose or poetry, realism or symbolism, and so on, now became equally valid abstractions, and the 'drama' unfolded in a void between them, tense to bursting-point with pent-up feeling. It was a development which had the effect of reviving a more self-conscious acting style in reaction to Naturalism's preference for 'natural' acting. Stereotyped facial expressions and physical gestures were 'in' again, as they were in the silent cinema. Names were replaced by types. There was even a craze for masks. German Expressionist drama was finding inspiration in classical Greece, Japan, and in primitive cultures, sensing that they all had contributions to make to the theatre of the twentieth century.

Ernst Toller was one of the most effective new playwrights of this innovating era. In 1924 he emerged from five years' imprisonment for his pacifist activities when in the army, but during his term in gaol he had already made his name with three highly original plays, *Masse-Mensch* ('Masses and man'), *Die Maschinenstürmer* ('The machine-wreckers') and *Der deutsche Hinkemann* ('Hinkemann the German'), which were performed to tumultuous acclaim, the first two abroad as well as in Germany because their message struck home in other industrialized societies too. In each of them commitment struggles with disillusion and abstract dialectic with violent action. In the first, an idealistic woman hoping to achieve a fair and peaceful society comes up against a nameless opponent who claims that it takes violent action to achieve freedom. The second takes up where Hauptmann's *Die Weber* left off in 1892: set in England in the days of the Luddite movement, it argues that progress can only be brought about by organized political action and industrial and social conflict. In *Der deutsche Hinkemann* (1923) and *Hoppla, wir leben!* ('Oops, we're alive!', 1927) disenchantment predominates: a mutilated soldier returns from the front, a grotesque figure of fun, and a man is released from an asylum into a corrupt world clearly identifiable with the Germany of its day. Meanwhile *Der entfremdete Wotan* ('Odin alienated', 1923), which called itself a comedy, had already painted a frightening picture of an even worse state to come, when a little man sets himself up as Germany's saviour.

Hitler made his first bid for power, the Munich *putsch*, in November of that year. There was a strong prophetic strain in Expressionist writing.

## Social and Satirical Comedy: Sternheim and Horváth

In the early years of the period, the comedies of Carl Sternheim had looked at contemporary society from a different angle, but the picture they presented as he unmasked its subterfuges and pretences was no more flattering, though more entertaining. *Die Hose* ('The knickers') brought Sternheim notoriety in 1911. It was a deft exercise in social comedy with a middle-class hero, a genre he borrowed from Molière and made his own with *Bürger Schippel* (1913) and *Der Snob* (1914). The return of satirical comedy to centre stage, which Hauptmann had inaugurated in 1893 with *Der Biberpelz* ('The beaver coat'), a send-up of obtuse prejudice and incompetence, continued well into the 1920s; it represents the lighter foil to the dark, agonized visionary drama of writers such as Ernst Barlach; it culminated with the revival of the Austrian *Volksstück* or popular play by Ödön von Horváth, which began in 1931 with productions of *Italienische Nacht* and *Geschichten aus dem Wiener Wald* ('Tales from the Vienna woods'), the two plays most readily associated with him. Both were written in Berlin, and achieved the distinction of popularity and critical recognition both there and in Vienna until their author was forced into exile in 1934. Their diagnosis of the fatal weaknesses of the middle class – stupidity, shallowness, dishonesty and self-deceit – is reached by means that might be called hackneyed, yet which seemed almost new after a decade of Expressionist abstractions: and were theatrically effective as his rich gallery of characters reveal themselves or are shown up for what they are through the banalities they utter and the mean and trivial things they do. Cruelty, hypocrisy and amorality were laid bare with the lightest of touches, and the audience chuckled as the playwright held up his satirist's mirror to show it its own tarnished image with startling clarity. Sternheim did much to preserve the traditions and techniques of well-turned comedy by turning them to new and contemporary ends; Horváth went further. He was the first playwright to use words and, almost more effectively, silence, to convey the presence of repressed aggression in the intimate sphere of human relationships, and to reveal it as a major source of the public aggression which was already finding expression in street violence and was about to take on an even more threatening dimension in the institutionalized violence of the Third Reich. Horváth's warnings take on even darker tones in Jura Soyfer's *Der Lechner-Edi schaut ins Paradies* ('Edi Lechner looks into paradise'), a remarkable revival of the Viennese suburban 'magic' play created by Ferdinand Raimund in the 1820s: its unemployed hero, Edi, embarks in a time machine on a quest to discover who was responsible for the misery in which he lives, and ends up attempting to cancel the evolution of the human race. The attempt is, of course, futile, but the author of the play was arrested in 1938, sent to Dachau and last heard of in Buchenwald.

## Brecht in the Pre-war Years

The achievements of Kaiser and Toller, Sternheim and Horváth, were to be overshadowed by the towering figure of Bertolt Brecht, who, since 1945, has been widely and often unquestioningly accepted in and outside Germany as its greatest twentieth-century playwright. Brecht hit the theatre public first in 1923 with *Baal*, a strong play in Expressionist style. In a long line of dramatic works he went on to build a reputation as the single most innovative, influential and relevant force in twentieth-century theatre. His range is certainly wide, his memorable characters many, and the theatrical style he developed from *Trommeln in der Nacht* ('Drums in the night', 1922) to the masterpieces of the 1940s, *Der gute Mensch von Sezuan* ('The good person of Szechwan'), *Leben des Galilei* ('The life of Galileo') and *Der kaukasische Kreidekreis* ('The Caucasian chalk circle') was distinctive and inimitable enough to justify the key modern literary term 'Brechtian'. In his plays, as in Shakespeare's, elements can be found of virtually all the playwrights who were his immediate precursors or his contemporaries. Like Shakespeare's, they have influenced subsequent drama deeply, though, with the possible exception of Dürrenmatt, without producing any notable successors.

For all his unacknowledged borrowings and collaborations, Brecht stands alone, a dramatist often of genius whose seemingly simplistic theories on the nature of drama and apparently clear-cut left-wing politics seem increasingly to be contradicted by the inner life of his works: had they been as tendentious and as didactic as he made out, they would no longer be played. Yet they remain lynchpins of the repertoire and sure box-office draws, because Brecht, a hardened would-be intellectual and sworn opponent of so-called 'Aristotelian' empathy in drama, retains his appeal through his ability to move audiences to pity and indignation. This quality is evident as early as his hard-bitten reworking of *The Beggar's Opera* (a ballad opera first staged in London in 1728), now aptly transposed to the Berlin of 1928 under the title *Die Dreigroschenoper*, a theatrical success much helped by a brilliantly appropriate musical score by Kurt Weill. He followed it with *Aufstieg und Fall der Stadt Mahagonny* ('The rise and fall of the city of Mahagonny', 1930), another musical play, which now seems to be one of the few survivors of a period rich in musicals and operettas, just as *Furcht und Elend des Dritten Reiches* ('The fear and misery of the Third Reich', 1938) now stands almost alone as an explicit dramatic treatment of its unpleasant subject. The great plays of Brecht's war years in Finnish and American exile achieve and justify their high artistic status through their triumphant ability to transcend the topical by endowing what their author considered to be its burning issues with a timeless relevance. Their secret of success may, on the other hand, equally well be the simple fact that, even in amateur productions, they work.


## Modern Poetry

The sources of modern German poetry lie in the late nineteenth century, when Nietzsche called for a 'great disengagement' from outworn traditions and heralded a shift towards new objectives. Poets began to look to the future instead of harking back to the great classical-romantic era which had been institutionalized and anthologized during the course of the nineteenth century as an integral part of German culture. New subject matter was coming into view: life in the big cities, the modest delights of modern existence, the cause of social justice, and during the 1890s – the decade dominated by Naturalism – these seemed to define the poetry of the new age. Soon, however, the objects of such descriptive or tendentious verse started to become the subjects of a different conception of poetry and to turn into the absolute metaphors of a new mode of lyric expression. The change may be observed in the exciting new work produced by writers such as Georg Heym and Georg Trakl just before the First World War; it came into its own in the early poems of Gottfried Benn.

The subject matter associated with Naturalism had encouraged the idea that all subjects are in themselves poetic and that poetry is therefore to be found everywhere, not least in the humdrum world all around us. But soon the shift away from the ideology of Naturalism made it possible to see poetry not just on the visible surface of life but also beneath and behind it. An emphasis on 'things' rather than 'moods' was indicative of the new trend; so, too, was the tendency to focus on the concrete and specific rather than on generalities. Soon 'things' revealed themselves to be the images of a new poetry, their apparently random juxtapositions suggesting analogies with collage rather than with formal composition, while their sequences generated a dynamism and momentum which carried the reader forward and seemed to possess a logic of their own. But the intellectual element – so often a key component in German lyric poetry – was not to be easily suppressed. Images succeeding one another assumed associations in a way that came close to the stream of consciousness technique being explored by some of the prose writers of the period. Sequences of impressions could suggest some form of esoteric and hermetic argument and reinforce the view – a legacy of Romanticism – that the poet inhabits a world of his own creation, and with its own coherence, even if it is only partly accessible to the reader. Sometimes this tendency manifested itself in a quasi-religious conception of the poet's function which bordered on self-indulgence and encouraged the unquestioning veneration of admirers and disciples: Stefan George is a good example, and so, to some extent, is Rainer Maria Rilke. Both writers enjoyed a large and appreciative following who regarded their work as little short of revelation, though to others it might appear nonsense. The status claimed for poetry by Rilke and George and the respect accorded them as poets by the broad mass of cultured Germans was the last manifestation in the twentieth century of the cherished concept of Germany as the 'Land der Dichter und Denker' ('the nation of poets and thinkers').

As the twentieth century opened, it was clear that Rilke and George were the dominant creative voices in German poetry: George's *Das Jahr der Seele* ('The year of the soul') appeared in 1897, Rilke's *Das Stunden-Buch* ('The book of hours') in 1905. At the other end of the scale, as in the Dada movement which sprang up in Zurich in and around 1916, poets chose instead to shed their outworn image entirely, and turned to nonsense verse; surrealism was equally successful in baffling its readers, but was less apt to be taken over-seriously. Yet the trend represented by Dadaism is worth taking seriously because it reveals the fundamental importance for modern poetry of linguistic and verbal experimentation in order to open up new expressive potential, seen to particularly striking effect in the work of Hans Arp.

The way in which poetry was developing in the early decades of the twentieth century encouraged a preoccupation with the problem of communication and communicability. This could trace its origins back to Naturalism: but then it had been essentially a social and psychological matter. Now, however, it was fast becoming a stylistic hallmark as well as an anxiety underlying the poet's creativity and sense of purpose. Not surprisingly, in view of the cultural and political vortex in which they were writing, some of the most original forms this preoccupation could take may be seen in the work of Else Lasker-Schüler, and, in mid-century, in that of Gertrud Kolmar and Paul Celan, Germany's three finest twentieth-century Jewish poets. In their poems and those of many others, the desire to communicate meaning remained paramount and triumphed over personal malaise and the dictates of fashion: they had too much to say. It is equally characteristic of German literature that in the twentieth century, the kind of poetry that communicated most readily still tended to be nature poetry. With a tradition behind it going back to the young Goethe and the *Sturm und Drang*, as well as to Eichendorff and Mörike, modern German nature poetry provides a rare but central instance of continuity. Loerke leads to Lehmann and Langgässer: Eich hands the legacy on to Krolow. To a lesser degree the 'Naturalist' mode of urban poetry (*Großstadtlyrik*) provides another example of continuity in what has turned out to be a prolonged period of experimentation, aesthetic uncertainty and constant change. But urban poetry was more affected than nature poetry by the vogue for functionalism (*Neue Sachlichkeit*) which swept the writing of the 1920s, the decade of art-deco which made the concept 'modern' its own. While the cultured German reader could relax over nature poetry from the mental and spiritual rigours of Rilke, a new readership responded more readily to the explosion – especially in Berlin – of down-to-earth, essentially urban verse, which concealed its potentially wide appeal under an air of wry detachment nowadays associated with Brecht. Erich Kästner was the master of this genre, which deserves recognition in its own right and on its own terms as a significant contribution to twentieth-century German poetry. Intended for 'low-brow' readers, Kästner's humorous and humane poems can trace their origins back to the comic and curious cabaret verse of Christian Morgenstern (*Galgenlieder*, 'Gallows songs', 1905) and influenced the observant, sardonic verse written by the Munich author Eugen Roth between 1918 and 1968.

Georg Heym died in 1912, having written *Der Krieg*, a horrendous apocalyptic vision of war. It is strangely significant that in Germany a poet had so prophetically anticipated the First World War, the outbreak of which generated a surge of exuberant but often reckless patriotic verse by writers such as Gustav Falke, who tried his best, and Stefan George, who could and should have done better. As in Britain, the war's four long years inspired much verse, as men, most of them young and many doomed, tried to adapt the phrases and images of late nineteenth-century lyric poetry to a new and searing experience for which they were unprepared. With their evocations of heroism, their anger and their melancholy, many sound like late imitators of the *Sturm und Drang*: few could find new words to give voice to what so many felt. Trakl was one, another was August Stramm, killed on the Russian Front in 1915, another Anton Schnack, who lived on until 1973. Schnack's compassionate lyricism is appealing, but can seem almost too self-indulgent when compared with the urgent laconic directness of Stramm in poems such as 'Angststurm', with their echoes of the disjointed exclamatory poetry of the Thirty Years War and their pre-echoes of concrete poetry to come. Trakl's war lyrics, for their part, are no more and no less than a further, starker dimension of his art, in which his images and visions are given even further weight to bear. Thematically the German war poets of 1914–18 are akin to their British counterparts such as Siegfried Sassoon, Wilfred Owen and Rupert Brooke: the differences between the poetic traditions of the two nations were never clearer than in the way their respective war poets responded to the bloody experience they shared and is an object-lesson in the mismatches which abound in comparative literature.

By the outbreak of the First World War Rilke and George had been joined by two other younger writers whose influence did much to shape the century's conception of its poetry and who opened up new vistas and traumas unknown to them in their serener, more subjective worlds. Both Georg Trakl and Gottfried Benn – just one year apart in age – rose rapidly to fame in the immediate prewar years. Trakl, the Austrian, did not survive the first year of the war. His output, the product of a brief creative lifespan (1909–14), presents a strident, sometimes meditative, often moving view of a world etched in bold outlines and painted in strong colours, in which narrative sequences make patterns that create a sense of shape which is reinforced by a skilful use of assonances, pauses and alliterations, and convey a sense of deeper meaning, of personal, even religious symbolism through juxtapositions that are only superficially haphazard. Indeed the formal quality of Trakl's poetry underlines his instinctive sense of the coherence of his apparently fragmented vision and gives deep resonance to images which on the surface seem primarily pictorial.

Benn, too, came to the fore suddenly, in 1910, with a set of nine poems, *Morgue* (1912), which brutally reflected his experiences and observations as a young hospital doctor. Behind a façade of imperturbable sang-froid was a man who served in both world wars as an army medical officer, a survivor who knew that only behind such an exterior could he hold fast to his unerring belief that artistic creation was the only valid occupation in a world of twisted and compromised values heading for catastrophe. Benn's quality entitles him to be regarded as the major German poet of the first half of the twentieth century, a pre-eminence reinforced by the length of his creative life; he had already achieved a collected edition of his poetry in 1927 and of his prose in 1928, but rejected the image of the socially committed writer during the Weimar years and kept aloof from the Nazi regime after initial sympathy with its objectives. He was the only major German writer to emerge from the Third Reich with his stature tainted but not diminished. In the 1950s he found himself the mentor of a new age with the collections *Statische Gedichte* (1948), *Fragmente* (1951) and *Destillationen* (1953), and with his penetrating analysis of the state of lyric poetry at mid-century, *Probleme der Lyrik* (1951), which became an *ars poetica* for the postwar generation.

Alongside the four 'great' poets, George, Rilke, Trakl and Benn, the first half of the twentieth century produced a large number of other distinguished lyric voices, some of them notable for their originality and individuality, others working within the traditions their predecessors and major contemporaries had created. The vatic seriousness of Rilke and George – and of Hölderlin too – can be found in the poems of the Austrian Josef Weinheber, for whom the conception of poetry as grace reinforced a sense of isolation which he often succeeded in presenting as the only valid stance for the poet in troubled times. But there are also times when Weinheber in more outgoing, life-loving mood has much in common with the nature poets. Foremost among these was Wilhelm Lehmann, whose personality and writings made a deep impact during the interwar years on the nature-loving religious symbolism of Elisabeth Langgässer and less directly on Johannes Bobrowski, a poet inspired by his particular East Prussian Baltic landscape; there are links too with Karl Krolow, who during the 1960s came to occupy a position almost as central as Benn's in the preceding decade. Weinheber's and Lehmann's highly serious conception of the poet's craft is also evident in the poetry, both traditionalist and innovative, of Marie Luise Kaschnitz and on a more modest, introspective level in that of her close contemporary, Gertrud Kolmar, a victim in 1943 of the Holocaust, whose reputation has grown steadily during the second half of the century. Here, too, the sense of isolation and vulnerability is offset by images full of life and by formal patterns which almost conceal their marked individuality.

The vein of nature poetry is relatively easy to follow in twentieth-century German literature; it is equally easy to isolate, if not so easy to evaluate, those writers who appeared to follow 'traditionalist' paths, and whose reputations have brought them into critical disrepute because they do not conform to the view that experimentation is a greater guarantee of true poetry than continuity and that personal expressiveness is a greater achievement than approachability and popularity. Yet the popularity enjoyed by some poets outside the mainstream should not be underestimated. For instance, there were those, such as Hans Carossa and Hermann Hesse, who emphasized the favourite German virtue of *Innigkeit* – a deep, intense yet undemonstrative sincerity – and favoured poetry of the evocative, atmospheric sort. And there have been sporadic successes for those who sought to revive traditional forms such as the ballad and the sonnet in the hope of reintegrating them into the literature of the century: Agnes Miegel and Börries von Münchhausen are examples in the domain of the ballad; Rudolf Hagelstange, Albrecht Haushofer and Johannes R. Becher, with widely differing aims and life stories, all made their names with their sonnets. That traditional forms can take on new life was also demonstrated by Bertolt Brecht, who reinvented popular verse traditions and effectively revived unfashionable rhyme and regular rhythms in poems whose social and political message was as central to them as their author's unique and immediately recognizable tone of voice. He was also receptive to another strand in twentieth-century German and European poetry: the Chinese or Japanese manner with its cult of economy and its clear eye for fleeting yet meaningful images. This vein owed much to the example set by the adaptations from the Chinese by Benn's close friend Alfred Klabund, and it has deeply affected poets ever since, notably Brecht and Günter Eich.

The oriental manner helped to make concision fashionable, a development which had a fundamental effect on the very nature of modern poetry. The verbal self-indulgence of post-Romantic poetry, which was widespread and much admired at the turn of the century, has continued to tend to give way to the laconic, detached utterance which marks most of what is currently regarded as the century's best poetry. Sometimes impressionistic, but more often intellectually motivated, evocative sometimes, but usually expressing and encouraging less 'romantic' responses, such poetry can degenerate into meaningless and repetitive gestures in its efforts to express a fragmented existence devoid of coherent meaning: the risk was frequently taken by poets such as Eich, the major exponent of the art of distillation. Consistency of meaning was rejected entirely by another grouping which traced itself back to the Dada movement's artistic revolution during the 1914–18 war and which enjoyed considerable esteem after the 1939–45 war: in Austria Friederike Mayröcker (born 1924) and Ernst Jandl (born 1925) experimented with language to achieve the most unlikely effects, while their exact contemporary Eugen Gomringer, the leading exponent of concrete poetry in German, showed what could be achieved by rejecting the notions of semantic function and grammatical logic.

## Prose Fiction between the Wars

In all three German-speaking countries the First World War and its aftermath provoked a reinterpretation of national stereotypes and called into question the values and attitudes of pre-1914 society. German reactions to the war, the horrors of it, and the defeat that ended it – for the Armistice of 1918 meant defeat – were bound to be many and varied. The loss of national confidence, which had been slowly built up during the second half of the nineteenth century, left a lasting impression of the work of a generation of writers who had gone into the war as if it were the testing ground and ultimate challenge to their nation's sense of imperial destiny. The war had already become a subject for literature while it was still raging. Graphic first-hand accounts did their best to convey to their readers the feel of what it was like at the front. One of the best of these was *Opfergang* ('Sacrifice'), written in 1916 during the Battle of Verdun by Fritz von Unruh, a man of military background who had made his name before the war with his Expressionist dramas *Offiziere* and *Prinz Louis Ferdinand*, a somewhat exalted treatment of a Prussian prince who had fallen in the Napoleonic wars. Unruh's Expressionist approach was ideal for capturing the hectic urgency and the boredom of modern warfare: but the book's lack of heroics and patriotic commitment caused it to be withheld from publication until the war was over. *In Stahlgewittern* ('In storms of steel'), by Ernst Jünger, has greater detachment, and for that very reason is even more powerful: written in retrospect, it appeared in 1920. More successful at the time, and the first to appear, was *Der Krieg im Westen* (1915), a much more emotive war book by Bernhard Kellermann, a journalist who had already made a name for himself on the eve of the war with *Der Tunnel*, a best-selling futurist story about the construction of a transatlantic tunnel which became an international best-seller in the aftermath of the *Titanic* disaster.

When the war ended with the defeat of Germany and Austria in 1918, uncertainty loomed large particularly for the men, young most of them, streaming back from the western, southern and eastern fronts and frontiers. At home they found a mood vastly different from the patriotic euphoria that had accompanied their departure. Inevitably the return from the front became a dominant theme in the literature of the 1920s and early 1930s, as it was to be again after 1945: the analogies between the post-1918 and post-1945 literature are often more striking than the differences. But it took some time for the classic novels of the First World War to appear. Erich Maria Remarque's *Im Westen nichts Neues* ('All Quiet on the Western Front'), first published in 1929, quickly established itself as *the* novel of the First World War because of its remarkable success in capturing the physical horror of trench warfare and its psychological traumas in a blend of narrative and description that achieves vivid realism without lapsing into sentiment or indulging in an excess of authentic detail. In 1931 another internationally best-selling war book brought home the trauma of the 'Great War' from a woman's angle. This was *Die Katrin wird Soldat* (1930) by Adrienne Thomas (1897–1980), published in English in 1931 as *Cathérine Joins Up*, and giving an equally vivid portrayal of the experiences of a young auxiliary nurse in Lorraine as she copes with the injured returning from the front and begins to see war for what it really is. Unlike Vera Brittain's *Testament of Youth* (1933), which could be seen as its English counterpart, it has failed to retain its hold on the reading public, a symptom of the fact that the 1914–18 war, for all its historical importance and national trauma, has been relegated to a more distant past by later events and preoccupations.

The outcome of the war was also a sobering shock to writers of the same generation in Austria, for whom it marked the end of an empire. That empire was now reduced to its German-speaking areas and transformed into a small European state, a republic deprived of much of its cultural hinterland. Understandably, this collapse (rather than the war itself) was the principal concern of Austrian novelists of the time, with the exception of Alexander Lernet-Holenia, who was later able to draw on his personal experience as a cavalry officer in his novel *Die Standarte* (1934) and in his surrealistic war tale *Der Baron Bagge* (1936), the account of a wounded officer's compressed and vivid experience of living his life out to the full in the split second of near death. If Lernet-Holenia drew on his memories to write, his contemporary, Joseph Roth, wrote because he was unable to forget. He had grown up in Galicia, on the outermost periphery of German-speaking Europe, where pre-1914 Austria shared a border with Tsarist Russia, but an Austrian grammar-school education enabled him to leave his then still largely Jewish home background to study in Vienna and become a notable war journalist. He made his name in 1927 with an aptly entitled novel, *Flucht ohne Ende* ('Flight without end'), followed by *Hiob* (1930), the story of the tribulations of Mendel Singer, a modern Job *cum* wandering Jew. Roth, too, could never escape his origins although his assimilation into the mainstream of Austrian literature meant that he lost his roots. His discovery of valid new ones came too late. He became an ardent Habsburg monarchist after the monarchy had ceased to exist, an experience which underlies his most famous novel, *Radetzkymarsch* (1932), his vast panorama of the Austrian Empire from 1859, when Lieutenant Trotta saves Emperor Franz

Joseph's life in battle, to 1914, when his grandson Carl Friedrich von Trotta loses his in the first weeks of the 1914–18 war. What happens in between is an extraordinary evocation of a vanished world which Roth's authentically realistic descriptions did much to turn into an almost fabulous yet potent twentieth-century Austrian myth.

As non-belligerents the Swiss experienced the First World War and its aftermath in a different way. For them it was not a question of victory or defeat but of patient inactivity and armed neutrality. The rural idyll of a harmonious, placid, perhaps rather self-satisfied community which nineteenth-century Swiss writers had made the characteristic feature of its German-language literature was beginning to be undermined, while neutrality in the modern world called into question received ideas of nationhood and national purpose, and demanded a response: it was a challenge which had never before faced them in such a stark and uncompromising way. The most effective record of the Swiss experience of the war was slow in coming. Meinrad Inglin's *Schweizerspiegel* (1938) is a novel of heroic proportions which covers a timespan from 1912, when the Swiss army manoeuvres were attended by the German Emperor as guest of honour, to the period of political and social destabilization that followed the Armistice in 1918, during which Switzerland began its long slow transformation from a traditionally agrarian society to a modern industrial economy.

## The Revival of the *Bildungsroman*

In the meantime, however, during the decade which elapsed between the end of the war and its literary recreation by authors such as Thomas and Remarque, German prose fiction was dominated by works which addressed different and more immediate themes. Defeat was hard to accept, demoralization was rife, and authors responded in various ways to the challenge of attempting to make some coherent sense of a harsh new world. The most effective means for approaching this challenge was to hand: Germany's well-established *Bildungsroman* tradition could be put to new use. Not surprisingly, it was to this genre that many post-1918 authors reverted in their efforts to find a way through the scattered remains of Germany's late-nineteenth-century dream of power and the vanished Austro-Hungarian Empire, now disintegrated into a patchwork of central European and Balkan states. Inevitably the nature of the genre began to change. Instead of the unfolding pattern of life associated with the classical *Bildungsroman*, writers now reinvented the Romantic concept of the genre as a narrative of the individual's spiritual journey into the unknown in quest of some distant and perhaps elusive goal. Almost invariably, the major German novels of the post-1918 period are novels of search and struggle, in which disoriented individuals attempt with more or less success to make their way in a difficult world. One of the most impressive appeared in 1922: *Johannes* by Jakob Schaffner. *Johannes* is an autobiographical *Bildungsroman*, and the first and best part of a tetralogy. It was immediately compared to Gottfried Keller's mid-nineteenth-century masterpiece *Der grüne Heinrich*, but the similarity was deceptive, for Schaffner's novel is less the portrayal of its author's development than an analysis of the social and moral forces which condition it and which Schaffner makes tangible through his compelling description of Demutt, the church-run institution for children in care in which he was himself brought up. It is a microcosm of a society in which Johannes, a boy without family or background, has humility and respect for authority drummed into him. Dominated by its well-meaning but tyrannical governor, always addressed as 'Herr Vater', Demutt is also on a deeper level an image of the

Christian world view which Johannes reluctantly comes to accept. The roots of Schaffner's willing later acceptance of National Socialism as a necessary discipline – while paradoxically retaining his fiercely Swiss sense of freedom-loving individuality – are clear to see in a neglected work which has much to tell modern readers about the apparent contradictions of the German-speaking world in the interwar years.

The institutional setting of *Johannes* brings Schaffner into the proximity of a whole group of writers who focused their attention on the experience of school as a microcosm of adult life and a first stage in the human being's quest for a meaningful role in society. School stories of this serious sort raise questions of authority, hierarchy, obedience, defiance and grudging acceptance of a feared and impersonal system. Throughout the early decades of the twentieth century, school is a frequent simile for the school of life, so that it is not surprising that school stories developed into a sub-genre of the traditional *Bildungsroman*. A fascinating variation on this theme is provided in *Jakob von Gunten* (1909) by the Swiss writer Robert Walser, who had used his own experience to depict the goings-on in a training school for butlers and manservants, men trained to serve. In retrospect it is impossible to overlook the note of warning in Walser's entertainingly satirical study of the dangers of unquestioning deference.

## Franz Kafka

The subject of Kafka's first and unfinished novel was fairly typical of its time. Feeling rejected, a young man emigrates to America, there to work out a new identity and purpose for himself. Twelve years later, by the end of his short career, Kafka had produced a unique body of work which has come to be regarded as a compellingly consistent, though profoundly enigmatic, representation of twentieth-century experience. No modern author in the German language has equalled Kafka's international status, if only because none has succeeded so well in extracting a commonly shared human relevance from his own personal experience of a particular time and place and from his own complicated responses to the pressures of modern life. A great admirer of Dickens, Kafka too was a realist who needed to look no further than his immediate surroundings to find all he needed. His imagination could provide the rest. Prague is his London, never explicitly named, but no less palpable for that. Few German authors of his time were as ready as he was to penetrate behind the surface of his everyday reality, and none was more adept at laying bare its deeper paradoxes and implications.

Kafka is a highly subjective writer, but one who instinctively transmutes the autobiographical elements and psychological insights in his fiction into images and patterns which take on the detached quality of myth. This tendency is already clear in his early short stories such as *Das Urteil* ('The verdict') and *Die Verwandlung* ('The metamorphosis'), both written in 1912. In the first story a son is driven to kill himself, in the other he wakes up to find himself turned into a bug: in this way Kafka's fraught relationship to his family background and especially to his own father is turned into hauntingly intense explorations of the individual human being's relationship to the superior forces which finally get the better of him or reject him. The short stories are thought-provoking parables rather than autobiographical fragments. The two great novels which followed them, *Der Prozeß* ('The trial') and *Das Schloß* ('The castle'), both published posthumously in 1925 and 1926, are epic myths which give new meaning to the word 'suspense' as they involve their readers in an individual's attempts to explain a riddle which seems to hold the key to the meaning and purpose of his life. Arrested for no apparent reason, Josef K., the central character of *Der Prozess*, tries, ultimately in vain, to ascertain the precise nature of his guilt. His story, with its echoes of Sophocles' *Oedipus* and Dostoevsky's *Crime and Punishment*, unfolds in a world of trivial Austro-Hungarian bureaucracy and everyday personal anxieties, yet insidiously confronts the reader with questions of inescapable though inexplicable importance. The quest for explanation and the hope of certainty is even more compelling in *Das Schloß*, for here K., an average individual, attempts to discover the true nature of the apparently omnipotent authority vested in the castle. Whatever Kafka's own understanding of his inconclusive masterpiece may have been, it soon became accepted as a close and penetrating metaphor of the impersonal and inscrutable power arbitrarily wielded by the totalitarian regimes which in the interwar years were beginning to dominate many countries as western society found its optimistic dreams of modern progress turning into living nightmares.

## The Sanatorium, the Desert Island and the Hotel

As is often the case when a literature changes direction, anticipations of what is to come can be observed in works written in the years leading up to the crucial new departure. Thus in 1912 Thomas Mann's *Der Tod in Venedig* had depicted a successful German author's gradual discovery of his unknown inner self and the destructive consequences of his abandonment of the late nineteenth-century cult of self-mastery of which he and his works are the epitome, but which shows itself to be a façade liable to crack when exposed to alien impulses. After the war, Mann followed up this long short story with *Der Zauberberg* ('The magic mountain', 1924), an ambitious attempt to confront a contemporary character with a microcosm of modern society seen from a variety of different angles. Its central figure, the young Hans Castorp of Hamburg, enters a Swiss mountain sanatorium of his own free will simply in order to visit an ailing friend, but his escape from the banality of the 'normal' world is no escape at all; slowly he is persuaded to stay on because he, too, is unwell; a spot is discovered on his lung and so he too becomes a citizen of this self-contained replica of a sick but not necessarily terminally ill society. In this most discursive of German novels (its models go back to Goethe's *Wilhelm Meister* and Stifter's *Der Nachsommer*, 'Indian summer'), the patients in the sanatorium, notably the Italian idealist Settembrini and Naphta, the nihilist Jew, discuss the human predicament at length with Hans and with one another, each embodying a standpoint – idealistic, escapist, fatalistic – in such a way that Mann's microcosm is able to convey multiple differing interpretations of an age and society which embraces and concerns them all. Here, then, was the great novel which summed up the intellectual atmosphere of a whole generation, but which outlives it because its discursive, rather outdated intellectualism is underscored by a sophisticated narrative structure which is in essence a study of the relative dimensions of time and space as experienced from different angles by people of widely differing intellects, temperaments and psychological make-up.

Mann's study of modern souls in limbo resurrected and adapted elements of the classical German novel of identity, and its stylistic and narrative approach endeared it to the cultivated German reading public, though it reinforced its perplexing quality for readers more accustomed to the realism with which novelists in other literatures treated even mythical and philosophical subjects. But the way had been prepared for it by works such as Gerhart Hauptmann's *Atlantis*, a novel published just before the *Titanic* disaster in 1912, in which Friedrich von Kammacher, a man disenchanted with modern European society and its values and in the grip of marital breakdown, embarks for the United States, and discovers on the way that the liner is a self-contained replica of the world from which he is trying to escape. From the first-class passengers and their spoilt lifestyle to the immigrants stowed out-of-sight below deck, all are bound, like Friedrich himself, for what they hope are new opportunities in the New World. When the ship strikes an iceberg and sinks – an episode which gave the novel unexpected topicality and boosted its sales – what will be the nature of the new life its passengers will experience in death or washed up on the shores of the land of promise, Utopia? The questions raised by this entertaining novel, like its satirical range, have been overlooked, as has its relationship to Kafka's first novel, *Amerika*, begun in 1912, and to Hauptmann's other essay in utopian fiction, *Die Insel der Großen Mutter* ('The island of the Great Mother', 1924), a brilliantly contrived social satire in which a lifeboat-load of women who have survived a maritime disaster are cast ashore on a desert island. There they create a female society which blossoms, proving that the male is the sole cause of all the troubles of selfish violent modern civilization. But will their ideal utopia survive? One by one they become mysteriously pregnant, which ensures the future of their south-sea vision of harmony and peace, or does it? Thanks to the survival of a small boy amongst their number, normality is preserved.

The island motif in interwar German fiction did not have to be exotic, however. It lies much nearer home in Hauptmann's *Im Wirbel der Berufung* ('In the vortex of vocation') and in *Das einfache Leben* ('The simple life'), a finely grained but ultimately flawed novel published two years after it in 1939 by Ernst Wiechert, an opponent of the National Socialist regime who elected to stay on in Germany. The central figure of Hauptmann's novel is a theatrical producer who tackles *Hamlet* in the small theatre of an unspoilt island uncannily like Rügen in the Baltic, and in the process discovers a great deal about the out-of-joint world that is his own in 1937: the potential of Shakespeare's most problematic play in the context of a *Bildungsroman* had of course already been recognized by Goethe, in whose *Wilhelm Meister* it also plays a central part. *Das einfache Leben* traces the attempt of a veteran First World War naval officer, Thomas von Orla, to find the sense of purpose and peace of mind which have eluded him in postwar civilian life. He regains them on an island in a lake in Wiechert's native East Prussia in communion with one or two trustworthy people and the vast unchanging North German landscape. Here the simple life is the only viable alternative to modern anxiety and uncertainty: it was of course a case of coded self-censorship in 1939.

A sanatorium or a desert island: each could be a metaphor for life threatened, in *Der Zauberberg* by death, or by the harsher facts of life in the novels by Hauptmann and Wiechert. A third and equally effective metaphor inspired another group of novels including *Savoy Hotel* (1924) by the Austrian writer Joseph Roth, *Grand Hotel Excelsior* (1928) by the Swiss Meinrad Inglin, and the best-seller *Menschen im Hotel* (1929) by the Viennese authoress Vicki Baum. One of the most famous novels to come out in German in the interwar years, *Menschen im Hotel* is a vivid evocation of 1920s Berlin which achieves the balance and constraint of great literature by focusing on the intermingling yet essentially isolated lives of a handful of people from very different walks of life who for a variety of personal reasons find sanctuary in a luxury hotel. The hotel thus becomes a powerful symbol of society seen as unstable and transitory but also characterized less by affluence than by shared human longings and weaknesses. Baum's unobtrusive artistry is at its most apparent in her recurring references to the hotel's revolving doors, which become a modern counterpart of the ever-turning wheel of fortune in medieval literature and remind us time and again of the equality of all humans in fortune's eyes, and of the short step it is to the cold pavement outside. With its connotations of casual romance and brief encounters, Baum's luxury hotel, like Mann's sanatorium, is a place of transit and unreality.

Within three years its potent visual quality had been transferred to celluloid: *Grand Hotel*, an American film starring Greta Garbo, brought Berlin to the notice of cinema-goers worldwide. Cinema and fiction had discovered their links and embarked on a fraught yet fruitful relationship.

## The New Novels of 1929–32

The period 1929–32 was one of severe economic crisis, yet it also saw the publication of a spate of remarkable novels. German society seemed to be lurching towards disaster, an atmosphere captured in graphic detail in Erich Kästner's satirical novel *Fabian* (1931), in which the central character, overwhelmed by the breakdown of political stability, financial security and traditional moral values, finds death by jumping into a river to save a drowning boy. Symbolically, in this 'sink or swim' era, Fabian is a non-swimmer: in the same year the philosopher Karl Jaspers published his *Die geistige Situation der Zeit* ('The intellectual and spiritual situation of our time'), a study of man in the modern age, which gave intellectual focus to the challenge of change and the need to find effective responses to it. Meanwhile the Viennese writer Hermann Broch was setting out to retrace the route which society had taken during his lifetime by recording the shifts of values which had taken place since the golden years of the 1880s, an era which now seemed distant history. The trilogy of novels entitled *Die Schlafwandler* ('The sleepwalkers'), which he chose to have published by the firm which had just brought out the German translation of Joyce's *Ulysses* in 1929, was a calculated effort to recreate and reinterpret three precise periods in recent history by carefully observing how they impinged on the trilogy's three different protagonists and how they each reflect a prevailing temper. *Pasenow oder die Romantik* ('Pasenow or romanticism'), set in 1888, centres on the old Prussian military tradition of self-discipline from which by 1903 Esch, the leading figure of the second volume (subtitled *Die Anarchie*), has moved away without finding a stable alternative. Esch's loss of direction is presented as symbolic of the mood as the twentieth century opens; by November 1919 that mood has given way to the cool efficiency of Huguenau, a survivor whose ruthless struggle to achieve status and supremacy in the third novel (subtitled *Die Sachlichkeit*, 'Objectivity') takes place against the backdrop of postwar unrest, which it implicitly links to the new Germany which would soon try to replace the nation's earlier value system with a new ideology claiming to be the fulfilment of long-standing aspirations. The trilogy was in the bookshops by 1932.

Broch is a writer of dense narratives rich in ambiguity: they are demanding, yet they are also marked by a conscious rejection of the articulate intellectualism which had characterized Thomas Mann's *Der Zauberberg*. In some respects the sum of *Die Schlafwandler*'s three parts comes closer to *Der Mann ohne Eigenschaften* ('The man without qualities'), the vast novel which Broch's fellow Austrian Robert Musil had already been working on for some three decades: the first volume had appeared in 1930. Like Esch in Broch's trilogy, Ulrich, the central figure in Musil's monumental novel, is a man all at sea in his day-to-day life in Vienna during the First World War. There he has to face the confusion and the questioning and collapse of values to which his only response is to live from hand to mouth in a chronic state of non-committal moral ambivalence. That Ulrich has strong similarities to his creator almost goes without saying; yet the carefully calculated narrative complexities of the novel's structure and style cocoon him in a web of detail at once graphic and ironic which far transcends his own limited perception and deficient sensibility.

The year that introduced readers to *Der Mann ohne Eigenschaften* also saw the publication of two other major novels whose tone and narrative approach illustrate the breadth of serious fiction in Germany at this time. Ina Seidel's first great success, *Das Wunschkind*, had also taken many years to write, and was greeted with acclaim on its publication in 1930. It is set during the Napoleonic wars, at a time when history was being made by men, but Seidel's novel concentrates instead on a woman's story, focusing on her as she sets about leading her own life in a localized world which the men have left to her, having evacuated it for greater things. Her husband is a casualty of the war; the doctor, with whom she had an intense relationship, is unable to marry her; her Prussian father disowns her; and her only son, the 'wish-child' of the title, falls in battle. But Cornelie does not give in. Passive she may be – she is a creature of her historical period – but she has no intention of being a victim and her author does not make her one. No rescuer arrives to bring about the happy end which would restore male supremacy while pleasing Seidel's readers: her fictional world is made of sterner stuff. Written between two disastrous wars and set in a third, longer ago, her novel is a notable attempt by a German woman writer to carve out her own territory and to take further the rare example set sixty years before by Louise von François in her novel *Die letzte Reckenburgerin*.

In the eyes of many American and British readers the most important German novelist of the 1930s period was Hermann Hesse. Hesse had made his name as early as 1904 with *Peter Camenzind*, an 'artistic' novel in a Swiss setting. But *Der Steppenwolf* (1927), his study of a lone outsider, had revealed a starker dimension of his imagination. *Narziß und Goldmund*, the long novel which followed in 1930, went back on the hardbitten tone of *Der Steppenwolf* by offering contemporary readers the solace of a conciliatory tale of the deep friendship between a monk, Narziß, and a gifted young artist, Goldmund, whom he sends out into the world – the novel takes place in an unspecified Middle Ages – to fulfil his artistic calling. Finally, however, Goldmund returns to the abbey to die in the arms of Narziß, who is now its abbot. There is an artificiality about this book which frequently calls popular romantic historical fiction to mind, though its true cause lies in Hesse's conscious attempt to write a 'psychoanalytic' novel revolving round the antitheses and polarities of Freud and Jung, as reflected in the relationship betweeen the extrovert Goldmund and Narziss, the introvert, and which it relates to its central themes, the different 'planes' of art, love, life and spirituality. The up-to-date ideas of psychological science were thus made readily accessible to a wider readership than the great German, Swiss and Austrian psychologists could reach. Readers took to Hesse's novel much as they were to take to Umberto Eco's semiotic romance *The Name of the Rose*, half a century later.

The escapist dimension of Hesse's *Narziß und Goldmund* had an understandable appeal at a time when the present was as unpleasant as much contemporary writing claimed. The late 1920s saw the brief emergence of a group of writers who were the opposite of escapist; mostly from a journalistic background and with left-wing liberal views, they took as their subjects some of the period's more disturbing trends. In his novel *Union der festen Hand* ('Power in safe hands', 1931) the sharp-sighted journalist-author Erik Reger (1893–1954) took up the theme of Freytag's classic novel of German business life, extending it to cover the whole unwholesome spectrum of contemporary economic and industrial life in the Ruhr, while Gabriele Tergit, in her Berlin novel *Käsebier erobert den Kurfürstendamm* ('Käsebier conquers the Kurfürstendamm', 1932), described the unholy power of the press to make and break images and careers when partnered by American-style public relations. Novels such as these anticipated the work of Heinrich Böll and other writers about Germany's postwar economic miracle. Meanwhile Hans Fallada was pointing to a nearer and more malign future in *Bauern, Bonzen und Bomben* ('Farmers, bigwigs and bombs', 1931), his fictional study of small-town political intrigue in Schleswig-Holstein, where the electoral successes of the National Socialist Party had already anticipated a disturbing trend in other parts of Germany. The future was certainly clouded, but the present was bad enough, as Alfred Döblin's 1929 masterpiece, *Berlin Alexanderplatz*, had just shown. It describes events taking place in Berlin at the time which present a challenge to the ex-convict Franz Biberkopf, its central figure, as he makes his painful way back into society. How, the novel asks its readers, can an intelligent person preserve his integrity and freedom of judgement yet at the same time participate in collective action against the growing threat of contemporary events? Döblin's novel is realistic in an exactingly Naturalist manner, but alternates this approach with passages of visionary Expressionist intensity, interspersed with speech and text in everyday registers which all combine to recreate the kaleidoscopic cacophony of Berlin in the late 1920s, the brash, exciting era which has given the city its most lasting image. *Kleiner Mann – was nun?* asked the title of Hans Fallada's best-selling novel in 1932. The financial anxieties of Johannes Pinneberg, its lower middle-class 'hero', were to receive an answer of sorts within the year: Adolf Hitler was appointed Reichskanzler on 30 January 1933.

## Historical Fiction Long and Short

Disturbed and alarmed by what was happening around them, many writers turned to history for analogies. The result was a wave of new and fascinating historical fiction more or less consciously geared to the present, though artistically often inspired by earlier precedents such as the novellen of Conrad Ferdinand Meyer, in which the psychological traumas and physical horrors of events such as the massacre of St Bartholomew's Eve in sixteenth-century France (in *Das Amulett*, 1873) are simultaneously distanced and brought into sharper focus by means of narrative frames. Even long historical novels such as Gertrud von le Fort's *Die Magdeburgische Hochzeit* (1938) and Ina Seidel's *Lennacker* (1938) adopted narrative techniques which are often reminiscent of Meyer; others, such as Werner Bergengruen's *Der Großtyrann und das Gericht* (1935) and *Im Himmel wie auf Erden* (1940), let past history speak for itself, allowing any resemblances to the contemporary situation in Germany to be purely coincidental.

The novel was popular with the reading public, but it was not necessarily the narrative genre preferred by the more serious authors in the interwar years. Many of them preferred to cultivate the more highly rated form of the novelle which they had inherited from the nineteenth century, and to put it to new uses. The genre's smaller compass and characteristic fusion of brevity and precision allowed writers in a time of change and tension to disregard the minutiae of contemporary life and concentrate instead on the crucial issues that mattered to them. There is no outstanding contemporary depiction in novel form of life in Germany in the period leading up to the Nazi seizure of power: Lion Feuchtwanger's *Der Wartesaal* ('The waiting-room'), a sequence of four novels subtitled *Ein Zyklus aus dem Zeitgeschehen* ('A cycle from contemporary events') and published between 1930 and 1944, is the closest any German writer came to achieving this aim. It is in the novellen of the period that we come closest to its deeper concerns, and this despite the fact that, true to the rarefied aesthetic tradition of the genre, the finest of them appear to relate only obliquely to immediate concerns.

The author of *Der Tod in Venedig* turned to Italy again for the banal yet alarming events in *Mario und der Zauberer*. Mann's impeccably constructed novelle of 1930 reflects the mounting sense of crisis surrounding the rise of fascism. Right up to its last page, the hypnotist Cipolla carries everything before him, assuming in his audience's eyes an aura of invincible infallibility. Yet at the height of his power he is laid low by Mario, the lovesick waiter he has made fun of: in violating Mario's privacy, the magician triggers off a defence mechanism which brings to an end his reign of terror. The reaction of Mann's German tourists watching the show in a small Italian coastal resort is strangely ambivalent. They experience the liberal's sense of guilt at having been drawn into an alien experience against their better judgement, but that is all. As in Goethe's poem 'Der Erlkönig', realistic circumstances are used to bring out the appeal of the irrational for civilized self-controlled people which both Goethe and his admirer, Thomas Mann, instinctively understood but profoundly mistrusted.

Shortly after the publication of Mann's novelle, another hauntingly prophetic example of the genre turned back to historical events to draw attention to the profound paradoxes and menacing perils which, in the eyes of Gertrud von le Fort, were facing her fellow Germans. In *Die Letzte am Schafott* ('The last on the scaffold', 1931) a meek and timorous young nun goes singing to her death at the guillotine; Le Fort uses this episode from the French Revolution's Reign of Terror to demonstrate that under extreme conditions abject fear can become a form of courage as valid and formidable as bravery itself. For a moment literature had overtaken reality; but the future it foresaw was not a safe or pretty sight. Comparably disturbing insights are to be found in many other shorter prose works of these years, such as the vivid depiction of a young boy's misapprehensions in the story *Der Eisläufer* ('The skater') by Georg Britting, a now underrated poet and prose writer of remarkable visual power, and Werner Bergengruen's chilling tale of pent-up passion and guilt, *Die Feuerprobe* ('The ordeal by fire'), set in Riga during the Middle Ages. In both these stories the finely chiselled descriptions of ice and snow add further layers of realism and metaphor to tales which were already clearly saying more than meets the casual reader's eye.

## Literature and the Third Reich

The lifetime of the Third Reich (1933–45) in no sense forms a natural division in terms of German literary history. But the psychological consequences of the twelve years of National Socialist dictatorship both for literature in the German language for the second half of the twentieth century and for the lives of hundreds of German and Austrian writers who happened to be Hitler's contemporaries were such that it is appropriate to examine the literature of that short period in its own context.

For almost forty years following the defeat of Nazi Germany, the evaluation of its recent literary history was shaped and guided by the work of its exiled writers. And, in terms of creative achievement, this was right and proper. But recent research into the psychology of readers, and a broadening definition of the concept of literature, have revived interest in writing which received the Third Reich's official approval, characterized as it was by the irrationality of its values and the powerful emphasis it placed on the affirmative responses it aroused in its 'consumers'. German literature in the Third Reich is more a matter of ideological manipulation than creative writing; its ideological basis was laid by *Der Mythus des 20. Jahrhunderts* by the party's leading 'cultural thinker', Alfred Rosenberg. Conceived as the First World War was ending, Rosenberg's diagnosis of the twentieth century sought to counteract the cultural pessimism of Spengler's *Der Untergang des Abendlandes* ('The decline of the West') by asserting a more positive solution to the perceived crisis in Western or, rather, Aryan German culture. The struggle for racial supremacy, he argued, would be an ineluctable concomitant of the struggle to revitalize the soul of the German race, and must therefore replace the outdated concepts of class and religious struggle which underlay so much of the German literature of the past. Rosenberg pinpointed the obvious enemies of national renewal – international Communism and Jewish high finance – but his most hostile tone is reserved for Roman Catholicism. Such views may partly account for the recurrent emphasis on Catholic nuns and priests, and on episodes and figures from Catholic history in the work of non-Nazi authors writing in the 1930s and 1940s, such as Gertrud von le Fort, Reinhold Schneider, Stefan Andres and Bertolt Brecht.

After 1933 there was a radical change in the policy governing the publication and distribution of books. The Third Reich was a pioneer in the way it used culture, including literature, as an essentially political instrument. Cultural life was rapidly reorganized, and control was imposed on it on quasi-military lines. Almost immediately after Hitler's seizure of power on 30 January 1933, lists of officially approved writers were issued, which also extended to Austrian sympathizers. Then, in April, lists of officially prohibited authors – among them Brecht, Döblin, Schnitzler and Toller – were issued, and libraries and bookshops 'cleansed' of their works. The dead were not spared any more than the living. The notorious burning of 'decadent' works followed on 10 May: it was a deeply symbolical event which threw a long shadow over the future: as Heine prophesied a century earlier: 'Wherever books are burnt, the burning of human beings will follow.' Germany's distinguished galaxy of Jewish classics, among them Heine and Auerbach, fell foul of the regime on pseudo-literary ethnic grounds. Jewish writers were excluded from the official new writers' organization, the *Reichsschrifttumskammer*, membership of which became obligatory for all the rest. As the brilliant Jewish satirist Tucholsky bitingly observed in May 1933, nonentities, ready to prostitute themselves, were crawling out of the woodwork now that Jewish competition was eliminated. In June 1935 Hanns Johst was made president of the writers' organization, not least as an expression of appreciation for his 'martyr drama', *Schlageter*, based on the life and death of a Nazi shot by the French in 1923. Hitler had conferred on him the status of martyr in *Mein Kampf* ('My struggle'), the autobiography and political manifesto he had published in 1925–6, and Johst presented the play to Hitler on his birthday on 20 April 1933: it was duly performed in over a thousand German towns and cities. In August the first exiled writers were stripped of their German citizenship.

## The Literature of National Socialism

Curiously enough, Nazi writers never managed to find a convincing focus for their new ideology; indeed, there is a considerable degree of artificiality in the very term 'Nazi literature', given the fact that the most prominent authors promoted by the regime actually wrote relatively little after its seizure of power in 1933. They included the writers of classic *Blut- und Bodenliteratur* ('blood and soil' fiction) – a populist genre which emphasized the rootedness of human beings in their native soil more overtly even than the fiction with a regional setting which had been popular in Germany and in other western countries since the late nineteenth century. *Volk ohne Raum*, the classic of the genre, had appeared in 1926 and had soon become a best-seller. Hans Grimm's saga is a spacious account of the experiences of Cornelius Friebott, a young man who leaves Germany to farm in South Africa and fight in the Boer War, returns to Germany where he seeks to apply his hard-won notion of living space to eastern Europe and then returns to Africa to farm and fight the British in the First World War. It offered escapism, harsh realism (the author knew South Africa well) and political pipe-dreams in equal measure to readers who felt hemmed in by economic constraints and lack of opportunities, and Grimm was content to live on the financial and literary proceeds, writing little else after Germany passed into National Socialist hands and his hero's passionate pleas for more *Lebensraum* became a pet theme of Nazi ideology. The other classic author of *Blut und Boden* fiction was Hans Friedrich Blunck, a more enthusiastic collaborator, whose profuse output of novels and stories extolled the heroic qualities of German folk and won him the grateful approval of the regime. Significantly, his most original work, a collection of stories drawing on North German folklore and entitled *Märchen von der Niederelbe* ('Tales from the Lower Elbe'), had appeared between 1923 and 1931.

Another group of favoured writers, at least in the early stages of the regime, were the authors of the cultic dramas which claimed respectability by tracing their lineage back to Klopstock's dreams of German bardic drama. They were intended to enhance the solemnity of National Socialist gatherings: two of the most important were Eberhard Möller, author of the impressive *Frankenburger Würfelspiel* ('The Frankenburg dice-game') premièred at the 1936 Olympic Games in Berlin, and Hanns Johst, the former Expressionist poet and pacifist who became a Nazi cultural official. The massive pomp and ceremony accompanying the staging of Nordic dramas and so-called *Thing-Spiele* (*Thing* being the Old Norse word for an assembly of the people) was ridiculed in *Mephisto*, the brilliant novel published in exile in 1936 by Klaus Mann, Thomas Mann's son. Yet Hitler's much-vaunted vision of the rebirth of drama in the new Reich failed to take place. Nor, as far as can be judged, did the mass of the German public develop a marked preference for the *völkisch* or 'ethnically correct' literature officially encouraged by the regime. Even the one area of genuine artistic creativity commonly associated with the Third Reich, namely the film industry, began in time to cater for mass entertainment rather than the indoctrination originally intended by its patron, Joseph Goebbels, the Reich's minister for propaganda and *Volksaufklärung* or the 'enlightenment of the people'.

The *Blut und Boden* novel can be seen as an attempt to fulfil the function of the nineteenth-century *Bildungsroman* by giving it greater topical relevance and promoting it into a major and innovative national German genre which would also provide a kind of armchair political arena. However, by the early 1940s the weekly reports on public morale by the Security Service were noting a growing resistance to literature of a propaganda type and an increased demand for good novels by women and for historical dramas. Certainly women writers such as Kuni Tremel-Eggert in Franconia and Josefa Berens-Totenohl in Westphalia found a ready market for their portrayals of women in a localized setting, German women not just as the helpmates of their men, but as their muse and political conscience: indeed, as Berens-Totenohl pointed out in 1934 in a lecture entitled *Die Frau als Schöpferin und Erhalterin des Volkstums*, women are the true creators and preservers of the racial stock. Such fusions of good country fare with unwitting parodies of German idealistic philosophy went down well. Their success drew on well-established reading habits and the long-standing fondness of German readers for *Heimatliteratur* and the utopian idylls promoted in many nineteenth-century German tales of unspoilt village life. Another key feature of the favourite National Socialist type of novel can be traced back as far as *Soll und Haben*, the best-seller of the nineteenth-century book market, and the dithyrambic passages in which its author, Gustav Freytag, evokes the deep kinship between the archetypal ordinary German, the soil he treads and the work he so industriously performs.

Did the literature which National Socialism inspired leave nothing of itself behind when the regime committed political and military suicide? Few of its major works are now available in print, so it is hard to judge. What is certain is that some of those who welcomed it survived its demise with their reputations tainted but not destroyed. One of these was Agnes Miegel, the East Prussian poet already famous for having given new life to Germany's long tradition of ballad-writing. Another was Erwin Guido Kolbenheyer, a Bohemian German born in Budapest and a prominent representative of the intellectuals who welcomed the new ideology of national rebirth with more or less cautious enthusiasm. In his case too, his literary reputation had already been made, especially by his absorbing but pretentiously profound trilogy of novels centring on the sixteenth-century physician Paracelsus published between 1917 and 1926.

There are a number of major writers who gave their open or tacit support to the regime, at least at the beginning, and whose reputations suffered accordingly as a result after 1945. The most notable of these were the poet and essayist Gottfried Benn, Gerhart Hauptmann, Germany's most celebrated dramatist at the time, the powerful Silesian mystical novelist Hermann Stehr, and Ina Seidel, admired for her originality as a novelist. All three became increasingly aware of the inherent danger of allowing their intense love of their country to impair their judgement. In 1938 Seidel published her most important and deeply considered book, *Lennacker*, a sequence of episodes set in different periods of Germany's history, when the ancestors of a young man facing the future after the defeat of 1918 were each confronted with moral dilemmas and worked out their own solutions to them. Seidel provides no solutions to the problems of the present: they are for each individual to work out in his own way. Her approach is schooled in the pedagogic tradition of the *Bildungsroman* and the detachment of the nineteenth-century novelle, but the message was clear. Hauptmann's half-hearted and, perhaps, naïve political stance soon changed. By 1939 he, too, was in trouble with a regime which had no sympathy with the compassionate element in his philosophy. Any thought of collaboration was over when his novelle *Der Schuß im Park* ('The shot in the park') was denounced as 'racially incorrect'. Eighty in 1942, he was officially fêted along with his nationalistic and anti-Semitic contemporary Adolf Bartels, an exponent of the theory and practice of *Heimatliteratur*. By then he had retired into the fastness of his Silesian home and buried himself in the composition of the *Atriden-Tetralogie*, a four-part drama based on the darkest and most brutal story in Greek mythology, the curse of Atreus, and not published complete until 1949, after his death. Of all the contemporary responses to what was happening, this, the most detached yet most intensely concentrated, may well grow in stature as the Third Reich recedes into past history.

Moral ambiguities in the work of other writers, such as Ernst Jünger, author of *In Stahlgewittern* ('In storms of steel', 1920), an enormously influential first-hand account of the psychology of war, caused them to be mistakenly associated with the Nazi regime long after 1945. Jünger's elusive anti-Nazi parable *Auf den Marmorklippen* ('On the marble cliffs', 1939) displayed what some have called a deficient sensibility in the treatment of violence, but he liked to adopt an élitist if not cynical indifference towards the strictures of his critics; as the only major writer of his generation to live on into the 1990s, he awaits the final critical verdict on his long oeuvre.

Many of the writers who gave tacit support to the National Socialists in the early months of the new regime were former Expressionists who believed that it would bring a new vitality and sense of direction to culture, the arts and especially literature. Like the futurist writer Marinetti in Fascist Italy, even Gottfried Benn, who was selected to meet him on an official visit to Germany in 1934, was initially ready to believe that a Fascist state was an appropriate instrument to impose form and discipline on society and on the arts. The process of disillusionment was not long in coming. By 1935 he had opted for what he chose to term the aristocratic form of emigration: he joined the Wehrmacht because its commissioned ranks were relatively free from party influence and seemed to embody a purer and nobler German tradition. Three years later, when his writings were proscribed, he too found himself forced into a form of 'inner emigration'. Like many another, he no longer wrote with a view to immediate publication, confining his work to the drawer of his desk instead.

## Exile and Inner Emigration

Erich Kästner's urgent plea to his refugee compatriots in Zurich on the morning of the Reichstag fire of 28 February 1933 to return to Germany, as he proposed to do, was grounded in the view that the country needed its intellectuals if it was to survive. Fortunately for them – and for Kästner's own conscience – his plea went unheard; he survived arrest but his writing was prohibited. From then on his only way to 'bear witness' was to publish abroad. Kästner's novel *Fabian* was one of the works ceremoniously burnt by the Nazis on 10 May 1933, yet, despite his otherwise sensitive political antennae, he failed to understand the true nature of modern totalitarianism. In this, however, he was like many German intellectuals and indeed the majority of informed observers across the globe. Despite the massive research effort expended on the Third Reich since 1945 by historians, political scientists and social psychologists, the same failure after the event to appreciate the realities of life under Nazism has affected the way we today regard those writers and artists who chose to stay on in Germany after 1933 and to continue, as best they could, to publish in passive or secret opposition to the regime. As the time gap separating us from the Third Reich grows longer, this disparate group is in danger of falling into oblivion in people's memories, and in literary histories too. They tend to be subsumed under the title 'inner emigration', a term coined as early as 1933 by Frank Thiess and used by Thomas Mann in his essay *Dieser Friede* (1938) to draw a distinction between the inner and overt emigration of his German contemporaries.

The genres favoured by this miscellaneous and often eclectic group of writers were those which lent themselves best to the survival strategies they adopted. Jochen Klepper and Werner Bergengruen chose the historical novel, Ernst Wiechert the lyrical novel of landscape; nature poetry was the natural medium for Wilhelm Lehmann and Oskar Loerke, the sonnet for Rudolf Alexander Schröder and Reinhold Schneider. As in the case of the *Jungdeutsch* writers of the 1830s, the choice of other times and places as settings for works of fiction proved a popular method for camouflaging their topical relevance. Thus Klepper's successful novel of 1937, *Der Vater*, a portrait of the authoritarian king Frederick William I of Prussia, father of Frederick the Great, could be and indeed was read by the Nazi reviewers as a helpful attempt to establish the historical legitimacy of the new regime; his intended readership, by contrast, appreciated the book's double aim, which was to explain the genesis of authoritarian political systems in German history and to draw a clear distinction between legitimate and illegitimate authority. Bergengruen's novels were set in his native Baltic state of Latvia: the transparently topical *Der Großtyrann und das Gericht* ('The great tyrant and the verdict', 1935), with its solemn epigraph (in Latin) 'Lead us not into temptation', continued to command the attention of critics of the regime well into the postwar period. So, too, did *El Greco malt den Großinquisitor* ('El Greco paints the Grand Inquisitor', 1936) and *Wir sind Utopia* ('We are Utopia', 1942), two intellectually and morally intense novellen by the Roman Catholic writer Stefan Andres, both set in Spain. The first takes place during the dark sixteenth-century days of the Inquisition, when the painter El Greco is asked to portray the sinister and terrifying Grand Inquisitor for posterity and comes to realize the full implications of an artist's duty; the second is set during the recent Spanish Civil War, when a captured officer regains the state of grace he had once had as an ordained priest when just before his execution he is asked to hear his captor's confession. Even more urgent in its moral challenge is the story *Las Casas vor Karl V* by Klepper's friend Reinhold Schneider – another work ostensibly set in sixteenth-century Spain, and grounded, as was all his work, in his tragic view of human history.

The elusive figure of Schneider, the variety of his oeuvre, the dexterity of his publishing strategies, his towering moral stature during and immediately after the Third Reich, followed by his almost total eclipse in modern German literary histories, is an object lesson in the problematic nature of inner emigration. Perhaps more than any other writer of the time, he illustrates the significance of what such writing was attempting at the time and its importance for its readers. Schneider's so-called *Feldbriefe*, cyclostyled on poor-quality paper and distributed usually with the help of military chaplains and notably on the Russian front, exceeded an estimated 1 million copies. Part poetic, part pastoral, part homiletic, they contained Schneider's short anonymous religious meditations and also his formally sophisticated and emotionally charged sonnets, and elicited some 70,000 letters of gratitude; sent to the author's Freiburg home, they are a record of his readers' appreciation for the way his work was helping ordinary people to cope. Early on in the Third Reich he had made a name for himself with a short story, *Der Tröster* ('The comforter'), written immediately after he received news in 1934 of what was actually happening in the concentration camps: it drew a poignant and pointed comparison between the cruel misogyny of the seventeenth-century witch-hunts and the equally heinous treatment of Germany's Jews.

More short-lived were the texts which Werner Bergengruen and his wife helped to type and distribute at night on their bicycles without knowing who their authors were: they were in fact members of a Christian student resistance group at Munich University whose names were Hans, Sophie and Inge Scholl, Willi Graf, and Kurt Huber, who was their professor. They were put to death in 1943 when their activities were discovered. Now more famous under their pseudonym *Weiße Rose*, they were inspired by Schneider's work and by Huber's discussions with Carl Muth, the editor of the Catholic literary journal *Hochland*, and the theologian and Kierkegaard scholar Theodor Haecker. Haecker's own illicit night-time broadcasts during the last years of the war (published in 1947 as *Tag- und Nachtbücher*) went undetected, and exercised a similar function to Schneider's writing. In the last weeks of the war, inner emigration found another champion in Albrecht Haushofer, a former protégé of Hitler's deputy, Rudolf Hess. After Hess's mysterious flight to England in 1941, Haushofer's loyalty became increasingly suspect. After the attempted assassination of Hitler on 20 July 1944, he was arrested and, in April 1945, shot. On his corpse was found the manuscript of a set of sonnets now called the *Moabiter Sonette* after the Berlin jail in which he died. They dwell questioningly on his country's atrocities in the context of the cultural and human heritage it shared with the rest of Europe. Parallels with the sonnet writers of the baroque era, such as Paul Fleming and Andreas Gryphius, who had wept over the fate of Germany during the Thirty Years War, mirror the rediscovery of German baroque literature and, more broadly, a changing view of Germany's relationship with its past, which was taking place during the dark years of Nazi dictatorship and postwar despondency.

The writers who opted for inner emigration were, for obvious reasons, anything but a cohesive or focused group. By contrast, those writers who were forced to leave Germany overnight after Hitler's seizure of power and the Reichstag fire soon found that their mission was to demonstrate to the world the difference between the 'true' Germany and its present masters, as Toller put it with courageous logic in his speech to the PEN conference in Ragusa/ Dubrovnik in May 1933. Only days before, his books, along with those of some forty other German authors, had been publicly burnt. People might accuse him, he declared, of attacking Germany, but that was untrue: 'I am attacking the methods of those men who today rule Germany but have no right to call themselves Germans.' But the realities of exile, and deep-seated ideological differences between them, soon led to the formation of cliques in the émigré communities. As Anna Seghers later showed in *Transit*, a novel set in Marseilles in 1940 and published in 1944, the anxieties and aggressions of the exiles could not be directed at their true cause, and turned back instead in a self-destructive manner on themselves.

What became of all these 'corpses on leave', to use Goebbels's sinister phrase? How did they set about earning a living, and who published their work? Their first destinations were almost always German-speaking cities outside the Reich: Vienna, Prague, Zurich. Some, such as Heinrich Mann and Anna Seghers, went to Paris; others, like Klaus Mann, to Amsterdam or, like the leading Berlin critic Alfred Kerr, to London: in her perennially popular children's story *When Hitler Stole Pink Rabbit*, Kerr's daughter Judith provides one of the most vivid accounts of the sheer incoherence of life in exile seen from a child's perspective. Once Hitler had entered Austria in March 1938 and the appeasement policies of the Allies had left Czechoslovakia defenceless six months later, the intellectuals moved on, the left-wing intellectuals to Moscow or, in the cases of Brecht and Tucholsky, to Denmark or Sweden, the rest generally westward. The fall of France in 1940 and the occupation of the Netherlands struck a fatal blow to the haphazard though effective publishing network on which the leading exiled writers depended, for it was in Paris that Heinrich Mann and Seghers had created the *Schutzverband deutscher Schriftsteller* in 1933, an organization for the protection of German writers, and in Amsterdam that Querido, the most influential publisher of German exile literature, was set up. Here, in the best centuries-old tradition of illicit and subversive literary publication, Klaus Mann inaugurated his journal *Die Sammlung* (1933–5) and published the novel *Mephisto*, a key anti-fascist text. Politics continually intervened to smash courageous endeavour: the left-wing periodical *Das Wort in der Zeit*, located in Moscow from 1936, was closed following the cynical German–Soviet pact of August 1939. Yet it would be wrong to see 1933 or 1938 as a clean break. The history of one of the leading Jewish publishing houses in Berlin, S. Fischer, illustrates the unpredictable nature of Nazi tyranny. S. Fischer managed to continue publishing in Frankfurt in 1936, where he brought out Thomas Mann's novels. When he moved to Vienna and then to Sweden after Switzerland refused him entry for fear of competition, he was able to take with him some three-quarters of a million copies of books by the Mann brothers, Döblin, and other modern 'classics' including Franz Werfel, author of the once famous artist novel *Verdi* (1924). Meanwhile Wieland Herzfelde had successfully established the avant-garde publishing house of Malik, later renamed Aurora, in London in 1933, moving later to New York.

The existential situation of writers who only a short time before had regarded themselves as the intellectual elite of their country or circle is reflected in their authorial stance when writing in exile and in their choice of genre. Role-play, epitomized in Lion Feuchtwanger's historical novel *Der Tag wird kommen*, a historical novel about the Jews in Roman times, and in Thomas Mann's ironic narrative style, is a common characteristic of exile literature, reflecting the constantly changing role each new beginning demanded of the refugee; it is also evident in many of the political lyrics they wrote, and nowhere more so than in Brecht's poem 'Über die Bezeichnung Emigranten' ('On the designation "emigrants"', 1937), probably the best-known single work of German exile literature. As for genre, the tradition of Expressionist poetry offered opportunities to sublimate naked fear while conveying a sense of human dislocation: a topical instance was *Schnellzug Berlin (Anhalter Bahnhof)–Prag* by Johannes R. Becher, a Communist writer who emigrated to Russia via Austria and France. Recognition of the full achievement of an older poet such as Else Lasker-Schüler, who emigrated in 1933, and of her younger contemporary Nelly Sachs, who escaped later still, in 1940, two of the most prominent Jewish women authors to escape the Holocaust, could not take place until after the war, because their experience of exile and survival had added immeasurably to the depth of their work.

Although Brecht wrote much of his finest dramatic work in exile, including *Mutter Courage und ihre Kinder*, *Der gute Mensch von Sezuan*, *Leben des Galilei* and *Der kaukasische Kreidekreis*, and managed to see most of it produced at the Schauspielhaus in Zurich during the war years, the problems of access to a theatre represented a major barrier for most German dramatists in exile. Ödön von Horváth was one of the most keenly affected: his exile plays, notably *Figaro läßt sich scheiden* ('Figaro gets divorced'), were not rediscovered until decades later. Brecht's *Furcht und Elend des Dritten Reiches* had had its première in Paris in 1938, and a two-volume edition of his works appeared in London and Prague in the same year; nevertheless resonance was lacking. There may have been an element of envy in the view that novelists came off best. But the novel was not just the representative and dominant genre of German exile literature, as Thomas Mann asserted. It was also felt to be the most appropriate in which to record the panorama of the age and endow its victims with the sense of cultural cataclysms which lent exemplary status to their individual fates. Moreover the epic tendencies of German drama since the 1920s worked in favour of the narrative genre. Among the epic works depicting the perennial story of human exile was Lion Feuchtwanger's anti-fascist novel *Die Geschwister Oppenheim*, one of the best-sellers of 1933, which told the topical story of the persecution of a Jewish family by the National Socialist regime. Thomas Mann's *Joseph in Ägypten* (1936), part of his cycle of four novels on the Old Testament subject of Joseph, belongs in the same context, but treats the subject of exile with greater detachment by turning to a famous biblical prototype: Joseph, his exile and tribulations in Egypt and his ultimate triumph. Heinrich Mann's two historical novels on the subject of Henry of Navarre, though equally historical in subject matter, were even more clearly a commentary on the events of his own day. So too, but less overtly, is Hermann Broch's best-known novel *Der Tod des Vergil*, written during his American exile. Meanwhile in Switzerland a huge, enthralling novel of very different provenance was being brought to its fragmentary conclusion: *Der Mann ohne Eigenschaften* ('The man without qualities') by Robert Musil.

One of the most enduring literary monuments to the suffering of those left behind, and one of German exile literature's finest works, is Anna Seghers's *Das siebte Kreuz* ('The seventh cross'). Seghers, a central figure of that literature, rises above the ideological labels, such as 'left-wing intellectual', which are so often applied to her and which act as an exclusive filter for its content. Born with the new century, and a proletarian by choice rather than birth, she was the highly educated daughter of well-to-do Jewish parents in Mainz. She achieved fame in 1928 with her short story *Der Aufstand der Fischer von Santa Barbara* ('The uprising of the fishermen of Santa Barbara') and joined the Communist party in the same year. After Hitler's seizure of power she fled to Prague and later to Paris, but unlike so many of the figures she portrays in her classic account of émigré life, *Transit*, she managed to find a safe haven in Mexico. *Der siebte*

*Kreuz* is not only a revealingly graphic account of life in and around a Nazi concentration camp. Its impact on the reader is grounded in what Seghers herself, referring to the novel's first dust jacket, described as the 'woodcut' approach: a laconic narrative style using a cinematographic technique inspired by the work of the American writer John Dos Passos. The story of the horrific conditions in the fictitious Westhofen camp from which seven escape and six are caught and then crucified, is told without sentimentality through the mind's eye of the protagonists, their tormentors and their friends: its extraordinary authenticity has been attested by victims, historians, psychologists and readers ever since. Ironically, yet in keeping with the sordidness of the international environment in which the Third Reich operated, the serialization of *Das siebte Kreuz* in Moscow in 1939 was summarily broken off after the German–Soviet pact was signed, but even without that intensely divisive event, and even after the outbreak of war in September 1939, what had been true of the German exiles in London in Karl Marx's day, eighty years before, was equally characteristic of the years 1933–45: the exiles used up more energy quarrelling with each other than they directed at the real enemy, as Feuchtwanger showed in his novel *Exil* (1940), another part of his *Wartesaal* cycle, to which *Die Geschwister Oppenheim* (renamed *Die Geschwister Oppermann* in 1949) also belongs.

The collapse of the Third Reich did not end this; it could even be said to have exacerbated it. The postwar alignments retrospectively applied to exile literature were less the result of the outbreak of the Cold War than of the public stance adopted by Thomas Mann, who as a professor at Princeton University had enjoyed growing international stature as the war was coming to an end. His speeches, and indirectly his great novel *Doktor Faustus* too, gained credence for the notion that all Germans had to share a collective guilt for the crimes of the Third Reich, a view to which Brecht responded with bitter anger. From the outset the achievement of Germany's exile literature had a very different profile in West and East Germany as a subject of focused academic study. Relatively few exiles had returned to settle in the West: suicide, perhaps the exiles' most insidious enemy, had claimed many of them including Ernst Toller, Kurt Tucholsky, Walter Benjamin and Stefan Zweig. Conspicuously and deliberately absent from among those returning was Thomas Mann, who made matters worse by settling in Switzerland rather than Germany.

Things turned out very differently in the East. The German Democratic Republic (GDR) started out from totally different premises, claiming to be something entirely new: the first socialist state on German soil. What better cultural legitimacy could it acquire for itself than the prominence it gave to returning exiles and those who had tasted suffering under the Third Reich, yet had survived? The ground had been well prepared. Even before the collapse of Germany in May 1945 the political exiles had been sent from Moscow in the wake of the Red Army to help set up a new administration in Soviet-occupied Germany. Those with Communist and socialist sympathies were promised and indeed given a warm welcome. Notable amongst them was Heinrich Mann, who died before his planned return but not before completing a valedictory essay *Ein Zeitalter wird besichtigt* ('An era revisited'), which is one of the best introductions to the period. Brecht returned to become an enormously influential but at times uncomfortable citizen of the GDR. He was soon installed with the Berliner Ensemble (founded by his former wife, the actress Helene Weigel), which became a byword for sophisticated staging and where forty years later the playwright Heiner Müller recreated the best traditions of GDR drama. Anna Seghers returned in 1947 to lend or, some would say, to bend her talent to the dictates of the Socialist Unity Party. She published regularly and became the long-serving president of the GDR writers' union; if she disagreed with the party, she kept it to herself, and by the end of her life had become something of a grand old lady of East German literature. Johannes R. Becher, however, like Hanns Johst before him, left his credentials as an Expressionist poet well behind him when he returned to become a high-up cultural official of a totalitarian regime in which he ultimately attained the post of Minister of Culture and bard of Stalin. However, the GDR not only cultivated the memory of German writers exiled during the Third Reich (including some who did not hold socialist views); it actively fostered knowledge of their works through publication. Here the Aufbau publishing house based in Berlin and Weimar, and still active today in privatized form, played a central role thanks not least to the copyright it held of so many major authors.

In West Germany the ideology of the Cold War required that 'all who are not for us are against us'. The blackening of the work of German exiles with Marxist sympathies became the order of the day. Even Heinrich Mann became a victim of unofficial censure (as, ironically, Heinrich Heine had also been) and was scarcely read, let alone published, until the political climate changed after 1968. By contrast with the GDR, cultural legitimacy was not consciously sought in the Federal Republic partly because American culture, and to a lesser extent British and French culture, supplied this need during the years of the Adenauer administration. For a while in the late 1940s and during the 1950s a number of the Christian writers who had chosen 'inner emigration' and remained in Germany were able to offer role models, notably Reinhold Schneider, until he publicly opposed rearmament and made contact with East German authorities in support of his campaign. The situation did not change significantly until centres for the documentation of exile literature were set up, notably in Hamburg in 1969 and in London in 1995 with the creation of the Research Centre for German and Austrian Exile Studies.

Under the impact of the commemorative symbolic dates 1938, 1939 and 1945, the two 'halves' of Germany's exile literature began to converge. Meanwhile a new sub-genre began in the 1980s to supplement the popular genre of diaries and reminiscences by exiles and survivors of the Nazi death camps. This was feminist autobiography, which offered a fundamental reappraisal of twentieth-century civilization by presenting it as the work of the male mind. A celebrated example is *weiter leben – Eine Jugend* (1992) by a Viennese-born American professor of German literature, Ruth Klüger. The extraordinary reception accorded to this subtle work by men and women alike is testimony to the continuing interest readers are ready to take in German life and literature during the era of National Socialism.

# 9

## *Literature after 1945*

The relevance of historical and political geography to German literature did not cease with the loss of almost one-third of Europe's German-speaking territories in consequence of the Second World War. It would thus be absurd as well as inaccurate to speak of German literature between 1945 and 1990 without reference to Switzerland, Austria or indeed the German Democratic Republic. In the 1950s the Swiss writers Friedrich Dürrenmatt and Max Frisch dominated two genres poorly represented in the work of the Federal Republic's writers, drama and the novel. Some of the finest poetry and some of the most original experimental work of the postwar era was produced by Austrians. Despite the totalitarian policies implemented by the regime of the German Democratic Republic and summed up in the words of the Party Secretary, Erich Honecker, when he observed in 1972 that culture is a struggle to influence the awareness of men and women, its writers made a sustained contribution to German literature throughout the period, even though many of them, including Uwe Johnson, Reiner Kunze, Sarah Kirsch, Heinar Kipphardt and Wolf Biermann, found themselves forced to emigrate to the West.

The exemplary places of German literature in the postwar era were radically different from the ones which had exemplified the previous seventy years or so of its history. Berlin had been the metropolis *par excellence* of the 1920s, but it had been physically destroyed in the last year of the war; now, like the other former imperial capital, Vienna, it was divided into occupation zones by the victors, and in the immediate postwar years the exigencies of the Cold War were to deny their populations access to the vibrant centres of international cultural life. For decades they were little more than islands surrounded by Soviet zones of occupation and, despite the various efforts of the West German and Austrian governments, they were in danger of sinking to the status of provincial cities. German literature was deeply affected by the political division of the German-speaking territories. This was true not only of the two new German states, the Federal Republic (consisting of the postwar British, American and French occupation zones) and the German Democratic Republic (GDR), which was created out of the Soviet zone in 1949; the new postwar divisions were also felt in Austria, which in 1945 became the 'Second Austrian Republic', while Switzerland was now more conscious than ever of the differences which separated it from its German-speaking neighbours. The GDR soon began to claim East Berlin as its capital, something which Berlin's four-power status explicitly prohibited; but after the Berlin Wall was erected in 1961, the city's Soviet sector actually became what the government of the GDR claimed it to be: its capital. Along with the East German cities of Leipzig and

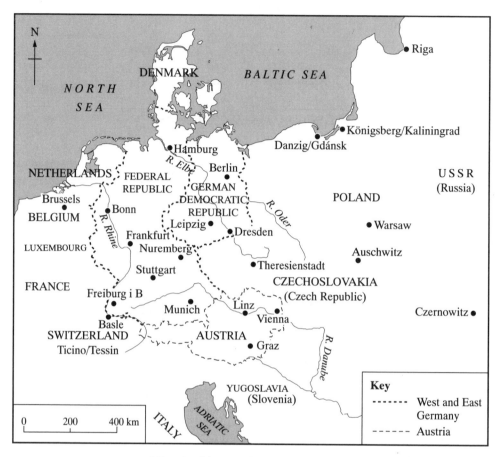

**Map 6**    Literary Germany after 1945

Weimar, it also became a lively centre of literary activity. There was not a little irony in the fact that the first socialist state on German soil, so conscious of its 'new beginnings', should so easily have located its literary focus in three of the most important centres of German literary life in the past. But exemplary status could equally be claimed for quintessentially socialist towns such as Bitterfeld, associated with the campaign to teach factory-workers to create their own literature, and Chemnitz, renamed Karl-Marx-Stadt during the socialist era and a showpiece of the drably functional environment in which Ulrich Plenzdorf's modern Werther (in the novel *Die neuen Leiden des jungen W.*, 1972–7) sets out on his tragi-comic destiny.

Bonn, the new capital of the Federal Republic, has less claim to be an exemplary place for post-1945 literature than Berlin. It had once been the seat of the Archbishops of Cologne; now it was nicknamed the 'federal village', and was home to ever-increasing numbers of civil servants. It had no literary pretensions, though Heinrich Böll's Cologne, the cultural capital of the Rhineland, was only half an hour away by train. The true exemplary places of West German literature in the second half of the twentieth century were the towns in which Germany's media industry was based: Munich, Hamburg, Frankfurt. In Switzerland, assured of greater continuity by its non-participation in the war, the main centre of literary life and the location of some of its main publishing houses was Zurich, its financial capital and the home of Max Frisch. Yet many Swiss writers chose, as did their Austrian counterparts, to get their works published in Germany, notably with the Frankfurt firm of Suhrkamp, which specialized in contemporary literature. The most remarkable shift of literary activity occurred in Austria. Here Graz, the capital of the south-eastern province of Styria and a former centre of National Socialist support familiarly known as 'Pensionopolis' because it was a favourite retirement place for Austrian officials, placed itself firmly in the forefront of experimental literature from the early 1960s on. Its celebrated group of avant-garde authors and its journal *manuskripte* gave substance to Graz's claims to regard itself and to be regarded as the true capital of the Austrian republic of letters.

In the half-century since the end of the Third Reich the central issue of literature in the German language has been identity. The work of Swiss writers has chiefly focused on the identity of the individual in the modern world. The literature inspired by the New Women's Movement after 1968 – in particular its experimental prose – has sought to discover the roots of the suppression of women's identity in the grammar, syntax, semantics and even the punctuation of patriarchal male language, a stance exemplified in 1972 by Ingeborg Bachmann's collection of stories, *Simultan*. Many of the most influential authors in this debate about identity have come from Austria, where, almost from the beginning of the Second Republic in 1945, young radical writers born between the 1920s and 1940s have chosen to make their medium, language, a weapon with which to attack the moral legitimacy of a society and state which were trying to create a new identity for themselves without reference to Austria's Nazi past. Austrian writers, among them Ingeborg Bachmann, Paul Celan, Ilse Aichinger and Milo Dor, also made a signal contribution to the achievement of the group of writers known as *Gruppe 47*, which with much justification but also some foreshortening has been identified with German literature in the Federal Republic between 1947 and 1968. The group provided postwar writers not just with an organization but also, in time, with their principal critical readership. From among its ranks were to come, in the late 1950s and 1960s, the authors of the first major novels to address the issue of German identity in and after the Nazi Reich: Heinrich Böll, Günter Grass, Martin Walser and Siegfried Lenz.

The Strasburg humanist, Jakob Wimpheling, once described the nation which invented printing as the 'benefactor of mankind'. Like Christ's disciples of yore, he wrote, the disciples of this sacred art went out from Germany as missionaries to the whole world. Four hundred years later, the situation was very different. West German authors and Austrian authors, too, such as those associated with the Vienna and Graz Groups of writers, struggled to find ways to overcome the dark legacy of the recent past. The psychological impact of the Second World War and what had preceded it was much more damaging to literary production than the enormous physical destruction it had left in its wake, yet for the first two decades of the postwar era the German literary market was largely shaped by more practical considerations. The Allies' fire-bombs had destroyed vast quantities of publishers' stocks as well as the archives of some of Germany's oldest publishing houses in Leipzig and elsewhere. Some archives and book collections had been prudently evacuated during the war, but their whereabouts had been forgotten or they had been stored in territories which now no longer belonged to Germany. The rediscovery of lost items in the 1970s and 1980s was to have a profound influence on the reception of some authors and to contribute to major new directions in literary criticism. Practical considerations also played their part in choice of genre. In the late 1940s and early 1950s the shortage of paper was a factor in the revival of lyric poetry, the essay and the short story, and in the vogue for the radio play, a newer genre which attracted many talented writers, among them Günter Eich, Ilse Aichinger, Ingeborg Bachmann and Friedrich Dürrenmatt.

The internationalization of German literature and the German book trade in the second half of the twentieth century was in part a consequence of economic forces, but it also offered a parallel to the efforts of German politicians to anchor the vulnerable new Federal Republic in a network of supranational alliances. A translation industry flourished in the postwar years which was in many ways comparable to the spate of translations in the early decades of the nineteenth century. But now German readers had a lot of catching up to do. If contemporary English-language, and especially American, authors were the main focus of attention, French authors were also admired and avidly read; thus German readers caught up with the literary developments they had missed out on during the Third Reich. In the years that followed, German writers and their reading public also had easy access to translations of contemporary Latin-American, Russian and Polish poets and writers. But, each in its own very different way, the two German states on either side of the Iron Curtain also promoted their own writers to a degree previously unknown in Germany. Foreign visits and international travel on an unprecedented scale brought new themes to German literature and at the same time provided a more detached perspective on the central theme of virtually all postwar German literature: Germany with all its problems, 'das schwierige Vaterland', as President Walter Scheel put it.

The currency reform of 1948 brought a radical reorganization of the German literary market not known since the expansion of the book trade in the eighteenth century. Admittedly popular interest focused much more on books of general or technical interest than on *belles-lettres* and lyric poetry, but so many people had lost their books during the war or when they had fled from their homelands in the East or, later, from the new German Democratic Republic, that the book market was able to benefit from the surge of purchasing power even in the literary sphere. By the early 1970s there was on average one bookshop for every 17,000 inhabitants in the Federal Republic, and in some cities, such as Hamburg, as many as one for every 10,000. Interestingly enough, the expansion and internationalization of the German literary market was accompanied by a paradoxical process of regionalization, which offered a parallel of sorts to the federal policy of the new German state. The loss of Berlin and Leipzig as centres of publishing for West Germany – they continued to be important publishing centres within the GDR – assisted the continuation and growth of a number of other cities and university towns as cultural and publishing centres, for example Munich, Stuttgart, Tübingen and Hamburg, all of which had already played important parts in the literary and publishing history of Germany in previous centuries. With some historical irony, the autumn book fair at Frankfurt am Main replaced the Leipzig book fair (which had overtaken it two centuries before) as the central event of the literary calendar not only for Germany but also for Austria and Switzerland, because so many of their authors preferred to see their books published in Germany for commercial reasons and the larger readership they would then enjoy. On the other side of Germany's southern border, Zurich became the centre for literary agencies, as once it had been for politically suspect writers in the 1840s, while in Bavaria in the 1970s, Munich, often called the 'secret' capital of the Federal Republic, established itself alongside Hamburg as a 'media city' and home of the film industry, the press, television and radio, as well as of some of the most powerful publishing combines. Though critics and writers spoke disparagingly of the 'culture industry', it was and still is a major employer of literary talent in the German-speaking countries. In 1969 Heinrich Böll declared that the postwar world heralded the end of the 'era of modesty' for German writers; in the same year the chairman of the newly constituted German Authors' Association, Dieter Landmann, made a case for the 'poet in the supermarket'. Imaginative literature may not be to the taste of the majority of people buying books in German, but German-speakers continue to be substantial 'consumers' of literature, whether original or in translation. Today's writer in German is the beneficiary of the nineteenth-century tradition which associated reading and the purchase of books with pleasure, self-improvement and social status.

## The Challenge of the Present

The Second World War ended in 1945. The immediate postwar period was dominated by an urgent need to come to terms with the recent past and establish the foundations for a new and viable literature for the future. As in the spheres of economics, politics and education, the keynotes in the literary world were reconstruction and denazification. Understandably, the concept of *Kahlschlag* or *tabula rasa* seemed particularly relevant and played a prominent part at first: the notion of a fresh start was an appealing one, for Germany had reached an all-time low and her culture had been bankrupted. Noble traditions had been effaced or undermined by the enormities of the National Socialist dictatorship and by the traumatic experience, for the second time in less than thirty years, of military defeat. Now the onus was on writers and on their publishers and readers to construct a new literary culture aware of what had happened, yet untainted by the past and open to the challenges posed by the immediate future. Parallels and links with the past existed, however, whether or not they were consciously felt and acknowledged. As soldiers returned from the front or from prisoner-of-war camps, a literature of returnees (*Heimkehrerliteratur*) began to flourish which had its obvious parallels in the literature of the 1920s: indeed fifty years on it is becoming more and more difficult for readers to distinguish between them. Yet there are perceptible differences of tone, for this second German catastrophe in the twentieth century was also the defeat of an oppressive and inhuman dictatorship. Would literature be equal to the challenge of facing up to what had happened?

One of the most successful and widely read books of the immediate post-1945 period was Wolfgang Borchert's radio and stage play *Draußen vor der Tür* ('Outside the door', 1947). Borchert's own hopes and ambitions had been thwarted by events: he had fought on the Russian front and been imprisoned for his anti-Nazi views. The coming together of these strands of experience which he shared with so many young Germans of his generation made him the most representative writer of the immediate post-1945 period. *Draußen vor der Tür* expresses the anxieties and fragile hopes of a whole generation with a compelling tragic immediacy because its author, by then terminally ill, sensed that the golden future for which his contemporaries longed was not for him or for Beckmann, the soldier who returns from Russian captivity to find himself excluded from his own home. Highly relevant though it was at the time, both the subject and the style made *Draußen vor der Tür* a backward-looking work with clear links with post-1918 treatments of the same theme, such as Ernst Toller's dramatization of an ordinary soldier's sense of postwar betrayal, *Der deutsche Hinkemann* (1923), and Gerhart Hauptmann's unfinished play *Herbert Engelmann* (1924), completed, significantly, by Carl Zuckmayer in 1951. Zuckmayer was a writer of an older generation than Borchert and had been one of Germany's most successful playwrights during the interwar years. Now that the war was over, he seized the opportunity to cast his eye back over recent events: *Des Teufels General* ('The Devil's General', 1946), written in American exile, daringly presents as its central character a

First World War *Luftwaffe* officer, General Harras, who, in the Second World War, compromises his conscience in order to be a hero again, but redeems himself in the end. In Germany the concept of heroism had already become tainted during the First World War, but it was still an important preoccupation, even though it had been irredeemably contaminated by the ideology and actions of the National Socialist regime. Its cynical exploitation by the Nazis was now joined by the realization that many millions had suffered and died both as champions and as victims of a cause which was now seen to be worthless at the very least. Moral bankruptcy was rapidly establishing itself as a major theme in postwar literature, and as it did so, it is not surprising that its corollary was a progressive disenchantment with the values which many German writers had extolled during the previous 200 years. Grimmelshausen's disillusioned satire on the Thirty Years War, *Simplicissimus Teutsch*, now seemed to be more relevant to the situation in which the German nation found itself. Though there was heroism in Hitler's Germany, the deeds and deaths of his opponents found no Schiller to write a modern equivalent to *Wilhelm Tell*. Was this because their heroism produced no happy ending?

It was inevitable that *Heimkehrerliteratur* should share with other aspects of post-1945 literature a tendency to evaluate German behaviour and attitudes during the Third Reich and the war years and to pass judgement on them. In this sense it was a literature of retribution as well as, sometimes, of exculpation; yet it could also be a literature of sympathy and understanding born of the knowledge that there were glimmers of hope amongst the dark clouds of fanaticism, misunderstanding and prejudice. Another successful postwar play exemplifies this: Max Frisch's aptly titled *Als der Krieg zu Ende war* ('When the war was over', 1948), which focuses on the tense personal triangle which develops when the husband of a Berlin woman returns from the front and she is forced to hide him because of her relationship with an officer in the Soviet army of occupation. The tension between present expediency and past normality was familiar to many people at the time, and the fact that it was presented by an outside Swiss observer made it even more glaring.

Drama was not the only medium in which the pressing themes of the postwar period were treated. Prose fiction played its part, too, most notably in the early short stories and novels of Heinrich Böll. He, too, had seen military action during the war and been taken prisoner; a 'homecomer' himself, he owed his initial success to his vividly laconic treatment of topical themes in the short stories which made up his early collection, *Wanderer, kommst du nach Spa . . .* ('Wayfarer, are you coming to Spa . . .', 1950), the semi-autobiographical long short story *Der Zug war pünktlich* ('The train was on time', 1949) and in *Wo warst du, Adam?* ('Adam, where were you?', 1951), the novel, or rather the set of interlinked episodes which depicts the ambivalences of growing demoralization on the front and the confused emotional responses and, often, also the sardonic stoicism involved in coming to terms with a society not only defeated but also disoriented. It was a topic to which Böll was to return in many of his later works.

These were also the challenges and ambivalences which the *Gruppe 47* set out to face in its critical and literary crusade. The group was founded in semi-satirical frame of mind by two writers, Hans Werner Richter and Alfred Andersch, who together with their ever-widening circle of associates made a concerted effort to turn away from the past which had marked them all in order to focus attention on the contemporary state of Germany as it underwent its gradual transformation from being an occupied country still unified, but subdivided into four occupation zones, to being a country divided into two states: the Federal Republic of Germany in the west and the German Democratic Republic in the east. Andersch, a man of Communist sympathies in the 1930s, had served in Italy during the war, deserted in 1944, and in 1945 had returned to become one of his generation's most influential spokesmen as joint editor, with Richter, of the radical literary and political journal *Der Ruf*, which was prohibited by the American military government in 1947. Richter had also been a soldier and a prisoner of war. For both men, topical comment took precedence over creative writing in the early postwar years, and it was not until the late 1940s that they began to make their names as novelists. Andersch did so with the autobiographical *Die Kirschen der Freiheit* ('The cherries of freedom', 1952), an apologia for a decisive action – desertion – in relation to his own inner development and his country's recent history, and in relation, too, to the tenets of the wartime philosophy of existentialism associated with his French contemporary Albert Camus. Andersch and many like-minded Germans welcomed a clear intellectual framework and explanation for the moral and intellectual crises they had personally experienced and which they were now trying to depict in their writing. The longing for personal freedom which underlies it provides the unifying element in Andersch's most admired work, *Sansibar oder der letzte Grund* ('Zanzibar or The final reason', 1957), a novel which evokes with extraordinary clarity the atmosphere of North Germany in the early war years as it follows the movements of six characters converging on a small Baltic seaport to find the boat which they hope will take them to Sweden and the freedom each of them longs for in his or her particular way.

The literature of postwar *Vergangenheitsbewältigung* was not confined to male authors who had seen active service. Women had their own voices to add and their own experiences to share, though only Ilse Aichinger in her novel *Die größere Hoffnung* ('The greater hope', 1948) managed to create a work of classic stature out of what so many millions had been through, though it was not in the realistic manner enjoyed by the majority of readers. Hers was the story of a half-Jewish child hoping to escape to America, who lives out her vision of freedom in her imagination as reality closes in around her. The first woman to find her own personal way of coming to terms with her experience of dictatorship and war was Elisabeth Langgässer, a Holocaust survivor who had experienced at first hand the intrusion of Nazism on her personal and artistic life. Already a writer of some prominence in prewar days, she now stood out as a major postwar figure for her violent and visionary depiction of the struggle between good and evil in *Das unauslöschliche Siegel* ('The indelible seal', 1946), a novel she had begun in 1937 after the Nazi authorities had forbidden her to publish; it is a realistic yet cryptic account of cosmic spiritual struggle acted out through the life and experiences of Lazarus Belfontaine, a converted Jew like herself, a narrative which enthrals yet disconcerts its reader because it never explicitly refers to the tribulations its author was experiencing as she wrote it. The year 1945 was to be both the subject and the setting of her last novel, *Märkische Argonautenfahrt* ('A Brandenburg argosy', 1950), which traces the efforts of a group of Berlin survivors to live 'beyond' the war and the effect which their personal experience of it has had on them. Luise Rinser also experienced Nazi censorship and the harshness of war at first hand, and came to prominence in 1946 with her dispassionate day-by-day account of Nazi imprisonment in *Gefängnistagebuch* and, two years later, with her less autobiographical *Jan Löbel aus Warschau*, the story of a Jewish prisoner on the run. For Langgässer such reckonings with the past marked the summation of her creative life, whereas for Rinser they were the necessary springboard for her subsequent career as a committed and critical commentator on contemporary life in postwar Germany.

In retrospect it is clear that the immediate postwar literature of Germany was one which concentrated on a number of themes which its authors presented from viewpoints almost always based on personal experience and ranging from apocalyptic vision and nightmare to impressionistic sketches and other forms of autobiographically grounded realism attractive to many younger writers whose primary aim was to capture the mood of the moment and with it a new postwar readership which shared the experiences they were depicting. This approach is graphically evident in Heinrich Böll's *Und sagte kein einziges Wort* ('And said not one word', 1953), a first-person narrative set in the then only too familiar world of chronic shortages. The war itself, so problematic in its causes and objectives, and so searing in its consequences, was from the German point of view a subject which the major writers of the postwar period preferred to leave to authors less complicated and perhaps less conscientious – notably Theodor Plievier, whose epic trilogy of war novels *Stalingrad* (1945), *Moskau* (1952) and *Berlin* (1954) achieved postwar international best-seller status, as did the war novels of Heinz Konsalik, such as the effectively clichéd *Der Arzt von Stalingrad* (1956), which gained much of its popularity in Germany by providing a heart-warmingly positive account of the heroism and self-sacrifice of German army medical prisoners of war in the Soviet Union. Not all had been bad, after all, and the deaths of millions of young Germans in the war had not been utterly in vain. It seems that only the writers of popular fiction were able and ready to reconcile the traumas of Germany's wartime history with the type of storyline preferred by the vast majority of people who had survived, and who now, in the growing prosperity and stability of their postwar leisure, wanted to read stories which made sense of the past and which worked on the assumption that heroism still existed and that not all Germans were villains and war criminals.

## The Return of the Exiles

There was another important group of writers who coincided with the new postwar generation, and like them claimed public attention and critical recognition: an older generation of writers who had spent the long years of the Third Reich in voluntary exile, or who had been expelled from Nazi Germany and Austria for political and ethnic reasons. As they returned, some for good, some only provisionally, they experienced their own forms of homecoming and of coping with a present still overshadowed by the past. Amongst them was Thomas Mann: he had spent the war years in the United States and now decided to take up residence in Switzerland. It was from the outside, therefore, that Mann undertook his searching analysis of his nation's protracted disease and final crisis in his last major novel, *Doktor Faustus* (1947). The essentially German quality of Mann's art is at its most evident here: his approach to the challenge of charting and probing Germany's darkest hours reassures and disconcerts because the text may be read as a *tour de force* of highbrow culture-sodden escapism redolent with allusions to Goethe's masterpiece and to modern musicians such as Reger, Schoenberg and Hindemith, yet turns out to be a compelling diagnosis of a cultured German's enthralment to the powers of darkness. The central myth dominating and controlling the whole work is that of Faust, the scholar and would-be necromancer who sold his soul to the devil. But here Faust manifests himself in the figure, career and artistic aspirations of Mann's composer protagonist Adrian Leverkühn. His life-story is told – and it is a *tour de force* – by his largely uncomprehending and humdrum friend, Zeitblom, whose average middle-class values are totally at odds with those of the man who fascinates him, but whose true *raison d'être* eludes him. As a student, Leverkühn contracts syphilis: this is his curse, but it allows him a creative span of twenty-four years in which to experience the ecstasy of creativity and the disappointments of a series of personal relationships as a great culture, Germany's, careers towards catastrophe. Adrian Leverkühn is one of the most profoundly conceived portrayals of a creative artist in the literature of a nation whose contribution to musical culture has been enormous. Moreover, Mann's ability to make the reader both admire and mistrust a man who is ready to sell his soul to the devil to achieve artistic pre-eminence commands respect because it does not take the easy route and exonerate him from guilt. It may seem strange, almost uncanny, that the novel contains such scant reference to the débâcle of democracy and the rise of Nazi dictatorship: such allusions as there are suggest the existence of a paratext which Mann assumed his readers would read between the lines of a work which, though a product of its age and a response to it, was intended to have a wider relevance. It retains its value as a profound commentary on Germany's darkest years, yet, like the myth on which it is based, its resonance will continue to haunt its readers. By avoiding any overt reference to the political context of this new version of the Faust story, Mann also succeeds in the double aim of showing how human beings can remain oblivious of what is going on around them and how this unawareness is itself a major contributory cause of what is taking place.

Hermann Hesse had been firmly established in Switzerland since before the First World War, using it as a neutral vantage-point to survey what was happening in the world outside and to keep the lamp of sanity burning: *Das Glasperlenspiel* ('The glass bead game'), his apologia for the values of the spirit, was published in 1943. Elias Canetti, another important émigré writer, settled in London. Canetti had already made his name in 1935 with a remarkable novel, *Die Blendung* (translated into English as *Auto da Fé* in allusion to the conflagration of its protagonist's library and his own self-immolation in the blaze which ends the novel), in which intelligent observation and grotesque incident are fused in a post-Kafka Austrian tradition subtly attuned to the urgency of contemporary events. More cosmopolitan than his major postwar German contemporaries (he was born into a Sephardic Jewish family in Bulgaria, and educated in Zurich, Frankfurt and Vienna), Canetti then used his personal experience of life in a complex and dangerous period to write his own fascinating record of it in the form of an autobiography, the first volume of which, *Die gerettete Zunge* ('The tongue set free'), appeared in 1977, four years before he was awarded the Nobel Prize for Literature; the two other volumes, *Die Fackel im Ohr* ('The torch in the ear') and *Das Augenspiegel* ('The mirror of the eye'), covering the years 1921 to 1937, followed in 1980 and 1985.

Some writers did return to postwar Germany, however, among them Bertolt Brecht, who settled in East Berlin in 1949. He had left Germany in 1933 and spent the war years in Finland and the United States. During this prolonged exile he wrote most of the plays which were to make him the most famous German dramatist of the mid-twentieth century: an oeuvre which constitutes an unbroken continuity throughout that turbulent period. *Mutter Courage und ihre Kinder*, *Der gute Mensch von Sezuan* and *Leben des Galilei* were given their first performances in the only major German-language theatre to escape the artistic incubus of the Nazi dictatorship: the Zurich Schauspielhaus. In them the close links between earlier German literary movements – notably Expressionism – and postwar literary developments are particularly clear. At the same time they also draw attention to the more or less constant tension in mid-twentieth-century German writing between aesthetic and imaginative freedom and the constraints and responsibilities of ideologically and politically conditioned writing. Because the left-wing ideology espoused by Brecht advocated change as the most effective means for improving society, it proved particularly congenial to drama: the prospect or occurrence of change makes for good theatre. In theatrical terms, too, the dramas of Brecht provided visible continuity with the artistic and technical experimentation associated with the playwrights and directors of the 1920s

and reaffirmed the theatre as an art form clearly and defiantly different from the photographi-
cally realistic cinema. The supreme merit of Brecht's plays is their sheer theatricality, achieved
through his deliberate renewal of the *Verfremdungseffekte* or alienation techniques which had
been characteristic of the theatre of Niklas Manuel and the other playwrights of the Reformation period, and were born of a similar wish to fuse entertainment with ideological debate and
indoctrination in order to make people think. But Brecht had other strengths besides, not least
his ability to create great roles for actors and actresses and great opportunities for stage directors
and producers. When he returned to East Berlin under the aegis of its new 'socialist' administration and set up the Berliner Ensemble in 1949 with his wife, the actress Helene Weigel, he
acquired the status of the internationally most-respected literary figure of the German Democratic Republic. Whatever the final verdict on the life and work of this provocative political
playwright, his postwar presence in Berlin certainly restored something of the city's sense of
creative theatrical continuity.

## The Swiss Take Centre Stage

In Zurich, meanwhile, Max Frisch had been making a more modest name for himself with the
six plays he wrote between 1945 and 1953, such as *Die chinesische Mauer* ('The Great Wall of
China', 1947), which owed increasingly much to Brecht's example and paved the way for his
emergence in 1961 as a major dramatist in his own right with *Andorra*, which soon became an
international success. *Andorra* took the theme of *Vergangenheitsbewältigung* to new heights, and
it did so for two reasons: in the first place Frisch adopted and adapted a Brechtian alienation
technique to create a striking antithesis between 'then' and 'now', 'former complicity' and
'present exculpation'; second, it focused explicitly on the subject of anti-Semitism while
interpreting it in such as way that it becomes a common human phenomenon bound up with
social prejudice and xenophobia rather than with specific events in Germany in the 1930s. In
the context of post-1945 literature, however, perhaps the most remarkable thing about *Andorra*
is that it is the work of a Swiss writer able to see recent events from close to, yet objectively and
with no need to exculpate himself. His drama thus achieves a timeless quality without forfeiting
the almost Expressionistic immediacy guaranteed by the primary colours of its stage-sets and
verbal images, its sequences of short, closely focused and deliberately juxtaposed scenes, and
the implicit equation of theatre audience and jury whenever its chief characters appear as in a
court of law to explain in retrospect why they failed to live up to the moral principles which
Frisch implies his play shares with all mankind.

Switzerland's contribution to postwar literature had already been demonstrated when, in
1956, Friedrich Dürrenmatt's so-called 'comic tragedy' *Der Besuch der alten Dame* ('The visit of
the old lady') was premièred in Zurich and met with outrage and derision. Dürrenmatt's most
famous play presents a society which is so avid to enjoy prosperity that it is ready to sacrifice the
life of one of its members to achieve it. But in this remarkable play concerns have clearly shifted:
the legacy of the war is no longer the centre of attention – though the guilt and complicity of
individuals and society still are – and economic considerations have displaced politics and
ideologies. Dürrenmatt's masterpiece embraces the evolution of a whole era which witnessed
the transformation of western Europe in one short decade. It opens with a caricature of apathy
and economic stagnation and comes to its climax in a phantasmagoria of economic recovery and
hovers between a sense of earthy realism that might well be described as Swiss and the

heightened surrealism of tragedy and farce which betrays both its rootedness in ancient Greek drama and its closeness to the theatre of the absurd. The old lady of its title, played in the première by the great interwar Berlin actress Therese Giehse, is a memorable personification of retribution, but her relationship to its object Alfred Ill, the man who stayed at home, is a personal one between one victim and another; the context she creates for her vengeance on Ill is, for its part, the most graphic depiction in German literature of the effects of wealth on moral standards and human conduct, and a bitingly satirical indictment of postwar society.

## Literature and the Economic Miracle

The première of *Der Besuch der alten Dame* was a proclamation of the fact that the emphasis of contemporary writing was moving away from the trauma of defeat and the challenges of reconstruction and was now beginning to fall on the state of contemporary society. The German economic miracle was at its height, Switzerland had become an enviable model of stable prosperity, and hopes were rising for the improvement of Austria's standard of living after the departure of the Soviets in 1955. But serious writers tended not to share the plutocratic values that were replacing the ideologies of the past; they peered behind the surface of West Germany's miraculous economic recovery, probing and asking awkward questions, and the result was a return to that Naturalist concept, the literature of exposure. Now, however, the approach was more cynical and less idealistic than that of writers fifty years before, and the means used to lay bare the underlying truths of the contemporary situation and to reveal its unpleasant implications were more complex and sophisticated.

The change of direction that occurred in German literature in the 1950s gave new life to the satirical mode as a traditionally effective means of unmasking hypocrisy and restoring a moral sense to values going astray. As a rule, satire's closest ally is humour; but the literature produced during the decade between 1955 and 1965 is deficient in this respect. Its chief authors were more intent on demonstrating what they had learnt from a reading of authors such as Proust and Joyce: multilayered narrative texts, streams of consciousness, cunningly encapsulated incidents and semi-symbolical patterns were now more highly prized by writers such as Martin Walser, whose *Ehen in Philippsburg* (1957) stands interesting comparison with John Braine's *Room at the Top*, published in the same year, as a subtly orchestrated study of the workings of upward mobility in a provincial social setting and, by implication, a scathing attack on the readiness of the newly affluent generation to hunt with the wolves and further their own careers and interests whatever the price. The complexities of Walser's narrative style did not please everyone. Max Frisch's *Homo Faber*, also published in 1957, presented a sensitive, though more straightforward, analysis of an analogous subject, the mental and emotional development of a simplistic and insensitive technician, a new type of working man who is only gradually made aware of the stratified, interlinked complexities of life in their broader dimensions of space and time. Heinrich Böll meanwhile had been building up his reputation as a novelist. In *Und sagte kein einziges Wort* (1953) he used the topical phenomenon of a disintegrating marriage to present an analysis of a society uncertain of its direction. But he harboured a more ambitious view of the novelist's responsibilities, as became evident in *Billard um halb zehn* ('Billiards at 9.30', 1959). This story of a family over a span of three generations from 1907 to 1959 marked the re-emergence of the family saga as one of the most potent ways of tracing the gradual changes which a society undergoes, but which can so easily go undetected. It was a narrative formula that had been used to similar effect half a century before by Thomas Mann in *Buddenbrooks* to portray the rise and fall of the upper middle class: here Böll uses it in order to demonstrate that the 'new' Germany of the Federal Republic during the Adenauer era was directly descended from an empire conditioned by factors both similar and very different. It was not so much the materialist values of the new age as its mindless banality that earned it the scorn of serious authors. Though some of the novels they wrote achieved critical esteem and success with a minority of readers, their failure to make much impact with the readership at large suggests that the gulf between writer and reader was getting wider: people who hitherto had turned to books for entertainment and improvement were beginning to find television an attractive alternative.

The large-scale novel's return to favour was demonstrated by Martin Walser's so-called 'Kristlein' trilogy, *Halbzeit* ('Half-time', 1960), *Das Einhorn* ('The unicorn', 1966) and *Der Sturz* ('The fall', 1973), which provides a panorama of West German life through the eyes of a versatile but ordinary 'little' man told in a manner which suggests Fallada's *Kleiner Mann – was nun?* retold by James Joyce. It was an undertaking that reflects in aesthetic terms the paradoxes underlying German culture at the time it was written. With the appearance in 1959 of Günter Grass's *Die Blechtrommel* ('The tin drum') German postwar literature had already produced its most impressive classic. Here the traumatic legacy of the Nazi past and the uneasy stability erected upon it had found an author who was capable of making coherent sense of them and of combining fact and fiction in a way which did justice to the claims of both. The novel owed much to the example of a predecessor whom Grass much admired: the seventeenth-century novelist Grimmelshausen, whose *Simplicissimus Teutsch*, published in 1668, had managed to make some sense of the Thirty Years War through its bold blend of autobiography, imagination and artistic manipulation. Like his precursor, Grass places an observant simpleton in the midst of incidents and characters whose significance would escape the notice and comprehension of a more adult but therefore also more partial observer, an observer who is also clearly related in part to himself, the self who experienced the past and who is now, in his fiction, coming to terms with it and exorcizing its memories. Oscar Matzerath, Grass's *alter ego*, is a case of retarded development, yet with his toy tin drum he can drum up significant fragments of a past which his adult contemporaries have suppressed: the simpleton can face the truth although it is often as unpleasant as the many graphic episodes in the novel relating to what was happening in Grass's home town, Danzig, between 1930 and 1950, that span of a mere twenty years which stretched from the slump to the economic miracle, and from the Weimar Republic to the Cold War. Significantly, what is depicted is not presented from a knowing and involved point of view: the sophistication and subtlety of the novel are to be found instead in Grass's masterly handling of the rhetoric of language and imagery, symbolism and register. The result is at once a fantasy bordering on nightmare and a graphic account of lived reality; it is profoundly serious yet rich in many sorts of humour, bawdy, verbal, ironic, surrealistic, yet characterized by Grass's sure eye for naturalistic detail. *Die Blechtrommel* unfolds with an imaginative verve which succeeded in reclaiming for German narrative literature the storytelling qualities of the Grimm fairy tales and Till Eulenspiegel's pranks without forfeiting the intellectual depth and moral seriousness of the German classics. Art had been used to tell the truth. It was a hard act to follow, even for its author.

By the early 1970s it was becoming clear that German literature was consolidating itself round a number of topical themes to which writers were bringing their individual approaches. The infringement of personal privacy by the ever more intrusive media, which was arousing widespread disquiet, was given classic treatment in 1974 in Böll's novelle *Die verlorene Ehre der*

*Katharina Blum* ('The lost honour of Katharina Blum'), a well-timed exposure of the lengths and the depths to which investigative reporting is prepared to go in search of a good story, which also homed in on its disregard for the apparently insignificant yet intrinsically important rights and feelings of human beings. Always particularly responsive to what was in the wind – it was his strength as an author, though perhaps also in the long run an artistic weakness – Böll, who had been awarded the Nobel Prize for Literature in 1972, continued his Dickensian survey of contemporary society and social issues by turning to the negative aspects of the welfare state. In the novel *Fürsorgliche Belagerung* ('Under solicitous siege', 1979) he set out to show how the authorities were again intruding on the private lives of men and women, this time in the name of security, an issue given added immediacy in the Federal Republic by the increasingly violent activities of terrorist movements such as the Baader-Meinhof Group and the Red Army Faction, which were causing mounting fear and anxiety between 1972 and 1977.

There were other threats to postwar stability and complacency in the West: the deep-seated fear of sudden nuclear destruction and the growing awareness, especially among the young intelligentsia, of the long-term dangers of ecological disaster posed by the pollution of the environment as a direct result of the industrial and economic miracle of the postwar years. This was leading to the formation of pacifist, green alternative movements in all the German-speaking countries, a trend often reflected in 'green' themes and imagery in literature, too. Prior to that, however, Dürrenmatt's 'comedy' *Die Physiker* ('The physicists', published and first performed in 1962) established itself overnight as an entirely original and indeed idiosyncratic treatment of a profound new *angst*, or rather as an exorcism of it through the medium of theatre. Dürrenmatt's ability in comedy to use exaggeration and bathos make audiences all over the world laugh at the threat looming over them, a response which reduced tension and helped remove the individual's sense of helplessness and vulnerability in the face of doom. Locked away in a private psychiatric clinic, three nuclear scientists pretend to be mad in order to keep a scientific secret – the key to total annihilation – from falling into the wrong hands; but their undertaking has disastrous results, for the secret has indeed fallen into such hands: the woman doctor who runs the clinic has already appropriated it – or claims she has – for her own insane ends. The return in Dürrenmatt's black comedy of deft stagecraft, dramatic irony and laughter proved welcome in an era characterized by its loss of a sense of fun. That its darkest dread should have stimulated the creation of one of the great comedies of twentieth-century literature was a timely illustration of the artist's ability to illuminate present-day reality while at the same time transcending it.

## The Curse of the Past

Underneath these topical issues, a malaise was continuing to prey on the minds and imaginations of German authors, and that was the curse of the not so distant past. Despite its frequent excellence, especially in the domains of the short story and the autobiographical novelle, the literature of *Vergangenheitsbewältigung* in the early postwar years had not succeeded in banishing it, so now a second wave of younger writers set about doing their best to come to terms with it artistically. This they did by adopting a less personal but more considered and deliberate approach. Grass had already anticipated this second wave of *Vergangenheitsbewältigung* in the two works which had followed the success of *Die Blechtrommel*: *Katz und Maus* (1961) and *Hundejahre* ('Dog years', 1963). The first of these uses material drawn from his own boyhood memories in order to probe the actual meaning of those solemn, daunting abstracts – patriotism, honour, duty, loyalty – which had been imposed on the minds of so many Germans in the past, and to elucidate their often uncomfortably close relationship to notions such as prejudice, chauvinism and cruelty. The second, *Hundejahre*, a much longer book, extends the range of Grass's inquiry in *Die Blechtrommel* by creating an even stranger, even more idiosyncratic picture of Germany from the war years onwards. In its intentions and implications the work is deadly serious, but it is told with a narrative verve and disregard for realism except in its graphic described detail and underlying purpose which both owe more than a little to the stimulating example of Jean Paul Richter, the little-read but much-admired novelist of Goethe's era, whose technical brilliance exerted an influence on many other writers of Grass's generation, most notably Arno Schmidt, the dauntingly allusive author of *Zettels Traum* ('Zettel's dream', 1970).

Boyhood experiences during the Nazi period also form the basis for Siegfried Lenz's novel *Deutschstunde* (1968), a story which wrestles with the moral dilemmas posed by the concept of duty in the life of Siggi Jepsen, a North German boy whose school punishment, an essay on that topic, turns into a full-scale account of his life during the war. In all these works, and many more besides, the memory of the author and his characters is probed and stimulated to come up with those often 'forgotten' and repressed yet decisive and telling incidents and impressions which are in effect the missing pieces of the great puzzle which had been perplexing so many German readers and writers during the postwar decades. A rather different approach to this same objective underlies Böll's novel *Gruppenbild mit Dame* ('Group photograph with lady', 1971), a fictional reconstruction or piecing-together of the past of a group of people caught by a photograph in a moment in time; gradually the novel builds up a rounded picture of them and of the enigmatic woman in their midst, Leni Pfeiffer née Gruytens, and in the process Böll convinces his readers that their own past experience has many close similarities with that of his fictitious characters. Common to all the fictions written by the second wave of postwar writers to concern themselves with the recent past and its literary potential is a compulsive urge to circumvent straightforward conventional storytelling; instead they indulge in narrative techniques such as concurrent storylines, flashbacks, inset texts and supporting references in order to create a textured sense of lived reality vivid and authentic enough to convince, grip and disturb the reader in the moment of reading. Overt interpretations of the past are not what these writers offer. Their purpose was to rekindle memory, stimulate reflection and thereby clarify the baffling complexity of what had happened in Germany by laying it to rest for the elderly while keeping it alive for the young.

Complex, extremely long-drawn-out narrative had already earned critical acclaim if not a widespread readership for *Mutmaßungen über Jakob* ('Conjectures about Jacob'), the fascinating novel by Uwe Johnson published in 1959 when he left the German Democratic Republic for the West, and which he followed, after two other novels, with an ambitious four-volume sequel, *Jahrestage: Aus dem Leben der Gesine Cresspahl* ('Anniversaries'), which followed it in the years 1970 to 1983. Between them, these fictions create a vast narrative structure which constitutes a retrospective survey of Germany's mid-twentieth-century history told in the form of a multifaceted inquest of enormous breadth and detail into the motivations of people who may exist or have existed and into events which may or may not have taken place. Johnson's slow, forensic narrative strategy, with its multiple perspectives, time-shifts, cross-references and retarding digressions, was well suited to the author's self-imposed but almost impossible task, which was nothing less than the analysis of an age and the evocation of its atmosphere as well as its influence on people's minds and emotions, presented in such a way that it also reflects the workings of memory and the diverse ways in which people experience and respond to the same things. Such ambitiously complex narrative structures are much indebted to the experiments of Proust, Joyce and Jakob Wassermann, his own by then already almost forgotten compatriot, author of the great trilogy of novels which had opened in 1928 with *Der Fall Maurizius* ('The Maurizius case') and also includes *Etzel Andergast* (1931) and *Joseph Kerkhovens dritte Existenz* ('Joseph Kerkhoven's third existence', 1934). Johnson's *magnum opus* commands respect as one of its era's outstanding works of narrative fiction, even if most late-twentieth-century readers have neither the time nor the intellectual stamina to read it.

## Poetry after Auschwitz: Paul Celan

The poet Hilde Domin described poetry as an open sesame to the human being's most important experience, the encounter with the self; her younger contemporary Paul Celan once said that a poem is a message in a bottle, a message recording the human being's search for reality despite being hurt by it. A novel could narrate what happened, a play could bring it to life by dramatizing it; but poetry alone could express the otherwise inexpressible. Yet in his essay *Prismen: Kulturkritik und Gesellschaft* (1955) Theodor Adorno stated that to write a poem after Auschwitz was barbaric, a dictum that was to haunt critical discourse and cripple creativity for decades. In 1988 a congress of writers met in Frankfurt to discuss 'Writing after Auschwitz' (the name of this concentration and extermination camp had become synonymous with the Holocaust and with National Socialism at its worst) and in 1990 Günter Grass had used the same title for a lecture on his own work as a writer; by 1992 an interdisciplinary conference in Berlin had widened the topic to include art of every kind. The great postwar debate about the future of German literature in relation to the past thus resurfaced in all its controversial diversity at precisely the time when the *Wende* was taking place and German reunification was apparently the dominant issue of the day. *Vergangenheitsbewältigung* had still not been achieved; the ghost of the past had not been laid to rest.

Adorno, one of Germany's most influential thinkers in the postwar period, had not forbidden poems about Auschwitz, let alone lyric poetry in general; but with their characteristic flair for bypassing the obvious and seeking sanctuary in aesthetic theory, many writers, poets and academics chose to read his dictum as a general indictment of all postwar cultural and artistic endeavour. He was of course acutely conscious of the paradoxical nature of art after the Second World War, and of the problematic role of aesthetic values in a world which had just barely survived its own destruction. Like many other survivors he felt that the upheaval had been too elemental to allow a return to some pre-established harmony. But not all writers agreed. The poet Nelly Sachs had survived the Holocaust in Swedish exile, and she was now taken up by Hans Magnus Enzensberger, a controversially outspoken West German poet and literary figure, as the living antithesis of Adorno's view, while Paul Celan, another survivor, championed his own poetry and, with it, the purpose and role of art in the postwar era in his speech or *Preisrede* on receiving the coveted Büchner Prize for literature in 1960. Both he and Sachs centred their work on the horrors they had lived through, with the obvious implication that for them at least poetry was the means for expressing the otherwise inexpressible. As Hilde Domin and other, younger writers were emphasizing in the 1960s, poetry was the only verbal art form capable of registering and communicating the full implications of what had taken place. Immediacy and concentration, the traditional qualities of lyric poetry, were, they argued, the prerogatives of poets still, and poets cannot be silenced. What needed to be silenced was the recurrent tendency of German lyric poetry ever since the late seventeenth century to rely on tired clichés and conventionally anodyne echoes of what had once been exciting and new, a tendency that had characterized many of the later classical and Romantic writers and many more of the countless minor poets of the turn of the century who had successfully imitated the styles of their greater contemporaries, such as Rilke and George, without really having anything to say. As the GDR writer Stefan Heym put it in 1988, there is spring still, and the smiles of young women, and beauty, but they are all covered by a blood-stained coating of frost – our memory of all the terrible things human beings have done to others. It was the sheer magnitude of the numbers involved that turned the stark reality of 1933–45 into a monstrous abstraction.

Paul Celan had been scarred by that reality. He had lost both parents during the German occupation of his native Bukovina, but survived to show the world that lyric poetry was perhaps the medium best suited to expressing what he and so many others like him had been through. No poet of the postwar era conveys that trauma quite so graphically. The very fact that he persisted in writing the language he had grown up speaking at home in Czernowitz was a defiant reminder that it is more than just the language of the Third Reich. In 1947 he fled from Romania to Vienna, where his first published collection of poems, *Der Sand aus den Urnen* ('The sand from the urns'), appeared in 1948. He never lived in Germany, and spent the remainder of his life in Paris. *Mohn und Gedächtnis* ('Poppies and remembrance'), the collection which made his a voice to be reckoned with in postwar German poetry, appeared in 1952. Such writing seemed perplexingly surrealistic at first, but it gradually disclosed its deeper meanings as its critical admirers realized that Celan's images and rhythms were the fragmented residue of the great poetic traditions of European and German poetry, and that he was painfully trying to put together the pieces after the culture to which he, too, belonged had been smashed by the aesthetic equivocations that had accompanied the new barbarian age. The titles of both collections spoke for themselves to those who could pick up the similes in them: sand, urns and poppies say more than memory (*Gedächtnis*) itself even to English readers, since for them their associations with Shelley, Keats and Rupert Brooke are almost more powerful than any which Celan could rely on in German poetry. 'Todesfuge', the most celebrated poem in this first collection, is clearly an attempt to express an all but inexpressible personal grief; but it is also a lament on the passing of time and the transience of life that is shot through with verbal echoes of the Old Testament and written in the shadow of death, and also permeated by the cadences of classical poetry and of the German classicism of Hölderlin. These elements Celan handles like a fugue, the baroque musical form whose very name suggests the flight of life, love and time, but whose recurring verbal and melodic patterns simultaneously suggest their continuity. The mastery was evident and did much to restore the good name of German poetry.

Celan is a commanding figure in the postwar literary landscape. But he was not alone. Rose Ausländer also grew up in Czernowitz, and like Celan survived the Holocaust which reduced the Jewish population of the city from 60,000 to 5000. Before that, in the 1920s, she had lived in New York, and she wrote well in English as well as German, but it was the uncertainty, fear and suffering of the war years back in Romania that made her discard the mannerisms of her often eclectic and imitative prewar poetry in order to focus on what few certainties remained. Of these the central one was her abiding attachment to her mother tongue, which for her came to be a more than adequate substitute for the so-called 'fatherland' that had never recognized her and had done its utmost to exterminate her people. Less hermetic than Celan's, and more accessible, too, because its themes are more obviously related to everyday experience,

Ausländer's poetry was a remarkable demonstration of the creative vigour which survived in an area of German culture far removed from that of postwar West Germany and virtually obliterated by the Third Reich, yet which still had much of value to communicate to readers of German everywhere. Indeed with names of survivors like Nelly Sachs, Ilse Aichinger and Hilde Domin to add to those who perished but whose poetry was rediscovered after 1945, such as Gertrud Kolmar, it is clear that Adorno's dictum about writing poems after Auschwitz was disproved by the Jewish women poets who in the postwar years did more than anyone could have expected to bring German lyric poetry back to life and restore its reputation.

## Drama after Brecht

German drama reached a high-water mark in the immediate postwar period thanks to the reputation and achievement of Brecht, the international popularity of Frisch and Dürrenmatt, and the success of isolated plays such as *Das heilige Experiment* (1947) by the Viennese playwright Fritz Hochwälder, in which more or less well-intentioned Jesuits were shown trying – and failing – to build an ideal society in eighteenth-century South America. But Brecht died in 1956, and Frisch proved unable to build on his achievement in *Andorra* (1961) and the shorter play that preceded it, *Biedermann und die Brandstifter* ('Biedermann and the arsonists', 1958), a mercilessly funny but fundamentally problematical send-up of middle-class complicity and helplessness in the face of anarchic terrorism represented by the arsonists who move into the cosy home of the feckless Herr Biedermann, a stereotype of his generation and class. After *Die Physiker* (1962) Dürrenmatt's dramatic powers, though not his imaginative and moral vigour, went into rapid decline, although his writings on theatre (*Theater-Schriften und Reden*) were establishing themselves as classic treatments of their subject comparable to the writings of Lessing and Hebbel for their range and power and their ability to stimulate thought and discussion.

The course of drama in the German-speaking countries from the early 1960s onwards was to be erratic. Dramatic achievement was sporadic, names came and went, fashions changed and the stage increasingly tended to become the domain of producers and directors, and to be dominated by dramaturgical considerations, production techniques, experiments with lighting, film and sound-effects. Drama as literature was neglected; German plays became ever harder to read, and performance seemed to be primarily aimed at the informed minority audience member. There were isolated exceptions of course. In 1964 Heinar Kipphardt demonstrated the uses to which a documentary approach to theatre could be put in his dramatic analysis of the McCarthy phenomenon in contemporary America, *In der Sache J. Robert Oppenheimer* ('The Oppenheimer case'), while Grass, already famous as a major contemporary novelist, turned his attention to the stage in order to depict in fiercely critical mood the aspirations and failure of the Berlin uprising of June 1953 in the play he scathingly entitled *Die Plebejer proben den Aufstand* ('The plebeians rehearse an uprising', 1965), where the eventuality of political action is satirically seen as a mere rehearsal for a revolution that never happened.

In the 1970s new voices started to make themselves heard. Botho Strauss came to the fore with plays such as *Kleists Traum vom Prinzen Homburg* (1972), which presupposes an audience sufficiently cultured and conversant with Kleist's classic drama to be able to appreciate its deconstruction in Strauss's clever and often entertaining contrasts between historical fact, the constructs of the creative imagination and the desire of fictitious characters to break out of their textual framework and take on a life of their own. A similar approach underlies Strauss's reworking – or travesty? – of *A Midsummer Night's Dream* in *Der Park* (1983), a theatrical entertainment more notable for its intentions than its actual effect. The type of drama which Strauss, a prolific writer, chose to put forward owed a good deal to the later work of Strindberg, the turn-of-the-century Swedish dramatist whose work, long admired in Germany, was being retranslated at the time by Peter Weiss, a dramatist who scored a more lasting success with two plays in the mid-1960s: *Die Ermittlung* ('The inquiry', 1965) is a powerful documentary drama based on the trial of a group of people who had formerly worked in the concentration camp at Auschwitz, and drama's most significant contribution to the theme of settling up with the past. Even more famous is Weiss's *Die Verfolgung und Ermordung Jean Paul Marats dargestellt durch die Schauspielgruppe des Hospizes zu Charenton unter Anleitung des Herrn de Sade* ('The pursuit and assassination of Marat as performed by the players of the asylum at Charenton under the direction of Monsieur de Sade', 1964), the play which revealed most fully the theatrical potential of the new trends in contemporary literature and drama. Like many prose narratives of the period, it too makes use of the framework technique in order to juxtapose past and present, historical reality and its re-enactment and reinterpretation: the murdered revolutionary being recreated on stage by a maniac nihilist who is apparently his opposite, is both genuine and himself and a hypocrite impersonated by an actor pretending to be a lunatic in a flamboyant stage-show demanding extreme technical skill from all its participants. At last German theatre was again enjoying itself in its characteristically thought-provoking way.

The new subjectivity being promoted or exploited by Strauss in a string of more or less successful plays was almost immediately counterbalanced by a sudden and unexpected return to all-out realism of the type associated with German Naturalism when the Bavarian playwright Franz Xaver Kroetz started to make a name for himself with plays such as *Heimarbeit* (1971) and *Stallerhof* (1972), which took the uncompromising realism of the 1890s to new depths, to the shocked horror of many of the people on whom the theatre depended for its regular audiences. Strauss's plays were wordy and clever. Kroetz's by contrast were relatively short, laconic and dark, but not without a certain humour. They took the lid off contemporary goings-on in a section of the German population – the peasant farmers of Bavaria – which had missed out on the rise in living standards in postwar Germany and lacked the educational advantages of the urban audiences whose members watched aghast as Kroetz's often drastic down-to-earth dramas unfolded. The kitchen sink had scarcely impinged on postwar modern drama, but the same cannot be said of the trough. The new naturalism of Kroetz's so-called *Volksstücke* was crude, but it had something to say about the affluent modern society in which such goings-on as the undetected killing of a woman's unwanted child by her husband or the pathetic efforts of a retarded girl to survive in her deprived surroundings could be recognized as authentic and realistic. Moreover, Kroetz's dramas also marked a return to a style and subject matter rooted in the Naturalism of Gerhart Hauptmann and going back at least as far as the *Sturm und Drang*. For all its postwar openness to foreign influences German dramatic literature was still capable of renewing its links with the past and drawing new nourishment from its old source of subject matter and inspiration: the life and language of the common people.

Naturalism has its limitations, as Gerhart Hauptmann and Arno Holz had discovered almost a century before. By 1984 Kroetz was turning to a wider, less naturalistic canvas in *Furcht und Hoffnung der BRD*: the title is an allusion to Brecht's *Furcht und Elend des Dritten Reiches*, which had been premièred by a group of German exiles in Paris in 1938. But, despite the protracted and often tense conflict between West Germany's right-wing press and its intelligentsia in the

1970s and the wave of protest aroused by the West German government's anti-terrorist legislation, which was seen by many as a denial of human rights, the obvious prosperity the country was enjoying tends to make such querulous diatribes seem the work of fault-finding pessimists with a certain amount of talent but without anything better to write about.

## Literature before the *Wende*

West German literature had become almost obsessed by the notion of contemporary relevance. Relevant responses to contemporary problems, and contemporary characters caught up in topically problematic situations, were the staple of contemporary fiction. Fantasy was 'out' and so, too, was the power of the imagination to transport readers to fictional worlds, though this was provided by many of the countless foreign authors whose works in German translation were flooding the bookshops. Why was it that no writer in Germany seemed able to provide what so many French, English and American writers could? It was becoming ever more clear that the highbrow or quality writers of Germany were entering a period of imaginative stagnation.

The best-sellers of the 1980s reflect this state of affairs from another angle. In 1979 Michael Ende published *Die unendliche Geschichte* ('The never-ending story'), a children's story for adults in which a young dreamer called Bastian Balthasar Bux sets out on his adventures to rescue the threatened kingdom of Phantásie. The message here was that the modern poet, too, must enter the world of the imagination: to drag the imaginary and fantastical over into the modern world is a recipe for distortion, vulgarization and aesthetic disaster. Six years later Patrick Süskind came to the rescue of imaginative writing by scoring an even greater success with his best-selling novel *Das Parfüm* ('The scent'). Like Ende's tale, this too is the story of a boy. But Süskind's boy, Jean-Baptiste Grenouille, turns into a nineteenth-century Parisian serial murderer who kills in pursuit of the scent that rises from his victims' bodies. Imaginative writing had made a comeback hailed by readers in their thousands; two authors had returned to the never-never-lands of fairy tale and historical fiction which had once been the speciality of German writers, and if their modern yarns were more horrific or more obscure than theirs, no matter: there was reason to rejoice that the nation of E. T. A. Hoffmann had produced Ende and Süskind. The fact that Süskind's monodrama *Der Kontrabass* ('The double bass'), premièred in Zurich in 1984, was the most often performed German play during the 1984–5 season only seemed to emphasize what was happening. So, too, did the revival of interest in medieval themes and Arthurian subjects in the 1980s which was exemplified by works such as Tankred Dorst's long saga *Merlin oder Das wüste Land* ('Merlin or The waste land', 1981) and, in the related realm of classical myth, by *Die letzte Welt* ('The Last World', 1988), a novel by the Austrian Christoph Ransmayr (b. 1954), in which German readers were reintroduced to the mythical topography that had delighted readers in earlier periods and which was enhanced by the novel's evocation of Ovid's metamorphoses in exile on the shores of a Black Sea. Ovid needed to leave Rome behind him to regain his creative freedom; only by turning his back on the affluent banalities of modern society can the modern German poet regain the lost world of the imagination. It was a world that readers were apparently longing to rediscover, as they showed by buying the new best-selling novels of Ende, Süskind and Ransmayr in their millions.

The Berlin Wall was breached in November 1989; but does the reunification of Germany on 3 October 1990 represent a more significant caesura in its modern literary evolution than the deaths of Uwe Johnson in 1984 and of Böll in 1985, Dürrenmatt in 1990 and Frisch in 1991?

The literary impact of the *Wende* and the creative response to it entailed a major shift in literary attitude and subject matter, and the deaths of these four major postwar writers cleared the scene for new talents. Of the leading West German writers of the postwar era, only Günter Grass and Martin Walser remained. Walser was quick to respond to the new situation. His long novel *Die Verteidigung der Kindheit* ('In defence of childhood') was hailed on its appearance in 1991 as Germany's first major post-*Wende* work. But the novel's protagonist, Alfred Dorn of Dresden in the (former) GDR, who makes it to West Germany, is in reality an addict of failure who keeps his options open until he finally chooses to opt out. This was hardly the positive note the exciting new era called for, and Walser's reputation, already in decline, soon paled before the example of Grass, who approached the new era less abruptly but with infinitely greater imaginative command. First, he published his relatively short novel *Unkenrufe* ('The croaking of toads') in 1992. It is the story of a German art historian, Alexander Reschke, and his relationship with Alexandra Piatkowska, a Polish conservator, who work together in Grass's old home town of Danzig, hatching their brilliant idea of creating a 'cemetery of reconciliation' there to which all those exiled and expelled can now return to enjoy eternal rest in their native soil. This idea quickly catches on, but as German developers and the D-mark begin to turn their dream into a crass reality, we realize that the modern German economy has peacefully regained what war and violence had lost.

With *Unkenrufe*, this satirical idyll in which the modern themes of conservation, development, homesickness and the fourth age are ingeniously blended, Grass prepared the way for the narrative *tour de force* which conveys his understanding of the *Wende* and its implications. *Ein weites Feld* (1995) is not an easy book, but, as its title implies to any moderately well-read German reader, it is an intensely ironic attempt to come to terms with a topic with vast ramifications, a task made more possible by the author's readiness and ability to see it in the wider context of cultural landscape and national identity. Not only is the title the favourite expression of the heroine's father in Theodor Fontane's most famous novel, *Effi Briest*, published exactly 100 years before; in the novel itself his *alter ego* Theo Wuttke, known to his friends as 'Fonty' and born exactly a century after the great Prussian novelist, is an entertaining narrative device which allows Grass to explore the paradoxes and riddles of the new Germany in the light of its past, a past that is the sum total of its values, experiences and illusions, themselves once the object of his great precursor's acute powers of descriptive observation. The fact that the villain of the piece is called Hoftaller, a direct allusion to *Tallhover*, a novel published in 1986 by the former GDR author Hans Joachim Schädlich (1935– ), in which a long-lived secret police officer of that name, also born in 1819, works indefatigably to preserve the status quo, allows Grass to provide a telling if sometimes over-subtle counterpoint to his fictional exploration of Germany's discontinuities during the last 150 years. He had written nothing on so grand a scale since *Der Butt* ('The flounder') in 1977.

## The Literature of the German Democratic Republic

'Was bleibt von der DDR-Literatur?' – 'What of the GDR's literature will endure?' asked the writer Helga Königsdorf in 1990, the year of German reunification. *Was bleibt?* is also the haunting title of Christa Wolf's novelle about her surveillance by the GDR secret police or Stasi, written in 1979 but not published until 1990, after the fall of the Wall. The consequences were to haunt Wolf herself, who had been so long identified both in the East and the West as probably the most gifted and one of the most committed socialist writers in the German Democratic Republic. When her own activities as an 'unofficial collaborator' with the Stasi in the late 1950s and early 1960s came to light, they unleashed in their wake what came to be known as the *deutsch-deutscher Literaturstreit*, or 'German-German literary feud', a bitter conflict between East and West Germans about the function of the writer under a dictatorship. It was conducted by a number of West Germans with scant regard for human psychology and the realities of life in a totalitarian state, and has left its traces in the patronizing tone of much critical work written in the Federal Republic about the literature of the GDR. Yet both the explicit question 'what will endure?' and the implied question as to what may constitute the most lasting literary achievements of the postwar period are legitimate. Should a literary history of Germany treat this period and this part of the German-speaking countries as separate from the rest of German literature in the latter half of the twentieth century? The answer must surely be yes, and particularly in the present context, which sets out to draw the reader's attention to broad trends and to see literature in terms of the self-perception of those who created it and those who read it.

Initially GDR literature, which still plays a prominent role in the curricula of German university departments throughout the world, was largely the creation of what Franz Fühmann, one of its main lyric poets and short-story writers, called the 'Stalingrad' generation, a generation decimated when Germany suffered its major defeat on the Russian front in February 1943. This first generation of postwar writers in the Soviet zone of occupation also included older men and women, many of whom had been in exile during the Third Reich. Young or old, they devoted their attention to the construction of a new society, and it is understandable that they did so on the ideological basis of anti-fascism and a commitment to an egalitarian and proletarian concept of social progress and social order. Christa Wolf, born in 1929, was one of its leading representatives, as were the dramatists Heiner Müller, Heinar Kipphardt and Peter Hacks, and the poets and shorter prose writers Franz Fühmann, Günter Kunert and Reiner Kunze, whose ironic prose sketches, *Die wunderbaren Jahre*, constitute an accessible and original introduction to the issues this new literature raised. Their mentors were older writers who had chosen to return to East Germany rather than to the West: they included Anna Seghers, Bertolt Brecht, Arnold Zweig, Heinrich Mann, Stephan Heym, Stephan Hermlin and Johannes R. Becher, who became the new state's Minister of Culture from 1954 until his death in 1958, and, like Seghers, a prominent cultural representative of the regime. The 'Stalingrad' generation had been politically formed in and by the Third Reich; many of them had then experienced 'conversion' to socialism in prisoner-of-war camps, including Fühmann and Hermann Kant, the successor of Seghers as president of the influential Writers' Union and author of *Die Aula* (1965), one of the most successful 'affirmative' novels of the new society, which sold well over a million copies. One of the most probing and original works to come from this generation is Christa Wolf's experimental novel, *Kindheitsmuster* ('A model childhood', 1976), with its protagonist exploring her own formation by the Third Reich and her gradual awakening as an adolescent, and its eloquent motto 'Die Vergangenheit ist nicht tot; sie ist nicht einmal vergangen' ('The past is not dead; it isn't even past'). It was these writers who, in the middle years of the GDR, conveyed such a sense of the vibrancy and social relevance of its literature. Soon they were joined by younger contemporaries such as the poets Sarah Kirsch and Reiner Kunze, and Jurek Becker, author of that extraordinary product of the human spirit, *Jakob der Lügner* ('Jacob the liar', 1969), a comic novel of wartime life in a Polish ghetto. Among them, too, were the *chansonnier* and satirist Wolf Biermann, the poets and essayists Volker Braun

(b. 1939), Christoph Hein (b. 1944) and Gert Neumann (b. 1942), and the witty feminist Irmtraud Morgner.

It was never intended by the Communists, when the new state was founded in October 1949, that the poet would be king. But it was made evident that imaginative literature and its creators were to be given a special function in building up and underpinning the new socialist society. Under the Soviet occupying forces in 1945–9, structures had been set in place to manipulate the creative energies of the writer in the interests of the community, always subject to the authority of the SED ('Sozialistische Einheitspartei Deutschlands' or Socialist Unity Party), the product of a forced merger between the Social Democrats and the Communists in the Soviet zone of occupation in 1946. In practical terms this meant that writers enjoyed higher earnings from their work than did their counterparts in the West, and something akin to a privileged status in society. A special and prestigious institution was set up in Leipzig to train future writers, and some fifty literary prizes were created to support them financially. In contrast to what Karl Marx had called capitalism's hostility to poetry, the new regime promoted the GDR as a 'nation of readers' ('Leseland DDR'). And it was a fact that its citizens owned more books per head than those of any other country in the world. Particularly in the early years of Erich Honecker's leadership, between 1971 and 1976, GDR writers believed that they were creating a fundamentally open type of literature for a readership that was accessible and critically constructive. It was, as Volker Braun put it, 'a process between people', hence the role in public life of readings by authors, followed by discussion, televised debates, open letters and interviews given by artists of every kind. In the theatre, the practical work and theoretical writings of dramatists such as Heiner Müller, Peter Hacks and Volker Braun put the onus on the audience to 'constitute the work of art for themselves'; as Hacks declared in 1977, 'we work with a socialist public in our mind's eye'.

For the committed socialist the attraction of the new regime was its concept of the artist as co-architect of a new and different Germany, and this ideal was all the more appealing to those confronted with the reality of Auschwitz in the immediate aftermath of 1945: the difference between Höss, the commandant of that notorious concentration camp, and himself, so Franz Fühmann provocatively declared, was one of scale, not of kind, and all thoughts about the postwar process of transformation therefore had to start right in front of the gas chambers. Not only was the socialist writer part of a collective, which in a classless society embraced all: socialist writers also felt that they were actively helping to exorcize the horrors that had been committed in the name of the German nation. But in the course of the 1950s, the concept of 'nation' was sedulously and progressively marginalized as the GDR struggled to establish an identity fundamentally and permanently distinct from that of any other form of German state. Ironically, Becher's text for the national anthem, 'Auferstanden aus den Ruinen und der Zukunft zugewandt' ('Arisen from the ruins and facing the future'), with its emphasis on reconstruction and the future, was quietly dropped, and on state occasions only its tune, by Hanns Eisler, was played. Still more ironic, perhaps, was the fact that Eisler's own ambitious opera, *Johann Faustus*, written to celebrate the change in substance of the 'new' Germany while retaining its cultural entity, had been proscribed immediately after its publication in 1952.

Looking back from the vantage point of forty years after the end of the Third Reich, Günter Kunert, a former Nazi and Stalinist, and later dissident, recalled that 'we felt it to be a moral imperative to submit to the common good. Didacticism was the keynote of our new literature.' Now the writer's duty was to proclaim and put forward blueprints for change, an approach which encouraged an uneasy blend of utopianism and down-to-earth realism designed to show that literature was not the province of a socio-cultural elite but accessible to all members of society. The didactic function of the writer, which had often dominated German literature in the past – most notably during the Reformation period and the Age of Enlightenment, two eras in favour in the new East German state – was back in vogue, and writers found themselves entrusted or burdened with the obligation of getting a set of non-literary ideological principles across to a reading public increasingly dependent on books published with state approval by state-run publishing houses. By 1961, the year when the Berlin Wall was built, this change of emphasis and direction had become specific and insistent. A nationalized literature with a socialist message and purpose would from now on have to leave outgrown middle-class values behind and promote the Marxist view of social evolution and the concept of a socialist society in ways which, to outsiders at least, seemed to have much in common with the political manipulation of artistic policy during the Third Reich, yet which also clearly shared the concern which leading West German writers were showing for past and present failings and future remedies.

The effect of this didactic emphasis was seen by the authorities, and by many writers, too, to depend on the reader's ability to recognize his or her own 'reality' in literature. Thus, in the Stalinist era of the late 1940s and 1950s, 'socialist realism', or 'tractor literature', as it was later derogatorily though not unfairly styled, became the order of the day. Even an established and sophisticated writer of the calibre of Anna Seghers was ready to try her hand, true to her lifelong belief that a socialist literature must be 'of the people'. Several well-known authors answered the call put out at the so-called Bitterfeld Conferences between 1959 and 1964, to become part of the world of factory and dockside work and collective farming, and to write about it. A hundred and fifty writers came forward to encourage creative writing among working men and women, Fühmann went to work in the Rostock docks and Christa Wolf in a railway carriage factory in Halle. In his novel *Ole Bienkopp*, one of the GDR's early classics, Erwin Strittmatter portrayed an enthusiastic but ineffectual collective farmworker in a way which owed much to the humorous approach of the great nineteenth-century Low German novelist, Fritz Reuter. The Bitterfeld initiative may not have been a complete success. The problems of communication involved are tellingly exemplified in Gert Neumann's short story 'Reportage' in his collection *Die Schuld der Worte* ('The guilt of words'), which was published in 1979 in the West but not until November 1989 in the East. But as a social experiment it had a significant impact at the time, and re-established workers' literature as a genre in its own right with origins stretching back to the early days of the German industrial revolution in the mid-nineteenth century.

Bitterfeld, which was also the centre of the East German chemical industry, is now associated with some of the worst state-engineered environmental pollution in Europe, but the ideas which emanated from its literary debates may well have been indirectly responsible for Christa Wolf's first major success, *Der geteilte Himmel* ('The divided sky', 1963), her novel about the division of Germany, which captured the prevailing mood during the months leading up to the building of the Berlin Wall. A human relationship of some personal depth and value is broken when Rita Seidel's fiancé leaves East Berlin for the West, but the break and separation enable her to find her way back painfully and at an emotional cost to a society in which shared responsibilities and rewards, and the healing experience of the comradeship of the factory floor, take precedence over the pursuit of personal happiness. The novel seemed to come to no clear conclusion, yet it was the starting-point for a sequence of works in which Wolf pursued her theme of search and self-discovery in ever more penetrating and complex ways. *Nachdenken über Christa T.* ('Reflections about Christa T.', 1968) and *Kindheitsmuster* (1976) were hardly typical of the new and officially sanctioned concept of a nationalized socialist literature promoted after the erection of the Wall, for instead of looking to the future arising out of the present, they turn their back on it in order to unearth the past buried beneath it. In the first, the personal papers of a dead woman gradually lay bare her struggle to accommodate her private self to her public persona; in the second, Wolf uses her increasingly involved and introspective style to conduct an in-depth analysis of the multi-layered memories and motivations of an individual woman. The 'Romantic' tendencies already making themselves evident in these two books culminated in *Kein Ort: Nirgends* ('No place: nowhere', 1979), where her focus falls on two exceptional people on the periphery of their society. The fact that they are in the past – they are the early nineteenth-century poets Heinrich von Kleist and Karoline von Günderode – indicates a further retreat from topical socialist realism to the less clear-cut and dogmatic but infinitely more alluring approach associated with German Romanticism.

The appeal of the past, or of its hardly audible yet still potent and perhaps even relevant message, had already been the central theme of *Die neuen Leiden des jungen W.* by Ulrich Plenzdorf. Finally published, after protracted difficulties, in 1972–3, Plenzdorf's novel is remarkable for the way in which it draws attention to a cultural crisis, the implications of which are as evident for a modern capitalist society as for the one in which the novel was written. A battered copy of Goethe's once famous novel, *Die Leiden des jungen Werthers*, is discovered by chance by an uneducated working-class boy who has never heard of it, doesn't know what it is, but finds that it still has something to say even to him. So careful is the author to conceal his own superior knowledge and to concentrate on a graphic rendition of average East German juvenile life, that the result is unusually free from the cultural snobbery this type of writing often encourages.

Narrative prose held a particular appeal for both writer and reader in the postwar period of reconstruction. It lent a notional continuity to the GDR's reading of the past, as did the highly selective canon of older German literary texts prescribed for study in the GDR's schools and universities and thus available in print. From this canon 'decadent' bourgeois writers such as Kafka, Trakl and Musil were excluded, in ironic analogy to the Third Reich. The rediscovery of such authors or, in the case of Wolf in the late 1970s, of Kleist, Hölderlin and Klopstock and the Romantic women writers Bettine von Arnim and Karoline von Günderode, was an expression of the growing disenchantment of committed GDR writers with the system. Yet the building of the Wall, the 'protective wall against capital western imperialism' in party-speak, had paradoxically promoted a new solidarity among GDR writers and renewed their commitment to the socialist experiment. In the expectation of the role as genuine partners promised them by the Party in the so-called post-Stalinist age, they permitted themselves a greater degree of liberty to criticize their own society. Thus the mid- and late 1960s saw the emergence of such classics as Günter de Bruyn's *Buridans Esel* ('Buridan's ass') and Stefan Heym's hard-hitting *Der König-David-Bericht* ('The King David report') which, like Plenzdorf's novel, was proscribed and held back for years. These years also saw the publication of the first of Wolf's characteristically reflective and subjective works, the short story *Der Juninachmittag*, and her highly controversial *Nachdenken über Christa T.*

*Ankunft im Alltag* ('Arrival in the everyday'), the title of a novel written in 1961 by Wolf's friend Brigitte Reimann (1933–73), is an appropriate description of the period from the early 1960s to the mid-1970s during which GDR literature began to rely increasingly on themes from everyday life under socialism. Reimann's posthumously published unfinished last novel, *Franziska Linkerhand* (1974), documents the human cost of the GDR writers' efforts to bridge the credibility gap between political reality and society's vision of itself as seen by the writer. From the viewpoint of the authorities, literature was there to serve party policy. Writing considered 'unhelpful' or 'nugatory' fell foul of the censor. Failure to comply with party guidelines led to delays in publication (a fate which affected all the major GDR writers, even the most loyal ones), to fines, especially for having recourse to publication in the West, and even to imprisonment and loss of livelihood. In the 1970s the most common persecution was to strip a writer of GDR citizenship; release from jail and expulsion were often literally bought by the West German authorities, as in the case of the young Jürgen Fuchs (b. 1950). As the dedicated communist Heym ironically put it in *Der König-David-Bericht*, 'Castration involves only momentary pain; afterwards one feels so much better off, almost happy.' Self-censorship was widely practised, but it rarely satisfied the authorities.

The bitter disappointment which followed the expectations raised by Erich Honecker's speech at the eighth Party Conference in 1971 and his assurance that there would be 'no more taboos in art and literature' brought about a crisis from which, in a sense, the GDR as a society never really recovered. Although the full degree of the abuse of power by the secret police, the Stasi, was not revealed until after 1989, what made its machinations and those of the party bureaucracy so unbearable to committed Marxist writers in the 1970s was not so much its arbitrariness as the lack of trust it demonstrated. The cost in human terms and, more seriously, to the moral fibre of society, was well exemplified by the case of Reiner Kunze, who was forced to emigrate in 1977. After the fall of the Wall he gained access to the Stasi files on himself and published a sample of some of the 3491 documents they contained. He discovered that he had been given the codename 'Lyrik' and that his entire circle of relatives, friends and colleagues had been suborned to spy on him. When later asked whom he still felt he could trust, he replied, 'only my wife and children'. Some were not even as fortunate as he.

The theatre in the GDR attracted some major talents. Brecht had presided over its postwar artistic rehabilitation, and in Heiner Müller it produced a dramatist whose work attracted international attention. But party policy often prevented the dramatic gifts of its playwrights from realizing their full potential. Heinar Kipphardt, for instance, was a successful dramaturge at the Deutsches Theater in East Berlin and already known as an author of satirical comedies (*Shakespeare wird gesucht*, 'Shakespeare wanted', 1953) before he surrendered to political pressure and left his chosen country for the Federal Republic in 1959, exactly ten years after he had gone there for idealistic reasons. He did not achieve wide acclaim until 1964 when his most famous dramatic work, *In der Sache J. Robert Oppenheimer*, was premièred on television and in the theatre. Müller, a Saxon, stayed. He navigated the ups and downs of GDR cultural and political life, writing highly complex plays which often seemed to belie his claim to be the true successor of Brecht, and achieving at least a *succès d'estime* in the West with plays such as *Hamletmaschine* (1979); after the *Wende* he defended himself against accusations of Stasi collaboration by admitting to it in a way entirely in keeping with his lifelong mistrust of heroics and his sardonic view of his own nation's performance in *Germania Tod in Berlin* (1978, but written much earlier) and *Die Schlacht* (1975), in which economy of means maximizes the mental and physical impact in ways that are overtly avant-garde yet classical in a sense both ancient and very modern. A known coiner of *bons mots*, he once wryly observed, 'The division between stage and auditorium has been abolished. Now there are only participants, at least in theory.'

Lyric poetry, as often under dictatorships, proved a more resilient medium. As Heinz Czechowski, Kirsch's exact contemporary and a fellow-member of the so-called 'Saxon school' of poets, put it much later in the *Weimarer Beiträge*, one of the GDR's leading literary journals, 'Lyric poetry has the chance of being heard, when manipulation and silence inhibit every other genre.' Poetry certainly attracted many talented authors, who worked in a wide range of forms and modes: the 'Saxon school', inspired by the poet and teacher Georg Maurer, rediscovered the neo–classical power of Hölderlin and Schiller; nature and landscape became the predominant theme for Peter Huchel, a member of the same generation as Brecht and Seghers, and Johannes Bobrowski, who 'read' the historical landscape of eastern Europe as the voice of violated nature and of the peoples and cultures mutilated and destroyed over the centuries by German expansion and colonization. Sarah Kirsch's poetry spoke of another kind of triumphalist colonization: the destruction of nature by heedless industrialization. By contrast, the 'poetic activists' Wolf Biermann and Volker Braun used their songs and satires each in his own way to provoke change; from the mid-1960s, however, Biermann was no longer allowed to perform his songs to his own guitar in public. Kunert, with his fondness for the image of Icarus, was among those who focused on language in order to highlight the gulf between theory and practice in a regime caught between utopia and apocalypse. Once the credibility gap between the socialist utopia and what came to be known as 'real-life socialism' grew wider, and more and more writers were victimized by the secret police, the search was on for a different public role. The turning-point came in November 1976 with the expulsion of the immensely popular Biermann, whose language was so reminiscent of the 'Hauspoet der Deutschen', Martin Luther himself; this act elicited a hitherto unparalleled public protest by some 100 GDR writers. Three years later, nine dissident writers, once stalwart supporters of the regime, were expelled from the writers' union, among them the patriarchal Communist Stefan Heym, and Rolf Schneider, whose novel *November* (1979) subtly documented the Biermann affair. The problem was that Biermann had become identified by GDR readers with their own society: the very saltiness of his satire was a pledge of its underlying robustness and his dialogue formed evident proof of the existence of a genuine community in contrast to individualistic, 'self-indulgent' western writing. The Biermann affair was widely publicized by the West German media – and all regions except Saxony could now receive broadcasts and television programmes from the Federal Republic. Those who protested but stayed on were variously punished and victimized. By 1979 most of them (including Kunze, Kunert, Kirsch, Becker, and Schneider) had been more or less forced to leave. Not all of them could cope with the entirely different status and function awarded writers in the West.

One of those who chose to remain was Christa Wolf. Both at home and in West Germany, the author of *Nachdenken über Christa T.* and *Kindheitsmuster*, though frequently the butt of bitter criticism from the Party and some of her colleagues for the 'subjectivism' of her work, was regarded as perhaps the most important GDR writer and one of its most committed. The experiences of the years 1976 to 1979 – she had been expelled from the committee of the Berlin section of the Writers' Union after signing a protest letter in 1977 – left their mark on her in a particular way, namely by adding a new feminist dimension to her writing and to her public profile. It was no accident that the year 1980 saw her contribute a short story (as did Sarah Kirsch and Irmtraud Morgner) to a collection of three stories about changing circumstances entitled *Geschlechtertausch: Drei Geschichten über die Verwandlung der Verhältnisse* ('Swapping sexes: Three tales of changing circumstances'), in which she identified the ossified party system with patriarchy. This was also the year of her memorable speech on receipt of the Büchner Prize. Here, like some more robust Ingeborg Bachmann, she used Büchner's female characters and his story *Lenz* to suggest a new perspective on history. Then, in 1983, she assumed the mantle of the prophetess Cassandra in a novel of that name, and elaborated her ideas further in her influential Frankfurt lectures in 1985, the fourth of which referred in its subtitle to 'very ancient states of affairs and new ways of looking at them'. She consistently presented her critique of the GDR system as part of her wider campaign in defence of humanity in the nuclear age, as in the short novel *Störfall* ('Technical fault', 1987) published the year after the Chernobyl power-station disaster.

Marx once observed that philosophers had interpreted the world but that it was now a question of changing it. In common with other feminist writers in the GDR, Wolf subscribed to Irmtraud Morgner's ironic feminist paraphrase of Marx's dictum, 'The philosophers have hitherto interpreted the world in a masculine way, but, if it is to be changed humanely, it will have to be interpreted in a feminine way.' The constitution of 1949 had established the absolute equality before the law of men and women. Both communist ideology and the needs of the GDR economy (translated into education and labour policy in the course of Stalin's enforced industrialization of the GDR) meant that almost all women had a job outside the home. In contrast with the West, they were almost as likely as men to become engineers and technicians. 'She works like a man, that's progress. And it is progress. Standing day and night alongside him at the machine', as Wolf put it in her Büchner Prize speech. While still in her twenties, Wolf successfully combined motherhood with an influential job as editor of a leading literary journal and as principal reader of a powerful state publishing enterprise, as well as membership of the committee of the East German Writers' Union. One of the attractive aspects of literary life in the GDR was the high proportion of women amongst its leading writers, by contrast with West Germany.

Why then did the Honecker era witness the emergence of so many consciously feminist authors? The need for a women's movement was officially denied throughout the history of the regime and emancipation was a 'non-issue' in contrast to the situation in West Germany. But socialist theory was one thing, 'real-life' socialism another. The burdens imposed by the conflicting claims of work and domesticity and the appalling difficulties encountered in a command economy in the simple act of shopping were not generally shared between women and their partners, and the resultant tensions were reflected in high rates of divorce, family violence and alcoholism. Nevertheless, GDR feminist literature did not see itself as exclusive of men, as in the West, but inclusive, and as part of the humanist compass of socialist writing. In contrast to most Western feminist writers, many of its exponents drew liberally on eighteenth-century traditions of wit and humour as the most effective agents of enlightenment and change. Morgner was an early proponent of the comic and fantastic novel, and her inimitable achievement was the creation in *Leben und Abenteuer der Trobadora Beatriz nach Zeugnissen ihrer Spielfrau Laura* ('The life and adventures of Trobadora Beatrix based on the testimonies of Laura, her minstrel', 1974) of a picaresque central character who is a woman and incidentally also a GDR citizen. Morgner's preference for collage techniques in her novels was, she claimed, derived from her life as a single working mother. She displayed her imaginative gifts and her flair for reading the market when she followed up her first major success with a topical novel featuring a 'witch', *Amanda: Ein Hexenroman* (1983). Her special contribution to women's literature, it has been said, was a distinctive note of genuine humour.

In the 1980s GDR women writers such as Sarah Kirsch and Monika Maron focused with increasing urgency on the environmental pollution – the death of nature – caused and then covered up by the authorities. This was a theme of urgent interest on both sides of the Wall: Kunze had already made it the subject of a subtle fairy tale, *Was aus Schneewittchens Stiefmutter geworden ist* ('What became of Snow-White's stepmother'), in which the wicked queen causes every mirror to be broken, all the clear waters darkened, the ice covered with black cloth, and an artist executed because he had unwittingly offended her as a schoolboy by making a spelling mistake in answering that famous question, 'Who is the fairest of them all?' Kunze's allegory reflected an uncomfortable truth, and the volume containing it was remaindered by order from on high. The links between the East and West German women's peace and green movements provided maximum embarrassment to the authorities who, however, knew no weapon other than repression. Maron's work included the novel *Flugasche* ('Flying ashes', 1981), about state-fostered pollution, and *Die Überläuferin* ('The defector', 1986), the tale of a female Oblomov who lies daydreaming on her sofa, like her nineteenth-century Russian male counterpart, and refuses to have anything to do with the frenzied activity of the majority of East German working women. The GDR authorities forbade publication.

## Literature in Austria 1945–95

Neat divisions into 'Austrian' and 'German' literature can raise many a problem. This is brought home at once to readers and spectators by the similarities of subject matter, form, language and message between the contemporary plays or *Volksstücke* written by the Bavarian writers Franz Xaver Kroetz and Martin Sperr and those by their Austrian contemporaries such as Peter Turrini, Wolfgang Bauer and Felix Mitterer, from the provinces of Carinthia, Styria and the Tyrol respectively. Culturally Bavaria is closer to Austria than are the other provinces of Germany, and this cultural relationship is underlined by the linguistic relationship between them at the everyday spoken level, which is much closer than that between Bavaria and, say, the Rhineland or Saxony. Moreover, the relationship of Bavaria to the rest of Germany in cultural terms is a matter of constant debate. In the postwar period it is even more difficult to make distinctions between the literatures of the two countries because so many of Austria's established contemporary writers have their books published in Germany and live outside their native land. Yet despite the moral of the cautionary tale of the Austrian Germanist who met his untimely end by falling into a crevasse in a glacier while endeavouring to discover the 'Austrianness' of Austrian literature, the question remains a valid one. Perhaps an answer is that modern Austrian writing is analogous to that of twentieth-century Ireland in the context of literature in English: it is intrinsically part of the broad spectrum of literature in German, but it assuredly has its own voice.

Several issues arise in this connection. First, is it justifiable to speak of a specifically Austrian literature in the second half of the twentieth century? Second, is there any legitimacy in the notion of continuity between the literature of Habsburg Austria, the First Austrian Republic (1918–38) and the Second Republic, established in 1945? The question is politically highly fraught. From the moment it began to be discussed in postwar Austria, it had an evident though seldom transparent political context. Yet it should also be stressed that the exploration of this problem during the first half of this century, and, still more, the attempts at resolving it in the second half, have been of very great consequence for thinking Austrians and their sense of their own cultural identity. A third point concerns language. Though German publishers' readers and copy-editors busy themselves deleting typically Austrian turns of phrase from the manuscripts of books by Austrian authors which, simply for demographic reasons, will inevitably be bought in greater numbers by German readers than by Austrian ones, the vital impulse underlying almost all significant postwar Austrian writing has been generated from its self-conscious use of language – in particular the dynamic tension created by the differences between the dialect or dialect-influenced idiom of normal everyday Austrian usage and the standard written language Austria shares with the other German-speaking countries. Lastly, just as the Bavarian writer Kroetz has given a whole new meaning to the contemporary *Volksstück*, his immense popularity on the German stage attesting to its relevance to his audience's perceptions, so, too, his Austrian 'cousins', such as Wolfgang Bauer, Thomas Bernhard, Peter Handke and Friederike Mayröcker and many others, have long since discovered that literature can be effectively regenerated by allowing one genre to lend its features to another.

The political context of the debate about Austrian literature was bound up with the circumstances in which the Second Austrian Republic was born. The new republic was founded just before the end of the Second World War and immediately found itself confronted with a need to seek legitimacy by having recourse to myth and symbol. The historical context did not favour close scrutiny of Austria's National Socialist past, let alone a confrontation with it. The psychological problems associated with the widespread suppression of this past provided the dynamic impulse for much of postwar Austria's most innovative writing. In time the issue exacerbated relations between Austria's writers and their society to the point where one of the leading writers in the German language, the Salzburger Thomas Bernhard, was to denounce Austria in apocalyptic terms and impose his presence beyond the grave in a will which forbade performance of any of his plays by the state-run Austrian theatres or with the financial support of the state. The majority of Austria's writers reacted less histrionically but no less logically by preferring to live and work abroad.

The brittle edge of modern experimental Austrian writing, like the dynamic impulse which underlies it, derives from the determination of its creators to find appropriate forms in which to confront the past. It was a policy which for many years barred their access to the broad Austrian public. When Adolf Hitler marched into Austria in March 1938, he had been greeted in Vienna with wild enthusiasm by crowds intoxicated with a blend of patriotic fervour and Nazi propaganda as he addressed them from the former imperial palace on the Heldenplatz or 'Heroes' Square'. This event, commemorated in key postwar texts by Austrian authors, had already been adumbrated in literature, but *Die Blendung* ('Auto da Fé', 1935), the novel by Elias Canetti, a Bulgarian-born but Viennese-educated Jewish writer, did not make the impact on contemporaries which the work of a younger generation, writing in retrospect, would ultimately achieve. Nevertheless, Canetti's remarkable study of mass hysteria, *Masse und Macht* ('Crowds and power'), published after prolonged research in 1960, is a seminal response to events at a time when Austrian poets were celebrating their 'home-coming' to the Reich in dithyrambic hymns, where religious allusions to resurrection and renewal jostle blasphemously with protestations of revolutionary ardour. The eager celebrants of this mass hysteria included established Austrian writers of the day such as Max Mell, the religious dramatist, the much-admired stylist Josef Weinheber, and the novelists Gertrud Fussenegger, a German-speaker from Pilsen in Bohemia, and Maria Grengg, who also wrote for children. Their work in the late 1930s was not unique, but belonged in a peculiarly Austrian pan-German tradition. This tradition had already found literary expression in the early 1930s in the Sudetenland, where a substantial percentage of the German-speaking minority was receptive to National Socialism, as it had done earlier in the jingoistic lyrics of the 1914–18 war. Such lyrics had in their turn drawn for their language, rhetoric and imagery on the panegyrics of Bismarck written in the 1880s by Austrians with nationalist German sympathies who had been excluded from the new German Reich by reason of their membership of the multi-ethnic Habsburg empire.

The historic celebration of Austria's 'return' to the German Reich staged by Hitler on the Heldenplatz in Vienna on 13 March 1938 was etched on the minds of the countless Viennese Jews whose fate it sealed, some few of whom, however, survived to record it. It literally gave its name to two works which in due course were to challenge much more than just the complacency of the postwar Austrian folk memory with regard to the years 1938–45: Ernst Jandl's poem 'wien: heldenplatz' (1966) and Thomas Bernhard's last play, *Heldenplatz* (1988). The impact of the choreographed brutality of the National Socialist troops' entry into Austria – witnessed by the twelve-year-old Ingeborg Bachmann in Klagenfurt, the capital of the province of Carinthia – was a seminal experience in her own poetic development, and is presented obliquely in one of her most powerful short stories, *Jugend in einer österreichischen Stadt* ('Growing up in an Austrian town'), written in 1956 and added five years later to the collection *Das dreißigste Jahr* ('The thirtieth year').

In 1945, however, and for almost a generation to come, the literary landscape of Austria, as it presented itself to contemporaries, was rather different from the one which modern literary historians now project. These years witnessed the paradoxically easy transition of Hitler's 'Ostmark' or eastern boundary area (the name given to Austria during the years 1938–45) into the Second Austrian Republic, founded in April 1945 and confirmed in a general election in November of that year. In 1945 the novelist and dramatist Alexander Lernet-Holenia, an army officer in both wars and later president of the Austrian PEN Club, summed up the official view of Austria's relationship to its recent past when he made the dismissive comment, 'All we need to do is carry on from the point where we were interrupted by the dreams of a lunatic.' Even before the end of the war some Austrians had begun to present their country as the victim of Nazi aggression. The consummate diplomatic skills of a nation which had exercised them over a period of time and on a scale rivalled only by the Vatican itself succeeded in bringing about the withdrawal of the Allied occupying forces and the unification of Austria in 1955, thirty-five years before the same process was completed in Germany. Enshrined in international law, the resultant agreement, the Austrian State Treaty of 1955, anchored the concept of perpetual neutrality in the state constitution; in time this was to become a vital element in the formation of a new kind of Austrian political identity. Not unlike modern Belgium, postwar Austria evolved a social and political system designed to resolve conflict, but one which inevitably involved the suppression of differences. It has been the source of Austria's social stability ever since and an important factor in her economic success, but it also bred cynicism and opportunism in society as a whole. Patronage appeared to have all but supplanted the democratic process. Small wonder that such political success, shaped and directed as it was by ideological compromise on the party political front in the form of a succession of grand coalitions between Catholics and Socialists, made it relatively easy to foster what now appears a specious impression of literary and cultural continuity with pre-Hitler Austria. Many of those ostentatiously promoted and chosen for literary awards during the first decades of the Second Republic were writers and cultural functionaries under Hitler and in the proto-Fascist regimes of Engelbert Dollfuß (1932–4) and Kurt von Schuschnigg (1934–8), both of whom themselves became victims of the Nazis.

Looking back from the vantage-point of our own time, the postwar period in Austria was characterized by a kind of literary double life. In November 1955, one month after the departure of the Soviets, the Burgtheater reopened with a production of Grillparzer's most powerful patriotic Habsburg drama *König Ottokars Glück und Ende*, an event designed to build continuity with a happier past; meanwhile a group of Viennese writers, including the architect Friedrich Achleitner, Hans Carl Artmann, who had seen war service, the trained musician Gerhard Rühm, the linguist and mathematician Oswald Wiener and the short-lived Konrad Bayer, were already engaged in establishing a far more vital cultural linkage, through the medium of lyric poetry and cabaret, with the European avant-garde of the 1920s. Associated with this group, though not part of it, were Friederike Mayröcker, whose *Larifari*, a collection of experimental poems, appeared in 1956, and Ernst Jandl, whose first major collection of 'concrete' poems, containing 'wien: heldenplatz', first appeared ten years later under the title *Laut und Luise*.

Despite the extreme self-absorption which characterized the work of Jandl and Mayröcker and that of the group of Viennese writers who became known as the *Wiener Gruppe* or Vienna Group, they also had a clear cultural agenda. Rühm's celebrated anthology, *Die Wiener Gruppe*, appeared only in 1967, after its members had gone their different ways; characteristically, as one Austrian critic has remarked, most felt that their post-modernist honour had been slighted by being thus forcibly 'collectivized'. In what was to become something of a hallmark of modern Austrian writing, the work of the Vienna Group, like that of Hofmannsthal and the other Viennese poets half a century before them, presupposed an active, sophisticated readership. Much of their poetry is hermetic in character – not least that of Mayröcker – and makes considerable demands on those who read it. But it becomes much more accessible when the reader co-operates actively as listener. As Oswald Wiener put it in his ironically titled yet programmatic experimental novel *die verbesserung von mitteleuropa* ('The improvement of Central Europe'), the reader was offered the promise of emancipation from the 'system' of an authoritarian society, and indeed even from the shackles of the human condition, if he was prepared to oppose all forms of proof, continuity, contingency, all formulations, everything in other words that is 'right', inevitable, natural and self-evident. Wiener's use of the pronoun 'he' seems particularly ironic in view of the fact that a characteristic feature of postwar Austria from around 1950 to the present day has been for women to be in the vanguard of literary experimentation.

The questioning reader, working at the text, is part of the 'modernness' of postwar Austrian writing, rather than the essentially passive reader of anti-modernist literature, the characteristic recipient of so much 'officially' approved writing between 1930 and 1960. But a more specifically Austrian strand in that configuration is its rootedness in the social dimension of literature and its determination to restore it in the changed circumstances of the postwar period. The literary text highlights its capacity to create a public, to link theatre with life, as it were. From the outset, performance was a key feature, whether simply as readings and discussion within a narrow group, or as a recording aimed at a wider public, or as a deliberately engineered scandal or 'happening'. Sometimes it could take the form of presenting work in progress followed by discussion in a local municipal café, as the writers of the *Grazer Gruppe* (Graz Group) did in the 1960s. Even Bernhard's posthumous snook-cocking gesture alluded to above was part of a lifelong 'performance', as was his dialogue with one of the intellectual fathers of modern Austrian literature, the philosopher Ludwig Wittgenstein, in *Wittgensteins Neffe* (1982), his brilliant study of terminal disease and patriotic malaise, modelled on Diderot's satirical dialogue

*Le Neveu de Rameau*, which had been translated by Goethe and published in German, in 1805, sixteen years before it appeared in French.

The effectiveness of this approach was well attested by those who heard members of the Vienna Group 'perform'. Jandl's poem 'wien: heldenplatz' illustrates the point. When it is read aloud, the listener can reconstruct the scene in 1938 with the screaming crowds acclaiming Hitler, a scene which ultimately deranges the minds of the protagonist and his wife in Bernhard's play *Heldenplatz* fifty years later; the ostensibly familiar and reassuring dialectal diminutives underline the orgiastic nature of the event and, worse still, the malevolent humiliation of the women involved, who are represented as dog-like in their gratitude for the modicum of vicarious sexual pleasure meted out to them. Equally iconoclastic, for all the differences of theme and tone, were Handke's carefully staged and highly publicized attacks on the revered *Gruppe 47* in Princeton in 1966 and in his now 'classic' piece of anti-theatre, *Publikumsbeschimpfung* ('Insulting the audience'), published in the same year, an outrageously deliberate provocation of what many younger writers felt to be the insufferable bourgeois respectability of their audiences.

The writers of the Vienna Group tried to release words from what they called the 'hierarchy of syntax', a notion which Handke was to take up early in his career in the phrase 'in Sätzen steckt Obrigkeit', by which he meant that even syntax is an authoritarian conspiracy. Their deft use of dialect, notably in the black humour of Artmann's most famous collection *med ana schwoazzn dintn* ('With a black ink', 1958), and taken up a decade later by Bauer in his 'anti-*Volksstücke*', was part of their alienation technique. They enjoyed shocking and provoking the public and were less concerned with their subjects than with the ways human beings and especially society are 'programmed' by language – a theme taken up with great force by Handke in his early play, *Kaspar*, and in his prose works. In assessing their achievement, one should not overlook how seriously these writers, and the Graz Group which came after them, took Karl Kraus's insights into the political dangers of unguarded and mindless use of language. Almost all major Austrian writers during the postwar decades have in varying degrees linked their critique of language with the task of compelling their country to confront its own past and the authoritarian structures which imprison, deform and threaten the human being. But there is a lighter side to their art: the delight engendered by the language games they play. Like the polyglot Artmann, Jandl delights in associations of sound, including those of a foreign language. One of the fruits of his stay in England is somewhat reminiscent of English nonsense verse:

Stilton cheese
Cureth
Warts
Wormeth
Through needles
Calleth
BBC
Moist soulful.

Jandl's poetry, including his later collections *sprechblasen*, *die bearbeitung der mütze* and *der gelbe hund*, constantly invites the reader to enjoy the sheer fun of playing with words. The popularity of his phonetic and semantic metaphorical word games among student learners of German at university, including even gifted beginners, demonstrates how accessible and simple his texts are, for all their very considerable sophistication.

Established writers, such as the panoramic historical novelist Heimito von Doderer in the late 1950s and Gerhard Fritsch (1924–69) in the 1960s, discovered that they had encouraged their younger colleagues at a cost to themselves. Following their critical recommendation of the work of the *Wiener Gruppe* in the popular press, Doderer lost his post as cultural correspondent of the *Kurier* and Fritsch his editorial post with the semi-official paper *Wort in der Zeit*. Paradoxically, in view of the vitriolic treatment accorded them by their compatriots, it was the Vienna Group together with the Graz Group (the name was coined by Alfred Kolleritsch in 1967) who in the late 1960s succeeded in establishing the legitimacy of an Austrian literature. They showed it to be at once part of and distinct from that of Germany, a literature with its own formal and thematic identity. As editor of the literary journal *manuskripte* (founded in 1960, the same year as the *Forum Stadtpark*, the annual writers' forum named after the municipal park where they met), Kolleritsch had published Wiener's novel, *die verbesserung von mitteleuropa* in 1965 and Handke's *Publikumsbeschimpfung* in 1966. A novelist and school-teacher himself, as is evident from his sinister Austrian school story, *Allemann*, he saw the friendship between the individual authors in the Graz Group and their resultant group solidarity as a valid defence against the 'post-fascist' mood of the times.

By the 1970s the fame of Graz authors such as Wolfgang Bauer, Barbara Frischmuth, Peter Handke, Elfriede Jelinek, Gert Friedrich Jonke, Gerhart Roth and Werner Schwab (b. 1958) brought independence and with it a natural distancing from the notion of group or movement in favour of a new concept conveyed by the more general term *Grazer Autorenversammlung*, for they now saw themselves as an assembly of like-minded authors. Their fame did not come by chance, but as a result of a good deal of deliberate marketing at a time when the Austrian economy was largely dependent on Germany. They all published in Germany; even Bachmann, in her novel *Malina*, made one of her characters speak of the German book market as the only one for books in German. This flair for ironic self-propaganda still holds good today, just as it did when, in his novel *Die Stunde der wahren Empfindung* ('The hour of genuine feeling'), Handke created the figure of Gregor von Keuschnig, an Austrian diplomat in Paris whose task it is to 'sell' Austrian literature. Bauer spoke of 'marketing slogans', Kolleritsch expressed the hope that Graz should be seen as being not just in Styria but in Europe. Their efforts met with some success. By the late 1960s Bauer and Handke were the most often performed dramatists on the German stage; in the early 1990s they were joined by Jelinek and Schwab.

If the 'exemplary place' of both official and pioneeringly iconoclastic Austrian writing in the 1950s and early 1960s was Vienna, from the mid-1960s it was undoubtedly Graz. It was the Graz authors who explored and publicized experimental literature and attracted large numbers of readers to it. Their self-confident campaign to go out and take literature by storm was amply rewarded: their work was soon being featured in hundreds of German-language radio and television programmes and translated into dozens of languages. Indeed, such was their appeal that in the 1970s German critics began to speak of the 'Austrification' of German literature, and to complain that it was being 'colonized' by Austrians. As Kolleritsch remarked in an interview in the 1966–7 issue of *manuskripte*, the Graz Group had a clear-cut cultural and political agenda: aesthetic problems were politically relevant, but their solution was to be sought at the aesthetic level, and not, as Heine had once nastily remarked of the *Jungdeutsch* writers' literary efforts, at the level of rhymed newspaper articles.

The genres most closely associated with the Vienna and Graz Groups were those that lend themselves readily to 'performance' or 'exhibition', or which could be 'contaminated' or 'subverted' to do so. Besides stage plays, these included lyric poems to be read aloud and novels constructed like abstract paintings, such as Jonke's *Geometrischer Heimatroman* (1969). Other writers used visual techniques or montage to send typographical messages to their reader, as Handke does; Bernhard even employs the rhythmical patterns of language with the explicit intention of actually excluding the referential system of language upon which readers have come to depend. And starting with Handke, who since the 1960s has preluded each new publication with carefully staged press interviews and radio and television appearances, modern Austrian writers, like their counterparts in many English-speaking countries, know that even a negative review in the media can be good publicity. Since the German culture industry needs good copy, they are prepared to supply it.

Besides stage and radio plays, the second generation of postwar Austrian experimental writers has increasingly tended to favour the novel. Their preferred approach – the destruction of linear narrative – dates back as far as Ilse Aichinger's *Die größere Hoffnung* (1948); this novel was also the first longer postwar German literary work to approach the past in terms of its author's own manifesto, which she had published in 1946 under the title *Aufruf zum Mißtrauen* ('An appeal to mistrust'). Almost all Ingeborg Bachmann's poetry dates from the 1950s; from the 1960s up to her death in 1973 she worked predominantly on her novels, though these received little critical comment until they were rediscovered by feminists nearly twenty years later. Authoritarian structures and attitudes reinforced by the institutions of society such as school, family, church, political party and, above all, language, have continued to provide the most fertile themes of the modern Austrian novel. Although these novels are almost invariably located in a rural setting, their world, like that of the satirical *Volksstück* or 'popular' play, has almost nothing in common with the idylls traditionally presented by so much Austrian and German regional literature from the eighteenth century to the *Blut und Boden* school of the Third Reich, and even less with the Austrian countryside as depicted in the officially marketed image of a tourist paradise. On the contrary, the rural setting of modern Austrian novels and plays provides a background against which the deformation of the individual is exposed and its cost in terms of human happiness and human relations worked out. The victims may be labourers coming from the country to the city in search of work, as in Michael Scharang's *Charly Traktor* or the novels of Franz Innerhofer and Gernot Wolfgruber (b. 1944), or they may be the weak and marginalized, the people who lend themselves to systematic tyrannization, such as the schoolboy in Handke's *Der Ritt über den Bodensee* ('The ride across Lake Constance', 1971) and the mother in his *Wunschloses Unglück* ('Unhappiness without wishes', 1972). In *Der große Horizont* ('The wide horizon', 1974) and *Winterreise* (1978), the novelist Gerhard Roth uses his laconic prose to convey a pervasive sense of human isolation and desolation which in his impressive sequence of novels subsumed under the title *Die Archive des Schweigens* and published between 1980 and 1991 is widened out into a large-scale treatment of provincial life in Austria: their titles, such as *Der Stille Ozean* ('The Pacific Ocean'), *Landläufiger Tod* ('A common death'), *Am Abgrund* ('By the abyss'), *Der Untersuchungsrichter* ('The examining magistrate') and *Geschichte der Dunkelheit* ('A tale of darkness'), convey something of their bleak atmosphere and suffocating sense of mental and physical malaise.

But of all the authors of recent decades, it is Thomas Bernhard who has been most consistent in his use of the Austrian countryside as the location for his cancerous vision of the world, a vision in which language is endlessly stripped of its capacity to convey meaning, and people are separated from each other by it because, as he reminds the reader of his autobiographical volume *Der Keller* ('The cellar', 1976), the individual speaks a language which nobody understands except himself, because each individual only speaks his own language. And yet, paradoxically, as Barbara Frischmuth remarked in 1978 when she was completing the first of her two feminist novel trilogies, in which Austrian and oriental myths are blended, a feel for language and a sensitivity to the unique quality of Austria's countryside are recurrent characteristics of contemporary Austrian prose. Certainly this is borne out by Handke's later work, with its religious rediscovery of the authenticity of things and of the enduring presence of nature and ritual in the everyday world. However iconoclastic, programmatic and experimental the creative impulse in modernist Austrian writing may be, the works of its major authors are almost as securely anchored in a sense of location and landscape as the stories of Adalbert Stifter himself.

## German-Language Literature in Switzerland

A distinct Swiss tradition in modern German-language literature can be traced back at least as far as Albrecht von Haller's pioneering poem *Die Alpen* (1732) and to the influential roles played in mid-eighteenth-century Zurich by Johann Jacob Breitinger and his colleague Johann Jacob Bodmer in offsetting the rationalist approach to literature championed by Gottsched in Leipzig by promoting the superiority of the imagination. From then on, the Swiss element in German literature was to be associated with the rustic simplicity of an idyllic world created by a judicious fusion of realistic observation and imaginative freedom, in which man's moral nature was seen as an integral part of the natural order. This characteristically Swiss interpretation of reality was in harmony with the temper of the age, and affected the literatures of both Germany and France in equal measure. Jean-Jacques Rousseau's ideas on man, nature and society stimulated the *Sturm und Drang* and fired Goethe to undertake his eye-opening first tour of Switzerland in 1775; but so, too, did the prose *Idylls* of Salomon Gessner, a miniaturist whose work left many traces in the literatures of Europe and not least on Goethe's *Werther* (1774). But Switzerland's first major modern prose-writer was Heinrich Pestalozzi, the Zurich-born educationalist whose thinking and methods have exerted a greater influence on the twentieth century than on his own; his long novel *Lienhard und Gertrud* (1781–7) is in part a treatise on educational methods in fictional form, but it was deliberately aimed at a popular readership which responded delightedly to its graphic anecdotal style and the underlying seriousness of Pestalozzi's didactic purpose. From now on German literature was to have two distinct conceptions of the novel, each with its own characteristics, but both united in their emphasis on the centrality of the ethical dimension which manifests itself most clearly in human conduct, and the moral lessons its characters draw from experience. On the one hand there was the German *Bildungsroman* as inaugurated by Wieland and exemplified by Goethe's *Wilhelm Meister*, which focuses on the development of a central character; on the other there was the type of novel which centres on a group or community of people. Even when their protagonists seem to be the centre of interest, as in Gottfried Keller's *Der grüne Heinrich*, Jakob Schaffner's *Johannes* (1922) or E. Y. Meyer's *In Trubschachen* (1973), the major Swiss novels leave their readers in no doubt that what their authors are really most interested in is the real world their characters inhabit.

The publication in 1929 of the anthology *Geisteserbe der Schweiz* ('The Swiss spirit and its legacy') by Eduard Korrodi (1885–1955), with its excerpts from Gessner, Breitinger and

Pestalozzi and many later writers, was a landmark in twentieth-century Switzerland's discovery of its cultural identity and the 'Swissness' of its literature. One of the most obvious characteristics of modern Swiss narrative literature to emerge from it is that it is highly localized. Frequently a setting is named and a familiar topography is evoked. It may therefore give outsiders the impression of bordering on the parochial. But what may seem to outsiders a fatal narrowness of range and therefore also of vision is seen by Swiss writers themselves as a fact of life and a challenge. Switzerland is a small country, whose 4 million German speakers make up two-thirds of its total population. Moreover, its smallness is compounded by a strong sense of local identity and 'belonging' of a kind no longer felt so strongly in Germany or even in Austria, because the German-speaking part of Switzerland is itself subdivided into eighteen self-governing cantons and into a complicated patchwork of dialects and denominational allegiances. Regionalism is an integral element of the Swiss experience of life, and is its strength rather than its weakness. It is therefore no surprise that a sense of place is also a constant feature of its essentially realistic literature. These factors are transcended, however, by a strong sense of confederate unity reinforced by long-shared democratic values, a highly developed educational system and an inbred sense of being different from the two neighbouring countries whose language the Swiss Germans officially share, but whose political and national identities they find alien, a perception strengthened by German and Austrian membership of the European Union, to which Switzerland does not yet belong. In 1914, at the start of the First World War, when tension between the German-speaking and French-speaking Swiss was running high, the writer Carl Spitteler had forcefully reminded his compatriots that, despite their affinities with the cultures of neighbouring countries, neutrality was essential to their nation's unity and therefore to its own identity.

From the point of view of German literature there is another decisive factor. Throughout its history German-speaking Switzerland has existed in a state of diglossia: German dialects are the spoken language of everyday life, while what is significantly known in Switzerland as *Schriftdeutsch*, or 'written' German, is the medium of written communication at all levels. There is, it is true, a long-standing tradition of dialect writing which, in the hands of authors such as Rudolf von Tavel (1860–1934), Meinrad Lienert (1865–1933), Simon Gfeller (1868–1943) and Ernst Burren (1944– ), has produced poetry and prose of distinction. But such achievements are overshadowed by the many Swiss authors who have prided themselves on their subtle handling of a language they seldom actually speak, but which they know how to mould to the needs of their essentially realist conception of literature. As their German critics have conceded since the days of Johann Gottfried Herder, they may not speak it like Germans, but they write it with verve, originality and accuracy. In the nineteenth century Gottfried Keller and Conrad Ferdinand Meyer quickly achieved the status of German classics, as have Robert Walser, Max Frisch and Friedrich Dürrenmatt in the twentieth. Their success is all the more remarkable because they were all faced with the challenge of communicating their own characteristically Swiss perceptions of life and the world to the wider German readership on which the sales of Swiss authors depend, but with whom they had increasingly little in common, especially during the National Socialist period and its aftermath. The 'otherness' of Swiss life and Swiss perceptions of it has to be conveyed to a readership outside Switzerland itself and in a written language the Swiss do not speak, but which they share with their neighbours, while at the same time what they write will be read by an indigenous readership noted for its mistrust of imaginative make-believe and intellectual cleverness. One of the earliest attempts to articulate and define the situation of the twentieth-century Swiss writer was made in an article published in 1926 by Hugo Marti. Marti isolated two basic factors: a deep-seated, though often critical, allegiance to the country and its unique identity, and an acute awareness of its complacent values and intellectually constricting outlook. By then the traditional image of simple honest farming communities in delightful settings – the Swiss idyll – was already beginning to crumble under the creeping impact of industrialization and urbanization, and the contradictions between public and private morality were becoming ever more palpable. Indeed these tensions in a society caught between change and tradition, and increasingly conscious of the threat to its practical democratic values by the growth of 'value for money' materialism, had been noted with mounting anxiety much earlier by Jeremias Gotthelf (for instance in the great novel of 1843–4 he ominously entitled *Geld und Geist*) and Gottfried Keller, whose last novel *Martin Salander* (1886) was a sober warning that these new trends would upset the balance of Swiss society. Meinrad Inglin's novel *Schweizerspiegel* (1938) followed their example by holding up a mirror to life in Zurich during the First World War. The historian is a prophet, too, but in retrospect, as the Romantic writer Friedrich Schlegel observed.

During the early years of the twentieth century many Swiss authors, such as Heinrich Federer and Jakob Heer, were exploiting the literary potential of the opening up of the Alps to summer tourism and winter sports. But after the War some also began to look beyond their own small world and to explore human experience in more subjective and subtle ways. Hermann Hesse lived in Switzerland from 1912 until his death in 1962 and had located some of his early works in Switzerland, while making it quite clear that the human psyche was his true subject. His presence encouraged writers to look further afield or, in the case of Rudolf Jakob Humm's semi-autobiographical novel, *Die Inseln* (1936), to probe more deeply in order to piece together the mosaic of memories floating like semi-submerged islands in the enigmatic sea of the subconscious. Humm's novel was to be a major literary rediscovery of the 1980s: so, too, were the novels of his exact contemporary, Friedrich Glauser. Vienna-born and unsettled throughout his life, Glauser uses his chequered experience as a drug addict, psychiatric patient, and French Foreign Legion soldier to conjure up strange and exotic places which, in novels such as his North African *Gourrama* (1940), turn into images of the disintegration of his reader's familiar world; his detective stories use more familiar locations in order to probe deeply into the nature of crime while at the same time providing his readers with what they want: a good read. Dürrenmatt learnt much from Glauser, whose Bernese detective officer, Studer, ranks among the most memorable in a distinguished international company. But the 'Swiss Simenon' had to wait a long time before the German book market realized that in him it had a great crime novelist of its own to set alongside the countless German translations of British, French and American crime-writers.

A new dimension was given to what were already dominant themes in Swiss literature by Switzerland's experience of the Second World War or, rather, of its privileged position of neutrality between the Allied Powers fighting for the democratic values it traditionally shared, and the fascist dictatorships to its north and south: it was of course the only European country whose writers and readers needed no translators to understand what these dictatorships were saying, and which had it in its power to challenge them by keeping the humane ideals of Goethe and Schiller alive in the new dark age. In 1939, the poet and novelist Albin Zollinger published a remarkable novel, *Die grosse Unruhe* ('The great unrest'), which evokes and diagnoses the malaise pervading Swiss and indeed European society during the 1930s, but its appearance passed almost unnoticed because all eyes were on the present political situation and the outbreak of war. Aware that their compatriots were in danger of being taken in by the Nazis' appropriation of the idealistic sentiments expressed in Schiller's 'Swiss' drama, *Wilhelm Tell* ('Wir sollen sein ein einzig Volk von Brüdern!', the oath sworn by Schiller's rebels against Austrian oppression, was easily subverted by Hitler, the new Austrian dictator) and that the Party's *Blut und Boden* literature had much in common, at least superficially, with their own rich literature of peasant life, a wide spectrum of intellectuals and writers came together in defence of Switzerland's true values. Drawn from all shades of political opinion and ranging from the inward-looking and 'insular' to the cosmopolitan and outward-looking, the champions of *geistige Landesverteidigung* found a sympathetic outlet in the *Schweizer Spiegel*, a periodical which had been founded as early as 1925, and which now became the leading organ of Switzerland's intellectual and moral home guard. Its publishers achieved international success when in 1935 they broke silence by publishing *Die Moorsoldaten*, an account by Wolfgang Langhoff (1901–66) of its author's twelve-month internment in a Nazi concentration camp. The book was an international best-seller, but from then on, the *Schweizer Spiegel* was banned in Germany: Switzerland's German-speaking intelligentsia had declared war on the Third Reich. In this sense the wartime work of Swiss writers such as Max Frisch and Friedrich Dürrenmatt stands alongside, yet is intrinsically distinct from, the work of the many Germans and Austrians who created the Third Reich's rich literature of exile.

During the war years, despite German political pressures, the Zurich municipal theatre provided a stage and forum for dramatists such as Brecht to present their plays (it premièred *Mutter Courage und ihre Kinder*, *Leben des Galilei* and *Der gute Mensch von Sezuan*, as well as Georg Kaiser's *Der Soldat Tanaka*), even though the instinctive reaction of their potential audiences to what was happening just across the borders of their country was to keep a low profile. In the immediate postwar period Frisch devised highly original and effective ways of bringing home the legacy of National Socialism. In 1945 his play *Nun singen sie wieder* ('Now they are singing again'), eloquently and bitterly subtitled 'An Attempt at a Requiem', celebrated the end of the war by opening up the unending post-mortem debate about it; it took longer for him to tackle his compatriots' sense of complicity by default in the black radio comedy *Biedermann und die Brandstifter* (1958), and in his powerful neo-Expressionist play, *Andorra* (1961), which face the moral and social after-effects of complicity straight on. Before that, in *Der Verdacht* ('Suspicion', 1953), Dürrenmatt had already used his favourite narrative form, the detective novel, to set his Swiss detective, Inspector Bärlach, on the trail of Emmenberger, a former Nazi concentration camp doctor, who is also 'wanted' by Gulliver, one of his Jewish victims.

With the 'tragic comedy' *Der Besuch der alten Dame* (1956) and the novel *Homo Faber* (1957), Dürrenmatt and Frisch shifted attention to the contemporary world of postwar economic reconstruction and new-found prosperity and their human price, a theme which was to characterize Swiss literature for the rest of the century and which was later to coalesce with a renewed and more pronounced sense of the persistent narrowness of Swiss social attitudes despite or, maybe, because of its ever more evident postwar economic prosperity. The Swiss writer was feeling less and less at home in his once familiar setting as the scenes his predecessors had described so lovingly started to take on less attractive features, and the dangers of ecological disaster in the wake of modern pollution began to arouse the concern of a new generation apparently growing indifferent to the values its elders had cherished and claimed they upheld. Yet here, too, Keller had anticipated them when, in *Das verlorene Lachen*, the last story in the second volume of *Die Leute von Seldwyla* (1874), he shows how the smile has begun to vanish from the 'sonnige und wonnige' landscape of the earlier stories. Deforestation threatens the delightfully sunny countryside around Seldwyla, and in one of its taverns the wallpaper depicting a typical Swiss lake and mountain scene is soiled by the greasy hair of parochial politicians meeting in their proverbial smoke-filled room to plan and plot how they can manipulate the system to gain their own ends. Perhaps it was not so surprising that the heirs of the Swiss writers who had evoked the smiling idyll of rural life amidst mountains and lakes should have become preoccupied in the twentieth century with the ways in which nature is threatened by modern civilization. As early as 1935, Rudolf Schwarz (1879–1945), a little-known Basle author, had published one of the earliest attempts to face up to the situation. In his novel *Das Staunen der Seele* ('To the soul's amazement'), a modern young woman of high principles discovers to her outrage and dismay that the man she loves is largely responsible for the leak of chemical effluent which pollutes the Rhine as it flows past a chemical factory in Basle, a city now famous as the centre of the Swiss pharmaceutical industry. The ecological theme was taken up again in the 1970s. In *Dorf am Rebhang* ('The village in the vineyards', 1974) by Otto Frei (1924–90) the threatened scene is the Lake of Geneva, the romantic landscape given international currency by Jean-Jacques Rousseau in his novel *La Nouvelle Héloïse* (1761) and by the countless tourists and residents who have followed in his steps. In Frei's novel the author-narrator's own unintentional complicity in a potential environmental disaster drew attention to the complexity of an apparently clear-cut subject when it involves individual as well as corporate action. The theme is woven more subtly into the finer fabric of E. Y. Meyer's *In Trubschachen* (1973), a novel of deceptively simple outline covering a writer's brief winter break in a typical Swiss village, which turns into an extraordinarily sensitive and artfully constructed survey of the modern psyche written in such a way that it entertains its readers and gives them food for thought without ever seeming abstract and intellectual. Even here, the classic dual purpose of literature – namely that it should teach as well as please – which informed Swiss writing in the eighteenth century is still palpably present, though the disenchanted tone is that of its age.

Swiss postwar literature may be less good-humoured than that of earlier generations. It sometimes takes on a decidedly dark tone scarcely heard since the days of Jeremias Gotthelf and particularly dominant in the stories of Adolf Muschg, such as the collection ironically entitled *Liebesgeschichten* (1972), and in his novel *Albissers Grund* ('Albisser's reason', 1974), in which he uses forensic narrative techniques to diagnose the demoralization of the Swiss teaching profession which followed the student unrest of 1968 and which leads its central figure from optimism to resentment, psychiatric disturbance and aggression. But this preference for ironic detachment and black humour has not necessarily been a disadvantage: as they observe the world around them, younger Swiss authors have given a new lease of life to the traditional Swiss fondness for close observation of human behaviour and satirical comment on it. This is seen to particularly striking effect in Gerold Späth's *Commedia* (1980), an idiosyncratic yet richly suggestive modern 'answer' to the first two parts of Dante's *Divina Commedia*. Here 'Inferno' and 'Purgatory' (what has become of 'Paradise'?) are turned into, firstly, a cross-section of realistically conceived contemporary people all responding to the same topical questionnaire and, secondly, to a conducted tour through 'Switzerland', now just another theme-park saturated with historical reminiscences which are only half-understood; worse still, their guided tour ends in a windowless room from which there is no way out. As in *Die Geschichte der Anna Waser* (1913), Maria Waser's historical novel about a gifted woman hemmed in by the conventions of life in eighteenth-century Zurich, the sense of place has turned into claustrophobia.

Dürrenmatt died in 1990, Frisch in 1991. In that same year the Swiss Confederation celebrated its 700th anniversary, but the celebrations were boycotted by most of its writers. Disenchantment with the contemporary state of the nation had dominated Frisch's later work ever since his iconoclastic deconstruction of the national myth of Switzerland's founding father in *Wilhelm Tell für die Schule* (1971): now it was rife, and added a critical, almost negative asperity to the themes which were to dominate Swiss writing during the 1980s, a decade during which authors gravitated to the depiction of individuals in search of themselves and, paradoxically perhaps, of ways out of the sense of loneliness and disorientation in a once familiar setting which they diagnosed as the malaise of the present. Here, too, Frisch led the way with his ruminative study of an ageing individual's loss of identity and ultimate insignificance within the vastness of geological time in the novel *Der Mensch erscheint im Holozän* ('Man first appears in the Holocene', 1979), a work complemented in its way by Dürrenmatt's less 'scientific', more 'theological' and certainly more bewildering *Durcheinandertal* ('Valley of confusion'), ten years later, and in the fascinating plethora of uncompleted works and sketches he published under the title *Stoffe* between 1981 and his death. Introspective these works may be; but their introspection is still shot through by the delight in external detail characteristic of the Swiss narrative tradition, and equally typical of the work of many other highly regarded writers such as Peter Bichsel, Hugo Loetscher, Kurt Marti and, above all, Gerhard Meier, a late developer whose *Baur und Bindschädler* trilogy of novels (*Toteninsel*, 'The Isle of the Dead', *Borodino*, and *Die Ballade vom Schneien*, 'The ballad of snowing') was published between 1979 and 1985. Notable for their highly original and idiosyncratic reinterpretation of Robert Walser's stream-of-consciousness techniques and their double counterpoint of lyrical and humorous elements, these three novels are already regarded by readers and critics as perhaps Switzerland's outstanding and most original contribution to German prose fiction in the second half of the twentieth century.

The stylistic and narrative qualities of modern Swiss writing, like many of its themes, had achieved the status of high art in the work of Robert Walser, an author admired by many contemporary writers and now widely regarded as the finest Swiss writer to use the medium of German in the twentieth century. Walser's stature has become increasingly evident since his death in 1956, after a silence dating back to 1933, during which he came near to passing into oblivion along with many other minor writers of his period. Between 1906 and 1909 Walser wrote three full-scale novels, including *Jakob von Gunten*, but he is essentially a miniaturist, though a miniaturist of genius. His gift of compressing the maximum experience and insight into a minimum of words without lapsing into gnomic shorthand is evident in the many pieces – part essay, part anecdote, part prose-poem – composed between 1904 and his death, but in none is greater perfection achieved than in *Der Spaziergang* ('The walk'), published in 1917. The walk in question is taken by the author one sunny day. It has no immediate purpose, though a few trivial errands and chance encounters endow it with a superficial sense of purpose and direction. There is no storyline to speak of, though now and then a well-told anecdote reminds us that we are in the presence of a great storyteller. There are descriptions, but no grand set-pieces, and entertaining conversations with characters who disappear leaving no more than a fleeting impression. Small town gives way to countryside. At a level-crossing a train passes. The landscape is aglow with supernatural clarity. It comes on to rain. Images surface which suggest mutability and the transience of things, perhaps even death. Nothing happens, yet we come away sensing that we have had the simultaneous experience of living life and of having read a text which is at one and the same time a demonstration of the creative potential of the imagination and an object-lesson in the identity of reality and art. No great work of modern fiction seems more ephemeral or slight on the surface except perhaps James Joyce's novel *Ulysses*, published five years after it. But Joyce's masterpiece is long and Walser's very short indeed. They stand in relation to each other like the German novelle to the European novel, exemplifying in vivid form one of the most fundamental distinctions between German literature and that of other Western nations.

Robert Walser's miniatures place the reader in the presence of a poet, albeit one in prose. Swiss lyric poetry after Conrad Ferdinand Meyer had to content itself with much that was pleasing but not of the first rank, or which has proved too idiosyncratic to stand the test of time. Carl Spitteler is a case in point. The recipient of the Nobel Prize for Literature in 1919, he reworked the Prometheus story into a Greek mythological world of his own in which the aspirations and failings of mankind are given shape and form. But monumental art of this kind has become suspect, and even Spitteler's has proved to be no exception, despite its infectious inventiveness. There is no longer any market in German for large-scale epic verse to set alongside the *Omeros* of Derek Wallcott, 1992's Nobel Prize winner. Yet, as the poems of Kurt Marti and Gerhard Meier show, poetry is not dead. In 1953 Erika Burkart's first collection of poems, *Der dunkle Vogel*, revealed what her subsequent poetry has confirmed: namely that Switzerland, hitherto not noted for successful women authors apart from Johanna Spyri, the author of *Heidi*, has now produced one of the most original and distinctive lyric voices of the later twentieth century. Life is for Burkart a mystery and a joy which she explores, an eternal child, but one able to find the words to say so without ever sounding pretentious or contrived. She is quotable, but her lucid intensity prevents pretentiousness, and her unassuming subjects seem miraculously to avoid the clichés of late twentieth-century verse. She was a primary-school teacher and, like Pestalozzi, she knows that head, heart and hand, all three, are necessary for human development, and that reality is made up of dreams, memories and imaginings. Her sense of place is acute, her idyll is in her back garden, and nature's beauty but also its vulnerability are her recurring theme. If her language sometimes almost brings the *Sturm und Drang* or even Romanticism to mind, as in the poems of death and love in the collection *Schweigeminute* ('A minute's silence', 1988), it is only because, like Greiffenberg and Droste-Hülshoff before her, she is using the German language in ways we have not heard before.

# Postscript

—— · ——

Blackwell's *Companion to German Literature* begins with the Reformation and the Renaissance, both of which exercised formative influences on the mentality and literature of the German-speaking peoples. It closes half a millennium later, when Germany is once again at the forefront of momentous events. In 1990 the two postwar Germanies witnessed their political reunification, following the *Wende* or 'turning-point', the first successful revolution in German history. This bloodless revolution and its impact on people's lives, particularly in what was the GDR, have already become the stuff of literature.

Two recent works exemplify the unique nature of what has happened, while at the same time pointing to the strength of tradition inherent in Germany's literature. For *Der wilde Forst, der tiefe Wald* ('The wild forest, the deep wood', 1995) Elke Erb, a Berlin poet associated with the *Prenzlauer Berg*, chose as her title the old Romantic image of the German forest, while in *Ein weites Feld* (1995) Günter Grass views recent events and the history of twentieth-century Germany's dictatorships through the medium of the life and works of the great nineteenth-century Prussian novelist Theodor Fontane. Grass has been a persistent and vigorous critic of German reunification in both fact and form, and his long novel is part of a strategy to tease and provoke German readers and their political mentors. Before him, Uwe Johnson had already used Fontane as a central figure in his *Jahrestage IV* in 1983, and it seems that this nineteenth-century novelist, who was read and studied on both sides of the political divide, has been made into a national icon, a role that would have appealed to his sense of irony. Johnson's creative use of Fontane leaves much to the imagination of his readers; by contrast, Grass's novel seems to stifle that illuminating and invigorating process which modern critical theory has shown to be so central to the art of reading literature, namely the *re*-creation of the poetic text by the reader. But at least he had the courage to help Germans understand their age through the medium of the discursive novel, just as his precursors had done from Grimmelshausen to Gutzkow and on to Thomas and Heinrich Mann and Alfred Döblin, and which he himself succeeded in doing in *Die Blechtrommel*. We may have to wait until well into the next millennium for the great novel of the *Wende*, but there seems little doubt that the events we have witnessed in our own lifetime are the stuff of literature on an epic scale. In the meantime, as so often at key periods in German political and cultural history, such as the High Middle Ages, the *Sturm und Drang* of Goethe's youth, or the early years of the twentieth century, the voice of the lyric poet is heard giving expression and meaning to the feelings and experience of a whole generation.

It is too early to predict whether the *Wende*, which has had such a profound effect on the self-perception of contemporary Germans, will actually come to be seen in such epochal terms as the great events of the sixteenth century. What is clear is that modern technology is already having as profound an effect on literature and its reception as it did in Reformation times. Modern writers exploit the media to attract the public's attention by means of carefully engineered 'happenings', scandals or speeches on receipt of literary prizes, while the shorter concentration span of generations brought up on visual images rather than on the written word is having its impact on the choice of literary genres, though paradoxically the market for long novels is thriving. Of central importance is the way in which the literary market is concentrated in so few hands. In 1995, 8 per cent of German publishing houses owned 80 per cent of bookshops, and 8 per cent of bookshops had 60 per cent of the total turnover in their area – yet only 3 per cent of all books sold counted as literature, and these now have an ever-shrinking 'shelf life'. But, as the poet Uta Mauersberger (b.1952) wittily put it in a recent essay, remaindered books are to the writer what ashes are to a phoenix. True poets have always sought and will always find their material and their readers, come what may.

Across the border to the south-east, other more local issues dominate discussion. Economically, the *Wende* has brought great benefits to the Austrian Republic, but it has also strengthened its writers' impulse to define their own identity by emphasizing that they are distinct from German culture rather than part of it. This is exemplified by the project to write a new comprehensive history of 'Austrian' literature and establish a canon of major Austrian authors going back at least to 1918 and including some great writers hitherto assumed to be 'German'. This project is being undertaken just when, in a grand postmodern gesture, some intellectuals in the Federal Republic of Germany appear to have abandoned the notion of a 'canonical' or 'classical' German literature altogether. Sometimes amused, but more often irritated, by what is happening over the border, German observers anxiously note the 'loss' of authors who have provided some of the finest modern works in the German language, such as Paul Celan and Ingeborg Bachmann, or even Franz Kafka, Rainer Maria Rilke, Robert Musil and Karl Kraus. To the foreign observer, parallels suggest themselves with the relationship between the literature of England and the literatures of the other English-speaking countries. To those who share our practically minded English-language culture, the pragmatic solution to the problem is not far to seek. They are 'sowohl . . . als auch' – they are both one and the other.

Finally, where do the Swiss or, more specifically, the German-speaking Swiss, come in when cultural integration or differentiation among the German-speaking peoples is under discussion? Can we believe one of Switzerland's major contemporary writers, Adolf Muschg, when in 1980 he declared that there is no Swiss national literature? With characteristic Swiss self-irony he went on to explain that if there is, it is only because Swiss writers need their German friends to behave as though there were. What Switzerland's 'German friends' also need to remember is that Swiss literature in German is not merely an annexe of German literature: it is written in the context of a multilingual country with a culture of its own. In 1988 the Zurich Germanist Michael Böhler reminded a largely American audience of something which is of profound relevance to Blackwell's *Companion to German Literature*: literature is at one and the same time the voice of an individual, a nation's language in action in time and place, and the universal voice of mankind.

# Biographical Index

— . —

Entries marked * were written by Daragh Downes, undergraduate student and Scholar of Trinity College, Dublin.

## Abbreviations

| | | | |
|---|---|---|---|
| anon | anonymous, anonymously | lr | lower |
| autobiog | autobiography, autobiographical | N | North |
| biog | biography, biographical | NL | Netherlands |
| c | century | nr | near |
| *c.* | *circa* | perf | performed, performance |
| cf | compare | publ | published |
| E | East | RC | Roman Catholic |
| ed | edited, editor | S | South |
| edn | edition | tr | translated, translator |
| eg | for example | trn | translation |
| esp | especially | upr | upper |
| etc | *et cetera* | vol | volume |
| i a | *inter alia* | W | West |
| incl | include, including, included | wr | written |
| lang | language | yr | year |
| | | $^2$ | second edition |

## A

**Thomas Abbt** (Ulm 1738–66 Bückeburg)
Abbt elaborated the notion of a German national literature by identifying a free and patriotic German nation with the Prussia of Frederick the Great. His main work, *Vom Verdienste* (essay 1764, $^3$1772), offered a dispassionate assessment of the French Enlightenment and reminded contemporaries that educated individuals are never exclusively the citizens of a particular nation.

**Abraham a Sancta Clara** (= *Johann Ulrich Megerle*) (nr Messkirchen/Baden 1644–1709 Vienna)
A Capuchin friar and court preacher to Emperor Leopold I, he was a major writer of Catholic Counter-Reformation sermons. Their 'weird and wonderful kaleidoscope' of

rhetoric, wit, puns, colourful images and biting satire lambast the folly of the world against a background of plague (*Mercks Wienn, Das ist: deß wütenden Todts, ein umständige Beschreibung*, 1680, a source for Schiller's *Wallensteins Lager*) and of the Turkish wars (*Auff, auff, Ihr Christen! Das ist: Ein bewegliche Anfrischung der christlichen Waffen wider den Türckischen Bluet-Egel*, 1683). His energetic verbal creativity has latterly attracted the interest of 20thc language theorists.

### Friedrich Achleitner
(Schalchen/Upr Austria 1930– )
An architect associated with the *Wiener Gruppe*, Achleitner helped establish architectural criticism as a genre in its own right (*Nieder mit Fischer von Erlach*, 1986). His literary texts, such as *prosa, konstellationen, montagen, dialektgedichte, studien* (1970), are based on mathematical principles, their graphic images of spaces forming part of the 'text': in his *quadratroman* (novel 1973) the 'hero' is a rectangle.

### Herbert Achternbusch (Munich 1938– )
Achternbusch is a sometimes anarchic film-maker (*Das Gespenst*, 1982, on the life of Christ), playwright (*Linz*, 1987), poet (*Südtyroler*, 1966), prose writer (*Die Alexanderschlacht*, 1971, *Breitenbach*, 1986) and scourge of the Catholic Church and the Christian Social Union in Bavaria. His black humour, self-irony and capacity for scandal made him a darling of the critics. His work is often characterized by a contamination of genres (*Das Andechser Gefühl*, part of his novel *Die Stunde des Todes*, 1975, is both radio play and film). He challenges contemporary West Germany's *Kulturbetrieb*, in which art is merely a 'commodity'.

### Johann Christoph Adelung (nr Anklam/ Pomerania 1732–1806 Dresden)
Adelung produced the first German dictionary written according to modern lexicographical principles: *Versuch eines vollständigen grammatisch-kritischen Wörterbuchs der Hochdeutschen Mundart, mit beständiger Vergleichung der übrigen Mundarten, besonders aber der Oberdeutschen*, 5 vols, Leipzig 1774–86. He also wrote textbooks on German grammar, stylistics and orthography, which formed the basis for later scholars and lexicographers such as the Grimm brothers.

### *Theodor Wiesengrund Adorno
(Frankfurt/M 1903–69 Visp/Switzerland)
Co-founder (with Max Horkheimer) of the renowned *Frankfurter Institut für Sozialforschung*, Adorno returned from US exile in 1949. His esoteric and often pessimistic prose provoked complaints from Lukács and others that he had relinquished his Marxist credentials by taking refuge in the quietism of theory. A consistent critic of the homogenizing logic embedded in modernity (*Dialektik der Aufklärung*, with Horkheimer, 1947, *Minima Moralia*, 1951, and his important methodological statement, *Negative Dialektik*, 1966), he deployed his musical and literary expertise to isolate the aesthetic sphere as the fragile repository of authenticity in an increasingly commodified social world (*Philosophie der neuen Musik*, 1949, *Prismen: Kulturkritik und Gesellschaft*, 1955, *Ästhetische Theorie*, 1970).

### Ilse Aichinger (Vienna 1921– )
Her allusively poetic novel *Die größere Hoffnung* (1948) was an early attempt to address the issue of collective guilt for Nazi Germany, a theme she broached in *Aufruf zum Mißtrauen*, 1946, and explored in short stories (*Reden unter dem Galgen*, 1952, incl *Spiegelgeschichte*, which won her the *Gruppe 47* prize). In *Knöpfe* (radio play 1953, publ 1961), she 'atomized' language to show how modern industrial society reduces human beings to mere numbers. Her professed aim is to stimulate her readers to 're-learn' their mother tongue. Her works include prose dialogues (*Zu keiner Stunde*, 1957), stories (*Eliza Eliza*, 1965, *Schlechte Wörter*, 1976, *Meine Sprache und ich*, 1978) and poetry (*Verschenkter Rat*, 1978).

### Aegidius Albertinus (Deventer/NL 1560–1620 Munich)
Albertinus made influential translations and compilations of spiritual writings from French, Italian and Spanish sources. His main claim to fame is that he made the Spanish picaresque

novel known in Germany through his 1615 German adaptation of Alemán's *Guzmán de Alfarache*.

### Willibald Alexis (= Georg Wilhelm Heinrich Häring) (Breslau 1798–1871 Arnstadt/Thuringia)

Inspired by Scott, Alexis's historical novels helped to enhance Prussia's patriotic credentials (*Cabanis*, 1832, *Der Roland von Berlin*, 1840, *Der falsche Woldemar*, 1842, *Die Hosen des Herrn von Bredow*, 1846–8, *Ruhe ist die erste Bürgerpflicht oder Vor fünfzig Jahren*, 1852, *Isegrimm*, 1854). A Berlin lawyer, journalist and indefatigable traveller, he helped Hitzig to edit the 9-vol digest of modern criminal cases, *Der Neue Pitaval* (1842–62), a key source for the modern German detective story.

### Peter Altenberg (= Richard Engländer) (Vienna 1859–1919)

A typical *fin-de-siècle* bohemian, Altenberg created a new poetic genre with prose sketches in which he responds to the disintegration of the self by recording in 'telegram style' his fleeting impressions, as in *Wie ich es sehe* (1896) and *Was der Tag mir zuträgt* (1901).

### Johann Baptist Alxinger (Vienna 1755–97)

A leading exponent of the Josephinist Enlightenment, Alxinger was a freemason and a correspondent of Nicolai in Berlin. He strove to create in Vienna a metropolitan literary culture on the N German and Prussian model.

### Jean Améry (= Hanns (Chaim) Mayer) (Vienna 1912–78 Salzburg)

The assumption in 1955 of a French pseudonym by the Jewish-born baptized Catholic Mayer was a symbolical response to his experience of Fascism (cf his novel *Die Schiffbrüchigen*, 1935), his part in the Belgian resistance and his internment in Auschwitz, Buchenwald and Bergen-Belsen, and, not least, to survival. His radio talks (*Jenseits von Schuld und Sühne: Bewältigungsversuche eines Überwältigten*, 1966) proclaimed his belief that the intellectual has a duty to educate others, as do his essays in *Weiterleben – aber wie?* (1982) and *Der integrale Humanismus* (ed by Heißenbüttel in 1985).

### Günther Anders (= Günther Stern) (Breslau 1902–92 Vienna)

The experiences of exile in the National Socialist era and of the atom bomb are central to the work of the philosopher and poet Günther Anders. On his return from French and US exile, he came to believe in literature's power to remedy the causes of 20thc dehumanization (*Mensch ohne Welt*, 1984), which he saw as rooted in the general failure of humans to understand, let alone control, what they create: *Die Antiquiertheit des Menschen: Über die Seele im Zeitalter der 2. industriellen Revolution* (1956), *Kosmologische Humoreske* (1978), *Gewalt – ja oder nein: Eine notwendige Diskussion* (1987).

### Alfred Andersch (Munich 1914–80 Locarno)

A former member of the Communist Youth, Dachau inmate and American POW, Andersch was one of the founding fathers of postwar German literature and, until the early 1970s, one of its main representatives. Ed with H. W. Richter of the short-lived journal *Der Ruf*, he helped to create the *Gruppe 47*. The central themes of his autobiog *Die Kirschen der Freiheit* (1952) and his now classic novels *Sansibar oder der letzte Grund* (1957) and *Winterspelt* (1974) are moral choice and the flight to freedom. His novels *Die Rote* (1960) and *Efraim* (1967) focus on individual responses to the Third Reich.

### Sascha Anderson (Weimar 1953– )

The career of Anderson is representative of the GDR rock protest generation and the 'alternative scene' of the *Prenzlauer Berg* (*Jeder Satellit hat einen Killersatelliten*, poems 1982, and *Totenreklame: Eine Reise*, travelogue 1983). It may also be seen as an example of informal collaboration with the Stasi or secret police, and of how the moral condemnation in 1989–90 of GDR writers by W German intellectuals accentuated ideological and psychological differences between post-1989 E and W Germany.

### Johann Valentin Andreae (Herrenberg/ Württemberg 1586–1654 Stuttgart)

For literary historians seeking to reintegrate German literature into the European mainstream, Andreae is of particular interest. He favoured satirical and utopian modes for his (usually anon) neo-Latin and German works, such as *Allgemeine und General Reformation der gantzen weiten Welt* (1615), *Menippus* (1617), in which he confronted the so-called Christian establishment with the 'virtues' of heretics and witches, and *Reipublicae Christianopolitanae Descriptio* (1619, German 1741), his idealistic vision of a new Christian Jerusalem.

### *Lou Andreas-Salomé* (St Petersburg 1861–1937 Göttingen)

Her ability to set her own values made Andreas-Salomé the embodiment of Nietzsche's *Fröhliche Wissenschaft* (1882). A lifelong student of philosophy and religion, she had a natural independence of mind which may have provided Fontane with the model for Melusine in *Der Stechlin*, as she no doubt did for Musil's 'friend of famous men'. In her fiction (some 40 works incl *Fenitschka*, 1898, *Im Zwischenland: 5 Geschichten aus dem Seelenleben halbwüchsiger Mädchen*, 1902, *Ródinka*, 1923) and in her critical studies (i a on Ibsen, Nietzsche and Rilke) she explored the role of religion in emotional life and the sexuality of women. She studied and practised psychoanalysis with Freud.

### *Stefan Andres* (nr Trier 1906–70)

Time has not been kind to Andres, though his fame in the 1950s seemed to guarantee him classical status. A former monk, he made his name in the 1930s with prose fiction which perfectly conveyed the 'feel' of Italy (*Die Reise nach Portiuncula*, 1936) and Germany (*Moselländische Novellen*, 1937) and above all with the powerful story, *Wir sind Utopia* (1942), serialized in the *Frankfurter Zeitung* but confiscated by the Nazis. In the novel trilogy *Die Sintflut* (1949–59), he confronted the issue of German collective guilt before the *Vergangenheitsbewältigung* debate, but in terms of the age-old struggle between good and evil and without finding a literary form appropriate to the postwar generation's sense of the uniqueness of its experience.

### *Leopold Andrian-Werburg* (Vienna 1875–1951 Nice)

A diplomat, close friend of the young Hofmannsthal and member of *Jung Wien*, he won immediate and deserved recognition for his classic tale of identity crisis, *Der Garten der Erkenntnis* (1895). His mythologizing monarchist text, *Österreich im Prisma der Idee* (1937), served the cause of post-1945 Austrian nostalgia.

### *Angelus Silesius* (= *Johannes Scheffler*) (Breslau 1624–77)

Epigrammatic virtuosity matches the gnomic and laconic discourse of mysteries divine in the rhyming couplets of his *Geistreiche Sinn- und Schlußreime* (1657, 1675 as *Der cherubinische Wandersmann*). The *Heilige Seelen-Lust oder geistliche Hirten-Lieder* (1657) of this medical doctor and later Counter-Reformation priest exercised a powerful influence on Christian devotional literature and on Romantic poetry.

### Ruth Angress *see* Ruth Klüger

### *Mathilde Franziska Anneke* (nr Blankenstein 1817–84 Milwaukee)

A journalist and editor, she was a fearless feminist and revolutionary, as epitomized in her spirited pamphlet in defence of Louise Aston (*Das Weib im Conflict mit den socialen Verhältnissen*, 1847), her *Memoiren einer Frau aus dem badisch-pfälzischen Feldzuge* (1853), based on her own experiences, and, in American exile, her antislavery writings, reprinted 1983 as *Die Sclaven-Auction*.

### *Anton Ulrich* of **Brunswick-Lüneburg** (Hitzacker 1633–1714 nr Wolfenbüttel)

Duke (co-regent from 1685, sole ruler from 1704), he wrote some 60 hymns, masques, *Singspiele* and, with Birken's help, 2 vast baroque novels, *Die durchleuchtige Syrerinn Aramena* (1669–73) and *Octavia* (1677–1707), which his contemporaries, Greiffenberg and Leibniz, described as theodicies in novel form.

### Paul Antschel *see* Paul Celan

### *Ludwig Anzengruber* (Vienna 1839–89)

He was the first major exponent of the critical

Austrian *Volksstück*. Though it had an anti-clerical slant typical of the temper of the Viennese liberal era, *Der Pfarrer von Kirchfeld* (1871), his greatest stage success, drew on the Josephinist Catholic notion of the *pastor bonus* or good priest. It was followed by the peasant tragedy *Der Meineidbauer* (1871), the social drama *Das vierte Gebot* (1878), and the comedies *Die Kreuzelschreiber* (1872), *Der G'wissenswurm* (1874) and *Der Doppelselbstmord* (1876). He used stylized dialect effectively in his unsentimental village tales (*Dorfgänge*, 1879, *Letzte Dorfgänge*, 1894) and in the novels *Der Schandfleck* (1877) and *Der Sternsteinhof* (1885).

#### *Hannah Arendt
(Hanover 1906–75 New York)

Born into a progressive Jewish family, she was guided to intellectual maturity by intellectual giants such as Heidegger (with whom she was at one point romantically involved), Husserl and Jaspers. Rare insight and compassion inform her approach to philosophy and politics, two concerns which mesh in landmark texts such as *Elemente und Ursprünge totaler Herrschaft* (publ in English 1951, in German 1955), *Eichmann in Jerusalem* (chillingly subtitled *A Report on the Banality of Evil*, English/German 1963), *Vita activa oder Vom tätigen Leben* (English 1958, German 1960) and *Macht und Gewalt* (English 1970, German 1972). Her positive explorations of Jewish identity in her biog *Rahel Varnhagen: Lebensgeschichte einer deutschen Jüdin aus der Romantik* (wr 1929–38, English 1958–9) and *Die verborgene Tradition* (essays 1976) made her uniquely well suited to introduce *Illuminations* (1968), a selection of essays by her long-dead friend Walter Benjamin.

#### *Ernst Moritz Arndt*
(Rügen 1769–1860 Bonn)

Historical hindsight hampers an objective approach to this journalist, historian, travel writer and patriotic poet, an architect of the notion of the moral superiority of the Germanic-Nordic races (*Geist der Zeit*, 1806–18). Son of a former serf and inspired by the language of Luther, he provided the resistance to Napoleon with martial lyrics ('Was ist des Deutschen Vaterland?') whose sentiments, purveyed through schoolbooks, appealed to the chauvinistic nationalism of later generations. His *Erinnerungen aus dem äußeren Leben* (1840) paint a vivid picture of Napoleonic Germany.

#### *Johann Arnd(t)* (nr Ballenstedt/Anhalt 1555–1621 Celle)

Arndt's *Vier Bücher vom wahren Christentum* (1610) were formative devotional reading among educated Lutherans and Pietists until the 19thc. Drawing on German mystical writings, they offered a model of personal piety in an age of religious controversy. Writers from Gerhardt and Gotthelf were influenced by A's idea that creation interprets God for man.

#### *Achim von Arnim*
(Berlin 1781–1831 Wiepersdorf)

Arnim studied physics and law at Halle and Göttingen and co-authored the German folksong collection, *Des Knaben Wunderhorn* (1805 and 1808) with Brentano, his friend and brother-in-law. In his ability to transcend boundaries of genre and register he is the Romantic artist *par excellence*, as in his novellen (such as *Isabella von Ägypten*, 1812, *Der tolle Invalide auf dem Fort Ratonneau*, 1818, and *Die Majoratsherren*, 1820), his drama *Halle und Jerusalem* (1811), and the novels, *Armuth, Reichthum, Schuld und Buße der Gräfin Dolores* (1810) and *Die Kronenwächter* (1817). Much of his work has a historical setting, but it can also be read as an extended allegory of his own times. The letters between him and his wife, Bettine, are among the finest of their kind in German.

#### *Bettine von Arnim*, née *Brentano*
(Frankfurt/M 1785–1859 Berlin)

Goethe called her 'the strangest being in the world', Rilke spoke of 'the sensuality of her soul', but the histrionic Bettine had also, in her own words, a cool brain. Mother of 7, editor of her husband Arnim's collected works, she wrote novels, tracts, and above all letters, many of which she reworked as autobiography or biography, as in *Goethes Briefwechsel mit einem*

*Kind* (1835), the work which made her famous, *Die Günderode* (1840) and *Clemens Brentanos Frühlings Kranz* (1844). Her dislike of strict poetic forms mirrored her dislike of rigid social structures, exemplified in her spirited protest against poverty, *Dies Buch gehört dem König* (1843), and in *Gespräche mit Dämonen: Des Königsbuches 2. Band* (1852).

### Hans (also Jean) Arp
(Strasburg 1887–1966 Basle)

A key figure of German modernism, he was of mixed German/French parentage and developed a rare double talent as painter/sculptor and poet. He championed modern French painting in Germany, while his collections of poetry (*Die wolkenpumpe* and *der vogel selbdritt*, both 1920) helped to promote the Dadaist movement, which he had co-founded in the Zurich Cabaret Voltaire in 1916. His 'linguistic anarchy' and the rich metaphorical character of his essays and poems (*Sinnende Flammen*, 1961) made him a key influence on post-1945 concrete and hermetic poetry.

### H(ans) C(arl) Artmann (Vienna 1921– )

A self-taught poet and thriller-writer whose foreign languages include Assyrian and Welsh, A was a central figure of the *Wiener Gruppe* in the 1950s and pioneered the use of dialect in postwar poetry. His black humour, imaginative wit, and the variety of satirical genres he uses (as in *The Best of H. C. Artmann*, 1970, *Nachrichten aus Nord und Süd*, novel 1978, *Nachtwindsucher: 61 österreichische Haikus*, 1984, and *gedichte von der wollust des dichtens*, 1989) cast him in the role of a modern intellectual picaroon, 'purgative of the Left, irritant of the Right'.

### Louise Aston
(nr Halberstadt 1814–71 Wangen)

Aston wrote lyric poems (*Wilde Rosen*, 1846), a novel (*Aus dem Leben einer Frau*, 1847) and a personal manifesto (*Meine Emanzipation, Verweisung und Rechtfertigung*, 1846); in 1848 she also briefly edited a militant journal, *Der Freischärler*. Perhaps the most consistent 19thc German feminist, Aston, with her mannish dress and first-hand experience of early factory life, an arranged marriage, divorce, and the

revolutionary barricades in 1848 Berlin, offered a serious challenge to contemporary views of the role of women in society.

### Berthold (= Moses Baruch) Auerbach
(Nordstetten/Black Forest 1812–82 Cannes)

After he had been imprisoned for his liberal views, he could no longer hope to become a rabbi and began instead to explore his Jewish heritage in the novels *Spinoza* (1837) and *Dichter und Kaufmann* (1840). His close knowledge of the Black Forest and the liberal optimism of his world view lie at the heart of the immense success (up to 1933) of his *Schwarzwälder Dorfgeschichten* (1843–53), the short novel, *Barfüßele* (1856) and his multi-volume *Volkskalender* in the tradition of Hebel.

### Rose Ausländer
(Czernowitz 1901–88 Düsseldorf)

She was one of the few Czernowitz Jews to survive the Holocaust. Her first collection of poetry, *Der Regenbogen*, was impounded after publication in 1939; her second, *Blinder Sommer*, appeared in 1965 after her return to Romania from the US, where she had lived 1921–31 and 1946–61. Almost every year thereafter she published collections in which her laconic language exemplifies the existential problem of the Holocaust survivor writing in German. Her stature as a lyric poet has only belatedly been recognized.

# B

### Ingeborg Bachmann
(Klagenfurt 1926–73 Rome)

In Bachmann, Austria has given 20thc German literature one of its most distinguished writers. Her dense, highly charged poetry (*Die gestundete Zeit*, 1953, [2]1957, *Anrufung des Großen Bären*, 1956) and her radio plays (*Ein Geschäft mit Träumen*, 1952, *Die Zikaden*, with music by Hans Werner Henze, 1955, *Der gute Gott von Manhattan*, broadcast 1959) were followed by luminous essays on life and art (*Die Wahrheit ist dem Menschen zumutbar*, 1959, *Ein Ort für Zufälle*, 1965, *Frankfurter Vorlesungen*, 1959–60). Feminist studies have made her late prose accessible: the theme of

Fascism, transmuted into the threat to woman from patriarchal power structures, dominates her novel *Malina* (1971), the stories *Simultan* (1972) and the fragmentary novel cycle *Todesarten* (*Der Fall Franza: Requiem für Fanny Goldmann*, 1978).

*Hermann Bahr* (Linz 1863–1934 Munich)
A controversial writer, critic, dramatist, Bahr was the principal champion of the Vienna Secession and of modernism in Vienna in the 1890s (*Zur Kritik der Moderne*, 1890, and *Die Überwindung des Naturalismus*, 1891). He was a lifelong target of Karl Kraus's pen. His most successful comedy, *Das Konzert* (1909), featured the composer Richard Strauss.

*Hugo Ball*
(Pirmasens 1886–1927 nr Lugano)
Dramatist, novelist, Dadaist and co-founder of the Cabaret Voltaire, Ball wrote experimental verse (*Gesammelte Gedichte*, 1963), aphorisms (*Die Flucht aus der Zeit*, 1927) and polemical essays (*Zur Kritik der deutschen Intelligenz*, 1919). An associate of Wedekind and Kandinsky, his avant-garde writings and works on the philosophy of language make him a seminal figure in German modernism.

*Ernst Barlach* (Wedel/Holstein 1870–1938 Güstrow/Mecklenburg)
Barlach developed a double talent as a sculptor and radical religious dramatist: his plays include *Der arme Vetter* (1918), *Die echten Sedemunds* (1920) and *Die Sündflut* (1924). He wrote a novel, *Der gestohlene Mond* (1936–7, publ 1948), and one of the greatest autobiogs by a German artist (*Ein selbsterzähltes Leben*, 1928). The neglect of his writings and sculpture is a long-lasting consequence of Fascist fear of his expressive power.

*Adolf Bartels* (Wesselburen/Dithmarschen 1862–1945 Weimar)
This Germanist and writer championed the anti-modernist *Heimat* movement with texts set in his native region (eg *Die Dithmarscher*, historical novel 1898) and a *Geschichte der deutschen Literatur* (1901–2), which became a standard text in the Third Reich. Long before

1933 he stereotyped 'the Jew' as alien to German culture (eg *Jüdische Herkunft und Literaturwissenschaft*, 1925) and did his best to destroy Heine's reputation.

*Wolf Heinrich Baudissin*
(Copenhagen 1789–1878 Dresden)
He was a major contributor to the Schlegel-Tieck Shakespeare trn, as well as an influential tr of Molière and other French, Italian and Spanish literature into German.

*Wolfgang Bauer* (Graz 1941– )
A member of the *Forum Stadtpark*, he manages to synthesize the formative influences of the theatre of the absurd and the critical *Volksstück* in his work. He has acquired a reputation, based above all on *Party for Six* (1967) and *Magic Afternoon* (1968), as one of the most widely played and fiercely attacked dramatists on the late 20thc German stage (*Gespenster*, 1974, and *Herr Faust spielt Roulette*, 1987).

*Adolf Bäuerle* (Vienna 1786–1859 Basle)
As editor of the *Wiener Theaterzeitung* from 1806 to 1859, he was an influential figure in the history of Viennese popular comedy. He helped to revive it by creating in Parapluienmacher Staberl the 'typical' Viennese petty bourgeois, a stock character in his play *Die Bürger in Wien* (1813), acted by Raimund and Nestroy. *Die falsche Primadonna von Krähwinkel* (1818) contributed to the satirical topos of Vienna as a 'village'.

*Eduard von Bauernfeld* (Vienna 1802–90)
Bauernfeld created Viennese drawing-room comedy in the French manner of Scribe. His numerous plays, such as *Bürgerlich und Romantisch* (1834) or *Großjährig* (1846), were much admired for their lively dialogue and were relished by 19thc Austrian audiences.

*Vicki Baum*
(Vienna 1888–1960 Hollywood)
This popular novelist and journalist was one of the few German exiles to make a successful transition to another language and culture. Her best-selling novel, *Menschen im Hotel* (1929), identified the big-city hotel as a microcosm of modern society.

## Konrad Bayer (Vienna 1932–64)

A founder member of the *Wiener Gruppe*, Bayer, a modern *poète maudit*, ultimately became the victim of his own deliberate destruction of language as a medium of expression. The only work to appear in his lifetime was *der stein der weisen* (1963), but his key role was acknowledged by his former colleagues in their publication of his novel, *der sechste sinn* (1969), and *der kopf des vitus bering* (recording 1977).

## Johannes R. Becher
### (Munich 1891–1958 Berlin)

By writing for *Die Aktion*, co-editing *Die Neue Zeit* and publishing his antiwar novel *Levisite oder Der einzig gerechte Krieg* (1926), Becher identified himself as an Expressionist. He later edited *Die Linkskurve* (1929–32) and chaired the *Bund proletarisch-revolutionärer Schriftsteller*. Moscow exile during the Third Reich (*Abschied: Einer deutschen Tragödie erster Teil 1900–1914*, novel 1940, *Deutschland ruft: Gedichte*, 1942) led to the founding of the Aufbau publishing house, classic status as a GDR author (he wrote the text of its anthem, *Auferstanden aus Ruinen*) and his appointment as culture minister.

## Jurek Becker (Lódz/Poland 1937– )

A child of the Jewish ghetto and the concentration camp, Becker achieved the seemingly impossible by writing a comic novel of his generation's experience: *Jakob der Lügner* (1969). Subsequent novels (*Irreführung der Behörden*, 1973, *Der Boxer*, 1976, *Schlaflose Tage*, 1978, and above all *Bronsteins Kinder*, 1986) explore the mentality of persecution victims. He also writes extensively for film, TV and cabaret.

## Rudolf Zacharias Becker
### (Erfurt 1752–1822 Gotha)

As author of the *Noth- und Hülfsbüchlein für Bauersleute*, he became an influential advocate of popular enlightenment. He enhanced his reputation by editing a quality newspaper, the widely read *Deutsche Zeitung* (from 1796 *Nationalzeitung der Deutschen*).

## Johann Beer
### (Attergau/Austria 1655–1700 Weißenfels)

B's comic ingenuity in devising pseudonyms is paralleled by the exuberant variety of human types which people the pages of his numerous novels, incl the first about a musician in German: *Der Simplicianische Welt-Kucker* (1677–9), yet this court musician and composer evidently regarded novel-writing as a mere pastime.

## Richard Beer-Hofmann
### (Rodaun nr Vienna 1866–1945 New York)

He was an influential figure of the Viennese *fin de siècle*. His tale *Der Tod Georgs* (1900) was an early example of the use of interior monologue to reflect the fragmentation of the individual personality, a central theme in his historical drama *Der Graf von Charolais* (1904). His poetry (notably *Schlaflied für Mirjam*) and a later biblical dramatic trilogy (unfinished) reflect his rediscovery of orthodox Judaism.

## *Walter Benjamin
### (Berlin 1892–1940 Port Bou/Spain)

The secularized messianism many have detected behind Marx's socialist discourse is more openly evident in the thought of Benjamin, one of western Marxism's most original exponents. Strongly influenced by the Cabbala scholar Gerschom Scholem, his voluminous output included ground-breaking literary criticism (*Goethes Wahlverwandtschaften*, 1925, *Ursprung des deutschen Trauerspiels*, 1928) and intuitive political essays (*Einbahnstraße*, 1928, *Das Kunstwerk im Zeitalter seiner Reproduzierbarkeit*, 1936, *Thesen über den Begriff der Geschichte*, 1940), which articulate a distinctively Jewish sense of a collective human past, saturated with untold suffering, which must be redeemed in a revolutionary *Jetztzeit* or here-and-now. A theorist of the dynamics of Fascism, B himself fell victim to it: his escape to the US was stymied at the French–Spanish border, whereupon he committed suicide.

## Gottfried Benn
### (Westprignitz 1886–1956 Berlin)

The son of a pastor, Benn served as an army doctor in the 1914–18 war (he was on duty at

Nurse Edith Cavell's execution). He achieved early fame with his harsh poetry (*Morgue*, 1912). The novellen collected as *Gehirn* (1916) were his response to his wartime experiences. He contributed to intellectual debate with *Über die Rolle des Schriftstellers in dieser Zeit* (1929) and other major essays. Benn initially identified with the National Socialist regime (*Antwort an die literarischen Emigranten, Kunst und Macht*, 1933, etc), and the anger of many fellow writers remained unrelenting, though his *Statische Gedichte* (1948) won him the respect even of his bitterest critics.

#### Josefa Berens-Totenohl
(Sauerland 1891–1969 Meschede)
A blacksmith's daughter, she wrote 'blood and soil' historical novels (*Der Femhof*, 1934, *Frau Magdlene*, 1935) which enjoyed a singular if ephemeral appeal, not least because of the author's sex.

#### Werner Bergengruen
(Riga 1892–1964 Baden-Baden)
B owed his reputation as 'inner emigrant' in the Third Reich to the dramatic intensity of his novellen (*Die Feuerprobe*, 1933, *Die drei Falken*, 1937), and to the allusive presentation of unjust authority in his novels (*Der Großtyrann und das Gericht*, 1935, *Der Starost*, 1938). His standing after 1945 grew with his promotion of Reinhold Schneider as a moral authority, while the setting of his often humorous prose fiction in the lost Baltic provinces won him a special popularity.

#### Thomas Bernhard (Heerlen/NL 1931–89 Gmunden/Upr Austria)
This nihilist offended Austrian readers by his provocative and negative image of their country in his first novels (*Frost*, 1963, and *Verstörung*, 1967). His idiosyncratic style is full of dark images, and his themes are illness (as in the brilliant monologue *Wittgensteins Neffe: Eine Freundschaft*, 1982), outsiders and above all artists (as in the novels *Das Kalkwerk*, 1970, and *Der Untergeher*, 1983). He is a harsh critic of Church, State and Austro-German Fascism in *Heldenplatz* (1988), his 'scandalous' contribution to the 50th anniversary of the *Anschluss*

of Austria to Nazi Germany. B's oeuvre also includes drama (*Ein Fest für Boris*, 1970, *Die Jagdgesellschaft*, comedy 1974, *Über allen Gipfeln ist Ruh*, 1982) and filmscripts, and he created his own genre of mockery (*Schimpfrede*) in the novel *Auslöschung* (1986), a human comedy of Austrian society.

#### Elsa Bernstein
(Vienna 1866–1949 Hamburg)
A former actress, celebrated hostess and octogenarian survivor of Theresienstadt, she wrote under the pseudonym of Ernst Rosmer. Her psychological sensitivity and technical assurance, seen at their best in *Dämmerung* (1894), *Johannes Herkner* (the tragedy of an artist, 1904) and *Maria Arndt* (in which a woman sacrifices her own fulfilment for her daughter's sake, 1908), make her 10 plays (all written between 1893 and 1910) the finest corpus of drama by a modern German woman writer. Her neo-Romantic fairy-tale drama, *Königskinder* (first perf 1897), won fame as the libretto of a Humperdinck opera.

#### Johann von Besser (Frauenburg/Courland 1660–1720 Dresden)
Though of middle-class origin, Besser became a diplomat and master of ceremonies at the court of the Elector of Brandenburg and was ennobled in 1701. He wrote official poetry (*Preußische Krönungsgedichte*, 1702), *Singspiele* and masques for court occasions. His less formal side is well represented in the famous anthology by Benjamin Neukirch (q.v.).

#### Werner Beumelburg (Traben-Trabach 1899– 1963 Würzburg)
The celebration of war as a national myth in his dramas and the presentation of the Third Reich as the apotheosis of German history in his novels made B one of its most admired authors.

#### Peter Bichsel (Lucerne 1935– )
A gifted exponent of the short prose text, he offered a graphically funny yet dehumanizing record of individual lives in *Eigentlich möchte Frau Blum den Milchmann kennenlernen* (1964). His subsequent stories (*Kindergeschichten*,

1969, *Geschichten zur falschen Zeit*, 1979, *Der Busant*, 1985) portray modern Switzerland as the epitome of materialism and alienation, themes also explored in the essays *Des Schweizers Schweiz* (1969) and *Das Ende der Schweizer Unschuld* (1985).

### Jakob Bidermann
#### (Ehingen/Swabia 1578–1639 Rome)
When still a student, this Jesuit dramatist produced his best-known work, *Cenodoxus* (1602), a kind of alternative *Faust*, a study of self-love and hypocrisy which exercised a powerful spell on his audience. A professor of rhetoric and a Jesuit censor at Rome, he went on to make imaginative use of allegorical figures in didactic dramas based on the Bible and church history.

### Horst Bienek (Gleiwitz 1930–90 Munich)
B was a young member of the Brecht Ensemble but became an inmate of the Soviet labour camp at Workuta, an experience recalled in *Traumbuch eines Gefangenen* (1957) and *Die Zelle* (novel 1968, film 1972). He then became the unsentimental poet of his lost Silesian homeland in *Gleiwitzer Kindheit* (poems 1976) and the *Gleiwitzer Tetralogie*, a cycle of 4 novels (*Die erste Polka*, 1975, *Septemberlicht*, 1977, *Zeit ohne Glocken*, 1979, and *Erde und Feuer*, 1982). The tetralogy reaches its powerful denouement with the 1945 bombing of Dresden. B's parable, *Der nicht verlorene Sohn*, and his sober *Reise in die Kindheit: Wiedersehen mit Schlesien* (1988), are witness to the power of literature to transcend horror.

### Otto Julius Bierbaum (Grünberg/Silesia
#### 1865–1910 nr Dresden)
B had a high profile as editor or promoter of influential literary journals, ranging from the *Freie Bühne* (1893– ) to *Pan* and *Die Insel* (with RA Schröder), a precursor of the Insel publishing house. Though he wrote verse and humorous novels (notably *Stilpe: Roman aus der Froschperspektive*, 1897), he would be a marginal figure today but for the impulse he gave to the production of beautifully designed books in *fin-de-siècle* Germany.

### Wolf Biermann (Hamburg 1936– )
A member of the Berliner Ensemble, he became a famous *chansonnier* in the Brecht tradition and writer of fairy tales, parables and dramas (*Der Dra-Dra*, 1971). His treatment by the GDR showed the perennial problems humour offers to totalitarian regimes. Petty persecution gave way to total proscription when *Die Drahtharfe* (songs) appeared in 1965 in W Germany. Expelled from the GDR, he developed as a lyric poet (*Verdrehte Welt – das seh' ich gern*, 1982), but has not spared his new environment (i a *Affenfels und Barrikade*, 1986, *Über das Geld und andere Herzensdinge: Fünf prosaische Versuche über Deutschland*, 1991).

### Richard Billinger (St Marienkirchen/
#### Upr Austria 1890–1965 Linz)
'One man's Brecht is another man's Billinger': Hofmannsthal's discovery of B's visionary plays for the Salzburg Festival, i a *Das Spiel vom Knecht* (1924), *Das Perchtenspiel* (1928), *Rauhnacht* (1931), won B wide popularity, deftly exploited by the Third Reich. Today he is remembered as an early prophet of the human and ecological catastrophe implicit in the mechanization of modern life.

### Charlotte Birch-Pfeiffer
#### (Stuttgart 1800–68 Berlin)
Heine and other contemporary caricaturists may have mocked her ability to produce plays of every kind, but few equalled B's success as an actress, notably as Schiller's Maria Stuart and Elisabeth, and as the enterprising artistic director of the Zurich theatre from 1837 to 1843. Her 23 vols of plays include dramatizations of Dickens, Charlotte Brontë and George Sand.

### Sixt Birck (Augsburg 1501–54)
He was an early Protestant scholar and schoolteacher in Basle who wrote plays in German on Old Testament subjects (*Susanna*, 1532, *Judith*, 1534), some of which he later reworked in Latin (*Dramata sacra*, 1547) when he became a headmaster in Augsburg.

### Sigmund von Birken
#### (nr Eger 1626–81 Nuremberg)
He suffered Counter-Reformation persecution, sought refuge in Nuremberg and gained

access to the influential literary organizations of the day, notably the *Fruchtbringende Gesellschaft*. He became a leading court poet, writing heroic pastorals in praise of the Habsburg and the Welf ruling houses (*Ostländischer Lorbeerhayn*, 1657, and *Guelfis oder Nidersächsischer Lorbeerhayn*, 1669). A copious letter-writer and religious poet (*Psalterium Betulianum*), he was the most prolific pastoral poet of the German baroque. His diaries and autobiog are being rediscovered.

#### Hans Friedrich Blunck
#### (Altona 1888–1961 Hamburg)

A former officer decorated with the Iron Cross and author of N German fairy tales (*Märchen von der Niederelbe*, 1923–31), he became president of the *Reichsschrifttumskammer* in 1933 and one of the Third Reich's most productive historical novelists, exalting the leadership principle, i a in *Werdendes Volk* (1934) and *Die große Fahrt* (1935).

#### Johannes Bobrowski
#### (Tilsit 1917–65 Berlin)

When Peter Huchel discovered B and published his elegy *Pruzzische Elegie* in 1955 in the leading GDR literary periodical, *Sinn und Form*, Germans were given access to the historic landscape of their E European colonial past. In his hermetically evocative lyrics in the collections *Sarmatische Zeit* (1961), *Schattenland Ströme* (1962), *Wetterzeichen* (1967), and his often deeply humorous novels (*Levins Mühle*, 1964, *Litauische Claviere*, 1966), landscape bears witness to lost cultures as B addresses the individual and collective guilt of his people towards those further to the E.

#### Friedrich (1867– von) Bodenstedt
#### (Peine 1819–92 Wiesbaden)

A member of Maximilian II of Bavaria's group of court poets, he was famous in his day as the author of the *Lieder des Mirza Schaffy*, purportedly tr from the Georgian (1851, [264]1917). He is now remembered for his writings about Russia and the Middle East and as a translator of Russian literature (Pushkin, Turgenev).

#### Johann Jacob Bodmer (Greifensee/Zurich
#### 1698–1783 nr Zurich)

Co-founder of the publishers Orell & Co. and of the moral weekly, *Discourse der Mahlern* (1721–3), B, together with his close collaborator Breitinger, helped to establish the role of the literary periodical in the critical culture of 18thc Germany and Switzerland. He also championed the English verse epic (Milton, Pope etc) and pioneered medieval German studies by editing the *Große Heidelberger Liederhandschrift* and parts of the *Nibelungenlied*.

#### Helene Böhlau (Weimar 1859–1940
#### Widdersberg nr Munich)

Daughter of the publisher of the authoritative *Sophienausgabe* of Goethe's works, she enjoyed ever-increasing sales of her humorous *Rathsmädelgeschichten* (1888 on) whose narrator invites the reader's identification with her own infantile view of adolescent girls; but she also wrote some highly provocative Naturalist novels such as *Der Rangierbahnhof* (1895) and *Halbtier!* (1899), which showed middle-class women to be prisoners of convention and legal discrimination.

#### Jakob Böhme
#### (nr Görlitz 1575–1624 Görlitz)

The influence of this visionary cobbler, born, like so many other German mystical writers, in religiously heterodox Silesia, is as surprising as it is extensive, reaching admirers as diverse as the Pietists and the Romantics (notably Novalis and Schelling). His nature mysticism appealed to poets because he assigned to the very sound or echo of language ('*Halle des Wortes*') the role of 'Nature's voice', through which God reveals Himself through His supreme creation, man (*Von der Menschwerdung Jesu Christi*, wr 1620). Although only *Der Weg zu Christo* (1624) was publ in his lifetime, his other works, such as *Drey Principien* (wr 1618–19), *Sechs theosophische Punckte* (wr 1620) and *Mysterium Magnum* (wr 1623), were circulated in manuscript form and later publ in Amsterdam, and were brought by the Pietists to the New World, notably to Philadelphia.

### Heinrich Christian Boie
(Meldorf/Holstein 1744–1806)
Boie earned Gleim's description as the 'manager of Germany's Parnassus' by creating a network of contacts to serve his journals. His *Göttinger Musenalmanach* (1770–5) and *Deutsches Museum* (1776–88, 1789–91) gave budding writers (i a members of the *Göttinger Hain*) access to a wider public and thus contributed to the creation of a national literature.

### Heinrich Böll
(Cologne 1917–85 Langebroich)
Even if his reputation does not stand the test of time, there is little doubt about B's immense influence in projecting a new image of Germany after 1945 and in provoking the W German authorities and his fellow citizens with his distinctive brand of anarchic Roman Catholicism. His massive output of prose fiction took as its central theme the moral cost of the Third Reich and the 1939–45 war. It includes short stories (*Der Zug war pünktlich*, 1949, *Wanderer, kommst du nach Spa...*, 1950, *Dr Murkes gesammeltes Schweigen*, 1958), and novels (*Wo warst du, Adam?*, 1951, *Und sagte kein einziges Wort*, 1953, *Haus ohne Hüter*, 1954, *Billard um halbzehn*, 1959). In later years, B turned his attention to W German consumerist society in novellen such as *Die verlorene Ehre der Katharina Blum oder: Wie Gewalt entstehen und wohin sie führen kann* (1974) and in novels (*Ansichten eines Clowns*, 1963, *Gruppenbild mit Dame*, 1971, *Frauen vor Flußlandschaft*, 1986). In his essays (*Aufsätze, Kritiken, Reden*, 1967) and controversial works such as *Will Ulrike Meinhof Gnade oder freies Geleit?* (1972), *Fürsorgliche Belagerung* (1979) and *Was soll aus dem Jungen bloß werden?* (1981), he elaborated his favourite themes. His famous travelogue, *Irisches Tagebuch* (1957), created the German tourist trade with Ireland.

### Wilhelm Bölsche
(Cologne 1861–1939 Riesengebirge)
Co-founder of the *Freie Bühne* and co-ed of its eponymous journal, programmatic Naturalist and author of *Die naturwissenschaftlichen Grundlagen der Poesie: Prolegomena einer realistischen Ästhetik*, 1887, B achieved bestseller status with his popular scientific works on Darwinism, such as *Die Abstammung des Menschen* (1904).

### Wolfgang Borchert
(Hamburg 1921–47 Basle)
Borchert lived out his short life as a cabarettist, soldier and Nazi prisoner with rare singleness of mind. His stories (*Traurige Geranien*, 1962), with their characteristic narrative dislocations, were mainly written during his last illness, occasioned by his treatment during the war; the moral character of his resistance to Nazism and his famous radio play/drama, *Draußen vor der Tür* (1947), made him the eloquent representative of the 'lost' generation of Nazi victims and war veterans.

### Ludwig Börne
(Frankfurt/M 1786–1837 Paris)
Born Juda Löw Baruch in the Frankfurt ghetto, he was both beneficiary and victim of changes in the civic and political status of German Jews in the Napoleonic era. The pungent satire and witty *aperçus* of his journals, *Die Waage* (1818–21) and *Zeitschwingen* (1819), his celebrated *Briefe aus Paris 1830–31* (1833) and his revolutionary republican views did much to make Germans politically aware.

### Otto Brahm (Hamburg 1856–1912 Berlin)
Brahm was primarily responsible for establishing Naturalist drama, through productions of Ibsen, Strindberg and Hauptmann. His training as a businessman and as a Germanist – he wrote major studies of Kleist and Schiller – equipped him for his role as first chairman of the *Freie Bühne* (1889), chief editor of its eponymous journal and of the *Neue deutsche Rundschau* (1904).

### Sebastian Brant (Strasburg 1457–1521)
Professor of civil and canon law at Basle and a high-ranking functionary in his native city, he was a prolific author who delighted intellectuals while at the same time aiming at educating the lower orders. With *Das Narrenschiff* (1494) he created one of the great satirical works of world literature: its apt integration of text and image inaugurated a new type of literary and visual communication which has found countless imitators to this day.

## Lily Braun
### (Halberstadt 1865–1916 Berlin)

One of Germany's most articulate bourgeois feminists, she co-ed *Die Frauenbewegung* (1895–1916). Her 'authentic voice' made her a focus of interest for the New Women's Movement in the 1970s and 1980s. The self-stylization of her work (*Im Schatten der Titanen*, biog 1908, and esp in her autobiog novel, *Memoiren einer Sozialistin*, 1909–11) does not diminish the impact of her energetic activism.

## Volker Braun (Dresden 1939– )

Miner, factory hand, lyric poet, playwright and author of fiction, Braun identified himself from the outset with the socialist regime of the GDR and is still regarded today as a quintessentially E German writer. As one of the initiators of the protest action in support of Wolf Biermann who chose to remain in the E, he suffered more than most from state harassment – his drama *Die Kipper* waited a decade to be performed in 1972. His finest – and at the time most controversial – work is the satiric novel of a GDR functionary, *Hinze-Kunze-Roman* (1985), a brilliantly topical and witty version of Diderot's *Jacques le Fataliste*.

## Bertolt Brecht
### (Augsburg 1898–1956 Berlin)

Like his models, Luther and Heine, he was one of German literature's great communicators. His dramatic oeuvre includes *Trommeln in der Nacht* (1922), *Baal* (1923), *Mann ist Mann* (1926), his operas with Kurt Weill (*Die Dreigroschenoper*, first perf 1928, and *Aufstieg und Fall der Stadt Mahagonny*, 1930), as well as didactic plays such as *Der Jasager und der Neinsager* (1930). B had several close (women) collaborators and controversy surrounds the authorship of some of his most famous plays. Among those first perf during his exile were *Die Gewehre der Frau Carrar* (1937), *Furcht und Elend des Dritten Reiches* (1938), *Mutter Courage und ihre Kinder* (1941), *Leben des Galilei* (1943), *Der gute Mensch von Sezuan* (1943). Yet his splendid comedy, *Herr Puntila und sein Knecht Matti* and one of his most celebrated epic dramas, *Der kaukasische Kreidekreis*, did not have their first perf until 1948, *Der aufhaltsame Aufstieg des Arturo Ui* followed in 1958, while his first great Marxist play, *Die heilige Johanna der Schlachthöfe*, wr 1929–31, only reached the stage in 1959. B's theoretical writings on the theatre won wide publicity: the *Schriften zum Theater* run to 7 vols and incl his *Kleines Organon für das Theater* (1948). B excelled in diverse genres, among them film (*Kuhle Wampe*, 1931), the novel (*Dreigroschenroman*, 1934), short stories in the manner of Hebel (*Kalendergeschichten*, 1949), and above all lyric poetry which may well prove to be his most enduring achievement: *Bert Brechts Hauspostille* (1927), *Svendborger Gedichte* (1939), *Buckower Elegien* (1953), *Die Kriegsfibel* (1955).

## Johann Jacob Breitinger
### (Zurich 1701–76)

The collaborator of Bodmer on the latter's influential moral weekly, *Discourse der Mahlern* (1721–3), he was also a historian of the Swiss Confederation (*Helvetische Bibliothek*, 1735–41 and *Historische und Critische Beiträge zu der Historie der Eidgenossen*, 1739), and the author of *Critische Dichtkunst* (1740), a treatise on the literary imagination which attracted the interest of Klopstock.

## Clemens Brentano (Ehrenbreitstein
### 1778–1842 Aschaffenburg)

B was the son of a Frankfurt merchant and the maternal grandson of the writer Sophie von La Roche. The death of his mother in 1793 and the consequent loss of a happy childhood paradise may account for the themes of losing and searching which permeate his works, and for the emotional instability and spiritual turmoil of his adult life. The wayward brilliance of his novel *Godwi oder Das steinerne Bild der Mutter* (1801) is characteristic: like most of his works it is fascinating but flawed by mercurial shifts of mood and direction. B achieved a prose masterpiece with the complex novelle *Geschichte vom braven Kasperl und dem schönen Annerl* (1817); he was also a master of the Romantic fairy tale (*Gockel, Hinkel und Gackeleia*, 1838). His great lyrical gifts contributed in large measure to the quality and popularity of *Des Knaben Wunderhorn* (3 vols, 1805–8), the folksong collection he issued in collaboration with his friend and brother-in-law Achim von Arnim.

### Georg Britting
(Regensburg 1891–1964 Munich)
B ed *Das Innere Reich*, the journal of the 'inner emigration'. During the Third Reich he was a much-read lyric poet (*Der irdische Tag*, 1935, *Rabe, Ross und Hahn*, 1939, *Lob des Weines*, 1944) whose poems and short prose works are characterized by their eye for telling detail.

### Hermann Broch
(Vienna 1886–1951 Connecticut)
It was only in the last third of his life that this mathematician, businessman and political philosopher turned to literature to counter what he saw as a collapse of European value systems with potentially terrifying political consequences. He chose the novel and the essay (*Logik einer zerfallenden Welt*, 1930, *Hofmannsthal und seine Zeit*, 1955), as likely to be the most influential genres. His works incl the *Schlafwandler* trilogy (wr 1931–2, publ 1932), *Die unbekannte Größe* (1933), and the anti-Hitler novel, *Die Verzauberung* (wr 1934–6; cf his theory of Kitsch as a key to understanding Nazism, and his designation of Hitler as 'der Kitsch-Mensch'). The elegiac novel, *Der Tod des Vergil* (1945), his finest work, is the product of disillusionment, while his late novels, *Die Schuldlosen: Roman in 11 Erzählungen* (1950) and *Der Versucher* (1953, 1967), sought to address the spiritual failure of postwar reconstruction in Germany and Austria.

### Barthold Heinrich Brockes
(Hamburg 1680–1747)
B helped to make his native city of Hamburg a centre of early Enlightenment by co-founding the *Teutsch-übende Gesellschaft zur Pflege von Sprache und Literatur* (1715) and the pioneering moral weekly, *Der Patriot* (1724–6). His oratorio *Der für die Sünden der Welt gemarterte und sterbende Jesus* (1712) was set to music by Telemann, while his equally admired 9-vol *Irdisches Vergnügen in Gott, bestehend in physikalisch- und moralischen Gedichten* (1721–48) testified to his belief in the harmony of creation and reason.

### Max Brod
(Prague 1884–1968 Tel Aviv)
Brod was a seeker after truth whose sense of Jewish identity carried with it a powerful ethical impulse. The author of the pioneering Expressionist novel *Schloss Nornepygge* (1908) and the historical novel *Tycho Brahes Weg zu Gott* (1916), he was also a patron of young talent incl Werfel, Jaroslav Hasek, Janáček, and, above all, though not unproblematically, Kafka.

### Friederike Brun
(Thuringia 1765–1835 Copenhagen)
A correspondent of Caroline von Humboldt, she wrote verse in the tradition of the *Göttinger Hain* – Mathisson publ her *Gedichte* in 1795 – and several travel books, incl *Briefe aus Rom, geschrieben 1808–10* (1816), containing an account of Pope Pius VII's imprisonment by Napoleon.

### Günter de Bruyn (Berlin 1926– )
B is an important figure in the GDR and post-GDR literary scene. Fontane's irony is an evident influence on his novels (*Buridans Esel*, 1968, *Preisverleihung*, 1972, *Märkische Forschungen: Erzählung für Freunde der Literaturgeschichte*, 1979), in which human conflicts and aspirations are located in a familiar landscape. *Das Leben des Jean Paul Richter* (1975) was an imaginative contribution to the GDR's attempt to establish its own identity within a wider German literary heritage. In his post-*Wende* work, he has promoted literature as an element of psychological and social cohesion.

### *Georg Büchner
(nr Darmstadt 1813–37 Zurich)
His existential sensitivity, political radicalism and analytical rigour find rich fusion in his literary productions: *Dantons Tod* (wr 1835), a startlingly unromantic drama set in the heart of Jacobin France, *Leonce und Lena* (wr 1836, publ 1838), a Shakespearean comedy with a marked political undertow, and *Lenz* (novelle 1839), an anatomy of psychic disintegration which anticipates much European modernist prose. *Woyzeck* (1836, publ as *Wozzeck* 1913) aims at a linguistic and thematic democratization of the tragic genre. B's 1836 medical trea-

tise *Sur le système nerveux du barbeau* led to the award of an MD and an appointment at Zurich University shortly before his death from typhus.

**Luise Büchner** (Darmstadt 1821–77)
Georg B's sister, she became an effective advocate of women's education and training despite – or because of – her own perfunctory formal education (*Die Frauen und ihr Beruf*, 1855). She publ her lectures (*Deutsche Geschichte von 1815–70*, 1875), given to the women's adult education institution she founded in collaboration with Princess Alice of Hesse-Darmstadt, Queen Victoria's daughter, and known as the *Alice-Verein für Frauenbildung-und Erwerb*. She also wrote verse and children's stories.

**Jakob Burckhardt** (Basle 1818–97)
The synchronic and diachronic approach to art criticism he adopted did much to establish art history as an academic discipline: *Der Cicerone: Eine Anleitung zum Genuß der Kunstwerke Italiens* (1855), and *Die Cultur der Renaissance in Italien* (1860) soon became classics. His lectures, publ posthumously as *Weltgeschichtliche Betrachtungen* (1905), are a worthy monument to an original and ironic mind.

**Gottfried August Bürger** (nr Halberstadt/ Harz 1747–94 Göttingen)
B was a typical 'poor poet' despite the efforts of his many literary friends. Schiller's notorious attack on his 'naturalness' and popular aspirations denied him the place he has held since the mid-19thc as one of Germany's greatest ballad writers (*Lenore, Der wilde Jäger, Des armen Suschens Traum*, 1773, etc). He is appreciated too for his political poetry (*Der Bauer: An seinen Durchlauchtigen Tyrannen*, 1773), the immediacy of his language, and his German trn of *Baron Münchhausen's Narrative of his Marvellous Travels and Campaigns in Russia* (1786).

**Erika Burkart** (Aarau 1922– )
She publ her first collection of poems in 1953, and since then has won a growing readership with 15 further collections (incl *Rufweite*, 1975, and *Die Zärtlichkeit der Schatten*, 1991) and 4

semi-autobiog novels (most notably, *Die Spiele der Erkenntnis*, 1985), all marked by her empathy with the countryside and her gift for expressing sophisticated insights in simple yet graphic language.

**Wilhelm Busch**
(nr Hanover 1832–1908 nr Seesen)
His failure to become a painter led B to become Germany's favourite armchair philosopher. No middle-class social gathering was complete without its plethora of quotations from B, few human follies escaped without reference to his verse caricatures, whose originality resides in their unlikely rhymes and the tension between message and picture. *Max und Moritz* (1865), his verse tales about two ghoulishly punished bad boys, are a forerunner of the modern comic. He adopted the anti-Catholic and especially anti-Jesuit polemics of the *Kulturkampf* in *Der heilige Antonius* (1870), *Die fromme Helene, Pater Filucius* (1872), *Fipps der Affe* (1879); and there is covert anti-Semitism in *Plisch und Plum* (1882). *Balduin Bählamm, der verhinderte Dichter* (1884) sends up all would-be poets.

# C

**Elias Canetti** (Bulgaria 1905–94 Zurich)
C's novel *Die Blendung* (1935) enjoyed a *succès d'estime*, but his postwar rediscovery, esp in Britain, centred on his probing studies of power (*Masse und Macht*, 1960) and revived interest in his plays (i a *Die Komödie der Eitelkeit*, 1965, but wr in 1934). His later work, crowned by the Nobel Prize in 1981, incl the powerful *Die Stimmen von Marrakesch* (1968), essays, and his great 3-part autobiog (1977–85).

**Friedrich Rudolph Ludwig von Canitz** (Berlin 1654–99)
A diplomat at the court of the Great Elector and his son, ennobled for his services by Emperor Leopold I, he aroused the admiration of educated Germans by his skilful application of Boileau's poetics to the fashioning of elegant verse in their native tongue. His posthumously publ collection of verse, *Neben-Stunden*

*Unterschiedener Gedichte* (1700), reached its 19th edn in 1719.

### Carmen Sylva
(Neuwied 1843–1916 nr Bucharest)

Even today one can still chance upon English translations of the once hugely popular but now forgotten work of Carmen Sylva, or Queen Elizabeth of Romania. She wrote historical novels (*Aus 2 Welten*, 1884), dramas (*Anna Boleyn*, 1886, *Frauenmuth*, 1890) and poetry (*Die Wacht an der Donau*, 1877).

### Hans Carossa
(Bad Tölz 1878–1956 nr Passau)

Goethe's dictum that all writing is essentially autobiographical applies aptly to this doctor and poet. In *Rumänisches Tagebuch* (1924), *Der Arzt Gion* (short stories 1931), *Eine Kindheit* (1922) and *Verwandlungen einer Jugend* (1928) his imagination, with its powerful sense of place, is shaped by biological thinking, in which sickness and decay are transformed by the 'healing' power of poetry. This, and his faith in the humane value of culture, made it difficult for the National Socialists to exploit him, as he explained in *Ungleiche Welten* (1951).

### Karl Heinrich Caspari
(Eschau 1815–61 Munich)

C made his name with popular novels for boys such as *Der Schulmeister und sein Sohn*, set during the 30 Years War and owing something to Grimmelshausen, and *Christ und Jude*, a far-fetched yet readable tale of 16thc Hungary's struggle against the Turks.

*Ignaz Franz Castelli* (Vienna 1780–1862)

The postwar reissue of his 4-vol Memoirs (1861) revived interest in a writer who, without great poetic pretensions, enlivened the Viennese literary scene with his myriad writings in a host of genres, among them some 200 plays, dialect literature (*Gedichte in niederösterreichischer Mundart*, 1828), early anti-Napoleonic verse (*Kriegslied für die österreichische Armee*, 1809) and non-fiction (*Über die Cholera*, 1831). He founded the Austrian Society for the Protection of Animals (1847).

### Paul Celan ( = Paul Antschel)
(Czernowitz 1920–70 Paris)

Celan tried to say the unsayable. This Romanian-born, German-speaking polyglot Jew tried to change Germans' relationship to their language and past. His early poetry *Typoskript* (1944, incl the famous lament 'Todesfuge'), *Der Sand aus den Urnen* (1948) and *Mohn und Gedächtnis* (1952), uses sound, imagery and rhythm to convey the guilt incurred by the culture which had once produced the poetry of his revered Hölderlin. His later poetry, with its composite nouns, oxymorons and silences (the much-criticized *Von Schwelle zu Schwelle*, 1955, and *Sprachgitter*, 1959, which his friend Nelly Sachs compared to the *Sohar*, a key work of the Jewish Cabbala), seems to withdraw from the communication process. *Die Niemandsrose* (1963) and *Atemwende* (1967) seek to 'hammer truth out of the wall of words'. He tr poems from 7 languages. C took his own life shortly after the savagely sarcastic *Fadensonnen* (1968) appeared. Posthumous vols (*Lichtzwang*, 1970, *Schneepart*, 1971, *Zeitgehöft*, 1976, *Eingedunkelt*, 1991) have enhanced his reputation, as did his *Büchner Preisrede*, publ in 1960 as *Der Meridian*.

*Conrad Celtis* (Wipfeld nr Schweinfurt 1459–1508 Vienna)

The 'arch-humanist' Celtis, Germany's leading neo-Latin poet during the Renaissance, was a typical humanist scholar who studied and taught in Italy, Cracow, Prague, Vienna, Nuremberg, Ingolstadt and Regensburg, a sequence reflected in the 4 love affairs of his *Amores* (1502). In 1500 he ed Tacitus's *Germania*, and in 1501 the works of Hrotsvit of Gandersheim, which he rediscovered: like Caritas Pirckheimer, she personified for him the key role of women in humanist society. His vision of the Germans as the Romans' true heirs underlies his reconciliation of classical antiquity and Christianity.

### Adelbert von Chamisso (Boncourt/ Champagne 1781–1838 Berlin)

French aristocratic refugee, army cadet, associate of Mme de Staël at Coppet, and student of philosophy and the sciences, Chamisso, the creator of that masterpiece of self-alienation, *Peter Schlemihls wundersame Geschichte* (1814), was also a botanist of note, a social poet in the manner of Béranger and an arbiter of poetic taste in the 1830s. He joined an expedition to circumnavigate the globe: his *Reise um die Welt in den Jahren 1815–1818* (1836) explores the impact of technology on the human sense of time, a theme in his once immensely popular poetry.

### Lena Christ (Glonn/Upr Bavaria 1881–1920 Munich)
C's poignant semi-autobiog novel *Erinnerungen einer Überflüssigen* (1912), the (dialect) tale of a rural servant girl *Rumpelhanni* (1916) and the short stories *Bauern* (1920), offer a graphic, down-to-earth and occasionally humorous portrayal of Bavarian peasant and petty-bourgeois life.

### Ada Christen (Vienna 1844–1901)
She was an early chronicler of the plight of the inner city in her 'shockingly' explicit *Lieder einer Verlorenen* (1868) and *Aus der Tiefe* (1878). Her play, *Die Häuslerin* (1867), *Aus dem Leben* (short stories 1876) and the novel *Jungfer Mutter: Eine Wiener Vorstadtgeschichte*, 1892) contributed to the literature of social criticism during the liberal era in Vienna.

### Matthias Claudius (Reinfeld/Holstein 1740–1815 Hamburg)
With his newspaper *Der Wandsbecker Bothe* (1771–5), Claudius created a medium of popular Enlightenment read all over the German-speaking world, with contributors such as Lessing, Klopstock, Goethe and Herder. *Asmus* (1775–1812) was his ongoing potpourri of essays, poetry, reflections and trns from major thinkers. He also wrote some of the most often sung and recited German poems, such as *Der Mond ist aufgegangen*.

### Heinrich Joseph von Collin (Vienna 1771–1811)
The neo-classical tragedies *Regulus* (1801), *Coriolan* (1802), *Polyxena* (1803), *Balboa* (1805) and *Horatier und Curiatier* (1810) earned Collin the title of 'Austrian Corneille'. He also wrote opera libretti, patriotic ballads

and martial songs (*Lieder Öesterreichischer Wehrmänner*, 1809).

### Matthäus von Collin (Vienna 1779–1824)
Ennobled, like his brother Heinrich, in 1803, tutor to Napoleon's son, the Duke of Reichstadt, Collin was early 19thc Vienna's leading literary and dramatic critic, publishing in F. Schlegel's *Deutsches Museum* and in the *Jahrbücher der Litteratur* which he ed 1818–21. His fine historical drama cycle on the medieval ruling house of Austria, the Babenbergs, marks him as a precursor of Grillparzer, but it never reached the stage.

### Michael Georg Conrad (Unterfranken 1846–1927 Munich)
He brought wide experience incl contact with Zola in Paris and Reichstag membership, to his editorship of his influential Naturalist journal, *Die Gesellschaft*, founded 1885 in Munich. He wrote an unfinished novel cycle (*Was die Isar rauscht*, 1888 etc) and dramas, but is best known for his essays and the semi-autobiog *Von Emile Zola bis Gerhart Hauptmann* (1902).

### Hedwig Courths-Mahler (Nebra 1867–1950 Tegernsee)
Once a servant girl and companion, she is still a successful beneficiary and manipulator of the mass market, with over 200 popular novels. Their titles, such as *Die Bettelprinzess* and *Unser Weg ging hinauf* (both 1914), invited her myriad women readers to identify with 'moral' heroines in pursuit of love and happiness through the fantasy of successful ascent of the social ladder.

### Heinz Czechowski (Dresden 1935– )
He belongs to the so-called 'Saxon school' of poets in the GDR (*Wasserfahrt*, 1967, *Schafe und Sterne*, 1974); deeply committed to the society in which they lived, they attempted to give poetry under socialism an authentic personal voice. This was associated by the authorities with subversion. He remained in the GDR after the Biermann affair, expressing an increasingly critical stance his readers shared.

# D

**Simon Dach** (Memel 1605–59 Königsberg)
Rector of Königsberg University and member
of the poetic circle known as the *Kürbishütte*,
he wrote some 1000 occasional poems
(*Gelegenheitsgedichte*) and songs celebrating
important events in the life of his friends
and city, in a style admired for its amiable
simplicity.

**Felix Dahn** (Hamburg 1834–1912 Breslau)
He was active in several genres but is identified
above all with the patriotic 'professorial novel':
*Ein Kampf um Rom* (1876) was a best-seller in
Wilhelmine Germany.

**Theodor Däubler**
(Triest 1876–1934 St Blasien)
Däubler's poetic oeuvre belongs at one level
to the German tradition of fascination with
Greece and 'Attic' clarity, at another to a contemporary search for a 'new mythology' and
philosophy of life; both inform his monumental 30,000-line epic *Das Nordlicht* (1910).

**Max Dauthendey**
(Würzburg 1867–1918 Java)
The powerful imagery of his early poetry anticipated literary Expressionism (*Ultra-Violett*,
1893, and *Schwarze Sonne*, 1897); his impressions of the Far East and the Pacific colour his
verse epic, *Die geflügelte Erde* (1910), and his
later more pretentious *Das Lied der Weltfestli-
chkeit* (1918). More appealing today are his stories in *Lingam* (1909) and *Die acht Gesichter am
Biwasee* (1911) and his *Raubmenschen* (1911), a
blend of travelogue and adventure novel.

**Jakob Julius David** (Weisskirchen/
Moravia 1859–1906 Vienna)
He made the immigrant's experience of life in
Vienna a central theme of his work, as in his
*Vier Geschichten* (1899), the novels *Am Wege
sterben* (1900) and *Der Übergang* (1902), and his
village tales of Moravian life.

**Franz Josef Degenhardt**
(Schwelm/Westphalia 1931– )
This West German *chansonnier* and ballad
writer prominent in the era of the 1968 stu-

dents' revolt pioneered the use of electronic
media in his work (LPs incl *Väterchen Franz*,
1966, *Im Jahr der Schweine*, 1969, *Die Joss-
Fritz-Ballade*, 1974), and helped revolutionize
the form and concept of 'literature' in W Germany in the 1970s. His novels dealt with issues
of topical protest, which partly explains his
later marginalization (*Brandstellen*, 1975, *Die
Mißhandlung oder Der freihändige Gang über
das Gelände der S-Bahn-Brücke*, 1979, *Der
Liedermacher*, 1982).

**Richard Dehmel** (Wendisch-Hermsdorf/
Mark Brandenburg 1863–1920
Hamburg-Blankenese)
He was a co-founder of the influential art
magazine *Pan* (1895). In *Erlösungen: Eine
Seelenwanderung in Gedichten und Sprüchen*
(1891), *Aber die Liebe* (1893), *Weib und Welt*
(1896) and *Zwei Menschen: Roman in
Romanzen* (1903) he made himself the poetic
arbiter of his age and a representative author of
the literary *Jugendstil*, with its cult of the body
and of Eros as 'new' religion. In later years he
was a successful dramatist (*Michel Michael*,
comedy 1911) and co-author, with his 1st wife,
**Paula Dehmel** (Berlin 1862–1918), of children's classics (*Fitzebutze*, 1900).

**Franz von Dingelstedt**
(Halsdorf 1814–81 Vienna)
This 'Young German' used the ploy of the
fictitious travelogue to castigate the political
system in his novel *Die neuen Argonauten*
(1839); his virtuoso (anon) collection of satirical verse *Lieder eines kosmopolitischen
Nachtwächters* (1840) won fame throughout
Germany. As director of the *Burgtheater*
(1870–80) he was renowned for his spectacular
productions.

**Alfred Döblin** (Stettin 1878–1957
Emmendingen/Brandenburg)
His early career as a neurologist and psychologist coincided with his debut as a major
Expressionist author. He focuses on the psychopathology of the authoritarian personality
in *Die Ermordung einer Butterblume* (short stories 1912), and in his historical novel
*Wallenstein* (1920) sides with history's under-
dogs. A supporter of the 1918 Revolution,

he worked as a satirical journalist and dramatist in the Weimar Republic (*Wissen und Verändern!*, 1931, and the trilogy of novels *November 1918*, completed and publ 1948–50). His masterpiece, the novel *Berlin Alexanderplatz: Die Geschichte vom Franz Biberkopf* (1929), filmed 1980 by Fassbinder, was his first popular success, not repeated until the novel of his and Germany's odyssey, *Hamlet oder Die lange Nacht nimmt kein Ende* (1956). Religion is central in his work, though portrayed indirectly, as in the exile novel *Babylonische Wanderung oder Hochmut kommt vor dem Fall* (1934).

#### Heimito von Doderer
(nr Vienna 1896–1966 Vienna)
In the narrative fiction of D, POW in 2 world wars, former Nazi and Catholic convert, the grotesque is central, as in the short novel *Ein Mord den jeder begeht* (1938). In his often mordantly witty panoramic novels *Die Strudlhofstiege* (1951), *Die Dämonen* (1956), the incomplete tetralogy *Roman No. 7* (*Die Wasserfälle von Slunj*, 1963) and the experimental *Die Merowinger oder Die totale Familie*, post-Imperial Austria's political condition is portrayed through the prism of multiple interlinked individual destinies. For him as for Canetti, the burning of the Palace of Justice in 1927 was a crucial event.

#### Hedwig Dohm (Berlin 1833–1919)
Wife of the proprietor of the satirical paper *Kladderadatsch*, and a successful writer of comedies, she developed a public profile as a pungently polemical feminist writer with *Was die Pastoren von den Frauen denken* (1873), *Die wissenschaftliche Emanzipation der Frau* (1884), her novel, *Christa Ruland* (1902) and, just before her death, her defence of pacifism, *Der Mißbrauch des Todes: Senile Impressionen*, which appeared (not without irony) in the same year as her grandson-in-law Thomas Mann publ *Betrachtungen eines Unpolitischen* (1918).

#### Hilde Domin (Cologne 1912– )
She began to write poems after nearly 20 years of exile and helped to get lyric poetry taken seriously in the W Germany of her day: *Nur eine Rose als Stütze* (1959), *Rückkehr der Schiffe* (1962), *Nachkrieg und Unfrieden* (anthology 1970), *Das Gedicht als Augenblick von Freiheit* (1988). Her theoretical writings explore the relationship between poem and reader, eg *Wozu Lyrik heute? Dichtung und Leser in der gesteuerten Gesellschaft* (1968).

#### Milo Dor (Budapest 1923– )
Many of the works of this Serb author, former Communist resistance fighter, forced labourer, and influential Austrian critic are autobiographical, such as the novels *Tote auf Urlaub* (1952) and *Nichts als Erinnerung* (1959) and the short stories, *Meine Reise nach Wien* (1974). Latterly his work for the media has attempted to revive Central European culture after Nazi attempts to destroy it.

#### Tankred Dorst
(nr Sonneberg/Thuringia 1925– )
He is a versatile dramatist and film-maker, as shown by his play *Gesellschaft im Herbst* (1961). His post-1968 work centres on a critical assessment of the W German intellectual, as in the plays *Toller* (1968) and *Goncourt oder die Abschaffung des Todes* (1977). Medieval epics provided material for his *Merlin oder Das wüste Land* (drama 1981) and *Parzival: Auf der anderen Seite des Sees* (1987).

#### Annette von Droste-Hülshoff
(nr Münster 1797–1848 Meersburg)
The powerful tension in her work derives from the conflict between her theological view of society and history and an ethical pessimism born of experience and religious doubt, as exemplified in *Das geistliche Jahr in Liedern auf alle Sonn- und Festtage* (1851). The wonderfully exact observation of nature in her *Gedichte* (1838 and 1844) frequently focuses on themes not usually associated with well-bred women poets from sheltered backgrounds. Her capacity to awaken a sense of fearful ambivalence is present in her verse epics, *Das Hospiz auf dem großen St Bernhard*, *Des Arztes Vermächtnis*, and *Die Schlacht im Loener Bruch* (in *Gedichte*, 1838), her ballads, and her novelle, *Die Judenbuche* (1842).

*Friedrich Dürrenmatt* (Konolfingen/
Switzerland 1921–90 Neuchâtel)
When the playwright, moralist and painter
visited Zurich University after his greatest
success, the première of *Der Besuch der alten
Dame: eine tragische Komödie* (1956), few Swiss
students turned up. Yet he has reason to be
grateful to his native land for stimulating the
comic talents he displayed in radio plays (*Der
Prozess um des Esels Schatten*, 1951, *Herkules
und der Stall des Augias*, 1954, *Die Panne*,
1956), detective stories (*Der Richter und sein
Henker*, 1952, *Der Verdacht*, 1953, *Justiz*,
1985), and satirical comedies (*Die Ehe des
Herrn Mississippi*, 1952, *Ein Engel kommt nach
Babylon*, 1954). His later plays, such as *Die
Physiker* (1962) and *Der Meteor* (1966), treat
major topical issues, as do his prose
*Zusammenhänge* (1976) and *Stoffe I–IX* (1981–
90). Like Brecht, D was an influential theorist
of 20thc theatre: *Theater-Schriften und Reden*
(1966), *Dramaturgisches und Kritisches* (1972),
*Bilder und Zeichnungen* (1978).

# E

*Georg Moritz Ebers*
(Berlin 1837–98 Tutzing)
This Egyptologist was the much-read author
of over 20 novels including *Eine ägyptische
Königstochter* (1864). Older readers recall the
imaginative excitement generated by his ability
to bring history to life.

*Johann Arnold Ebert*
(Hamburg 1723–95 Brunswick)
A key figure in the history of sensibility
(*Empfindsamkeit*), he seems to have been a man
everyone liked. A tireless teacher of English,
he translated Young's *Night Thoughts* between
1751 and 1769. His circle of friends and admirers extended far and wide and spanned the
generations, and his advice in matters of taste
was much sought and generously given.

*Marie von Ebner-Eschenbach*
(Zdislavic/Moravia 1830–1916 Vienna)
15 years vainly attempting to establish herself
as a dramatist left their mark on her. Her
prose works, popularized by publication in

Rodenberg's *Deutsche Rundschau*, incl the
novelle *Božena*, 1876, the *Dorf- und
Schloßgeschichten* (1883–6), and the novels *Das
Gemeindekind* (1887), *Unsühnbar* (1890) and
*Glaubenslos?* (1893). Her diffident yet robust
view of herself as a woman writer is reflected
in her *Aphorismen* (1880) and her autobiog
writings *Meine Kinderjahre* (1906) and *Meine
Erinnerungen an Grillparzer: Aus einem
zeitlosen Tagebuch* (1916).

*Johann Peter Eckermann*
(Winsen/Luhe 1792–1854 Weimar)
He often seems an institution, rather than an
actual personality of German literature, in
his capacity as the self-effacing author of
*Gespräche mit Goethe in den letzten Jahren
seines Lebens 1823–32* (1836–48), which
Hofmannsthal called one of the world's great
books, unique in its ability to mediate and to
problematicize Goethe as man, poet and
thinker.

*Günter Eich* (Lebus/Mark Brandenburg
1907–72 Salzburg)
A Sinologist by training, he was a pioneer of
the radio play in the 1930s, a form he used with
sophistication and great popular success in
the 1950s (*Träume*, 1953). Associated with
Andersch's *Der Ruf* and Höllerer's *Akzente*
(1953), co-founder of *Gruppe 47*, his POW
poetry (*Abgelegene Gehöfte*, 1948) established
him as one of Germany's leading postwar
authors, whose vision of the poet as anarchist
was a significant influence on the 1968
generation.

*Joseph von Eichendorff*
(Lubowitz nr Ratibor 1788–1857 Neisse)
He was writing at a time when Europeans were
beginning to sense that freedom was being
bought at the cost of separation from nature.
Art, exemplified in the musicality of his poetry, can restore that lost unity, but only mo-
mentarily. In *Ahnung und Gegenwart* (1815), a
novel written against the background of the
Wars of Liberation in which he took part, and
in the shorter fictions *Aus dem Leben eines
Taugenichts* and *Das Marmorbild* (both 1826)
and *Schloß Dürande* (1836) the writer and poet
strives to teach humanity to read the 'hiero-

glyphic language' of Nature and art. His translations of Calderón and his critical works on Romantic and Christian poetry are masterpieces of their kind (*Die geistliche Poesie in Deutschland*, 1847, and *Geschichte der poetischen Literatur Deutschlands*, 1857).

### Elisabeth Charlotte (= Liselotte) von der Pfalz (Heidelberg 1652–1722 Saint-Cloud)

The court of Louis XIV may not have been amused by her colourful language and often scatological humour, and the circle of Monsieur, her disagreeable and homosexual consort, may have thought her silk-covered corpulence an easy target of their malice, but they provided her with ample material for several thousand witty letters, many still unpublished, which make her one of Germany's greatest epistolary talents.

### Michael Ende (Garmisch-Partenkirchen 1929–95 Stuttgart)

He became a cult figure in the 1970s and 1980s with his books for children, *Jim Knopf und Lukas der Lokomotivführer* (1960), *Momo oder Die seltsame Geschichte von den Zeit-Dieben und von dem Kind, das den Menschen die gestohlene Zeit zurückbrachte* (1973), and especially *Die unendliche Geschichte* (1979). These brought fantasy back to children's – and adults' – reading in a materialist consumer society.

### *Friedrich Engels (Barmen 1820–95 London)

He has long been the 'whipping-boy' for those attacking the tendency towards determinism in Marxist theory. Did such late works as *Herrn Eugen Dührings Umwälzung der Wissenschaft* (known as *Anti-Dühring*, 1878), *Die Entwicklung des Sozialismus von der Utopie zur Wissenschaft* (French 1880, German 1882) and *Der Ursprung der Familie, des Privateigentums und des Staats* (1884) corrupt the dialectical thought of his close friend and associate Karl Marx? E's involvement in his father's cotton-spinning business in Barmen and Manchester gave his nascent socialism its empirical moorings (see *Die Lage der arbeitenden Klasse in England*, 1845) and enabled him to keep Marx financially solvent.

They co-authored *Die Heilige Familie* (an attack on the Young Hegelians, 1845), *Die deutsche Ideologie* (wr 1845–6) and the *Communist Party Manifesto* (now credited largely to Marx, 1848).

### Hans Magnus Enzensberger (Kaufbeuren 1929– )

Founder of the journal *Kursbuch* (1965), author of powerful essays (*Deutschland, Deutschland unter anderem: Äußerungen zur Politik*, 1967, *Ach Europa! Wahrnehmungen aus sieben Ländern. Mit einem Epilog aus dem Jahre 2006*, 1987), he fused political commitment, colloquial and trendy language and sophisticated imagery in his poetry (*verteidigung der wölfe*, 1957, *landessprache*, 1960, *blindenschrift*, 1964) and did more than most to release German literature from the isolation of the Nazis' *Sonderweg* by drawing attention to other contemporary literatures; he has also produced much documentary work, as well as the apocalyptic comedy *Untergang der Titanic* (1978).

### Desiderius Erasmus (Rotterdam 1466–1536 Basle)

The greatest Renaissance humanist created a many-faceted oeuvre which incl pioneering edns, a trn of the Greek New Testament into Latin, and Latin works much tr into German by his contemporaries. These include *Adagia* (1500–36), a treasury of classical wisdom drawn on by intellectuals for 200 years, the *Enchiridion militis Christiani* (1503), a code of behaviour for the educated Christian, and the *Colloquia* (1524), a set of elegant model dialogues. His best-known work, *Morias encomion* or *In Praise of Folly* (1511), was dedicated to his English friend, Thomas More. E's name was given to the pioneering European Union university exchange programme which laid the foundation for a new concept of European citizenship, though he would not have been surprised at the failure of political will to implement it.

### Elke Erb (Vienna 1945– )

She collaborated with Sarah Kirsch after so many GDR writers moved to the West (*Musik auf dem Wasser*, Leipzig 1977, *Trost, Gedichte und Prosa*, Stuttgart 1982), but it is for her association with the *Prenzlauer Berg* writers, notably Sascha Anderson, that she has made her name in both parts of Germany (see also her collection of lyric poetry *Unschuld, du Licht meiner Augen*, 1994).

### Paul Ernst (Elbingerode/Harz 1866–1933 St Georgen/Styria)

An active if uncomfortable Social Democrat, he was a household name around 1900 as the theoretician of the neo-classical novelle and author of some 250 of them. Undeservedly neglected are his *Jugenderinnerungen* (1930) about growing up in a mid-19thc mining community.

### Dorothea Christiane Erxleben (Quedlinburg 1715–62)

She pioneered medical studies for women by becoming a practising doctor and wrote the ground-breaking inquiry into the state of women's education (or lack of it), *Gründliche Untersuchung der Ursachen, die das Weiblich Geschlecht vom Studiren abhalten* (1742, reprinted anon and in abridged form, at Frankfurt/M and Leipzig, 1749).

### Johann Joachim Eschenburg (Hamburg 1743–1820 Brunswick)

A leading contributor to Enlightenment periodicals, notably Nicolai's *Allgemeine deutsche Bibliothek* and *Allgemeine Literatur-Zeitung*, he was the first to tr the complete works of Shakespeare into German ([1]1775–82; [2]1780–1; [3]1798–1806).

# F

### Gustav Falke (Lübeck 1853–1916 Großorstel/Hamburg)

Falke was, like T Mann, a Lübeck merchant's son. He achieved his artistic ambitions by becoming a piano teacher and writing derivative turn-of-the-century poetry and novels which provide a context for Mann's early masterpieces (*Landen und Stranden*, 1895). His chauvinistic war poems ('Vaterland, heilig Land', 1915) were rewarded by Wilhelm II with the Order of the Red Eagle.

### Hans Fallada (= Rudolf Ditzen) (Greifswald 1893–1947 Berlin)

He wrote his immensely successful novels, *Bauern, Bonzen und Bomben* (1931) and *Kleiner Mann – was nun?* (1932), from the perspective of the 'little man'; his reader is invited to identify with politically ineffectual protagonists marginalized by society and politics. His later novels, *Wer einmal aus dem Blechnapf frißt* (1934) and *Der Trinker* (1950), draw on his experiences as an alcoholic, drug addict and jailbird; his last, *Jeder stirbt für sich allein* (1947), is more positive in its portrayal of working-class characters in the German Resistance.

### Heinrich Federer (Brienz 1866–1928 Zurich)

Federer was ordained in 1893. He engaged in religious journalism until his novel *Berge und Menschen* (1911) brought him financial and intellectual independence. His works give a rugged and unsentimental view of Swiss life, especially when they are based on his own often bitter experience (*Das Mätteliseppi*, 1916, and *Papst und Kaiser im Dorf*, 1924).

### Lion Feuchtwanger (Munich 1884–1958 Los Angeles)

After writing a doctorate on Heine, he worked for Theodor Wolff, the Jewish editor of the liberal *Berliner Tageblatt*. The phenomenal success of his political historical novel *Jud Süß* (1925) and the publication of *Erfolg: Drei Jahre Geschichte einer Provinz* (1930), a novel about the early years of the Hitler movement in Bavaria, made him a marked man for the Nazis. In US exile he completed the two trilogies for which he is best remembered: *Wartesaal* (*Erfolg, Die Geschwister Oppenheim*, 1933, *Exil*, 1940) and *Josephus* (*Der jüdische Krieg*, 1932, *Die Söhne*, 1935, *Der Tag wird kommen*, 1945).

### *Johann Gottlieb Fichte (Rammenau/Lausitz 1762–1814 Berlin)

By elevating the self-conscious subject to the supreme status of 'absolutes Ich' (the 'absolute ego') in the seminal system of knowledge or *Wissenschaftslehre* he based on his lectures at Jena University, F went beyond Kant's theory of subjectivity (*Über den Begriff der Wissenschaftslehre*, 1794, etc). There can be, he claimed, no higher philosophical act than for the ego to posit itself in the very act of thinking. Attacked as an atheist for his *Über den Grund unseres Glaubens an eine göttliche Weltregierung* (1798), he became an ardent nationalist, delivering his *Reden an die deutsche Nation* in Berlin under French occupation in 1807–8 (publ 1808). He was elected first Rector of the new University of Berlin in 1811.

### Johann Fischart
### (Strasburg 1546–90 Forbach?)

He travelled widely, qualified and practised as a lawyer, and wrote copiously, capping his extravagantly inventive *Aller Practic Großmutter* (1572), a phantasmagoria in Rabelaisian manner, with his brilliantly idiosyncratic trn of Book I of *Gargantua* (1575, expanded eds 1582 and 1590). Though one of the most verbally and syntactically creative of German authors, his oeuvre has attracted surprisingly little critical attention.

### Cäsar Flaischlen
### (Stuttgart 1864–1920 Gundelsheim)

He was determined to be a successful writer and succeeded in terms of royalties with *Von Alltag und Sonne* (1898) and *Aus dem Lehr- und Wanderjahren des Lebens* (1900). His short, rapturously impressionistic pieces caught the mood of the times. He ed the *Jugendstil* magazine *Pan*, produced a semi-autobiog collage novel *Jost Seyfried* (1905) and enjoyed renewed popularity with his jingoistic war poems (*Heimat und Welt*, 1916).

### Otto Flake
### (Metz 1880–1963 Baden-Baden)

This fine stylist was, like René Schickele, a member of *das Jüngste Elsaß* and then a Dadaist (novel *Ja und Nein*, 1920). A biographer, essayist, author of fairy tales, he was associated with the 'Inner Emigration'.

### Marieluise Fleißer (Ingolstadt 1901–74)

A critical sense of place and a blend of comedy and pathos characterize her work which incl stories such as *Die List* (wr 1925–7, publ 1995) and *Ein Pfund Orangen* (1929), a semi-autobiog

novel *Mehlreisende Frieda Geier* (1931) and plays of peasant life, such as *Fegefeuer in Ingolstadt* (1926) and *Pioniere in Ingolstadt* (1928), which have become a powerful influence on more recent exponents of the critical *Volksstück*.

### Paul Fleming (Hartenstein/Saxony
### 1609–40 Hamburg)

The discipline of Opitz's poetics, combined with his own literary talent and humanist education, helped this doctor and diplomat to produce one of 17thc Germany's finest poetic oeuvres. His posthumous *Teutsche Poemata* (1646) incl love poems which display his elegant wit (as in 'Wie er wolle geküsset seyn') and relaxed mastery of Petrarchan conceits, but also contains some of the finest neo-Stoical poems in German. After returning from a 6-yr diplomatic mission to Russia and Persia, and gaining his MD in Leyden, he died, celebrating his achievements in his own epitaph: '*Ich war an Kunst und Gut / und Stande groß und reich.*'

### Walter Flex (Eisenach 1887–1917 Ösel)

With his best-selling autobiog tale, *Der Wanderer zwischen beiden Welten* (1917), whose hero goes to the front equipped with the New Testament, Goethe and Nietzsche's *Zarathustra*, F provided his own generation, as well as that of the 1920s, with an icon of the 'youthful martyr in the people's cause', later exploited by the Nazis.

### Theodor Fontane
### (Neu-Ruppin 1819–98 Berlin)

He was for his contemporaries primarily a ballad-writer (*Der alte Dessauer* etc) and author of military and topographical works (*Ein Sommer in London*, 1854, *Jenseit des Tweed*, 1860, *Wanderungen durch die Mark Brandenburg*, 1862–82) and an only relatively successful novelist. His 'rediscovery' by post-1945 scholars (notably in the GDR) as late 19thc Germany's major novelist and letter-writer is one of the many surprises of German literary history. Beginning with the historical novel *Vor dem Sturm* (1878), written against the grain of Wilhelmine nationalist historiography, the works he wrote in his 60s and 70s incl the novellen *Schach von Wuthenow* (1883), *Graf*

*Petöfy* (1884), *Unterm Birnbaum* (1885), *Cécile* (1887) and *Stine* (1890) and the novels, *Irrungen, Wirrungen* (1888), *Unwiederbringlich* (1891), *Frau Jenny Treibel* (1892), *Effi Briest* (1895), *Die Poggenpuhls* (1896) and *Der Stechlin* (1898). He also produced two vols of autobiog, *Meine Kinderjahre* (1894) and *Von Zwanzig bis Dreißig* (1898).

### Friedrich Heinrich Karl de la Motte Fouqué (Brandenburg 1777–1843 Berlin)

Elemental spirits – generally in the form of seductive or even destructive women – populate F's works, such as the elusive heroine of his famous fairy tale *Undine* (1811). His complex evocation of the world of chivalry in *Der Zauberring* (1813) and *Sintram* (1815) exerted wide and international appeal, while his dramatic trilogy *Der Held des Nordens* (*Sigurd der Schlangentödter, Sigurds Rache, Aslauga*, 1808–10) is a thematic and metrical forerunner of Wagner's *Der Ring des Nibelungen* (1848–74). F was an energetic ed of periodicals who showed insight and critical taste in his promotion of younger talents, among them Chamisso, Eichendorff and Kleist.

### Caroline de la Motte Fouqué (nr Rathenow 1774–1831)

The wife of the Romantic author Friedrich de la Motte Fouqué, she was a relatively successful and sometimes consciously feminist historical and autobiog novelist (*Die Frau des Falkensteins*, 1810, *Feodora*, 1814). Despite an unconventional character and lifestyle, she propounded conservative views on the social and political role of women in *Briefe über Zweck und Richtung weiblicher Bildung* (1810).

### Sebastian Franck (Donauwörth *c.*1500–43 Basle)

F led a peripatetic life. He is remembered today for a collection of proverbs and sayings, publ in 1541, which incl the first reference to the German national stereotype, *der t(d)eutsche Michel*.

### August Hermann Francke (Halle 1663–1727)

This great Protestant reformer personally experienced that 'conversion', which became a central tenet of the Pietist movement he founded, documenting it in his autobiog in 1690–1 and elaborating it in sermons, beginning with *Buß-Predigten* (1699–1707). F combined a voluminous pastoral correspondence with imaginative, practical Christianity involving pioneering forms of education for the poor and for girls in his Halle schools, and extensive publishing; his missionary activity had a long-lasting impact on the US and on Russia. He was truly one of Germany's most innovative spirits.

### Louise von François (Herzberg/Elster 1817–93 Weissenfels)

Almost more than any other woman writer in 19thc Germany, she was a victim of her gender and of domestic circumstances. Unending and humiliating exploitation by her family and a lack of formal schooling did not prevent her from writing history (anon: *Geschichte der preußischen Befreiungskriege in den Jahren 1813 bis 1815*, 1874) and from bringing a high degree of authenticity to her intuitive understanding of the past in *Die letzte Reckenburgerin* (1871), her masterpiece, a novel which waited nearly a decade for a publisher. She also wrote collections of stories (publ 1868, 1871, 1874) and the novels *Stufenjahre eines Glücklichen* (1877) and *Frau Erdmuthens Zwillingssöhne* (1872).

### Karl Emil Franzos (Czortków/Galicia 1848–1904 Berlin)

Germanists researching the lost landscape of central E Europe in the aftermath of the Holocaust rediscovered the first ed of Büchner's *Woyzeck* as an author in his own right. His essays and novellen *Aus Halb-Asien: Kulturbilder aus Galizien, der Bukowina, Südrußland und Rumänien* and *Die Juden von Barnow* (both 1876, though the latter bore the year 1877) and the novels *Judith Trachtenberg* (1891), *Leib Weihnachtskuchen und sein Kind* (1896) and *Der Pojaz* (1905) evoke a multicultural world and epitomize the poignant irony of liberal Jewish self-identification with German idealism and culture.

### Ferdinand Freiligrath (Detmold 1810–76 Cannstadt)

His position in older German anthologies reflected the range of contradictory trends in mid-19thc German literature: exoticism, escapism from provinciality and oppression, the romanticization of the river Rhine, and revolutionary fervour (*Ein Glaubensbekenntnis, Zeitgedichte*, 1844, and especially *Ça ira!*, 1846, *Neuere politische und soziale Gedichte*, 1849–51). After 1871 his poetry struck a more chauvinistic note. The impressive sums F could command for his work in the 1840s illustrate the powerful role of literature in the pre-1848 or *Vormärz* period of political and social ferment. F was also a fine tr from English and other langs.

### Gustav Frenssen
### (Dithmarschen 1863–1945)
F was aware of contemporary fears of modernization, and his ability in his fiction to provide persuasive role models who successfully resist it, helps to account for the enormous sales (over 3 million copies) of his novels, notably *Jörn Uhl* (1901) and *Hilligenlei* (1905). In later years he became a convinced 'German Christian' and Nazi supporter (*Lebensbericht*, 1940).

### Gustav Freytag (Kreuzburg/Silesia
### 1816–95 Wiesbaden)
A Germanist by training, he ed the influential National Liberal periodical *Die Grenzboten* and wrote *Soll und Haben* (1855), the best-selling novel of the century. Author of a widely perf comedy, *Die Journalisten* (1854), and often-cited essays, his presentation of German history in the 5-vol *Bilder aus der deutschen Vergangenheit* (1859–67) and the novel cycle *Die Ahnen* (1873–81) had a formative influence on generations of German readers, amongst them the young T Mann.

### Erich Fried
### (Vienna 1921–88 Baden-Baden)
Despite 50 years in English exile, admired and vilified by turns as 'the house poet of the German Left', Fried became the most successful lyric poet since Brecht, selling over 150,000 copies of *Liebesgedichte* (1979). In this and the many other collections appearing from the mid-1960s to his death (i a *und Vietnam und*, 1966, *Gedanken in und an Deutschland*, essays

and speeches 1988), F, a political activist, moralist and Holocaust victim, offered his audience a chance to identify with their few remaining certainties as sentient human beings.

### Max Frisch (Zurich 1911–91)
'I try on stories like clothes,' says the narrator in *Homo Faber* (1957). His words characterize the work of F and the dialectic of self-concealment and self-revelation in the novels *Stiller* (1954), *Mein Name sei Gantebein* (1957), *Montauk* (1975) and the *Tagebücher 1946–1949* (1950), with which Suhrkamp launched its publishing programme. Role play also characterizes his drama, from the antiwar hostage play *Nun singen sie wieder* (1945) to his witty challenge to received role models in *Don Juan oder Die Liebe zur Geometrie* (1953), his much-played black comedy *Biedermann und die Brandstifter* (1958) and *Andorra* (1961), which exemplify the banality of evil. F provided a focus for debate with his ambivalent relationship to his nation in the parodistic *Wilhelm Tell für die Schule* (1971), the angrier *Schweiz ohne Armee? Ein Palaver* (staged as *Jonas und sein Veteran*, 1989) and *Schweiz als Heimat* (1990).

### Barbara Frischmuth (Altaussee 1941– )
A member of the Graz *Forum Stadtpark*, she is one of contemporary Austria's most prolific authors. Following her imaginatively humorous *Die Klosterschule* (1968) and *Amoralische Kinderklapper* (1969), she developed a feminist perspective in *Haschen nach Wind* (1974) and her novel trilogy, *Die Mystifikationen der Sophie Silber, Amy oder die Metamorphose* and *Kai und die Liebe zu den Modellen* (1976–9). Her more recent work incl *Mörderische Mörder und andere Erzählungen* (1989), *Einander Kindsein* (novelle 1990) and her Munich poetry lectures on literature and dreams (1991).

### Franz Fühmann (Rochlitz/
### Czechoslovakia 1922–84 Berlin)
A powerful moral impulse is evident in the work of F, a fine stylist whose lyric poetry (*Die Nelke Nikos, Die Fahrt nach Stalingrad*, both 1953) and prose fiction, often filmed, featured the relationship of Germans to their past (i a *Kameraden*, 1955, *Das Judenauto*, 1962); he brought his Czech background into *Der*

*Jongleur im Kino oder Die Insel der Träume* (1970) and took his readers to Hungary in the travelogue *Zweiundzwanzig Tage oder Die Hälfte des Lebens* (1973). F is a fine essayist, notably in *Der Sturz des Engels* (1982).

**Gertrud Fussenegger** (Pilsen 1912– )
She was a typical *Anschluß* writer with her antimodernism and idealization of the Reich as a racial community, exemplified in her Sudetenland novels (*Böhmische Verzauberungen*, 1944, *Die Brüder von Lasava*, 1948) and her poems to Hitler. A prolific postwar author, she was also one of the first Austrians to breach the silence about their Nazi past in *Ein Spiegelbild mit Feuersäule: Lebensbericht* (autobiog 1979).

# G

**Gerd Gaiser** (Oberriexingen/
Württemberg 1908–76 Reutlingen)
He owed his popularity in the postwar years to his portrayal of the German experience of war and reintegration into civil life in his short stories *Zwischenland* (1949) and the semi-autobiog novel, *Eine Stimme hebt an* (1950); his place in that elusive entity, the 'canon' of W German fiction promised by *Schlußball* (1958), his once-successful experimental novel attacking consumerism, has not materialized.

**Amalia Princess Gallitzin**, née *von Schmettau* (Berlin 1748–1806 Münster)
Friend of Claudius, F H Jacobi and Leopold Stolberg, she was the separated wife of the Russian ambassador to the Netherlands and became the focus of the so-called Münster Circle, which achieved a unique degree of integration between the Catholic Enlightenment and major contemporary German writers such as Goethe (briefly), Herder, Kant and Hamann. She introduced the Romantics to the tradition of Catholic devotion from Thomas à Kempis and St John of the Cross to Pascal, François de Sales and Johann Michael Sailer.

**Ludwig Albert Ganghofer** (Kaufbeuren
1855–1920 Tegernsee)
He grew wealthy on the profits from his plays

(such as the *Volksstück*, *Der Herrgottschnitzer von Amergau*, 1880) and fiction in a Bavarian setting (*Schloß Hubertus*, 1895), in which normality and goodness are rewarded and nature often takes a hand in punishing those who fall short. His attractive personality won him the friendship of Rilke, T Mann and Thoma.

**Emanuel Geibel** (Lübeck 1815–84)
The widely held 19thc notion of literature as the expression of public feeling explains the phenomenal success of G, protégé of Maximilian II of Bavaria and 'court poet of the Wilhelmine Empire'. His early *Gedichte* (1840) won him a Prussian stipend. His popularity with middle-class readers was reinforced by his attacks on the socio-political poetry of the 1840s (*Juniuslieder*, 1848) because of its threat to artistic values and by his celebration of German unification and the founding of the German Empire in 1871. The musicality of his verse is reflected in his trns from Greek, Latin, Spanish and French.

**Geiler von Kayserberg**
(Schaffhausen 1445–1510 Strasburg)
One of his age's great preachers, he reminds us that, in times past, sermons were not only a source of moral teaching but also a form of entertainment. Thus G expounded Brant's *Narrenschiff* in 110 sermons in Strasburg Cathedral which were later publ in Latin as *Navicula sive speculum fatuorum* (1510).

**Christian Fürchtegott Gellert**
(Erzgebirge 1715–69 Leipzig)
The 'apostle of friendship', he was the favourite writer and moralist of 18thc Germany (*Fabeln und Erzählungen*, 1746–8). His *Geistliche Oden und Lieder* (1757) struck a chord throughout Protestant Germany. He was an arbiter of good taste, which he saw as the prerequisite of the rational man of feeling (*Briefe, nebst einer Praktischen Abhandlung von dem guten Geschmacke in Briefen*, 1751). His successful comedies (*Die Betschwester*, 1745, *Die zärtlichen Schwestern*, 1747) were underpinned by his Latin treatise on sentimental comedy (*Pro comoedia commovente*, 1751), while his novel *Das Leben der schwedischen*

*Gräfin von G . . .* (1747–8, [2]1751) was the first in German to project a new ideal of bourgeois life and manners and to provide an idealized portrait of a Jew.

### Stefan George
(Büdesheim 1868–1933 nr Locarno)
Mallarmé introduced this young poet to the work of Baudelaire and Rimbaud: he responded by producing symbolist poetry of great formal beauty (*Algabal*, 1892, *Das Jahr der Seele*, 1897) which formed the starting-point of an aesthetic programme elaborated in the *Blätter für die Kunst* (1882–1919). G sedulously promoted his own beautifully printed work (*Der siebte Ring*, 1907, *Stern des Bundes*, 1914) through the *George Kreis*: poetry was seen as a way of life through which a sensitive elite sought to counter the destructive impact of 'Americanized' culture on 'European' literature (i a *Das neue Reich*, 1928).

### Paul Gerhardt
(nr Wittenberg 1607–76 Lübben)
Germany's greatest hymn writer (*Geistliche Andachten*, 1667) is famous both for his original hymns and for his German versions of great Latin hymns of the Christian tradition, such as 'O Haupt voll Blut und Wunden'. These still form part of the Protestant canon, while their presence in RC hymnals underscores the ecumenical character of the intention and reception of his work.

### Friedrich Karl Gerok
(Vaihingen/Enz 1815–90 Stuttgart)
His fame was legendary in the Wilhelmine Empire both for his Protestant religious lyrics (*Palmblätter*, 1857, [400]1900) and for his religious legitimization of war in *Deutsche Ostern: Kriegslieder* (1871).

### Friedrich Gerstäcker
(Hamburg 1816–72 Brunswick)
No doubt the experience of this inveterate traveller in all sorts of jobs in N, Central and S America and Australia, described with objectivity and good humour in *Die Flußpiraten des Mississippi* (1848), *Die beiden Sträflinge: Australischer Roman* (1856), *Gold! Ein californisches Lebensbild aus dem Jahre 1849*

(1858), accounts for the phenomenal success of his 80 travel tales and adventure stories among would-be German emigrants and those who stayed behind.

### Heinrich Wilhelm von Gerstenberg
(Tondern/Schleswig 1737–1823 Altona)
G wrote Anacreontic verse (*Tändeleyen*, 1759) and bardic poetry (*Gedicht eines Skalden*, 1766), but is now best remembered for his influential appreciation of Shakespeare's treatment of human feeling in *Briefe über die Merkwürdigkeiten der Litteratur* (1766–70), exemplified in his own stark tragedy, *Ugolino* (1768), based on an episode in Dante's *Inferno*.

### Salomon Gessner (Zurich 1730–88)
He was an influential publisher and an accomplished draughtsman (*Brief über die Landschaftsmahlerey*, 1770) whose mellifluous arcadian prose poems appeared anon (*Die Nacht*, 1753, *Daphnis*, 1754, *Idyllen von dem Verfasser des Daphnis*, 1756). Gessner's *Idyllen* were amongst the most reprinted and tr works of the 18thc. They offered an Enlightenment critique of the threat to 'idyllic' and virtuous nature posed by 'civilization' and put Germany on the literary map of Europe. His dramatic epic *Der Tod Abels* (1758) proved popular in England.

### Friedrich Glauser
(Vienna 1896–1938 Nervi/Italy)
He was almost forgotten, but his rediscovery had made him something of a cult figure by his centenary year. His unconventional life from foreign legionary to drug addict colours his novels: beneath their readable blend of excitement and suspense lie darker visions. His 6 crime novels brought this genre to rare literary heights (*Matto regiert*, 1936, *Die Fieberkurve*, 1938).

### Johann Wilhelm Ludwig Gleim
(Ermsleben/Harz 1719–1803 Halberstadt)
The contribution of the 'German Anacreon' to literary history incl his much-read *Versuch in Scherzhaften Liedern* (1744–58), the *Romanzen* (1756), which anticipated the German ballad, and the *Preußische Kriegslieder in den Feldzügen*

*1756 und 1757 von einem Grenadier* (1758), in which G stylized Frederick II of Prussia as a national hero. 'Father' Gleim's capacity for practical friendship succoured many other writers, including Anna Luisa Karsch.

**Babette Elisabeth Glück** *see* **Betty Paoli**

*Gulielmus Gnaphaeus* (The Hague 1492–1568 Norden/Friesland)
He studied in Cologne and became headmaster of a new school in Elbing, E Prussia. His influential Latin play *Acolastus* (1529) appeared in German in 1535 and in English in 1540 and was the epitome and model of the 16thc's countless dramatizations of the Prodigal Son parable. Later he held a chair at Königsberg University: he spent the years 1562–5 on a diplomatic mission to England.

*Karl Goedeke* (Celle 1814–87 Göttingen)
He is the founder and author of the first 3 vols of the *Grundriß zur Geschichte der Deutschen Dichtung* (1856–61), which is still one of the great bibliographical tools for the academic study of German literature.

*Reinhard Goering* (Fulda 1887–1936 Jena)
He made his name as the dramatist of the 1914–18 naval war with 2 plays: *Seeschlacht* (1917) and *Scapa Flow* (1919). He returned to the stage in 1930 with *Die Südpolexpedition des Kapitäns Scott*. He put an end to his drift towards National Socialism by committing suicide.

*Catharina Elisabeth Goethe* (Frankfurt/M 1731–1808)
Apart from her benign influence on her son, she deserves a place in literature for her letters to him and to Bettine von Arnim.

*Cornelia Goethe* (Frankfurt/M 1750–77 Emmendingen, Baden)
A mannered French diary and some poignant letters are her tragic memorial. She was excluded because of her sex (and possibly by her mother) from access to the world of letters and knowledge inhabited by her beloved and much more famous brother.

*Johann Wolfgang* (1782– *von*) *Goethe* (Frankfurt/M 1749–1832 Weimar)
G bestrides the crucial period of dynamic change and creativity which produced Mozart, Beethoven, Napoleon, the American War of Independence and the French Revolution, the first railways and steamships, smallpox vaccination, Byron's poetry, Hegel's philosophy and the decipherment of Egyptian hieroglyphics, and he is the European writer in whose works that extraordinary range is most fully reflected. A life-loving young man absorbed in love and art, he spent most of his life in Weimar, becoming the scientist and sage whose Olympian presence dominated the 19thc in Germany. The profoundest achievements of his maturity, such as *Zur Farbenlehre* (scientific treatise 1810), *West-östlicher Divan* (poetry 1819), *Wilhelm Meisters Wanderjahre* (novel 1821) and *Faust Part II* (poetic drama 1832), should not blind present-day readers to the originality and perfection of earlier works such as *Urfaust* (*c*.1776) and *Faust Part I* (drama 1808), *Wilhelm Meisters Lehrjahre* (novel 1795–6) and the 'Sesenheimer Lieder' (lyric poems 1770–1). The historical play *Götz von Berlichingen* (1773) made his name in Germany; with the epistolary novel *Die Leiden des jungen Werthers* (1774) he became world-famous. *Iphigenie auf Tauris* (prose drama 1779, verse drama 1800) and the *Römische Elegien* (elegiac/erotic poems 1795) came to represent German classicism (or neo-classicism) at its finest, yet to non-German readers and admirers G has always been a Romantic icon. His novel *Die Wahlverwandtschaften* (1809) is an experimental novel decades before its time. He travelled to Switzerland and Italy (*Italienische Reise*, travelogue 1787), yet unlike Mozart he never visited Paris, London or Vienna. Instead he made the modest township of Weimar into the intellectual epicentre of Europe and produced a corpus of work in many fields (including optics, botany, anatomy and art criticism) and a sequence of literary masterpieces which exemplify every facet of the drama, lyric poetry and narrative fiction of his era.

*Clare Goll* (Nuremberg 1891–1977 Paris)
She made her name with antiwar essays and reports in pacifist papers; she went to Paris

with Ivan Goll, where their *Poèmes d'amour*
and *Poèmes de jalousie* appeared in 1925–6
(*Zehntausend Morgenröten: Geschichte einer
Liebe*, 1954). On returning from exile in 1947
she acted as his pugnacious advocate in her
autobiography, *Ich verzeihe keinem* (1978).

### Ivan or Yvan Goll (= Isaac Lang)
(St Dié/Alsace 1891–1950 Paris)

Born of Alsace-Lorraine Jewish parents whose
mother tongue was French, he co-founded the
surrealist movement and was associated with
the Zurich Dadaists. From Paris he denounced
Expressionism in the surrealist manifesto, *Der
Expressionismus stirbt* (1921). His essays and
culture-critical novels *Der Mitropäer* (1928)
and *Sodome et Berlin* (1929) were followed by
his ballad/self-portrait, *La Chanson de Jean
sans Terre* (3 vols 1936–9), and by exile.
*Traumkraut* (lyric poems 1951) was written on
his return to Germany.

### Bogumil Goltz (Warsaw 1801–70 Thorn)
He wrote *Buch der Kindheit* (1847): with its
wonderfully vivid recall of moments of child-
hood, it is a classic autobiog. His other works
(*Zur Charakteristik und Naturgeschichte der
Frauen*, 1859, *Die Deutschen: Ethnographische
Studie*, 1860) are of anecdotal interest for their
age.

### Eugen Gomringer
(Cachuela/Bolivia 1925– )

Commonly known as the father of concrete
poetry (*konstellationen constellations constel-
aciones*, 1953; *konkrete poesie – poesia concreta*,
1960–5, *worte sind schatten*, ed H Heißenbüttel
1969), he has exercised a formative influence
on his own generation and the next as an art
critic, teacher and writer, not least by virtue
of his own cosmopolitan Swiss and Bolivian
background.

### Johann Joseph von Görres
(Koblenz 1776–1848 Munich)

The brilliant editorship of G's anti-
Napoleonic *Rheinischer Merkur* (1814–16) provoked Napoleon to remark that the press was
the 'fifth great power'. An influential
Heidelberg teacher and close associate of
Arnim and Brentano (his Romantic pupils included Eichendorff), G directed one of Ger-

many's most powerful pamphlets, *Athanasius*
(1838), against Prussian attacks on Rhineland
Catholicism; his intensive studies of medieval
mysticism (*Die christliche Mystik*, 1836–42)
helped to give his German co-religionists access to the European Catholic cultural tradition at a time when Prussian liberal nationalism
was threatening to marginalize them.

### Jeremias Gotthelf
(Murten 1779–1854 Lützelflüh
nr Berne)

Few novelists in German can match the epic
power of Albert Bitzius, better known as
Jeremias Gotthelf, but the stylized dialect of
his characters has denied him his rightful place
alongside the great 19thc European realists. A
Swiss Protestant parson, he adapted his homiletic training to treating topical moral and political issues in novellen and novels of Swiss
rural life, such as the 'Uli' novels (*Uli der
Knecht*, 1841, *Uli der Pächter*, 1849), *Wie Anne
Bäbi Jowäger haushaltet* (1843–4), *Käthi die
Grossmutter* (1847), about what hunger is really
like, and *Die Käserei in der Vehfreude* (1850),
where the village families are a collective hero.
Though he is fond of biblical imagery and sustained allegory, his utopian vision and rationalist reforming impulse focus on the ills of his
own day. His rich humour offsets his deep
sense of mankind's fallen but redeemable nature. Today his best-known and most relevant
works are *Die schwarze Spinne* (1842), his
mythical novelle of the plague, and *Geld und
Geist* (1843–4), a complex study of greed and
goodness. The 'Swiss Homer' also wrote excellent stories (*Wie Joggeli eine Frau sucht*, 1841,
*Elsi, die seltsame Magd*, 1843, *Das Erdbeeri
Mareili*, 1850).

### Rudolf von Gottschall
(Breslau 1823–1909 Leipzig)

A versatile journalist and author of a once-
standard literary history, *Die deutsche
Nationallitteratur in der ersten Hälfte des 19.
Jahrhunderts* (1855), he began as a radical
in 1848 (*Barrikaden-Lieder*, 1848), became a
nationalist (cf his anti-English plays *Pitt
und Fox*, 1854, and *Der Nabob*, 1866) and, despite his dislike of Naturalism, addressed contemporary social issues in his novels (*Das

*goldene Kalb*, 1880, *Verkümmerte Existenzen*, 1892).

### Johann Christoph Gottsched (Juditten/ E Prussia 1700–66 Leipzig)

Dogmatism and an overtly didactic approach to literary and linguistic reform (*Versuch einer critischen Dichtkunst*, 1729, [4]1751, and *Grundlegung einer Deutschen Sprachkunst*, 1748, [6]1762) permanently injured the reputation of this professor of poetry and philosophy at Leipzig. Yet he is a key figure in the cultural and theatrical history of Germany and the evolution of a self-aware and literate middle-class German public. Of central interest are his editorship of influential moral weeklies, *Die vernünftigen Tadlerinnen* (1725–6) and *Der Biedermann* (1727), his model tragedy *Der sterbende Cato* (1732) and his foreword to the 6-vol drama anthology *Die Deutsche Schaubühne* (1741–5) stressing the moral function of the stage.

### Luise Adelgunde Victoria Gottsched (Danzig 1713–62 Leipzig)

Stylized as his 'domestic muse' by her husband, J C Gottsched, she may have aroused his opposition to her development as a writer. Yet theirs was a formidable partnership which incl trns of Bayle's *Dictionary* and of plays by Molière, Corneille, Racine and Voltaire for their (joint) publication *Die Deutsche Schaubühne*. She made Addison and Steele known in Germany, co-edited moral weeklies, and wrote notable comedies (i a *Die Pietisterey im Fischbeinrocke*, 1736) and letters (*Briefe*, 1771–3).

### Christian Dietrich Grabbe (Detmold 1801–36)

Though he enjoyed the generous literary patronage of Tieck and Immermann, his historical dramas, *Herzog Theodor von Gothland* (wr 1827), *Kaiser Friedrich Barbarossa*, *Kaiser Heinrich der Sechste*, *Die Hermannsschlacht* (wr 1829, 1830 and 1838), were not staged during his lifetime; *Don Juan und Faust* (1829) is an exception. In personality and his best work, G approximates to the notion of 'original genius', not least in his eminently performable black

comedy, *Scherz, Satire, Ironie und tiefere Bedeutung* (wr 1823) and his masterly dramatic presentation of volatile popular favour creating the traditional heroes of world history in *Napoleon, oder die hundert Tage* (1831, but not perf uncut until 1895) and *Hannibal* (1835, perf 1918).

### *Günter Grass (Danzig-Langfuhr, then Free State of Danzig 1927– )

Novelist, dramatist (the absurdist *Noch zehn Minuten bis Buffalo*, 1959, *Die bösen Köche*, 1961), poet (*Gleisdreck*, 1960, *Ausgefragt*, 1967), painter, cook and sculptor, Grass refused to gloss over Germany's past and thus became a master of *Vergangenheitsbewältigung*. His *Danzig*-trilogy (*Die Blechtrommel*, novel 1959, filmed 1979, *Katz und Maus*, novelle 1961, *Hundejahre*, novel 1963), with its idiosyncratic multi-perspectival treatment of the pathologies which brought Germany to catastrophe, is to the Third Reich what Heinrich Mann's *Kaiserreich*-trilogy was to the Wilhelmine era: a crucial settling of accounts. Joining the *Gruppe 47* in 1955 (mirrored in his 17thc story, *Das Treffen in Telgte*, 1979), he was preoccupied with the writer's role in society (*Die Plebejer proben den Aufstand*, verse play, perf 1965, publ 1966). A prominent figure in leftist SPD politics (*Aus dem Tagebuch einer Schnecke*, 1972; essays and speeches *Über das Selbstverständliche*, 1968, *Der Bürger und seine Stimme*, 1974, *Denkzettel*, 1978; *örtlich betäubt*, novel 1969) he voiced fierce criticism of the terms of the 1990 Unification (speeches *Deutscher Lastenausgleich: Wider das stumpfe Einheitsgebot*, 1990, *Ein Schnäppchen namens DDR: Letzte Reden vor dem Glockenläut*, 1990). His novel *Ein weites Feld* (1995) is an idiosyncratic gloss on German history 1930–95 grafted on to the life and works of T Fontane. G's novels incl *Der Butt* (1977), *Die Rättin* (1986) and *Unkenrufe* (1992).

### Georg Greflinger (nr Regensburg 1620–71 Hamburg)

Author of 100s of occasional poems and a poetic history of the 30 Years War which so affected his own life, he ed the early German newspaper *Der Nordische Mercurius* and influenced German literature with his trn of Henry Neville's utopian satire *The Isle of Pines*.

### Catharina Regina von Greiffenberg
#### (nr Amstetten/Lr Austria 1633–94 Nuremberg)

A staunch Protestant faith underlay the works of this lyric and mystical poet, whom Birken called the 'marvel of our age' and Duke Anton Ulrich portrayed as a new Urania in his novel *Aramena*. Her *Geistliche Sonnette, Lieder und Gedichte* (1662) express her intense spirituality, *Sieges-Seule der Buße und Glaubens* (1675) is a robust attack on the Turkish 'Infidel'. RC persecution finally drove her out of Austria in 1680, but she was received in Lutheran Nuremberg with an admiration and enthusiasm unprecedented for a woman writer.

### Maria Grengg
#### (Stein 1889–1963 Rodaun nr Vienna)

She was an artistically gifted woman whose work is characterized by strong autobiog impulses and vivid description. She tarnished the reputation she made with her 'green' novel *Die Flucht zum grünen Herrgott* (1930) by her toadying identification with National Socialist values. She became a noted Austrian children's author; reassessment of her adult fiction has not yet taken place.

### Franz Grillparzer (Vienna 1791–1872)

He deserves to be called the 'Austrian Shakespeare' for his sense of theatre, his finely modulated blank verse, and the psychological realism of his characters and situations. His tragedies draw on Greek mythology (*Sappho*, 1818, the dramatic trilogy *Das Goldene Vlies*, 1821, *Des Meeres und der Liebe Wellen*, 1831), and on Austrian and especially Habsburg history (*König Ottokars Glück und Ende*, 1825, *Ein treuer Diener seines Herrn*, 1830, and *Ein Bruderzwist im Hause Habsburg*, publ posthumously in 1872 along with *Die Jüdin von Toledo* and *Libussa*). They are borne on his profound knowledge of English, Spanish, French, Italian and classical drama, as well as that of Schiller. He also achieved distinction in several other genres: the 'Gothic' fate drama (*Die Ahnfrau*, 1817), comedy (in his still underestimated *Weh dem, der lügt*, 1838) and the novelle (*Der arme Spielmann*, 1848, beloved of Kafka). He also wrote some fine poetry, a celebrated autobiog (1872), diaries, theatre criticism, and a moving funeral oration on Beethoven, whom he had known, as he had Schubert.

### Hans Grimm (Wiesbaden 1875–1959 Lippoldsberg/Weser)

A leading representative of German colonial literature, he spent the years 1896–1911 in South Africa, and wrote compellingly about it (*Südafrikanische Novellen*, 1911, *Lüderitzland*, 1934). His best-known novel, *Volk ohne Raum* (1926), also set largely there, provided Nazi Germany with both a slogan and a programme.

### Jakob Grimm (Hanau 1785–1863 Berlin), Wilhelm Grimm (Hanau 1786–1859 Berlin)

'Always under one roof', wrote Jakob in his obituary on his much-loved brother, Wilhelm. It is as 'the brothers Grimm' that we rightly think of the founding fathers of our discipline, *Germanistik*. Both trained as lawyers, and were imbued with Herder's notion of the *Volksgeist*, the spirit of the ordinary people whose collective memory stored the heritage they now set out to explore. W was the more sensitive, as is shown by his contributions to their most widely known work, the *Kinder- und Hausmärchen* (1812–14) and to their *Irische Elfenmärchen* (1826), and by his account of their expulsion from Göttingen in 1837 for political reasons; J inclined more to philology, wrote a *Deutsche Grammatik* (1819–37) and gave his name to 'Grimm's Law'. 'If pedantry did not exist', he wrote in his own brand of dry humour, 'the Germans would invent it': together the Grimms raised it to an art. Their *Deutsche Sagen* appeared 1816–18, (J's) *Deutsche Mythologie* in 1835, besides innumerable editions of German (and Scandinavian) medieval texts, incl the *Hildebrandslied* and Hartmann's *Der arme Heinrich*. Their most famous scholarly undertaking, the *Deutsches* (or *Grimms*) *Wörterbuch*, was commissioned in 1838 and completed long after them in 1960: it is a monument to their lifelong belief in the role of Germany's language and literature as the central elements of their nation's identity.

### Hans Jacob Christoffel von Grimmelshausen (Gelnhausen 1621/2–1676 Renchen/Baden)

The extraordinary pseudonyms G used to conceal his identity reflect his imaginative range. His great novel, *Der abentheuerliche Simplicissimus Teutsch* appeared in 1668, its *Continuatio* in 1669: a sequence of shorter narratives in the 'Simplician' manner followed, incl the picaresque *Satyrischer Pilgram* (1666–7), *Der seltsame Springinsfeld* (1670), *Trutz Simplex: oder Ausführliche und wunderzeltsame Lebensbeschreibung der Ertzbetrügerin und Landsstörtzerin Courasche* (1670), and *Das wunderbarliche Vogel-Nest* (1672–3).

### George Grosz (Berlin 1893–1959)

The searing social criticism G directed against the unreformed conservative establishment in *Das neue Gesicht der herrschenden Klasse* (1921), *Ecce Homo* (1922–3), *Stützen der Gesellschaft* (1926) is made visible in his work as a graphic artist and caricaturist, which has had a formative influence on English-speaking students' perception of the Weimar Republic, so widely – and aptly – has it been used to illustrate lectures and publications on that period.

### Klaus Johann Groth (Heide/Holstein 1819–99 Kiel)

He publ his celebrated lyric volume, *Quickborn* (1852), just when the Schleswig-Holstein question had invested his native region with intense topicality. He can be said to be both the re-creator of Low German as a literary language, and a major influence on its dialect poetry to this day.

### Anastasius Grün (Ljubljana-Laibach 1808–76 Graz)

Under this pseudonym Count Anton Alexander Auersperg produced in *Spaziergänge eines Wiener Poeten* (1831) a pioneering and hugely popular collection of political poetry which exposed the brutal nature of the repressively reactionary Metternich regime.

### Durs Grünbein (Dresden 1962– )

'As a virus, I am far too benign. What literature needs today, when literary criticism has become a self-referential system, are dangerous viruses of the Baudelaire kind,' declared this former GDR poet in 1996 in an interview after his receipt of the Büchner Prize. The author of *Falten und Fallen* ([2]1994), *Grauzone morgens* (1988), *Schädelbasisselektion* (1993), *Von der üblen Seite: Gedichte 1985–1991* (1994) is regarded since the *Wende* as one of Germany's leading lyric talents.

### Andreas Gryphius (Glogau 1616–64)

Immensely erudite and many-sided, but scarred as a boy by the bitter experiences and brutality of Germany's 'religious' 30 Years War, G brought to his public career as municipal secretary of his home town in Silesia and to his literary output the benefits of many years of education at the Dutch Protestant university of Leyden (1637–44) and of travels in France and Italy. In his poetry, *Sonnete* (1637), *Son- undt Feÿrtags Sonnete* (1639), *Teutsche Reim-Gedichte* (1650), *Freuden und Trauer-Spiele, auch Oden und Sonnette* (1663), German acquired a sonority and intensity rarely surpassed. His tragic dramas of state and martyrdom (*Leo Armenius, Catharina von Georgien, Carolus Stuardus,* and *Papinianus*) were all publ by 1659. He also wrote *Singspiele* (*Majuma,* publ 1659; *Piastus,* publ 1698), a love tragedy (*Cardenio und Celinde,* publ 1657) and eminently stageworthy comedies such as *Absurda Comica: Oder Herr Peter Squenz* (publ 1658), *Horribilicribrifax Teutsch* (publ 1663) and the bipartite *Verlibtes Gespenste/Die gelibte Dornrose* (publ 1661), as well as epigrams and funeral orations (*Leichenreden*).

### Christian Gryphius (Glogau 1649–1706 Breslau)

Son of Andreas, he was himself a poet (*Poetische Wälder,* 1698), and an author of Latin and German school dramas and an esteemed arbiter of good taste. He ed his father's poetry in *Andreae Gryphii um ein merkliches vermehrte Teutsche Gedichte* (1698).

## H

*Karoline von Günderode* (Karlsruhe
1780–1806 Winkel/Rhineland)
Life was difficult for her less because of her
genteel poverty than because of her hyper-
sensitive and painful shyness. Her poetry
(*Gedichte und Phantasien*, 1804, *Poetische
Fragmente*, 1805) has done less than Bettine
von Arnim's creative edn of her letters and
Christa Wolf's novel, *Kein Ort: Nirgends*
(1979) to give her a prominent place in the
female literary canon which is emerging in
Germany today.

*Johann Christian Günther*
(Striegau/Silesia 1695–1723 Jena)
It is symptomatic of the cultural reputation of
Leipzig that G, medical student, author of
some 500 lyric poems, a school drama (on jealousy) and a heroic ode to the Habsburg Emperor Charles VI (1718), should have wished to
move there in 1717. In the poetic *persona* of
his love poetry and laments (*Leonorelieder,
Klagelieder*) G achieved a subjectivity and intensity of feeling new to German poetry, while
still embodying the range and formal mastery
of the Augustan age.

*Karl Ferdinand Gutzkow*
(Berlin 1811–78 Frankfurt/M)
From the perspective of the late 20thc, this
gifted journalist seems something of a might-
have-been. He left no major work, though
his controversial novel, *Wally, die Zweiflerin*
(1835) has often aroused interest from a political and/or feminist perspective. Yet he produced an oeuvre of great range, and was a
significant and encouraging critic who early
recognized the genius of Droste-Hülshoff and
Büchner. His potential as a humorist is evident
in the comic novels, *Seraphine* (1837) and
*Blasedow und seine Söhne* (1838), his once
much-perf comedies, *Zopf und Schwert* and
*Das Urbild des Tartüffe* (1844), and his too
little-known stories. His fine tragedy, *Uriel
Acosta* (1846) addressed the issue of tolerance,
while his epic novels *Die Ritter vom Geiste*
(1850–1) and *Der Zauberer von Rom* (1858–61)
dealt with contemporary issues. His sensitive
autobiog *Aus der Knabenzeit* (1852), like his
essays and much else in his work and life, still
merits attention.

*Peter Hacks* (Breslau 1928– )
This dramatist wrote historical materialist
plays (*Die Schlacht bei Lobositz*, 1956, *Der
Müller von Sanssouci*, 1958) then, in the late
1960s and 1970s, 'classical' socialist works such
as *Ein Gespräch im Hause Stein über den
abwesenden Herrn v. Goethe* (1976), intended to
secure for socialist Germany a '*literarisches
Erbe*' or literary continuity appropriate to an
established state and community, a concern
expressed in his theoretical writings, notably
*Das Poetische: Ansätze zu einer postrevo-
lutionären Dramaturgie* (1972) and the ironical
*Schöne Wirtschaft: Ästhetisch-ökonomische
Fragmente* (1989).

*Theodor Haecker* (Eberbach 1879–1945
Usterbach/Augsburg)
Who today recalls H, author of *Christentum und
Kultur* (1927)? Yet in the last years of the
war the illicit broadcasts of the *Tag- und
Nachtbücher* (1947) by this proscribed tr of
Kierkegaard and John Henry Newman pro-
vided many Germans with an elixir of life.

*Friedrich von Hagedorn*
(Hamburg 1708–54)
Connoisseur of English and French literature,
and Germany's leading rococo poet and stylistic innovator, he brought to the literary language of 18thc Germany musicality, wit and
simplicity in the short forms he favoured in his
*Versuch in Poetischen Fabeln und Erzählungen*
(1738) and *Sammlung Neuer Oden und Lieder*
(1742–52), his didactic *Moralische Gedichte*
(1750–3) and epigrams.

*Rudolf Hagelstange*
(Nordhausen/Harz 1912–84 Hanau)
The need for escapism on the part of readers,
and his own considerable talents as lecturer
and organizer, help to explain the success of
H's lyric collections *Venezianisches Credo*
(1946) and *Meersburger Elegie* (1950) in the first
two postwar decades.

*Ida von Hahn-Hahn* (Tressow/
Mecklenburg 1805–80 Mainz)
A 'one-eyed man-eater' according to the other-
wise charitable Elizabeth Barrett Browning,

Countess Hahn-Hahn wrote erotic poetry and provocative feminist novels (*Gräfin Faustine*, 1841, *Clelia Conti*, 1846, etc.), and showed a flair for the market when, after her spectacular conversion to Catholicism in 1850, she supplied the growing demand for Catholic novels (*Maria Regina*, 1860, *Peregrin*, 1864) and became a standard author for Catholic lending libraries. Her *Bilder aus der Geschichte der Kirche* (4 vols 1856–66) provided a quarry for authors of 'catacomb novels'.

### Max Halbe (Güttland nr Danzig 1865–1944 Neuötting/Bavaria)

Halbe enjoyed stage success on a par with that of Hauptmann and Sudermann for his Naturalist dramas *Eisgang* (1892), and especially *Jugend* (1893), a tragedy of adolescence. He wrote folk drama (*Der Strom*, 1904) but perhaps his most original work is *Die Tat des Dietrich Stobäus* (novel 1911), the analysis of a crime by the criminal.

### Albrecht von Haller (Berne 1708–77)

A doctor, botanist and one of the German language's most prolific scientific writers, he 'discovered' Switzerland for German literature and the European tourist with his discursive poem *Die Alpen* (1732), the fruit of a botanizing tour, and his immensely successful *Versuch Schweizerischer Gedichten* (1732). He turned down an Oxford chair and became ed of the influential scientific *Göttingische Gelehrten Anzeigen*, but in Switzerland the prophet was without the honour which Enlightenment Europe enthusiastically bestowed on him.

### Johann Christian Hallmann

Thought to have been born in 1640 and to have died in either Vienna in 1716 or Breslau in 1704, he is the author of much occasional funeral and panegyric verse (*Leich-Reden und Grab-Schriften*, 1682, *Der Triumphirende Leopoldus*, 1689) and a number of overblown dramatic works in the high baroque manner (*Mariamne*, 1669).

### Friedrich Halm (= Eligius Franz Joseph Baron von Münch-Bellinghausen) (Cracow 1806–71 Vienna)

He established his fame in Vienna with his first play *Griseldis* (1835), and remained a firm favourite with the Viennese public with *Der Sohn der Wildnis* (1842) and *Der Fechter von Ravenna* (1854); he later briefly became director of the Burgtheater. Now he is better remembered for his novellen, the best known being *Die Marzipan-Lise* (1856).

### *Johann Georg Hamann (Königsberg 1730–88 Münster)

The 'magus of the North' was a radical seeker after God in the 'book' of nature and history, and in many ways an antipole to Enlightenment rationalism. Yet it would be mistaken to describe him as an 'irrationalist'; his deliberately 'difficult' writings compel the reader to 'deconstruct'. His vision of poetry as the 'mother tongue of mankind' influenced both Goethe and Herder, and his correspondences with Herder and Jacobi are among the most important of their day.

### Joseph von Hammer-Purgstall (Graz 1774–1856 Vienna)

The monumental oeuvre of this orientalist, first president of the Austrian Academy of Science, incl a translation of the *Divan* by the Persian poet Hafiz (1814: an important source for Goethe), oriental fairy tales (*Rosenöl oder Sagen und Kunden des Morgenlandes*, 1813), a 4-vol *Osmanische Dichtkunst bis auf unsere Zeit* (1836–8) and a 7-vol *Literaturgeschichte der Araber* (1850–6).

### Enrica Handel-Mazzetti (Vienna 1871–1955 Linz)

Her immense success derived mainly from her ability to establish a 'counter-landscape' for Austria (and Germany), which appealed to a new type of self-conscious Catholic readership in the post-*Kulturkampf* era: *Meinrad Helmpergers denkwürdiges Jahr* (1900), *Jesse und Maria: Ein Roman aus dem Donaulande* (1906), *Die arme Margaret: Ein Volksroman aus dem alten Steyr* (1910).

### Peter Handke (Griffen/Carinthia 1942– )

In assessing H, it is important to distinguish between the early and mature works. He showed he understood the art of self-salesmanship with his plays *Publikumsbeschimpfung*

(1966), *Kaspar* (1968) and *Der Ritt über den Bodensee* (1971), the story *Wunschloses Unglück* (1972) and the novels *Die Angst des Tormanns beim Elfmeter* (1970) and *Die Stunde der wahren Empfindung* (1975). After what he terms an *Einweihung* or religious initiation process, he began to explore the interaction of image and language in *Langsame Heimkehr* (story 1979) and the novels *Die Lehre der Sainte-Victoire* (1980) and *Die Kindergeschichte* (1981); the revelation of transcendence is a central theme of his subsequent work, such as *Die Wiederholung* (1986) or *Das Spiel vom Fragen* (1989).

### Eberhard Werner Happel
### (Kirchhain 1647–90 Hamburg)

He settled in Hamburg in the 1680s, where he produced what are in effect forerunners of the 19thc serial novel and late-20thc 'faction' in an apparently successful bid to give new relevance to the classical terms *prodesse* and *delectare*. A good example is *Fortuna Britannica* (1690), which is almost as interesting today as it was for H's late 17thc readers.

**Friedrich von Hardenberg** *see* **Novalis**

### Ernst Hardt (Graudenz/W Prussia, now
### Poland 1876–1947 Ichenhausen)

Hardt became a leading playwright of the pre-1914 era with his neo-Romantic *Tantris der Narr* (1907) based on an episode in the Tristan legend. His postwar efforts to bring culture to the masses via the wireless, and his productions as director of the Weimar National Theatre, were viewed askance by the Nazis.

### Georg Philipp Harsdörffer
### (Nuremberg 1607–58)

Of the works of H, Nuremberg city father and prolific writer, 2 stand out: the 8-vol *Frauenzimmer-Gesprächsspiele* (1641–9), in which conversations between representatives of the sexes and the upper classes function as examples of instructively edifying entertainment, and *Poetischer Trichter* (1647–53), which is much more than just the mechanistic training in poetics which its ironic title and subsequent literary history might suggest.

### Peter Härtling (Chemnitz 1933– )

His works offer their reader, as H writes in his autobiog *Meine Lektüre: Literatur als Widerstand* (1981), a concept of literature in which individuals gain through the creative imagination a vision of their own humanity. He exemplified this in the novels *Niembsch oder Der Stillstand* (1964), *Hölderlin* (1976) and *Waiblingers Augen* (1987). In *Das Windrad* (1983) he demonstrates the potential of literature to serve the cause of the peace and ecological movements.

### Walter Hasenclever (Aachen 1890–1940
### Les Milles/Aix-en-Provence)

The Expressionist poet of *Städte, Nächte und Menschen* (1910) and *Der Jüngling* (1913) and celebrated dramatist of *Der Sohn* (1914), he became a pacifist during the war, as documented in his drama *Antigone* (1917) and his political poetry (*Die Mörder sitzen in der Oper*, wr 1917). H was a scriptwriter for silent films (*Die Pest: Ein Film*, 1920) and in late Weimar produced politically sophisticated comedies: *Ein besserer Herr* (1927), *Ehen werden im Himmel geschlossen* (1929), the anti-Nazi *Napoleon greift ein* (1930) and *Der Froschkönig* (a skit on Goebbels wr 1930). His attempt as a Jew to dramatize Nazi treatment of his people in *Konflikt in Assyrien* (London première 1937) brought expulsion and, later, French internment and suicide.

### Wilhelm Hauff (Stuttgart 1802–27)

Ed of Cotta's *Morgenblatt* and *Taschenbuch für Damen*, he showed a unique capacity to cater for the phenomenon of the emerging mass reader. He left behind a substantial oeuvre: the anthology *Krieg- und Volkslieder* (1824), which incl his *Morgenrote! Leuchtest mir zum frühen Tod* (1824), the stories *Der Mann im Mond* (1826), *Lichtenstein* (1826), and *Das Bild des Kaisers* (1828), and the satire *Mittheilungen aus den Memoiren des Satan* (1826–7).

### Gerhart Hauptmann (Obersalzbrunn
### 1862–1946 Agnetendorf/Silesia)

T Mann's portrait of Hauptmann as Mynheer Peeperkorn in *The Magic Mountain* may have irritated but also flattered the 1912 Nobel Prize winner. Contact with the Naturalists gave him direction and he achieved early fame with the drama *Vor Sonnenaufgang* (1889), followed by *Das Friedensfest* (1890), *Einsame Menschen* (1891) and *Die Weber* (1893). His capacity to give tragic pathos to those who do not command lang is evident in *Fuhrmann Henschel* (1898), *Rose Bernd* (1903), and *Hanneles Himmelfahrt* (1893), a play which displays the religious element so characteristic of this Silesian author, and central to his novelle *Der Apostel* (1892) and the novels *Der Narr in Christo Emanuel Quint* (1910) and *Der Ketzer von Soana* (1918). Contemporaries loved the neo-Romantic make-believe of the verse drama *Die versunkene Glocke* (1896), and warmed to his humour in the incomparable comedy of character and milieu, *Der Biberpelz* (1893) and the tragi-comedy *Die Ratten* (1911). H revived a central German literary tradition by creating in his verse epic *Till Eulenspiegel* (1927) an image of modern Germany, and another by reverting during the war years to classical myth in his *Atriden-Tetralogie*, the towering product of his own inner emigration: unwisely, perhaps, he rejected exile, thus witnessing the abandonment of liberal and humane values which his 1932 play, *Vor Sonnenuntergang*, foresaw.

### Albrecht Haushofer
#### (Munich 1903–45 Berlin)

After he was killed by the SS, the so-called *Moabiter Sonette* (1946) written in Berlin's Moabit prison were found on him. His career as a political geographer had been advanced by Rudolf Hess, whose adviser he became: after Hess's flight to England in 1941 H's loyalty to the Nazi regime became suspect even to those who had overlooked the oblique criticism in his Roman plays *Scipio* (1934), *Sulla* (1938) and *Augustus* (1939).

### Marlen Haushofer (Frauenstein/Upr
#### Austria 1920–70 Steyr)

Known in her lifetime merely as the author of children's books, this 'ordinary housewife' conveys in short stories (*Das fünfte Jahr*, 1952) and novels, *Himmel, der nirgendwo endet* (1966) and *Die Mansarde* (1969), the dehumanizing and hermetic isolation of some women's lives. Her stylistic power was only recognized after her death.

### Friedrich Hebbel (Wesselburen/
#### Dithmarschen 1813–63 Vienna)

The single-mindedness of H, who literally starved his way to an education, is reflected in the inhuman demands his dramatic characters make on each other in his tragedies *Judith* (1840), *Genoveva* (1843), *Maria Magdalene* (1844, publ 1846), *Herodes und Mariamne* (1849, publ 1850), *Agnes Bernauer* (1851), *Gyges und sein Ring* (1854) and *Die Nibelungen* (1861). The unique contribution he made to classical German drama lies in the magnificent female roles which he wrote for his wife, the Burgtheater actress Christine Enghaus, such as that of Mariamne. His wonderfully observant and introspective diaries (*Tagebücher*, 1835–63, 1885–7), fluid lyric poetry and taut *Erzählungen und Novellen* (1855) are undeservedly neglected.

### Johann Peter Hebel
#### (Basle 1760–1826 Schwetzingen)

His literary career only began in his 40s and he owes his reputation as a 'naïve' poet to Goethe and Jean Paul. His *Alemannische Gedichte* (1803) became a model for German dialect poets, while the apparently artless tales of *Das Schatzkästlein des Rheinischen Hausfreundes* (1811), written for his almanac *Der rheinische Hausfreund* (1808–15) and aimed at both the cultivated and the unlettered, conceal a highly sophisticated narrative technique.

### Jakob Christoph Heer
#### (Töss nr Winterthur 1859–1925 Zurich)

He opened up the Swiss Alps to a mass readership with his novels *An heiligen Wassern* (1898) and *Der König der Bernina* (1900) and other best-selling works which have a harder centre than their reputation suggests.

### *Georg Wilhelm Friedrich Hegel
#### (Stuttgart 1770–1831 Berlin)

'Contradiction is the root of all movement and life.' This insight in H's *Wissenschaft der Logik* (3 vols, 1812–16) underlies his philosophy (*Phänomenologie des Geistes*, 1807, *Enzyklopädie der philosophischen Wissenschaften*, 1817, *Vorlesungen über Ästhetik*, 1835–8). H's insistence on viewing reality 'dialectically' transformed the discourse of German Idealism. It had a galvanizing effect on the young Marx and offered much of lasting value to thinkers in psychoanalysis, theology and law (see *Grundlinien der Philosophie des Rechts*, 1821). It also anticipated existentialism. Friendly as a young man with Hölderlin and Schelling, and (like Kant) a cautious supporter of the French Revolution, H was appointed Fichte's successor at Berlin University in 1818.

### *Martin Heidegger* (Messkirch/Baden 1889–1976 Freiburg)

In *Sein und Zeit* (1927) he launched his 'fundamental ontology', an attempt to capture the tang of life as experienced, not by the transcendental subject but by *Dasein-in-der-Welt*. In the 1930s he embarked on a broader, more mystical 'quest for Being'. Alarmed at the loss of *Bodenständigkeit* (rootedness) in modern industrialized society and moved by Hölderlin's evocation of a hidden Germany, H proved susceptible to the lure of the Nazi regime. His discussion of 'pre-understanding' as central to interpretation opened the way for the literary investigations of Hans-Georg Gadamer and of Wolfgang Iser and the Konstanz school of *Rezeptionsästhetik*, while his recognition of the constitutive role of language in shaping 'reality' anticipated many of the issues central to Jacques Derrida's deconstructionism. Other major works are *Was ist Metaphysik?* (1929), *Der Ursprung des Kunstwerkes* (1935), *Beiträge zur Philosophie* (1936–8), and *Unterwegs zur Sprache* (1959).

### Christoph Hein (Heinzendorf/Silesia 1944– )

One of the GDR's most sophisticated and elegant essayists, he is the author of psychological studies of historical figures, periods and incidents, such as *Cromwell* (1978–81), *Die wahre Geschichte des Ah Q* (1984), and *Passage* (1988). He made his name with the much-anthologized novelle *Drachenblut* (1983, [9]1985) and the novels *Horns Ende* (1985) and *Der Tangospieler* (1989).

### Heinrich Heine (Düsseldorf 1797–1856 Paris)

'What a tool the German language is in his hands,' marvelled Nietzsche. H was a master of metrics, rhyme and rhetoric whose work incl lyric poetry which made him the favourite of countless composers (*Buch der Lieder*, 1827, *Neue Gedichte*, 1844, *Romanzero*, 1851, and *Gedichte 1853 und 1854*). He also created a new type of wittily allusive yet critical journalism in the guise of travelogues such as *Briefe aus Berlin*, *Über Polen* (1823), *Die Harzreise* (1824) and the *Reisebilder* 1–IV (1826–31) and wrote some of Germany's greatest political poetry (the mock-heroic epics *Deutschland: Ein Wintermärchen*, 1844, and *Atta Troll*, 1847). A brilliant and feared, if often shameless, polemicist (*Die Bäder von Lukka*, 1827, in which he exposed Platen's homosexuality, *Heine über Ludwig Börne*, 1840), he also publ penetrating artistic and literary criticism (i a *Französische Maler*, 1831, *Französische Zustände*, 1832, *Die romantische Schule*, 1835, *Shakespeares Mädchen und Frauen*, 1838, *Geständnisse*, 1854) which was shaped by his perspective as a poet in (voluntary) exile in Paris from 1831 until his death. Though baptized in 1825, he never forgot the suffering of the Jewish people (*Der Rabbi von Bacherach*, 1840) and returned to their cultural traditions, if not their religion, in his last years.

### Heinrich Julius, Duke of Brunswick (Brunswick 1564–1613 Prague)

Brother-in-law of James VI of Scotland, he was a man of many parts, who publ ten dramas wr for his English strolling players in 1593–4. His integration of the clown into German-language comedy, as in *Vincentius Ladislaus*, constitutes his most lasting literary achievement.

### Wilhelm Heinse (Langewiesen/Thuringia 1746–1803 Aschaffenburg)

He owed his career to the Saxon education system and the patronage of Wieland and Jacobi for whom he ed the periodical *Iris*. H publ his main work, *Ardinghello* (1787), the 'bible of sensualism', after his journey, mainly on foot, to Rome. H's *Aufzeichnungen*, wr over 3 decades but publ only in 1925, are a compendium of insights into fundamental issues of, and contemporary debates on, aesthetics.

### Karl Henckell (Hanover 1864–1929 Lindau)

In the 1880s the poetry of this exact contemporary of Wedekind gave powerful voice to his generation's social conscience (*Poetisches Skizzenbuch*, 1882). When his work was banned in the German Empire, he chose, like Georg Herwegh 50 years before him, to go into exile in Switzerland, where he became a pivotal figure in Naturalist avant-garde circles in Zurich. After his return at the turn of the century, his tone changed (*Neues Leben*, 1990); by the end of the 1914–18 War he was *passé*.

### *Luise Hensel* (Linum/Brandenburg 1798–1876 Paderborn)

Friend of Annette von Droste-Hülshoff, she was a religious poet, whose poems, such as 'Müd geh' ich zur Ruh', were much anthologized in the 19thc. She had a vital influence on Brentano, and some of her work is indistinguishable from his. She was the sister-in-law of the musician Fanny Mendelssohn.

### *Karl Friedrich Hensler* (Vaihingen/Enz 1759–1825 Vienna)

Director of the Leopoldstädter and Josephstädter theatres and the Theater an der Wien, he wrote many plays, the most popular being his *Kasperl* comedies, wr for the great comic actor Laroche, incl *Kasperl, der Besenbinder* (1787), *Kaspar der Schornsteinfeger* (1791) and *Das Judenmädchen von Prag, oder Kaspar der Schuhflicker* (1792).

### *Johann Gottfried Herder* (Mohrungen/ E Prussia 1744–1803 Weimar)

Herder is a key figure in 18th and 19thc German literature and thought. His lifelong insistence on the importance of intuition and emotion, and his emphasis on the close ties between man and nature, made him prominent in the *Sturm und Drang* movement (*Über die neuere deutsche Literatur*, 1766–7, *Kritische Wälder*, 1769, the essay on Shakespeare in *Von deutscher Art und Kunst*, 1773). A prime mover in the development of historic relativism as a concept (*Auch eine Philosophie der Geschichte zur Bildung der Menschheit*, 1774, *Ideen zur Philosophie der Geschichte der Menschheit*, 1784–91), and in the emergence of psychology

as a field of inquiry (*Über den Ursprung der Sprache*, 1772, *Vom Erkennen und Empfinden der menschlichen Seele*, 1774), he was a key mediator between the Enlightenment and German Romanticism, and a wide-ranging tr of folk-poetry.

### *Stephan Hermlin* (Chemnitz 1915– )

The son of wealthy Jewish parents, he entered the Communist youth organization in 1931 after contacts with Berlin workers, whose lives he celebrated in poetry rich in allusion: *12 Balladen von den großen Städten* (1945), *Die Straßen der Furcht* (1947) and *22 Balladen* (1947). His prose texts recall the memory of victims of terror, notably the Warsaw ghetto in *Die Zeit der Gemeinsamkeit* (1950). His was a key role in introducing world literature to E Germany; he was also a high political functionary of the GDR up to 1963, after which he mainly wrote essays and articles. His collected stories appeared as *Lebensfrist* in 1980, his poems in 1990.

### *Georg Herwegh* (Stuttgart 1817–75 Baden-Baden)

The 'iron lark', as Heine maliciously called him, won nationwide acclaim for his rhetorical political verse (*Gedichte eines Lebendigen*, 1841–3). He fought, somewhat ingloriously, on the battlefields of the 1848 revolution, but, unlike many, he remained true to his socialist ideals after he returned from Swiss exile in 1866, and worked for Ferdinand Lassalle's *Arbeiterverein*.

### *Henriette Herz* (Berlin 1764–1847)

The personality of this celebrated and highly educated Jewish beauty was such that she could promote literary discourse in her salon while in an adjoining room her doctor husband **Markus Herz** (Königsberg 1747–1803 Berlin) presided over philosophical discussions. Members of her circle included Alexander and Wilhelm Humboldt (her not very grateful pupil in Hebrew), Schleiermacher and F Schlegel, who met Dorothea Veit, his future wife, there. Her individual voice is audible in her informative memoirs, *H. H. Ihr Leben und ihre Erinnerungen* (1850).

*Theodor Herzl* (Pest 1860–1904
Edlach/Lr Austria)

The father of Zionism, he tirelessly sought literary fame as an assimilated Viennese Jew, and managed to get his *Unser Käthchen* (1899) perf at the Burgtheater. His novel *Der Judenstaat* (1896) changed his life and ideas: aiming at a liberal Jewish audience, he found himself transformed into the champion of the E European ghetto Jews. His novel *Altneuland* (1902) was acclaimed as providing the blueprint of a future Jewish homeland.

*Rudolf Herzog* (Wuppertal-Barmen
1869–1943 Rheinbreitbach)

Herzog worked as a newspaper editor until he discovered 'his' subject, German industry, and grew wealthy on the proceeds of family sagas which caught the mood of Germany's pre-1914 economic prosperity (*Die Wiskottens*, 1905, *Die Stoltenkamps und ihre Frauen*, 1917).

*Hermann Hesse* (Calw/Swabia, 1877–1962
Montagnola/Ticino)

'*La donna è mobile*' (woman is fickle), they say: so too is public taste. For decades the works of Hesse enjoyed the status of modern classics, and during the Vietnam war he became the guru of the hippy movement and the flower people of American campuses (notably for his novel, *Der Steppenwolf*, 1927), yet now he is neglected. A poet and the author of justly admired stories of childhood and adolescence (*Unterm Rad*, 1906, *Demian*, 1919) and student of Jungian psychology and Indian philosophy (*Siddhartha*, 1922), he wrote *Das Glasperlenspiel* (1943), perhaps his major work, as a 'counter-utopia' to the Third Reich.

*Georg Heym*
(Hirschberg/Silesia 1887–1912 Berlin)

His well-to-do background was a burden to him, from which he sought refuge by writing poems from the age of 12, taking as his models Hölderlin and Rimbaud, Büchner and Nietzsche. Contact with like-minded artists unleashed his visionary creativity (*Der*

*Gott der Stadt*, 1910, *Der ewige Tag*, 1911, *Der Krieg*, 1912). His poems are characterized by objectivity, close structure, the intense colour of their imagery, and their prophetic quality. He died in a skating accident before his worst nightmares came true.

*Stefan Heym* (Chemnitz 1913– )

A Jew and Communist like Hermlin, he fled via Prague to US exile. An American citizen, soldier and author of the best-selling exile novel *Hostages* (1942, *Der Fall Glasenapp*, 1958, based on the assassination of Heydrich and its aftermath), he returned to E Germany in the MacCarthy era (*Reise ins Land der unbegrenzten Möglichkeiten*, 1954). A committed democrat, he often fell foul of the GDR authorities for his witty and sophisticated critique of Stalinism (*Fünf Tage in Juni*, 1974, W Germany), especially in novels secularizing Jewish myth such as *Der König-David-Bericht* (publ 1972/GDR 1973) and *Ahasver* (1981, GDR 1988). He was an ardent advocate of the right of a reformed GDR to survive the fall of the Berlin Wall but, in one of the abundant quirks of modern German history, was elected a member of the reformed Communist Party (*Partei des Demokratischen Sozialismus*) and became Speaker of the Bundestag in 1994.

*Paul Heyse* (Berlin 1830–1914 Munich)

Historical justice, if it exists, is well exemplified by H, Germany's first literary Nobel laureate (1910). Author of some 150 carefully crafted novellen, 60 dramas, novels and exquisitely-wrought verse, and owner of a Renaissance villa, H was a darling of the Muses, with whose success Fontane often ruefully contrasted his own. Yet even H's finest works, such as the novellen *L'Arrabbiata* (1855), *Das Mädchen von Treppi* (1855) and the novel *Kinder der Welt* (1873), are now little read. Perhaps the lasting monument to a man generous in his prosperity will prove to be his *Deutscher Novellenschatz* (24 vols 1870–6, with Herman Kurz), the anthology of novellen which helped to found the fame of Droste-Hülshoff's *Die Judenbuche*.

## *Rolf Hochhuth*
(Eschwege nr Kassel 1931– )

It is no longer easy today to imagine the political scandal unleashed by *Der Stellvertreter*, the documentary drama by H, at its Berlin première in 1963 under Piscator's direction. Subtitled *Ein christliches Trauerspiel*, it dramatized the Pope's alleged appeasement of Hitler. H differs from most postwar exponents of documentary theatre in his view of the individual's role in the moral conflicts of society (*Soldaten*, 1967, *Juristen*, 1979, *Lysistrate und die NATO*, 1974).

## *Fritz Hochwälder*
(Vienna 1911–86 Zurich)

*Das heilige Experiment* (1947), about the attempt of Paraguayan Jesuits to create a utopian state, is his best-known play. Like much of his drama, it explores the relationship between idealism and the realities of political power systems. H, whose parents died in a concentration camp, treated the persecution of the Jews in *Esther* (drama, wr 1940, publ 1960) and Austria's relationship with Nazism in *Der Himbeerpflücker* (comedy 1965).

## *Ernst Theodor Amadeus Hoffmann*
(Königsberg 1776–1822 Berlin)

Writers and critics have long been fascinated by H, poet, lawyer, composer (i a of the early Romantic opera, *Undine*, 1816), conductor, poet, graphic artist, literary and music critic and theorist, and caricaturist in line and word. Freud marvelled at H's insight not just into psychopathology but into the complex psychology of ordinary people, while modern critical interest in narratology has renewed interest in his multi-perspective narrative techniques. His tales incl *Fantasien in Callots Manier* (4 vols 1814–15, incl *Ritter Gluck, Kreisleriana, Don Juan, Der goldne Topf*), *Nachtstücke* (2 vols 1816–17, incl *Der Sandmann, Das steinerne Herz*), *Klein Zaches, genannt Zinnober* (fairy tale 1819), *Die Serapions-Brüder* (1819–21, incl *Rath Krespel, Die Bergwerke zu Falun, Nussknacker und Mäusekönig, Die Automate, Der unheimliche Gast, Das Fräulein von Scuderi*), and the tales *Prinzessin Brambilla* (1821) and *Meister Floh* (1822). In his most original work, *Lebensansichten des Katers Murr*

(2 vols, unfinished 1820–2), a send-up of the *Bildungsroman*, the self-reflexivity of the Romantic artist is at its most sophisticated, yet, typically of H, it is entertainingly accessible to 'ordinary' readers who also enjoy the tales of his admirer Edgar Allan Poe and Offenbach's opera *The Tales of Hoffmann*.

## *August Hoffmann von Fallersleben*
(Fallersleben 1798–1874 Corvey)

*Deutschland, Deutschland über alles*, the German national anthem since 1922, was written by H in 1841 as a counterpart to *La Marseillaise*, and cost him his university post. His *Unpolitische Lieder* (1840–1) made him the first political lyricist to attract a mass readership. His tragedy was to be a liberal in a revolutionary age, a fact reflected in *Mein Leben* (1868), his dull but informative account of the writer's life in mid-century.

## *Christian Hoffmann von Hoffmannswaldau*
(Breslau 1617–79)

Educated in Breslau, Danzig, Leiden and on the Grand Tour, he was a Breslau city father whose work was publ posthumously (mainly by Benjamin Neukirch). He is the leading German exponent of late baroque Marinism, and his erotic poetry, notably *Helden-Briefe* (1690), fulfils Marino's dictum that poetry should 'tickle the ear of the readers with the charm and stimulus of novelty'.

## *Hugo von Hofmannsthal*
(Vienna 1874–1929 Rodaun nr Vienna)

'Whom do I write for?' asked H, poet, dramatist, essayist, letter-writer and author of the great comedies *Der Schwierige* (1917) and *Der Unbestechliche* (1921). A schoolboy poetic genius (he used the pseudonym *Loris* for *Ballade des äußeren Lebens*, 1892, and other early works), he composed impressionistic lyrical dramas of great beauty (incl *Der Tor und der Tod, Der Tod des Tizian, Das kleine Welttheater*, publ in 1892, 1893 and 1897, some staged in Berlin by Otto Brahm, and all publ in book form as *Die Gedichte und kleinen Dramen*, 1911). His shorter prose incl *Das Märchen der 672. Nacht*, and *Reitergeschichte*, publ in 1895–8, and a novel, *Andreas oder die Vereinigung*, 1930. H's view of the 1890s as a 'reactive self-image' led to his famous elaboration of the *fin-de-siècle* crisis of language: *Ein Brief des Lord Chandos* (1901). His morality play *Jedermann* (1911) became a central feature of the festival he helped to create at Salzburg (cf *Das Salzburger große Welttheater*, 1922), and he collaborated with Richard Strauss in the operas *Salome* (1903), *Elektra* (1909), *Der Rosenkavalier* (1911), *Ariadne auf Naxos* (1912), *Die Frau ohne Schatten* (1916), and *Arabella* (1933). A distinguished essayist, H later addressed the political cost of the destruction of European culture ('out of the poet's mouth 10,000 dead speak') in lectures (*Das Schrifttum als geistiger Raum der Nation*, 1927) and in his tragedy *Der Turm* (1927).

### Wolfgang Helmhard von Hohberg
#### (Ober-Thumritz/Austria 1612–88 Regensburg)
This Protestant nobleman wrote devotional literature but is chiefly remembered for his massive pseudo-mythological Habsburg verse epic, *Habspurgischer Ottobert* (1664) and for his *Georgica Curiosa* (1682), an encyclopaedic compendium and contemporary record of estate and household management.

**Theophrastus Bombast von Hohenheim see Paracelsus**

### Friedrich Hölderlin (Lauffen/Neckar 1770–1843 Tübingen)
Unlike many of his gifted contemporaries, H failed to find a foothold in the literary market of the day, though many of his uniquely powerful poems were publ in his lifetime, as were his trns from Pindar, to whom his own poetic diction ` owed much (eg his elegy 'Brot und Wein', 1800–1, and the hymns *Patmos* and *Der Rhein*, wr 1800–2). Many of his best poems had to wait long for publication, among them 'An die Parzen', 'An die Deutschen', the novel *Hyperion oder Der Eremit in Griechenland* (wr 1797–9), the verse tragedy *Empedokles* (wr 1797–1800), and the late hymns ('Der Einzige', 'Mnemosyne', 'An die jungen Dichter', 'Dichtermut', 'Dichterberuf' and 'Friedensfeier' (publ 1954). A so-called 'complete' edn of his works appeared in 1846, 40 years after he was declared mentally ill and 3 years after his death.

### Walter Höllerer
#### (Sulzbach-Rosenberg 1922– )
Poet (*Der andere Gast*, 1952, *Systeme: Neue Gedichte*, 1969) and member of the *Gruppe 47*, Höllerer has been a major promoter of poetic and critical talents other than his own, notably in his capacity as (co-)ed of *Akzente* (1954–67) and *Sprache im technischen Zeitalter* (1961– ).

### Karl von Holtei (Breslau 1798–1880)
Best remembered for his dialect *Schlesische Gedichte* (1830, [18]1883), H was an officer turned poet, theatre director, and author of vaudevilles and patriotic songs. His memoirs, *Vierzig Jahre* (1843–50), are a useful compendium of the literary life of his generation.

### Hans Egon Holthusen (Rendsburg 1913– )
Through his study *Der unbehauste Mensch* (1951), this poet and critic gave reflective Germans of the immediate postwar generation a sense of the potential of poetry to help them express and come to terms with the human and moral desolation of their nation.

### Ludwig Heinrich Christoph Hölty
#### (Mariensee nr Hanover 1748–76 Hanover)
He was the most gifted poet of the *Göttinger Hain*. The musicality of his language is evident in the classical verse forms he adopted and renewed, such as the idyll, ode and elegy. Many of his poems retain their popular appeal, such as 'Üb immer Treu und Redlichkeit', 'Die Mainacht', or 'Lied eines befreiten Türkensklaven'.

### Arno Holz (Rastenburg/E Prussia 1863–1929 Berlin)
It is difficult at first to relate H, the pioneer of Naturalism in *Papa Hamlet* (prose sketch 1889) and *Die Familie Selicke* (social drama 1890, both with Johannes Schlaf), with the experimental poet who wrote *Phantasus* (1898), with its endlessly inventive, associative, onomatopoeic language, disregard for strophic convention, and beautiful *Jugendstil* lettering and presentation. The story of the poet since the birth of time, *Phantasus* became his lifework and obsession: it appeared in 1924–5 in 3 vols containing over 1300 pages.

*Ödön von Horváth*
(Fiume, now Rijeka 1901–38 Paris)
Few playwrights have so clearly identified the role played in the rise of Fascism by the petite bourgeoisie and its sentimental and brutal language as did H. His early explorations of the sordid world of small-time politics (*Die Bergbahn* and *Sladek der schwarze Reichswehrmann*, plays, both 1929, *Der ewige Spießer*, novel 1930) led to a sequence of comedies or *Volksstücke* which constitutes one of the most original dramatic and political statements of his inevitably political age: *Italienische Nacht* (1931), *Geschichten aus dem Wienerwald* (1932), *Kasimir und Karoline* (1932) and *Glaube, Liebe Hoffnung*, that 'dance of death', the Berlin première of which was cancelled in 1933 by the Nazi seizure of power. Lack of access to theatres persuaded him to follow his two exile comedies (*Figaro läßt sich scheiden* and *Don Juan*, 1936) with two studies of the Fascist personality, the novels *Jugend ohne Gott* and *Ein Kind unserer Zeit* (both Amsterdam 1938). He was killed by a branch which fell off a tree in the Champs-Elysées during a storm.

*Anna Ovena Hoyers* (Koldenbüttel/
Schleswig 1584–1655 Stockholm)
A doughty opponent of Protestant as well as Catholic religious orthodoxy, she included polemical broadsides and dialect (*Plattdeutsch*) satirical poems in her *Geistliche und weltliche Poemata* (Amsterdam 1650), and was the author of many (still unpubl) hymns.

*Therese (Forster-)Huber*, née *Heyne*
(Göttingen 1764–1829 Augsburg)
She was married to the ethnographer and Jacobin, Georg Forster, and from 1794 to 1804 to the journalist, **Ludwig Ferdinand Huber** (Paris 1764–1804 Ulm), a number of whose works she ed. She even publ her novel *Die Familie Seldorf* (1795–6) under his name. A contributor and from 1816 to 1823 the literary ed of Cotta's *Morgenblatt für gebildete Stände*, she tailored her fiction to the demands of the market by portraying dutiful, self-abnegating heroines. She herself was resolute, ingenious and always short of cash. In her writings and 3800 extant letters she created a 'secondary' women's network and addressed the problems of unmarried, ill or ambitious women.

*Ricarda Huch* (Brunswick 1864–1947
Schönberg/Taunus)
Students of German studies would benefit from an acquaintance with the fine historical monographs and novels of H, one of the first German women to obtain a doctorate (1891 from Zurich) and the first to be elected to the Prussian Academy of Arts (from which she resigned in protest at the persecution of the Jews). Her best-known works, *Blütezeit der Romantik* (1899), *Ausbreitung und Verfall der Romantik* (1902) and *Der große Krieg in Deutschland* (1912–14), display a well-differentiated sense of historical time and her awareness of belonging to the 1st generation of autonomous women writers. They are but a fraction of her remarkable oeuvre which incl contributions to the leading literary and artistic periodicals of the *Jahrhundertwende*, studies of German writers, novels, biogs, religious works and some impressive poetry.

*Peter Huchel*
(Berlin-Lichterfelde 1903–81 Staufen)
The ed (1949–62) of the internationally esteemed GDR journal *Sinn und Form*, where his important poem 'Der Garten des Theophrast' appeared, Huchel made his name in the 1930s for the veiled political critique of his radio plays (*Margarethe Minde*, 1935 etc). H is one of Germany's major lyricists: *Lenz* (1927), *Gedichte* (1948), *Chausseen, Chausseen* (1963), and a 'poet's poet', not least for the hermetic quality of *Gezählte Tage* (1972) and *Die neunte Stunde* (1979).

*Richard Huelsenbeck* (Frankenau/
Hesse 1892–1974 Ticino)
A co-founder of Dadaism, his recitations of his poetry (*Schalaben, Schalomai, Schalamezomai*, and *Phantastische Gebete*, 1916) exemplified the movement's efforts not simply to '*épater les bourgeois*' but to revitalize art by exposing people to the vital and sensual character of language. His *Dada: Eine literarische Dokumentation* (1964) played an important role in reviving interest in the movement, and forms part of the history of pop art.

### Alexander von Humboldt
### (Berlin 1769–1859)

Humboldt was, as Goethe recognized, one of the age's most influential men. A founder of modern ethnography and human geography, his 30-vol *Voyage aux regions équinoxiales du Nouveau Continent* (1804–27) was the fruit of profound theoretical and empirical research, while his Berlin lectures, publ as *Kosmos: Entwurf einer physischen Weltbeschreibung* (1845–62), became the mid-century best-seller for the last generation of readers for whom the modern division between the 'sciences' and the 'humanities' did not exist. His *Ansichten der Natur* (1808), with its quintessentially 'German' feeling for nature, conveys a lively sense of the man and his work.

### *Wilhelm von Humboldt* (Potsdam 1767–1835 Schloss Tegel Berlin)

Alexander's elder brother, Wilhelm, was a universal genius and practical man of affairs who interacted with many of the greatest minds of his time. He left his reforming mark on the German education system up to the 20thc: Berlin's Humboldt University is named after him. A distinguished diplomat who represented Prussia at the Congress of Vienna, a (minor) poet and great letter-writer, he was the author of influential works on politics, anthropology and aesthetics, incl brilliant essays on Schiller and Goethe. A founding father of comparative linguistics, to which he devoted much of his life (*Über das vergleichende Sprachstudium in Beziehung auf die verschiedenen Epochen der Sprachentwicklung*, 1820), H's ideas on the philosophy of language, such as his stress on the individual speaker's inherent creative linguistic ability, have influenced Saussure, Chomsky, Heidegger, Wittgenstein and Gadamer.

### *Rudolf Jakob Humm*
### (Modena/Italy 1895–1977 Zurich)

He grew up in Italy, and his boyhood, an archipelago of half-remembered experiences, is recalled in his impressionistic masterpiece, *Die Inseln* (1936). A key contact for writers fleeing Nazi Germany, he caught the atmosphere of the period in his novel *Carolin* (1944).

### *Christian Friedrich Hunold*
### (Wandersleben 1681–1721 Halle)

He provided Augustan German readers with reading matter disapproved of by their stricter mentors. His popular manual, *Die allerneueste Art höflich und galant zu schreiben* (1703), taught them how to write, but few rivalled his ability to blend fact and fiction in novels that brought the glamour and intrigue of court life to ordinary people (*Die verliebte und galante Welt*, 1700, *Die liebenswürdige Adalie*, 1702, *Der Europäischen Höfe Liebes- und Helden-Geschichte*, 1705).

### *Ulrich von Hutten* (Burg Steckelberg nr Fulda 1488–1523 Ufenau nr Zurich)

Hutten is an emblematic figure in German history. A humanist, Reformation polemicist and follower of Luther, imperial knight (and pioneer of herbal treatment for syphilis), he was stylizd during the 1871–1918 Second Empire as a doughty Protestant nationalist freedom-lover, who (in his *Arminius*, 1529) first 'patented' Hermann the Cheruskan as the heroic opponent of Roman tyranny. His other memorable contributions to German literature are his *Gespräch büchlin*, his German version of his Latin prose dialogues, and his famous song 'Ich habs gewagt mit Sinnen' (both 1521).

# I

### *August Wilhelm Iffland*
### (Hanover 1759–1814 Berlin)

He was an actor, theatre manager and author of numerous well-turned comedies and 'family dramas', who, together with Kotzebue, dominated the stage in the age of Goethe and Schiller. I's *Die Jäger: Ein ländliches Sittengemälde* opened the Weimar theatre in 1791 under Goethe's direction. Later he became the powerful director of Prussia's royal theatres.

### *Karl Immermann*
### (Magdeburg 1796–1840 Düsseldorf)

A veteran of the Napoleonic wars, and friend of Tieck, he was a generous patron as founder director of the Düsseldorf theatre. His novels *Die Epigonen* (1836) and *Münchhausen: Eine*

*Geschichte in Arabesken* (1838–9) captured his generation's experience of being born 'too late' and their mistrust of industrialization and its human and social dimensions. His idealization of rural life in the *Oberhof* section of *Münchhausen* is concealed by its surface realism: it remained a paradigm of a German ideal up to the Third Reich. I's satirical verse epic *Tulifäntchen* (1830), was, he said, a parody of both its genre and age.

### Meinrad Inglin (Schwyz 1893–1971)

He drew on his own early experiences in a sequence of Swiss novels before making his breakthrough to the German market with *Der graue March* (1935), a rugged peasant story, and *Schweizerspiegel* (1938), a panoramic novel of Zurich life at the time of the 1914–18 war. His work provided a basis for Max Frisch, but deserves recognition in its own right.

### Franz Innerhofer
#### (Krim nr Salzburg 1944– )

He belongs to the generation of Austrian writers who initiated the disillusionment of their readers as regards the carefully nurtured rural idyll of their Austrian 'Heimat'. He employs sophisticated narrative perspectives in his novel trilogy *Schöne Tage* (1974), *Schattseite* (1975), *Die großen Wörter* (1977), and in *Der Emporkömmling* (short stories 1982) to portray life as a farm and factory worker and as a working-class student in a closed, status-bound, brutal society.

# J

### Friedrich Heinrich Jacobi
#### (Düsseldorf 1743–1819 Munich)

He wrote two influential novels, the epistolary *Aus Eduard Allwills Papiere* (1775), fruit of his friendship with Goethe, and *Woldemar* (1779), a sentimental exploration of love and friendship. His advocacy of feeling and intuition as central to human understanding, and of dialogue as a form of intellectual discourse, had a profound impact on German early Romanticism. His home near Düsseldorf provided a meeting-place for a whole generation of writers.

### Karoline Jagemann, later von Heygendorf
#### (Weimar 1777–1848 Dresden)

In her own day a celebrated actress and singer and mistress of Duke Karl August of Weimar, she is chiefly remembered for her memoirs (*Die Erinnerungen der K. J.*, publ 1926), her directorship of the Weimar opera (1808–17) and her influence on its theatre up to the duke's death in 1828.

### Friedrich Ludwig (= 'Turnvater') Jahn
#### (nr Prignitz 1778–1852 Freyburg/Unstrut)

The author of *Deutsches Volkstum* (1810) and (with Ernst Eiselen) of *Die deutsche Turnkunst* (1816), he founded the patriotic athletic movement (1811) as part of grassroots resistance to Napoleon and then (1815) the *Burschenschaft* or university fraternity, thereby profoundly influencing nationalist ideology in Germany. He was himself the victim of the 1819 Karlsbad Decrees, and of his own unreflective, verbally violent rhetoric. Championed by the Nazis, he was reviled by post-1945 Germany.

### Hans Henny Jahnn (Hamburg 1894–1959)

He fled conscription in 1914 to Norway, became a celebrated organ-builder, and wrote dramas (*Pastor Ephraim Magnus*, 1919) and the Joycean novel, *Perrudja* (1929). The works of his Danish exile (1933–45), *Fluß ohne Ufer* (novel trilogy 1949–61) and *Bornholmer Tagebuch* (1986), and his early advocacy of animal rights and ecological issues, constitute his major achievement.

### Ernst Jandl (Vienna 1925– )

Partner of Mayröcker, he is the pioneering exponent of concrete poetry, which has inspired endless imitators, *Andere Augen* (1956), 'wien: heldenplatz' (1962), *Laut und Luise* (1966), *Der Gigant* (radio play 1969), *sprechblasen* (1968), *der künstliche Baum* (1970), *dingfest* (1973), *selbstporträt des schachspielers als trinkende uhr* (which contains his poetological and 'confessional' foreword, 1983). Between 1976 and 1995 J wrote some 20 vols of poetry, among them *lechts und rinks* (1991), in what he terms 'heruntergekommene sprache'.

*Karl Jaspers* (Oldenburg 1883–1969 Basle)
He was a doctor whose *Psychologie der Weltanschauungen* (1919) brought him a chair in philosophy at Heidelberg (where Hannah Arendt was his pupil). *Philosophie* (3 vols 1932) established his reputation as a Christian existentialist, confirmed by his searching essays (*Zur Schuldfrage*, 1946; *Wohin treibt die Bundesrepublik?*, 1966, [4]1988). J has been a major influence on postwar political thought in western Germany.

*Jean Paul* (= *Jean Paul Richter*)
(Wunsiedel 1763–1825 Bayreuth)
The cultural gap separating our age from the 1800s is perhaps nowhere more evident than in Jean Paul. His humour – he is one of Germany's outstanding humorists and also its leading theorist of humour in *Vorschule der Ästhetik* (1804) – allusive style and recondite learning made him the delight of a generation used to being read to aloud. Today, to anyone who has not studied him in depth, *Die unsichtbare Loge* (1793), *Hesperus* (1795), *Quintus Fixlein* (1796), *Siebenkäs* (1796–7), and *Titan* (1800–3), *Flegeljahre* (1804–5) seem elusive and 'difficult'; up to 1850, this child of his pedagogic age (see especially *Levana, oder Erziehungslehre*, 1807), was deservedly regarded by women and men alike as one of the greatest writers of German.

*Elfriede Jelinek*
(Mürzzuschlag/Steiermark 1946– )
She writes prose, drama, and lyric poetry combining in an almost unique degree radical feminist social criticism with aesthetic sophistication and stylistic provocation, most notably in her novels, *Die Liebhaberinnen* (1975), *Die Klavierspielerin* (1983), *Die Ausgesperrten* (1980; as radio play 1978), and *Lust* (1989). In her 'anti-*Heimat*' novel *Die Kinder der Toten* (1995) she uses her abundant moral energy to undermine the carefully-nurtured commercial image of Austria as a tourist paradise.

*Uwe Johnson* (Kammin/Pomerania
1934–84 Kent/England)
The son of staunch Nazis, he set his hopes on the GDR, but the authorities proscribed his (autobiog) novel of the first generation of committed socialists: *Ingrid Babenderde: Reifeprüfung 1953* (wr in the 1950s, publ 1985). The same fate threatened *Mutmaßungen über Jakob* (1959), so he left for W Germany to write *Das dritte Buch über Achim* (1961), *Karsch, und andere Prosa* (1964) and *Zwei Ansichten* (1965), novels of a new kind of inner exile. J's prose, particularly in his ambitious *Jahrestage* (novel tetralogy 1970–83), blends personal experience with postwar German history. He is emerging as one of the great German fiction-writers of the 2nd half of the 20thc.

*Hanns Johst* (nr Oschatz/Saxony
1890–1978 Ruhpolding/Bavaria)
He advocated the Germanic *Thingspiele* in Nazi Germany: his cultic drama *Schlageter* (1929–32) was staged in 1933 in more than 1000 towns and cities of the Reich. A former Expressionist (*Die Stunde der Sterbenden*, drama 1914 etc), J was made president of the Writers Association and the German Academy of Literature after Hitler came to power.

*Gert Friedrich Jonke* (Klagenfurt 1946– )
His best-known novel, *Geometrischer Heimatroman* (1969), combines linguistic analysis with parody of a favourite Austrian genre. The sophisticated narrative technique of his later stories (*Schule der Geläufigkeit*, 1977, and *Der Kopf des Georg Friedrich Händel*, 1988) and novel (*Der ferne Klang*, 1979) reflects his training as a musicologist.

*Ernst Jünger* (Heidelberg 1895– )
He was deeply marked by the 1914–18 war, reflected in his cult book, *In Stahlgewittern* (1920, [26]1961). A key figure of the so-called conservative revolution of the 1920s, his elitism distanced him from the National Socialists, who first courted him for his *Der Arbeiter: Herrschaft und Gestalt* (1932), then persecuted him. His elliptical and stylistically polished novel *Auf den Marmorklippen* (1939) was widely read as a major document of resistance, a view not always shared by later readers, who see his postwar works, such as the war diaries, *Strahlungen*, the utopian novel, *Heliopolis: Rückblick auf eine Stadt* (1949), and *Siebzig*

*verweht* (1980) as expressions of J's amoral aestheticism.

### *Johann Heinrich Jung-Stilling* (Grund/ Rothaargebirge 1740–1817 Karlsruhe)

The fame of this Pietist author, doctor, political scientist and publicist derives mainly from his highly individual account of his own childhood in his memoirs (*Heinrich Stillings Jugend*), publ 1777 by Goethe, then his fellow-student, without his authorization (sequels 1778–1817). The many contradictions in J-S's life and work exemplify the intense intellectual ferment of his age.

# K

### *Franz Kafka* (Stuttgart 1883–1924 Kierling nr Vienna)

The worlds depicted in his novels (*Der Verschollene*, 1911–14, publ 1927 as *Amerika; Der Prozeß*, 1925, and *Das Schloß*, 1926) and his stories (*Das Urteil*, publ 1913, *Vor dem Gesetz*, 1915, *Die Verwandlung*, 1915, *In der Strafkolonie*, 1919, *Ein Hungerkünstler*, 1922) continue to confront readers in all their forbidding strangeness and disconcerting familiarity. K, who 'could dream only nightmares' (JL Borges), wrote at night, working by day as an insurance clerk in Prague (see *Tagebücher und Briefe*, 1937, *Brief an den Vater*, 1919). Despite intensive attempts – critical existentialist, theological, psychoanalytical and Marxist – to penetrate the 'Kafkaesque', his texts retain their tangible yet elusively puzzling quality.

### *Georg Kaiser* (Magdeburg 1878–1945 Ascona/Switzerland)

'Tell me', asks one of the protagonists in a play by K, 'where is Man? When will he appear – and call himself by name?' This question, with its unmistakably post-Nietzschean theme of apocalypse and regeneration, hovers over many of the works of this leading Expressionist dramatist (*Die jüdische Witwe*, 1911, *König Hahnrei*, 1913, *Die Bürger von Calais*, *Von morgens bis mitternachts*, *Die Koralle*, 1917, *Gas*, 1918, *Gas II*, 1920, *Der gerettete Alkibiades*, 1920, *Nebeneinander*, 1923, *Der Soldat Tanaka*, 1940, *Das Floß der Medusa*, 1948 etc), and

essayist (*Vision und Figur*, 1918) who also wrote novels (*Es ist genug*, 1932, *Villa Aurea*, 1940). His art is an often luminous (though sometimes crudely programmatic) attempt to grapple with the implications of modernity itself.

### *David Kalisch* (Breslau 1829–72 Berlin)

The founder of the Berlin farce, he was one of Germany's most successful authors for the comic stage during and after the 1848 revolution, with *Einmalhunderttausend Thaler!* (1848) and the tongue-in-cheek *Faust, der zu spät bekehrte Demokrat* (1855). With Ernst Dohm, he founded Germany's *Punch*, the Berlin satirical magazine *Kladderadatsch* (1848–1944).

### *Hermann Kant* (Hamburg 1926– )

He created in his novel *Die Aula* (1965) a kind of collective autobiog of the first generation of GDR socialist intellectuals. Here and in *Das Impressum*, his portrait of journalistic life under socialism (1972), his witty, fluent and provocative lang established him as one of the GDR's most widely read and representative writers. A high party functionary, he succeeded Anna Seghers in 1978 as President of the GDR Writers' Association, but was dismissed in December 1989 by his fellow writers for his denunciations to the Stasi of colleagues during his term of office.

### *Immanuel Kant* (Königsberg 1724–1804)

Western man's understanding of his own status in the scheme of things undergoes a 'second Copernican revolution' in the thought of Kant. He set out his intellectual revolution in a monumental triad of critiques: *Kritik der reinen Vernunft* (1781), *Kritik der praktischen Vernunft* (1788) and *Kritik der Urteilskraft* (1790), whose respective epistemological, ethical and aesthetic systems grant the human subject an unprecedented centrality. It is *our* inbuilt cognitive capacity which supplies the world 'out there' with its cohesion, just as it is 'the moral law *within*' which gives us our ethical bearings. In the third critique (which Goethe admitted was the only one he found readable) K's pioneering treatment of such categories as 'genius' and 'the sublime' established the co-ordinates for subsequent German aesthetic theory, while the idealism of Fichte, Schelling and Hegel owed its origins to K's deductions. See also: 'Was ist Aufklärung?' (*Berlinische Monatsschrift*, essay 1783), *Prolegomena zu jeder künftigen Metaphysik, die als Wissenschaft wird auftreten können* (1783), *Grundlegung der Metaphysik der Sitten* (1785), *Die Religion innerhalb der Grenzen der bloßen Vernunft* (1793), *Zum ewigen Frieden* (1795) and *Die Metaphysik der Sitten in zwei Teilen* (1797).

### Anna Louisa Karsch
(Dürbach/Lr Silesia 1722–91 Berlin)
Karsch was not a Sappho but a Mother Courage, who used her talent for occasional verse to address all strata of society, from the king downwards, to earn money to feed her family. Promoted by Gleim and by the distinguished aesthetician Johann Georg Sulzer (who saw in her the living epitome of his theories of the relationship of nature to poetry), her *Auserlesene Gedichte* (1764) and *Gedichte* (1792) belong to the pre-*Sturm und Drang* tradition of poetry as a craft. Perhaps even more telling are her little-known letters, which paint a portrait of her age as women experienced it.

### Hermann Kasack
(Potsdam 1896–1966 Stuttgart)
He worked for leading publishers: Kiepenheuer, S Fischer, Suhrkamp, and in the 1920s pioneered the radio play (*Stimmen im Kampf*, 1930). *Die Stadt hinter dem Strom* (1947), wr 1942–6, was one of the most influential novels of the immediate postwar years, an important factor in its success being the distancing effect created by the author's surrealist and symbolic presentation of the Third Reich.

### Marie Luise Kaschnitz
(Karlsruhe 1901–74 Rome)
'If I earn my place in literary history, it will be as the eternal autobiographer, and rightly so.' She wrote novels (*Liebe beginnt*, 1933, *Elissa*, 1937) and poems (*Gedichte*, 1947, *Neue Gedichte*, 1957) as well as autobiog (*Das Haus der Kindheit*, 1956, and *Beschreibung eines Dorfes*, 1966) and diary extracts (*Wohin denn ich*, 1963, and *Tage, Tage, Jahre*, 1968), and was an early proponent and analyst of subjectivity as an intrinsic characteristic of women's writing.

### Erich Kästner
(Dresden 1899–1974 Munich)
Influential journalist and satirist in the Weimar years, he used a variety of genres to promote the political education of the German middle-class reader and voter. Best known are his parodistic poems, his children's story *Emil und die Detektive* (1928), and his satires of city life, notably *Fabian: Geschichte eines Moralisten* (1931).

### Minna Kautsky (Graz 1937–1912 Berlin)
Known for her success and the facility with which she wrote for working-class women as 'die rote Marlitt', she was a former actress who through the help of her son, the socialist **Karl Kautsky**, became the chronicler of proletarian life in Austria. The socialist press and workers' libraries helped to publicize her plays and novels (*Die Alten und die Neuen*, 1885, *Viktoria*, 1890, *Helene*, 1894), whose central theme and function is the awakening and development of political awareness among working women.

### Gottfried Keller (Zurich 1819–90)
Central to the narrative manner of Keller, poet (*Gedichte*, 1846, *Neuere Gedichte*, 1851) and sometime city clerk of Zurich, is his capacity to question the patterns underlying the culture in which his works are located. Anarchy, an at times grotesque humour, self-irony and sensuousness underlie the surface 'poetic realism' of his autobiog novel, *Der grüne Heinrich* (1854–5, 2nd version 1879–80), and of his novellen cycle *Die Leute von Seldwyla* (I: 1856: *Pancraz der Schmoller, Romeo und Julia auf dem Dorfe, Frau Amrain und ihr Jüngster, Spiegel das Kätzchen, Die drei gerechten Kammacher*; and II: 1873–4: *Kleider machen Leute, Der Schmied seines Glückes, Die mißbrauchten Liebesbriefe, Dietegen, Das verlorene Lachen*). The *Züricher Novellen* (1878: *Hadlaub, Der Narr auf Manegg, Der Landvogt von Greiffensee, Das Fähnlein der sieben Aufrechten, Ursula*) adopt a more historical perspective, while *Das Sinngedicht* (novellen cycle 1882) takes a witty epigram as the point of departure for a subtle study of love from many angles. His last novel, *Martin Salander* (1886), failed because it offered his readers a darker and more bitter vision of humanity and modern society.

### Bernhard Kellermann
(Fürth 1879–1951 Potsdam)

He attracted notice in 1913 with *Der Tunnel*, a utopian/American novel. His patriotic First World War novels (*Der Krieg im Westen*, 1915) have dated, but *Totentanz* (1948) is interesting as an analysis of the German middle class's abandonment in 1933 of the democratic ideals K championed.

### Friederike Kempner (Opatov/Posen
1836–1901 Reichthal/Silesia)

An energetic philanthropist and author of *Gegen die Einzelhaft* ($^2$1885), she does not merit inclusion in a literary history on the basis of her slight novellen and tragedies; but in her time 'the Silesian swan' was the notorious author of poems (*Gedichte*, 1873, $^8$1903) whose involuntary humour and whose recitation formed the staple diet of social gatherings in pre-television days; today no anthology of comic and curious verse would be complete without her.

### Walter Kempowski (Rostock 1929– )
He was a political prisoner of both the Nazi and Soviet regimes, and his experiences form the theme of his 6-vol novel *Tadellöser & Wolff* (1971), based on contemporary diaries, letters, and radio and newsreel scripts. His use of the comic mode as the means of transmitting the reality of the Third Reich to later generations has made him one of the Federal Republic's most widely read authors. Subsequent vols include *Uns geht's ja noch gold* (1972) and *Ein Kapitel für sich* (1975).

### Johannes Kepler (Weil der Stadt
1571–1630 Regensburg)

Despite the adversity with which the noble-minded 'crypto-Calvinist' mathematician had to contend all his life, he was able to draw on his studies on astronomy and music to elaborate a bold and inspiring vision of an ecumenical order for the disturbed society of his day.

### Justinus Kerner
(Ludwigsburg 1786–1862 Weinsberg)

A doctor, authority on animal magnetism and leading member of the Swabian school of Romantics, he was a poet (*Gedichte*, 1826, $^5$1854) and the influential publisher of the younger Romantics: *Poetischer Almanach für das Jahr 1812* (with Uhland and Schwab) and *Deutscher Dichterwald* (1813, with Uhland and Fouqué). His high reputation among contemporaries, which Heine undermined for later generations, rested on his practical, typically *biedermeier* understanding of literature as a promoter of human and social bonds.

### Alfred Kerr
(Breslau 1867–1948 Hamburg)

He edited the influential impressionist literary journal *Pan* (1912–13), and was Berlin's most influential critic 1919–33. His theatre reviews in the *Berliner Tageblatt* and elsewhere constitute a major contribution to the political literature of the Weimar Republic and gained acceptance for the literary review as an art form in itself. He fled to Paris in 1933 and then in 1936 to London, where he and his daughter **Judith Kerr** (Berlin 1923– ) conveyed a vivid sense of the everyday reality of exile in their work, she as a highly acclaimed children's author, notably of *When Hitler Stole Pink Rabbit* (1971).

### (Count) Harry Kessler
(Paris 1868–1937 Lyons)

The diaries of this diplomat and *homme de lettres*, only parts of which have been publ, are a vital source for understanding the literary life of the early decades of the century. As founder and director of the Cranach press, he was one of the most influential of a diverse group of patrons of the arts from whom Germany's literature derived much benefit. Among his auto/biog writings were *Walter Rathenau* (1928), *Gesichter und Zeiten* (1935) and *Tagebücher* (1961).

### Irmgard Keun (Berlin 1910–82 Cologne)
Döblin provided this erstwhile actress with the impetus to write her first 2 best-selling novels, *Gilgi, eine von uns* (1931) and *Das kunstseidene Mädchen* (1932), wittily told from the subjective perspective of 'ordinary' girls naïvely 'on the make'. Decried as 'anti-German' by the

Nazis, she went into exile in 1935, returning with forged papers in 1940. The novels she wrote in 1936–8 were rediscovered in the 1980s: through a series of often unconnected scenes and events they offer vivid insights into the everyday world of the Weimar Republic, the Third Reich and exile: *Das Mädchen, mit dem die Kinder nicht verkehren durften, Nach Mitternacht, Kind aller Länder*.

#### *Eduard von Keyserling* (Hasenpoth/ Courland 1855–1918 Munich)

He was a déclassé Baltic baron and central figure of Munich's *fin-de-siècle Bohème*, whose novels of life on the great Baltic estates, including *Beate und Mareile* (1903), *Dumala* (1908), *Fürstinnen* (1917) and the unusually explicit novelle, *Schwüle Tage* (1906), established his reputation as the impressionistic and ironic portraitist of a decadent aristocratic culture.

#### *Johanna Kinkel* (Bonn 1810–59 London)

This concert pianist and composer combined the role of valiant wife to the 1848 radical author and art historian **Gottfried Kinkel** (Oberkassel/Bonn 1815–82 Unterstrass/Zurich) with that of journalist and music teacher (*Acht Briefe an eine Freundin über Clavier-Unterricht*, 1852) to fellow German exiles in London, whose lives and relationships she portrayed in her abundant letters and in her *roman à clef*, *Hans Ibeles in London: Ein Familienbild aus dem Flüchtlingsleben* (1860).

#### *Heinar Kipphardt* (Heidersdorf/Silesia 1922–82 Munich)

A victim of the Nazis, soldier on the Russian front, psychiatrist, author and dramaturge, who subscribed to a view of the artist as social revolutionary, he wrote his early plays in E Berlin, among them, *Shakespeare wird gesucht* (1953). For political reasons he returned to the W in 1959, where he became one of the leading proponents of documentary theatre with the dramas *Der Hund des Generals* (1962), *In der Sache J. Robert Oppenheimer* (1964) and *Bruder Eichmann* (1983). A significant component of K's influence derived from the adaptability of his work for TV, as in *Mär* (film 1975, novel 1976, drama 1980).

#### *Sarah Kirsch* (= *Ingrid Bernstein*) (Limlingerode/Harz 1935– )

A biologist, later student of literature, journalist and broadcaster, she is a major exponent of the modern lyric in Germany: *Zaubersprüche* (1973), *Rückenwind* (1976), and, following her leaving the GDR, *Drachensteigen* (1979), *Katzenleben* (1984). Her prose, such as *Irrstern* (1986), is also haunted, as she phrased it in an interview in 1983, by the sense of being the 'chronicler of the end of the world'.

#### *Klabund* (= *Alfred Henschke*) (Crossen/Oder 1890–1928 Davos)

K packed an incredibly productive oeuvre and an often scandal-ridden public career into his short life. He wrote with verve and often great originality in the manner of the French *chansonnier* Villon (*Der himmlische Vagant*, 1919), and was famed for his Chinese poems, such as *Li tai-pe* (1916). In 1925 his *Kreidekreis*, a model for Brecht, was a huge stage success. K, who performed his own compositions in Max Reinhardt's cabaret *Schall und Rauch*, exemplified for the Nazis the typical decadent *Asphaltliterat*.

#### *Ludwig Klages* (Hanover 1872–1956 Kilchberg)

Influential art philosopher and proponent of the conservative revolution (whom Musil pilloried in *Der Mann ohne Eigenschaften* as Meingast), he was, until the breach in 1903/4, an intimate member of the *George-Kreis* and author of the influential monograph: *Stefan George* (1902).

#### *Johann Klaj* (Meissen 1616–56 Kitzingen)

He founded with Harsdörffer the Nuremberg-based language society *Pegnesischer Schäferorden*. In his *Pegnesisches Schäfergedicht* (1644), he applied H's theories to his own poetry, and by use of rich metrical forms, notably the dactyl, anapaest and internal rhyme, helped publicize the intrinsic musicality of the German language.

#### *Ewald Christian von Kleist* (Königsberg 1715–59 Kunersdorf)

Author of the much-praised didactic poem in

hexameters, *Der Frühling* (1749), he embodied for Lessing the 18thc ideal of friendship and may have provided the model for the noble officer Tellheim in his *Minna von Barnhelm*.

### Heinrich von Kleist
#### (Frankfurt/O 1777–1811 nr Berlin)

A Prussian army officer, Kleist was also a keen student of philosophy (*Über die allmähliche Verfertigung der Gedanken beim Reden*, 1805/6?, and the incomparable essay *Aufsatz über das Marionettentheater*, 1810), mathematics, physics and political economy, a civil servant, French POW and journalist in Berlin (ed of *Berliner Abendblätter*, 1810–11). He wrote the tragedies *Die Familie Schroffenstein* (1803, publ 1822), *Penthesilea* (wr 1806–7, publ 1808, perf 1876), and the incomplete *Robert Guiskard*; the comedies *Amphitryon: Ein Lustspiel nach Molière* (wr and publ 1807, perf 1898), *Der zerbrochene Krug* (1808), and the historical dramas *Das Käthchen von Heilbronn* (1810), *Die Hermannsschlacht* (wr 1808, publ 1821, perf 1839) and *Prinz Friedrich von Homburg* (wr 1808–10, publ and perf 1821). K's novellen are also among the most formally sophisticated in the German language: *Erzählungen* (1810–11: vol 1: *Das Erdbeben in Chili*, *Die Marquise von O.*, *Michael Kohlhaas*; vol 2: *Die Verlobung in St Domingo*, *Das Bettelweib von Locarno*, *Der Findling*, *Die heilige Cäcilie oder die Gewalt der Musik*, *Der Zweikampf*). He shot himself in a suicide pact on the shore of the Wannsee.

*Jochen Klepper* (Beuthen 1903–42 Berlin)
In his best-known novel, *Der Vater* (1937), this Lutheran pastor, a leading exponent of Christian 'inner emigration', used a revaluation of Frederick William I of Prussia to explore the paternalist tradition of authority in Prussia in a manner designed to pass the Nazi censorship, yet offer comfort to members of the Confessing Church.

### August Klingemann
#### (Brunswick 1777–1831)

A journalist, man of the theatre, author of widely-performed historical dramas incl in 1811 *Faust* (publ 1815), he is particularly remembered as director of the Brunswick theatre, where in 1829 he put on the first public perf of Goethe's *Faust*.

### Friedrich Maximilian Klinger
#### (Frankfurt/M 1752–1831 Estonia)

Energy and magnetism characterized the life and work of K, student in Giessen, theatre director with the Seyler troupe, officer, later major general in the Russian army. His play, written during the year of his breach with Goethe, gave the name to the literary movement: *Sturm und Drang* (1776). He wrote tragedies, incl *Das leidende Weib* (1775) and two *Medea* dramas (1791), a novel (*Fausts Leben, Thaten und Höllenfahrt*, 1791) and the much-played comedy *Prinz Seiden-Wurm* (1780). K exemplifies the European dimension of the German Enlightenment (e.g. *Betrachtungen und Gedanken über verschiedene Gegenstände der Welt und der Literatur*, 1803–5, and his many philosophical novels).

### Friedrich Gottlieb Klopstock
#### (Quedlinburg 1724–1803 Hamburg)

He studied theology at Jena and Leipzig, and exercised a decisive influence on the form (*Vom dt. Hexameter*, 1779) as well as on the content of German poetry in his age; he also made a major contribution to the development of the German writer's identity, by focusing, like Lessing, on the importance of a sound financial basis of the professional writer's life (*Die deutsche Gelehrtenrepublik*, 1774). Besides his celebrated epic masterpiece, *Der Messias* (1749–73), he wrote the biblical tragedies *Der Tod Adams* (1757), *Salomo* (1764) and *David* (1772), *Geistliche Lieder* (1758, 1769), drama (*Hermanns Schlacht*, 1769) and immensely influential odes (*Oden*, 1771, incl 'Der Zürcher See', 'Die Frühlingsfeier', 'Der Eislauf').

### Meta Klopstock *see Margareta Moller*

*Alexander Kluge* (Halberstadt 1932– )
This lawyer and film-maker is the creative and formally innovative chronicler in literary and media texts of the impact of the 1939–45 war on Germans' lives, as in the narrative prose, *Lebensläufe* (1962) and *Schlachtbeschreibung* (1964), in which Stalingrad takes on exemplary character as a piece of *Kulturkritik*, or

*Lernprozesse mit tödlichem Ausgang* (1983). K is a vigorous contemporary representative of the Enlightenment tradition of political education of society through aesthetic means.

### *Ruth Klüger* (Vienna 1931– )

History, the history of the Holocaust, determined that K, at 11 an inmate of Auschwitz, would always be a nomad and a loner. A distinguished German scholar in California (under the name of **Ruth Angress**), she established herself as a writer in 1992 with *weiter leben – Eine Jugend*, one of the finest late 20thc autobiogs in German, which is also a study of discontinuous time from a Jewish feminist point of view.

### *Adolf Freiherr von Knigge* (Bredenbeck/ Hanover 1752–96 Bremen)

Current scholarly interest in late Enlightenment anthropology assigns significant influence to the work of K, tr of Rousseau, who helped popularize British empirical philosophy in Germany, was actively involved in the masonic-type *Illuminatenorden* (1780–4) and wrote one of late 18thc Germany's most widely read and frequently reissued works of popular philosophy: *Über den Umgang mit Menschen* (1788). His novels, such as the picaresque *Geschichte Peter Clausens* (1783–5), offer practical examples of his social utopia.

### *Oskar Kokoschka* (Pöchlarn 1886–1980 Montreux)

Although primarily a painter, he was an Expressionist dramatist whose plays, *Sphinx und Strohmann* (later as *Eine Groteske*, and in expanded form, *Hiob*, 1909) and *Mörder, Hoffnung der Frauen* (1910), *Der traumhafte Dornbusch* (1913), *Orpheus und Eurydike* (1919), also focus on the central theme of his oeuvre, the battle of the sexes; cf also his autobiog, *Mein Weg* (1971).

### *Annette Kolb* (Munich 1875–1967)

'Jeannette Scheurl' in T Mann's *Doktor Faustus*, she drew much of her creative energy, but also much anguish in her life, from her mixed German and French origin. It expressed itself in politically engaged essays, newspaper articles, trns and autobiog writings (*Briefe einer Deutsch-Französin*, 1916, publ in France 1917). Her stylish and witty novels: *Das Exemplar* (1913), *Daphne Herbst* (1927) and *Die Schaukel* (in exile 1934), link very different stages in her own life to parallel stages in the evolution of German society.

### *Erwin Guido Kolbenheyer* (Budapest 1878–1962 Munich)

A former student of zoology and psychology, he was a high Nazi functionary and once-popular author of historical-philosophical dramas based on a biological reading of German history (*Gregor und Heinrich*, 1934), novels including a *Paracelsus* trilogy (1917–26) and *Meister Joachim Pausewang*, based on the mystic, Jakob Böhme (1920), and a work of topical philosophy, *Die Bauhütte: Elemente einer Metaphysik der Gegenwart* (1925).

### *Alfred Kolleritsch* (Brunnsee/Styria 1931– )

This Graz schoolteacher and Heidegger scholar founded the Austrian avant-garde *Forum Stadtpark* and its influential literary journal *manuskripte* in 1960. His novel *Die Pfirsichtöter: ein seismographischer Roman* (1972) deconstructed traditional narrative as a form of critique of Austria's rigid social hierarchies and their political consequences in the Hitler era. K's subsequent novels *Die grüne Seite* (1974), *Allemann* (1989), and his poetry (*Einübung in das Vermeidbare*, 1978) centre on the capacity of youth to oppose and subvert power structures.

### *Gertrud Kolmar* (= *Gertrud Chodziesner*) (Berlin 1894–1943?)

The life and work of 'Kafka's sister in spirit', poet, author of the short stories, *Susanna* (1939–40, publ 1993), interpreter, teacher of deaf mutes and student of Asian culture, and forced labourer, offers a paradigm of the fate of the Jews under the Nazis. Her poem, *Wir Juden*, publ in *Die Frau und die Tiere* (1938), the whole of which was pulped after the 'Kristallnacht', recorded the first stage of the process to isolate them within society. Between 1938 and her transportation in 1943, probably to Auschwitz, her highly artistic poetry gave voice to the suppressed and silenced.

*Leopold Kompert* (Mnichovo Hradiste/
Bohemia 1822–86 Vienna)
He was not rich enough to complete his studies
but earned money as a private tutor until 1848,
when *Aus dem Ghetto* (5 stories) established
him as the creator of a specifically Jewish brand
of topical literature. His novel *Zwischen Ruinen*
(1875) sought to demonstrate the mutual benefits of Jewish assimilation and pointed towards a society achieved in the US and Britain
rather than in Austria or Germany.

*Johann Ulrich König*
(Esslingen 1688–1744 Dresden)
After initial encouragement in Augustan Hamburg, he moved on to rococo Dresden, where
he succeeded Johann von Besser as court master of ceremonies. His early flair for occasional
verse in every mode (*Theatralische, geistliche,
vermischte und galants Gedichte*, 1713) stood
him in good stead as he set about glorifying
Augustus the Strong of Saxony, revising
Opitz's views on poetry (*Untersuchung von dem
guten Geschmack in der Dicht- und Rede-kunst*,
1727) and reconciling baroque traditions with
Augustan aesthetics.

*Helga Königsdorf* (Gera 1938– )
A mathematician and physicist, K is the author
of coolly stylized feminist prose which focuses
on contemporary life, as in *Meine ungehörigen
Träume* (1983), *Der Lauf der Dinge* (1983),
*Respektloser Umgang* (1986), and which
brought her almost immediate recognition. K
has managed the transition of the feminist
writer to post-1990 Germany perhaps more
effectively than most.

*Heinz Günther Konsalik*
(Cologne 1921– )
He worked as a war reporter, then made his
name with a flood of novels of which *Der Arzt
von Stalingrad* (1956) remains the best-known.
His flair for publicity has helped him to survive
and prosper in the face of translated US pulp
fiction.

*Theodor Körner*
(Dresden 1791–1813 nr Gadebusch)
Körner, who fell in battle in the early stages of
the Wars of Liberation, Burgtheater dramatist,

had already had several plays perf (notably the
historical drama *Zriny*, publ 1814). Popular
mythology and later nationalist history stylized
K as the young bard who gave his life for the
Fatherland. His patriotic poems *Leier und
Schwert* were publ in 1814 by his father, the
aesthetician and close friend of Schiller,
**Christian Gottfried Körner** (Leipzig 1756–
1832 Berlin).

*August von Kotzebue*
(Weimar 1761–1819 Mannheim)
What makes K remarkable is that he dominated the German-speaking theatre in the age
of Schiller and Goethe. Abroad, too, he overshadowed them: *Menschenhaß und Reue* (1789)
was played (in trn) to audiences in London,
Dublin and New York. In the German-
speaking world his comedy *Die deutschen
Kleinstädter* (1803) lasted longest and had some
influence on Viennese popular comedy.

*Karl Kraus*
(Gitschin/Bohemia 1874–1936 Vienna)
Kraus soon became notorious for the power
of his satirical and polemical pen (*Die
demolierte Literatur*, 1897, *Eine Krone für
Zion*, 1898). From 1899 to 1936 he ed his
journal *Die Fackel*, from 1912 as its sole
author, unfolding his masterly revelation of
the power of manipulative language. He was
an inventive deconstructionist of corruption,
notably in the press, but also in the justice
system (*Sittlichkeit und Kriminalität*, 1908).
He was also a brilliant aphorist, eg in the
collection *Sprüche und Widersprüche* (1909),
and the author of an apocalyptic drama, *Die
letzten Tage der Menschheit: Tragödie in 5
Akten mit Vorspiel und Epilog* (1918–19). He
was amongst the earliest to focus openly on the
role of language in Hitler's seizure of power
(*Die dritte Walpurgisnacht*, wr 1933, publ
1952).

*Max Kretzer* (Berlin 1854–1941)
Kretzer was the author of a naturalist novel,
*Meister Timpe* (1888), portraying the tragedy of
the craftsman as victim of the Industrial Revolution. *Das Gesicht Christi* (1896) explores the
theme of religious utopia among the working
classes.

*Franz Xaver Kroetz* (Munich 1946– )
He is a leading exponent of the modern critical *Volksstück: Heimarbeit* (1971), *Stallerhof* (1972), *Das Nest* (1975), *Bauern sterben* (1985). The often wordless brutalities of the creatures of his peasant world are deliberately intended as extreme provocation to the audience. He has also tried to revive domestic tragedy with modernizations of Hebbel: *Maria Magdalena* (1973), *Agnes Bernauer* (1977).

*Karl Krolow* (Hanover 1913– )
Krolow started to publ during the war. A fine translator from French, he aims in his poetry to be open and transparent, and combines the semi-romantic nature tradition of Lehmann and Loerke with surrealistic experimentation. The first vol of his collected poems was publ in 1965.

*Quirinus Kuhlmann*
(Breslau 1651–89 Moscow)
He was a messianic figure and author of some 40 religious publications in German, Latin, Dutch and English, the best known being the ecstatic poetic cycle *Kühlpsalter* (1684–6); he studied law in Jena and experienced religious conversion in Leyden (1673). Abortive missions to Turkey, Palestine and Moscow in pursuit of his utopian vision finally led to his death at the stake.

*Günter Kunert* (Berlin 1929– )
The fate and heritage of Germany's Jews was addressed by K in his novel *Im Namen der Hüte* (W Germany 1967); his subsequent works in satirical, utopian and grotesque mode have focused on contemporary issues. His shorter prose, as in *Die Beerdigung findet in aller Stille statt* (1968) and *Tagträume in Berlin und andernorts* (essays/short stories 1972), exemplifies the role of humour in GDR literature and K's ability to engage the reader in sophisticated dialogue; so, too, does his ironically titled collection of poetry, *Unterwegs nach Utopia* (1977).

*Reiner Kunze*
(Oelsnitz/Erzgebirge 1933– )
Forced into exile in W Germany in 1977, he uses associative techniques to give subjective

experience exemplary status as 'political' literature in *Poesiealbum 11* (1968) and *sensible wege* (1969, shaped by his experience of Czechoslovakia in the 'Prague Spring'), *zimmerlautstärke* (1972) and *Die wunderbaren Jahre* (1976). His prose style demands rational and intuitive responses from the reader. In post-Unification Germany K is more concerned than ever with the moral and political position of the writer in society.

*Ferdinand Kürnberger*
(Vienna 1821–79 Munich)
This former 1848 revolutionary and political exile wrote a successful novel, *Der Amerika-Müde* (1855). Today his contribution to the feuilleton as an art form is central to his reputation. His work constitutes an important link between *Vormärz* and *fin-de-siècle* Vienna and affords illuminating insights into life under the Habsburg monarchy.

*Hermann Kurz*
(Reutlingen 1813–73 Tübingen)
The reputation of the author of the novel *Der Sonnenwirt* (1854) suffers from having been associated, not least by his daughter, Isolde, with patriotic local *Heimatliteratur*. He was preoccupied with the shortcomings of the educational system for the underprivileged classes. In his antihero's criminal career we see the workings of a legal system of social control from its victim's perspective.

*Isolde Kurz*
(Stuttgart 1853–1944 Tübingen)
For this polished stylist the Italian Renaissance, with its recognition of the social role of gifted women, represented both a moral refuge and an alternative to a brutalized 'modern' culture. Business acumen helped her to achieve success with her lyric poetry and prose: *Gedichte* (1888), *Neue Gedichte* (1905), *Florentiner Novellen* (1890), *Italienische Erzählungen* (1895), *Der Ruf des Pan* (1928). Her aphorisms, *Im Zeichen des Steinbocks* (1905), had wide appeal, as did her autobiog writings, esp the best-selling semi-autobiog novel, *Vanadis: Der Lebensweg einer deutschen Frau* (1931).

# L

### Samuel Gotthold Lange
(Halle 1711–81 Laublingen)

L extolled friendship as he experienced it with Jakob Immanuel Pyra (1715–44). Their poems were publ by Bodmer (*Thyrsis' und Damons freundschaftliche Lieder*, 1745) and created a fashion which marks the transition from Augustan rationality to the pre-*Sturm und Drang* cult of sensibility. An inspector of schools by profession, L devoted himself doggedly but unsuccessfully to translation.

### Elisabeth Langgässer (Alzey/Rheinhessen 1899–1950 Rheinzabern)

A Catholic with a Jewish father, she wrote poetry (*Der Wendekreis des Lammes*, 1924, *Proserpina*, verse novelle 1933, *Die Tierkreisgedichte*, 1935). Banned from publishing in 1936, her novel of 'inner emigration', *Das unauslöschliche Siegel* (1946), was partly written when doing forced labour; *Märkische Argonautenfahrt* (1950) was a remarkably successful effort to find a modern appropriate narrative form in which to express belief in salvation in an extreme historical situation. Widely read in the post-1945 period, her urgent focus on the need for judgement, penance and the purging of Nazi crimes came to seem out of touch with the consumer society of the 1950s and the new political certainties of 1968.

### Sophie von La Roche
(Kaufbeuren 1730–1807 Offenbach)

As author of *Geschichte des Fräuleins von Sternheim* (1771), *Rosaliens Briefe an ihre Freundin Mariane von St . . .* (1779–81) and the partly autobiog *Melusinens Sommer-Abende* (1806), she exercised a formative influence on women's writing. In her work as ed of a (women's) journal, *Pomona: Für Teutschlands Töchter* (1782–84), and in her *Briefe an Lina* (1785–87, 1789–94), she aspired to educate women readers in enlightened values and to provide role models acceptable, within strictly circumscribed conventions, to the male establishment.

### Berta Lask
(Galicia 1878–1967 Berlin/GDR)

L, whose husband was a Berlin slum doctor, was an influential socialist poet and agitprop dramatist (*Auf dem Hinterhof, 4 Treppen links*, tragedy 1912, *Leuna 1921 – Drama der Tatsachen*, documentary drama 1927). A member of the German Communist Party from 1923 and co-founder of the *Bund proletarisch-revolutionärer Schriftsteller*, she also wrote children's fiction (*Wie Franz und Grete nach Rußland reisten*, 1926), poetry (*Rufe aus dem Dunkel*, 1921) and an autobiog novel, *Stille und Stürme* (1955).

### Else Lasker-Schüler (Elberfeld/Wuppertal 1869–1945 Jerusalem)

'I was born in Thebes, though I came into the world in Elberfeld,' wrote this poet and painter. In terms of personality if not work she was part of the anarchic artistic world of Expressionism. Writer of passionate love poems to Benn and correspondent of Kraus, she celebrated Berlin in her novel, *Mein Herz* (1912), as befitted a writer who wrote much of her later work in the insecurity of a hotel room. *Konzert*, a collection of essays and poems, appeared 1932 on the eve of Hitler's rise to power, as did her play, *Arthur Aronymus und seine Väter*, about Jewish persecution and Christian intervention. In Zurich she became one of the earliest exponents of exile literature; she found final refuge in Israel, but never got over her loss of homeland, the theme of her travelogue, *Das Hebräerland* (1937) and the poems of *Mein blaues Klavier* (1943).

### Heinrich Laube
(Sprottau/Silesia 1806–84 Vienna)

L exemplifies the achievement of the Young Germans in forging a new relationship with the reading public with his novel *Das junge Europa* (1833–7), the essays in *Das neue Jahrhundert* (1833), his *Reisenovellen* (1834–7), and his work as editor of *Aurora* and *Zeitung für die elegante Welt*. The latter half of his life was spent in the theatre, as author of *Die Bernsteinhexe* (after Meinhold), *Struensee* (1846) and the 'literary' plays *Gottsched und Gellert* and *Die Karlsschüler* (on Schiller, both

1847), and as director of the Vienna Burgtheater (1849–67) where he reformed every aspect from finance to repertoire.

### Johann Caspar Lavater
#### (Zurich 1741–1801)

Current interest in anthropology has restored to Lavater something of the centrality he enjoyed among his contemporaries and reflected in his huge personal correspondence; he owed this to the importance for empirical psychology of his innovative focus on the introspective self in *Geheimes Tagebuch von einem Beobachter seiner Selbst* and *Tagebuch eines Beobachters seiner Selbst* (1771 and 1773). His greatest international success was his richly illustrated *Physiognomische Fragmente zur Beförderung der Menschenkenntniß und Menschenleben* (1775–8) in which he aimed to provide a scientific basis for the ancient idea of judging human character by physical appearance.

### Gertrud von le Fort
#### (Minden 1876–1971 Obersdorf)

She was, like Louise von François and Fontane, of Huguenot origin, but converted to Roman Catholicism in 1926 (*Hymnen an die Kirche*, 1924, *Das Schweißtuch der Veronika*, novel 1928–46). She helped create a (non-polemical) Catholic reading culture with her short intense narratives *Die Letzte am Schafott* (1931, dramatized 1949 by Bernanos), *Der Papst aus dem Ghetto* (1930), *Die Magdeburgische Hochzeit* (1938) and *Das Gericht des Meeres* (1943), and was a resolute member of the Christian opposition to Hitler (*Die Consolata*, wr 1943, publ 1947). Her work was widely popular during the immediate postwar period.

### Wilhelm Lehmann (Puerto Cabello/Venezuela 1882–1968 Eckernförde)

One of 20thc Germany's major exponents of nature poetry, he publ his first poetry volume, *Antwort des Schweigens*, in 1935, followed by *Der grüne Gott* in 1942. His 'nature magic' (i a *Entzückter Staub*, 1946, *Noch nicht genug*, 1950, and the essays, *Dichtung als Dasein*, 1946, *Kunst des Gedichts*, 1961) fascinated poets ac-

tive after 1945, such as Huchel and Eich, Krolow, Fried and Hermlin.

### Gottfried Wilhelm von Leibniz
#### (Leipzig 1646–1716 Hanover)

'We have no Descartes', lamented Loen in 1744, 'but we do have Leibniz.' He was an infant prodigy and polymath, member of the French Academy, and a thinker whose European connections are documented in his immense correspondence. A friend of Sophie Charlotte, the gifted Queen of Prussia, he profoundly influenced his contemporaries. His optimism, recorded in his *Theodicée* (1710) and *Monadologie* (wr 1716, publ 1840) and famously ridiculed by Voltaire in *Candide* (1759), is guided by his belief in the unity of divine and human reason.

### Johann Anton Leisewitz
#### (Hanover 1752–1806 Brunswick)

Leisewitz studied at Göttingen, and later became a civil servant with particular competence in taxation, who helped implement a social welfare programme in the duchy of Brunswick. His only surviving literary work is *Julius von Tarent* (1776), a tragedy of fratricide, and an important influence on Schiller's *Die Räuber*.

### Nikolaus Lenau (Nikolaus Franz Niembsch, Edler von Strehlenau)
#### (Csatád/Hungary 1802–50 Oberdöbling/Vienna)

The 'Austrian Byron' was not simply an older contemporary of Büchner, Kierkegaard and Baudelaire, but closely akin to them. In *Faust: Ein Gedicht* (1836) and in his poetry (*Gedichte*, 1832, *Neuere Gedichte*, 1838) he expressed, often in lang of utter simplicity (as in his *Schilflieder*), the anxieties of a whole generation and, long before Nietzsche, articulated modern man's alienation from God. In philosophy (Spinoza), Christian mysticism (Heinrich Suso) and contemporary thought (Franz von Baader, Hegel) he searched for answers to a lifelong dread of man's obliteration at death, expressed in his central images of decay, destruction and emptiness. He sought utopia in America in 1832, and was so deeply marked by his generation's politicization that Engels and later socialist critics hailed the author of *Savonarola* (1837, [2]1842) and *Die Albigenser* (1842, [3]1849) as the voice of revolution.

### Jakob Michael Reinhold Lenz (Seßwegen/ Livonia 1751–92 Moscow)

His unconventional plays *Der Hofmeister, oder Vortheile der Privaterziehung* (1774), *Der neue Mendoza* (1774) and *Die Soldaten* (1776), together with his *Anmerkungen übers Theater* (1774), made this 'transient meteor' (Goethe) the programmatical pioneer of *Sturm und Drang* theatre focused on contemporary social abuses and without a hero. 'Rejected by heaven . . . a vagrant, rebel and cheap satirist' (L to Herder), he spent his last restless years after a breakdown in 1777 travelling. Büchner based his brilliant novelle *Lenz* (1839) on incidents from his life in 1778. *Pandämonium Germanikum*, a satire on Enlightenment rationalism, was publ posthumously in 1819.

### Siegfried Lenz (Lyck/E Prussia 1926– )

A journalist with *Die Welt*, he wrote deservedly popular, witty stories about his lost homeland in *So zärtlich war Suleyken* (1955). A founder-member of the *Gruppe* 47, his novel *Deutschstunde* (1968) was influential in changing public perceptions of the Third Reich in the media, educational policy, and the school and university curriculum. His novel *Heimatmuseum* (1978) called into question contemporary attitudes to a favourite German cultural concept.

### Alexander Lernet-Holenia (Vienna 1897–1976)

He served in the 1914–18 war as an Austrian cavalry officer, then wrote light plays, poetry and fiction, drawing on his war experiences for much of his best work (*Die Standarte*, novel 1934, *Der Baron Bagge*, novelle 1936). The novel he based on service in Hitler's war in Poland in 1939–40 (*Mars im Widder*, 1941) was promptly withdrawn from sale. He survived to become a major postwar Austrian author of nostalgic fiction such as *Mayerling* (stories 1960) and *Die Geheimnisse des Hauses Oesterreich: Roman einer Dynastie* (novel 1971).

### Gotthold Ephraim Lessing (Kamenz/ Oberlausitz 1729–81 Brunswick)

A leading exponent of the Enlightenment and one of Germany's greatest critical minds, Lessing studied theology and medicine in Leipzig, and tried his hand at writing comedies (notably his enlightened and witty send-up on endemic anti-Jewish prejudice in *Die Juden*, 1749), before becoming an influential literary journalist in the 1750s. His friendship with Moses Mendelssohn proved to be a central intellectual and personal influence, while his domestic tragedy *Miß Sara Sampson* (1755) gave a new direction to German theatre, as his *Laokoon, oder Über die Grenzen der Malerei und Poesie* (1766) did to aesthetics. The works of L's later years retain their central importance for an understanding of German drama: *Minna von Barnhelm oder Das Soldatenglück* (comedy 1767), *Hamburgische Dramaturgie* (his major achievement in drama criticism 1767–69), *Emilia Galotti* (domestic tragedy 1772) and his 'dramatic poem' *Nathan der Weise* (1779), a noble plea for tolerance.

### Fanny Lewald (Königsberg 1811–89 Dresden)

Lewald exemplifies the development of liberal bourgeois Jewish emancipation in 19thc Germany: her parents decided to have her christened, her schooling was restricted, but she achieved an independent existence through writing. Her first (anon) novels (*Clementine*, 1842, *Jenny*, 1843) were marked by a guarded feminism. Her initial enthusiasm for the liberal revolution of 1848 gave way to disillusionment and later identification with Bismarck's Empire. In some 50 vols of novels, travelogues and reminiscences, most notably the vividly-told *Meine Lebensgeschichte* (1861–2), L's shrewd assessment of the market helped her to cater for her educated middle-class readers' interest in historical figures (*Prinz Louis Ferdinand*, novel 1849), topical issues (*Die Kammerjungfer*, novel 1856) and holiday destinations (*Italienisches Bilderbuch*, 1847).

### Georg Christoph Lichtenberg (Oberramstadt/Darmstadt 1742–99 Göttingen)

The first publ work of L, a favourite author of

Tolstoy, Albert Schweitzer and Karl Kraus, concerned the use mathematics might be to a man of taste; his last (1799) ranged from the magnetic needle and the telegraph to a 'mechanical theory of the kiss'. To the literary historian, the man who introduced modern science and technology to a backward Germany is at his best in his aphorisms. Not meant for publication, they offer, like his letters, a witty critical distillation of the knowledge and experience of his age.

### *Friedrich Lienhard* (Rothbach/Alsace 1865–1929 Eisenach)

Lienhard, the self-styled crusader against 'urban cosmopolitan intellectualism', was, with Adolf Bartels, the founder of the *Heimatkunstbewegung* and a popularizer of the terms *Heimatkunst*, *Heimatschutz* and *Heimatpflege* which have exerted such profound positive (and also negative) effects on our modern *Weltanschauung*.

### *Detlev von Liliencron* (Kiel 1844–1909 Alt-Rahlstedt/Hamburg)

*Bunte Beute* (1903), a lyric collection ranging from doggerel to terzinas, would be a good general title for all the poetry of Liliencron, an army officer whose talent for impressionistic protomodern verse matured late, notably in collections such as *Adjutantenritte und andere Gedichte* (1883), *Gedichte* (1889), *Der Haidegänger* (1890) and *Neue Gedichte* (1893). His *kunterbuntes Epos*, *Poggfred* (dedicated to Dehmel: 1896 and extended in 1906) is a vast and whimsical survey of the contemporary world as seen from his fictitious country estate, the name of which means 'frog-peace' in Plattdeutsch.

### Liselotte von der Pfalz *see* Elisabeth Charlotte von der Pfalz

### *Johann Michael von Loen* (Frankfurt/M 1694–1776)

Goethe's wealthy and generous great-uncle produced his political novel *Der redliche Mann am Hofe* in 1740, the year Richardson's *Pamela* was publ. Like his teacher Thomasius, L helped to spread a knowledge of French civic culture in Germany. Author of some 40 books, he was a typical Augustan moralist, whose favourite concern, the promotion of tolerance between Lutherans and Calvinists, got him into serious trouble with the authorities.

### *Oskar Loerke* (Jungen/W Prussia 1884–1941 Berlin)

He worked from 1917 to 1941 as an ed for the publisher S Fischer. The wooded landscape of his E German homeland provides the backdrop for lyric poetry in which time is suspended and the self is obliterated (*Wanderschaft*, 1911, *Gedichte*, 1916, *Die heimliche Stadt*, 1921, *Der längste Tag*, 1926, *Die Abschiedshand: Letzte Gedichte*, 1949).

### *Hugo Loetscher* (Zurich 1929– )

Being a journalist, Loetscher's view of the world and of his own country is more sanguine than that of most Swiss writers of his post-Frisch/Dürrenmatt generation: perhaps this is because he has seen more of the outside world than they have. His first novel (*Abwasser: Ein Gutachten*, 1963) concerned a sewer-inspector who keeps one of society's most essential yet least valued amenities going; in later novels (*Der Immune*, 1975; *Die Papiere des Immunen*, 1986) he explores the subtle tensions between turning a blind eye and taking active personal responsibility.

### *Friedrich von Logau* (Nimptsch/Silesia 1605–55 Liegnitz)

He was the major epigrammatist of his age (*Deutscher Sinn-Getichte Drey Tausend*, 1654). His reputation survived into the 18thc thanks to Lessing's admiration for his laconic style and enlightened religious and moral attitudes.

### *Daniel Casper von Lohenstein* (Nimptsch/Silesia 1635–83 Breslau)

The metaphor of 'all the world's a stage' is central to his virtuoso oeuvre. He wrote his first tragedy *Ibrahim Bassa* as a schoolboy in Breslau, studied law in Leipzig and Tübingen, travelled to the Netherlands, Switzerland and Hungary and from 1670 to his death held the influential post of Secretary to the city of Breslau. Prior to this he wrote his baroque tragedies *Cleopatra* (1661), *Agrippina* and

*Epicharis* (1665), *Sophonisbe* (1665), celebrating Emperor Leopold I's first wedding, and *Ibrahim Sultan*, on the then highly topical subject of Turkish menace and human corruption, on the occasion of the Emperor's second marriage in 1673. L's *Gedichte* (1685) and his 5000-page novel *Großmütiger Feldherr Arminius* (1689–90), a fiction simultaneously topical and historical, were published posthumously.

### Otto Ludwig
#### (Eisfeld/Werra 1813–65 Dresden)

The ambition of this would-be operatic composer was centred on the stage (see his posthumous *Shakespeare-Studien*). In his powerful domestic tragedy *Der Erbförster* (1850) his psychological presentation of human beings trapped in their milieu anticipates Naturalism, as does *Zwischen Himmel und Erde* (1856), his poetic realist story of a small-town Cain and Abel, a precursor of the modern psychoanalytical novel.

### Ludwig, Prince of Anhalt-Köthen
#### (Dessau 1579–1650 Köthen)

He founded Germany's first language society, the *Fruchtbringende Gesellschaft*, in 1617. Modelled on the Florentine Accademia della Crusca, of which he became a member on his Grand Tour, it became a vital agent in spreading the poetic reforms of Opitz.

### *Georg Lukács (Budapest 1885–1971)

He is remembered for two things: his rehabilitation of Hegelian dialectic within Marxist theory in the brilliant essay, *Geschichte und Klassenbewußtsein* (1923), and his critique of the 'subjectivist' bias in modernist art (especially Musil, Kafka, Joyce, Gide, Beckett) in favour of a more socio-historically sensitive 'critical realism' (eg Tolstoy, Balzac, T and H Mann) but not to be confused with Naturalism or crude 'Socialist Realism' (*Theorie des Romans*, 1920, *Der historische Roman*, 1936, *Essays über den Realismus*, 1948, *Wider den mißverstandenen Realismus*, 1958, *Ästhetik*, 1963).

### Martin Luther
#### (Eisleben 1483–1546 Wittenberg)

L's language, shaped by his own forthright, colourful personality, his training as a theolo-

gian and his teaching experience, lies at the heart of his impact as Germany's greatest religious reformer. As a writer in Latin and German (113 vols of collected works) he did much to change the mentality of his fellow countrymen in the 16thc. His sermons, homilies, open letters, tracts (most notably *Von der Freiheit eines Christenmenschen* and *An den christlichen Adel deutscher Nation*, 1520) and hymns ('Ein feste Burg ist unser Gott', 'Vom Himmel hoch da komm ich her') laid the basis for the German Protestant tradition which has shaped and moulded German literature ever since. His Bible translation (*Neues Testament*, 1522, *Altes Testament*, 1534) was the greatest creative achievement of the age, and helped to transform the Christian believer from passive recipient to active apostle of God's word.

# M

### Erika Mann (Munich 1905–69 Zurich)

The daughter of T Mann, she worked as an actress and cabarettist, married WH Auden in 1935, and became an energetic counter-propagandist of the Third Reich as a radio journalist and war reporter. She was the only woman reporter present at the Nuremberg trials. In 1940 she publ *The Lights Go Down* and *The Other Germany* (with Klaus M).

### *Heinrich Mann (Lübeck 1871–1950 Santa Monica/California)

M felt uncomfortable with his German identity. His early novels satirized the repression and hypocrisy pervading the Wilhelmine bourgeoisie: *Im Schlaraffenland* (1900), *Die kleine Stadt* (1910, Germany's first novel using a montage technique); the trilogy *Die Göttinnen oder Die drei Romane der Herzogin von Assy* (1903); *Professor Unrat oder Das Ende eines Tyrannen* (1905, filmed 1930 as *Der blaue Engel*, starring Marlene Dietrich); the *Kaiserreich*-trilogy (*Der Untertan*, delayed by censorship, caused a sensation in 1918, *Die Armen*, 1917, *Der Kopf*, 1925). A pre-First World War advocate of democratic European co-operation (essays: *Geist und Macht*, 1910, *Diktatur der Vernunft*, 1923, *Sieben Jahre Chronik der Gedanken und Vorgänge*, 1929), M spent 1933 to 1940 in exile in France, working on his 2-part novel *Die Jugend und die Vollendung des Königs Henri Quatre* (1935, 1938), in which his opposition to Nazism is condensed in the idealized figure of his historical Bourbon namesake, Henry IV of France.

### Klaus Mann
(Munich 1906–1949 Cannes)

Son of T Mann, he was a child of his time: his early autobiog *Kind dieser Zeit* (1932) focused on the dehumanizing influences of social and political developments on the individual. These are the theme of his novels *Der fromme Tanz: Das Abenteuerbuch einer Jugend* (1926), *Kindernovelle* (1926), *Alexander: Roman der Utopie* (1929). In *Mephisto: Roman einer Karriere* (1936) M paints a macabre portrait of the Nazi artistic scene; and *Der Vulkan* (1939), his incomparable portrayal of exile, is an apocalyptic picture of a self-destructive civilization: he himself committed suicide. His essays on German writers, i a Benn and Rilke, his *Tagebücher* (1936–49, publ 1990–1) and his autobiog, *Wendepunkt* (1953, as *The Turning Point*, 1942), are key sources for M's time and paradigmatic fate.

### Thomas Mann
(Lübeck 1875–1955 Kilchberg/Zurich)

Mann grew up in the milieu depicted in his family saga *Buddenbrooks* (1901), and put much of his complex self into finely-tuned novellen (*Tristan*, 1903, *Tonio Kröger*, 1903, *Wälsungenblut*, wr 1905, publ 1921, and *Der Tod in Venedig*, 1912). *Königliche Hoheit* (1909) brought out the lighter side of his narrative art. *Betrachtungen eines Unpolitischen* (1918) coincided with a split with his brother, Heinrich M, whose political sympathies he could not share, but *Der Zauberberg* (1924), a novel on the grand scale, probes deeply into conflicts the 20thc had inherited, while the novelle *Mario und der Zauberer* (1930) anticipates those to come. The four 'Joseph' novels *Joseph und seine Brüder* (1933–43: *Die Geschichte Jaakobs*, 1933, *Der junge Joseph*, 1934, *Joseph in Ägypten*, 1936, *Joseph der Ernährer*, 1943) marked an unexpected return to a subject popular in the troubled 17thc, whereas in *Lotte in Weimar* (1939) M sought the essence of Goethe's Weimar. His

lifelong fascination for the artist as creator and victim culminated in *Doktor Faustus* (1947), a novel subtitled *Das Leben des deutschen Tonsetzers Adrian Leverkühn*, which daringly fused Germany's modern cultural crisis with its greatest myth: its composition is charted in *Die Entstehung des Doktor Faustus: Roman eines Romans* (1949). *Der Erwählte* (1951) retold the medieval legend of Gregorius; it appealed less strongly to postwar taste than *Bekenntnisse des Hochstaplers Felix Krull* (1922, 1937, 1954), Mann's final, often funny excursion into a world where, like the artist, the confidence trickster is king.

### Niklas Manuel (Berne *c.*1484–1530)

He used the monogram NMD on his paintings and was often surnamed 'Deutsch'. His masterpiece, a 'Dance of Death', painted for the Dominicans in Berne, has not survived, unlike his plays, which paint a vivid picture of the Reformation seen through contemporary eyes (*Vom Papst und seiner Priesterschaft*, 1524, *Der Ablaßkrämer*, 1525).

### *Herbert Marcuse
(Berlin 1898–1979 Starnberg)

A leading light of the Frankfurt School of Marxist critical theorists, he left Germany on Hitler's rise to power. Denouncing both Western capitalism and Soviet Communism as profoundly dystopian, the one for its provision of 'manipulated comforts' to an anaesthetized population (*One-dimensional Man*, 1964), the other for its betrayal of Marxian humanism (*Soviet Marxism*, 1958), he called for the emancipation of humanity from the 'surplus-repression' inherent in a consumerist *Überfluß-gesellschaft* (affluent society). Aesthetic theory is a central strand in M's philosophy: from his 1922 dissertation on *Der deutsche Künstlerroman* through to his final work, *Die Permanenz der Kunst* (1977), he emphasizes the role of art in the anticipatory release of utopian energies.

### Eugenie Marlitt
(Arnstadt/Thuringia 1825–87)

'*Marlitteratur*', as Fontane described the phenomenon of serialized love stories for the mass market, was created by this former opera singer. Beginning with *Goldelse* (1866), the family weekly *Die Gartenlaube* carried the best-selling novels, such as *Das Geheimnis der alten Mamsell* (1868) and *Reichsgräfin Gisela* (1870), which made her a household name and an immensely wealthy woman.

### Monika Maron (Berlin 1934– )

Stepdaughter of a GDR Interior Minister and herself a party activist, she became identified in the 1980s as the voice of GDR women's protest at the ecological devastation and the repression of its patriarchal regime, documented esp in her novels *Flugasche* (1981) and *Die Überläuferin* (1986). After her emigration to W Germany in 1988 she appeared as the ideal female embodiment of challenge to the unreformed GDR, writing in the columns of *Der Spiegel*. Yet it was *Der Spiegel* that in a much-publicized 'revelation' in 1995 drew attention to M's brief (and inevitable?) involvement with the Stasi in 1976–8.

### Hugo Marti (Basle 1893–1937 Davos)

Editor of the Berne daily *Der Bund*, Marti wrote brilliant articles under the pseudonym 'Bepp' and sensitive, evocative prose (*Das Haus am Haff*, novelle 1922, *Ein Jahresring*, novel 1925, and *Rumänische Mädchen*, novellen 1928) inspired by his experience of other countries. His *Davoser Stundenbuch* (1935) is a countdown to death anticipating his own.

### Kurt Marti (Berne 1921– )

M exemplifies the continuities that characterize Swiss literature. Like Gotthelf he is both a creative writer and a Bernese Protestant parson, a patriot, yet also a critic of his country (*Heil-Vetia: Poetischer Discurs*, 1981), and he shares his feel for the layers and registers of language in German-speaking Switzerland. He is an experimental poet in dialect (*rosa loui*, 1967) and in High German (*Leichenreden*, 1969; *Mein barfüssig Lob*, 1987), a probing theological author (*Das Aufgebot zum Frieden*, 1969), a topical essayist (*Die Schweiz und ihre Schriftsteller – die Schriftsteller und ihre Schweiz*, 1966) and a notable exponent of traditional narrative genres (*Dorfgeschichten*, 1960; *Bürgerliche Geschichten*, 1981; *Nachtgeschichten*, 1987).

### *Karl Marx (Trier 1820–83 London)

The collapse of the Soviet bloc notwithstanding, insights continue to ramify in immensely significant ways. M's diagnosis of the alienation, exploitation and antagonism at the heart of capitalism marks the opening salvo in the socialist project of reclaiming from the 'financial soul' of commodity production the 'soul of man' with its innate impulse towards autonomous creativity. The *Kommunistisches Manifest* (with Engels, 1848) and M's principal work *Das Kapital* (3 vols 1867, 1885, 1895) are perhaps best read against the backdrop of M's earlier, more 'humanistic' texts (especially *Ökonomisch-philosophische Manuskripte*, 1844, not publ until the 1930s), if the charge of economic reductionism is to be tempered. M's distinction between the (socio-economic) 'base' and the (ideologico-cultural) 'superstructure' was to be paradigmatic for subsequent Marxist theoreticians of the aesthetic.

### Friedrich Matthisson
### (Magdeburg 1761–1831 Wörlitz)

His career was advanced by his patroness, Princess Luise of Anhalt-Dessau, whose reader and companion he became. Imitative rather than original, his poetry was appreciated by the generation for whom he wrote it: being a product of Germany's classical golden age, its standard is remarkably high (*Schriften*, 1825–9).

### Emperor Maximilian I
### (Wiener Neustadt 1459–1519 Wels)

Grandfather of Emperor Charles V, he has a double claim on the student of German literary culture: on the one hand, by his marriage to the heiress Mary of Burgundy he linked Austria to the dominant culture of his age and with his own subsequent dynastic marriage policy created the Spanish-Austrian Habsburg connection; on the other, as author of the first New High German novel, *Der Weißkunig* (1514, but first publ in 1775), and of the last medieval verse epic, *Theuerdank* (1517), his literary efforts place him at the cultural watershed between two ages.

## Karl May
### (Erzgebirge 1842–1912 nr Dresden)

Not only Adolf Hitler, but millions of Germans, including Ernst Bloch, regarded May's best-selling adventure stories as their favourite adolescent reading (in some cases adolescence lasts longer than in others). His 'westerns' featured Old Shatterhand, prototype of the technologically advanced European, and Winnetou, the Red Indian 'gentleman' (*Winnetou*, 1893 etc); others successfully transported their readers to his equally vividly evoked Near East.

## Friederike Mayröcker (Vienna 1924– )

An experimental lyricist in the surrealist tradition, she is the prolific author of widely-translated concrete poetry and of a pioneering type of experimental novel. Her 100 publications (to 1995) include: *Ausgewählte Gedichte 1948–78* (1979), *Gute Nacht, guten Morgen: Gedichte 1978–81* (1982), *Winterglück: Gedichte 1982–85* (1986), as well as prose works such as *je ein umwölkter gipfel* (1973), *Die Abschiede* (1980), *mein Herz mein Zimmer mein Name* (1988) and several radio plays, among them *5 Mann Menschen* (with Jandl, 1968, publ 1971).

## Gerhard Meier
### (Niederbipp/Solothurn 1917– )

He worked in a lamp factory until the time was ripe for him to emerge as one of Switzerland's leading contemporary authors and poets (*Das Gras grünt*, 1964, and *Im Schatten der Sonnenblumen*, 1969: poetry collections); a number of prose works such as *Der schnurgerade Kanal* (novel 1977) led up to his acclaimed novel trilogy *Baur und Bindschädler* (1979–85: complete 1987). *Land der Winde* (novel 1990) provides a retrospective farewell to M's towering achievement.

## Wilhelm Meinhold (Netzelkow/Usedom
### 1797–1851 Charlottenburg)

He was a literary pastor of conservative leanings whose works, of unequal quality, include religious and nature poetry (*Gedichte*, 1835) and two highly original works of historical fiction, *Maria Schweidler, die Bernsteinhexe*

(1843) and *Sidonia von Bork, die Klosterhexe* (1847–8) which were widely admired in Pre-Raphaelite circles in England.

## Philipp Melanchthon (Bretten/Palatinate
### 1497–1560 Wittenberg)

This distinguished humanist, praised for his edn of Terence's comedies at 16, Professor of Greek at Luther's Wittenberg at 21, became known as *Praeceptor Germaniae* or 'Germany's teacher'. His contribution to Lutheran theology and the organization of the new church and its educational institutions was systematic and far-reaching. Always a mediator, he devised the justly famous 1530 Augsburg Confession, a milestone in the acceptance of the reformed religion.

## Max Mell (Maribor/Slovenia
### 1882–1971 Vienna)

He was a friend of Hofmannsthal who worked in the tradition of the (Catholic) Styrian popular theatre (*Das Apostelspiel*, 1923, and *Nachfolge-Christi-Spiel*, 1927), and can be seen in terms of H's own postwar efforts to revive a 'European Christian culture'. He harmed his reputation by too readily accepting status as an establishment writer during the Third Reich.

## Moses Mendelssohn
### (Dessau 1729–86 Berlin)

Even across the centuries the attractive personality of this great Enlightenment scholar and critic has the power to move. The model for Lessing's Nathan, and the father of Jewish–Gentile understanding (exemplified in *Jerusalem oder über religiöse Macht und Judentum* and his trn of and commentary on the Pentateuch in 1783 in Hebrew script in order to make the German language more accessible to his fellow Jews), his contribution, at once scholarly and popular, to the German Enlightenment was enormous. It incl his *Philosophische Gespräche* and *Über die Empfindungen* (1755), *Phädon oder über die Unsterblichkeit der Seele* (1767), the work which made him a household name, and his essay: *Über die Frage: was ist Aufklärung?* (1784), which appeared in the *Berlinische Monatsschrift*, one year after Kant's essay on the same topic.

*Wolfgang Menzel* (Waldenburg/Silesia
1798–1873 Stuttgart)
The 'literary pope' of the *biedermeier* era and
the once influential author of *Die deutsche
Literatur* (1828), he suffered the deserved fate
of many such vindictive critics, namely:
oblivion.

*Sophie Mereau* née *Schubart*
(Altenburg 1770–1806 Heidelberg)
Most literary histories enter after her name the
words: 'see Brentano'. Yet her first husband,
Mereau, encouraged her to write the novels
*Das Blüthenalter der Empfindung* (1794) and
*Amanda und Eduard* (1803) and poems
(*Gedichte*, 1800–2). She ed a literary journal,
*Kalathiskos* (1801–2). She married Brentano in
1803 and thereafter concentrated on translat-
ing Boccaccio, Mme de la Fayette, and Italian
and Spanish short stories.

*Conrad Ferdinand Meyer*
(Zurich 1825–98 Kilchberg)
The reputation of this Swiss author has
fluctuated over the years, but he is now recognized as a key figure in the revaluation of the
post-1870 era. His work reflects the complex
cultural relationship between Germany and
Switzerland, though this is less evident in his
*Zwanzig Balladen von einem Schweizer* (1863)
and *Romanzen und Bilder* (1869) than in his
verse epic *Huttens letzte Tage* (1872) or his
historical novel *Jürg Jenatsch* (1874), a study in
17thc Swiss politics told with half an eye on
contemporary developments in Germany. M's
lyric poetry (*Gedichte*, 1882, incl the poems
'Der römische Brunnen', 'Eingelegte Ruder',
'Das Wetterleuchten') suggests analogies to
the French symbolists and influenced Rilke's
*Dinggedichte*. His novellen, like many of their
time, beautify history, at least on the surface.
Yet in *Das Amulett* (1873), *Der Heilige* (1879)
and *Gustav Adolfs Page* (1882), *Das Leiden eines
Knaben* (1883), *Die Hochzeit des Mönchs*
(1884), *Die Richterin* (1885), *Die Versuchung des
Pescara* (1887) and *Angela Borgia* (1891) their
central images suggest the dichotomies of his
characters and of his age.

*E Y* (= *Peter*) *Meyer* (Liestal 1946– )
He made his name in the 1970s with his explo-

rations of the relationship between fiction and
reality in stories (*Ein Reisender in Sachen
Umsturz*, 1972, *Eine entfernte Ähnlichkeit*,
1975) and novels (*In Trubschachen*, 1973, *Die
Rückfahrt*, 1977).

*Malwida von Meysenbug*
(Kassel 1816–1903 Rome)
A committed radical all her life, she had a capacity for friendship which was attested by
men and women as different as Mazzini,
Garibaldi, Nietzsche, Wagner and Lou
Andreas-Salomé. Though not an innovative
thinker, she lived according to her ideals, and
was widely admired, as was shown by the reception given her anon *Memoiren einer
Idealistin* (1876, [43]1927). A second vol, entitled
*Der Lebensabend einer Idealistin* (1898, [7]1907),
showed her still questioning the foundations of
19thc society.

*Agnes Miegel* (Königsberg 1879–1964
Bad Nenndorf )
Her literary origins lay in *Heimat* literature
and ballads, *Gedichte* (1901, 1939 as *Frühe
Gedichte*), *Balladen und Lieder* (1907),
*Geschichten aus Altpreußen* (1926) and
*Herbstgesang* (1932); after 1933 she accepted
membership of the *Dichterakademie* and the
role of major woman author of the Third
Reich, exemplifying many of its central tenets,
incl eugenics, in *Gang in die Dämmerung* (short
stories 1934) and *Ostland* (lyric poetry 1940).

*Johann Martin Miller* (Ulm 1750–1814)
'Utterly devoid of art' was Goethe's verdict on
*Siegwart: Eine Klostergeschichte* (1776), M's
best-selling novel: 2 generations of Germans
evidently did not share his view. M went on to
become a successful popular preacher, leaving
posterity to debate the literary value of his
observant and readable, if lachrymose,
novels.

*Felix Mitterer* (Achenkirch/Tyrol 1948– )
He is the author of critical *Volksstücke* in a
Tyrolean setting, which have been highly successful on stage. They feature the marginalized
in contemporary Tyrol society and in Austria's
past, and move audiences to identify with the
victims, as in *Kein Platz für Idioten* (1977),

*Stigma: Eine Passion* (1982), *Besuchszeit* (1985), *Die wilde Frau* (1986), *Kein schöner Land* (1987), *Die Kinder des Teufels* (1989). He appears to have become the victim of his own calculated destruction of language as a means of communication.

### Eberhardt Möller
(Berlin 1906–72 Bietigheim)

He made his name with semi-historical dramas such as *Rothschild siegt bei Waterloo* (1934) which reflected National Socialist thinking and brought him Goebbels's commission to write a drama for the 1936 Olympic Games in Berlin: *Das Frankenburger Würfelspiel*. M handles his 16thc subject impressively in the manner of Georg Kaiser, whom the Nazis had silenced.

### Meta or Margareta Moller
(Hamburg 1728–58)

Klopstock's wife and the author of a variety of writings, publ posthumously by K as *Hinterlassene Schriften* (1759), is perhaps unique in the history of German literature. Highly educated, her personality and family circumstances enabled her to enjoy an untypical measure of independence. Her vigorous and intimate letters, spontaneous in expression yet studied in intention, exemplify a new, more flexible relationship to the German lang, closer to its spoken form.

### Alfred Mombert
(Karlsruhe 1872–1942 Winterthur)

He conjured up a cosmic vision of the origin and destiny of man in lyric and epic verse (*Der Glühende*, 1896, *Die Schöpfung*, 1897, *Der Denker*, 1901) and his main work, *Aeon* (1907–11), a dramatic trilogy. A Jewish writer deeply influenced by Nietzsche, M refused to leave Germany after 1933 and went on writing. He was rescued and taken to Switzerland just in time to die a natural death.

### Christian Morgenstern
(Munich 1871–1914 Merano)

Like Lewis Carroll and Hilaire Belloc, M was one of a relatively select band to recognize the ability of humour to engender delight in the possibilities of language. He exploited the potential of German in two famous books of

nonsense verse, the *Galgenlieder* (1905) and *Palmström* (1910).

### Irmtraud Morgner
(Chemnitz 1933–90 Berlin)

Perhaps being a train driver's daughter gave her the idea of making a train driver the hero of *Die wundersamen Reisen Gustav des Weltfahrers* (1972), the first of her satirical fantasies on GDR life. Her major feminist works are the picaresque novel *Leben und Abenteuer der Trobadora Beatriz nach Zeugnissen ihrer Spielfrau Laura* (1974) and its grotesque sequel, *Amanda: Ein Hexenroman* (1983).

### Daniel Georg Morhof
(Wismar 1639–91 Lübeck)

He was a wide-ranging scholar at the new university of Kiel, who wrote mainly in Latin. His main work in German bore the imposing title *Unterricht von der teutschen Sprache und Poesie, deren Ursprung, Fortgang und Lehrsätze* (1682, 1700) and was the first comprehensive account of Germany's language and literature.

### Eduard Mörike
(Ludwigsburg 1804–75 Stuttgart)

He was the author of two major fictional studies of artistic creativity, the post-Romantic artist novel, *Maler Nolten* (1832) and the novelle *Mozart auf der Reise nach Prag* (1856), one of the finest of its kind in German literature. He retired early from being a country parson (1843) to devote himself to literature, excelling in genres favoured by contemporaries, such as the fairy tale (*Das Stuttgarter Hutzelmännchen*, 1853), the neo-classical epic in hexameters (*Idylle von Bodensee*, 1846), and its whimsical modern counterpart (*Der alte Turmhahn*, 1852), while giving the term 'idyll' a new and highly-charged meaning (as in his incomparable poem, 'Die schöne Buche'). M was an exquisite craftsman and his work is distinguished by its unique sense of rhythm, play with intertextual allusions, vowel colours and sense of humour, ironic and relaxed by turns.

### Karl Philipp Moritz
(Hameln 1756–93 Berlin)

His 'psychological relentlessness' is evident in

*Anton Reiser* (1785–90), aptly subtitled 'ein psychologischer Roman' and a masterly autobiog account of its author's childhood. It was written concurrently with his 10-vol *Magazin für Erfahrungsseelkunde* (1783–93), a key document of late 18thc anthropology. To Goethe M was 'like a younger brother, whom fate, which blessed and favoured me, neglected and ill-used', and it was thanks to Goethe that M publ his important contribution to aesthetics, the essay *Über die bildliche Nachahmung des Schönen* (1788) and gained a post in the Berlin Academy of Arts.

### Johann Michael Moscherosch
(nr Kehl/Alsace 1601–69 Worms)
In the *Wunderliche und wahrhafftige Gesichte Philanders von Sittewalt* (1642–3), an allegorical and visionary novel based on Quevedo's *Sueños* (1635) but adapted to contemporary Germany, M produced the most influential satire of his age. He was probably the author of the first illustrated account of the 'typical German', in the doggerel *Der Teutsche Michel* (*c*.1641).

### Friedrich Carl von Moser
(Stuttgart 1723–98 Ludwigsburg)
The model for Philo in Goethe's novel *Wilhelm Meisters Lehrjahre*, he was an enlightened civil servant who made a wide-ranging contribution to the pre-nationalistic debate on the political future of Germany with *Der Herr und der Diener* (1759), a critique of the absolutism of princes and a revaluation of the moral and practical role of their ministers and advisers. His political ideas are further developed in *Patriotische Briefe* (1767) and *Von dem Deutschen National-Geist* (1765) and, more obliquely, his political fables *Der Hof in Fabeln* (1762) and his prose poem in 6 cantos, *Daniel in der Löwen-Grube* (1763), in which the prophet Daniel figures as the ideal counsellor to a king.

### Justus Möser (Osnabrück 1720–94)
One of the fathers of German journalism, he used his pen in a manner not previously associated with middle-class politicians in Germany, that is with wit, cogency and style, to win support for the policies of his paternalist state of Osnabrück. He is best known for two forward-looking and thought-provoking works: *Harlekin, oder Verteidigung des Grotesk-Komischen* (1761), his rebuttal of Gottsched's no-nonsense rationalism, and *Patriotische Phantasien* (1774–86), in which M drew attention to the interdependence of economic and political factors.

### Luise Mühlbach
(Neubrandenburg 1814–73 Berlin)
She spotted a market for historical novels and successfully targeted her bourgeois readership with almost 300 patriotic works featuring kings and princes such as Frederick II, Joseph II and Kaiser Wilhelm I.

### Heinrich Mühlpfort (Breslau 1639–81)
A product of the Breslau Elisabethanäum and a lawyer by profession, he was a successful writer in the Hoffmannswaldau manner whose poems were of the kind that circulated anon among friends during his lifetime. A collected edn appeared in 1686–7.

### Adam Müller (Berlin 1779–1829 Vienna)
Göttingen played a key role in shaping this Romantic political thinker, Catholic convert and co-ed of Kleist's *Phönix*, in which his *Dramatische Poesie und Kunst* appeared. M's *Die Elemente der Staatskunst*, the key document of early 19thc conservative thought, appeared in 1808–9. Settling in Metternich's Vienna, he gave his celebrated *12 Reden über die Beredsamkeit und deren Verfall in Deutschland* in 1811 (publ 1816), his classic study of the roles of listening and hearing in private and public life.

### Friedrich 'Maler' Müller
(Bad Kreuznach 1749–1825 Rome)
He was discovered by *Sturm und Drang* writers as a 'child of nature' whose original talent was evident in his *Balladen* (1776) and his idylls in the tradition of Theocritus, *Die Schaaf-Schur* (1775) and *Das Nußkernen* (*c*.1781, publ 1811). He publ Part I of his *magnum opus*, *Fausts Leben*, in 1778 before going into permanent exile in Rome, where he painted and worked as a tourist guide, completing his *Faust* drama in 1825, only to have it rejected by Goethe's publisher, Cotta.

## Heiner Müller

(Eppendorf nr Chemnitz 1929–95 Berlin)
Despite the fact that he treated approved contemporary socialist themes and gained prizes for his plays such as *Traktor* (1975), *Die Umsiedlerin oder Das Leben auf dem Lande* (1961), *Die Bauern* (1976), *Der Lohndrücker* (1958), *Die Korrektur* (1958), *Der Bau* (1980), Müller experienced difficulty in having them perf in the GDR, and publication often came years after completion. The same applied to his *Lehrstücke* in Brecht's manner (i a *Mauser*, 1975) and his equally controversial, deeply pessimistic plays on classic themes (*Philoktet*, 1968, *Macbeth*, 1972, *Hamletmaschine*, 1979). M's best-known play, *Germania Tod in Berlin* (wr 1956–71, 1978), challenged the hope of establishing a socialist Germany. Ironically, his determination after the *Wende* to restore the tradition of socialist drama on the Berlin stage in his capacity as director of the Schauspielhaus was cut short by his death just before his planned staging of his last drama, *Germania 3 – Gespenster am Toten Mann*. It was publ in 1996.

## Herta Müller

(Nitzkydorf/Romania 1953– )
She chronicled life among the German minority in Ceaucescu's Romania in lyrical prose writings such as *Niederungen* (1982), *Drückender Tango* (1984) and *Der Mensch ist ein großer Fasan auf der Welt* (short stories 1986). She finally managed to emigrate to Germany, where she offered a new perspective on life in her estranged 'motherland', the Federal Republic (*Reisende auf einem Bein*, short stories 1989) and novels (*Der Fuchs war damals schon der Jäger*, 1992, *Herztier*, 1995).

## Wilhelm Müller (Dessau 1794–1827)

He earned his nickname 'Greek Müller' for his *Lieder der Griechen* (3 vols 1821–4) and *Missolunghi* (1826), which echo Byron's enthusiastic response to the Greek war of independence and his death in that cause. M championed political liberty in a period of reaction: a darker side of his personality is evident in his lyrics, which are often grouped in cycles such as *Die Winterreise*, from *Gedichte aus den hinterlassenen Papieren eines reisenden Waldhornisten* (1821–4), a title which reflects his affinities with Eichendorff.

## Börries, Baron von Münchhausen

(Hildesheim 1874–1945 Windischleuba/
Thuringia)
He was popular because he adapted to the taste of his day: thus his *Balladen und ritterliche Lieder* (1908) praise old-world chivalry and were popular among members of the youth movement. His initial enthusiasm for National Socialism gave way to horror at the Holocaust (he had denounced such atrocities in his early *Balladen*, 1901): he committed suicide as the Allies drew near.

## Theodor Mundt

(Berlin 1808–61 Hamburg)
A member of the *Junges Deutschland*, author of *Moderne Lebenswirren* (1834) and later husband of Luise Mühlbach, he proclaimed the emancipation of women and the flesh in his novel *Madonna* (1835). Its heroine bears a resemblance to Charlotte Stieglitz, whose suicide, designed to inspire her husband's 'muse', was a *cause célèbre* in 1832. The novel and his *Charlotte Stieglitz, ein Denkmal* (1835) won him notoriety and a ban by the Prussian censorship.

## Thomas Murner

(Oberehnheim/Alsace 1475–1537)
He got scant reward for entering the Reformation controversy by translating *Assertio septem sacramentorum*, Henry VIII's riposte to Luther's *De captivitate*, but made his own rich contribution to it with his sprawling but brilliant mock epic *Von dem großen lutherischen Narren* (1522). A devoted Franciscan from the age of 15 and a fine satirist in the Brantian manner in his pre-Reformation days (*Narrenbeschwörung* and *Der Schelmen Zunft*, both 1512; *Die Geuchmatt*, 1515), he was the only major German writer of his generation not to go over to the Lutheran side.

## Adolf Muschg

(Zollikon/Switzerland 1934– )
A Germanist at the world-famous Swiss polytechnic, the ETH, and as such a particularly self-conscious writer, he has written dramas, incl one on Gottfried Keller and one on

Ferdinand Raimund, several vols of short stories featuring problematical human relationships, novels which explore group relationships in the contemporary world, a detective story, *Albissers Grund* (1974), and a monumental Parsifal novel, *Der rote Ritter* (1993). Like Frisch, M has offered his compatriots a thoughtful and provocative exploration of 'Swissness': *Die Schweiz am Ende: Am Ende die Schweiz* (1990).

### Walter Muschg
#### (Witikon/Zurich 1898–1965 Basle)

Stepbrother of the writer Adolf M, he wrote two scholarly works which made a profound contribution to the sensibility of postwar readers. His *Tragische Literaturgeschichte* (1948) proclaimed his belief in the inherent morality of great art; *Die Zerstörung der deutschen Literatur* (1956) diagnosed the consequences of the destructive impact of the Third Reich on the German language.

### *Robert Musil
#### (Klagenfurt 1880–1942 Geneva)

'We have gained in terms of reality and lost in terms of dream,' laments the narrator of *Der Mann ohne Eigenschaften* (3 vols 1930, 1933, 1943), the Austrian M's massive (and unfinished) novel. Set in 1913 Vienna, it depicts a society clamped between the anachronistic trappings of (Austro-Hungarian) empire and the materialistic, positivistic imperatives of modernity. An earlier novel, *Die Verwirrungen des Zöglings Törless* (1906), is memorable not just as an account of sadistic bullying at school but also for its daring juxtaposition of the physical and metaphysical in the sensitive adolescent figure of Törless. Like his novel, M's stories (*Vereinigungen*, 1911, *Drei Frauen*, 1924, *Die Amsel*, 1928) show a striking degree of narrative self-reflexivity, while his training in engineering, psychology, philosophy and mathematics lends authority and texture to his work.

## N

### Marie Nathusius
#### (Magdeburg 1817–57 Neinstadt/Harz)

The name of this poet and novelist became synonymous with Christian fiction for girls. Her successful strategy in *Tagebuch eines armen Fräuleins* (1854), *Rückerinnerungen eines Mädchens* (1855) and *Elisabeth: Eine Geschichte, die nicht mit der Heirat endet* (1858, [14]1886) of making her reader identify with her poor but thoroughly self-assured heroines was widely imitated and exploited.

### Benedikte Naubert
#### (Leipzig 1756–1819)

She wrote some 50 historical, 'family' and sentimental novels in which women were seen to play a key role, and may have influenced the historical novel in Germany through her technique of locating the story of an individual life against a background of contemporary conflict. She was a prolific contributor to literary journals for women such as the *Frauenzimmer Almanach* and *Journal für deutsche Frauen* and to those aimed at the general public, such as Cotta's *Zeitung für die elegante Welt*.

### Johann Nepomuk Nestroy
#### (Vienna 1801–62 Graz)

N, 70 of whose plays survive, made his name with the 'magic farce' *Der böse Geist Lumpacivagabundus oder Das liederliche Kleeblatt* and *Robert der Teuxel* (1833), a parody of a fashionable grand opera by Meyerbeer. These were followed by a satirical Viennese farce with an experimental 2-storey staging, *Zu ebener Erde und erster Stock oder Die Launen des Glückes* (1835) and its sequel, *Eine Wohnung ist zu vermieten* (1837). In the 1840s N's work was dominated by his most famous 'classic' farces such as *Der Talisman* (1840), *Das Mädl aus der Vorstadt* (1841), *Einen Jux will er sich machen* (1842), *Der Zerrissene* (1844) and *Der Unbedeutende* (1846); during the 1848–9 revolution his satirical comedy *Freiheit in Krähwinkel* (1848) was perf uncut by the censor. Parodies (of Hebbel: *Judith und Holofernes*, 1849, of Wagner: *Tannhäuser*, 1857, *Lohengrin*, 1859) were followed by two of his finest farces,

*Frühere Verhältnisse* and *Häuptling Abendwind* (1862), a skit on colonialism provocatively based on the Atreus legend.

### Benjamin Neukirch (Reinecke/Silesia 1665–1729 Ansbach)

He tr Fénelon's *Télémaque* and produced a socially useful manual on letter-writing, *Unterricht von Teutschen Briefen* (1707) but, an able versifier himself, he owes his place in literary histories to the so-called *Neukirchsche Sammlung* (1695–1727), the 7 vols of which illustrate the evolution of German verse from the high baroque to Augustan urbanity.

### Friedrich Nicolai (Berlin 1733–1811)

A friend of Lessing and Moses Mendelssohn and leading representative of Enlightenment rationalism, he was a major contributor to normative aesthetics in Germany. He helped to institutionalize literary criticism with his *Briefe, die Neueste Litteratur betreffend* (1759–65) and *Allgemeine deutsche Bibliothek* (1765–1805). He was no stranger to public controversy, as was shown by the reception given to *Das Leben und die Meinungen des Herrn Magister Sebaldus Nothanker* (1773–6), his novel attacking religious orthodoxy, and for his send-up of Goethe's *Werther* in *Freuden des jungen Werthers* (1775). His 12-vol *Beschreibung einer Reise durch Deutschland und die Schweiz im Jahre 1781* (1783–96) is a rich source of statistical information filtered through his rationalist perspective.

### Ernst Elias Niebergall (Darmstadt 1815–43)

He wrote two successful comedies in the dialect of his home town in Hesse, most notably *Datterich* (1841) which, with its pioneering episodic form, has something in common with Büchner's approach in *Woyzeck*.

### *Friedrich Nietzsche (Röcken nr Lützen 1844–1900 Weimar)

'I am no man, I am dynamite,' wrote the philosopher in his autobiography, *Ecce Homo*, completed shortly before the mental breakdown from which he never recovered. The 'prophet of European nihilism', he instigated a revaluation of all values (*Jenseits von Gut und Böse*, 1886, *Zur Genealogie der Moral*, 1887) and a relentless assault on the 'slave morality' of Christianity, which he saw as fundamentally at odds with his tragic philosophy of life (*Also sprach Zarathustra*, 1883–5, publ 1892 in full, *Der Antichrist*, 1888, publ 1895); he set out the more optimistic facets of his new philosophy in *Die fröhliche Wissenschaft* (1882). N's retrieval of the paradigmatic Greek antithesis of Apollonian and Dionysian elements (*Die Geburt der Tragödie aus dem Geiste der Musik*, 1872) strongly influenced the aesthetic bearings i a of T Mann. He cultivated a pungent, aphoristic style which rendered his texts deceptively accessible and hence vulnerable to grotesque oversimplifications at the hands of National Socialist ideologues and misunderstandings by unwitting readers.

### Novalis (= Friedrich von Hardenberg) (Oberwiederstadt/Mansfeld 1772–1801 Weißenfels)

He distinguished himself as a law student at Jena, Leipzig and Wittenberg, and then took further practical qualifications at the school of mining in Freiberg in Saxony. This promising career was cut short by tuberculosis in 1800. N packed intense intellectual and emotional experience into his short adult life, recording it in aphorisms and 'fragments' (*Blütenstaub*, 1798) and the six *Hymnen an die Nacht* (1802), a reinvention of Germany's hymn traditions inspired by his love for his 12-year-old fiancée Sophie von Kühn, who died in 1797. The long essay *Die Christenheit oder Europa* (1797: not publ until 1826) evoked a picture of medieval Christian civilization which marked the 19thc deeply, while the unfinished novels *Die Lehrlinge von Sais* and *Heinrich von Ofterdingen* (both 1802) confirmed German Romanticism's anti-classical aesthetic distinction between perfection and completion. N's equally far-reaching contributions to the movement's philosophical, religious and psychological thinking were ensured by the efforts of his posthumous eds, F Schlegel and Tieck, who recognized his unique status and perpetuated his image as youthful magus and romantic icon.

# O

### *Adam Oehlenschläger*
### (Copenhagen 1799–1850)

The career of this major Danish Romantic writer reminds us of the role of Denmark in the German literary landscape. Strongly influenced by German Romanticism, his works, many of them rediscoveries of his Scandinavian heritage, appeared in an 18-vol German edn in 1829–30. Sometimes O wrote in German, notably his Renaissance artist-drama *Correggio* (1809) based on his own relationship to Goethe, whose *Hermann und Dorothea* he tr into Danish. His *Lebenserinnerungen* (1850–1) are a useful source for the temper of the age.

### *Wilhelm Oertel*
### (Horn/Hunsrück 1798–1867 Wiesbaden)

He agreed with his many satisfied readers that *Friedel: Eine Geschichte aus dem Volksleben* (1845) was his best book. His stories for ordinary readers (often publ under the pseudonym WO von Horn) dealt with topical mid-19thc issues, promoted Christian family life and made him a best-seller. Many were tr into English.

### *Rudolf Oeser* (Gießen 1807–59 Lindheim)

He based his most popular tale on local fact: *Anna, die Blutegelhändlerin* (1842) tells of a young leech-gatherer's tribulations and teaches its readers the rewards of stoicism and endurance. It was considered a suitable gift for domestic servants.

### *Martin Opitz* later *von Boberfeld*
### (Bunzlau 1597–1639 Danzig)

When still at school he wrote a treatise (in Latin) on the German language (*Aristarchus*, 1617), a subject which was to have a formative influence on his career as teacher, personal secretary, imperial poet laureate, diplomat and court historiographer. In addition to his immensely influential poetics (*Buch von der deutschen Poeterey* or *Prosodia Germanica*, 1624, and numerous later edns) and his own wide-ranging verse in a variety of genres (*Acht Bücher Deutscher Poematum*, 1625, and other

later collections), he made a vital contribution to German literary history by editing the now lost ms. of the 11thc *Annolied*. Everywhere he went, he came back with work that made him famous: in Denmark in 1621 he wrote his sombre *TrostGedichte in Widerwertigkeit deß Krieges* (1633), in the bucolic simplicity of Romania his colourful discursive poem *Zlatna, Oder von der Ruhe des Gemütes* (1623). Contemporaries were unanimous in regarding him as the 'father' of modern German poetry: he is a much more interesting figure than conventional literary history would suggest.

### *Carl von Ossietzky*
### (Hamburg 1889–1938 Berlin)

Before 1914 he was attacking German militarism; as a soldier in 1917 he protested against the continuation of the war. A radical democratic journalist in the Weimar years and briefly secretary to the Peace Movement, he became ed of Tucholsky's *Weltbühne* in 1926. His attack on Germany's illicit rearmament led to imprisonment in 1932 and 1934; Nobel Peace Prize winner in 1936, he was released under international pressure to die in a Berlin hospital.

### *Luise Otto-Peters*
### (Meissen 1819–95 Leipzig)

The co-founder of the first German professional organization for women, the *Allgemeine deutsche Frauenverein* (1865), and ed of its journal, *Neue Bahnen*, O wrote some 50 novels incl *Schloss und Fabrik* (1846) and fought a protracted but losing battle with the censor to edit her *Frauen-Zeitung* (1849–52), a political journal for women. *Drei verhängnisvolle Jahre*, her autobiog account of the 1848 revolution, appeared in 1867.

# P

### *Oskar Panizza*
### (Kissingen 1853–1921 Bayreuth)

The son of a Protestant mother in Catholic Bavaria, and ardent exponent of modernism in Munich and an energetic supporter of its leading periodical, Conrad's *Die Gesellschaft*, Panizza, a qualified medical doctor, systematically (and blasphemously) exploited Catholic iconography and imagery, directing his ire against the papacy (*Die unbefleckte Empfängnis der Päpste*, 1893, and *Das Liebeskonzil*, 1894, a cabaret-type drama) and against the state and esp Wilhelm II, whom he saw as the 'enemy of mankind' (*Parisjana: deutsche Verse aus Paris*, 1899). For doing so the paranoid author served prison sentences, lost his job and worldly goods, and was confined to an asylum, attributing his fate to the Kaiser (*Selbstbiographie*, 1904). Some of his powerful stories (*Dämmerungsstücke*, 1890) were publ posthumously (*Der Korsettenfritz*, 1981; *Die Menschenfabrik*, 1984).

### Betty Paoli (= Babette Elisabeth Glück)
(Vienna 1815–94 Baden/Vienna)
Allegedly the illegitimate daughter of a high Hungarian aristocrat and companion i a to Princess Schwarzenberg (both of whom Stifter portrayed in *Der Nachsommer*), Paoli wrote well-received reviews and essays for Austrian newspapers and became, in Grillparzer's view, Austria's leading lyric poet with *Nach dem Gewitter* (1843), *Die Welt und mein Auge* (1844) and *Neueste Gedichte* (1870). P was the friend and mentor of Ebner-Eschenbach, who ed her *Gedichte: Auswahl und Nachlaß* in 1895.

### Paracelsus (= Theophrastus Bombast von Hohenheim) (Maria Einsiedeln 1493/4–1541 Salzburg)
A peripatetic scholar like Faust himself, whose massive oeuvre was wr almost wholly in German, he fascinated contemporaries by his empirical, anthropocentric approach to knowledge, incl medicine. A lay theologian, he opposed the death penalty and war, and was in the forefront of modern methods of healing.

### Johann Pauli (?–after 1520)
His name is synonymous with *Schimpf und Ernst* (1522), a collection of some 700 anecdotes drawn from many sources and designed by this Franciscan preacher as a compendium of apt illustrations of every aspect of the human being and society as he and his generation saw them. Its appearance at the outset of the Reformation gives it added interest.

### Friedrich Christoph Perthes
(Rudolstadt 1772–1843 Gotha)
The son-in-law of Matthias Claudius, he played an important role in the German literary market as co-founder of the *Börsenverein des deutschen Buchhandels* (1825), the professional organization of the book trade, and author of an influential report, *Der deutsche Buchhandel als Bedingung des Daseyns einer deutschen Literatur* (1816).

### Leo Perutz (Prague 1882–1957 Bad Ischl)
In his novel *Zwischen neun und neun* (1918), he wrote one of the best-sellers of early post-World War I Germany. His post-World War II novel, *Nachts unter der steinernen Brücke* (1953), is an illuminating and complex portrayal by the returned exile of the Prague Jewish literary circle to which he had belonged.

### Johann Heinrich Pestalozzi
(Zurich 1746–1827 Brugg/Aargau)
He was one of the most famous and influential educational thinkers and practitioners of modern times. In his widely-read novel *Lienhard und Gertrud* (1781–7) and his major theoretical writings, such as *Meine Nachforschungen über den Gang der Natur in der Entwicklung des Menschengeschlechts* (1797), he elaborated his holistic concept of education as the key to a well-functioning society.

### Ida Pfeiffer (Vienna 1797–1858)
Acknowledged by Alexander von Humboldt both for her intrepidness as a traveller and for the scientific objects she collected, P was the best-selling author of *Eine Frauenfahrt um die Welt* (1851; *Meine zweite Weltreise*, 1856), describing an expedition financed by the sales of her *Reise einer Wienerin in das Heilige Land* (1844).

### Karoline Pichler, née Greiner
(Vienna 1769–1843)
She was a pianist taught by Haydn and Mozart and author of some 50 works, of which the most successful were her patriotic historical dramas and her novels (*Agathokles*, an Austrian Catholic 'answer' to Gibbon's *Decline and Fall of the Roman Empire*, 1808), wr during and in the aftermath of Austria's humiliation by Napoleon. Her salon was a meeting place

for intellectuals, artists and civil servants in Restoration Austria and her memoirs *Denkwürdigkeiten aus meinem Leben* (1844) an informative source.

### Kurt Pinthus (Erfurt 1886–1975 Marbach)

He was the creator of an important 20thc text, the Expressionist anthology *Menschheitsdämmerung: Symphonie jüngster Dichtung* (1920), which he reissued in 1959. P edited Büchner and Hasenclever and film texts of Expressionist writers, such as Lasker-Schüler.

### Caritas Pirckheimer
#### (Eichstätt 1467–1532 Nuremberg)

She was an exemplary representative of the *virgo docta* or learned virgin. An abbess from 1503 until her death, she corresponded with, among others, the humanist poet Celtis. Her *Denkwürdigkeiten* (1528) are a monument to the quality of her mind and her courageous life in Reformation Nuremberg.

### Willibald Pirckheimer
#### (Eichstätt 1470–1530 Nuremberg)

Erasmus called Willibald, brother of Caritas P, the 'ornament of Germany'; the Emperor Maximilian referred to him as the Reich's 'most learned doctor'. A diplomat and humanist, P was a key figure of the German Renaissance, known for his distinguished trns and commentaries on classical antiquity, and as the author of neo-Latin and German works; his greatest achievement is probably his topical account of the Swiss War (*Bellum Helveticum*, 1519) in which he had participated as commanding officer of the Nuremberg contingent.

### Erwin Piscator
#### (nr Wetzlar 1893–1966 Starnberg)

An experimental poet and one of the 20thc's most original stage directors, he worked in the 1920s and early 1930s with Wedekind, Sternheim, Toller, and in Moscow with Seghers. Founder in 1920 of the Proletarian Theatre in Berlin and influential proponent of the stage as tribune, he aimed, by contrast with Brecht, at the emotional identification of actor and public in the service of the proletarian

cause. The influence of his political concept of theatre bore fruit in his teaching in US exile (Tennessee Williams and Arthur Miller were students of his) and in the dramas of Hochhuth, Weiss and Kipphardt, which he produced in Berlin in the 1960s.

### August, Graf von Platen-Hallermünde
#### (Ansbach 1796–1835 Syracuse)

Modern students of literature are wary of pathos, which may explain the unjustifiable neglect of one of 19thc Germany's great poets, a master of form and renewer of the sonnet, ghazal, idyll, ballad, classical ode, *terza rima* etc, who helped 'discover' Venice as part of the German literary landscape, not least for Nietzsche and T Mann, in *Sonette aus Venedig* (1824), and who anticipated Mann's aestheticism with his key poetic statement, the poem 'Tristan'. P also wrote satirical comedies (*Die verhängnisvolle Gabel*, 1826, *Der romantische Oedipus*, 1829), political poetry and diaries (publ 1896–1900).

### Ulrich Plenzdorf
#### (Berlin-Kreuzberg 1934–  )

A graduate of the GDR film university at Babelsberg, he won fame for his Goethe travesty, *Die neuen Leiden des jungen W.* (1972–3, as drama 1974), modelled on JD Salinger's *Catcher in the Rye* (1951), which did much to win respect for GDR literature in the W, as well as to politicize young readers at home; among his many films are *Die Legende von Paul und Paula* (1974) and *Buridans Esel* (1986), based on de Bruyn's novel.

### Theodor Pli(e)vier
#### (Berlin 1892–1955 Avegno/Ticino)

He worked his way up, seeing naval service before becoming involved with anarchist groups: *Des Kaisers Kulis* (1930) was the major (critical) naval novel to come out of the 1914–18 war. *Der Kaiser ging, die Generale blieben* (1932) took as its subject the failed 1918 revolution. An exile throughout the Nazi period, P returned to (Eastern) Germany with his bestselling novel *Stalingrad* (1945), expanded to the trilogy *Der große Krieg im Osten* (1966) with *Moskau* (1952) and *Berlin* (1954). No other German author made such a literary success of both world wars or was prepared to face up to their implications in such a readable way.

### Wilhelm von Polenz
(Oberlausitz 1861–1903 Bautzen)

A novelist whose work covers a wide range of contemporary issues (*Sühne*, 1890, *Der Pfarrer von Breitendorf*, 1893, *Thekla Lüdekind*, 1899), Polenz was a leading Naturalist whose masterpiece *Der Büttnerbauer* (1895), with its powerful evocation of its milieu, owes much of its force to the agrarian depression in Germany (1875–*c*.1900) and the social impact of industrial capitalism on its peasantry, to which it is dedicated.

### Wolfgang Caspar Printz
(Waldturm 1641–1717 Sorau)

Printz broke off his mathematical studies in 1661 to become a professional musician. After a visit to Italy he settled in Sorau as its cantor for half a century. His music has vanished, not so his musicological writings (his *Historische Beschreibung der Sing- und Kling-kunst*, 1690, was the first history of music in German) or his novels. An early work bore the title *Satyrischer Komponist* (1676): it could also serve for the three picaresque 'musical novels' he publ in 1690–1.

### Robert Eduard Prutz (Stettin 1816–72)

He worked on the *Hallische Jahrbücher* and became a prominent *Vormärz* critic and political poet – both his *Gedichte: Neue Sammlung* (1843) and the comedy *Die politische Wochenstube* (1845) are close in manner and content to contemporary broadsheet cartoons; his novel *Das Engelchen* (1851) treats the 1844 Silesian weavers' revolt. He wrote a much-cited history of literature and a *Geschichte des deutschen Journalismus* (1845).

### Prince Hermann Ludwig von Pückler-Muskau (Muskau/Oberlausitz 1785–1871 Branitz nr Cottbus)

He was a gifted landscape architect and consciously eccentric author of the anon bestseller *Briefe eines Verstorbenen* (4 vols 1830–2); its extensive critical account of life in Britain and Ireland in the 1820s established his fame

and popularized the travelogue as a genre. *Vorletzter Weltgang von Semilasso* (1835) and *Semilasso in Afrika* (1836) recount his travels in Africa.

### Samuel von Pufendorf
(Chemnitz 1632–94 Berlin)

He was the first professor of natural and international law in Germany (at Heidelberg). In the (Latin) work for which he is best known, *The State of the German Empire* (1667), he identified the idiosyncratic character of its constitution and government. P's importance lies in the influence he exercised on subsequent German political thought and practice with his rationalist apologia for the absolutist state, stressing as it did the protective function it exercised over its citzens.

# R

### Wilhelm Raabe
(Brunswick 1831–1910)

He became a professional writer after the success of his early novel, *Die Chronik der Sperlingsgasse* (1856), and identified himself to a unique degree with 19thc Germany – its economy and social progress and its post-1871 self-contradictory retrogressions – portraying it with increasing narrative sophistication over some 40 novels and stories: *Der Hungerpastor* (1864), *Abu Telfan, oder Die Heimkehr vom Mondgebirge* (1868), *Der Schüdderump* (1870), *Horacker* (1876), *Alte Nester* (1880), *Pfisters Mühle* (1884), *Das Odfeld* (1888), *Die Akten des Vogelsangs* (1896), *Hastenbeck* (1899) etc. A favourite device is his use of the (eccentric) perspective of the outsider, most notably in his masterpiece, *Stopfkuchen: Eine See- und Mordgeschichte* (1891). R's interest for students of modernity lies in his artistry in writing consciously 'literary' texts and teasingly involving the alert and informed reader in their reconstruction.

### Gottlieb Wilhelm Rabener
(nr Leipzig 1714–71 Dresden)

His much-discussed *Sammlung satirischer Schriften* (1751–5) spanned a variety of genres and advocated the view that manners, not political abuses, should be the proper object of satire – a view challenged by his successors, the generation of the *Sturm und Drang*.

### Ferdinand Raimund
### (Vienna 1790–1836 Pottenstein)

He worked for the theatre from his boyhood, aspiring despite a speech impediment to be a tragic actor. His success as the violinist Adam Kratzerl in Gleich's *Die Musikanten vom hohen Markt* started his successful career at the Leopoldstädter theatre in roles blending humour with pathos, such as he created so successfully in his own 8 comedies: *Der Barometermacher auf der Zauberinsel* (1823), *Der Diamant des Geisterkönigs* (1824), *Das Mädchen aus der Feenwelt oder Der Bauer als Millionär* (1826), *Moisasurs Zauberfluch* (1827), *Die gefesselte Fantasie* (1828), *Der Alpenkönig und der Menschenfeind* (1828), *Unheilbringende Zauberkrone* (1829), *Der Verschwender* (1834). A comic entertainer who suffered from depression, he shot himself believing he had contracted rabies.

### Karl Wilhelm Ramler
### (Colberg 1725–98 Berlin)

A translator and imitator of Roman poetry (*Oden*, 1767), he was a respected if pedantic authority on metrics in late 18thc Germany who made a useful contribution to the evolution of German national literature in his programmatic edn of Friedrich von Logau's *Sinngedichte* (with *Lessing*, 1759). His own lighter verse appeared in *Lieder der Deutschen* (1766), a 2nd edn of which appeared with melodies in 1767–8.

### Leopold (1865– von) Ranke
### (Unstrut 1795–1886 Berlin)

He is associated with a concept of history based on the systematic critical analysis of archival sources, both in research and teaching, exemplifed in his early *Geschichte der romanischen und germanischen Völker von 1494 bis 1514* (1824) and esp in his famous *Die römischen Päpste, ihre Kirche und ihr Staat im 16. und 17. Jahrhundert* (1834–6), but also in his multi-vol *Deutsche Geschichte im Zeitalter der Reformation* (1839–47) and his *Neun Bücher Preußischer Geschichte* (1847–8). Later he

found time to turn to 17thc French and British history. His projected history of the world did not get much beyond the fall of Constantinople, and its last 3 vols were publ posthumously.

### Walther Rathenau (Berlin 1867–1922)

The model for Dr Paul Arnheim in Musil's *Der Mann ohne Eigenschaften*, he was an industrialist and thinker (*Zur Mechanik des Geistes*, 1913); he wrote numerous other socio-political books incl *Der Kaiser* (1919), a study of servility and its consequences in the Wilhelmine Empire, and *Von kommenden Dingen* (1917, [65]1919), an analysis of the relationship between the public and private sectors, as shrewd as it was successful. He became the Weimar Republic's (Jewish) foreign minister and was murdered by right-wing radicals.

### Ernst Raupach
### (nr Liegnitz/Silesia 1784–1852 Berlin)

After many years teaching German in St Petersburg, Raupach established himself in Berlin as an author of comedies (*Kritik und Antikritik*, 1825 etc) and as a patriotic dramatist with his 16-drama cycle, *Die Hohenstaufen* (1829–37), *Der Nibelungen-Hort* (tragedy 1828) and a Cromwell trilogy (1829–33), in all of which the powerful style of Schiller is reduced to blandness.

### Paul Rebhuhn (Waidhofen *c*.1500–46
### Oelsnitz, Saxony)

He was a grammar-school teacher whose plays, *Susanna* (1536) and *Die Hochzeit zu Cana* (1538) are paradigmatic of the didactic aims and values of the first generation of Protestant writers but also reveal the aesthetic sense of a Renaissance humanist. He also publ a successful marriage guidance manual in which the new ethos is clearly evident: *Hausfried: Was für Ursachen den christlichen Eheleuten zubedencken, den lieben Hausfriede in der Ehe zu erhalten* (1546, [7]1571). It was still in print as late as 1662.

### Elise von der Recke
### (Schönberg in Courland, now Latvia
### 1754–1833 Dresden)

Despite having published her *Geistliche Lieder*

*einer vornehmen kurländischen Dame* (1780) anon, she used her own name for her *Nachricht von des berüchtigten Cagliostros Aufenthalt in Mitau, und von dessen dortigen magischen Operationen* (1787). It provided innumerable writers with a basic text for their versions of the Don Juan myth. The forthright character of her writing, here as in her travel journals (1815–17) and diaries (1927) etc, reveals a stalwart representative of Enlightenment attitudes and values.

### Oskar von Redwitz (Lichtenau nr Ansbach 1823–91 nr Bayreuth)

He established his fame at 26 with a verse epic *Amaranth* (1849; [44]1904), romanticizing medieval Christendom. His later 'conversion' to anti-Catholic liberal nationalism, evident in the aptly-named novel *Hermann Stark* (1869) and in his *Lied vom neuen deutschen Reich: Eines ehemaligen Lützow'schen Jägers Vermächtniß an's Vaterland* (1871), a narrative couched in sonnets, ensured him a place in the Parnassus of the new German Reich.

### Hermann Samuel Reimarus (Hamburg 1694–1768)

He taught Oriental languages at the *Akademisches Gymnasium* in Hamburg, already a centre of the Enlightenment. He was a radical critic of traditional religion from a secular viewpoint whose *Apologie oder Schutzschrift für die vernünftigen Verehrer Gottes* (parts of which Lessing publ as the *Wolfenbütteler Fragmente* in 1774 and 1777) gave rise to an intense debate to which Lessing memorably contributed.

### Max Reinhardt (Baden/Vienna 1873–1943 New York)

He was a legend in an age of great actors and directors (many trained by himself), and of stimulating theatre critics such as Alfred Kerr. He transformed theatre management into a major commercial enterprise, starting in Berlin, then moving on to Vienna. His gala performances and productions pioneered new technology such as revolving stages, gauzes, electric lighting etc. He was always ready to put on new plays or revive old ones to satisfy his audiences' thirst for 'cultural experience' and lavish entertainment: with Hofmannsthal

and Richard Strauss he founded the Salzburg Festival. US exile in 1937 did not fulfil his hopes of doing for cinema in the New World what he had done for theatre in the Old.

### Erich Maria Remarque (= Erich Paul Remark) (Osnabrück 1898–1970 Locarno)

He was the author of the world's best-selling (anti-)war novel, *Im Westen nichts Neues* (1929), which sold millions of copies worldwide. The campaign of vilification against him and his work by the right-wing parties between 1929 and 1933 showed up the deep ideological divisions in the late Weimar Republic.

### Johannes Reuchlin (Pforzheim 1455–1522 Stuttgart)

A lawyer and humanist in the service of Duke Eberhard of Württemberg and of the university towns of Heidelberg, Tübingen, Ingolstadt and Basle, he tr Hebrew, Greek and Latin works and compiled a Hebrew grammar. His courageous protest at the burning of Hebrew books gave rise to a notorious quarrel between obscurantist scholastic philosophers and open-minded humanists like himself.

### Christian Reuter (nr Halle *c*.1665–*c*.1712 unknown)

Relatively little is known about this Leipzig student, except that he was constantly in trouble for his comic portrayal of local life in his plays (*L'Honnête Femme Oder die Ehrliche Frau zu Plißine*, 1695, *Der Ehrlichen Frau Schlampampe Krankheit und Tod*, 1696, and *Graf Ehrenfried*, 1700). His main work was the comic novel, *Schelmuffskys warhafftige curiöse und sehr gefährliche Reisebeschreibung zu Wasser und Lande* (1696). He belongs to the early Augustan age in his determination to unmask through satire the foolishness of those lacking 'honour' and 'integrity', and his ability to conceal his adroit Horatian didacticism under the guise of exuberant entertainment.

### Fritz Reuter (Stavenhagen 1810–74 Eisenach)

He was one of Germany's great comic geniuses. After serving a 7-year sentence for his part in student demonstrations, he began to write in *Plattdeutsch* (Low German), beginning with humorous verse (*Läuschen un Riemels*, 1853, and the verse tale *Kein Hüsung*, 1858). His 7-vol novel cycle, *Olle Kamellen* (1860–8), which includes his autobiog *Ut de Franzosentid* (1859), *Ut mine Festungstid* (1862), *Ut mine Stromtid* (1862–4), made him both famous and rich; *Dörchläuchting* (1866, part VI of *Olle Kamellen*) offers a comic view of his native Mecklenburg, long the most reactionary of German principalities. He is still popular in N Germany.

### Gabriele Reuter
#### (Alexandria 1859–1941 Weimar)
*Aus guter Familie: Leidensgeschichte eines Mädchens* (1895, [18]1908) made Reuter one of the best-known women writers of her time, and deservedly so. Here, as in her novellen in the Naturalist manner (eg *Frauenseelen*, 1902), she uses her characteristic blend of 'objective' and 'subjective' narratorial voices to analyse the psychological and physical harm done to middle-class German girls by their education and experience of life, comparing and contrasting it with the cynical exploitation of working-class women. Her later work, incl stories for girls (eg *Großstadtmädel*, 1920), links her, like Böhlau and Viebig, to the moderate wing of the women's movement.

### Franziska, Gräfin zu Reventlow
#### (Husum 1871–1918 Muralto/Ticino)
She portrayed in her first novel *Ellen Olestjerne* (1903) the impact of the cult of Nietzsche and Ibsen and a variety of often conflicting issues which dominated the women's movement at the turn of the century. In *Viragines oder Hetären?* (1901), an essay criticizing the view that women's distinctive identity would be lost in the struggle for emancipation, she stressed their subjectivity and right to sexual freedom. The irony and the studied disorganization of her 'fragmentary' novel, *Herr Dame's Aufzeichnungen oder Begebenheiten aus einem merkwürdigen Stadtteil* (1913), build up a picture of the Munich *Bohème* and create a specifically 'female' form of subjective writing.

### Hans Werner Richter
#### (Bansin 1908–93 Munich)
It is often forgotten today that the editor of *Der Ruf* and literary mentor of the 1950s and early 1960s, a former member of the KPD Resistance, was also an influential writer and moralist in his own right, notably in *Sie fielen aus Gottes Hand* (1951), a concentration-camp novel in the style of a report. The novels *Spuren im Sand* (1953) and *Du sollst nicht töten* (1956) analyse the causes and effects of the war.

## Jean Paul Richter *see* Jean Paul

### Wilhelm Heinrich Riehl
#### (Biebreich/Rhine 1823–97 Munich)
He was in his time an influential cultural anthropologist advocating a corporate view of society (*Die bürgerliche Gesellschaft*, 1851, *Die Familie*, 1855). He wrote some 50 novellen; the set entitled *Kulturgeschichtliche Novellen* (1856) influenced the development of the genre, and his descriptive approach to milieu was adopted by many historical and social novelists later in the 19thc.

### Johannes Riemer
#### (Halle 1648–1714 Hamburg)
He was Weise's successor at the Weißenfels Gymnasium and, like him, a serious author with a sense of humour whose 'political' novels on the way of the world embodied the new ethos of the Augustan era, as is shown by the popularity of his 3rd and last, *Der Politische Stockfisch* (1681, [9]1734).

### Rainer Maria Rilke
#### (Prague 1875–1926 nr Montreux)
This Prague-born Austrian poet won his reputation as the major German lyric poet of the early 20thc with two lyric volumes (*Das Buch der Bilder*, 1902; *Das Stunden-Buch*, 1905). His poetic prose narrative *Die Weise von Liebe und Tod des Cornets Christoph Rilke* (1904) won him a popular readership usually denied the kind of fastidiously 'difficult' modern poet whose German prototype he became. In *Neue Gedichte* (2 vols 1907 and 1908), the *Duineser Elegien* (1923; named after the Adriatic castle of Duino, where he began them), and the *Sonette an Orpheus* (1923), his uniquely recognizable

fusion of reality and expressive subjectivity gave renewed meaning to the forms and images of European poetry since classical antiquity, thanks to his ability to recreate them and endow them with a new and communicable though essentially esoteric personal coherence.

### Joachim Ringelnatz
(Wurzen/Saxony 1883–1934 Berlin)

Not even the most enterprising modern student can boast the range of experience in casual labour on which R drew when he became the 'local poet' of Munich's *Café Simpl* in the early 20thc. His nonsense verse and tales appeared in several collections, among them *Die Schnupftabakdose: Stumpfsinn in Versen und Bildern* (1912). A brilliant cabaret performer, whose work Kästner described in 1924 as 'die Groteske als Zeitgefühl' (the grotesque as mood of our times), R was banned by the Nazis in 1933.

### Luise Rinser
(Pitzling/Upper Bavaria 1911– )

A teacher imprisoned when she refused to join the Nazi party, she achieved world best-seller status with her *Gefängnistagebuch* (1946) and the novels *Mitte des Lebens* (1950) and *Mirjam* (1983), a feminist slant on the Gospel story through the eyes of Mary Magdalene. An RC convert, Green Party presidential candidate in 1984 and prolific author, R has been an influential voice in W German political and moral debate (*Gespräche über Lebensfragen*, 1966).

### Johann Rist
(Ottensen 1607–67 nr Hamburg)

He wrote several hundred hymns (*Himmlische Lieder*, 1641–2), a drama (*Perseus*, 1634), and masque-like plays (*Festspiele*) commemorating the end of the 30 Years War (*Das Friedewünschende Teutschland*, 1647, and *Das Friedejauchtzende Teutschland*, 1653): a Lutheran pastor, he did not put his name to the amorous pastoral poem *Des Daphnis aus Cimbrien Galathee* (1642). He is best known for his advocacy of Opitz's reforms in northern Germany, as exemplified by his own lyric collection, *Musa Teutonica* (1634), and the founding of the *Elbschwanenorden* to promote them.

### Otto Roquette
(Korotschin 1824–1896 Darmstadt)

He wrote a verse epic, *Waldmeisters Brautfahrt* (1851), which ran to 80 edns by 1900. But today few remember the author of the Faustian novel, *Gevatter Tod* (1873), which once seemed so representative of its age.

### Peter Rosegger
(Alpl/Styria 1843–1918 Krieglach)

He exemplifies some of the most important secular trends of his age. Patrons and publishers helped launch his dialect poems *Zither und Hackbrett* and *Tannenharz und Fichtennadeln* (1870), while his early realistic novels of harsh life in beautiful countryside (*In der Einöde*, 1872, *Die Schriften des Waldschulmeisters*, 1875) drew on the popular traditions of the *Kalendergeschichte* and village tales. The extraordinary acclaim given to his *Waldheimat* tales (1877 and continually reissued) was symptomatic of an urbanized readership's sense that it had lost touch with the countryside, and reflected the mass-market appeal of the concept of '*Heimat*'.

### Peter Rosei (Vienna 1946– )

This gifted stylist and lawyer has written novels and stories about brutal, socially marginalized egoists (*Landstriche*, 1972, *Wer war Edgar Allen?*, 1977, *Von Hier nach Dort*, 1978, *Die Milchstraße*, 1981 and the 6-vol *15,000 Seelen*, 1985) in which he explores the theme of human identity in a society alienated from itself.

### Alfred Rosenberg (Reval = Tallinn/
Estonia 1893–1946 Nuremberg)

He championed the supremacy of the German race and was a senior functionary in the National Socialist party responsible for its ideology and educational policies. His *Der Mythus des 20. Jahrhunderts* attracted scant attention when publ in 1930: by 1933 it ranked 2nd only to Adolf Hitler's *Mein Kampf* itself. R was tried and executed by the Allies for his crimes as minister for the Nazi-occupied Eastern territories.

**Ernst Rosmer** *see* **Elsa Bernstein**

*Eugen Roth* (Munich 1895–1976)
Roth is 20thc Germany's past master of comic
and satirical verse. Some of his best work is in
*Dinge, die unendlich uns umkreisen* (1918),
*Heitere Verse* (1959) and *Ins Schwarze: Limer-
icks und Schüttelreime* (1968).

*Gerhard Roth* (Graz 1940– )
He is the author of experimental prose (*die
autobiographie des albert einstein*, 1971), dramas,
and novels of identity (*Der Stille Ozean*, 1980,
*Landläufiger Tod*, 1984).

*Joseph Roth*
(Brody/Galicia 1894–1939 Paris)
*Flucht ohne Ende* ('Flight without End', 1927)
was the ominous title of an early novel of his. A
successful journalist across the political spectrum in both Austria and Germany, he later
chronicled the psychoses of those returning
from the Great War in which he too had fought
(novels, *Das Spinnennetz*, 1967, *Rechts und
links*, 1929, *Der stumme Prophet*, 1966) and
the political and human consequences of
the decay and collapse of Habsburg
Austria (*Radetzkymarsch*, 1932, and *Die
Kapuzinergruft*, 1938). In his most famous
novel, the Hasidic parable *Hiob* (1930), the Old
Testament Jew is the mythical chronicler of
homelessness and persecution (see also his
essay *Juden auf Wanderschaft*, 1927).

*Friedrich Rückert*
(Schweinfurt 1788–1866 Coburg)
Professor of Oriental languages at Erlangen
University, he was not just one of the
biedermeier age's most prolific and popular
lyricists and a household name throughout
Germany (*Haus- und Jahreslieder*, 1838). He
was also a genuine experimenter in poetic
forms, particularly in his many fine trns
of Arabic and Persian poetry, and a favourite
with great composers: Schubert set him and
he provided Mahler with the text of
*Kindertotenlieder*.

*Gerhard Rühm* (Vienna 1930– )
A key figure of the *Wiener Gruppe*, Rühm is a
musician and writer for stage and film as well

as author of concrete poetry (*Ideogramme*,
1961, *konstellationen*, 1961) and 'auditive' poetry (*Schriftzeichnungen*: 1956–1977, 1982),
prose texts such as *fenster, texte* (1968), and the
drama *Ophelia und die Wörter* (1969). His experimental poetry attempts to extend the expressiveness of language beyond the wr and
spoken sign while remaining within a living
tradition embracing the German and European
avant-garde and the macabre vigour of Viennese dialect.

*Peter Rühmkorf* (Dortmund 1929– )
He contributed to the recovery of a sense of
the autonomy of literature and culture in
Adenauer's Germany, both as lyric poet (*Heiße
Lyrik*, 1956 with W Riegel, *Walther von der
Vogelweide, Klopstock und ich*, 1975, *131
expressionistische Gedichte*, 1976) and as a pro-
vocative satirist of the consumer society
(*Haltbar bis Ende 1999*, poems 1979, *Der Hüter
des Misthaufens: Aufgeklärte Märchen*, 1983).

*Philipp Otto Runge*
(Wolgast 1777–1810 Hamburg)
The career of this Romantic painter, poet and
colour theorist, to whom painters such as Paul
Klee and Franz Marc have acknowledged their
debt, received stimulus from many literary
groupings, such as those associated with
Friederike Brun in Copenhagen and with
Tieck in Dresden, whose *Minnelieder aus dem
Schwäbischen Zeitalter* (1803) he illustrated.
Besides his graphic work, R's interest lies in his
Low German fairy tales, esp *Von den Mahandel
Bohm* (1808) and *Von dem Fischer un syner Fru*
(1812).

# S

*Ferdinand von Saar*
(Vienna 1833–1906 Döbling/Vienna)
Like Marie von Ebner-Eschenbach, he sought
fame in drama and lyric poetry (*Wiener Elegien*,
1893), and equally vainly. Although, like
Grillparzer, he was appreciated in high circles,
he enjoyed only a *succès d'estime* in his lifetime
for his now much-admired *Novellen aus
Österreich* (1877, expanded edn 1897). These
contained i a the stories *Innocens, Marianne,*

*Die Steinklopfer, Die Geigerin* and *Vae Victis!*, *Leutnant Burda, Die Troglodytin, Ginevra* and *Seligmann Hirsch.* S's later novellen include *Schloß Kostenitz* (1892) and the collections *Herbstreigen* (1897), *Camera obscura* (1901), and *Tragik des Lebens* (1906), an appropriate title for a deeply pessimistic writer who took his own life, as his wife had done before him.

### Leopold Sacher-Masoch
(Lemberg 1836–95 nr Frankfurt/M)
Though not himself a Jew, he helped to popularize the genre of ghetto story (*Galizische Geschichten*, 1875, *Judengeschichten*, 1878). He also gave his name to the term 'masochism', portraying its exemplary type, a man dominated by a woman, in his notorious story, *Venus im Pelz* (1870), one of an ambitious but incomplete collection of novellen with the projected title *Das Vermächtniß Kains*, and a classic of German 19thc soft-pornographic literature.

### Hans Sachs (Nuremberg 1494–1576)
A cobbler by trade, this poet and playwright followed his grammar-school education and 5 years as a journeyman by making his name as a vernacular poet. He welcomed Luther in the resonant lines of his poem 'Die wittenbergisch Nachtigall' (1523) and supported the Reformation with his prose dialogues (notably *Disputation zwischen einem Chorherrn und einem Schuhmacher*, 1524). His exuberantly prolific output includes 85 entertaining *Fastnachtspiele* or carnival plays drawn from the humorous tradition of the *Schwank*, and 130 comedies and tragedies which dramatized subjects taken from classical antiquity, Germanic myth and Italian *novella*. Despite Goethe's early admiration (*Hans Sachsens poetische Sendung*, 1776) and his important place in German Renaissance and Reformation literary culture, S's 4275 *Meisterlieder* and other lyric and narrative verse, like much else in his oeuvre, have yet to be fully appreciated.

### Nelly Sachs (Berlin 1891–1970 Stockholm)
One of the 20thc's major poets, who escaped from Germany in 1940 with the help of Selma Lagerlöf, she was almost 60 when, drawing on her reading of Jewish mystical writings, she began to give voice to her people's memory in lyric poetry and her celebrated *Eli: Ein Mysterienspiel vom Leiden Israels* (wr 1943, perf 1962). The crematorium at Auschwitz is at the core of her poetry. The twin images of star and dust inform her work, which she saw as the task of infusing with soul what has been turned into dust ('Durchseelung des Staubes'). Her titles are laconic yet eloquent: *In den Wohnungen des Todes* (1947), *Flucht und Verwandlung* (1959), *Fahrt ins Staublose* (collected poems 1961), *Noch feiert der Tod* (1961), *Die Suchende* (1966) etc. Paul Celan, her friend and correspondent, regarded *Und Niemand weiß weiter* (1957) as one of the 'truest' of books.

### Georg Saiko (Seestadtl/Bohemia
1892–1962 Rekawinkel/Lr Austria)
A man of many parts, he was proscribed in 1938 and publ the body of his work after 1945, notably *Auf dem Floß* (1948), his novel on the political/moral collapse of the Austro-Hungarian Empire, and *Der Mann im Schlaf*, a historical novel on the Fascist Putsch in Vienna in July 1934.

### Johann Michael Sailer
(nr Schrobenhausen/Upr Bavaria
1751–1832 Regensburg)
He was a pioneering spirit in modern Catholic pastoral theology, whose personality, writings and trn (1794) of Thomas à Kempis's *Imitation of Christ* brought about the spiritual renewal of many members of both the RC and Protestant Churches, among them C. Brentano.

### Hans Salat (Sursee 1498–1561 Fribourg)
He conducted the foreign affairs of the city of Lucerne, wrote a history of the Reformation from the RC angle and produced his one extant play on the theme of the Prodigal Son in 1537: 3 years later a conviction for fraud led to his banishment.

### Wilhelm Schäfer
(Ottrau 1868–1952 Überlingen)
He made his name with his short prose anecdotes (*Dreiunddreißig Anekdoten*, 1911) which figured large in German course books. His

novel *Der Hauptmann von Köpenick* (1930) appeared the year before Zuckmayer's classic play, but S's reputation has been even more overshadowed by the ease with which he played into Nazi hands.

### Jakob Schaffner
(Basle 1875–1944 Strasburg)
He was T Mann's exact contemporary, and for him, too, adolescence and the search for meaning are fundamental to his writing from *Konrad Pilater* (novel 1910) to the *Johannes* tetralogy of novels (1922–39) which reflects S's career as it traces its protagonist's progress from institutionalized orphan to Nazi author. It cost S his nationality: expelled from Switzerland, he was killed in an air raid in German-occupied Strasburg, an end in keeping with the life and work of this powerful maverick of an author whose rediscovery is yet to come.

### Edzard Schaper
(Ostrowo/Poland 1908–84 Berne)
His novels treated contemporary issues in the context of life in the Baltic states and from a Christian perspective, often choosing extreme existential situations to highlight their moral and emotional dimensions, as in *Die sterbende Kirche* (1936) and its sequel, *Der letzte Advent* (1949), and the revealingly titled best-selling novels *Die Freiheit des Gefangenen* with its sequel *Die Macht der Ohnmächtigen* (1950–1), in which his innocent protagonist comes to find inner peace.

### Michael Scharang
(Kapfenberg/Styria 1941– )
He disturbed his Austrian readers with his short stories *Schluß mit dem Erzählen und andere Erzählungen* (1970), his novels, *Charly Traktor* (1973) and *Der Sohn eines Landarbeiters* (1976), and his radio play, *Der Beruf des Vaters* (1985). The dialectical character of his writing and his fondness for parables are evident in *Das Wunder Österreich: Essays, Polemiken, Glossen* (1989), a fine example of his efforts to re-establish the role of the essay in the Kraus-Musil tradition as a medium for social and cultural criticism in post-Nazi Austria.

### Josef Viktor (1876– von) Scheffel
(Karlsruhe 1826–86)
He was the author of the narrative poem *Der Trompeter von Säckingen* (1854), and the historical novel *Ekkehard* (1855), one of the favourite books in German in the mid-19thc.

**Johannes Scheffler** *see* **Angelus Silesius**

### *Friedrich Wilhelm Joseph (1808– von) Schelling* (Lemberg 1775–1854 Bad Ragaz/Switzerland)
This philosopher helped to build a bridge between German Idealism and Romanticism. In *Ideen zu einer Philosophie der Natur* (1795), *Von der Weltseele* (1798) and in his centrally important *System des transzendentalen Idealismus* (1800), he reacted against the subjective idealism of Fichte. The influence of his friend Hölderlin helped S to relate his nature philosophy to an early Romantic appreciation of art in his 1802–3 lectures (publ as *Philosophie der Kunst*, 1809). The young S held the chair of philosophy at Jena from 1798 to 1803 (an appointment he owed in no small part to Goethe and Fichte), in which year he married Caroline, former wife of AW Schlegel. He spent his later years in Munich and Berlin.

### Max von Schenkendorf
(Tilsit/E Prussia 1783–1817 Koblenz)
He has a special place in the galaxy of 19thc liberal German patriots for his *Freiheitsgesänge* (1810) celebrating Prussia's abolition of serfdom. Many of his *Sieben Kriegslieder* (with Fouqué 1813) and *Gedichte* (1805) were set to music and sung by male-voice choirs and in drawing-rooms (eg 'Die Freiheit, die ich meine') and reflect the love of group activities which was such an appealing feature of German life in the first half of the 19thc.

### Wilhelm Scherer
(Schönborn/Lr Austria 1841–86 Berlin)
Despite his relatively early death, he put his mark on the history of German studies with *Über den Ursprung der deutschen Literatur* (1864) and *Geschichte der deutschen Literatur* (1880–3, [16]1927). In his work he argued that texts should be interpreted in the context of literary tradition, the market and the personal-

ity of the poet. Himself a professor of German at Vienna, Strasburg and Berlin, he successfully 'managed' appointments to chairs in German, thus ensuring the perpetuation of his ideas.

### René Schickele (Obernai/Alsace 1883–1940 Vence/France)

He was a man of many facets who called himself a 'citoyen français und deutscher Dichter'. A leading Expressionist, he ed the pacifist journal, *Die weißen Blätter*, from Switzerland during World War I. His sense of the antitheses between the French and German cultures in his native Alsace (German when he was born, but French 1918–40) is expressed in terms of the split personalities and existential dualities in his novels *Der Fremde* (1907) and *Symphonie für Jazz* (1929) and particularly in his major work, the novel trilogy *Das Erbe am Rhein* (1925–31).

### Emanuel Schikaneder (Straubing 1751–1812 Vienna)

A musician and strolling player, he did much to popularize the *Singspiel* or play with music. He met Mozart in 1780, and was the librettist of his *Magic Flute* (1791). He briefly managed various companies and theatres incl the new *Theater an der Wien*; his *Der Tiroler Wastl* (1796) helped to develop the *Volksstück* genre, and his *Die Fiaker in Wien* (1813) was equally successful. In 1777 he had been Munich's first Hamlet.

### Friedrich (1802– von) Schiller (Marbach 1759–1805 Weimar)

For 19thc German-speakers he was *the* poet of freedom. Modern literary criticism has led to a renewed respect for the sheer range of his intellect, already evident in the dissertation he wrote as a medical student (*Über den Zusammenhang der thierischen Natur des Menschen mit seiner geistigen*, 1780), and in the psychological insights and structural mastery of his novelle *Der Verbrecher aus verlorener Ehre* (1789). Admiration for the master architect of the German tragedy remains undiminished. His plays include *Die Räuber* (1781), *Die Verschwörung des Fiesko zu Genua* (1783), *Kabale und Liebe* (1784), *Don Carlos* (1787), the

*Wallenstein* trilogy (*Ws Lager*, 1798, *Die Piccolomini* and *Ws Tod*, 1799), *Maria Stuart* (1800), *Die Jungfrau von Orleans* (1801), *Die Braut von Messina* (1803), *Wilhelm Tell* (1804). He never wrote comedy but he achieved widespread popularity with his virtuosic poem 'Das Lied von der Glocke' (1800). His 'philosophical' poetry, such as 'Die Götter Griechenlands' (1788) and his ballads, 'Die Kraniche des Ibykus' and 'Der Ring des Polykrates' (both 1798) illustrate his remarkable ability to synthesize antiquity and the contemporary and exemplify the complex arguments which underlie his aesthetic writings, notably *Über die ästhetische Erziehung des Menschen*, *Über naïve und sentimentalische Dichtung*, publ 1795–8 in his journal *Die Horen*. He wrote two major historical studies, *Geschichte des Abfalls der vereinigten Niederlande von der spanischen Regierung* (1788) and *Geschichte des 30jährigen Kriegs* (1790–3), and was appointed professor of history at Jena in 1789. His 10-yr friendship and intellectual collaboration with Goethe is highlighted in their correspondence.

### David Schirmer (Freiberg 1623–87 Dresden)

He was a protégé of the Elector of Saxony who made his mark as a love poet with *Die Rosen-Gepüsche* (1650). In his collection of *Singende Rosen* (1654) the musicality of his verse was enhanced by settings provided by the Saxon court composer Philipp Stolle.

### Johannes Schlaf (Querfurt/Saxony 1862–1941)

Joint author with Arno Holz of the Naturalist prose piece *Papa Hamlet* (1889) and the drama *Die Familie Selicke* (1890), he also wrote much-admired lyrical impressionist prose (*In Dingsda*, 1892) and a second Naturalist drama *Meister Oelze* (1892). His biological cast of mind remained a constant feature of his work, as in the novel *Das dritte Reich* (1900), which won him favour in the Third Reich.

### August Wilhelm (1815– von) Schlegel (Hanover 1767–1845 Bonn)

August Wilhelm may have been less dynamic than his brilliant younger brother Friedrich, but he was a man of clear vision, whose lectures *Über schöne Litteratur und Kunst* (1801, publ 1884) and *Über dramatische Kunst und Litteratur* (1808, publ 1809–11) won him a deserved international reputation. A great ed and tr, notably of Shakespeare (1797–1810) and i a of Dante in his *Blumensträuße italienischer, spanischer und portugiesischer Poesie* (1804), he helped to establish the concepts of Romance literature and of comparative literature and had a formative, if often contested, influence on the whole discipline of literary history and criticism.

### Dorothea (Veit-)Schlegel
#### (née *Mendelssohn* Berlin 1764–1839 Frankfurt/M)

Mother of the Nazarene painters, Johannes and Philipp Veit, she was the author of the novel *Florentin* (1801), reviewer and tr, notably from the French (Mme de Staël's *Corinne*, 1807), and the assiduous and practical collaborator of her second husband, F. Schlegel.

### Friedrich (1815– *von*) Schlegel
#### (Hanover 1772–1829 Dresden)

'What a restless genius he was!' wrote August Wilhelm on the death of his brother, Friedrich. The gifted youngest child of a large family, he indulged himself as an *enfant terrible* long into adulthood (as, in a sense, he did in his provocative novel, *Lucinde*, 1799). Much of what he undertook remained unfinished, yet he opened up new areas of human thought and endeavour, such as historical and comparative linguistics (*Über die Sprache und Weisheit der Indier*, 1808) and was a uniquely potent catalyst of new ideas in many disciplines. He was most at home with fragments and aphorisms, and irony was his favourite mode. A leading theoretician (i a on Romantic irony), he made his journals, *Athenäum* (1798–1800) and *Europa* (1803–5), the repository of early Romantic ideas; the later *Deutsches Museum* (1812–13) and *Concordia* (1820–3) documented the dogmatic conservatism of his middle age. His acute sense of history expressed itself as a sense of lost continuity (*Über die neuere Geschichte*, lectures 1810, publ 1811; *Geschichte der neueren Litteratur*, 1812, publ 1815); this and the intel-

lectual quality of his aesthetic and philosophical criticism has ensured the relevance of his work for the 20thc.

### Johann Elias Schlegel
#### (Meissen 1713–44 Sorø/Denmark)

He was recognized as 18thc Germany's leading dramatist before Lessing. He wrote several tragedies in the Augustan manner incl *Hermann* (1743) and *Canut* (1746) which introduced Germanic subjects to the mid-18thc stage. He was at his best in comedy (*Die stumme Schönheit*, 1747) and in his pioneering writings on the aesthetics of drama.

### Caroline Schlegel (-Schelling)
#### (Göttingen 1763–1809 Maulbronn)

Though she collaborated with AW Schlegel and Schelling, her second and third husbands, she belongs at the forefront of early Romanticism for her letters, as was recognized by Georg Waitz in his 1871 edn and by Erich Schmidt in *Briefe der Frühromantik* (1913), and, for different reasons, by late 20thc feminist critics.

### Friedrich Schleiermacher
#### (Breslau 1768–1834 Berlin)

Dialogue characterizes his writings and identifies this charismatic Pietist theologian and preacher as a quintessential Romantic. He was the author of *Über die Religion: Reden an die Gebildeten unter ihren Verächtern* (*Reden Über die Religion*, 1799), the central text of Romantic philosophy of religion and of a celebrated German trn of Plato's *Dialogues* (1804–28); here, as in his writings on pedagogy and hermeneutics and the famous *Monolog* (1800) on ethics (still a major influence on 20thc theology and literary criticism), he invariably creates a 'partnership' with his readers.

### August Ludwig Schlözer (1803– *von*)
#### (Kirchberg/Jagst 1735–1809 Göttingen)

He was renowned as a teacher of princes and senior civil servants at Göttingen University, and was the father of the first woman to take a Dr phil. in Germany, Dorothea S. During the French Revolution period the journal he edited, the *Staats-Anzeigen* (1782–93), provided a public forum for discussing current affairs.

Tirelessly productive as a historian and journalist, he offered Germany an eclectic yet also original reform plan on the eve of the French revolutionary wars with his main work, *Allgemeines Statsrecht und Statsverfassungslehre* (1793).

### Christoph (1828– von) Schmid
#### (Dinkelsbühl 1768–1854 Augsburg)

The moral tales for children by this rural parish priest, such as *Genovefa* (1810), *Die Ostereier* (1816), *Wie Heinrich von Eichenfels zur Erkenntnis Gottes kam* (1817), *Das Blumenkörbchen* (1823) etc, provided staple reading in the German-speaking countries until well into the 20thc and in trn had immense success in England, the US and Brazil.

### Arno Schmidt
#### (Hamburg-Hamm 1914–79 Celle)

He wrote short stories (collected as *Leviathan*) which reflect his generation's experience of war, but it is his 'meta-literary' novels *Kaff auch Mare Crisium* (1960) and *Zettels Traum* (1970) that give him his unique place in modern German literary studies. Why? Partly because of his fervent concern, translated into a 'new' syntax and lexis, to counter what he saw as the dangerous discontinuity of German culture by rescuing neglected poets from undeserved oblivion (i a Fouqué, Tieck, and Brockes), partly too for the fervour his own work inspires among leading Germanists.

### Johann Gottfried Schnabel
#### (nr Bitterfeld 1692–1751/8?)

Journalist and author of a once much-reprinted anthology of erotic poetry, *Der im Irrgarten der Liebe herumtaumelnde Kavalier* (1738), he is now remembered for his 4-vol 'German Robinson Crusoe', *Die Insel Felsenburg* (1731–43, [5]1768), in which sailors create a utopian community based on active Christianity on a remote island.

### Peter Schneider (Lübeck 1940– )

He was a student activist in 1968 (*Schon bist du ein Verfassungsfeind*, 1975) who made his name with a modern version of Büchner's *Lenz* (short story, 1973) and, particularly with the

picaresque story on the schizophrenic impact of the Wall, *Der Mauerspringer* (1982); like many of his contemporaries in the W, his more recent work has been in the area of social and cultural comment, eg *Extreme Mittellage: Reise durch das deutsche Nationalgefühl* (1990).

### Reinhold Schneider
#### (Baden-Baden 1903–58 Freiburg i B)

A leading member of the Inner Emigration, he wrote widely-admired historical novels (notably *Das Inselreich*, 1936, and *Las Casas vor Karl V*, 1938) and essays (*Macht und Gnade*, 1941) which reflect his tragic view of history. He became a lifeline for literally hundreds of thousands of soldiers on the Russian front and for victims of Nazi persecution thanks to his clandestine letters and poems. His life was changed by his discovery of the existence of the concentration camps: in 1934 he had written a powerful novelle, *Der Tröster*, on Friedrich von Spee, who 300 years earlier countered tyranny by his ministry to its victims. His autobiog works, *Verhüllter Tag* (1954) and *Winter in Wien* (1958), are richly rewarding.

### Rolf Schneider (Chemnitz 1932– )

He made his name as author of the novel, *November* (1979 in W, 1989 in E Germany), on the impact on the GDR public of the 'Biermann affair'. His satirical novel, *Jede Seele auf Erden* (1988), focused on the clash of two cultures within Germany; his post-Unification views of the workings of capitalist society are illuminating for his W German as well as his E German readers.

### *Arthur Schnitzler
#### (Vienna 1862–1931)

Vienna was the focus of his life and work. His early dramas (*Anatol*, 1910, publ 1892, *Liebelei*, 1895, *Reigen*, 1921, publ 1903) explore the dynamics and consequences of ephemeral erotic experience and provoked scandal by identifying the libido as an element linking all Viennese social classes. The psychologizing and sociological impetus behind S's plays (*Der grüne Kakadu*, 1899, *Der einsame Weg*, 1904, *Professor Bernhardi*, 1912), short stories (*Sterben*, 1893, *Leutnant Gustl*, 1901,

*Casanovas Heimfahrt*, 1918, *Fräulein Else*, 1924) and novels (*Der Weg ins Freie*, 1908, *Therese: Chronik eines Frauenlebens*, 1928) bears witness to his energetic participation in the tireless inquiry into human nature which characterized intellectual life in *fin-de-siècle* Vienna. Small wonder, then, that Freud, writing in 1922 to S, his fellow upper-middle-class Viennese Jew, admitted to a certain *Doppelgängerscheu* towards a writer who was in many ways his intimidating double.

### *Laurentius von Schnüffis* (Schnüffis/ Vorarlberg 1633–1702 Constance)

S, whose real name was Johann Martin, worked as a strolling player before being ordained and becoming a Capuchin friar (1663–5). Literary success came with the semi-autobiog novel *Philotheus, oder Deß Miranten [= Martin] wunderlicher Weg* (1665) which retold his spiritual odyssey in terms of pastoral romance. It was followed by *Mirantisches Flötlein*, which employs the same conceit to express S's relationship to Christ. They won him the recognition of Emperor Leopold I himself.

### *Wolfdietrich Schnurre* (Frankfurt/M 1920–89 Keil)

He was a co-founder of *Gruppe 47* whose early work challenged the notion that reconciliation was the answer to German 'collective guilt' (*Der Rohrdommel ruft jeden Tag*, short stories 1950, *Sternstaub und Sänfte: Aufzeichnungen des Pudels Ali*, aphorisms 1953). A prominent left-wing intellectual in the 1960s and 1970s, he made the issue of restitution a feature of his later work (*Der Schattenfotograf*, essays, reflections and reminiscences, 1978, and *Ein Unglücksfall*, novel 1981).

### *Arthur Schopenhauer (Danzig 1788–1860 Frankfurt/M)

No doubt the dividend of a masterly prose style inherited from his mother helped S to refresh the often stiflingly abstract philosophical discourse of his time. His masterpiece, *Die Welt als Wille und Vorstellung* (1819), which identifies the 'blind incessant impulse' of the Will as the impersonal motive force of life and downgrades the Intellect as its anaemic deriva-

tive, was to steer German Idealism away from Hegel's teleological faith in progress towards an unexpected pessimism. For S the only means of escape is art and, more lastingly, resignation, renunciation and compassion. These ideas, which came to general notice only after the publication in 1851 of the essay collection, *Parerga und Paralipomena*, were to set the keynote for much post-1848 German thought, art and literature. Among those whose creative imaginations owed much to S were Wagner, Nietzsche, Raabe and T Mann.

### *Johanna Schopenhauer* (Danzig 1766–1838 Bonn)

The mother of the philosopher, she became a successful biedermeier period writer with travel books and fiction: her strategy, notably in the novel *Gabriele* (1819–20), was to appear to promote an ideal of womanly duty. Like many another woman she wrote because she needed the money. Her major literary achievement is her autobiog *Jugendleben und Wanderbilder* (1839), posthumously ed by her daughter, Adele (Hamburg 1797–1849 Bonn), whose own sad life is recorded in her *Tagebücher*, publ in 1909.

### *Justus Georg Schottelius* (Einbeck 1612–76 Wolfenbüttel)

Tutor to Duke Anton Ulrich of Brunswick and a member of both influential societies for language reform, the *Fruchtbringende Gesellschaft* and the Nuremberg *Pegnesischer Blumenorden*, he wrote festival plays, satires and religious poetry in addition to his more celebrated *Teutsche Sprachkunst* (1641), *Teutsche Vers- und Reimkunst* (1645) and *Ausführliche Arbeit von der teutschen Haubtsprache* (1663). In suggesting that German, like Hebrew, Greek and Latin, was close to the so-called '*Ur-Sprache*' or 'Adam's language', S made a significant contribution to German national myth-making as well as to the history of German linguistics.

### *Josef Schreyvogel* (Vienna 1768–1832)

He made his literary debut in Viennese Enlightenment journals and was for a time a reviewer for Nicolai's Berlin *Allgemeine Literatur-Zeitung*; he wrote a number of comedies (notably *Samuel Brucks letzte*

*Liebesgeschichte*, 1820), but his most influential years were those when he directed the Vienna Burgtheater, bringing Calderón to the attention of the Viennese (and German) public and helping Grillparzer to gain access to the stage.

### Friedrich Ludwig Schröder
(Schwerin 1744–1816 nr Hamburg)
He was the son of the actress Sophie S and stepson of the theatre director Ackermann, in whose troupe he as a child played the role of Arabella in Lessing's *Miß Sara Sampson*; appropriately, he took leave of the stage as Odoardo in *Emilia Galotti* in 1796. A key figure in the German theatre life of his day, S pioneered the natural style of acting favoured by Garrick and familiarized German audiences with their own contemporary drama, including Lenz and Goethe, and with Shakespeare. He wrote eminently stageable adaptations of French and Italian and especially English lighter dramas.

### Rudolf Alexander Schröder
(Bremen 1878–1962 Bad Wiessee)
Hofmannsthal's close friend, this architect and poet was a man of parts. He co-founded the Insel publishing house, wrote *Deutsche Ode* (1910) and became one of 20thc Germany's great translators (the classics, Shakespeare, Pope, Aubrey Beardsley, and, later in life, TS Eliot). He was involved with Bierbaum, Wedekind and Wolzogen in the Munich cabaret *Überbrettl*, yet also wrote hymns and spiritual works (*Das Wunder*, 1925, *Mitte des Lebens*, 1930, *Gedichte*, 1935) which provided solace to Christians in the Third Reich.

### Christian Friedrich Daniel Schubart
(Obersontheim 1739–91 Stuttgart)
He was both the victim and a scourge of tyrants, not least 'Schiller's' Duke Karl Eugen of Württemberg, who incarcerated him for 10 yrs in the fortress of Hohenasperg; here this pugnacious and witty journalist, founded ed of the *Teutsche Chronik* (1774–8) and virtuoso pianist, wrote some of his best-known poetry of liberation: 'Die Fürstengruft' (1781), 'Die Forelle' (1783) and 'Kaplied' (1787).

### Gotthilf Heinrich (1853– von) Schubert
(Hohenstein/Erzgebirge 1780–1860 Laufzorn)
He came under Schelling's influence while studying medicine in Jena and in 1808 publ the work which made him the leading natural philosopher of the German Romantic movement, *Ansichten von der Nachtseite der Naturwissenschaften*, which he followed up with his equally seminal *Die Symbolik des Traumes* (1814). Together they provide a bridge from Romanticism to the rise of psychoanalysis in the late 19thc.

### Levin Schücking
(Meppen 1814–83 Bad Pyrmont)
Liberal journalist for the *Allgemeine Zeitung* and the *Kölnische Zeitung*, he was a close friend and the first biographer of Annette von Droste-Hülshoff, whose intense affection for him inspired some of her finest poetry. His Westphalian topographical book, *Das malerische und romantische Westfalen* (1841), is of interest for its role in the genesis of her story *Die Judenbuche*.

### Gustav Schwab (Stuttgart 1792–1850)
This aptly named Swabian poet combined a successful career in the Lutheran Church with a job as classics master at the Stuttgart Gymnasium and an unremitting zest for literature, writing, translating, reviewing, anthologizing and editing the works of Hölderlin, Müller and others. His retellings of German and classical myths and legends have held the attention of the reading public. A student friend of Uhland and Kerner, he compiled one of Germany's many student song-books (*Neues deutsches allgemeines Kommers- und Liederbuch*, 1815).

### Brigitte Schwaiger
(Freistadt/Upr Austria 1949– )
She followed her best-selling treatment of the well-worn theme of conventional but unhappy bourgeois marriage in *Wie kommt das Salz ins Meer?* (novel 1977) with her semi-autobiog *Mein spanisches Dorf* (1978) and *Der Himmel ist süß* (1986). Her success derives from her ability, much in evidence in *Die Galizianerin* (1982), a moving biog of a Galician Jewess and

sole survivor of her family, to write with the voice of her protagonists.

*Sibylle Schwarz* (Greifswald 1621–38)
She died at the age of 17, but her command of the whole range of poetry as outlined by Opitz was revealed when her *Poetische Gedichte* were publ in 1650.

*Charles Sealsfield* (= *Carl* or *Karl Postl*)
(Poppitz/Moravia 1793–1864
nr Solothurn)
The 'literary pioneer of the American prairies', he fascinated readers with his vivid novels of American and Mexican life: *Lebensbilder aus beiden Hemisphären* (1835–7), which includes *Nathan, der Squatter-Regulator, Lebensbilder aus der westlichen Hemisphäre* (1839–40), and especially *Das Kajütenbuch, oder Nationale Charakteristiken* (1841). How much more intrigued they would have been to know that in reality he was an Augustinian monk of liberal views who had fled Metternich's Austria in 1823, wrote about it in English (*Austria as it is: or, Sketches of continental courts*, 1828), and led an adventurous transatlantic life under a number of aliases.

*Anna Seghers* (= *Netty Reiling*)
(Mainz 1900–83 Berlin)
She was already world-famous for her stories and novels of revolution (*Der Aufstand der Fischer von Santa Barbara*, 1928, *Die Gefährten*, 1932, and *Der Weg durch den Februar*, 1935) and of exile and death (*Der Ausflug der toten Mädchen*, 1946, *Das siebte Kreuz: Roman aus dem Hitlerdeutschland*, 1942, *Transit*, 1948, and *Die Toten bleiben jung*, 1949) when she returned to E Germany in 1947. Whether she actively embraced the 'partisanship' required by the Party is unclear, but as influential president (1952–78) of the GDR Writers Union and author of affirmative novels (*Die Entscheidung*, 1959, and *Das Vertrauen*, 1968) and stories (*Die Kraft der Schwachen*, 1965), she remained publicly committed to the authority of the SED Party, even after the Biermann affair.

*Ina Seidel*
(Halle 1885–1974 Ebenhausen nr Munich)
She was the niece of a popular 19thc author Heinrich S. Her conventional early war poetry (*Gedichte*, 1914) soon took on a critical tone, rare in her circle and determined by her perspective as a woman. She developed these insights in her novels, *Brömseshof* (1928) and *Das Wunschkind* (1930); but the matriarchal social utopia evoked in these appealed to readers in the Third Reich, to which she appeared to give allegiance despite the courageous support she gave to those who resisted. Her Christian masterpiece *Lennacker* (1938) and her short stories made her a favourite author in Adenauer's Germany.

*Johann Gottfried Seume*
(Poserna/Saxony 1763–1810 Teplitz)
Autobiographer, aphorist (*Apokrypha*, 1811) and poet (*Gedichte*, 1801, [4]1815), he made his name with his avidly read 'travelogue', *Spaziergang nach Syrakus im Jahre 1802*, which, under its disarming title, was a paean of democracy and a prime example of the way literary genres can be appropriated for political criticism in the absence of a public sphere.

*Sibylle Ursula of Holstein-Glücksburg*
(Hitzacker 1629–71 Glücksburg)
The highly educated daughter of Duke August of Brunswick-Wolfenbüttel was taught by Schottelius, wrote occasional poetry and tr widely from Spanish and French literature. Her posthumous *Himmlisches Tagebuch* (1674) was based on the spiritual diaries she kept for more than 20 years.

*\*Georg Simmel*
(Berlin 1858–1918 Strasburg)
'I see philosophy as my life-task and engage in sociology only as a subsidiary discipline,' wrote S in 1889. Posterity, however, honours him as one of the founders of modern sociology. His seminal *Über sociale Differenzierung* (1890), publ at the height of the Naturalist era, put his academic grounding in history, psychology, ethnology and philosophy to good use. His *Philosophie des Geldes* (1900) was a response to modern life in terms of economics. His other works include *Soziologie* (1908) and

*Grundfragen der Soziologie* (1917), as well as monographs on Kant (1904), Goethe (1913) and Rembrandt (1916).

### Johannes Mario Simmel (Vienna 1924– )

Even if one is not a fan of S, one cannot help admiring his sustained capacity to captivate the German reading public ever since his first novel, *Mich wundert, daß ich so fröhlich bin* (1949). Is it his flair for a catchy title, such as *Es muss nicht immer Kaviar sein* (1967), and a deadpan humour not normally characteristic of German light literature? At all events he commands sales comparable to those of Marlitt in her heyday.

### Reinhard Johannes Sorge
(Rixdorf/Berlin 1892–1916 Somme)

Sorge, who began his career with Nietzschean lyric poetry and sketches in neo-Romantic vein, is remembered as the author of the first Expressionist drama, *Der Bettler*, publ in 1912 but first staged by Reinhardt in 1917.

### Jura Soyfer
(Kharkov 1912–39 Buchenwald)

The son of a Russian Jewish industrialist who fled to Vienna after the Revolution, he became a committed Communist after 1933. He revived the *Volksstück* tradition with light satirical plays which he saw as a means of communicating humanist values to those outside the privileged intellectual elite. They embrace a variety of genres (*Broadway-Melodie 1492* was an adaptation of Hasenclever's and Tucholsky's *Kolumbus; Weltuntergang*, 1936); he also wrote songs and the novel fragment *So starb eine Partei* (1934) on the socialist rising of 1934.

### Kerstin Specht
(Kronach/Upr Franconia 1966– )

She has described the characteristically laconic statements of her highly successful critical *Volksstücke* in lyrical Franconian dialect (*Das glühend Männla, Lila, Amiwiesen*, all 1990) as 'social criticism conveyed through the senses'. The figures of her plays are unpredictable and generally violent characters, trapped in their narrow worlds, and incl the old and the marginalized who vainly pursue their particular utopia, described in Beckett-like monologues.

### Gerold Späth (Rapperswil 1939– )

He created something of a new Seldwyla in his satirical novels *Unschlecht* (1970), *Balzapf oder Als ich auftauchte* (1977) and *Barbarswila* (1988); they are told with a colourfully baroque verve which takes on darker, more caustic hues in *Die heile Hölle* (1974) and *Commedia* (1980).

### Friedrich Spee von Langenfeld
(Kaiserswerth 1591–1635 Trier)

He was a Jesuit priest who wrote love songs to Jesus and in 1631 publ one of the earliest and most systematic attacks on witch hunts (*Cautio criminalis*). An apostle of tolerance in a harsh age, he influenced the Romantics (notably Brentano) with the musical poetry of his *Trutznachtigall* (1649). S's *Güldenes Tugend-Buch* (1649) was based on his work as a confessor to women (incl alleged 'witches').

### Philipp Jakob Spener
(Rappoltsweiler 1635–1705 Berlin)

In a learned age this charismatic reformer was a man distinguished for the range of his knowledge. He held many of the highest posts in the Lutheran Church but lost his belief in its capacity to renew itself. His most celebrated work, *Pia desideria* (1675), has been aptly described as the 'manifesto of Pietism': with Francke, S is a central figure in the history of a Protestant reform movement which influenced Germany's life and literature profoundly.

### Oswald Spengler
(Blankenburg/Harz 1880–1936 Munich)

The author of the manifesto of cultural pessimism, *Der Untergang des Abendlandes*, he became the most widely read philosopher of history of his day. Its first part, completed during the war, appeared in 1918, the notoriously prophetic 2nd part, with its vivid vision of the coming dictatorship, in 1922.

### Martin Sperr (Steinberg/Bavaria 1944– )

An actor and short-story writer (*Landshuter Erzählungen, Bayerische Trilogie*, 1967), he was one of the first to rediscover the richness of dialect for his essentially middle-class audience, as in his 'new' *Volksstück, Jagdszenen aus Niederbayern* (1972) and those with historical subjects such as *Koralle Meier* (1970) and *Die Spitzeder* (1977).

### Hilde Spiel (Vienna 1911–90)

A poet, essayist and journalist, she worked during her English exile for the *New Statesman*. With *Fanny Arnstein oder die Emanzipation* (1962) she gave German scholars their first informed account of 18thc Viennese cultural life from the perspective of a female protagonist, Moses Mendelssohn's daughter. S's witty and provocative memoirs *Die hellen und die finsteren Zeiten 1911–1946* and *Welche ist meine Welt? Erinnerungen 1946–1989* (1989–90) constitute her most lasting work.

### Friedrich Spielhagen
#### (Magdeburg 1829–1911 Berlin)

Only his *Theorie des Dramas* (1883), a work which also influenced Naturalist narrative prose, is now in print, but in his day he was the immensely successful author of novels featuring 'bourgeois' heroes in their topical but ineffective struggle against the neo-feudal Prusso-German society of the day: *Problematische Naturen* (1861), *In Reih' und Glied* (1866), *Hammer und Amboß* (1869), *Sturmflut* (on the subject of the notorious stock exchange crash of 1873, 1877). Endlessly re-printed, they graced the glass-fronted book-case of every self-respecting liberally minded Wilhelmine middle-class citizen.

### Christian Heinrich Spieß (nr Freiberg/
#### Saxony 1755–99 nr Klattau/Bohemia)

This prolific writer was, with Jean Paul, one of late 18thc Germany's most widely read authors. He also collected and edited *Biographien der Selbstmörder* (1786–9) and *Biographien der Wahnsinnigen* (1795–6) with a view to further-ing a better understanding of human pathology and its treatment.

### Karl Spindler (Breslau 1796–1855
#### Bad Feiersbach/Baden)

He led a restless life as an actor until his break-through with his historical novel *Der Bastard* (1826), followed by *Der Jude* (1827) and *Der*

*Jesuit* (1829), which made him Germany's best-selling author by 1830. Over-production led to a decline in quality, but his gripping storylines retained a hold on readers through-out the 19thc.

### Baruch Spinoza
#### (Amsterdam 1632–77 The Hague)

The influence of this learned optician, a de-scendant of Portuguese Jewish refugees, on Lessing, Mendelssohn, Jacobi and esp Goethe, lay in his pantheism: God, he said, is Nature. A pioneer of textual critical exegesis, he refused a chair in Heidelberg on the grounds that he would not be free to teach what he believed it the duty of the state to be, namely to promote freedom, and felt constrained to publ almost all his work anon, notably his *Tractatus Theologico-Politicus* (1670).

### Carl Spitteler
#### (Liestal 1845–1924 Lucerne)

Author of the novelle *Konrad der Leutnant* (1898), the remarkably forward-looking psy-choanalytical novel *Imago* (1906) and the verse epic, *Olympischer Frühling* (1905), he was more widely read in Germany than in his native Switzerland before the 1914–18 war, but can be regarded as one of the architects of Swiss cultural identity: his famous speech, *Unser Schweizer Standpunkt*, made on 14 December 1914, advocated the healing of the divisions between French-speaking and German-speaking Switzerland. He received the Nobel Prize in 1919.

### Johanna Spyri
#### (Hirzel/Zurich 1827–1901 Zurich)

She gained her first success as a children's au-thor with *Heimatlos* (1878), but it was *Heidis Lehr- und Wanderjahre* (1880) and *Heidi kann brauchen, was es gelernt hat* (1881) which made her one of the world's best-known writers for girls and made her little Swiss girl a perennial favourite, especially in Britain, the US and Japan, shaping readers' views of Switzerland for the next 100 years.

### Ernst Stadler (Colmar 1883–1914 Ypres)

Akin to Hofmannsthal in the precocity of his

literary talent (*Präludien*, 1904), his training as a comparatist and his disillusionment with aestheticism, Stadler established himself on the eve of the 1914–18 war as one of Expressionism's most influential and admired essayists, critics and poets: *Der Aufbruch* (1914) contains one of its paradigmatic poems, 'Fahrt über die Kölner Rheinbrücke bei Nacht'.

*Germaine de Staël* (Paris 1746–1817)
Schiller published an essay by S in his journal *Die Horen* (*Versuch über die Dichtung*, 1796) and she was seen as a pioneer of the socio-historical approach to literature with her *De la littérature considérée dans ses rapports avec les institutions sociales* (1800). But it is for the influence of her *De l'Allemagne* (1813) in promoting a new and positive image of Germany and its literature that she deserves a place in a history of German literature.

*Hermann Stehr* (Habelschwerdt 1864–1940 Oberschreiberhau/Silesia)
The rhapsodic evocations of Silesia in his works, and his stereotyping of women as maternal or irrational beings mediating Nature to 'Faustian' man, may make it hard for the modern (woman) reader to see his best-selling novel, *Der Heiligenhof* (1918), as anything more than an overblown example of the *Blut und Boden* fiction which the Nazis so eagerly acclaimed. Yet his work is not without social concern and is deeply permeated with the Silesian mystical tradition.

*Rudolf Steiner* (Kraljevec/Croatia 1861–1925 Dornach)
The founder of the anthroposophical movement with its view of the spiritual interdependence of man and the cosmos (*Theosophie*, 1904), he exercised an influence on artists and writers as diverse as Morgenstern, Kandinsky, Hesse, Lasker-Schüler and Ende, as well as Albert Schweitzer. Perhaps his most enduring legacy is his idea of the 'whole child' (*Die Erziehung des Kindes vom Gesichtspunkte der Geisteswissenschaft*, 1907), as expressed in the many Waldorf Schools today. His views on wholeness and ecology and the role he accorded Goethe in a movement whose

headquarters is the Goetheanum near Basle have also exerted a pervasive influence on the 20thc.

*Carl Sternheim*
(Leipzig 1878–1942 Brussels)
He sought to provide a portrait of his age, warts and all, in what he later called his 'comedies on the heroic life of the German bourgeoisie', such as *Die Hose* (1911), *Bürger Schippel* (1913) and *Der Snob* (1914). The 'warts' ensured him a *succès de scandale* at the time, but neglect afterwards. His comedies lacked the traditional 'moral message', or even a clear satirical and hence normative viewpoint.

*Adalbert Stifter*
(Oberplan/Bohemia 1805–68 Linz)
One of the greatest prose writers in the German language, he was also a painter and educator, and thoroughly versed in modern science. A man of his times, yet at odds with them, he was unsuccessful in his career as an inspector of schools and writer of educational works, yet *Der Nachsommer* (1857) is one of the greatest of *Bildungsromane*. S grew up close to nature (in the Bohemian forest), and landscape is central to his *Studien* (1844–50) which include the novellen *Abdias* and *Brigitta*, and to *Bunte Steine* (1853, which incl the stories *Granit*, *Bergkristall* and *Kalkstein*), as it is to his historical novel *Witiko* (1865–7). Yet, unsentimental countryman that he was, he portrays nature as indifferent to human destiny, and infuses the relationship of some human beings to it with cosmic fear.

*Julius Stinde* (Kirchnüchel/Holstein 1841–1905 Olsberg/Ruhr)
He created an extremely funny pastiche of middle-class post-1870 German society in the person of the domineering and smug Frau Wilhelmine Buchholz (forerunner of Fontane's *Frau Jenny Treibel*). She is the fictitious protagonist and narrator of the novels *Buchholzens in Italien* (1883) and *Die Familie Buchholz* (3 vols 1884–6). His success suggests that even Wilhelmine society was capable of laughing at itself.

*Friedrich-Leopold, Count Stolberg*
(Bramstedt/Holstein 1750–1819
Sondermühlen nr Osnabrück),
*Christian, Count Stolberg* (Hamburg
1748–1821 Windeby/Eckernförde)
Friedrich-Leopold and his brother Christian
were Goethe's companions on his Swiss journey in 1775. F-L's conversion to Roman Catholicism in 1800 proved a cultural milestone
and was the first of many, both on the periphery and at the centre of Romanticism, incl
those of Friedrich Schlegel, Adam Müller and
Zacharias Werner. It caused a violent reaction
among his erstwhile friends, which his bigoted
statements in his 15-vol *Geschichte der Religion
Jesu Christi* (1806–18) did little to abate. F-L
wrote classical tragedies with choruses and tr
Aeschylus and Homer; C often collaborated
with him but was an able poet in the manner of
Hölty and Bürger. Both brothers deserve
greater recognition as fine representatives of
the culture of the German classical age.

### Theodor Storm
(Husum 1817–88 Hademarschen)
He was a magistrate who wrote his lyric poetry
(*Gedichte*, 1852, [7]1885), stories and novellen in
his leisure time. Beginning with *Immensee*
(1849), his greatest success, most of his
novellen first appeared, as was then customary,
in literary journals, notably *Westermanns
illustrierte Monatshefte* (*Viola tricolor*, 1873–4,
*Carsten Curator*, 1878, *Hans und Heinz Kirch*,
1882–3, *Zur Chronik des Grieshuis*, 1884–5,
*Ein Festtag auf Hadlershuis*, 1885–6, *Ein
Bekenntnis*, 1887–8) and in Rodenberg's
*Deutsche Rundschau* (*Aquis submersus*, 1876,
*Eekenhof*, 1879, *Der Schimmelreiter*, 1888).
Virtually all his stories feature tense, even
destructive, family relationships and are told
with narrative sophistication embedded in a
living oral tradition. His early rejection of any
transcendental dimension in life informs a concern for social and moral issues particularly
evident in his later work, and is reflected in the
pessimistic undertone of much of his writing.

*Moritz von Strachwitz* (Frankenstein/
Silesia 1822–47 Vienna)
He was, like Fontane, a ballad writer (*Das Herz
von Douglas*) and a member of the influential
Berlin literary circle, *Der Tunnel über der Spree*,
and, like Platen, a master of complex verse
forms. Schumann and Brahms set his poems to
music, but the ideal of virile heroism they embody has become suspect and fallen out of
fashion since the Third Reich.

### August Stramm
(nr Münster 1874–1915 Gorodec)
He was killed at the scene of Trakl's great
poem *Grodek*. Yet his posthumous cycle *Du:
Liebesgedichte* (1915) and the war poems,
*Tropfblut* (1919), make him the first great abstract poet of German Expressionism and a
forerunner of many later 20thc poets in the
visual quality he gives to words, his 'destruction' of metre, grammar and syntax, and his
characteristic single-word lines.

### Joseph Anton Stranitzky
(Graz or Prague 1676–1726 Vienna)
Toothpullers were famous for telling jokes to
distract their 'customers', and the same was
said of S, who combined dentistry with the
management of a troupe of actors in Vienna.
By 1710 he had managed to displace the Italian
comedians from the Kärntnertor theatre; there
he created the role of the vulgar Salzburg peasant, Hans Wurst, who comments, incongru-
ously yet aptly, on the doings of the mighty in
the 14 melodramas S adapted from Italian
operas.

### Botho Strauss
(Naumburg/Saale 1944– )
Did the affluent society of W Germany get the
scourge it deserved in Strauss? There has been
no lack of adulation and demonization of this
disciple of Foucault and Wittgenstein and author of the acerbic short story, *Die Widmung*
(1977), the novel *Der junge Mann* (1984), the
prose text, *Paare, Passanten* (1981) and the dramatic *Trilogie des Wiedersehens* (1977) which
began his domination of the W German stage
for over a decade. His other plays include *Groß
und klein* (1978), *Kalldewey, Farce* (1982), *Die
Zeit und das Zimmer* (1988), *Angelas Kleider*
(1991) and the '*Wende*'-trilogy, *Schlußchor*
(1991), with its central image of the 'castrated
chimera', the (German) griffin/eagle. Vilified
in recent years for his 'neo-conservatism' and

'cultural pessimism', Strauss has the polemical vigour of one who sees the poet as the only reliable guardian of a nation's culture, as he made abundantly clear in *Anschwellender Bocksgesang*, his notorious interview in *Der Spiegel* of February 1993.

### David Friedrich Strauss
(Ludwigsburg 1808–74)

His *Das Leben Jesu* (1835–6) galvanized Protestant thinking with its presentation of the 'historical' Jesus, which had a profound impact on its tr Mary Ann Evans (George Eliot), among others. With *Der alte und der neue Glaube* (1873) he found a ready audience for his advocacy of a new humanist and secularized Protestantism appropriate to the new Reich.

### Lulu von Strauß und Torney
(Bückeburg 1873–1956 Jena)

She is a central figure in the history of the German ballad: *Balladen und Lieder* (1902), *Neue Balladen und Lieder* (1907), and *Reif steht die Saat* (1919), a title which provides a link with her prose fiction about peasant life (*Judas*, 1911, reissued as *Der Judashof*, 1937). This made her a popular and supportive author of the Third Reich.

### Erwin Strittmatter
(Spremberg/Niederlausitz 1912–94 Dollgow/Brandenburg)

This undogmatic working-class writer became a national figure for people in the GDR, whose familiar world he portrayed in his semi-autobiog writings, from the early novel, *Ochsenkutscher* (1950) and *Katzgraben* (a comedy staged by Brecht, 1954) to his first major success, *Ole Bienkopp* (1963), a novel about GDR collectivization. His public readings in post-1989 E Germany, notably from his 3-part novel *Der Laden* (1983–92), drew thousands, for whom he represented continuity and familiarity. His work owes much to Jean Paul and Raabe, and has been tr into 38 languages, though 'not into West German'. His wife **Eva Strittmatter** (Neuruppin 1930– ) writes verse in traditional forms, which may account for her popularity.

### Hermann Sudermann
(Matzicken/E Prussia 1857–1928 Berlin)

Author of the Naturalist novel *Frau Sorge* (1887), he took his place alongside Hauptmann with his first stage success, *Die Ehre* (1889). This was followed by *Sodoms Ende* (1991) and *Heimat* (1893). His later work includes a wide range of dramas, such as the political comedy *Der Sturmgeselle Sokrates* (1903), novels critical of contemporary or past society (*Das Hohe Lied*, 1908, *Der tolle Professor*, 1926), and realist fiction set in his eastern homeland, notably *Litauische Geschichten* (1917), a set which incl his finest novelle, *Die Reise nach Tilsit*.

### Peter Suhrkamp (Kirchhatten/Oldenburg 1891–1959 Frankfurt/M)

He managed the section of the S Fischer publishing house which remained in Germany after 1933 from 1936 until his arrest in 1944. In 1950 he set up his own firm, Suhrkamp Verlag, taking with him major authors such as Hesse and Frisch, and identifying it with modern German literature, featuring authors silenced under Nazism such as Adorno, Benjamin and Brecht, and newer names such as Enzensberger and M Walser.

### Patrick Süskind
(Ambach/Starnberger See 1949– )

The phenomenal success of his comedy *Der Kontrabaß* (1984), and his stylishly written novel *Das Parfüm: Geschichte eines Mörders* (1985), made S one of Germany's leading authors. He also writes short stories (*Die Taube*, 1987, *Die Geschichte des Herrn Sommer*, 1992), and freelances for TV.

### Bertha von Suttner
(Prague 1843–1914 Vienna)

Her celebrated novel *Die Waffen nieder!* (1889) became the manifesto of pacifism, a cause she actively promoted as founder member of the German Peace Movement and for which she was awarded the Nobel Peace Prize in 1905, the first woman to receive it.

# T

### Fanny (Franziska) Tarnow
(Güstrow 1779–1862 Dessau)

She must have been a tiresome friend, clinging as she did to anyone who would help her financially. She made valiant efforts on her own behalf, running a girls' school in Hamburg and translating George Sand's *Indiana* as well as Balzac and the Irish novelist, Lady Morgan. Her own romantic fiction made much reference to the 'womanly heart', and she set something of a fashion by investing the 'acceptable' female types in her *Gallerie weiblicher Nationalbilder* (1838) with a 'national' aura.

### Gabriele Tergit (Berlin 1894–1982)

The literary merits of her brilliant crime reports for the *Berliner Tageblatt* have been rediscovered by modern feminist literary historians, as has her novel, *Käsebier erobert den Kurfürstendamm* (1932). In exile she wrote *Effinger* (1951), a German saga along Galsworthy lines. Her arresting memoirs, *Etwas Seltenes überhaupt*, were publ in 1983.

### Ludwig Thoma
(Oberammergau 1867–1921 Rottach)

His oeuvre encompasses a wide and contradictory range. As a journalist and editor of *Simplicissimus*, he wrote satirical poems and stories (*Assessor Karlchen*, 1901) under the pseudonym 'Peter Schlemihl'. He also wrote satirical comedies (*Die Medaille*, 1901, and *Die Lokalbahn*, 1902) and (tragic) novels of peasant life, notably *Der Wittiber* (1911). He is best known for his *Lausbubengeschichten* (1905), masterly examples of the humorous school-story genre. Under the impact of the 1914–18 war, he underwent a 'conversion' to extreme right-wing politics, epitomized in the often viciously anti-Semitic articles he wrote during his final illness.

### Christian Thomasius
(Leipzig 1655–1728 Halle)

He is still closely identified with the beginnings of modernity in German life through his unremitting advocacy of tolerance and the role of reason in developing the individual's moral autonomy for the good of society as a whole. His attacks on orthodox Lutheranism while a university teacher in Leipzig damaged his reputation and his purse, but he escaped disciplinary proceedings by turning to the Elector of Brandenburg (1701), who allowed him to shape the ethos of the new university of Halle. He was an opponent of torture and capital punishment, and a flavour of his character is conveyed by his simple and genial response to those advocating witch-trials: witchcraft is neither provable – nor possible.

### Ludwig Tieck (Berlin 1773–1853)

Tieck, who, chameleon-like, 'became' the characters he read in his celebrated dramatic readings, notably of Shakespeare, was a central figure of German Romanticism. An allusive yet transparent style marks his early novellen (*Der blonde Eckbert*, 1797, *Der Runenberg*, 1804) and artist novels (*Geschichte des Herrn William Lovell*, 1795–6 and *Franz Sternbalds Wanderungen*, 1798); he wrote idiosyncratic Romantic comedies (*Die verkehrte Welt*, *Der gestiefelte Kater*, *Prinz Zerbino*, 1797) and the poetic drama *Leben und Tod der Heiligen Genoveva* (1800), and was the ed both of medieval texts and the works of Novalis, Kleist, Lenz and Shakespeare. Later he became a leading *biedermeier* prose writer admired for his historical novellen, such as *Der Aufruhr in den Cevennen* (1826) and *Der Hexen-Sabbath* (1832), the stylish novel *Vittoria Accorombona* (1840) and novels and novellen set in the present, such as *Der junge Tischlermeister* (1836) and *Des Lebens Überfluß* (1839), whose first paragraph so perfectly encapsulates his age's fear of revolution.

### Christoph August Tiedge (Gardelegen/ Brandenburg 1752–1841 Dresden)

The companion of Elise von der Recke, he was the author of *Urania; über Gott, Unsterblichkeit und Freiheit* (1800, [18]1862), one of the most admired didactic poems of the classical era.

### Ernst Toller (Smotschin nr Bromberg 1893– 1939 New York)

This great Expressionist dramatist fought and became a pacifist in the 1914–18 war and was a leading figure in the short-lived revolutionary government in Bavaria in 1918–19. Condemned to 5 years' imprisonment, he wrote many of his most celebrated plays in custody: *Die Wandlung* (dramatic monologue with *Vorspiel*, 1919), *Masse-Mensch* (verse drama 1921), *Die Maschinenstürmer* (drama 1922) and *Der deutsche Hinkemann* (tragedy 1923). *Hoppla, wir leben!*, staged by Piscator in 1927, is a prime example of political theatre. He emigrated in 1933, the year his wonderfully vivid *Eine Jugend in Deutschland* was published.

### Georg Trakl
### (Salzburg 1887–1914 Cracow)

The 'Austrian Rimbaud' is a poet's poet, as writers as different as Rose Ausländer and Celan, Eich, Huchel, Bobrowski and Nelly Sachs have shown. Yet even uninitiated readers respond to the brilliant images and slow melodic lines in *Gedichte* (1913) and the free verse of *Elis, Helian,* and *Sebastian im Traum* (1915), in which leitmotifs and images are stripped of their traditional associations, underpinning the extreme sense of isolation and cosmic desolation of his late work such as 'Grodek', a poem recording the Austro-Russian battle whose carnage indirectly led to his death, perhaps by suicide.

### B. Traven (San Francisco or Chicago 1882 or 1890–1969 Mexico City)

His is now a name to be reckoned with in terms of sales and popularity, though the identity of T, also known as **Ret Marut**, remains obscure. *Das Totenschiff* (1926) and *Der Schatz der Sierra Madre* (1927, filmed by John Huston in 1928) made him world-famous. T's *Mahagoni* novels (1931–40) are set amidst the deforestation and exploitation of the Latin-American rain forest.

### Heinrich von Treitschke
### (Dresden 1834–96 Berlin)

He was the author of an influential (though unfinished) history of Germany, *Geschichte Deutschlands im 19. Jahrhundert* (1879–94), distinguished for its style, its author's interest in literature, and for establishing the notion of Prussia's historical destiny to rule Germany. As professor of history at Berlin from 1873, he lent his considerable authority to the anti-Semitism of his students, as in *Ein Wort über unser Judentum* (1880).

### Kuni Tremel-Eggert
### (Burgkunstadt 1889–1957)

She was an author of regional fiction set in Franconia, but the success of her novels, *Barb: Der Roman einer deutschen Frau* (1934) and especially of *Freund Sansibar* (1939), endowed her with the status of party propagandist during the Third Reich.

### Kurt Tucholsky
### (Berlin 1890–1935 Gothenburg/Sweden)

A feuilletonist and journalist for newspapers and magazines such as *Vorwärts, Ulk* and *Berliner Tageblatt*, Tucholsky transformed *Die Weltbühne* after 1918 to one of the principal intellectual arenas of the Weimar Republic. 'The satirist is a disappointed idealist,' he wrote: after the Nazis stripped him of citizenship and burnt his writings, he publ nothing more, and took his own life in Swedish exile.

### Peter Turrini
### (St Margarethen nr Klagenfurt 1944– )

His early dialect dramas are characterized by violent language and action (*Rozznjogd*, 1971, *Sauschlachten*, 1972, *Kindsmord*, 1973). Updated versions of Beaumarchais and Goldoni preceded his politically controversial career as a TV script writer; his series *Alpensaga* (1976–80) and *Arbeiterjagd* (1988–90) aimed with some effect to use drama to attack and reform the Austrian political system, as do his plays *Die Bürger* (1982), *Die Minderleister* (1988) and *Tod und Teufel* (1990).

# U

### Ludwig Uhland (Tübingen 1787–1862)

No anthology of German poems between the 1830s and 1930s was complete without Uhland, a medievalist, university professor, lawyer and democratic parliamentarian admired for his integrity and loved for the melodic appeal and ready accessibility of his poems and ballads, some of which (such as 'Der gute Kamerad') are still part of traditional

German culture. His early *Gedichte* appeared with Cotta in 1815 ([19]1851, [42]1867).

### *Fritz von Unruh*
(Koblenz 1885–1970 Diez nr Limburg)
An officer turned pacifist, he attempted to use literature (*Opfergang*, short stories 1919, and *Ein Geschlecht*, 1917) in the service of the Peace Movement. He was more successful abroad in exile than at home, especially with his apocalyptic novel *The End Is Not Yet* (1947, *Der nie verlor*, 1948).

### *Johanna Charlotte Unzer*, née *Ziegler*
(Halle 1725–82 Altona)
Her *Versuch in Scherzgedichten* (1751) in Gleim's manner earned Unzer the accolade of a crown of laurels in 1753, so she promptly followed it with a collection of 42 *Sittliche und zärtliche Gedichte* (1754). The attribution to her of many didactic texts for women written by her uncle was simply a publisher's marketing stratagem.

### *Johannes Urzidil*
(Prague 1896–1970 Rome)
A habitué of the Prague literary circle of the Café Arco, Expressionist poet (*Sturz der Verdammten*, 1919) and Goethe scholar, he was a journalist, diplomat and, after the Nazi invasion of Czechoslovakia, a refugee. His *Prager Triptychon* (1960) and *Das Elefantenblatt* (1962) contributed to postwar Western awareness of Prague's unique cultural role in Central Europe.

### *Johann Peter Uz* (Ansbach 1720–96)
One of his period's most competent authorities on poetics, this rococo poet wrote much anacreontic and didactic verse (*Lyrische Gedichte*, 1749, *Lyrische und andere Gedichte*, 1755).

# V

### *Karl Valentin* (Munich 1885–1948)
This endlessly inventive cabaret artist was the delight of writers as different as Brecht, Adorno and Ionesco. Starting with *Der Kuß* (1913) he also made films (some 3 dozen of

which survive). His central comic theme was the inadequacy of language as a means of social intercourse or for conveying 'truth'.

### *Karl August Varnhagen von Ense*
(Düsseldorf 1785–1858 Berlin)
He fought in the Austrian and Russian armies in the Napoleonic wars, was wounded at Wagram, and became a Prussian diplomat until 1819 when he was prematurely retired for his liberal views. An aristocrat who knew everybody from Napoleon, Beethoven and Goethe downwards, he counted himself fortunate when in 1814 Rahel Levin, a vivacious Jewish woman 14 years his senior, accepted him. His chief interest lies in his idiosyncratic (auto)biog writings, notably *Rahel: Ein Buch des Andenkens für ihre Freunde* (1834) and his (somewhat gossipy) 9-vol *Denkwürdigkeiten* (1837–59) and 14-vol *Tagebücher* (1861–70).

### *Rahel Varnhagen von Ense*
(Berlin 1771–1833)
The spoken word dominated the life of this clever daughter of a Berlin Jewish merchant. Her 'attic salon' brought together personalities such as Prince Louis Ferdinand, W von Humboldt, F Schlegel, Brentano and Jean Paul; later her drawing room as the wife of V was attended by Heine and other notables. Her personality comes over in her correspondence, a 'dialogue in letters' which feminist scholars have identified as a paradigm of *weibliches Schreiben*.

### *Will Vesper* (Barmen 1882–1962 Gifhorn)
He was an established lyric poet and popularizer of German literature of every century and almost every genre, when he became a prominent Nazi functionary, helping direct the burning of 'degenerate' books in 1933 and supervising the media industries of the Third Reich.

### *Clara Viebig* (Trier 1860–1952 Berlin)
She was influenced by the French Naturalists in her novellen about lower-class life (*Kinder der Eifel*, 1897) and her comic novel *Das Weiberdorf* (1900), both set in her home area, the Eifel mountains. Her novels *Das tägliche Brot* (1900) and *Einer Mutter Sohn* (1906) fea-

tured the migrant domestic servant and the unmarried mother; others, such as *Die Wacht am Rhein* (1902), present a detailed panorama of life and attitudes in later 19thc Germany. V's little-known plays (*Der Kampf um den Mann*, 1903) show her rare mastery of the one-acter.

### Friedrich Vieweg
(Halle 1761–1835 Brunswick)

The long history of this Brunswick firm founded in 1786 by this publisher, bookseller and printer epitomizes the development of the book trade in Germany. Vieweg publ Goethe's *Hermann und Dorothea* and works by W von Humboldt and the Schlegels; Keller's novel *Der grüne Heinrich* was publ by his son Eduard V. In the later 19thc Vieweg's was a major supplier to lending libraries and a publisher of periodicals; today it is a leading scientific publisher and part of the Bertelsmann group.

### Friedrich Theodor (1870– von) Vischer (Ludwigsburg 1807–87 Gmunden/Upr Austria)

He was professor of aesthetics at Tübingen, Zurich and Stuttgart (*Die Aesthetik oder Wissenschaft des Schönen*, 1846–57, 6 vols). A member of the Frankfurt Parliament and a powerful speaker (*Frisch gewagt!* speeches, 1863), he wrote a Faust parody (1862) and a best-selling comic novel *Auch Einer* (1879), and invented the phrase '*die Tücke des Objekts*', which is the German equivalent of Murphy's Law.

### Helene Voigt-Diederichs
(nr Eckernförde 1875–1961 Jena)

She married the nationalist publisher Eugen Diederichs and won popularity as a writer of beautifully presented books about her native region (*Schleswig-Holsteiner Landleute*, 1898), which made perfect gifts, and admiration for her powerful treatments of women's lives (*Dreiviertel Stund vor Tag*, 1905, and *Regine*, 1923). Her 'strong silent women' were acclaimed by the Third Reich, which explains her neglect today.

### Karl Gustav Vollmoeller
(Stuttgart 1878–1948 Los Angeles)

He started out as a disciple of Stefan George but won international acclaim with his neo-Romantic *Das Mirakel*, first perf in London in 1911. His later work has its admirers.

### Johann Heinrich Voss (Sommersdorf/ Mecklenburg 1751–1826 Heidelberg)

He edited the *Göttinger Musenalmanach* and was a member of the *Göttinger Hain* whose idylls in the tradition of Theocritus, notably *Die Leibeigenen* (1775), *Die Freigelassenen* (1776) and the utopian *Die Erleichterten* (1801), were characteristic expressions of *Sturm und Drang* hostility to feudalism. His family idyll *Der siebzigste Geburtstag* (1781) and the rural epic *Luise* (1795) sustained his 19thc popularity, as did his pioneering trns of Homer.

### Christian August Vulpius
(Weimar 1762–1827)

Brother of Goethe's partner and later wife, **Christiane** (Weimar 1765–1816), he achieved fame, not to say notoriety, with his 'romantic robber novel', *Rinaldo Rinaldini, der Räuberhauptmann* (1799); today his chief interest lies in his versatile career as a much-translated and plagiarized popular author in a whole variety of genres, incl opera.

# W

### Wilhelm Heinrich Wackenroder
(Berlin 1773–98)

His meditations on medieval and Renaissance art (notably Raphael, Dürer and Michelangelo) publ as *Herzensergießungen eines kunstliebenden Klosterbruders* (1797, incl the artist novelle *Joseph Berglinger*) and *Phantasien über die Kunst, für Freunde der Kunst* (1799), constitute a central contribution to early Romantic aesthetics, as does his correspondence with Ludwig Tieck, his close friend and collaborator on both works.

### Heinrich Leopold Wagner
(Strasburg 1747–79 Frankfurt/M)

He is a kind of seismograph of the literary life of his age. He translated *Macbeth* for performance rather than literary fame, adroitly advertised his early work by giving false places of publication, and is best known for his tragedy on the topical *Sturm und Drang* theme of infanticide, *Die Kindermörderin* (1776), a play ahead of its time in its realistic depiction of a petty-bourgeois milieu.

### *Richard Wagner
(Leipzig 1813–83 Venice)

The musical genius of Wagner made him Germany's towering cultural figure in the second half of the 19thc. His landmark tragic music dramas *Tannhäuser* (1845), *Lohengrin* (1850), *Tristan und Isolde* (1865), *Parsifal* (1882) and the *Ring des Nibelungen* cycle (*Das Rheingold*, 1869, *Die Walküre*, 1870, *Siegfried*, *Götterdämmerung*, 1876) and his comic masterpiece *Die Meistersinger von Nürnberg* (1868) were conceived as a revolutionary attempt to concentrate the power of music, literature and spectacle into one tremendous aesthetic experience or *Gesamtkunstwerk*. Whether idolized or spurned (as by Nietzsche in *Der Fall Wagner*, 1888), W was able to obsess such key 20thc cultural mediators as T Mann and Adorno: he was also appropriated by Hitler. The Bayreuth Festival, which W created in 1876, remains to this day a major event in Europe's cultural calendar.

### *Burkhard Waldis* (Allendorf/Werra *c*.1490–?1556 Abterode)

He worked in Riga as a Protestant agent and author. His carnival play *De Parabell vam verlorn Szohn* (1527) was an innovative attempt to make the *Fastnachtspiel* serve the Reformation. His 'topical' German rendering of Aesop's fables (*Esopus*, 1548) was designed to appeal to young people; his adaptation of Emperor Maximilian's chivalric allegory *Teuerdank* (1553) proved equally popular throughout the 16thc.

### *Hans Günter Wallraff*
(Burscheid nr Cologne 1942– )

W occupies a central place in the post-1968 politicization of W German literature: he brought wit and humour to his 'Till Eugenspiegel' role of working in disguise in institutions which he then exposed in his

*13 unerwünschte Reportagen* (1969) and *Der Aufmacher, Der Mann, der bei 'Bild' Hans Esser war* (1977), directed at the Axel Springer press empire. His autobiog works *Von einem der auszog und das Fürchten lernte* (1970) and *Ganz unten* (1985) were best-sellers.

### *Martin Walser* (Wasserburg/Lake Constance 1927– )

Walser, whom his left-wing opponents frivolously dismissed as conservative, brought the perspective of a S German democrat to his critical vision of Federal Republic society in novels such as *Ehen in Philippsburg* (1957), *Halbzeit* (1960), *Das Einhorn* (1966), *Der Sturz* (1973) and the novelle *Ein fliehendes Pferd* (1978). His dramas include *Eiche und Angora* (1952), *Überlebensgroß* (1963), *Die Zimmerschlacht* (1967) and *In Goethes Hand* (1982). In the novelle *Dorle und Wolf* (1987) and the long novel *Verteidigung der Kindheit* (1991) he portrays the deformation of people and politics brought about by the division of Germany.

### *Robert Walser*
(Biel 1878–1956 Herisau/Appenzell)

This Swiss writer, long a literary outsider, today enjoys classical status as one of the great ironists of German literature. Drawing on the tradition of Swiss self-mockery, W wrote his major novels (*Geschwister Tanner*, 1907, *Der Gehülfe*, 1908, and *Jakob von Gunten*, 1909) during his Berlin years (1905–13), concentrating for the rest of his career on what he called his '*Prosastückligeschäft*', writing hundreds of short texts which add up to an impressive œuvre: these incl *Der Spaziergang*, *Prosa Stücke* and *Kleine Prosa* (1917), *Poetenleben* (1918), *Seeland* (1919), *Die Rose* (1925), *Mikrogramme* (not all deciphered or publ yet) and the unfinished novel *Der Räuber* (publ 1972). His silence from 1933 onwards has fascinated numerous writers since.

### *Maria Waser*
(Herzogenbuchsee 1878–1939 Zurich)

She studied history, made her name as Switzerland's leading woman writer in the interwar years with her historical novel *Die Geschichte der Anna Waser* (1913) and went on to champion Switzerland's literary and cultural independence from Nazi Germany.

### Jakob Wassermann
(Fürth 1873–1934 Altaussee/Styria)

His experience as an assimilated Jew confronted with the realization that emancipation had failed to change the consciousness of his fellow citizens enabled W, as a prolific S Fischer author of internationally best-selling novels and essays, to articulate the existential experience of the German Jew (*Die Juden von Zirndorf*, and its sequel; *Die Geschichte der jungen Renate Fuchs*, novels 1897 and 1900; *Mein Weg als Deutscher und Jude*, autobiog essay 1921). He also portrayed the outsider (*Caspar Hauser oder Die Trägheit des Herzens*, novel 1908) and German middle-class society in the novels *Das Gänsemännchen* (1915: 300,000 copies sold) and, most successfully, *Der Fall Maurizius* (1928), his most ambitious and sophisticated work.

### *Max Weber (Erfurt 1860–1924 Munich)

The 'bourgeois Marx' lent his support to the Weimar Republic. He gave modern sociology its normative foundations by insisting on strict empirical controls and avoidance of ideological bias – a methodological integrity which he sought to exemplify in works such as *Politik als Beruf* (1919) and *Wirtschaft und Gesellschaft* (1922). In *Die protestantische Ethik aus dem Geist des Kapitalismus* (1904–5) he probed the *Entzauberung* (demystification) of life associated with the modern industrial world and traced it back i a to the asceticism of an earlier 'Protestant work ethic'. He co-founded the *Deutsche Gesellschaft für Soziologie* in 1909.

### Georg Rudolf Weckherlin
(Stuttgart 1584–1653 London)

He set out to anchor German poetry in the European Renaissance. He led an interesting life as a diplomat in the service of Württemberg and as a long-serving English civil servant under Charles I. He became Secretary for Foreign Tongues in 1644 but resigned after the King's execution; later he briefly acted as assistant to his successor, the poet Milton. W was a versatile writer of occasional poetry (collected in *Oden und Gesänge*, 1618–19). His *Gaistliche und Weltliche Gedichte* appeared in Amsterdam in 1641, by which time his conception of modern German poetry had been overtaken by the poetic reforms of Martin Opitz.

### Frank Wedekind
(Hanover 1864–1918 Munich)

He was brought up in Switzerland, worked in advertising for Maggi Soups, then became an actor and producer in Berlin and a famous cabaret singer in Munich. His breakthrough as a playwright came with *Frühlings Erwachen* (1891) followed by the 'Lulu' plays *Erdgeist* (1898) and its sequel *Die Büchse der Pandora* (1902). Other plays incl *Der Marquis von Keith* (1901), *Hidalla* (1904) and *Musik* (1908). Their experimental approach and strong satirical sense have had far-reaching effects on 20thc drama.

### Georg Weerth
(Cologne 1822–56 Havana/Cuba)

He was, in Engels's phrase, the first major poet of the German proletariat. He employed humour and irony in its cause, combining business with writing for the *Kölnische Zeitung*. His *Humoristische Szenen aus dem deutschen Handelsleben* (1847–8), the first German novel to be serialized in a newspaper, appeared in Marx's *Neue Rheinische Zeitung*, as did his satirical *Leben und Thaten des berühmten Ritters Schnapphahnski* (1849). He worked in textiles in Bradford in 1843–6 and became Germany's most noted commentator on England during the Industrial Revolution. Prophesying global conflict over limited resources, he died of yellow fever while travelling on business in the US and Latin America.

### Josef Weinheber (Ottakring/Vienna
1892–1945 Kirchstetten/Lr Austria)

A poet schooled in Hölderlin's poetry and himself the author of poems of great formal beauty (i a *Adel und Untergang*, 1934) as well as wit and humour (*Wien wörtlich*, 1935), his reputation sadly but inevitably suffered after he prostituted his gifts in the service of the Nazi regime in Austria.

*Otto Weininger* (Vienna 1880–1903)
His *Geschlecht und Charakter* (1903), a precocious work notorious for its vehement hatred and fear of Jews and women, has provided its admirers and detractors with abundant material for stereotyping misogyny and Jewish self-hatred.

*Christian Weise* (Zittau 1642–1708)
He taught at the Weißenfels grammar school and then became *Rektor* (headmaster) of the Gymnasium at Zittau, where he wrote some 55 comedies, biblical dramas and historical tragedies for performance by his boys. Prior to that he made his name with entertainingly satirical novels which laid the basis for the practical rationalism of his numerous works on stylistics, poetics, educational theory and political studies.

*Peter Weiss* (Nowawes nr Berlin 1916–82 Stockholm)
He was nearly 50 when, as the author of what became one of the manifestos of 1968, he produced in 1964 his masterly example of 'total theatre': *Die Verfolgung und Ermordung Jean Paul Marats dargestellt durch die Schauspielgruppe des Hospizes zu Charenton unter Anleitung des Herrn de Sade*, a work combining tragedy, pantomine and the theatre of the absurd with a marvellous command of the stage. The role of art in the political struggle against human cynicism was evident in *Die Ermittlung: Oratorium in elf Gesängen* (1965) on the Eichmann trial, and in his *Hölderlin* drama of 1971; *Die Ästhetik des Widerstands* (novel 1975–81) offers a unique analysis of 20thc European socialism.

*Christian Felix Weiße* (Annaberg 1726–1804 Leipzig)
Librettist and writer of tragedies 'after' Shakespeare (*Richard der Dritte*, 1745) and *Singspiele* such as *Die verwandelten Weiber oder Der Teufel ist los* (1751) and *Die Liebe auf dem Lande* (1767), and books for children, he is best known today as ed of the early children's paper, *Der Kinderfreund* (1775–82).

*Wilhelm Weitling* (Magdeburg 1808–71 New York)
Son of a French army officer and a German cook, journeyman apprentice tailor, utopian socialist (*Die Menschheit, wie sie ist, und wie sie sein sollte*, 1839) and member of the *Bund der Gerechten* (League of the Just), W attempted in his most influential work, *Das Evangelium des armen Sünders* (1845), to reconcile early Christianity and Communism.

*Dieter Wellershoff* (Neuß/Rhineland 1925– )
His career and work can be seen to typify the W German literary scene. An influential ed for Kiepenheuer & Witsch and 1960s essayist who attacked normative language as the expression of outmoded authority crippling human potential, he has written novels (*Die Schattengrenze*, 1969, *Einladung an alle*, 1972), stories and opera libretti (*Doppelt belichtetes Seestück und andere Texte*, 1974), radio plays, poems, literary theory (*Das Verschwinden im Bild*, 1980) and autobiog (*Die Arbeit des Lebens*, 1985, *Blick auf einen fernen Berg*, 1991).

*Diederich von dem Werder* (Werdershausen 1584–1657 Reinsdorf)
He wrote a cycle of 100 sonnets in which the words 'Krieg' and 'Sieg' appear in every line (*Krieg und Sieg Christi*, 1631), but a greater achievement was his trn of Tasso's Christian epic poem *Gerusalemme liberata* (*Gottfried von Bulljon, oder Das Erlösete Jerusalem*, 1626, [2]1651), which put him at the centre of his period's literary awareness.

*Franz Werfel* (Prague 1890–1945 Beverly Hills)
Whereas many baptized Jews came back to their Jewish roots through the experience of persecution, W converted to R Catholicism. The international success of the film of his novel, *Das Lied von Bernadette* (1941), has obscured his other work such as the drama *Spiegelmensch* (1920), the novel trilogy *Magische Trilogie* (*Nicht der Mörder, der Ermordete ist schuldig*, 1919, *Barbara oder die Frömmigkeit*, 1929, *Der veruntreute Himmel*, 1939), and the novels *Verdi: Roman der Oper* (1924) and *Stern der Ungeborenen* (1946).

**Zacharias Werner**
(Königsberg 1768–1823 Vienna)
An E Prussian and a minor Prussian civil servant, he was portrayed by his friend ETA
Hoffmann in *Die Serapionsbrüder*, and scored a
success in Berlin on the eve of Prussia's cata-
strophic defeat by Napoleon at Jena with his
patriotic drama *Martin Luther, oder die Weihe
der Kraft* (1806), with his mentor Iffland in the
title role. He followed it with his very actable
fate drama *Der vierundzwanzigste Februar* (perf
1810, publ 1815) and with his conversion and
ordination as a RC priest in 1814. A brilliant
preacher to the Congress of Vienna (1814–75),
he played an influential secret role as a crusader against enlightened Reform Catholicism
in Metternich's Austria.

**Jörg Wickram** (Colmar *c*.1500–55/60)
A mastersinger and town clerk in Burkheim/
Alsace, he was the author of romances (*Ritter
Galmy*, 1539, *Gabriotto und Reinhart*, 1551)
and novels (*Von guten und bösen Nachbarn*,
1556, *Goldtfaden*, 1557), and *Der jungen
Knaben Spiegel* (1554), an early prototype
of the *Bildungsroman*. He also wrote dramas
(*Der verlorene Sohn*, 1540) and the famous
collection of mainly farcical anecdotes, *Das
Rollwagenbüchlein* (1555).

**Ernst Wiechert** (Kleinort/E Prussia
1887–1950 Uerikon/Switzerland)
He won acclaim in the Third Reich for his
*völkisch* stories, *Der Totenwolf* (1924), *Die
Majorin* (1934), and *Hirtennovelle* (1935).
However, his courageous protest at Pastor
Niemöller's imprisonment led to a sojourn in
Buchenwald. His subsequent novels, combin-
ing evocative 'harmless' portraits of the E
German landscape with a powerful sense of
unseen evil (*Das einfache Leben*, 1939, *Die
Jeromin-Kinder*, 1945–7, *Missa sine nomine*,
1950), won him a large readership.

**Martina Wied** (Vienna 1882–1957)
Wied, who had contributed before the 1914–18
war to the Expressionist journal *Der Brenner*,
was one of the first Austrian writers implicitly
to subvert the utopian image of the Austrian
village (*Rauch über St Florian*, 1937). Most of
her novels, including the semi-autobiog *Die*

*Geschichte des reichen Jünglings* (1952), were wr
in English exile.

**Christoph Martin Wieland** (Oberholzheim
nr Biberach 1733–1813 Weimar)
He offers a kaleidoscope of 18thc German
writing: a parson's son and Pietist, he was influenced by Brockes and Haller, by Klopstock,
Wolff's philosophy and Bayle's *Dictionary*.
He was invited to Zurich by Bodmer following
the publication of his incomplete national
epic, *Hermann* (1751), became professor of
philosophy at Erfurt, and tutor to the future
Duke Karl August of Weimar by virtue of
his novel of state, *Der goldene Spiegel oder
Die Könige von Scheschian* (1772). As editor
of *Teutscher Merkur* (1773–89, 1790–1810)
W exercised a formative influence on German
journalism and wrote in a wide range of
genres: *Comische Erzählungen* (verse travesties
1765), *Der Sieg der Natur über die Schwärmerei,
oder Die Abenteuer des Don Silvio von Rosalva*
(burlesque novel 1764), *Die Geschichte des
Agathon* (novel 1766–7), *Musarion, oder Die
Philosophie der Grazien* (verse tale 1768),
*Alceste* (*Singspiel* 1773), *Die Abderiten, eine sehr
wahrscheinliche Geschichte* (comic novel 1774–
80) and the Romantic heroic epic *Oberon*
(1780).

**Oswald Wiener** (Vienna 1935– )
Membership of the *Wiener Gruppe* may have
only been an episode in the life of this poet,
cyberneticist, mathematician and student of
African langs, but it was a critical one. His
'anti-novel', *die verbesserung von mitteleuropa*
(book publ 1969), confronted but failed to
find an answer to the paradox of the group's
critique of lang: namely, that despite their
extraordinary command of lang and their
understanding of text as extending far beyond
the boundaries of the wr and spoken word,
the discrepancy between their need to express
reality and the inadequacy of their poetic
medium remained unresolved. Logically,
if absurdly, W destroyed most of the texts he
wrote as member of the *Wiener Gruppe*.

**Ernst von Wildenbruch**
(Beirut 1845–1909 Berlin)
The 'dramatist of the Hohenzollerns', he wrote

patriotic historical dramas of which the best known is *Die Quitzows* (1888). He enjoyed a dominant position in the Berlin court theatre, and the ironic exploitation of this play by Fontane in the novel *Die Poggenpuhls* provides modern readers with a sophisticated insight into the phenomenon of official culture in the Second Empire.

#### *Ottilie Wildermuth* (Rottenburg/Swabia 1817–77 Tübingen)

Humour and self-irony characterized W, one of the most successful (Protestant) Christian writers of 19thc literature for young people (*Bilder und Geschichten aus dem schwäbischen Leben*, 1852, and *Bilder und Geschichten aus Schwaben*, 1857).

#### *Bruno Wille* (Magdeburg 1860–1928 nr Lindau)

He was a principal architect of the Free Stage or *Freie Bühne* and the *Neue freie Volksbühne* which aimed to bring drama to working-class people. His lyric poetry veers between Naturalism and neo-Romanticism (*Einsiedler und Genosse*, 1894).

#### *Marianne von Willemer* (Linz? 1784–1860 Frankfurt/M)

Illegitimate daughter of a Viennese actress, she was brought up by a Frankfurt widower who married her in 1814. In 1815 she and Goethe developed a relationship which released her poetic gifts, not fully recognized until after her death. A fine musician herself (Brentano taught her the guitar), her poems were set by Beethoven, Schubert and Mendelssohn.

#### *Johann Joachim Winckelmann* (Stendhal 1717–68 Trieste)

He played a decisive part in opening up the civilization of classical Greece and shifting the emphasis of 18thc classicism away from Roman antiquity. His seminal art-historical works affected neo-classicism profoundly esp in French translation: *Gedanken über die Nachahmung der griechischen Werke in der Mahlerey und Bildhauer-Kunst* (1755, French 1755) and *Die Geschichte der Kunst des Altherthums* (1764, French 1766). His murder in Trieste has become a myth in itself.

#### *Gabriele Wohmann* (Darmstadt 1932– )

An author of radio and TV scripts, she is the German chronicler of the human cost of modern life and of the lack of meaningful interaction between the private sphere and contemporary society in her novels *Abschied für länger* (1965), *Die Bütows* (1967), *Ernste Absicht* (1970) and *Schönes Gehege* (1975), and the story *Kassensturz* (1989).

#### *Christa Wolf* (Landsberg a.d.Warthe 1929– )

She personifies the achievements and complex public face of GDR literature throughout most of its 40-yr history. An official of the *Deutscher Schriftstellerverband*, reader for publishing houses and ed of the journal *Neue Deutsche Literatur*, she wrote *Der geteilte Himmel* (novel 1963) to advocate a new, post-Berlin Wall GDR patriotism, while *Nachdenken über Christa T.* (1968) was intended to create a literary continuity between the GDR and (a selective reading of) earlier German literature, as were *Till Eulenspiegel* (short story/film text 1972, wr with her husband **Gerhard Wolf**, Bad Frankenhausen 1928– ), *Unter den Linden: Drei unwahrscheinliche Geschichten* (1974), *Kein Ort: Nirgends* (novel 1979), *Der Schatten eines Traumes* (essays 1979), *Kassandra* (novel) and *Voraussetzungen einer Erzählung: Kassandra* (both 1983). Her celebrated autobiog novel *Kindheitsmuster* (1976) had offered a way of coming to terms with the past; by contrast *Störfall* (novel 1987) took issue with the Chernobyl disaster and official refusals to acknowledge massive ecological destruction, while *Was bleibt?* (1990) addressed Stasi tyranny without accepting her own and other GDR writers' complicity, (also *Auf dem Weg nach Tabou*, 1990–4). W has written essays and lectures on the role of the (woman) writer, collected notably in *Die Dimension des Autors 1959–1985* (1986).

#### *Friedrich Wolf* (Neuwied 1888–1953 nr Oranienburg)

Wolf was a doctor and Communist activist in film and theatre, eg his play *Cynkali* attacking the anti-abortion Para. 218 (1929, film version 1930) and *Professor Mamlock* (first perf in Yiddish in Warsaw and German in Zurich, 1934,

Soviet film version in 1938). In the GDR he was active as a film scriptwriter, ambassador to Poland and leading Stasi member (*Im eigenen Auftrag*, 1991).

### Christian von Wolff
#### (Breslau 1679–1754 Halle)

He was a pupil of Christian Gryphius at the Breslau Magdalenäum before studying at Jena and Leipzig. He developed his rationalist philosophy early and expounded it as professor of mathematics at Halle, influencing generations of students and becoming the first German philosopher to dominate his period intellectually. His numerous works in Latin and German brought him wide recognition and culminated in his 5-vol *Philosophia moralis sive Ethica* (Halle 1750–3).

### Karl Wolfskehl
#### (Darmstadt 1869–1984 Auckland/ New Zealand)

The life and work of Wolfskehl, an early disciple of Stefan George, is a tragic monument to the failure of his hoped-for symbiosis of Jew and German (as in *Saul*, 1908). *Die Stimme spricht* (1934), *An die Deutschen* (1947), *Hiob* and *Sang aus dem Exil* (both 1950) were written in Swiss and New Zealand exile.

### Johann David Wyss
#### (Berne 1743–1818 Köniz)

He studied theology, spent 2 years in Sardinia as a military padre and ended his career as minister at Berne Cathedral. In the 1790s he wrote a story for his children which, when reworked by his son **Johann Rudolf Wyss** (Berne 1782–1830), became the international children's classic *The Swiss Family Robinson* (4 vols: vols 1 & 2 1812–13, English and French 1814). JRW wrote the words of the Swiss national anthem 'Rufst du, mein Vaterland' in 1811.

# Z

### Friedrich Wilhelm Zachariä
#### (Frankenhausen 1726–77 Brunswick)

He specialized in burlesque poems in the Boileau-Pope manner such as 'Der Renommiste' on university life and 'Phaeton'

on country life (both 1744). He represents Augustan poetry in lighter vein.

### Sidonia Hedwig Zäunemann
#### (Erfurt 1716–40 nr Plaue)

At only 24 she was crowned 'imperial poet laureate' by Göttingen, the university whose foundation in 1737 she had commemorated in verse. A proto-feminist, she disputed the view that literature was a male preserve by writing on such themes as mining and war.

### Philipp von Zesen
#### (nr Dessau 1619–89 Hamburg)

One of the baroque era's most versatile and productive writers, Zesen aimed to enrich German literature through his knowledge of other literatures, particularly that of the Dutch Republic, where he lived for several years and where his novel *Die Adriatische Rosemund* (1645) is partly set. *Assenat* (1670) a thoughtful study of conduct in public and private life, anticipates T Mann's *Joseph* novels.

### Christiane Marianne Ziegler
#### (Leipzig 1695–1760 Frankfurt/Oder)

She was a young widow who graced Leipzig society and became the first female member of Gottsched's *Deutsche Gesellschaft*. She publ two vols of poetry (1728–9 and 1739) and was crowned imperial poetess at Wittenberg in 1733. In 1741 she married a professor of philosophy and quitted Leipzig and literary life for good.

### Julius Wilhelm von Zincgref
#### (Heidelberg 1591–1663 St Goar)

He ed the first vol of the poems of Martin Opitz in 1624 and publ a collection of German maxims (*Der Teutschen Scharpfsinnige kluge Sprüch*, 1626–31). His own verse tended to be of the topical kind and was often anon.

### Erdmuth Dorothea von Zinzendorf
#### (Ebersdorf/Vogtland 1700–56 Herrnhut)

She married NL v Z in 1722 and managed his financial affairs and those of their Pietist community. She spent a substantial part of her middle age journeying across northern Europe to spread the gospel, after having produced a dozen children and written several hymns still sung today.

*Nikolaus Ludwig von Zinzendorf*
(Dresden 1700–60 Herrnhut)
The widely-travelled and well-connected Z
gave a home to persecuted Protestant radicals
on his estate, thus founding the immensely
influential religious community, the Pietist
Herrnhut *Brüdergemeine* better known as the
Moravian Brethren. His missionary efforts
extended to England and N America, but
he suffered persecution in his native Saxony.
Z promoted his ideas of tolerance and
fervour in innumerable hymns and religious
writings.

*Albin Zollinger* (Zurich 1895–1941)
He was a gifted poet, journalist and unremitting champion of democratic values whose
topical novel *Die große Unruhe* (1939) evokes
the unsettled mood of 1930s Europe. In his
later novels *Pfannenstiel* (1940) and *Bohnenblust*
(1941) he diagnoses the near-disillusionment of
a contemporary sculptor and his regained sense
of direction as war looms.

*Heinrich Daniel Zschokke*
(Magdeburg 1771–1848 Aarau)
He had a turbulent literary apprenticeship, i a
writing plays for a company of strolling players,
notably his highly successful *Aballino der große
Bandit*, 1795, based on an earlier novel. Settling
in Switzerland, he developed his practical philosophy in novels whose idealized protagonists
counter current abuses (*Das Goldermacherdorf*,
1817, *Die Branntweinpest*, 1837). A fine storyteller, he became one of the most widely read
authors and journalists of his day.

*Carl Zuckmayer* (Nackenheim/Rhine
1896–1977 Visp/Switzerland)
He became one of the most successful dramatists of the Weimar Republic. He dramatized
the story of Germany's legendary bandit in
*Schinderhannes* (1927); wrote 2 much-played
comedies, *Der fröhliche Weinberg* (1925) and
*Der Hauptmann von Köpenick* (1930) and the
drama *Des Teufels General* (1946, film 1955).
Both he (*Als wär's ein Stück von mir*, 1966) and
his wife **Alice Herdahn-Zuckmayer** (*Die
Farm auf den grünen Bergen*, 1949) wrote
memorable autobiogs through the perspective
of exile.

*Hermine Zur Mühlen*
(Vienna 1883–1951 Radlett/England)
Research into exile literature is only beginning
to do justice to this author of the influential
*Proletarische Märchen* (illustrated by Grosz and
Heartfield), the semi-autobiog novels *Das
Riesenrad* (1932), *Reise durchs Leben* (1933) and
*Ein Jahr im Schatten* (1935), children's books
and of exile literature in both German and
English, incl *Unsere Töchter, die Nazinen*
(1935) and *We Poor Shadows* (1943).

*Arnold Zweig* (Groß-Glogau/Silesia
1887–1968 Berlin)
As early as his student days he was exploring
his own identity as a Jew (as in the tragedy,
*Ritualmord in Ungarn*, 1914, *Die Umkehr des
Abtrünnigen*, drama 1925) and developing his
views in essays such as *Caliban oder Politik und
Leidenschaft* (1927) on the pathology of anti-
Semitism. He made his name with his psychological *Die Novellen um Claudia* (1912). After
initial war enthusiasm he became a pacifist; his
international best-seller, *Der Streit um den
Sergeanten Grischa* (novel 1927) was followed
by a series of antiwar novels, eg *Junge Frau von
1914* (1931). He returned from exile in Palestine in 1948 to become president of the (E
German) *Deutsche Akademie der Künste*, at
once an opportunist and a victim of his circumstances as a Jew whose language was unwanted
in Israel.

*Stefan Zweig*
(Vienna 1881–1942 Petropolis/Brazil)
He is best remembered for *Schachnovelle*
(1941), a classic of exile literature, and for his
kaleidoscopic evocation of *fin-de-siècle* and pre-
Fascist Vienna in *Die Welt von Gestern:
Erinnerungen eines Europäers* (1944). He was an
immensely successful writer whose range included the pacifist drama *Jeremias* (1918), novels and stories featuring sexual repression and
its social impact (eg *Amok: Novellen einer
Leidenschaft*, 1922, and *Verwirrung der Gefühle*,
novel 1927). He also wr biogs, anti-heroic historical essays and biog miniatures, of which
*Sternstunden der Menschheit* (1927) became a
world best-seller.

# General Index

———— · ————

This General Index refers to the main text only, and should be used in conjunction with the Biographical Index (pp. 259–358), which provides further information about authors and their works.

Abraham a Sancta Clara, 18
Achleitner, Friedrich, 245
actors and acting, 9, 18, 27, 77–8, 86, 130, 168, 190
Addison, Joseph, 36
Adelung, Johann Christoph, 54
Adenauer era, 90, 121, 214, 226
adolescence *see* youth
Adorno, Theodor, 188, 229, 231
   *Prismen: Kultur und Gesellschaft*, 229
aesthetics, 55, 77, 229
aestheticism *see* art for art's sake
Aichinger, Ilse, 217, 218, 221, 231, 248
   *Aufruf zum Mißtrauen*, 248
   *Die größere Hoffnung*, 221, 248
*Die Aktion* (journal), 161
Albertinus, Aegidius, 47
alexandrine, 26–7
Alexis, Willibald, 99
   *Die Hosen des Herrn von Bredow*, 99
   *Isegrimm*, 100
   *Ruhe ist die erste Bürgerpflicht*, 100
alienation *see Verfremdungseffekt*
*Allgemeine deutsche Bibliothek*, 51
*Allgemeine Literatur-Zeitung*, 52
*Allgemeine Zeitung*, 127
almanacs, 12
Alps in literature, 42, 55, 108, 142, 157, 200, 251

Alsace, 11, 141
Altenberg, Peter, 162
Amsterdam, 34, 35, 211
anacreontic poetry, 61
Andersch, Alfred, 220–1
   *Die Kirschen der Freiheit*, 221
   *Sansibar oder der letzte Grund*, 221
Andreas-Salomé, Lou, 164
Andres, Stefan, 209–10
   *El Greco malt den Großinquisitor*, 209–10
   *Wir sind Utopia*, 209–10
anecdote as genre, 4, 9, 142
Angelus Silesius (Johannes Scheffler), 18, 24
Anna Amalia, Duchess of Weimar, 50, 56
*Anschluß* (annexation of Austria by Hitler in 1938), 211, 243, 244, 246
anthology, 24, 119, 129, 162
anti-Semitism, 19, 117, 121, 143, 175, 210, 212, 224
Anton Ulrich, Duke of Brunswick, 19
Anzengruber, Ludwig, 135, 173
  as dramatist, 173
  as novelist, 135
Aristophanes, 110
Arminius *see* Hermann
Arndt, Ernst Moritz, 119
   *Geist der Zeit*, 119
   'Was ist des Deutschen Vaterland', 119
Arnim, Achim von, 93